JAN 2 0 2018

P9-ELT-157

Laos

Northern
Laos
p64

Luang
Prabang &
Around
p34

Vientiane, Vang
Vieng & Around
p126

Central
Laos
p174

Southern
Laos
p200

THIS EDITION WRITTEN AND RESEARCHED BY

Kate Morgan, Tim Bewer, Nick Ray, Richard Waters

Contents

PLAN YOUR TRIP

ON THE ROAD

WAT HO PHA BANG (P36), LUANG PRABANG

SIMON IRWIN/LONELY PLANET ©

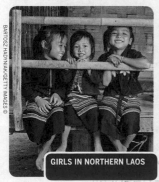

GIRLS IN NORTHERN LAOS

BARTOSZ HADYNIAK/GETTY IMAGES ©

SIMON IRWIN/LONELY PLANET ©

BUDDHAS AT WAT SI SAKET (P130), VIENTIANE

Contents

Welcome to Laos

A land of the lotus eaters amid the bloated development of its neighbours, Laos brings together the best of Southeast Asia in one bite-sized destination.

An Authentic Asia

Laos retains many of the traditions that have disappeared in a frenzy of development elsewhere in the region. It's hard to believe somnolent Vientiane is an Asian capital, and there's a timeless quality to rural life, where stilt houses and paddy fields look like they are straight out of a movie set. Magical Luang Prabang bears witness to hundreds of saffron-robed monks gliding through the streets every morning in a call to alms, one of the region's iconic images. Intrepid travellers will discover a country untainted by mass tourism and Asia in slow motion – this is Lao People's Democratic Republic (Lao PDR), or 'please don't rush' as the locals like to joke.

A Kaleidoscope of People

Laos is one of the most ethnically diverse countries in the region, reflecting its geographic location as a crossroads of Asia. The hardy Hmong people live off the land in remote mountain communities of the north, remote Kahu and Alak communities of the south have the last remaining traditional face tattoos, and the Katang villages of central Laos sleep with the spirits of the forest. Whether it is the cities of the lowlands or the remote villages of the highlands, Laos offers some wonderful opportunities for local interaction.

Fifty Shades of Green

With its dark and brooding jungle, glowing emerald rice fields, and the glistening tea leaves that blanket the mountains, the landscape in Laos changes shades of green like a chameleon. But it's not just the luscious landscapes that are green: when it comes to ecotourism, Laos is leading the way in Southeast Asia. Protected areas predominate in remote areas of the country, and community-based trekking combines these spectacular natural attractions with the chance to experience the 'real Laos' with a village homestay.

Eclectic Asia

Travellers rave about Laos for a reason. Adventure seekers can lose themselves in underground river caves, on jungle ziplines or while climbing karsts. Nature enthusiasts can take a walk on the wild side and spot exotic animals such as gibbons or elephants. Culture lovers can explore ancient temples and immerse themselves in Lao spiritual life. Foodies can spice up their lives with a Lao cooking class or go gourmand in the French-accented cities. And if all this sounds a little too strenuous, then unwind with a spa session or yoga class. Laos has something for everyone.

Why I Love Laos

By Nick Ray, Writer

I first came to Laos as a backpacker in 1995 and quickly succumbed to the natural charms of the landscape, not to mention ice-cold Beerlao while overlooking the Mekong River. Fast forward more than two decades and Laos still delivers adventures. On my latest visit, I explored the pristine province of Khammuan, took a trip into the underworld of Tham Kong Lor, got a buzz motorbiking the Loop, and spent time trawling the authentic eateries and lively bars of Vientiane, Laos' underrated capital. A travel tonic to slake your thirst for the real Asia, Laos will leave a lasting impression long after you return home.

For more about our writers, see p320

Above: Hot air balloon over the Nam Song, Vang Vieng (p163)

Laos

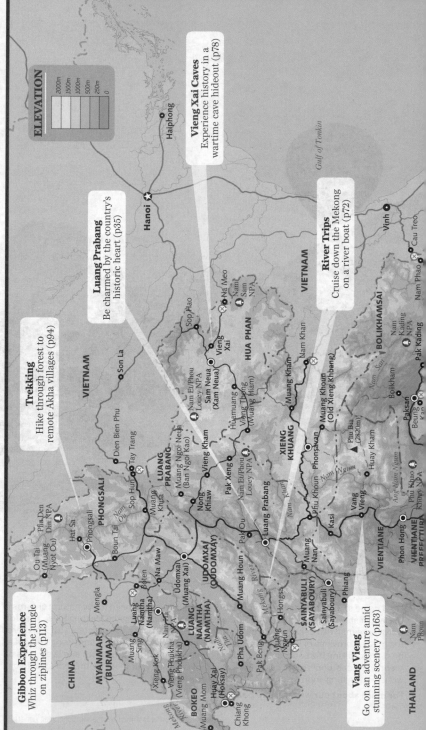

Gibbon Experience
Whiz through the jungle on ziplines (p113)

Trekking
Hike through forest to remote Akha villages (p94)

Luang Prabang
Be charmed by the country's historic heart (p35)

Vieng Xai Caves
Experience history in a wartime cave hideout (p78)

River Trips
Cruise down the Mekong on a river boat (p72)

Vang Vieng
Go on an adventure amid stunning scenery (p163)

ELEVATION

	2000m
	1500m
	1000m
	500m
	250m
	0

100 km
60 miles

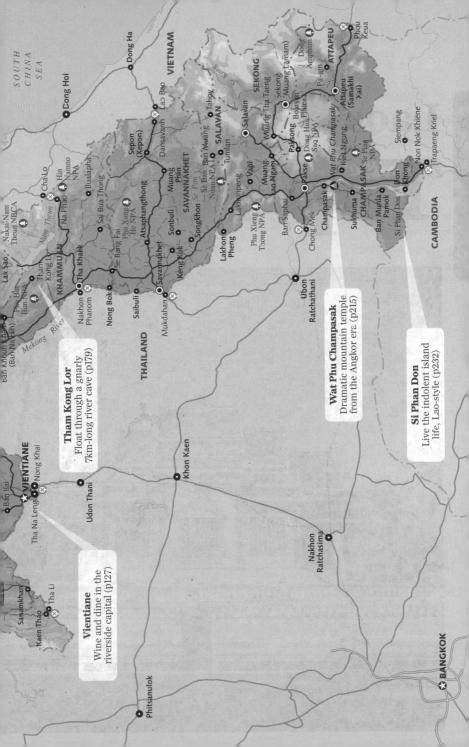

Tham Kong Lor
Float through a gnarly
7km-long river cave (p179)

Vientiane
Wine and dine in the
riverside capital (p127)

Wat Phu Champasak
Dramatic mountain temple
from the Angkor era (p215)

Si Phan Don
Live the indolent island
life, Lao-style (p232)

Laos'
Top 10

Luang Prabang

1 Bordered by the Mekong River the Nam Khan (Khan River), this timeless 'city of temples' (p35) is the stuff of travel legends: rich in royal history, saffron-clad monks, stunning river views, world-class cuisine and some of the best boutique accommodation in the region. Hire a bike and explore the tropical peninsula's backstreets, take a cooking class or just ease back with a restful massage at one of the many affordable spas. Prepare to adjust your timetable and stay a little longer than expected. Below left: Wat Ho Pha Bang, Royal Palace museum (p36)

Vang Vieng

2 The riverine jewel in Laos' karst country, Vang Vieng (p163) sits under soaring cliffs beside the Nam Song (Song River) and is the undisputed adventure capital of Laos. Since the party crowd moved on, tranquillity reigns again with more family-oriented visitors dropping in to soak up such well-organised activities as hot-air ballooning, trekking, caving and climbing. And don't forget the original draw: tubing down the river. Where once there were only budget guesthouses and same-same traveller cafes, now they have been joined by smarter boutique hotels and restaurants serving delicious food. Below right: Hot air balloon over the Nam Song

AVIGATOR THAILAND/SHUTTERSTOCK ©

THANACHET MAIJANG/SHUTTERSTOCK ©

Si Phan Don

3 Laos' hammock-flopping mecca has been catering to weary travellers for years. While these tropical islands (p232) bounded by the waters of the Mekong are best known as a happy haven for catatonic sun worshippers, more active souls are spoilt for choice. Between tubing and cycling through paddy fields, grab a kayak, spot rare Irrawaddy dolphins, and then round off your day with a sunset boat trip.

Vientiane

4 Meandering along the banks of the Mekong, Vientiane (p127) is surely Southeast Asia's most languid capital. The wide streets are bordered by tamarind trees and the narrow alleys conceal French villas, Chinese shophouses and glittering wats. The city brews a heady mix of street vendors, saffron-clad monks, fine Gallic cuisine, boutique hotels and a healthy vibe that sees visitors slinking off for spa treatments and turning their time to yoga and cycling. It may not have Luang Prabang's looks, but Vientiane has a certain charm all of its own. Top right: Spa treatment in Vientiane

Trekking & Homestays

5 Laos is famous for its wide range of community-based treks, many of which include a traditional homestay for a night or more. Trekking is possible all over the country, but northern Laos is one of the most popular areas. Trekking (p94) around Phongsali is considered some of the most authentic in Laos and involves the chance to stay with the colouful Akha people. Luang Namtha is the most accessible base for ecotreks in the Nam Ha National Protected Area (NPA), one of the best-known trekking spots in the Mekong region. Bottom right: Akha woman near Luang Namtha (p103)

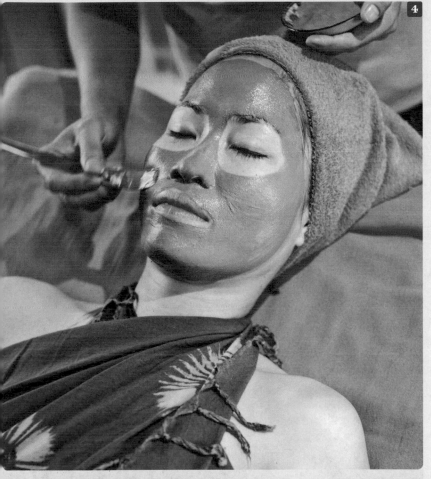

Vieng Xai Caves

6 This is history writ large in stone. An area of outstanding natural beauty, Vieng Xai (p78) was home to the Pathet Lao communist leadership during the US bombing campaign of 1964–73. Beyond the breathtaking beauty of the natural caves, it is the superb audio tour that really brings the experience alive. When the bombers buzz overhead to a soundtrack of Jimi Hendrix you'll be ducking for cover in the Red Prince's lush garden.

Gibbon Experience

7 Whiz high above the forest floor attached to a zipline. These brilliantly engineered cables – some more than 500m long – span forest valleys in the lush Bokeo Nature Reserve (habitat of the black-crested gibbon and Asiatic tiger). Some of the proceeds go towards protecting the eponymous endangered primate and guides are former poachers turned rangers. Zip into and bed down in vertiginously high tree houses by night, listening to the call of the wild. The Gibbon Experience (p113) is Laos' premier wildlife and adventure playground.

Tham Kong Lor

8 Imagine your deepest nightmare: the snaggle-toothed mouth of a river cave beneath a towering limestone mountain, the boatman in his rickety longtail taking you into the heart of darkness. Puttering beneath the cathedral-high ceiling of stalactites in this extraordinary 7.5km-long underworld (p180) in remote Khammuan Province is an awesome experience. You'll be very glad to see the light at the other end of the tunnel. The village of Ban Kong Lor is now the most convenient base for visiting the cave, after an explosion of guesthouses and small resorts in the last few years.

9

River Trips

9 River trips (p72) are a major feature of travel through Laos. One of the most popular connects Luang Prabang and Huay Xai, the gateway to the Golden Triangle, via Pak Beng. From local boats to luxury cruises, there are options to suit every budget, including floating through sleepy Si Phan Don in the far south. Beyond the Mekong, many important feeder rivers such as the Nam Ou and Nam Tha connect places as diverse as Nong Khiaw and Muang Khua (for Phongsali). As well as boat trips, it is also possible to kayak some of these regional rivers in multiday activity trips. Left: Nam Ou, Nong Khiaw (p82)

Wat Phu Champasak

10 Not as majestic as the temples of Angkor, but just as mysterious, this mountainside Khmer ruin (p215) has both the artistry and the setting to impress. Once part of an important city, it now sits forlorn on the side of Phu Pasak. You'll discover something special at each level as you walk up to the summit where the views are vast and the crowds are thin. Other related ruins can be found in the rice paddies and forest down below.

10

Need to Know

For more information, see Survival Guide (p281)

Currency
Lao kip (K)

Language
Lao

Visas
Thirty-day tourist visas are readily available on arrival at international airports and most land borders.

Money
The official national currency in Laos is the Lao kip (K). Although only kip is legally negotiable in everyday transactions, in reality three currencies are used for commerce: kip, Thai baht (B) and US dollars (US$).

Mobile Phones
Roaming is possible in Laos but is generally expensive. Local SIM cards and unlocked mobile phones are readily available.

Time
Indochina Time (GMT/ UTC plus seven hours)

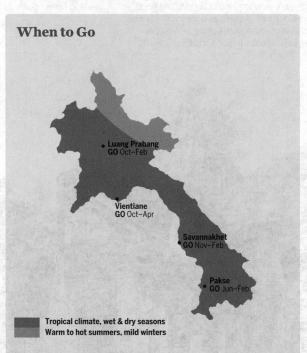

When to Go

Luang Prabang
GO Oct–Feb

Vientiane
GO Oct–Apr

Savannakhet
GO Nov–Feb

Pakse
GO Jun–Feb

Tropical climate, wet & dry seasons
Warm to hot summers, mild winters

High Season
(Nov–Mar)

➡ Pleasant temperatures in much of Laos, though it's cold in the mountains.

➡ The best all-round time to visit.

➡ Book accommodation in advance during the peak Christmas and New Year period.

Shoulder Season
(Jul & Aug)

➡ Wet in most parts of Laos with high humidity, but the landscapes are emerald green.

➡ Popular time for European tourists to visit from Italy or Spain, plus backpacking students with a long summer break.

Low Season
(Apr–Jun, Sep & Oct)

➡ April and May brings the hot season to Laos when the thermostat hits 40°C and visitors wilt.

➡ September and October can be very wet, but there are some incredible cloud formations to accompany the deluge.

Useful Websites

Lonely Planet (www.lonely planet.com/laos) Destination information, hotel bookings, traveller forum and more.

Ecotourism Laos (www. ecotourismlaos.com) Information about the Lao environs, focusing on trekking and other ecotourism activities.

lao*miao* (www.laomeow. blogspot.com) Up-to-date transportation details, mostly regarding northern Laos.

Lao National Tourism Administration (www.tourismlaos.org) Mostly up-to-date travel information from the government.

RFA (Radio Free Asia; www.rfa. org/english/news/laos) Unbiased, censorship-free news on Laos from Asia-based journalists.

Important Numbers

To dial listings from outside Laos, dial your international access code, the country code and then the number (minus '0', which is used when dialling domestically).

Laos' country code	☏856
International access code	☏00
Ambulance	☏195
Fire	☏190
Police	☏191

Exchange Rates

Australia	A$1	6152K
Canada	C$1	6110K
Euro zone	€1	8788K
Japan	¥100	7729K
Thailand	10B	2289K
UK	UK£1	9838K
US	US$1	8005K
Vietnam	10,000d	3524K

For current exchange rates, see www.xe.com.

Daily Costs

Budget: Less than US$50

➡ Cheap guesthouse room: US$3–10

➡ Local meals and street eats: US$1–2

➡ Local buses: US$2–3 per 100km

Midrange: US$50–US$150

➡ Air-con hotel room: US$15–50

➡ Decent local restaurant meal: US$5–10

➡ Local tour guide per day: US$25

Top End: More than US$150

➡ Boutique hotel or resort: US$50–500

➡ Gastronomic meal with drinks: US$15–50

➡ 4WD rental per day: US$60–120

Opening Hours

Bars and clubs 5pm–11.30pm (later in Vientiane)

Government offices 8am–noon and 1pm–5pm Monday to Friday

Noodle shops 7am–1pm

Restaurants 10am–10pm

Shops 9am–6pm

Arriving in Laos

Wattay International Airport (Vientiane; p292) Buses and jumbos run to/from the airport. Taxis/minibuses cost a flat fare of US$7/8.

Luang Prabang International Airport (p292) Taxis to/from the airport cost a standardised 50,000K.

Savannakhet International Airport (p292) Jumbos cost 30,000K from the airport, but drivers may start higher.

Pakse International Airport (p292) A *săhm-lór* or tuk-tuk to the airport will cost about 50,000K.

Getting Around

Transport in Laos is generally very good value, but journeys can take a lot longer than distances on a map might suggest.

Air Laos has an extensive domestic flight network and this can save considerable time on a short visit.

Boat Rivers are the lifeblood of Laos, making boat journeys an important element of the transport network.

Bus Laos has some smart buses operating on major routes out of Vientiane, but venture into remote areas and vehicles are as old as the hills.

Car For those with a more flexible budget, a rented car with driver is the smoothest way to cover a lot of ground in a limited amount of time.

For much more on **getting around**, see p297

If You Like...

Outdoor Activities

Vang Vieng An adventure playground for river tubing, kayaking, caving, climbing and cycling. (p163)

Tha Khaek The karst limestone peaks are home to deep caves and soaring overhangs. (p182)

Bolaven Plateau Impressive waterfalls, motorcycle trips and the Treetop Explorer zipline adventure. (p219)

Luang Namtha Gateway to northwest adventures, Luang Namtha offers trekking, cycling, kayaking and, further down the jungle trail, the Gibbon Experience. (p103)

Culinary Experiences

Vientiane The culinary capital of the country, with Laotian home cooking, Gallic gastronomy and flavours as diverse as Indian and Italian. (p127)

Luang Prabang Dine on the Mekong side of the peninsula for sunsets or on the Nam Khan (Khan River) for sophisticated set menus. (p35)

Luang Namtha Luang Namtha has several excellent restaurants that specialise in ethnic minority cuisine. (p103)

Si Phan Don Skip the tourist menus and dig into a variety of fresh Mekong River fish dishes. (p232)

River Trips

Huay Xai to Luang Prabang One of the more conveniently accessed river trips in Laos, with an overnight stop at the dramatically situated town of Pak Beng. (p59)

Si Phan Don With a name that means 'Four Thousand Islands', it's not surprising that boat trips feature strongly in this beautiful southern stretch of the Mekong in Laos. (p232)

Tham Kong Lor A river trip with a difference, passing through a 7km cave that is straight out of Greek mythology. (p180)

Vang Vieng River tubing on the Nam Song is a young backpacker rite of passage, but there are kayaking trips here too. (p163)

Old Temples

Luang Prabang The royal city is home to more than 30 gilded wats, including the soaring roofs of Wat Xieng Thong. (p35)

Wat Phu Champasak The ancient Khmers once held sway over much of the Mekong region and Wat Phu was one of their hilltop temples. (p215)

Vientiane The Lao capital is home to some fine temples, including Pha That Luang, the golden stupa that is the symbol of a nation, and Wat Si Saket, which houses thousands of revered buddha images. (p127)

Savannakhet Home to That Ing Hang, one of the holiest temples in all of Laos, plus the ancient Khmer ruin of Heuan Hin. (p190)

Off the Beaten Track

Vieng Xai Caves These underground caves were the Pathet Lao's base during the US bombing campaign. (p78)

Phongsali Province The remote far north of Laos is the location for some of the most authentic hill-tribe village treks in the country. (p88)

Khammuan Province This rugged central province is peppered with karst limestone peaks and rewards two-wheeled adventurers prepared to head off-piste on the Loop. (p175)

Nam Nern Night Safari A nighttime boat tour through Nam Et/Phou Louey National Protected Area (NPA) spotlighting for wildlife and tigers – fingers crossed! (p80)

Top: Sunrise at Si Phan Don (p232)
Bottom: Noodle dish, Luang Prabang

Memorable Markets

Handicraft Night Market
Night markets, day markets, they come in every flavour in Luang Prabang, including the Handicraft Night Market on the main street and an affordable food market. (p56)

Vientiane's Talat Sao The Talat Sao (Morning Market) is more like a department store or shopping centre in parts, but it is still one of the best places in Laos to shop for handicrafts and textiles. (p153)

Sam Neua's Main Market This huge market has some interesting textiles from this remote region, as well as proving a crossroads for imported goods from China and Vietnam. (p76)

Savannakhet Plaza Food Market The central square comes alive by night, as local street stalls cook up a storm. (p193)

Talat Dao Heuang The largest market in Pakse, and the country, is packed to the gunnels with goods. (p202)

Wellness Centres

Luang Prabang The spiritual home of wellness in Laos, there are lots of impressive spas at the leading hotels and resorts in town. (p35)

Vientiane The capital is home to many sumptuous spas, some international standard fitness centres and a yoga school. (p127)

Champasak Home to the eponymous Champasak Spa, which helps create a sustainable living for young women in this small town. (p211)

Nong Khiaw Get in shape with a yoga session at Mandala Ou Resort or a scrub at Sabai Sabai. (p82)

Month by Month

January

Peak season in much of Laos. It's a pleasantly chilled time to be in the main centres and downright cold at higher altitude.

✨ International New Year

A public holiday in sync with embassy and aid workers resident in Laos.

✨ Bun Khun Khao

The annual harvest festival in mid-January sees villagers perform ceremonies offering thanks to the land spirits for their crops.

February

The weather is usually still relatively cool and dry at this time, when Chinese and Vietnamese New Year often fall.

✨ Makha Busa

Also known as Magha Puja or Bun Khao Chi, this full-moon festival commemorates a speech given by Buddha to 1250 enlightened monks. Chanting and offerings mark the festival, and celebrations are most fervent in Vientiane and at Wat Phu Champasak. (p217)

✨ Vietnamese Tet & Chinese New Year

Celebrated in Vientiane, Pakse and Savannakhet with parties, fireworks and visits to Vietnamese and Chinese temples. Chinese- and Vietnamese-run businesses usually close for several days.

March

Things are starting to warm up and this can be a good time to step up to the higher altitudes of Xieng Khuang and Phongsali.

✨ Bun Pha Wet

This is a temple-centred festival in which the Jataka (birth tale) of Prince Vessantara, the Buddha's penultimate life, is recited. This is also a favoured time for Lao males to be ordained into the monkhood.

April

April is the hottest month of the year when the thermometer hits 40°C.

✨ Bun Pi Mai

Lao new year is the most important holiday of the year. Houses are cleaned, people put on new clothes and Buddha images are washed with lustral water. Locals douse one another, and sometimes random tourists, with water, which is an appropriate activity as April is usually the hottest month of the year. This festival is particularly memorable in Luang Prabang, where it includes processions and lots of traditional costumes. There are public holidays on 14, 15 and 16 April, and the vast majority of shops and restaurants are closed. (p48)

May

Events go off with a bang this month, as rockets are fired into the sky. 'Green' (low) season kicks in and prices drop accordingly.

✨ Visakha Busa

Visakha Busa (also known as Visakha Puja) falls on the 15th day of the sixth lunar month, which is considered the day of the Buddha's birth, enlightenment and *parinibbana* (passing away). Country-wide celebrations are centred on the wat, with beautiful candlelit processions by night.

✵ Bun Bang Fai

The Rocket Festival is a pre-Buddhist rain ceremony now celebrated alongside Visakha Busa in Laos and northeastern Thailand. It can be one of the wildest festivals in the whole country, with music, dance and folk theatre, processions and general merrymaking, all culminating in the firing of bamboo rockets into the sky. The firing of the rockets is supposed to prompt the heavens to initiate the rainy season and bring much-needed water to the rice fields.

July

The wet season is winding up with some heavy rains, but it only pours for a short time each day, making this a lush time to explore.

✵ Bun Khao Phansa

Also known as Khao Watsa, this full-moon festival is the beginning of the traditional three-month 'rains retreat', during which Buddhist monks are expected to base themselves in a single monastery. This is also the traditional time of year for men to enter the monkhood temporarily, hence many ordinations take place.

August

Summer holidays in Europe see a mini peak during the off season, which

brings French, Italian and Spanish tourists, as well as university students to the country.

✵ Haw Khao Padap Din

This sombre full-moon festival sees the living pay respect to the dead. Many cremations take place – bones being exhumed for the purpose – and gifts are presented to the Buddhist order (Sangha) so monks will chant on behalf of the deceased.

October

It is all about river action this month. Choose between racing dragon boats in the capital or floating candles across the country.

✵ Bun Awk Phansa

At the end of the three-month rains retreat, monks can leave the monasteries to travel and are presented with robes and alms bowls. The eve of Awk Phansa (Ok Watsa) is celebrated with parties and, near any river, with the release of small banana-leaf boats carrying candles and incense in a ceremony called Van Loi Heua Fai, similar to Loy Krathong in Thailand. Luang Prabang is a popular place to witness this festival. (p49)

☆ Bun Nam

In many river towns, including Vientiane and Luang Prabang, boat races are held the day after Awk Phansa. In smaller towns the races are often postponed until National Day (2 December) so residents aren't saddled with two

costly festivals in two months. Also called Bun Suang Heua. (p139)

November

Peak season begins in earnest and accommodation prices rise once more.

✵ Bun Pha That Luang

The That Luang Festival, centred around Pha That Luang in Vientiane, lasts a week and includes fireworks, music and drinking across the capital. Early on the first morning hundreds of monks receive alms and floral offerings. The festival ends with a fantastic candlelit procession circling That Luang. (p140)

December

Christmas may not be a big Lao festival, but it certainly sees a lot of foreigners arrive in country. Book ahead and be prepared to pay top dollar.

✵ Lao National Day

This public holiday on 2 December celebrates the 1975 victory over the monarchy with parades and speeches. Lao national and Communist hammer-and-sickle flags are flown all over the country.

☆ Luang Prabang Film Festival

This festival in early December sees free screenings at several venues around town. The focus is on the blossoming work of Southeast Asian production houses and all films have English subtitles. (p48)

Itineraries

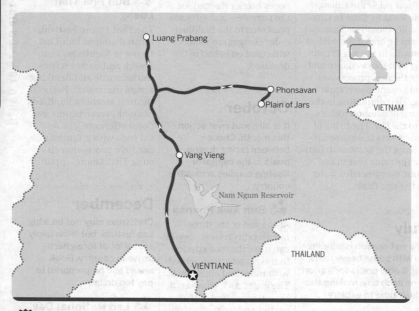

Luang Prabang

Phonsavan
Plain of Jars

VIETNAM

Vang Vieng

Nam Ngum Reservoir

THAILAND

VIENTIANE

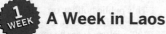

1 WEEK — A Week in Laos

Start out your classic Laos adventure in **Vientiane**, the atmospheric Lao capital. There are few must-see sights beyond a handful of temples, but the Mekong riverside setting is dramatic and there are some excellent cafes, restaurants and bars to enjoy and some of the best shopping in the country.

Head north to **Vang Vieng**. Once a sort of backpacker Xanadu where anything goes, it has reinvented itself as the adventure centre of Laos with caving, rock climbing, ziplining, kayaking, mountain biking and trekking, not forgetting the infamous river tubing that put this place on the map.

Continue north on Rte 13, making a side trip to **Phonsavan**, gateway to the **Plain of Jars** and its mysterious vessels, one of the more popular destinations in Laos.

The highlight of this trip is **Luang Prabang**, the historic capital of Lan Xang and a worthy Unesco World Heritage Site. Plan a few days here to soak up the timeless atmosphere of the old town, including the *tak bat* (dawn call to alms) for the city's many monks. Save some time for outdoor adventures, with waterfalls, mountain-bike trails, kayaking trips and jungle treks all on offer.

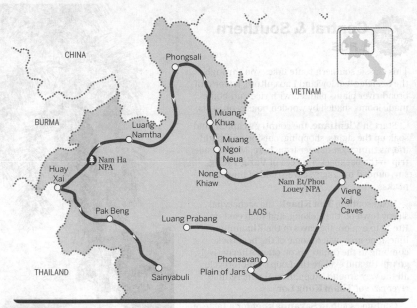

3 WEEKS Hit the North

Northern Laos is one of the most popular regions of the country for adventure activities, coupled with an authentic dose of ethnic minority lifestyles. Right at the heart of the region lies Luang Prabang, the perfect place to start or finish a road trip through the remote north.

Lovely **Luang Prabang** is a destination in itself. Spend your time exploring the old town and its myriad temples, traditional buildings and galleries, cafes and shops.

Head southeast from Luang Prabang to **Phonsavan**, the base from which to see the impressive **Plain of Jars**. It is then time to leave the tourist trail and head to the **Vieng Xai Caves**. The setting is spectacular amid the karst caves and the historic audio tour is one of the most compelling experiences in Laos.

Swinging west, head to the remote protected area of **Nam Et/Phou Louey National Protected Area (NPA)** for a night-time wildlife-watching safari. Continue to **Nong Khiaw**, a beautiful village on the banks of the Nam Ou (Ou River) with striking limestone crags looming all around. This is the embarkation point for an adventurous boat trip to Phongsali Province via the small villages of **Muang Ngoi Neua** and **Muang Khua**. **Phongsali** is considered the most authentic trekking destination in Laos and it is possible to experience homestays with Akha villagers.

Head on to **Luang Namtha**, a friendly base for some northwesterly adventures. Trek into the **Nam Ha NPA** or try a cycling or kayaking trip in the countryside beyond.

From Luang Namtha head down to **Huay Xai**, a Mekong River border town and gateway to the Gibbon Experience. If time is tight, bail out here, but it is better to continue the loop back to Luang Prabang by river. The two-day boat trip from Huay Xai to Luang Prabang via **Pak Beng** is one of the most conveniently accessed river trips in the country.

Or take just a one-day boat trip to Pak Beng and then leave the river behind to head to **Sainyabuli** and the superb Elephant Conservation Center on the Nam Tien lake. This can also be visited out of Luang Prabang.

2 WEEKS Central & Southern Laos

This classic southern route takes you through the heartland of lowland Lao culture, a world of broad river plains planted with rice and homemade looms shaded by wooden houses on stilts.

Start in **Vientiane**, the country's capital, and soak up the sights, shopping, cuisine and nightlife, as things get quieter from here. Make a side trip to the backpacker mecca of **Vang Vieng**, surrounded by craggy, cave-studded limestone peaks.

Head south to **Tha Khaek**, the archetypal sleepy town on the Mekong, and then east on Rte 12 to explore the caves of the Khammuan limestone area, where some of the best rock climbing in the country is on offer. Alternatively, go full tilt and explore the Loop by motorcycle all the way around, stopping at the incredible river cave of **Tham Kong Lor**.

Continue south to **Savannakhet** for a taste of how Vientiane looked before it received a makeover from the Lao government and international aid money. Explore the somnolent streets of old French architecture and surf the street stalls at the Savannakhet Plaza Food Market.

Roll on southward to **Pakse**, gateway to the southernmost province of Champasak. **Champasak** town is a more relaxed alternative to Pakse and is the base for seeing Laos' most important archaeological site, Wat Phu Champasak, an Angkor-style temple ruin spread across the slopes of sacred Phu Pasak.

A rewarding side trip takes you up onto the **Bolaven Plateau** and to some impressive waterfalls, including Tat Fan. This is also the place to try the adrenaline-fuelled Treetop Explorer experience, a jungle zipline adventure. Pass through the coffee capital of **Paksong** to buy some java before heading to beautiful Tat Lo. This is a great place to hang out and swim in the falls, undertaking gentle treks through local villages.

Continuing south, consider stopping at the village of **Kiet Ngong** to visit the elevated archaeological site of Phu Asa or try bird-spotting in the nearby forest and wetlands. This is a logical stop on the route south to **Si Phan Don** (Four Thousand Islands), an archipelago of idyllic river islands where the farming and fishing life have not changed much for a century or more. Swing in a hammock and relax, before moving on to Cambodia or heading to Thailand via Chong Mek.

Top: Patuxai monument (p130), Vientiane
Bottom: Sun-dried coffee beans, Bolaven Plateau (p219)

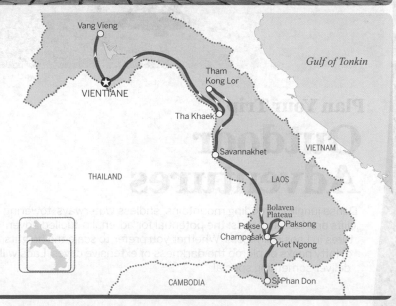

Cyclist on a valley road

Outdoor Adventures

Dense jungles, brooding mountains, endless waterways, towering cliffs and hairpin bends: the potential for adrenalin-fuelled adventures in Laos is limitless. Whether you prefer to scale the heights of lofty peaks or plumb the darkness of extensive caves, Laos will deliver something special.

©MARK WATSON/HIGHLUX/GETTY IMAGES/FLICKR RF/LONELY PLANET ©

When to Go

November to February

This is the cool, dry season and considered the best time for activities like trekking, cycling and motorbiking. Trekking in higher altitude places like Phongsali may be better in spring or autumn, as the winter can be very cold at 1500m, but it is a great time of year to trek in central and southern Laos.

March to May

Temperatures regularly hit 40°C during the hot season. Common sense dictates that this is a good time to go underground and do some cave exploring around Vang Vieng or Tha Khaek or cool off with some kayaking on the Nam Ou (Ou River) or tubing on the Nam Song (Song River).

June to October

The wet season is the time for water-based activities such as rafting or kayaking, as even the smaller rivers have a bit more volume at this time of year.

jungle hikes to pristine waterfalls and village walks in remote areas. The scenery is often breathtaking, featuring plunging highland valleys, tiers of rice paddies and soaring limestone mountains.

Treks are mostly run by small local tour operators and have English-speaking guides. Prices, including all food, guides, transport, accommodation and park fees, start at about US$25 per person per day for larger groups. For more specialised long treks into remote areas, prices can run into several hundred dollars. In most cases you can trek with as few as two people, with per person costs falling with larger groups.

Where to Go

➡ **Nam Ha NPA** (p104) Luang Namtha has developed an award-winning ecotourism project for visits to local ethnic-minority villages in the national park.

➡ **Phongsali Province** (p88) Explore fascinating hill-tribe terrain in one of the most authentic trekking destinations in the region. Mountainous and chilly in winter, multiday treks include traditional homestays with the colourful Akha people.

➡ **Phu Hin Bun NPA** (p185) A karst of thousands, this national park offers sublime scenery with towering limestone peaks and snaking rivers.

➡ **Se Pian NPA** (p219) Community-run trekking trips provide easy access to some deep forest.

➡ **Dong Natad** (p197) Treks through beautiful landscapes, organised by Savannakhet's eco-guide unit.

Trekking

Trekking in Laos is all about exploring the National Protected Areas (NPAs) and visiting the colourful ethnic-minority villages, many of which host overnight trekking groups. Anything is possible, from half-day hikes to weeklong expeditions that include cycling and kayaking. Most treks have both a cultural and an environmental focus, with trekkers sleeping in village homestays and money going directly to some of the poorest communities in the country. There are now a dozen or more areas you can choose from. Less strenuous walks include

Cycling

Laos is slowly but steadily establishing itself as a cycling destination. For hard-core cyclists, the mountains of northern Laos are the ultimate destination. For those who like a gentler workout, meandering along Mekong villages is memorable, particularly in southern Laos around Si Phan Don.

In most places that see a decent number of tourists, simple single-speed bicycles can be hired for around 20,000K per day. Better mountain bikes will cost from 40,000K to 80,000K per day or US$5 to US$10. Serious tourers should bring their own bicycle. The choice in Laos is fairly limited compared with neighbouring Thailand or Cambodia.

Several tour agencies and guesthouses offer mountain-biking tours, ranging in duration from a few hours to several weeks.

Where to Go

➡ **Luang Namtha** (p103) Cycle through ethnic-minority villages.

➡ **Luang Prabang** (p35) Biking is a great way to get around the old town or explore some of the surrounding countryside.

➡ **Si Phan Don** (p232) Cycle past peaceful rice paddies and raging waterfalls.

➡ **Udomxai** (p97) Three-day cycle challenge to Chom Ong Caves.

Motorbiking

For those with a thirst for adventure, motorbike trips into remote areas of Laos are unforgettable. The mobility of two wheels is unrivalled. Motorbikes can traverse trails that even the hardiest 4WD cannot follow. It puts you closer to the countryside – its smells, people and scenery – compared with getting around by car or bus. Just remember to watch the road when the scenery is sublime. Motorbiking is still the mode of transport for many Lao residents, so you'll find repair shops everywhere. If you are not confident riding a motorbike, it's comparatively cheap to hire someone to drive it for you. For those seeking true adventure there is no better way to go.

Tham Kong Lor (p179)

Where to Go

➡ **The Loop** (p182) Tame the back roads of uncharted central Laos in this motorbike circuit out of Tha Khaek.

➡ **Southern Swing** (p230) Explore some off-the-beaten-path places in southern Laos with this motorbike adventure up on to the Bolaven Plateau and beyond.

SAFETY FOR HIKERS

➡ Don't stray from established paths, as there is unexploded ordnance (UXO) in many parts of the country.

➡ Hire a local guide; they're inexpensive, speak the language and understand indigenous culture.

➡ Dogs can be aggressive; a stout stick can come in handy.

➡ Invest in a pair of boots with ankle support.

➡ Carry a mosquito net if trekking in malarial zones of the region.

➡ Wear quality socks and repellent to reduce the likelihood of leeches.

➡ Carry water-purification tablets.

➡ Take along some snack bars or energy snacks to avoid getting riced out on longer treks.

Tubing on the Nam Song (p164), Vang Vieng

→ **West Vang Vieng** (p168) Delve deep into the limestone karsts that pepper the west bank of the Nam Song (Song River) with this scenically stunning motorbike ride.

Boat Trips, Kayaking & Tubing

With the Mekong cutting a swathe through the heart of the country, it is hardly surprising to find that boat trips are a major drawcard here. There are also opportunities to explore small jungled tributaries leading to remote minority villages.

Kayaking has exploded in popularity in Laos in the past few years, particularly around Luang Prabang, Nong Khiaw and Vang Vieng, all popular destinations for a spot of paddling. Kayaking trips start from around US$25 per person and are often combined with cycling.

Tubing down the river has long been a popular activity in Vang Vieng and is now a more sedate affair with the clamp down on riverside bars, rope swings and aerial runways. Tubing is a lot of fun, but it's a safer experience sober.

Where to Go

→ **Huay Xai to Luang Prabang** (p112) Down the mighty Mekong from the Golden Triangle via Pak Beng to the old royal capital of Laos.

→ **Nong Khiaw to Muang Ngoi Neua** (p82) A short but very sweet ride passing through a striking landscape of karst limestone.

→ **Si Phan Don** (p232) A kayak trip or boat is the only way to see the Four Thousand Islands, where the Mekong spreads its girth to around 13km.

→ **Tham Kong Lor** (p180) Cruise through this otherworldly 7km cave system – the Lao answer to the River Styx.

→ **Vang Vieng** (p163) Go with the flow on the Nam Song in the tubing capital of Laos.

Rock Climbing & Caving

When it comes to organised climbing, Vang Vieng and Tha Khaek have some of the best climbing in Southeast Asia, along with excellent instructors and safe equipment. Climbing costs from about US$25

ZIPLINING

Ziplining has, well, quite literally taken off in Laos. The Gibbon Experience (p113) in Bokeo Nature Reserve pioneered the use of ziplines to glide through the forest where the gibbons roam. Stay overnight in tree houses and test drive the Gibbon Spa for a massage in the most memorable of locations.

Ecotourism pioneer Green Discovery (p203) now offers an alternative zipline experience for thrill seekers in southern Laos. Its Treetop Explorer tour is an exciting network of vertiginous ziplines passing over the semi-evergreen canopy of the south's Dong Hua Sao National Protected Area (NPA). Ride so close to a giant waterfall you can taste the spray on your lips.

Vang Vieng has recently emerged as a zipline centre with several companies offering aerial adventures among the karst, including the Vang Vieng Challenge (p166).

per person for a group of four and rise for more specialised climbs or for instruction.

Real caving of the spelunker variety is not really on offer unless undertaking a professional expedition. However, there are many extensive cave systems that are open to visitors.

Where to Go

➡ **Vang Vieng** (p163) More than 200 rock-climbing routes – many of them bolted – up the limestone cliffs, plus some impressive caves to explore.

➡ **Vieng Xai Caves** (p78) Underground base and wartime capital of the Pathet Lao communists, these caves are set beneath stunning limestone rock formations.

➡ **Tham Kong Lor** (p180) This river cave is not for the faint-hearted, but offers one of the most memorable underground experiences in Laos.

➡ **Tham Lot Se Bang Fai** (p189) The most impressive of Khammuan's cave systems; a river plunges 6.5km through a limestone mountain and can only be explored between January and March.

Animal Encounters

While wildlife-spotting may not be quite as straightforward as on the Serengeti, it is still possible to have some memorable encounters in Laos.

Where to Go

➡ **Gibbon Experience** (p113) Take to the trees to live like a gibbon in the jungle canopy at this celebrated ecotourism project.

➡ **Elephant Conservation Center** (p276) Learn about the life of the Laotian elephant at this superb conservation centre near Sainyabuli.

➡ **Si Phan Don** (p232) The freshwater Irrawaddy dolphin is one of the rarest mammals on earth, with fewer than 100 inhabiting stretches of the Mekong. View them in their natural habitat off the shore of Don Khon in southern Laos.

➡ **Nam Nern Night Safari** (p80) The Nam Et/ Phou Louey NPA is the last official home of tigers in Laos, and this exciting night trip by boat uses torchlight to scope out forest animals coming to the river to drink.

➡ **Kuang Si Rescue Centre** (p61) Tat Kuang Si is a must-visit destination thanks to its iconic menthol-blue waters, plus the chance to see Asiatic Wild Moon bears saved from the wildlife trade.

Regions at a Glance

For many short-stay visitors, Luang Prabang is their Laos experience. And a mighty impressive one it is too, thanks to its deserved World Heritage Site status. Laos' other main city, its capital Vientiane, may be bucolic for an Asian city, but it hits home on the charm stakes, with attractive cafes, stylish restaurants and lively little bars.

Beyond lies northern Laos, a landscape of towering mountains and dense forests that is home to extensive national parks, rare wildlife and some of the most colourful minorities in the region.

The middle of the country is one of the least travelled regions. Some of the most dramatic cave systems in Asia are found here, together with spectacular scenery and crumbling colonial-era towns. Head south to live life in the slow lane. The Mekong islands of Si Phan Don suck people in for longer than expected, and there is a real buzz on the Bolaven Plateau – not just from the coffee.

Luang Prabang & Around

Food
Activities
Shopping

Wining & Dining

World-class dining is on the menu, with many impressive eateries set in beautifully restored colonial-era properties. As the evening moves on, there are some bohemian little bars and swanky watering holes.

Outside Luang Prabang

It's not all temples and monks in Luang Prabang, despite the iconic imagery. Just beyond the 'burbs lie action and adventure, including inviting waterfalls, mountain-bike trails and ziplines.

Art & Antiquities

The night market on the main drag is lit up with fairy lights and draws visitors to browse its textiles and trinkets. Around town are art galleries and antique shops that reward the curious shopaholic.

p34

Northern Laos

Adventure
Boat Trips
History

Massive Jungle

The jungle is massive in northern Laos. This region is home to rewarding national parks and the best trekking in the whole country, not to mention cycling, kayaking and ziplining.

All Aboard

The Mekong meander from the Golden Triangle down to lovely Luang Prabang is one of the most iconic river trips in the region. Smaller rivers reward with fairy-tale scenery, particularly the Nam Ou (Ou River) around Nong Khiaw.

On the Trail of War

The convoluted history of modern Laos comes alive here. Discover the Vieng Xai Caves where the Pathet Lao based their underground government while dodging US bombs, or explore the Plain of Jars, one of the most contested areas in the country in the 1960s.

p64

Vientiane, Vang Vieng & Around

Food
Activities
Shopping

Fine Dining

Vientiane's spectrum of global cuisine ranges from Italian to Japanese. But perhaps its ace card is its chic French restaurants, so redolent of Indochina they could make the Seine glow green with envy.

Healthy Living

Vientiane has great bike tours, yoga classes, running clubs, swimming pools and, come the early morning, free Mao-style mass exercises by the Mekong riverfront.

Tailor-Made Shopping

Expect tasteful locally sourced soap shops and silk boutiques hawking made-to-measure chemises, boho dresses and pashminas. You can still buy lacquer Tintin prints or old Russian watches if that's your thing.

p126

Central Laos

Caves
Architecture
Adventure

Going Underground

Central Laos is honeycombed with caves ranging from small, Buddha-ornamented grottoes with green lagoons, to monstrous river caves, such as Tham Kong Lor, which is cloaked in preternatural darkness.

Colonial-Era Towns

French colonials left not just boule and baguettes here, but also some elegant architecture, still seen today in cities like Tha Khaek and Savannakhet, and ranging from beautifully restored to ghostly decrepit.

Two-Wheeled Touring

Hit the Loop on a motorbike or, if training for the Tour de Laos, bicycle, and experience sublime scenery and destinations a world away from the tourist trail of mainstream Southeast Asia.

p174

Southern Laos

Rivers
Activities
Adventure

Mekong Islands

Zoning out in Si Phan Don is the quintessential southern Laos experience, but do prise yourself away your hammock to engage with laid-back locals or kayak around this sublime slice of the Mekong.

Walks & Waterfalls

Jungle walks in a clutch of national parks lead to minority villages, crumbling temples and some of Laos' highest waterfalls. Combine your trek with a village homestay for the ultimate experience.

Bike Trips

Southern Laos is ripe for exploration by mountain bike or motorbike. New pavement has spread beyond the main highways making exploration as easy as ever, including the legendary Ho Chi Minh Trail.

p200

On the Road

Luang Prabang & Around

Best Places to Eat

➡ Dyen Sabai (p54)
➡ Le Banneton (p53)
➡ Coconut Garden (p54)
➡ The Apsara (p54)
➡ Tamarind (p54)

Best Places to Sleep

➡ La Résidence Phou Vao (p53)
➡ The Apsara (p50)
➡ Satri House (p52)
➡ Amantaka (p52)
➡ Sofitel Luang Prabang (p52)

Why Go?

Luang Prabang slows your pulse and awakens your imagination with its combination of world-class comfort and spiritual nourishment. Sitting at the sacred confluence of the Mekong River and the Nam Khan (Khan River), nowhere else can lay claim to this Unesco-protected gem's romance of 33 gilded wats, saffron-clad monks, faded Indochinese villas and exquisite Gallic cuisine.

Over the last 20 years Luang Prabang has seen a flood of investment, with once-leprous French villas being revived as fabulous – though affordable – boutique hotels, and some of the best chefs in southeast Asia moving in. The population has swollen, and yet still the peninsula remains as sleepy and friendly as a village, as if time has stood still here.

Beyond the evident history and heritage of the old French town are aquamarine waterfalls, top trekking opportunities, meandering mountain bike trails, kayaking trips, river cruises and outstanding natural beauty, the whole ensemble encircled by hazy green mountains.

When to Go

Luang Prabang

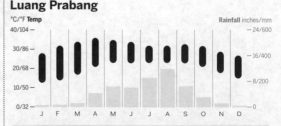

Nov–Feb The ideal season to visit weather-wise, but as this is no secret it's also peak tourist season.

Mar–May Hot season with some hazy skies from slash-and-burn cultivation; some like to join in the Pi Mai celebrations.

Jun–Oct The wet season sees numbers and prices, plummet – great if you don't mind the odd downpour and extreme humidity.

LUANG PRABANG
ຫລວງພະບາງ

POP 55,000 / ☎ 071

History

Legend has it that Luang Prabang's founder was Phunheu Nhanheu, a sexually ambiguous character with a bright-red face and a stringy body. His/her ceremonial effigies are kept hidden within Wat Wisunarat, only appearing during Pi Mai (Lao New Year), but models are widely sold as souvenirs.

Known as Muang Sawa (Muang Sua) from 698, then Xiang Dong Xiang Thong (City of Gold) from the 11th century, a city-state here passed between the Nanzhao (Yunnanese), Khmer and greater Mongol empires over

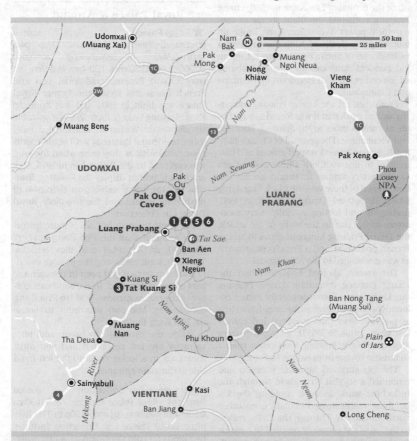

Luang Prabang & Around Highlights

❶ Luang Prabang (p35) Watching the dawn call to alms as locals give their daily offering to the monks.

❷ Pak Ou Caves (p60) Cruising up the Mekong River to this holy site brimming with buddha images.

❸ Tat Kuang Si (p61) Plunging into menthol-blue waters, some of the most beautiful in all of Laos.

❹ Wat Xieng Thong (p40) Marvelling at the sweeping roof of the oldest and most beautiful temple in Luang Prabang's centre.

❺ Handicraft Night Market (p56) Seeking out memorable souvenirs in Luang Prabang's famous night market and old curiosity shops.

❻ Bamboo Tree Cooking Class (p48) Learning a few memorable Lao dishes after a half-day's lesson, which includes a takeaway cookbook and visit to the market.

several centuries. It flourished at the heart of Lan Xang, following that kingdom's creation in 1353 by Khmer-supported conqueror Fa Ngum. In 1512, Lan Xang's King Visoun accepted the Pha Bang, a celebrated Buddha image, as a gift from the Khmer monarchy. The city was renamed in its honour as Luang (Great/Royal) Prabang (Pha Bang).

Although Viang Chan (Vientiane) became the capital of Lan Xang in 1560, Luang Prabang remained the main source of monarchical power. When Lan Xang broke up following the death of King Suriya Vongsa in 1695, one of Suriya's grandsons set up an independent kingdom in Luang Prabang, which competed with kingdoms in Vientiane and Champasak.

From then on, the Luang Prabang monarchy was so weak that it was forced to pay tribute at various times to the Siamese, Burmese and Vietnamese. The reversal of China's Taiping Rebellion caused several groups of 'Haw' militias to flee southern China and reform as mercenary armies or bandit gangs. The best known of these was the Black Flag Army which devastated Luang Prabang in 1887, destroying and looting virtually every monastery in the city. In the wake of the attack, the Luang Prabang kingdom chose to accept French protection, and a French commissariat was established in the royal capital.

The French allowed Laos to retain the Luang Prabang monarchy. Luang Prabang quickly became a favourite post for French colonials seeking a refuge as far away from Paris as possible. Even during French Indochina's last years, prior to WWII, a river trip from Saigon to Luang Prabang took longer than a steamship voyage from Saigon to France.

The city survived Japanese invasion and remained a royalist stronghold through the Indochina wars, as such avoiding the US bombing that destroyed virtually every other northern Lao city. Through the 1980s, collectivisation of the economy resulted in a major exodus of business people, aristocracy and intelligentsia. With little money for or interest in conserving the city's former regal-colonial flavour, Luang Prabang became a ghost of its former self. But after 1989, the return of private enterprise meant that long-closed shops reopened and once-dilapidated villas were converted into hotels and guesthouses. The city received Unesco World Heritage status in 1995, accelerating the process, raising the city's international profile and, in principle, ensuring that any new development in the old city remains true to the architectural spirit of the original. Such has been the city's international popularity in the 21st century that in some quarters, guesthouses, restaurants, boutiques and galleries now outnumber actual homes.

⊙ Sights

⊙ Royal Palace & Around

★ **Royal Palace**   MUSEUM
(ພະຣາຊະວັງຫຼວງແກວ, Ho Kham; Map p44; ☏ 071-212470; Th Sisavangvong; admission 30,000K; ⊙ 8-11.30am & 1.30-4pm Wed-Mon, last entry 3.30pm) Evoking traditional Lao and French beaux-arts styles, the former Royal Palace was built in 1904 and was home to King Sisavang Vong (r 1905–59), whose statue stands outside. Within are tasteful, decidedly sober residential quarters, with some rooms preserved much as they were when the king was captured by the Pathet Lao in 1975. Separate outbuildings display the **Floating Buddha photography exhibition** (Map p44) of meditating monks and the five-piece Royal Palace Car Collection.

No single treasure in Laos is more historically resonant than the **Pha Bang** (ພະບາງ; Map p44), an 83cm-tall gold-alloy buddha. To find it, walk east along the palace's exterior or southern terrace and peep in between the bars at the eastern end. In the southeast corner of the palace gardens, **Wat Ho Pha Bang** (ວັດຫໍພະບາງ; Map p44) was built to house the Pha Bang Buddha.

Inside the museum, footwear and photography are not permitted and you must leave bags in a locker room to the left-hand side of the main entrance.

Royal Palace Car Collection   MUSEUM
(Map p44; Royal Palace Grounds; ⊙ 8-11.30am & 1.30-4pm Wed-Mon, last entry 3.30pm) The five-piece Royal Palace Car Collection includes two 1960s Lincoln Continentals, a rare winged-edged 1958 Edsel Citation and a dilapidated Citroën DS. Plus a wooden speedboat the king used to take upriver to visit his vegetable garden.

Wat Mai Suwannaphumaham   BUDDHIST TEMPLE
(ວັດໃໝສຸວັນນະພູມອາຣາມ; Map p44; Th Sisavangvong; 10,000K; ⊙ 8am-5pm) Wat Mai is one of the city's most sumptuous monasteries, its wooden *sĭm* (ordination hall) sporting a

LUANG PRABANG IN...

Two Days

After breakfasting on coffee and croissants at **Le Banneton** (p53), immerse yourself in the **old town** of Luang Prabang with a stroll around the temples and historic buildings. Make sure you include the striking temple of **Wat Xieng Thong** (p40) and the **Royal Palace**, where you can now see the fabled **Pha Bang buddha statue**, as well as some of the small alleyways that link the Mekong and Nam Khan riverfronts. Try lunch at **Joma Bakery Cafe** (p54) on the slow-flowing Nam Khan and dinner after sunset on the banks of the mother Mekong. On your second day, rise early to observe the **tak bat** as the monasteries empty of their monks in search of alms (to avoid the scrum of photographers on the main road, follow it through the peninsula's interior). Continue to the lively **morning market** (p53) before taking a boat trip upriver to the **Pak Ou Caves** (p60). If time allows, spend the afternoon trekking, ziplining and swimming around the lush waterfalls at **Tat Kuang Si** (p61). Round things off with a delicious Laotion dinner at **Tamarind** (p54) followed by a night on the town at buzzing **Utopia** (p55).

Four Days

Once you've explored the old town and the headline attractions, it's time for an adrenaline buzz or some cultural immersion. For adrenaline seekers, choose from hiking, biking or kayaking in the surrounding countryside. **Tiger Trail** (p48) or **Green Discovery** (Map p44; ☑071-212093; www.greendiscoverylaos.com; 44/3 Th Sisavangvong; ⊗8am-9pm) are reliable tour operators to hook up with. For more culture than adventure, consider a cooking class at **Tamarind** (p47) or **Bamboo Tree** (p48), a weaving class at **Ock Pop Tok** (p47), or a visit to the excellent **Traditional Arts & Ethnology Centre** (p39). Definitely try a gastronomic blowout at one of the classy international restaurants in town such as **Tangor** (p54) or **Blue Lagoon** (p55). Still want more? Check out **La Pistoche** (p56) for the equivalent of a beach experience in town. And if you want a day trip that includes a boat ride and ziplines, head to the recently opened **Green Jungle Flight** (p60).

five-tiered roof in archetypal Luang Prabang style, while the unusually roofed front verandah features detailed golden reliefs depicting scenes from village life, the Ramayana and Buddha's penultimate birth. It was spared destruction in 1887 by the Haw gangs who reportedly found it too beautiful to harm. Since 1894 it has been home to the Sangharat, the head of Lao Buddhism.

★**Phu Si**   HILL
(ພູສີ; Map p44; 20,000K; ⊗8am-6pm) Dominating the old city centre and a favourite with sunset junkies, the 100m-tall Phu Si (prepare your legs for a steep 329-step ascent) is crowned by a 24m gilded stupa called **That Chomsi** (ທາດຈອມສີ; Map p44; admission incl with Phu Si). Viewed from a distance, especially when floodlit at night, the structure seems to float in the hazy air like a chandelier.

Beside a flagpole on the same summit there's a small remnant anti-aircraft cannon left from the war years.

Ascending Phu Si from the northern side, stop at Wat Pa Huak (ວັດປາຮວກ; Map p44; admission by donation). The gilded, carved front doors are usually locked but an attendant will open them for a tip. Inside, the original 19th-century murals show historic scenes along the Mekong River, including visits by Chinese diplomats and warriors arriving by river and horse caravans.

Reaching That Chomsi is also possible from the southern and eastern sides. Two such paths climb through large Wat Siphoutthabat Thippharam (ວັດສີພຸດທະບາດ; Map p44) FREE to a curious miniature shrine that protects a Buddha Footprint (Map p44) FREE. If this really is his rocky imprint, then the Buddha must have been the size of a brontosaurus. Directly southwest of here a series of new gilded buddhas are nestled into rocky clefts and niches around Wat Thammothayalan (Map p44); this monastery is free to visit if you don't climb beyond to That Chomsi.

Luang Prabang

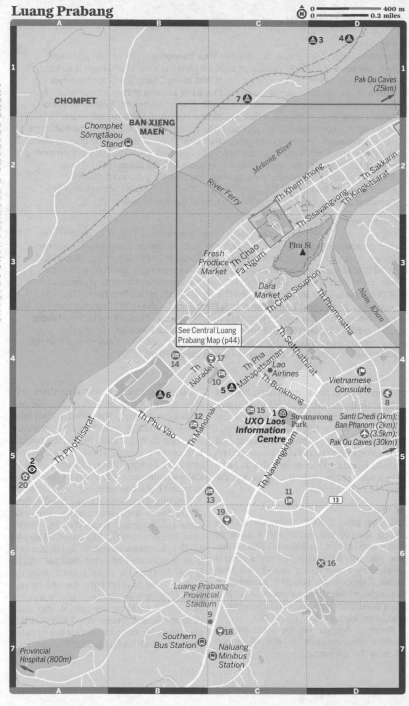

CHOMPET

BAN XIENG MAEN

Chomphet
Sŏrngtăaou
Stand

Pak Ou Caves
(25km)

Mekong River

River Ferry

Th Khem Khong

Th Sisavangvong

Th Kingkitsarat

Th Sakkarin

Fresh
Produce
Market

Th Chao
Fa Ngum

Phu Si

Dara
Market

Th Chao Sisuphon

Th Phommatha

Nam Khan

See Central Luang
Prabang Map (p44)

Th Setthathirat

14

Th
Noradet

17

10

Th Pha
Mahapatsaman

Lao
Airlines

6

5

Th Bunkhong

Vietnamese
Consulate

8

Th Phothisarat

Th Phu Vao

Th Manomai

12

15

1

UXO Laos
Information
Centre

Suvanavong
Park

Santi Chedi (1km);
Ban Phanom (2km);
(3.5km);
Pak Ou Caves (30km)

2

20

Th Naviengkham

13

19

11

13

16

Luang Prabang
Provincial
Stadium

9

Southern
Bus Station

18

Naluang
Minibus
Station

Provincial
Hospital (800m)

0   400 m
0   0.2 miles

Luang Prabang

Wat Pa Phon Phao BUDDHIST TEMPLE
FREE An easy 3km walk or bicycle ride northeast of town is Wat Pa Phon Phao, a forest meditation wat famous for the teachings of the late abbot Ajahn Saisamut. Saisamut's funeral in 1992 was the largest and most well-attended monk's funeral Laos had seen in decades.

TAEC MUSEUM
(Traditional Arts & Ethnology Centre; Map p44; ☑071-253364; www.taeclaos.org; off Th Kitsarat; 25,000K; ☺9am-6pm Tue-Sun) 🖉 Visiting this professionally presented three-room museum is a must to learn about northern Laos' various hill-tribe cultures, especially if planning a trek. There's just enough to inform without overloading a beginner, including a range of ethnic costumes and a brilliant new exhibition, 'Seeds of Culture: From Living Plants to Handicrafts'. TAEC sits within a former French judge's mansion that was among the city's most opulent buildings of the 1920s. There's a cafe and a shop selling handicrafts and pictorials.

◉ Xieng Mouane Area

Wat Pa Phai BUDDHIST TEMPLE
(ວັດປ່າໄຜ່; Map p44; Th Sisavang Vatthana) Over the gilded and carved wooden facade, Wat Pa Phai has a classic Tai-Lao fresco depicting everyday scenes of late 19th-century Lao life.

Villa Xieng Mouane ARCHITECTURE
(ເຮືອນມໍລະດົກຊຽງມວນ; Map p44; Th Xotikhoumman) Footpaths lead back from the commercial main drag into a little oasis of palm-shaded calm around the Villa Xieng Mouane, an authentic traditional longhouse on tree-trunk stilts that is now partly used as an occasional exhibition centre.

Heritage House Information Centre GALLERY
(Map p44; ☺9am-5pm Mon-Sat) The Heritage House Information Centre has computers on which you can peruse a series of photos and descriptions of the city's numerous Unesco-listed historic buildings.

Wat Xieng Mouane BUDDHIST TEMPLE
(ວັດຊຽງມວນ; Map p44; Th Xotikhoumman; ☺8am-5pm) FREE In the old quarter, Wat Xieng Mouane's ceiling is painted with gold *naga* (river serpent) and the elaborate *háang thien* (candle rail) has *nagas* at either end. With backing from Unesco and New Zealand, the monks' quarters have been restored as a classroom for training young novices and monks in the artistic skills needed to maintain and preserve Luang Prabang's temples. Among these skills are woodcarving, painting and Buddha-casting, all of which came to a virtual halt after 1975.

Wat Choumkhong BUDDHIST TEMPLE
(ວັດຈຸມຄອງ; Map p44; Th Xotikhoumman) FREE The garden around the little Wat Choumkhong is particularly attractive when its poinsettia trees blush red. Built in 1843, the monastery takes its name from a Buddha statue that was originally cast from a melted-down gong.

◉ The Upper Peninsula

The northern tip of the peninsula formed by the Mekong River and the Nam Khan is jam-packed with glittering palm-fronded mon-asteries. Well before dawn they resonate mysteriously with drumbeats and as the morning mists swirl they disgorge a silent procession of saffron-clad monks. The most celebrated monastery is Wat Xieng Thong, but several others are quieter, less touristy, and intriguing in their own right.

A fine viewpoint overlooks the river junc-tion from outside Hotel Mekong Riverside. At the peninsula's far tip, a bamboo bridge (toll 5000K return) that's rebuilt each dry season crosses the Nam Khan, allowing access to a 'beach' and basic sunset-watching bar and offering a shortcut to Ban Xang Khong, 1km northeast.

★**Wat Xieng Thong**　　　BUDDHIST TEMPLE
(ວັດຊຽງທອງ; Map p44; off Th Sakkarin; 20,000K; ⊗8am-5pm) Luang Prabang's best-known monastery is centred on a 1560 *sĭm* (ordina-tion hall). Its roofs sweep low to the ground and there's a stunning 'tree of life' mosaic set on its western exterior wall. Close by are sev-eral stupas and three compact little chapel halls called *hŏr*. **Hŏr Đại**, shaped like a tall tomb, now houses a standing Buddha. The **Hŏr Đại Pha Sai-nyàat**, dubbed La Chapelle Rouge – Red Chapel – by the French, contains a rare reclining Buddha.

Wat Pakkhan　　　BUDDHIST TEMPLE
(ວັດປາກຄານ; Map p44; Th Sakkarin) **FREE**
Dated 1737 but rebuilt a century ago, Wat Pakkhan has a simple, appealingly archaic look with angled support struts holding up the lower of its two superposed roofs. Across the road, the ochre colonial-era villa that now forms **Unesco offices** was once the city's customs office.

Wat Souvannakhili　　　BUDDHIST TEMPLE
(ວັດສຸວັນນະຄີລີ, Wat Khili; Map p44; off Th Sakkarin) **FREE** The most prominent build-ing of Wat Souvannakhili looks more like a colonial-era mansion than a monastery, but the small *sĭm* is a classic of now-rare Xieng Khuang style.

Wat Sensoukaram　　　BUDDHIST TEMPLE
(ວັດແສນສຸກອາຮາມ; Map p44; Th Sakkarin) **FREE** Rich ruby-red walls with intricate gold overlay give Wat Sensoukaram one of the most dazzling facades of all of Luang Pra-bang's temples. The name reportedly refers

Wat Xieng Thong

to the initial donation of 100,000K made to build it, a handsome sum back in 1718.

◉ Wat Wisunarat (Wat Visoun) Area

Two of Luang Prabang's most historically im-portant temples lie amid palms in pleasant if traffic-buzzed grounds offering glimpses towards Phu Si.

Wat Wisunarat　　　BUDDHIST TEMPLE
(ວັດວິຊຸນ, Wat Visoun; Map p44; Th Wisunarat; admission 20,000K; ⊗8am-5pm) Though touted as one of Luang Prabang's oldest operating temples, it's actually an 1898 reconstruction built following the Black Flag raids. Peruse a sizeable collection of old gilded 'Calling for Rain' buddhas with long sinuous arms held to each side. These were placed here, along with some medieval ordination stones, for their protection, having been rescued from various abandoned or ravaged temples.

That Makmo　　　BUDDHIST SHRINE
(ທາດໝາກໂມ; Map p44; Th Phommatha) This lumpy hemispherical stupa is commonly nicknamed That Makmo, which translates as 'Watermelon Stupa'. Originally constructed in 1503, it was pillaged for hidden treasures during the 1887 destruction and the latest renovation in 1932 coated the stupa in drab grey concrete.

◉ South of the Centre

★**UXO Laos Information Centre**　　　MUSEUM
(Map p38; ☎071-252073, 020-22575123; www.uxolao.gov.la; off Th Naviengkham; admission by

donation; ⊘8-11.45am & 2-4pm Mon-Fri) The sobering UXO Laos Information Centre helps you get a grip on the devastation Laos suffered in the Second Indochina War and how nearly 40 years later death or injury from unexploded ordnance (UXO) remains an everyday reality in several provinces. If you miss it here, there's a similar centre in Phonsavan. In September 2016 President Obama announced that the US would provide an additional US$90 million to address the problem of UXO in Laos over the next three years.

Wat Manorom   BUDDHIST TEMPLE
(ວັດມະໂນລົມ, Wat Mano, Wat Manolom; Map p38; Th Pha Mahapatsaman) FREE Winding lanes to the west lead to Wat Manorom, set amid frangipani trees just outside what were once the city walls (now invisible). This is possibly the oldest temple site in Luang Prabang and the *sĭm* contains a sitting 6m-tall bronze Buddha originally cast in 1372. During the 1887 devastation the statue was hacked apart,

but surviving elements were reconstituted in 1919; the missing limbs were replaced with concrete falsies covered in gold leaf in 1971.

Wat That Luang   BUDDHIST TEMPLE
(ວັດທາດຫຼວງ; Map p38; 10,000K; ⊘8am-6pm) Traditionally the cremation site for Lao royalty, legend has it that Wat That Luang was originally established by Ashokan missionaries in the 3rd century BC. However, the current large *sĭm* (ordination hall) is an 1818 rebuild whose leafy column-capitals look more Corinthian than Indian. The *sĭm* is bracketed by two stupas, the larger of which reputedly contains the ashes of King Sisavang Vong, even though it was built in 1910, 50 years before his death.

Ock Pop Tok Living
Crafts Centre   ARTS CENTRE
(OPT; Map p38; ☑071-212597; www.ockpoptok.com; ⊘9am-5pm) 🏊 Set serenely close to the Mekong, this beautiful, traditionally styled

---

TAK BAT: THE MONKS' CALL TO ALMS

Daily at dawn, saffron-clad monks pad barefoot through the streets while pious townsfolk place tiny balls of sticky rice in their begging bowls. It's a quiet, meditative ceremony through which monks demonstrate their vows of poverty and humility while lay Buddhists gain spiritual merit by the act of respectful giving.

Although such processions occur all over Laos, old Luang Prabang's peaceful atmosphere and extraordinary concentration of mist-shrouded temples mean that the morning's perambulations along Th Sakkarin and Th Kamal create an especially romantic scene. Sadly, as a result, tourists are progressively coming to outnumber participants. Despite constant campaigns begging visitors not to poke cameras in the monks' faces, the amateur paparazzi seem incapable of keeping a decent distance. Sensitive, non-participating observers should follow these guidelines:

➡ Stand across the road from the procession or better still watch inconspicuously from the window of your hotel (where possible).

➡ Refrain from taking photos or at best do so from a considerable distance with a long zoom. Never use flash.

➡ Maintain the silence (arrive by bicycle or on foot; don't chatter).

If it's genuinely meaningful to you, you may take part in the ceremony – meaningful in this case implies not wanting to be photographed in the process. Joining in takes some preparation and knowledge to avoid causing unspoken offence. Don't be pushed into half-hearted participation by sales-folk along the route. Such vendors contribute to the procession's commercialisation and many sell overpriced, low-grade rice that is worse than giving nothing at all. Instead, organise some *kao kai noi* (the best grade sticky rice) to be cooked to order by your guesthouse. Or buy it fresh-cooked from the morning market before the procession. Carry it in a decent rice-basket, not a plastic bag. Before arriving, dress respectfully as you would for a temple (covered upper arms and chest, skirts for women, long trousers for men). Wash your hands and don't use perfumes or lotions that might flavour the rice as you're handing it out.

Once in situ, remove your shoes and put a sash or scarf across your left shoulder. Women should kneel with their feet folded behind them (don't sit) while men may stand. Avoid making eye contact with the monks.

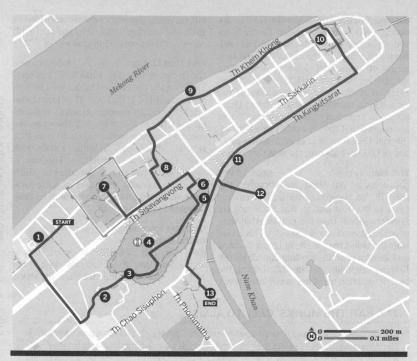

🚶 City Walk
Old Luang Prabang

START MORNING MARKET
END UTOPIA
LENGTH 4.5KM; FOUR TO FIVE HOURS

This walk meanders through the heart of the historic city in a leisurely half-day, assuming plenty of stops. We suggest starting bright and early to miss the afternoon heat on Phu Si, and avoiding Tuesday to fit in with museum opening times. But if you accept that it's the overall atmosphere and cafe scene that makes Luang Prabang special rather than any particular sights, the walk can work any time.

After an early stroll through the **①Morning Market** (p53) and a local breakfast, arrive at **②TAEC** (p39) where you can peruse the excellent little exhibition on northern Laos' ethnic mosaic. Suitably fuelled, try to weave your way through the untouristed little maze of residential homes to reach the southern flank of **③Phu Si** (p37). Climb to **④That Chomsi** (p37) before the day gets too hot. Or, if the air looks too hazy for city views, continue instead around the hill via Buddha's oversized **⑤footprint** (p37) and descend to the main commercial street through **⑥Wat Siphoutthabat Thippharam** (p37). If you can arrive by 11am, visit the **⑦Royal Palace Museum** (p36) to see how Lao royalty lived until 1975 and the Pha Bang Buddha statue. Afterwards meander through the palm-shaded footpaths of **⑧Xieng Mouane area** to reach the **⑨Mekong waterfront** with its inviting cafes and Lao-French colonial-era houses. If you didn't already explore them at dawn after the monks' alms procession, dip into a selection of atmospheric wats as you wander up the spine of the peninsula. Don't miss the most famous monastery of all, **⑩Wat Xieng Thong** (p40). Stroll back, taking in a stretch of the lovely **⑪Nam Khan waterfront** and, in the dry season, cross the bamboo bridge for a well-deserved lunch at delightful **⑫Dyen Sabai** (p54). If the bridge isn't there (June to November), or you are walking in the afternoon, seek the winding path to **⑬Utopia** (p55) for a drink and peaceful views of the Nam Khan.

workshop, where weavers, spinners and batik makers produce top-quality fabrics, offers free tours every half-hour. There's also a great riverside cafe serving drinks and excellent Lao food. Or try a cup of the surprisingly pleasant worm-poo tea – yes, a unique infusion made from silk-worm droppings. Better still, why not try a bamboo weaving course (p47).

◉ Across the Mekong River

For a very different 'village' atmosphere, cross the Mekong to Muang Chomphet. To get there, take a cross-river boat (local/foreigner 2000/5000K) from the navigation office (p59) behind the Royal Palace. Boats depart once they have a handful of passengers. Alternatively, boatmen at various other points on the Luang Prabang waterfront will run you across to virtually any point on the north bank for around 20,000K per boat. If water levels allow, a good excursion idea is to hire such a boat to the Wat Longkhun (p43) jetty then walk back via Ban Xieng Maen to the main crossing point. However, reaching Wat Longkhun by boat isn't always practicable due to seasonally changing sandbanks.

Above the ferry landing on the other side, a branch of **Jewel Travel Laos** (Map p44; ☏ 020-55687663; www.jeweltravellaos.com; Sisavangvong Rd, Ban Xieng Muane; ⊙8am-4pm; 🛜) rents mountain bikes (per day 50,000K). However, you'll need neither bike nor map to visit the series of attractive monasteries that are scattered east along the riverbank from the traffic-free village of Ban Xieng Maen.

Wat Xieng Maen   BUDDHIST TEMPLE
(ວັດຊຽງແມນ; Map p38; Ban Xieng Maen; 10,000K) First founded in 1592, Wat Xieng Maen gained a hallowed air in 1867 by housing the Pha Bang (p36) for seven nights while on its way back to Luang Prabang after 40 years in Thai hands. The monastery's current, colourful *sĭm* (ordination hall) contains an attractive 'family' of buddhas and has stencilled columns conspicuously inscribed with the names of US donors who paid for their renovation.

Wat Chomphet   BUDDHIST TEMPLE
(ວັດຈອມເພັດ; Map p38; Ban Xieng Maen; ⊙8am-5pm) Ban Xieng Maen's long, narrow, brick-edged 'street' slowly degrades into a rough track, eventually becoming little more than a rocky footpath. At about this point, climb an obvious 123-step stairway to find the 1888 Wat Chomphet fronted by greying twin

WORTH A TRIP

LIVING LAND FARM

Living Land (☏ 020-77778335, 020-55199208; www.livinglandlao.com; Ban Phong Van; tour per person 344,000K; ⊙8.30am-noon) 🚶 is about five clicks out of Luang Prabang, on the road to Tat Kuang Si. It's a brilliant rice farm co-operative, where you can spend half a day learning how to plant and grow sticky rice, the ubiquitous dish of Laos. This includes prepping the paddy with gregarious water buffalo Rudolph – expect to be knee-deep in glorious mud! You'll never taste rice in the same way. Kids love it.

Living Land helps educate children in disadvantaged families in the local community.

pagodas. The hilltop temple is little more than a shell, but the site offers undisturbed views of the town and river.

Wat Longkhun   BUDDHIST TEMPLE
(ວັດລອງຄຸນ; Map p38; Ban Xieng Maen; 10,000K; ⊙8am-5pm) When the coronation of a Luang Prabang king was pending, he spent three days in retreat at Wat Longkhun before ascending the throne. The central *sĭm* (ordination hall) features old murals, one of which depicts giant fish attacking shipwrecked sailors. Ask at the ticket desk for the key required to visit **Tham Sakkalin** (admission incl with Wat Longkhun), a humid, slippery 100m-long limestone cave. It's a three-minute walk further east then up a few stairs. A few Buddha fragments are kept here. Bring your own torch (flashlight).

◉ Across the Nam Khan

In the dry season, once water levels have dropped significantly, a pair of bamboo footbridges (2000K) are constructed, making for easy access to the Nam Khan's east bank and its semi-rural neighbourhoods. When the river is high (June to November), the bridges disappear.

Crossing the southern bamboo bridge, climb steps past the highly recommended garden cafe Dyen Sabai (p54), emerging beside **Wat Punluang** (Map p44; Ban Phan Luang). **FREE**. The road to the left leads to **Watpakha Xaingaram** (Map p44) **FREE** with its ruined shell of a temple, and

Central Luang Prabang

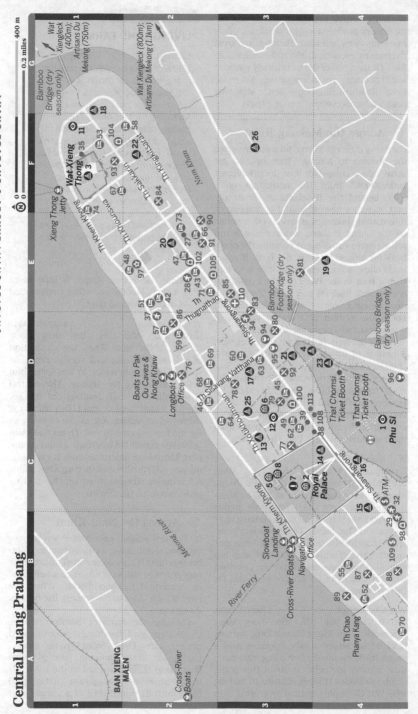

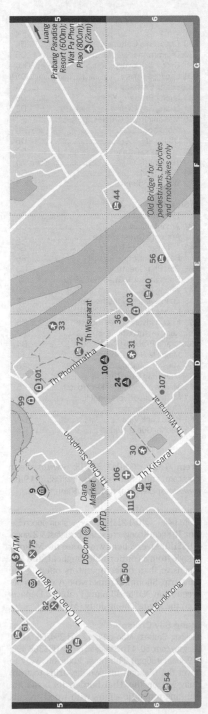

Wat Xiengleck FREE, in an Angkorian-style state of atmospheric dilapidation. Half a kilometre beyond, Ban Xang Khong has a 400m-strip of old houses and craft boutiques where you can watch weavers and papermakers at work. The most striking gallery-workshop is **Artisans du Mekong** (Ban Xang Khong; ⊙9am-4pm), behind a giant 'tusk' gateway, with its pleasant cafe.

🏃 Activities

Some of the most popular activities are based further outside of the city, but in Luang Prabang itself, it's all about yoga, massages and cookery classes.

Yoga

Luang Prabang Yoga   YOGA
(Map p44; www.luangprabangyoga.org; classes 1/1½hr 40,000/60,000K; ⊙classes usually at 7.30am & 5pm) Slow down, unwind and sync your spirit to the city's relaxed vibe with yoga classes taught at serene locations, from lush riverside garden decks at Utopia (p55), to rooftop sunset views. The city's yoga co-operative keeps up-to-date information on classes and venues on its website. In our experience this is a well-run network of qualified teachers. All levels welcome.

Luang Prabang Yoga also runs relaxing three-day yoga retreats at the delicious Mandala Ou Resort (p84) in Nong Khiaw. See www.laosyogaretreats.com

Massages & Saunas

Lao Red Cross   MASSAGE, SPA
(Map p44; ☑071-253448; Th Wisunarat; sauna 15,000K, 1hr traditional/aromatherapy massage 50,000/80,000K; ⊙7am-10.30pm) 🍃 Recently renovated, this traditional blue Lao house was the original place to come for a sauna and massage before all the fancy ones arrived. It might be no frills, but well-trained staff give first-rate massages and there's a terrific sauna infused with medicinal plants that will clear your respiratory system like mentholated Drano! Now with air-con.

Donations go directly to improving the lives of the poorest villages in Laos.

Dhammada   MASSAGE
(Map p44; ☑071-212642; www.dhammada.com; Namneua Lane; per hour foot/aromatherapy massage 100,000/160,000K; ⊙11am-11pm) One of the best in town. A stylish rustic place beside a meditative lotus pond. As ever with massage it depends on who you get and how enlivened they are, so Dhammada has both

Central Luang Prabang

strong and weak reviews. We personally enjoyed it. Run by Kranchit, it's chilled, clean and restful.

River Cruises

Mekong River Cruises   BOATING

(Map p44; ☑ 030-78600017, 071-254768; www.cruisemekong.com; 22/2 Th Sakkarin, Ban Xieng Thong; tours per person incl flights to/from Bangkok US$1650-2980) Mekong River Cruises and its gorgeous boat, the *Mekong Explorer,* offer an upmarket way to explore the Mekong River in Isan. Its weeklong voyages from Ubon Ratchathani to Nong Khai sail November to March, though trip length and other logistics may change with the river's seasonal variations (eg from April to October the cruise starts and ends in Nakhon Phanom).

Apart from sightseeing on the deck and an onboard massage, there are numerous onshore excursions. You can book through **Thai**

Drem Tours (☑ 043 332113; www.thaidreamtours.com) and **Isan Explorer** (☑ 085 354 9165; www.isanexplorer.com) in Khon Kaen.

Shompoo Cruise   BOATING

(Map p44; ☑ 071-213190; www.shompoocruise.com; Th Khem Khong; cruise incl breakfast & 2 lunches US$110) An excellent way to see the Mekong in style from a comfortable longboat, and less expensive than other operators offering the same trip, Shompoo runs two-day cruises between Huay Xai and Luang Prabang. Departs from the Xieng Thong Jetty (Map p44).

Luang Say Cruise   BOATING

(Mekong Cruises; Map p44; ☑ 071-254768; www.luangsay.com; 50/4 Th Sakkarin; cruise US$362-490; ⊙ 9.30am-9.30pm) The most luxurious way to travel the Mekong on two-day trips to/from Huay Xai on the Thai border. Its boats are stunning romantic affairs with wood accents and great service. Prices depend on the season. Departs from the Xieng Thong Jetty.

Banana Boat Laos BOATING
(Map p44; 071-260654; www.bananaboatlaos.com; Ma Te Sai, Th Sisavangvong) Picking up good reviews for their combo trips such as Pak Ou Caves and Kuang Si waterfalls, Sunset Cruise and Temple View, or, most popular, Kuang Si Sun Bear Rescue Area (for which you'll pay US$45 per person for a couple, less if there more of you). Comfortable boat; friendly staff with limited English.

Courses

★ Tamarind COOKING
(Map p44; 020-77770484; www.tamarindlaos.com; Ban Wat Nong; full-day/evening course 285,000/215,000K) Join Tamarind at its lakeside pavilion for a day's tuition in the art of Lao cuisine, meeting in the morning at its restaurant before heading to the market for ingredients for classic dishes such as *mok pa* (steamed fish in banana leaves). Evening classes don't include a market visit.

Ock Pop Tok COURSE
(Map p38; 071-212597; www.ockpoptok.com; half-/full-day bamboo-weaving course 240,000/284,000K, Hmong Batik class 480,000/640,000K, 3-day natural dyeing & weaving course 1,584,000K; 8.45am-4pm Mon-Sat) Learn to weave your own scarf and textiles or take a half-day bamboo-weaving course at Ock Pop Tok. Teachers are master craftspeople, you get to keep your handiwork and lunch is included. Situated 2km past Phousy market; a free tuk-tuk will pick you up and bring you back.

LUANG PRABANG FOR CHILDREN

While wats and museums may not seem a recipe for excited children, there are now plenty of attractions in and around Luang Prabang that will get their attention. Children of all ages will love **Tat Kuang Si** (p61) and **Tat Sae** (p61) for the natural swimming pools and ziplines; the former also offers a fascinating glimpse of Asiatic Wild Moon bears in their impressive enclosure. New to Kuang Si is the **Kuang Si Butterfly Park** (p61) and **Green Jungle Flight** (p60). Boat trips on the Mekong, such as to **Pak Ou Caves** (p60), are a nice diversion for budding explorers.

Older children will enjoy the activities on offer around town like cycling or kayaking. The younger ones can spend some time on the playground and ziplines at the **ABC School** (Map p38; ☑020-56920137; per child 20,000K; ⊗3-9pm Mon-Fri, 9am-9pm Sat & Sun). There are plenty of family-friendly cafes around town, but if it's a swimming pool they crave, then it's probably better to consider accommodation beyond the old town or make for the chilled out **La Pistoche** (p56) during the day.

Bamboo Tree Cooking Class & Restaurant
COOKING

(Map p44; ☑020-22425499; bambootreelp@live.com; Th Sakkarin; cookery class 250,000K; ⊗9am-10pm) A respected chef and teacher will teach you how to cook five or six Lao dishes, such as *láhp* (minced pork salad with shallots and coriander), at Bamboo Tree's spacious and airy restaurant. You'll also receive a cookbook to take home. Classes start at 9am and finish at 2pm.

🖙 Tours

★Motolao
ADVENTURE

(Map p44; ☑020-54548449; www.motolao.com; Ban Phone Peang Rd; ⊗9am-6pm) This excellent outfit is one of the country's best motocross tour operators and has terrific two-wheel odysseys exploring authentic Lao life in the boonies that you'd usually be hard-pressed to visit. Top kit and with well-maintained bikes, this outfit is owned by dependable **Tiger Trail** (Map p44; ☑071-252655; www.laos-adventures.com; Th Sisavangvong; tours from US$50; ⊗8.30am-9pm) 🏍. It also rents mountain bikes (per day 50,000K) and Honda 250cc motorbikes (per day US$50).

E-Bus Tour
BUS

(Map p38; ☑071-253899; www.laogreengroup.com; tour US$40, child under 10 free; ⊗tours morning 8.30am-12.30pm, afternoon 1-5.30pm) Lao Green Travel's E-Bus takes passengers (up to six) around the city on a guided tour. You'll visit the local market, the Royal Palace and learn about Lao architecture, between exploring Wat Xieng Thong and its quiet backstreets. Pick-up from your hotel is available. Its office is located across from the southern bus station.

White Elephant
HIKING

(Map p44; ☑071-254481; www.white-elephant-adventures-laos.com; Th Sisavangvong; ⊗8.30am-9pm) 🏍 White Elephant is hailed for its relationships with remote Hmong and Khamu villages, allowing a deeper insight into their way of life. You can get this on solid two- or three-day trekking and bike tours. Look out for the BMW motorbike and communist flag to find its main office.

Off Road Laos
ADVENTURE

(Map p44; ☑020-598144423, 071-254695; www.offroadlaosadventures.com; Th Phommatha; 3-day trips per person for a group of 2 from US$280; ⊗8.30am-5pm Mon-Fri, to noon Sat & Sun) Offering intrepid motorcycle enthusiasts a chance to really explore a side of Laos they will never get to see by public transport. Using experienced guides, and regularly serviced top-notch Honda 250cc dirt bikes, trips can be designed bespoke depending on your interests and level of confidence. And you can store your heavy luggage at the shop.

🎊 Festivals & Events

Luang Prabang Film Festival
FILM

(LPFF; www.lpfilmfest.org) At the start of every December, the Luang Prabang Film Festival hand-picks the best new films from 10 Southeast Asian countries, with screens set up alfresco all around the city. Better still it's free.

Bun Pi Mai
CULTURAL

(Lao New Year) Large numbers of visitors converge on Luang Prabang for this 'water throwing' festival in April. Be careful of your camera getting soaked and prepare to be drenched! Advanced bookings around this time are recommended (see box, right).

Bun Awk Phansa CULTURAL
(End of the Rains Retreat) Bun Awk Phansa sees boat races on the Nam Khan in September or October. Buddhists send little boats made of banana leaves with lit candles inside downriver by night, chiefly to send the bad luck of last year away, and to also make thanks to Mother Mekong and the sentinel *naga* (river serpents) who dwell within her watery arms. Pure magic.

🛏 Sleeping

🛏 Thanon Sisavangvong & Around

Bou Pha Guesthouse GUESTHOUSE $
(Map p44; ☎ 071-252405; Th Sisavangvong; r 60,000-100,000K; ☯) This takes us back to 1990s Luang Prabang – an old house in the heart of the city with rooms for less than a tenner. The cheapest rooms have a shared bathroom while the more expensive upstairs rooms include a street view. They also sell some very rare antiques in their dimly lit shop.

Paphai Guest House GUESTHOUSE $
(Map p44; ☎ 071-212752; Th Sisavang Vatthana; r without bathroom 50,000K; @) Did the owners forget to put the prices up at this rickety old wooden traditional house near the heart of the peninsula? Rooms are fan-cooled, rattan-walled and have padlocks on the doors. It's run by a lovely older couple. There's a nice garden out front, too.

★ **Chang Inn** BOUTIQUE HOTEL $$
(Map p44; ☎ 071-255031; www.burasariheritage. com; Th Sakkarin; r from US$150; ☯☯) This romantic bijou belle is stunningly tasteful with Indochinese style; think pendulums ticking away on walls covered with vintage Lao B&W photography, slatted wood mother-of-pearl-inlay furniture, rosewood floors, fragrant linen and chandeliers. The air-con units have been boxed in, preserving the conceit that you have travelled back 100 years. A leafy brick-floored garden lies behind.

Pack Luck Villa GUESTHOUSE $$
(Map p44; ☎ 071-253373; www.packluck.in; Th Thugnaithao; r US$55; ☯☯) This stunning boutique hotel has an eclectic feel of dark woods, paper lanterns, chrome fans and Persian rugs; by night, subtle lighting picks out flecks of gold leaf on its wine-red walls. Rooms are a little tight, but the three with upper balco-

BUN PI MAI (LAO NEW YEAR)

In the middle of April, when the dry season reaches its hottest peak, **Bun Pi Mai** marks the sun's passage from the zodiac sign of Pisces into Aries. The old year's spirit departs and the new one arrives amid a series of celebrations and a frenzy of good-hearted water throwing. Festivities are especially colourful in Luang Prabang where many people dress in traditional clothes for major events, which stretch over seven days.

Transport can be hard to find at this time and hotel occupancy (and prices) will be at a peak, especially in Luang Prabang.

nies overlook the monks' morning meander. Downstairs is the popular Pack Luck Liquor wine bar.

Khong Kham Villa HOTEL $$
(Map p44; ☎ 071-212800; off Th Sisavangvong; r US$45; ☯☯) Head down a side street off Th Sisavangvong and into a courtyard choking on palms to find small but stylish rooms with chess-tiled bathrooms (weak showers), dough-soft beds, reading lamps, flat-screens TVs with cable, safety deposit boxes and communal balconies. In low season you can easily talk the price down.

Oui Guesthouse GUESTHOUSE $$
(Map p44; ☎ 071-252374, 020-54349589; r with/without balcony US$35/45; ☯) In a peaceful setting at the end of the peninsula facing the Nam Khan, it's so quiet here you can almost hear the breeze. Downstairs rooms are simple wood-ceiling affairs with tile floors, ethnic curtains and swish bathrooms. For an extra 10 bucks you can get an upstairs room with verandah and riverine views.

Phounsab Guesthouse GUESTHOUSE $$
(Map p44; ☎ 071-212975; www.phoun-thavy-sab. jimdo.com; Th Sisavangvong; r US$30-40; ☯☯) Slap-bang in the heart of the old-city's commercial centre, the Phounsab's newer rooms are set back off a narrow courtyard and the great-value front ones are big and breezy with wooden trim and polished floorboards. Silent air-con that won't keep you awake, private balconies and en suite, helpful management, plus the night market begins almost outside your front door.

Villa Senesouk
HOTEL $$

(Map p44; ☑ 071-212074; www.luangphabang.com/senesouk; Th Sakkarin; r US$40-60; ❋ 🖢) The morning monks' procession passes right outside the cheaper rooms. The upper ones are brighter and share a balcony with a wat view. Wood-panelled rooms have full mod cons, with the US$40 options offering additional space. Rooms out back are more expensive.

Magic M Guesthouse
GUESTHOUSE $$

(Map p44; ☑ 020-98837237; off Th Sakkarin; r incl breakfast US$45; 🖢) Run by a friendly Chinese lady, these wood-floored rooms have carriage lamps on the walls, verandah, private bathroom and flat-screen TV. Down a quiet lane at the end of the peninsula.

Sackarinh Guest House
GUESTHOUSE $$

(Map p44; ☑ 071-254512; sackarinh888@hotmail.com; Th Sisavangvong; r 200,000-250,000K; ❋ 🖢) Easily missed down a side alley off the main street, this simple belle is something of a Tardis, with 14 scrupulously clean, spacious rooms with little interior decor but clean linen and comfy beds. Central, friendly and close to the action, this is a great place for travellers watching their budget.

Auberge les 3 Nagas
BOUTIQUE HOTEL $$$

(Map p44; ☑ 071-253888; www.3-nagas.com; Th Sakkarin; r from US$200; ❋ @ 🖢) Luang Prabang style was minted at this boutique hotel, bookended by mango trees and a 1950s Mercedes. The 100-year-old Lao-style building brims with old-world atmosphere and has recently been revamped under new management. Palatial suites sport sink-to-sleep four-poster beds, tanned-wood bathrooms and a modern Asian design fusing colonial-era French roots. The restaurant serves Lao-only food in a palm-shaded terrace.

Villa Santi
HISTORIC HOTEL $$$

(Map p44; ☑ 071-252157; www.villasantihotel.com; Th Sakkarin; r US$128-288; ❋ 🖢 🖢) This striking old royal building has three very different personalities. The original 19th-century villa, once home to King Sisavang Vong's wife, has just six vast 'royal' suites, plus an upstairs breakfast room with a road-view terrace. The standard rooms are in a central annexe behind, while the majority are in a well-appointed 'resort', 5km south of town.

Victoria Khoum Xiengthong Guesthouse
GUESTHOUSE $$$

(Map p44; ☑ 071-212906; www.khoumxiengthong.com; Th Sisalernsak; r US$90; ❋ 🖢) So close to Wat Xieng Thong you can hear the resonance of the prayer gong floating across its ornamental gardens bedecked in tea light. There's a fragrant whiff of Indo-chic and its stone-floored, white-walled rooms enjoy golden tapestries and chrome fans. Rooms 2 (lower floor) and 5 (upper floor) are vast and include four-poster beds and stylish modern en suite.

⌨ Nam Khan Riverfront

1989 Guesthouse
GUESTHOUSE $

(Map p44; ☑ 020-91701061; joannethinking@yahoo.com; off Th Phommatha; dm/r US$19/25; 🖢) This delightful boho joint is run by a lovely Chinese lady. There's a patio terrace to chill in, and the reception is scattered with Tibetan photos and travel memorabilia. Choose from two twin rooms or a double, and three well-spaced dorms.

Meune Na Backpacker Hostel
HOSTEL $

(Map p44; ☑ 071-260851; Th Phetsarath; dm 30,000K, r from 60,000K; 🖢) A real budget crash pad close to the old Nam Khan bridge, the dorms here only have five beds to a room, making it a little less crowded than some of the other backpacker hostels around town. There's a traditional costume place next door if you fancy a souvenir photo decked out in Lao wedding clothes.

Bel Air Boutique Resort
RESORT $$

(Map p44; ☑ 071-254969; www.lebelairhotels.com; r from US$60; ❋ 🖢) Bel Air's thatched cottages might look rustic from the outside, but inside it's all modern and tastefully fitted out, including curtained display-baths and sunset-facing private balconies. Standard rooms are large and similarly stylish in a complex that's widely spaced amid palm trees and beautifully manicured lawns. Note that it is on the opposite side of the Nam Khan.

Luang Prabang Paradise Resort
HOTEL $$

(☑ 071-213103; www.luangprabangparadiseresort.com; 13 North Rd, Ban Meuang Nga; r US$75; ❋ 🖢 🖢) Near the Nam Khan, but a long way out of town over the new bridge, this is a relaxing place to stay for those who want to get away from it all. Sun-filled bungalows are nicely finished with polished teak floors and colourful bed rugs and bathroom are huge. Outside there's a palm-surrounded swimming pool.

★ The Apsara
BOUTIQUE HOTEL $$$

(Map p44; ☑ 071-254252; www.theapsara.com; Th Kingkitsarat; standard/superior r incl breakfast US$81/123; ❋ 🖢) Apsara commands fine views of the sleepy Nam Khan. Its Indochinese lobby is peppered with silk lanterns and the bar springs from an old classic film, while each of the open-plan rooms is individually designed. From its turquoise walls to its coloured glass buddhas, everything about this place screams style. The restaurant (p54) and bar are romantic affairs best enjoyed at night.

🍴 Mekong Riverfront & Around

Boungnasouk Guesthouse GUESTHOUSE $
(Map p44; ☎071-212749; 1/3 Th Khem Kong; r US$10; 🛜) This cheap family-run guesthouse has an enticing location down on the Mekong riverfront. There are just six rooms here, three twins and three doubles, but no river views, as the family have bagged those. It can be noisy here at night.

Ammata Guest House GUESTHOUSE $$
(Map p44; ☎071-212175; pphilasouk@yahoo.com; Ban Wat Nong; r US$30-40; ❄🛜) A friendly, family-run place, this attractively timbered guesthouse has a low-key ambience, spotless and spacious rooms with polished wood interiors, and renovated bathrooms. Most rooms are upstairs, running off a shared and shaded balcony. Management is friendly and you're perfectly located to watch the morning alms procession pass by without all the snapping cameras.

Muang Lao Riverside Villa HOTEL $$
(Map p44; ☎071-252219; www.xandriahotels.com; Th Khem Khong; r US$25-45; ❄🛜) Set in a charming wooden property overlooking the Mekong, these small rooms are good value given the location, and include white quilts decked in Hmong bed runners, parquet floors, air-con, flat-screen TV, minibar, fridge, wardrobe and rain showers. A few rooms have balcony views over the river. Hot-water shower facilities are included in the en suites.

Kongsavath Guesthouse GUESTHOUSE $$
(Map p44; ☎071-212994; www.khongsavath.com; Th Khem Khong; r US$50-60; ❄🛜) This lovely, vine-choked villa has wood-panelled rooms reminiscent of a captain's bunk in an old schooner. Boasting a great Mekong-front location, the family suite overlooking the river is the best. Great breakfasts and very helpful management make this a safe choice for families and couples alike.

Villa Champa GUESTHOUSE $$
(Map p44; ☎071-260252, 071-253555; www.villachampa.com; Th Sisavang Vatthana; s/d US$35/49,

superior r US$56; ❄🛜) This tastefully renovated traditional house has a prime location between the Mekong River and the old temple district. The nine rooms include air-con, TV and minibar, plus some more traditional Laotian textiles to complete the picture. Fresh and airy, this is a good peninsula option.

Luang Prabang River Lodge HOTEL $$
(Map p44; ☎071-253314; www.luang-prabang-river-lodge.com; Th Khem Khong; r US$40-60; ❄🛜) This shuttered colonial-era corner house has an alluring patio draped in floral vines and framed by a lychgate and old bomb casings. Interiors have clean lines and restrained decor, with wood floors, white walls and cable TV. A few rooms offer Mekong views. It's one of a few places in town that welcomes pets.

Villa Chitdara GUESTHOUSE $$
(Map p44; ☎071-254949; www.villachitdara.com; Th Khounswa; r from US$55; ❄🛜) The monks' alms procession at dawn passes directly by Villa Chitdara, set amid a verdant garden in the heart of the old town. It's a charming base to explore the peninsula. Rooms include TVs, hot water and safes. Breakfast is pleasant. The friendly owners speak eloquent French and are warmth personified.

En Provence Guesthouse GUESTHOUSE $$
(Map p44; ☎071-212380, 071-212035; r incl breakfast 414,000K; ❄🛜) At the peaceful end of the peninsula, this handsome Lao villa is run by a pleasant Frenchman and has lemon-hued rooms with flat-screen TVs, dark-wood floors and furniture, and immaculate bathrooms with roomy bath. The Mekong River views... formidable!

Sala Prabang HOTEL $$$
(Map p44; ☎071-252460, 071-254087; www.salalao.com; 102/6 Th Khem Khong; r incl breakfast US$90-155; ❄🛜) Housed in an old French villa and another seven buildings closely joined together, Sala's rooms have lime-washed walls, guacamole-coloured linen and hardwood floors, and are separated from the bathrooms by Japanese-style screens. There are many variations of room size so make sure you shop around. Beautiful throughout, this is a tasteful option.

Xiengthong Palace HISTORIC HOTEL $$$
(Map p44; ☎071-213200; www.xiengthong-palace.com; Th Khem Khong; r US$200-500; ❄@🛜📧) This former royal residence has a striking setting overlooking the Mekong River next to Wat Xieng Thong. The 26 rooms

are luxuriously appointed and include open-plan Mekong suites with grandstand views and two-storey suites with their own private plunge pools and lounges.

🛏 Ban Hoxieng

Phonemaly Guesthouse   GUESTHOUSE $

(Map p44; ☎071-253504; Th Hoxieng; r from 100,000K; ❄️🛜) Close to the night market, this pair of traditionally styled wooden houses has very much the feel of a real home yet all the conveniences of a well-run guesthouse. The best timber-clad rooms are upstairs. Obliging family owners ensure a free supply of bananas, coffee and water refills. Decent air-con and wi-fi.

Sayo Naga Guesthouse   GUESTHOUSE $$

(Map p44; ☎071-252614, 071-212484; www.sayoguesthouse.com; Th Wat That; r US$35-80; 🛜) Guarded by *naga* (river serpents) this serene white, green-shuttered house boasts atmospheric rooms with polished wood floors, bathroom, mozzie nets, fine furniture and balcony. Add to this bedside lamps and Hmong throws and it seems a fair steal. There are also small rooms in a separate block at the back of the garden – skip these and go for the house.

Villa Pumalin   BOUTIQUE HOTEL $$

(Map p44; ☎071-212777; www.villapumalin.com; Th Hoxieng; r incl breakfast US$55-75; ❄️🛜) Rosewood steps lead across a tiny carp pool on the way up to this hotel, which has superbly finished rooms that combine stylish bathroom fittings with semi-traditional woodwork interiors and top-quality linens. The best room (201) has a private balcony with glimpses of the Mekong. For more privacy and better views, grab a room upstairs.

Manichan Guesthouse   GUESTHOUSE $$

(Map p44; ☎020-56920137; www.manichanguesthouse.com; off Th Khem Khong; r with/without private bathroom US$37/27; ❄️🛜) Run by Andy and Venus, Manichan is big on personality and warmth, with air-con rooms and terrific breakfasts – crêpes, homemade jams and wholemeal bread, fruit salads and yoghurt. Upper rooms share a bathroom worthy of a boutique hotel, plus a wide terrace with Phu Si views, while ground-floor rooms have en suite bathrooms with screened showers.

Ban Lao Hotel   HOTEL $$

(Map p38; ☎071-252078; www.banlaohotel.com; Th Thammamikalath, Ban Mano; r incl breakfast US$25-75; ❄️@🛜) Tasteful, comfortable rooms set behind a late-colonial-era mansion that's 'hollowed out' so that you can see the garden's palms and jackfruit trees while checking in. Deluxe rooms come on sturdy stilts over fountain walls and swing seats. Breakfast is served in a large pavilion perched over a pond. It's peaceful and good value.

★Amantaka   LUXURY HOTEL $$$

(Map p44; ☎071-860333; www.amanresorts.com; Th Kitsarat; ste from US$1000; ❄️🛜🏊) You can imagine Graham Greene writing under a wood-blade fan in the wicker-accented restaurant of this beautifully renovated French colonial-era building. Flanked by manicured lawns, a centrepiece jade swimming pool and dreamy spa and gym, suites here are capacious, with living room, four-poster beds and most feature a private pool in their back garden. Surely Luang Prabang's finest hotel?

★Satri House   HISTORIC HOTEL $$$

(Map p38; ☎071-253491; www.satrihouse.com; off Th Phothisarath; r US$192-384; ❄️🛜🏊) This beautiful villa, once the former house of the Lao Red Prince, has stunning rooms with huge beds, fine furniture and a decorative flair unmatched by any other boutique in the city. Imagine pathways through lush gardens lit by statues of Indian gods, ornamental lily pools, a stunning jade swimming pool and a maze of Indo-chic corridors. The spa is terrific.

★Sofitel Luang Prabang   SPA HOTEL $$$

(Map p38; ☎071-260777; www.accorhotels.com; r from US$250; ❄️🛜🏊) This former governor's residence hides a paradise of mature palms and exotic flowers within its high walls, the highlight of which is a stunning cherry-tiled swimming pool. In a fan-cooled pavilion the Governor's Grill turns out terrific Western food, and there's also a world-class spa. Rooms are huge, with battleship-grey walls, fine art and walk-in showers. It's superb.

Le Sen Boutique Hotel   BOUTIQUE HOTEL $$$

(Map p38; ☎071-261661; www.lesenhotel.com; 113 Th Manomai; r US$95-160; ❄️@🛜🏊) This stylish boutique hotel southwest of the town is exceptional value when compared with some of the heritage hotels crammed into the old quarter. Rooms are well appointed with modish bathrooms and flat-screen TVs, and all face the inviting central swimming pool and Jacuzzi. Extra touches include a well-equipped gym and free use of bicycles. Staff are super friendly and the place is well organised.

Maison Dalabua BOUTIQUE HOTEL **$$$**
(Map p44; ☑071-255588; www.maison-dalabua.
com; Th Phothisarat, Ban That Luang; r US$75-100;
❋⊛) Set in spacious grounds that include a
vast pond dotted with water lilies, Maison Da-
labua is a real hideaway. The 15 rooms are in
an attractive building and include flat-screen
TVs and generously proportioned beds, choice
furnishings and a sense of space. More expen-
sive rooms include a bathtub.

⌂ South of Phu Si

Villa Sayada HOTEL **$**
(Map p44; ☑071-254872; www.villa-shayada-laos.
com; Th Phommatha; r 120,000-200,000K; ❋⊛)
Opposite Wat Visoun, this welcoming nine-
room mini-hotel run by lovely Mr Takashi, a
gentle Japanese man who welcomes you with
a glass of rum, has generously sized cream
and cloud-white rooms, with hung fabrics,
handmade lamps and decent hot showers.
There are small private balconies with pleas-
ant views.

Khounsavanh Guesthouse GUESTHOUSE **$**
(Map p44; ☑071-212297; Ban Thongchaleum; dm
from 48,000K, r 80,000-140,000K, without bathroom
60,000K; ❋⊛) Khounsavanh sits on a qui-
et lane near Dara Market. There's a choice of
air-conditioned en suite rooms with views
of Phu Si's summit temple, as well as dorms
(one four-berth female only, and two mixed).
While toilets are lamentably dirty, on the plus
side there's a great swimming pool and it's a
good place to meet other travellers.

★ La Résidence Phou Vao LUXURY HOTEL **$$$**
(Map p38; ☑071-212530; www.belmond.com/
la-residence-phou-vao-luang-prabang; r incl breakfast from US$492; ❋@⊛) With its stunning
hilltop grounds, seamless service and stylish
wood rooms, Luang Prabang's first luxury
hotel minted revivalist Indo-chic. The infinity
pool reflects distant Phu Si and is flanked by
a top-notch Franco-Lao restaurant. The Mekong Spa is spectacular and has won several
global awards. No other hotel has such a spectacular view of the city and mountains. Bliss!

Free use of bikes and free limo shuttle to
the city five minutes away.

Luang Say Residence LUXURY HOTEL **$$$**
(Map p38; ☑071-260891; www.luangsayresidence.
com; Ban Phonepheng; ste incl breakfast from
US$170; ❋@⊛) Conjuring the colonial-era
heyday of Luang Prabang, this sophisticated
all-suite hotel consists of six French-accented

buildings set amid verdant gardens a short
tuk-tuk ride southwest of the city. Furnishings
are sumptuous and there's an inviting swim-
ming pool. The Belle Epoque Restaurant is
one of the top dining destinations in town;
eat on the terrace overlooking a lush garden.

✕ Eating

After the privations of the more remote areas
in Laos your stomach will be turning cart-
wheels at the sheer choice and fine execution
of what's on offer here. Aside from some very
fine Lao restaurants, the gastro scene is large-
ly French. Luang Prabang also has a terrific
cafe scene, with bakeries at every turn.

Archetypal dishes include ubiquitous lo-
cal sausages and a soup-stew called *orlam*
(*àw lám*) made with meat, mushrooms and
eggplant with special bitter-spicy wood chips
added for flavouring (don't swallow them!).
A great local snack is *kai bâan* (Mekong
riverweed).

Food markets are great for fresh fruit, while
self-caterers should check out the **morning
market** (Map p44; ☺5.30am-4pm Sat-Mon).

✕ Thanon Sisavongvong & Around

★ Le Banneton BAKERY **$**
(Map p44; Th Sakkarin; meals 20,000-40,000K;
☺6.30am-6pm; ❋⊛) It's the softness of
the melt-in-your-mouth pastry that keeps
us coming back to our favourite bakery in
Luang Prabang, which serves *pain au choc-
olat* (chocolate croissants), pizza, terrine, ba-
guette sandwiches, salads, crêpes and more.
The ceiling is a maze of arabesques, there's a
cool fan at every turn, and the white walls are
offset by a passing blur of orange outside –
monks from the monastery opposite.

Le Café Ban Vat Sene FRENCH **$**
(Map p44; http://elephant-restau.com/cafeban
vatsene; Th Sakkarin; mains 50,000-75,000K;
☺7.30am-10pm; ❋⊛) Luang Prabang's most
stylish stop for afternoon tea and scones.
Fans whirr above a serenely lit bar, while the
dessert cabinet purrs at you like a calorif-
ic temptress – think éclairs, lemon tart and
raspberry mousse. Beef steak, salads, pizza,
and grilled chicken and perch are also on the
menu. Eat outside or within the cool interior.

Xieng Thong Noodle-Shop LAOTIAN **$**
(Map p44; Th Sakkarin; noodle soup 20,000K;
☺7am-2pm) The best *kòw bĕeak sèn* (round

rice noodles served in a broth with pieces of chicken or deep-fried crispy pork belly) in town is served from an entirely unexotic shopfront well up the peninsula. It usually runs out by 2pm.

★**Coconut Garden**   LAOTIAN, INTERNATIONAL $$
(Map p44; ☑ 071-252482; www.elephant-restau. com/coconutgarden; Th Sisavangvong; meals 35,000-150,000K, set menu 100,000K; ☺8am-11pm; ☎⏚) An excellent vegetarian set menu includes five top-quality Lao dishes, allowing a single diner to create the subtle palate of flavours that you'd normally only get from a feast with many people. Coconut Garden has front and rear yards, and is a great spot for lunch or dinner. International favourites are also available.

Café Toui   FUSION $$
(Map p44; www.cafetoui.com; Th Sisavang Vatthana; mains 50,000-80,000K; ☺7am-10pm; ☎⏚) Elegant and bijou, candlelit Café Toui is a delight of Lao cuisine. Gold-stencilled ox-blood walls, great service and an Asian fusion menu with standout dishes such as *mok pa* (steamed fish wrapped in banana leaves) and zingy *láhp*, plus an inviting sampler menu.

Tangor   FUSION $$
(Map p44; ☑ 071-260761; www.letangor.com; Th Sisavangvong; mains 40,000-80,000K; ☺11am-10pm; ☎) Atmospheric with its low-lit interior of dark woods and tangerine-coloured walls peppered with old travel posters, Tangor boasts a menu of beautifully crafted fusion food, blending the best of seasonal Lao produce with French cuisine. Dishes include beef tenderloin, pork filet mignon and tapas and there's a decent wine selection.

✖ Nam Khan Riverfront & Around

★**Dyen Sabai**   LAOTIAN, INTERNATIONAL $
(Map p44; ☑ 020-55104817; http://dyensabai restaurant.wordpress.com; Ban Phan Luang; mains 20,000-35,000K; ☺8am-11pm; ☎) One of Luang Prabang's top destinations for fabulous Lao food. The eggplant dip and fried Mekong riverweed are as good as anywhere. Most seating is on recliner cushions in rustic open-sided pavilions. It's a short stroll across the Nam Khan bamboo bridge in the dry season or a free boat ride at other times.

Rosella Fusion   FUSION $
(Map p44; www.facebook.com/rosellafusion; Th Kingkitsarat; mains 35,000K; ☺9am-10.30pm) Es-

tablished by a former Amantaka bartender, this riverside restaurant offers an innovative selection of affordable fusion flavours. The owner is particularly proud of his bargain cocktails, so consider dropping by for a sundowner before dinner.

Joma Bakery Cafe   BAKERY $
(Map p44; www.joma.biz; Th Kingkitsarat; mains 40,000K; ☺7am-9pm; ☀☎) Joma's second branch in Luang Prabang has the usual tempting offering of sorbets, fruit salad, cookies, bespoke subs and fair-trade coffee. Eat in the cosy wood-accented interior, or on the fan-cooled terrace with sumptuous views of the Nam Khan.

★**Tamarind**   LAOTIAN $$
(Map p44; ☑ 071-213128; www.tamarindlaos. com; Th Kingkitsarat; mains 40,000K, set dinner 100,000-150,000K; ☺11am-10pm; ☎) On the banks of the Nam Khan, mint-green Tamarind has created its very own strain of 'Mod Lao' cuisine. The à la carte menu boasts delicious sampling platters with bamboo dip, stuffed lemongrass and *meuyang* (DIY parcels of noodles, herbs, fish and chilli pastes, and vegetables). There's also buffalo *láhp* and Luang Prabang sausage. Deservedly popular.

★**The Apsara**   FUSION $$
(Map p44; ☑ 071-254670; www.theapsara. com; Apsara Hotel, Th Kingkitsarat; mains 60,000-110,000K; ☺7am-10pm; ☎) This chic eatery fronting the Nam Khan offers fusion cuisine blending East and West. Choose from buffalo steak, stuffed *panin* fish to share, or braised pork belly for a main. Save some space for the divine desserts such as poached nashi pear in lime and ginger syrup served with coconut ice cream and a Lao poppadom.

Couleur Cafe   INTERNATIONAL $$
(Map p44; ☑ 071-254694; Th Kingkitsarat; mains 40,000-100,000K; ☺11am-10pm; ☀☎) Well regarded by long-term residents, Couleur Cafe has relocated to the Nam Khan side of the peninsula but continues to serve French-accented and creatively presented Laotian cuisine. Menu highlights include chicken casserole with ginger and lemongrass, and duck breast with honey and mango chutney.

✖ Mekong Riverfront & Around

Riverside Barbecue Restaurant   BARBECUE $
(Map p44; Th Khem Khong; all you can eat 60,000K; ☺5-11pm) Tabletop *sìn daat* (Lao hotpot barbecue) is pretty popular in Luang

Prabang and this lively Mekong riverfront restaurant may just be the most popular of all. Hygiene can be patchy so make sure you cook your shrimp, beef or chicken thoroughly.

Big Tree Cafe KOREAN, INTERNATIONAL $$
(Map p44; www.blgtreecafe.com; Th Khem Khong; mains 35,000-50,000K; ☺9am-9pm; 🔊🚲) Located in a stunning wooden house, Big Tree Cafe's Korean food is the best in the city and it's always packed with Koreans, as well as aesthetes who come to see photographer Adri Berger's work in the gallery (p56) upstairs. Eat inside or out on the terrace in the leafy, restful garden. There's also a choice of Western and Japanese dishes.

L'Elephant Restaurant FRENCH $$$
(Map p44; www.elephant-restau.com; Ban Wat Nong; mains 80,000-250,000K; ☺11.30am-10pm; 🌐) L'Elephant serves arguably the most sophisticated cuisine in the city in a renovated villa with wooden floors, stucco pillars, stencilled ochre walls and great atmosphere. The Menu du Chasseur includes terrines, soups, duck breast and other Gallic specialities.

✗ Royal Palace Museum & Ban Hoxieng

Joma Bakery Cafe BAKERY $
(Map p44; www.joma.biz; Th Chao Fa Ngum; mains 35,000K; ☺7am-9pm; 🌐🔊) This haven of cool with comfy chairs and a contemporary vibe is one of the city's busiest bakeries. It offers delectable comfort food in the form of soups, salads, bagels, creatives coffees and wholesome shakes. There's a second branch (p54) overlooking the Nam Khan.

Night Food Stalls LAOTIAN $
(Map p44; ☺6-10pm; 🚲) Food stalls emerge at dusk on a narrow street behind the tourist office with illuminated communal tables to sit at. There's no better place to taste a wide variety of cheap, well-cooked local food. There are plenty of vegetarian stalls offering a range of dishes for just 15,000K. Whole roast fish stuffed with lemongrass is a bargain at around 25,000K.

Baguette Stalls SANDWICHES $
(Map p44; cnr Th Kitsarat & Th Chao Fa Ngum; ☺7am-10pm) A variety of well-filled French-bread sandwiches are available at makeshift baguette stalls facing the tourist office. Lao pâté is a delight. Fresh fruit shakes are also a favourite here.

Blue Lagoon INTERNATIONAL $$
(Map p44; www.blue-lagoon-restaurant.com; Th Ounheun; mains 75,000-140,000K; ☺10am-10pm; 🔊) A favourite with expats for its lantern-festooned walls, leafy patio and jazz-infused atmosphere. The menu features Luang Prabang sausage, pasta, boeuf bourguignon, salads and very tasty *láhp*.

✗ South of Phu Si

Secret Pizza ITALIAN $$
(Map p38; 📱020-56528881; www.facebook.com/pizzasecret; Ban Nasaphanh; mains 50,000-60,000K; ☺from 6.30pm Tue & Fri) Alright, so the secret is out, but it's well worth sharing. Long the preserve of Luang Prabang residents, host Andrea prepares wood-fired pizzas, classic lasagne and homemade gnocchi in the garden of his lovely home. Profiteroles round things off nicely, plus a fine bottle of Italian wine.

🍷 Drinking & Nightlife

★**Icon Klub** BAR
(Map p44; www.iconklub.com; Th Sisavang Vatthana; ☺5pm-late; 🔊) Imagine a place in the afterlife where writers meet and conversation is as free flowing as the fabulous mixology cocktails. You pull up a pew next to Jack Kerouac, and Anaïs Nin is reading in a cosy chair nearby... Icon may just be this place. A sculpted angel rises out of the wall and there are poetry slams, jam sessions and kick-ass tunes.

Utopia BAR
(Map p44; www.utopialuangprabang.com; mains 30,000K; ☺8am-11pm; 🔊) Lush riverside bar with peaceful views of the Nam Khan; think recliner cushions, low-slung tables and hookah pipes. Chill over a fruit shake, burger, breakfast or omelette, play a board game or volleyball, or just lose yourself in a sea of candles come sunset. Brilliantly designed with faux Khmer ruins and creeper vines, surely the city's liveliest outdoor bar.

Bar 525 BAR
(Map p38; 📱071-212424; www.525.rocks; ☺5-11.30pm; 🔊) Parked down a quiet street, there's nothing retiring about this chic, urban bar. Sit outside stargazing on the terrace, inside at the long bar in low-lit style, or chill in the comfy lounge. Cocktails galore, glad rags, stunning photography on the walls and a sophisticated crowd.

Chez Matt
BAR

(Map p44; Th Sisavang Vatthana; ⏰7pm-late; 🗺) Ox-blood walls, low lights and a handsome bar glittering with polished crystal, this candlelit haunt is central and peaceful, adding a dash of upscale sophistication to the city's nocturnal landscape. With its cocktails, French and Italian wine cellar and chilled music, this makes for a good spot to dress up in your finest before going somewhere swish for dinner.

La Pistoche
BAR

(Map p38; http://lapistochepool.wordpress.com; Ban Phong Pheng; entry 30,000K; ⏰10am-11pm; 🗺🍴) The perfect medicine for landlocked Laos, La Pistoche offers two swimming pools set amid a spacious garden in the suburbs south of town. Entry includes pétanque and water volleyball if you're feeling active. Generous happy hours from noon to 7pm mean there's a bit of a hippy-trippy vibe by day, but full-moon parties are on the cards.

Lao Lao Garden
BAR

(Map p44; Th Kingkitsarat; mains 30,000K; ⏰5pm-late; 🗺) Lit up like a jungle Vegas, this garden bar on the skirts of Phu Si calls you to chill by candlelight, listen to easy sounds and warm the cockles of your heart by the firepit. Besides cocktails there's a wide range of foods, including *orlam* and buffalo stew, plus cook-it-yourself *sìn daat* (Lao hotpot barbecue).

Dao Fah
CLUB

(Map p38; Rte 13; ⏰9-11.30pm) A young Lao crowd packs this cavernous club, located just near the southern bus terminal. Live bands playing Lao and Thai pop alternate with DJs spinning rap and hip hop.

☆ Entertainment

Moonlight Cinema
CINEMA

(Map p38; http://ockpoptok.com/eat/moonlight-cinema; Ock Pop Tok Living Crafts Centre; ticket incl return tuk-tuk & dinner 70,000K; ⏰9am-10pm; 🗺) 🍴 The latest films are shown at the Ock Pop Tok centre every Thursday at 7.30pm, screened after 7pm dinner. Tuk-tuk is inclusive; pick-up is from in front of the Joma Bakery (p55) on Th Chao Fa Ngum at 6.45pm. Book online.

Garavek Storytelling
THEATRE

(Map p44; ☏020-96777300; www.garavek.com; Th Khounswa; tickets 50,000K; ⏰6.30pm) 🍴 Garavek means 'magical bird', and this enchanting hour-long show – comprising an old man

dressed in tribalwear playing a haunting *khene* (Lao-style lyre) alongside an animated storyteller (in English) recalling local Lao folk tales and legends – takes your imagination on a flight of fancy. Held in an intimate 30-seat theatre. Book ahead.

L'Etranger Books & Tea
CINEMA

(Map p44; www.facebook.com/booksandtea; Th Kingkisarat; ⏰8am-10pm Mon-Sat, 10am-10pm Sun; 🗺) 🍴 Order a drink and a bite to eat and then get comfy on a lounging cushion to watch the latest blockbuster and indie films shown nightly at 7pm. If it's quiet you usually get to choose the film. Run by a friendly cineaste (she's also a script writer in LA).

🛍 Shopping

The best areas for shopping are Th Sisavangvong and the Mekong waterfront, where characterful boutiques selling local art, gilded buddhas, handmade paper products and all manner of tempting souvenirs abound. Silver shops are attached to several houses in Ban Ho Xieng, the traditional royal silversmiths' district. And don't forget the night market where you'll find a cornucopia of handicrafts.

★Handicraft Night Market
MARKET

(Map p44; Th Sisavangvong; ⏰5.30-10pm) Every evening this tourist-oriented but highly appealing market assembles along Th Sisavangvong and is deservedly one of Luang Prabang's biggest tourist lures. Low-lit, quiet and devoid of hard selling, it has myriad traders hawking silk scarves and wall hangings, plus Hmong appliqué blankets, T-shirts, clothing, shoes, paper, silver, bags, ceramics, bamboo lamps and more.

Prices are remarkably fair but cheaper 'local' creations sometimes originate from China, Thailand or Vietnam – as a rule of thumb, if it's a scarf or bed runner, those with perfectly smooth edges are factory-made copies.

★Big Tree Gallery
ART

(Map p44; ☏071-212262; www.adriberger.com/general/luang-prabang; Th Khem Khong; ⏰9am-9pm; 🗺) Photographer and film-maker Adri Berger's compositions of rural Laos capture that honeyed afternoon light like no one else. His ochre-walled gallery-cum-restaurant is in a breezy wooden house with a delightful palm-shaded terrace to read in. Upstairs you'll find the bulk of his work. His prints can be safely sent home in protective containers. Exquisite souvenirs.

GIVING SOMETHING BACK

There are several ways in which travellers can give back to the local community in Luang Prabang.

Big Brother Mouse (BBM; Map p44; ☏ 071-254937, www.bigbrothermouse.com; Th Phayaluangmeungchan; ⊙ 9-11am & 5-7pm) 🍃 Travellers can buy books here to distribute to local children. As well as promoting literacy, the idea is that it's more beneficial for visitors to hand out books than candy.

Luang Prabang Library (Map p44; ☏ 071-254813; www.communitylearninginternational. org; Th Sisavangvong; ⊙ 8am-5pm Tue-Sun) 🍃 Collects donations to provide local books for a mobile library that sails to remote villages.

Children's Cultural Centre (Map p44; ☏ 071-253732; www.cccluangprabang.weebly. com; Th Sisavangvong; ⊙ 4-5pm Tue-Fri, 8-11.30am & 2-4pm Sat) Seeks donations of virtually anything recyclable or resalable to provide after-school activities for kids.

Lao Red Cross (p45) Travellers can donate used, washed clothing or even give blood, a precious commodity in Laos as anywhere.

★ **Queen Design Lao** CLOTHING
(Map p44; queendesignlao@gmail.com; Th Sakkarin, 1/17 Ban Khili; ⊙ 10am-6pm Mon-Sat; ☏) This stylish Aussie-run boutique has a choice selection of hand-woven linen, silk and cotton dresses, chemises, skirts, and beach shawls made by Chris Boyle, a renowned designer in Oz. Most are one-off pieces. As well as pashminas and scarves, it also sells organic face scrubs and wood designer glasses.

TAEC Shop ARTS & CRAFTS
(Map p44; www.taeclaos.org; Th Sakkarin; ⊙ 9am-8pm) 🍃 This new shop sister to the TAEC (p39) museum is a safe way to buy the finest handicrafts made in Laos – be it clothes, bags or bed runners – in the knowledge they are not fakes and your purchase is directly benefiting local people.

Ma Te Sai ARTS & CRAFTS
(Map p44; www.matesai.com; cnr Th Kingkitsarat & Th Phommatha) 🍃 The name means 'where is it from' in Lao, and all the silk, paper and gift items in this attractive boutique come from villages around Luang Prabang. A great selection of silk pashminas, cool T-shirts and linen chemises.

Luang Prabang Artisans ARTS & CRAFTS
(Map p44; ☏ 020-55571125; www.luangprabang artisanscafe.com; ⊙ 9am-6pm Mon-Sat; ☏) 🍃 Located in a 100-year-old wooden home on a narrow lane running from the main street, this great little shop sells handicrafts like naturally dyed cushions, silk purses and pashminas, handmade paper and kids' soft toys.

Pathana Boupha Antique House ANTIQUES
(Map p44; Th Phommatha; ⊙ 10am-5pm) Follow the sweeping stairs in the garden of this impressive old French mansion to discover an Aladdin's cave of antique buddhas, golden *naga,* silver betel-nut pots, Akha-style bracelets and Hmong necklaces. Also sells fine silk scarves from Sam Neua. It's not cheap but it is respected for its quality.

Kopnoi ARTS & CRAFTS
(Map p44; www.facebook.com/kopnoi; Th Kingkitsarat; ⊙ 9am-9pm; ☏) 🍃 Kopnoi sells stunning handicrafts from ethnic-minority craftsmen; Akha bracelets, silk pashminas, fine jewellery, packaged spices and teas, and local art. If you're 'shopped out' by the night market, this is a restful alternative; the quality is good, and there's no chance of you buying fake Chinese copies. Find it at L'Etranger Books & Tea.

Ock Pop Tok CLOTHING, HANDICRAFTS
(Map p44; ☏ 071-254406; www.ockpoptok.com; Th Sakkarin; ⊙ 8am-9pm) 🍃 Ock Pop Tok works with a wide range of different tribes to preserve their handicraft traditions. Fine silk and cotton scarves, dresses, wall hangings and cushion covers make perfect presents. Weaving courses (p47) are also available.

Orange Tree ANTIQUES
(Map p44; Th Khem Khong; ⊙ 10am-6pm Mon-Sat; ☏) 🍃 This riverfront antiques shop is a testament to its owners' magpie wanderings, with Hong Kong tea tins, Chinese retro alarm clocks, Mao revolutionary crockery, Bakelite inkwells, Vietnamese clocks and Burmese Buddhist statuary. Curio heaven!

Monument Books

BOOKS

(Map p44; www.monument-books.com; Th Khem Khong, Ban Wat Nong; ⊙9am-9pm Mon-Fri, to 6pm Sat & Sun) Part of a regional chain, this shop stocks guidebooks, maps, novels, magazines and books on Lao history.

❶ Information

DANGERS & ANNOYANCES

Luang Prabang is an incredibly safe and intimate city. But of course there are always exceptions. Beware of buying drugs; you'll probably be offered them by tuk-tuk drivers, but given they may well be undercover cops and the fine is around US$500 if you get caught, it's not worth it. Also, if you have a security box in your room, use it. Beware, too, of leaving valuables out in hostels; theft does sometimes point towards the owners as it does occasionally to other travellers.

INTERNET ACCESS

It's increasingly common to find wi-fi in guesthouses, hotels and cafes, but you'll need your own laptop or mobile device. Most guesthouses and hotels also include a desktop computer in the lobby area for the use of guests. If your laptop is playing up or your camera's flash memory has been zapped by viruses, **DSCom** (Map p44; ☑ 071-253905; Th Kitsarat; ⊙9.30am-noon & 1-6pm Mon-Sat) might be able to save the day; the owner speaks good English.

MEDICAL SERVICES

Chinese Hospital (Map p44; ☑ 071-254026; Ban Phu Mok) Modern medical equipment and supplies, but sometimes short of trained personnel.

Pharmacie (Map p44; Th Sakkarin; ⊙8.30am-8pm) Stocks basic medicines. On weekends, hours are variable.

Provincial Hospital (Map p44; ☑ 071-254023; Ban Naxang; doctor's consultation 100,000K) OK for minor problems but for any serious illnesses consider flying to Bangkok or returning to Vientiane and neighbouring hospitals across the Thai border. Note that the hospital in Luang Prabang charges double for consultations at weekends or anytime after 4pm.

MONEY

There are lots of ATMs in town. Several tour companies on Th Sisavangvong offer cash advances on Visa or MasterCard for around 3% commission. They'll also change money but rates tend to be poor.

BCEL (Map p44; Th Sisavangvong; ⊙8.30am-3.30pm Mon-Sat) Changes major currencies in cash or travellers cheques, has a 24-hour ATM and offers cash advances against Visa and MasterCard.

Lao Development Bank (Map p44; 65 Th Sisavangvong; ⊙8.30am-3.30pm Mon-Sat) Has a 24-hour ATM.

Minipost Booth (Map p44; Th Sisavangvong; ⊙7.45am-8.30pm, cash advances 9am-3pm) Changes most major currencies at fair rates and is open daily.

POST

Post office (Map p44; Th Chao Fa Ngum; ⊙8.30am-3.30pm Mon-Fri, to noon Sat) Phone calls and Western Union facilities.

TELEPHONE

Most internet cafes in town have Skype and can offer international calls at 2000K per minute or less. The **Minipost Booth** sells mobile phone SIM cards.

TOURIST INFORMATION

Provincial Tourism Department (Map p44; ☑ 071-212173; www.tourismlaos.org; Th Sisavangvong; ⊙8am-4pm Mon-Fri; ☎) General information on festivals and ethnic groups. Also offers some maps and leaflets, plus information on buses and boats. Great office run by helpful staff.

TRAVEL AGENCIES

All Lao Travel (Map p44; ☑ 071-253522, 020-55571572; www.alllaoservice.com; Th Sisavangvong; ⊙8am-10pm) One of the best ticketing agents in the city; it sells plane, boat and bus tickets.

Jewel Travel Laos (p43) Useful tour company offering a range of excursions.

Treasure Travel (Map p44; ☑ 071-254682; www.treasuretravellaos.com; Th Sisavangvong; ⊙8am-9pm) Organised and customised tours throughout Laos. Prices depend on duration and group size.

VISAS

Immigration office (Map p44; ☑ 071-212435; Th Wisunarat; ⊙8.30am-4.30pm Mon-Fri) It's usually possible to extend a Lao visa for up to 30 extra days (US$2 per day) if you apply before it has expired.

Vietnamese Consulate (Map p38; www.vietnamconsulate-luangprabang.org; Th Naviengkham, Luang Prabang; ⊙8-11.30am & 1.30-5.30pm Mon-Fri) Arrange your visas for Vietnam here.

❶ Getting There & Away

AIR

Around 4km from the city centre, **Luang Prabang International Airport** (☑ 071-212173; ☎) has a smart new building as of 2013 and an expanded runway. For Bangkok, Bangkok Airways (www.

bangkokair.com) and **Lao Airlines** (Map p38; 071-212172; www.laoairlines.com; Th Pha Mahapatsaman) both fly twice daily. Lao Airlines also serves Vientiane several times daily and Pakse, Chiang Mai, Hanoi and Siem Reap once daily. **Vietnam Airlines** (071-213049; www.vietnam airlines.com) flies to both Siem Reap (codeshare with Lao Airlines) and Hanoi daily.

BOAT

Though not always the quickest way to travel, journeying by river allows you to slow down and take in the city and surrounding country from a different angle.

Pak Beng & Huay Xai

For slowboats to Pak Beng (130,000K, nine hours, 8am), buy tickets from the **navigation office** (Map p44; 8-11am & 2-4pm) behind the Royal Palace. Through-tickets to Huay Xai (220,000K, two days) are also available, but you'll have to sleep in Pak Beng. This also allows you to stay a little longer in Pak Beng should you like the place. The main **slowboat landing** (Map p44) is directly behind the navigation office, but departure points can vary according to river levels.

The more upscale **Luang Say Cruise** (p46) departs on two-day rides to Huay Xai from the Xieng Thong jetty opposite Wat Xieng Thong. Rates include an overnight stay at the Luang Say Lodge in Pak Beng. A cheaper alternative is **Shompoo Cruise** (p46), a two-day cruise aboard a smart boutique boat; accommodation in Pak Beng is not included.

Fast, uncomfortable and seriously hazardous six-person speedboats can shoot you up the Mekong to Pak Beng (190,000K, three hours) and Huay Xai (320,000K, seven hours). However, there are no fixed departure times and prices assume a full boat, so unless you organise things through an agency, it's worth heading up to the speedboat station the day before to make enquiries. It's around 5km north of town: turn west off Rte 13 beside the Km 390 post then head 300m down an unpaved road that becomes an unlikely dirt track once you cross the only crossroads en route.

Thailand's Golden Triangle

River levels permitting, **Mekong River Cruises** (p46) makes lazy seven-day trips from Luang Prabang to Thailand's Golden Triangle on innovative new two-storey German-Lao riverboats with a sun deck and 16 cabins in which you sleep as well as travel (departs Thursday).

BUS & MINIBUS

Predictably enough, the **northern bus station** (071-252729; Rte 13) and **southern bus station** (Bannaluang Bus Station; Map p38; 071-252066; Rte 13, Km 383) are at opposite ends of town. Several popular bus routes are duplicated by minibuses/minivans from

the **Naluang minibus station** (Map p38; 071-212979; souknasing@hotmail.com; Rte 13), diagonally opposite the latter. Typical fares include Vientiane (170,000K, seven hours) with departures at 7.30am, 8.30am and 5pm; Vang Vieng (110,000K, five hours) at 8am, 9am, 10am, 2pm and 3pm; Luang Namtha (120,000K, eight hours) at 8.30am; and Nong Khiaw (70,000K, three hours) at 9.30am.

For less than double the bus fare, another option is to gather your own group and rent a comfortable six-seater minivan. Prices include photo stops and you'll get there quicker. Directly booked through the minibus station, prices are about 1,000,000K to Phonsavan or Vang Vieng and 500,000K to Nong Khiaw, including pick-up from the guesthouse.

Vientiane & Vang Vieng

From the southern bus station, there are up to 10 daily Vientiane services (115,000K, nine hours) via Vang Vieng between 6.30am and 7.30pm. Sleeper buses (150,000K, nine hours) leave at 8pm and 9.30pm.

Sainyabuli & Hongsa

Buses to Sainyabuli (60,000K, three hours) depart from the southern bus station at 9am and 2pm. The new Tha Deua bridge over the Mekong River is now open and has reduced the journey time to Sainyabuli to two hours or so by private vehicle. There is also a new minibus service to the Elephant Conservation Center in Sainyabuli, operated by **Sakura Tour** (074-212112) which picks you up outside the post office. For Hongsa, the new bridge means it is easiest to travel to Sainyabuli and connect from there.

Phonsavan & Vietnam

For Phonsavan (10 hours) there's an 9am minibus (120,000K) from Naluang minibus station and a 8.30am bus (ordinary/express 90,000/105,000K, 10 hours) from the southern bus station. You can get to Dien Bien Phu (220,000K, 10 hours, leaves 6.30am) and Hanoi (380,000K, 24 hours, leaves 6pm) in Vietnam.

Nong Khiaw & Sam Neua

For Nong Khiaw (55,000K, four hours), 9am minibuses start from Naluang minibus station. Alternatively, from the northern bus station take the *sǒrngtǎaou* (pick-up trucks fitted with benches in the back for passengers; 55,000K) at 9am, 11am and 1pm or the 8.30am bus that continues to Sam Neua (140,000K, 17 hours) via Vieng Thong (120,000K, 10 hours). Another Sam Neua–bound bus (from Vientiane) should pull in sometime around 5.30pm.

Northwestern Laos & China

The sleeper bus to Kunming (450,000K, 24 hours) in China departs from the southern bus station at 7am, sometimes earlier. Pre-booking, and checking the departure location, is wise. From the northern bus station, buses run to Udomxai (60,000K, five hours) at 9am, noon and 4pm; Luang Namtha (105,000K, nine hours) at 9am; and Huay Xai (Borkeo; 130,000K, 15 hours) at 5.30pm with a VIP service at 7pm (150,000K).

❶ Getting Around

BICYCLE

A satisfying way to get around is by bicycle. Numerous shops and some guesthouses have hire bikes for 15,000K to 30,000K per day.

Be careful to lock bicycles and motorbikes securely and don't leave them on the roadside overnight. Note that the peninsula's outer road is one-way anticlockwise: signs are easy to miss. Although you'll see locals flouting the rule (and riding without helmets), police will occasionally fine foreigners.

BOAT

Numerous **boats to Pak Ou Caves** (Map p44) depart between 8.30am and lunchtime; buy tickets at the easily missed little **longboat office** (Map p44; Th Khem Khong; ⊙ 9am-5pm Mon-Sat). **Banana Boat Laos** (p47) offers better organised boat trips for those who aren't worried about every last kip; boats leave from behind the Royal Palace.

BUS

New to Luang Prabang is Lao Green Travel's **E-Bus** (www.laogreengroup.com; trips from 5000K), an electric zero-emission tuk-tuk (green and yellow), which circulates around the old town. You can buy tickets in shops and guesthouses. It also offers an **E-Bus Tour** (p48), which takes passengers around the city on a guided tour.

CAR & MOTORCYCLE

Motorcycle rental typically costs 120,000K per day. **KPTD** (Map p44; ☏ 020-97100771, 071-253447; Th Kitsarat; semi-automatic 100,000K, automatic 120,000K, 250cc dirt bikes per day US$70; ⊙ 8am-5pm) has a wide range of bikes available, including Honda Waves (semi-automatic), Honda Scoopy (automatic) and a thoroughly mean Honda CRF (US$70) for motocross riders only. **Motolao** (p48) rents Honda 250cc motorbikes.

SŎRNGTǍAOU

Located on the opposite side of the Mekong to Luang Prabang, about 400m up from the river, the **Chomphet sŏrngtǎaou stand** (Map p38) serves local villages only.

TUK-TUK

Luang Prabang has no motorbike taxis, only tuk-tuks, plus the odd taxi-van from the airport charging a standardised 50,000K into town. These will cost more if more than three people share the ride. From town back to the airport you might pay marginally less.

Around town locals often pay just 5000K for short tuk-tuk rides, but foreigners are charged a flat 20,000K per hop. To the speedboat landing reckon on 50,000K for the vehicle.

AROUND LUANG PRABANG

Some of the most popular activities in Luang Prabang are based in the countryside beyond, including trekking, cycling, motocross, kayaking and rafting tours. A popular destination is the new forest attraction Green Jungle Flight, almost nearing completion when we passed, with its botanical gardens, swimming pool, cafe and ziplines.

Tours to waterfalls and the Pak Ou Caves are particularly popular and prices are generally competitive, but it still pays to shop around. The Pak Ou Caves and Tat Kuang Si are an odd combination, given that the sites are in opposite directions, but the advantage is that the vehicle to the Kuang Si waterfalls should be waiting when you return to the agency office from your boat trip. Note that tour prices don't include entry fees.

Thirty-two kilometres south of the city, **Green Jungle Flight** (☏ 071-253899, 020-58677616; Ban Paklueang; park entrance US$3, ziplining & ropes course US$28-45, trekking US$35, return boat transfer from Luang Prabang 10,000K) 🌿 is a slice of natural paradise reclaimed from a rubbish dump. It uses the forest and a stunning cascade as its backdrop for a spectacular cat's cradle of ziplines (900m), monkey bridges and rope courses. Also here is a cafe, a restaurant and flower gardens. There were also plans for an organic produce market, swimming pool, and elephant-viewing area where ex-logging jumbos can bathe and socialise.

To reach the park, you catch the boat by the navigation office (p59) in Luang Prabang; you'll ride downriver for 30 minutes and then be taxied the rest of the way by road.

Pak Ou Caves ຖ້ຳປາກອູ

Where the Nam Ou (Ou River) and Mekong River meet at Ban Pak Ou, two famous **caves** (Tham Ting; cave admission 80,000K, return boat tickets per person/boat 65,000/300,000K; ⊘ boats depart 8.30-11am) in the limestone cliff are crammed with myriad buddha images. In the lower cave a photogenic group of buddhas are silhouetted against the stunning riverine backdrop. The upper cave is a five-minute climb up steps (you'll need a torch), 50m into the rock face. Buy boat tickets from the long-boat office in Luang Prabang.

Most visitors en route to Pak Ou stop at the 'Lao Lao Village' Ban Xang Hay, famous for its whiskey. The narrow footpath-streets behind the very attractive (if mostly new) wat are also full of weavers' looms, colourful fabric stalls and a few stills producing the wide range of liquors sold.

An alternative is to go by road to Ban Pak Ou (30km, around 150,000K return for a tuk-tuk) then take a motor-canoe across the river (20,000K return). Ban Pak Ou is 10km down a decent unpaved road that turns off Rte 13 near Km 405.

Tat Kuang Si   ຕາດກວາງຊີ

Thirty kilometres southwest of Luang Prabang, **Tat Kuang Si** (20,000K; ⊘ 7.30am-5.30pm) is a many-tiered waterfall tumbling over limestone formations into a series of cool, swimmable turquoise pools; the term 'Edenic' doesn't do it justice. When you're not swinging off ropes into the water, there's a public park with shelters and picnic tables where you can eat lunch. Don't miss the **Kuang Si Rescue Centre** (www.freethebears. org.au; Kuang Si Waterfall; admission incl with Tat Kuang Si ticket; ⊘ 8.30am-4.30pm) **FREE** near the park entrance. Run by Free the Bears, this excellent centre cares for some 38 Asiatic Wild Moon bears – 15 have been saved in the last three years – confiscated from poachers who sell them to horrendous bile farms serving the appetites of Chinese traditional medicine. These happy little bears merit equal reason for your visit as the cascades themselves. The centre depends on donations and sponsorship: consider buying a T-shirt or adopting a bear.

Kuang Si Butterfly Park (www.facebook. com/laos.kuang.si.butterflypark; adult/child 30,000/ 15,000K; ⊘ 10.30am-4.30pm) ✐, 300m before the Kuang Si waterfall, was opened in 2014 as a breeding sanctuary for Laos' myriad butterflies. Open to travellers, it has a spa where you can have your feet nibbled by miniature fish, or wander the beautiful gardens on a tour.

Many cheap eateries line the entrance car park at the top end of the Khamu village of Ban Thapene.

Visiting Kuang Si by hired motorcycle is very pleasant now that the road here is decently paved and allows stops in villages along the way. By bicycle, be prepared for two long, steady hills to climb. A tuk-tuk from Luang Prabang costs 250,000K for one person, and 85,000K per person in group of three, so it's best to get a group together.

Tat Sae   ບ້ຳຕົກຕາດແສ

The wide, multi-level cascade pools of this menthol-hued **waterfall** (ຕາດແສ; 20,000K, child under 8 free; ⊘ 8am-5.30pm) 15km southeast of Luang Prabang are a memorable sight from August to November. Unlike Tat Kuang Si, there's no single long-drop centrepiece and they dry up almost completely by February. But several year-round gimmicks keep visitors coming, notably a loop of 14 **ziplines** (☑ 020-54290848; www.flightofthe nature.com; per person 300,000K) that allows you to 'fly' around and across the falls.

Part of the attraction of a visit is getting here on a very pleasant seven-minute boat ride (20,000K per person return, 40,000K minimum) that starts from Ban Aen, a peaceful Lao village that's just 1km east of Rte 13 (turn east at Km 371.5). A 30-minute tuk-tuk from Luang Prabang costs up to 150,000K return, including a couple of hours' wait.

Ban Phanom & Beyond   ບ້ານພະນົມ

If you climbed Phu Si you'll surely have spied a large octagonal stupa painted a dazzling golden hue near the 'New Bridge'. This is the 1988 **Santi Chedi** (ສັນຕິເຈຕິ, Peacefulness Pagoda; donation expected; ⊘ 8-10am & 1.30-4.30pm Mon-Fri); its five interior levels are painted with all manner of Buddhist stories and moral admonitions.

It's on a gentle rise, 1km off Rte 13 beside the road to **Ban Phanom**, a prosperous weaving and handicrafts village less than 1km further east. A mostly unpaved road initially follows the Nam Khan east and south, looping round eventually after 14km to **Ban Kok Gniew**, the 'pineapple village' at Km 372 on Rte 13, just 500m short of the turning to Tat Sae waterfall. The road is dusty and gently hilly but quiet and scenic with some attractive karst scenery and several points of interest.

River Life

The Mekong River is the lifeblood of Laos. It's like an artery cutting through the heart of the country, while other important rivers are the veins, breathing life into the landscape and providing transport links between remote landlocked communities. For many Laotians, the river is not just part of their life, it is their life.

LMSFENCER/SHUTTERSTOCK ©

JEAN-PHILIPPE BABU/SHUTTERSTOCK ©

1. Mekong River (p273)
Fishing on the river

2. Nam Song, Vang Vieng (p163)
Row of tourist bungalows along the river

3. River travel, Laos
Travelling in a traditional boat

4. Mekong River, Si Phan Don (p232)
Boats moored on the river

5. Near Vang Vieng
View of the river and karst limestone peaks

JOEB21943/BUDGET TRAVEL/ LONELY PLANET ©

Northern Laos

Best Places to Eat

➡ Lao Falang Restaurant (p71)

➡ Coco Home Bar & Restaurant (p84)

➡ Bamboo Lounge (p106)

➡ Riverside Restaurant (p87)

➡ Souphailin Restaurant (p99)

Best Places to Sleep

➡ Mandala Ou Resort (p84)

➡ Luang Say Lodge (p119)

➡ Zuela Guesthouse (p105)

➡ Nong Kiau Riverside (p84)

➡ Phou Iu III Guesthouse (p106)

Why Go?

Whether it's for trekking, cycling, kayaking, ziplining or a family homestay, a visit to northern Laos is for many the highlight of their trip. Dotted about are unfettered, dense forests home to tigers, gibbons and a cornucopia of animals, with a well-established ecotourism infrastructure to take you into their very heart.

In the north you will also find a tapestry of vividly attired ethnic tribes unlike anywhere else in Laos.

Here the Land of a Million Elephants morphs into the land of a million hellish bends and travel is not for the faint-hearted, as roads endlessly twist and turn through towering mountain ranges and serpentine river valleys. By contrast, most northern towns are functional places, rebuilt after wholesale bombing during the 20th-century Indochina wars.

But visitors aren't in northern Laos for the towns. It's all about the rural life. River trips are a wonderful way to discover the bucolic scenery at a more languid pace.

When to Go
Luang Prabang

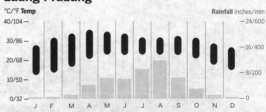

Nov–Feb The ideal season to visit, with little rain and clear skies; chilly at higher altitudes.

Mar–May This time of year is cooking at lower altitudes; lots of haze around from slash-and-burn cultivation.

Jun–Oct The wet season; accommodation is cheap but humidity is high.

ℹ Getting There & Away

The state of roads linking the north to the rest of Laos is steadily improving. By far the easiest, most popular and most spectacular is Rte 13 from Luang Prabang to Vang Vieng. The alternative, via Sainyabuli and Pak Lai, is now paved but less scenic. A third possibility, Rte 10 from Muang Khoun to Paksan, is now in good shape, but there are still some lingering security concerns along certain remote stretches. Finally, the hellish ordeal on what was an ulcerous and dangerously slippery road from Udomxai to Phongsali is now completely sealed, but sadly just as serpentine!

ℹ Getting Around

Road journeys in northern Laos are slow and exhausting. Only the key major routes are asphalted and even these are generally so narrow and winding that it's rare to average more than 30km/h, though many bus drivers push their weary steeds quicker than they are safely able to go. On unpaved roads progress is further hampered by mud in wet conditions, while in the dry season, traffic creates vast dust clouds making travel extremely unpleasant by bike or *sŏrngtăaou* (pick-up trucks fitted with benches in the back for passengers). Follow the local example and wear a face mask. Or consider engaging a private chauffeured minivan (roughly US$100 per day, available in major towns). Fortunately for adventure motorcyclists with decent trail bikes, many secondary roads have virtually no traffic.

A delightful, if often even slower, alternative to road travel is to use riverboats. Think twice before opting for a 'speedboat' – a surfboard with a strap-on car engine might be safer.

XIENG KHUANG & HUA PHAN PROVINCES

Long and winding roads run in seemingly endless ribbons across these green, sparsely populated northeastern provinces towards the mysterious Plain of Jars and the fascinating Vieng Xai Caves. Both are truly intriguing places to visit if you're en route to or from Vietnam. Those with the time can add stops in Nong Khiaw and Vieng Thong. The latter is a gateway to the Nam Et/Phou Louey National Protected Area (NPA) and its 'tiger treks'. All of the above feature on **Stray's** (www.straytravel.asia) ⓟ pricey *Long Thaang* bus loop. Almost anywhere else in either province is completely off the tourist radar.

The altitude, averaging more than 1000m, ensures a climate that's neither too hot in the hot season, nor too cold in the cool season. In December and January, a sweater or jacket is appropriate at night and early morning when seas of cloud fill the populated valleys and form other-worldly scenes for those looking down from passes or peaks.

History

Xieng Khuang's world-famous giant 'jars' along with Hintang's mysterious megaliths indicate a well-developed iron-age culture of which historical knowledge is astonishingly hazy. Whoever carved those enigmatic monuments had long since disappeared by the 13th century when Xieng Khuang emerged as a Buddhist, Tai Phuan principality with a capital at today's Muang Khoun. Both provinces spent subsequent centuries as either independent kingdoms or part of Vietnamese vassal states known as Ai Lao and Tran Ninh. In 1832 the Vietnamese captured the Phuan king of Xieng Khuang, publicly executed him in Hué and made the kingdom a prefecture of Annam, forcing people to adopt Vietnamese dress and customs. Chinese Haw gangs ravaged the region in the late 19th century, pushing both provinces to accept Siamese and French protection.

Major skirmishes between the Free Lao and the Viet Minh took place from 1945 to 1946, and as soon as the French left Indochina the North Vietnamese started a build-up of troops to protect Hanoi's rear flank. By the end of the 1960s the area had become a major battlefield. With saturation bombing by American planes obliterating virtually every town and village, much of the population had to live for their protection in caves, only emerging in 1973. At Vieng Xai, the most important of these caves also sheltered the Pathet Lao's anti-royalist government.

North Vietnamese troops did their share of damage on the ground as well, destroying once-magnificent Muang Sui and much of royalist-held western Xieng Khuang Province. After the conflict, infamous *samana* re-education camps appeared, notably in eastern Hua Phan, to 'rehabilitate' and punish former royalists with a mixture of hard labour and political indoctrination. Many continued into the 1980s and the possibility that a *samana* still remains near Sop Hao has never been officially confirmed nor denied. Meanwhile, decades after the conflict, unexploded ordnance (UXO) remains very widespread, especially in central and eastern Xieng Khuang, threatening local lives for generations to come.

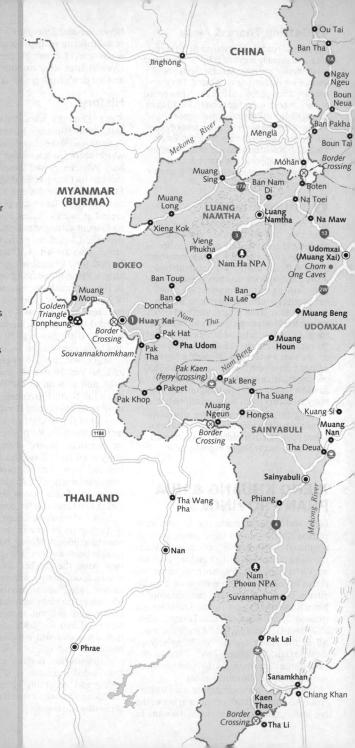

Northern Laos Highlights

1 Gibbon Experience (p113) Soaring through the jungle canopy on ziplines to remote tree houses on this unforgettable adventure near Huay Xai.

2 Nam Ou (p72) Karsting away on a boat ride or kayak trip down the Nam Ou (Ou River) between Muang Ngoi Neua and Nong Khiaw.

3 Phongsali (p91) Learning about the local lifestyle in homestays on a tribal trek in this remote region.

4 Vieng Xai Caves (p78) Discovering the history of the incredible limestone landscape where the Pathet Lao hid from US aerial assault.

5 Plain of Jars (p73) Exploring Xieng Khuang's mysterious archaeological sites.

Phonsavan ໂພນສະຫວັນ

☑ 061

Phonsavan is a popular base from which to explore the Plain of Jars. The town itself has an unfinished feel and is very spread out, with its two parallel main boulevards stretching for about 3km east–west. Fortunately a very handy concentration of hotels, restaurants and tour agents is crammed into a short if architecturally uninspired central 'strip'. More shops, markets and facilities straggle along Rte 7. But the town is best appreciated from the surrounding hills, several of which are pine-clad and topped with small resorts. Keep an eye out too for wooden powder-blue Hmong cottages on the mountain roads with firewood neatly stacked outside.

The region has long been a centre of Phuan language and culture (part of the Tai-Kadai family). There's also a strong Vietnamese presence.

◉ Sights

About 1km apart at the southern edge of town are two hilltop **memorials** (open sunrise to sunset) to Pathet Lao and Vietnamese soldiers lost in the war.

UXO Information Centre (MAG)   CULTURAL CENTRE

(Map p70; ☑ 061-211010; www.maginternational. org/laos; donations encouraged; ☺10am-8pm) **FREE** Decades after America's Secret War on Laos, unexploded bombs and mines remain a devastating problem throughout this region. Visit the thought-provoking UXO Information Centre, run by British organisation MAG (Mines Advisory Group) that's been helping to clear Laos' unexploded ordnance since 1994. The centre's information displays underline the enormity of the bomb drops, and there are also examples of (defused) UXO to ponder. Donations are encouraged: US$12 pays for the clearing of around 10 sq metres and a commemorative T-shirt.

Late-afternoon screenings show the powerful documentaries *Bomb Harvest* (4.30pm; www.bombharvest.com), *Surviving the Peace* (5.50pm) and *Bombies* (6.30pm; www. itvs.org/bombies/film.html). They are distressing but important, as they show the full scale of the trauma, from footage of US bombers in action to the ongoing casualties of their horrific legacy.

★ Xieng Khouang UXO-Survivors' Information Centre   CULTURAL CENTRE

(Map p70; www.laos.worlded.org; donations encouraged; ☺8am-8pm) **FREE** This unexploded ordnance (UXO) information centre and colourful, upbeat shop sells silk laptop bags, purses and handicrafts made by UXO survivors. Aside from displays including prosthetic limbs, wheelchairs and bomb parts, there's also a reading room with a wealth of information on the Secret War and the different kinds of UXO that still present a danger to Laos today. Ask to see the video *Surviving Cluster Bombs*. Note that 90% of your donations go towards the treatment of UXO survivors.

Mulberries   FARM

(ປັ່ສາ; ☑ 061-561271; www.mulberries.org; ☺8am-4pm Mon-Sat) This is a fair-trade silk farm that offers interesting free visits including a complete introduction to the silk-weaving process from cocoon to colourful scarves. It's off Rte 7 just west of the main bus station.

⊙ Tours

Several agents on the main drag and virtually every guesthouse will be ready to slot you into a one-day Plain of Jars tour visiting the three main sites. The going rate is 150,000K including a noodle-soup lunch and entry fees. This price is contingent on there being at least seven fellow passengers.

Other advertised tours include trips to places such as Muang Khoun, Muang Sui or Tham Piu, but these rarely garner enough customers for prices to be competitive. Try gathering your own group.

Lao Falang Travel Service   ADVENTURE

(Map p70; ☑ 020-55406868, 020-23305614; Rte 7; one-day trip US$108) Run by a dependable Italian guy, this outfit operates multiday and one-day motorbike tours, of which 70% to 85% are spent off-road (depending on your confidence). A one-day tour typically includes Jar Site 1, the Russian tank and Muang Khoun. Dinner is included at the excellent Lao Falang Italian restaurant. Solid, experienced guides ensure you don't go beyond your comfort zone.

Sousath Travel   TOURS

(Map p70; ☑ 020-55406868, 020-23305614; rasapet_lao@yahoo.com; Rte 7; ☺8am-8pm) Sousath offers very reliable tours to the Plain of Jars and the Ho Chi Minh Trail, as well as

UXO & WAR JUNK

During the Indochina wars, Laos earned the dubious distinction of becoming the most heavily bombed nation per capita in world history. Xieng Khuang Province was especially hard hit and even today, innumerable scraps of combat debris remain. Much of it is potentially deadly unexploded ordnance (UXO), including mortar shells, white phosphorous canisters (used to mark bomb targets) and assorted bombs. Some of the most problematic UXO comes from cluster bombs, 1.5m-long torpedo-shaped packages of evil whose outer metal casing was designed to split open lengthwise in mid-air, scattering 670 tennis-ball-sized bomblets ('bombies') over a 5000-sq-metre area. Once disturbed, a bombie would explode, projecting around 30 steel pellets like bullets, killing anyone within a 20m radius. Over 40 years after bombing ceased, almost one person a day is still injured or killed by UXO in Laos, 40% of them children. Tens of millions of bombies remain embedded in the land, causing an ever-present danger to builders, farmers and especially young children, who fatally mistake them for toys. And for impoverished villagers, the economic temptation to collect UXO to sell as scrap metal has caused numerous fatalities. Despite valiant ongoing clearance efforts, at current rates it would take an estimated 150 years to deal with the problem.

Cluster-bomb casings, which were not themselves explosive, have meanwhile found a wide range of more positive new uses. In some places you can see them reused as architectural features, feeding troughs, pots for growing spring onions or simply as ornaments around houses or hotels.

If you find any war debris, don't be tempted to touch it. Even if it appears to be an exhibit in a collection, beware that some hotels display war junk that's never been properly defused and might remain explosive. Even if it isn't live and dangerous, the Lao legal code makes it illegal to trade in war leftovers of any kind. Purchase, sale or theft of any old weaponry can result in a prison term of between six months and five years.

homestays in Hmong villages. For war obsessives he can organise trips to Long Tien, the clandestine runway in the Saisombun jungle created by the CIA during the Secret War. He also rents bikes (20,000K) and scooters (manual/automatic 70,000/90,000K).

Amazing Lao Travel HIKING
(Map p70; 020-22340005; www.amazinglao. com; Rte 7) Runs treks to the jar sites and two-day treks in the mountains, including a homestay in a Hmong village. As ever, the more the merrier, with prices falling for larger groups.

🛏 Sleeping

🛏 Central Strip

Kong Keo Guesthouse GUESTHOUSE $
(Map p70; 061-211354, 020-285858; www. kongkeojar.com; dm 40,000K, r in outside block 80,000K, chalets 120,000K; 🛜) Run by Veomany, at the time of writing he was doing a great job of replacing the shoddy wood huts with six balconied brick chalets. While the seven-berth dorm is cramped, the outdoor block has large clean rooms with mint-green walls and private bathroom. The UXO-

decorated restaurant-bar has nightly barbecues, and Veomany runs excellent tours to the Plain of Jars.

Anoulack Khen Lao Hotel HOTEL $$
(Map p70; 061-213599; www.anoulackkhenlao hotel.com; Main St; r incl breakfast 200,000K; ❄🛜) This glass Lego tower has easily the best rooms in town, with wood floors, thick mattresses, white linen, cable TV, fridges, kettles and swish hot-water en suites. There's a great restaurant on the 5th floor where you can take breakfast and use the wi-fi. Conveniently the hotel also has a lift. Worth the extra spend.

🛏 Around Town

Hillside Residence HOTEL $$
(Map p70; 061-213300; www.thehillside residence.com; Ban Tai; r incl breakfast US$30; 🛜) Set in a lush little garden, this replica half-timbered mansion looks like it belongs in a colonial-era hill town. Rooms are petite but attractive with all the trimmings, including blankets for the cool season. However, the beds are pretty hard. There's a shared upper sitting terrace and some upstairs rooms have their own balconies. Free wi-fi, and a lovely owner.

Phonsavan

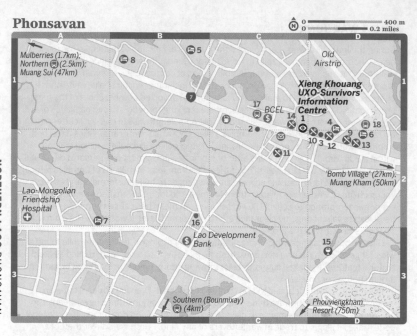

Phonsavan

Vansana Plain of Jars Hotel HOTEL $$
(Map p70; ☎061-213170; www.vansanahotel-group.com; r 400,000-500,000K) Opulent by Phonsavan standards, this grand hotel built in 2004 occupies its own small summit above town. Large, comfortable rooms have plush carpeting, aged TVs, minibars, tasteful decor and big tubs in the bathrooms. Each also has a small balcony with great views over town. The place is a little tired and in need of a shot in the arm, however.

Maly Hotel HOTEL $$
(Map p70; ☎061-312031; www.malyhotel.com; r incl breakfast US$25-60; ❇@☎) OK, so it's 15 minutes' walk or 20,000K in a tuk-tuk to the town centre; however, tangerine-coloured Maly excels, with wood beams and candlelit ambience. Rooms include weary en suites, TVs, hot water and Lao textiles. Room 8 is a spacious corner suite at the top of the range. Helpful staff, and a decent breakfast.

✕ Eating & Drinking

In case you want to avoid an unpleasant surprise, note that several Vietnamese restaurants serve dog (*thịt chó*).

Nisha Restaurant INDIAN $

(Map p70; Rte 7; meals 20,000 30,000K; ☻7am 10pm; 🛜🍴) Cream-interiored Nisha is tidy and simple but the real colour is found in its excellent cuisine. The menu includes all the usual suspects like tikka masala and rogan josh, curries and a wide range of vegetarian options. However, it's the perfect application of spice and the freshness of the food that'll keep you coming back.

Fresh Food Market MARKET $

(Map p70; ☻6am-5pm) This market stocks exotic fruits you won't typically see elsewhere in Laos, such as Chinese pear. Other local delicacies include *nok qen dąwng* (swallows stored whole in jars until they ferment) and *hét wâi* (wild matsutake mushrooms), which grow around Xieng Khuang and fetch high prices in Japan. Bring your camera.

Sanga Restaurant LAOTIAN $

(Map p70; Rte 7; mains 15,000-30,000K; ☻11am-10pm) The venue is a bland box of a front room but the meals are unexpectedly accomplished for such sensible prices. The chicken *láhp* (minced pork salad with shallots and coriander) is especially tasty and the steak and chips is a popular bargain at 30,000K.

★Lao Falang Restaurant ITALIAN $$

(Map p70; ☎020-5546868; mains 50,000-70,000K; ☻7am-4pm & 5-10.30pm; 🏵🛜🍴) Sister of Lao Falang Travel Service (p68), this spacious, stylish and impeccably clean Italian restaurant is run by a friendly Genoese man who speaks four languages. Highly recommended for alchemising sirloin steak, lamb and giant prawns into various delicious incarnations, plus its handmade pasta (carbonara and bolognese), thin-based pizza and homemade ice cream. Great wine choices, too.

Bamboozle Restaurant & Bar INTERNATIONAL $$

(Map p70; ☎030-9523913; Rte 7; meals 25,000-52,000K; ☻7-10.30am & 3.30-10.30pm, kitchen closes 9pm; 🛜) 🍴 True to its name, with bamboo walls plus pretty lanterns strung from its ceiling, Bamboozle dishes up thin-crust pizza, salads, pasta dishes, good-sized cheeseburgers and terrific Lao cuisine. Add to this chilled beers and a rock-and-roll soundtrack and it's a winner. A percentage of the profits goes towards the Lone Buffalo Foundation (www.facebook.com/lonebuffalo), which supports the town's youth.

Cranky-T Café & Bar FUSION $$$

(Map p70; ☎061-213263, 020-55504677; www.facebook.com/CrankyTLaos; Main St; mains 35,000-130,000K; ☻7am-11pm, food served 5-9pm, happy hour 4-7pm; 🏵🛜) Cranky-Ts has a stylish red-wine-coloured and exposed-brick interior, with the eponymous owner creating mouth-watering salads, sashimi, smoked-salmon crêpes and hearty fare like NZ sirloin with mash to fill you up after trekking the jar sites. Add to this cinnamon muffins, brownie cheesecake and a good selection of cocktails (35,000K), and you may spend all day here.

Barview BAR

(Map p70; ☻8am-11pm) Try this simple shack for sunset beers over the rice-paddy fields. Locals gather here to play guitars and munch on barbecued meat.

ℹ Information

DANGERS & ANNOYANCES

Don't underestimate the dangers of unexploded ordnance (UXO) in this most heavily bombed of provinces.

INTERNET ACCESS

Wi-fi is commonly available at accommodation and eating spots.

MEDICAL SERVICES

Lao-Mongolian Friendship Hospital (Map p70; ☎061-312166) May be able to assist with minor health concerns.

MONEY

Currency exchange is available at **Lao Development Bank** (Map p70; ☎061-312188; ☻8.30am-3.30pm Mon-Fri), at **BCEL** (Map p70; ☎061-213291; Rte 7; ☻8.30am-3.30pm Mon-Fri) and from several travel agents. There are two ATMs along Rte 7.

POST

Post Office (Map p70; ☻8am-4pm Mon-Fri, to noon Sat) Also has a domestic phone service.

TOURIST INFORMATION

Xieng Khuang Tourist Office (☎020-22340201, 061-312217; www.xiengkhouang tourism.com; Hwy 1E; ☻8am-4pm) While impractically located in the middle of nowhere (on the road to the airport), this helpful office has English-speaking staff, brochures and souvenirs recycled from war junk. Free maps

RIVER TRIPS

Until the 1990s, riverboats were an essential form of intercity passenger transport in Laos. Today, villagers in roadless hamlets still travel by river, while several longer-distance routes remain possible thanks in significant part to tourist interest. On riverboats the journey is an attraction in itself.

Mekong Slowboats

Huay Xai–Pak Beng or Pak Beng–Luang Prabang (one day) Both sectors are very pleasant one-day rides. Boats are designed for 70 passengers but are sometimes seriously overcrowded. The seats are usually very hard, but you can get up and walk around. There's a toilet on board and usually a stall selling snacks and overpriced beer.

Huay Xai–Luang Prabang (two days) Travel in relative luxury with Luang Say Cruise (p117) or Shompoo Cruise (p117). Both run boats that are similar in size to the Mekong slowboats but carry a maximum of 40 passengers. The Luang Say Cruise is not for the budget traveller, but includes meals, sightseeing stops and excellent overnight accommodation at the Luang Say Lodge.

Mekong Speedboats

Huay Xai–Luang Prabang (one day) Scarily fast, dangerous and excruciatingly uncomfortable if you're not small and supple. It's also best to avoid this trip when river levels have dropped after the wet season, giving boatmen less clearance of the underwater pillars of rocks.

Nam Tha Boats

Luang Namtha–Huay Xai or Na Lae–Huay Xai longboat (one day) You can now only take the boat as far as Ban Phaeng, where a dam has recently been built; from here you are picked up and driven the remaining route to Huay Xai. What was a two-day experience is now just a day, though you still have around eight hours of puttering downriver. The journey starts in Luang Namtha where you are driven by car to Na Lae to board the boat.

Hat Sa–Muang Khua is no longer possible since the Nam Ou (Ou River) was dammed, although **Muang Khua–Nong Khiaw** (six hours) still sees boats leave Muang Khua every morning, passing through Muang Ngoi Neua (five hours) before arriving in Nong Khiaw, and taking you through the country's most spectacular karst scenery.

Nong Khiaw–Luang Prabang (one day) Due to the damming of the Nam Ou, the boat trip to Luang Prabang was not possible at the time of writing, but will, like the other dam-affected river trips, be available in sections in the near future, and will involve hopping in and out of vehicles and boats to accommodate the obstacles.

---

for Phonsavan and Xieng Khuang district are available. Also, keep an eye out for its free photocopied sheet entitled 'What Do I Do Around Phonesavanh Town', for alternative ideas on things to do aside from the jar sites.

ℹ Getting There & Away

Airline and bus timetables usually call Phonsavan 'Xieng Khuang', even though that was originally the name for Muang Khoun.

AIR

Lao Airlines (Map p70; ☎ 061-212027; www.laoairlines.com) has daily flights to/from Vientiane (US$63). Sometimes a weekly flight to/from Luang Prabang operates in peak season.

BUS
International & Long Distance Buses

Longer-distance bus tickets presold by travel agencies typically cost around 40,000K more than standard fares but include a transfer to the confusingly named **Northern Bus Station** (☎ 030-5170148), located 4km west of the centre, also sometimes known as the Provincial Bus Station. From here Vietnam-bound buses depart to Vinh (150,000K, 11 hours) at 6.30am on Tuesday, Thursday, Friday and Sunday, continuing seasonally on Mondays to Hanoi (320,000K). For Vientiane (110,000K, 11 hours) there are air-con buses at 7.30am, 8.30am, 10.30am, 4.30pm, 6.30pm and a VIP bus (130,000K) at 8.30pm. These all pass through Vang Vieng, to where there's an additional 7.30am departure

(95,000K). The sleeper here (150,000K) leaves at 8pm. For Luang Prabang (10 hours) both minivans (95,000K) and VIP buses (120,000K) depart at 8.30am and 6.30pm. There's an 8am bus to Sam Neua (80,000K, eight to 10 hours) and a 6pm sleeper (100,000K), plus two Vientiane–Sam Neua buses passing through. A 7.30am bus is timetabled to Paksan (100,000K, 10 hours) on the new road.

The **Southern (Bounmixay) Bus Station** (Highway 1D), 4km south of town, has a 6am bus (four days a week) to Savannakhet (150,000K) that continues on to Pakse (180,000K). Buses to Paksan (100,000K, eight hours) via the newly completed road depart daily at 6.30am and 8am.

Phoukham Minibus and Bus Station (Map p70; ☑ 020-99947072; Th Xaysana; ⊙ 7am-8pm) in the east-central side of town has minibuses leaving at 8.30am for Luang Prabang (110,000K) and Vang Vieng (100,000K), with 6.30am, 8am and 5pm minibuses for Vientiane (110,000K). There's also a VIP bus for Vientiane (130,000K) leaving from here at 7.30pm.

Local Services

Local buses and *sŏrngtăaou* use the **Old Bus Station** (Map p70); destinations include Muang Khoun (20,000K, hourly), Muang Kham (25,000K, two hours, hourly) and Nong Haet (35,000K, four hours, four daily).

🛈 Getting Around

Tuk-tuks, if and when you can find them, cost from 15,000K for a short hop to about 30,000K to the airport. Lao Falang Restaurant (p71) rents bicycles (40,000K per day) and 100cc motorbikes (100,000K), ideal for reaching a selection of jar sites. It also has some Chinese quad bikes (160,000K) if you're feeling brave. Fill up at the **petrol station** (Map p70) in town.

Chauffeured six-seater vans or 4WDs can be chartered through most guesthouses and hotels; you're looking at US$150 to Sam Neua or US$120 to Luang Prabang.

Around Phonsavan

Plain of Jars   ທົ່ງໄຫຫິນ

Mysterious giant stone jars of unknown ancient origin are scattered over hundreds of hilly square kilometres around Phonsavan, giving the area the misleading name of Plain of Jars. Remarkably, nobody knows which civilisation created them, although archaeologists estimate they date from the Southeast Asian iron age (500 BC to AD 200).

Smaller jars have long since been carted off by collectors but around 2500 larger

Plain of Jars

jars, jar fragments and 'lids' remain. As the region was carpet-bombed throughout the Indochina wars, it's miraculous that so many artefacts survived. Only a handful of the 90 recorded jar sites have so far been cleared of unexploded ordnance (UXO), and then only within relatively limited areas. These sites, and their access paths, are delineated by easily missed red-and-white marker stones: remain vigilant.

Sites 1, 2 and 3 form the bases of most tour loops.

⊙ Sights

While the jars at Sites 2 and 3 aren't as large or as plentiful as at Site 1, they have their own charm. Set in very different locations, the journey to reach them offers glimpses of some typical local villages.

Jar Site 1   ARCHAEOLOGICAL SITE
(Thong Hai Hin; 15,000K) The biggest and most easily accessible, Site 1 of the Plain of Jars features over 300 jars relatively close-packed on a pair of hilly slopes pocked with bomb craters. The biggest, **Hai Jeuam**, weighs around 6 tonnes, stands more than 2.5m high and is said to have been the mythical victory cup of Khun Jeuam. The bare, hilly landscape is appealing, although in one direction the views of Phonsavan airport seem discordant.

There is a small cafe, a gift shop and toilets near the entrance.

Jar Site 2
ARCHAEOLOGICAL SITE

(Hai Hin Phu Salato; 10,000K) Site 2 of the Plain of Jars is a pair of hillocks divided by a shallow gully that forms the access lane. This rises 700m from the ticket desk in what becomes a muddy slither in wet conditions. To the left in thin woodlands, look for a cracked stone urn through which a tree has managed to grow. To the right another set of jars sits on a grassy knoll with panoramas of layered hills, paddies and cow fields. It's very atmospheric.

Jar Site 3
ARCHAEOLOGICAL SITE

(Hai Hin Lat Khai; 10,000K) The 150-jar Site 3 of the Plain of Jars sits on a scenic hillside in pretty woodland near Ban Lat Khai village. The access road to Lat Khai leads east beside a tiny motorbike repair hut just before Ban Xiang Di (Ban Siang Dii). The ticket booth is beside a simple local restaurant that offers somewhat overpriced *fĕr* (rice noodles; 30,000K). The jars are accessed by a little wooden footbridge and an attractive 10-minute walk across rice fields.

❶ Getting There & Away

All three main jar sites can be visited by rented motorbike from Phonsavan in around five hours, while Site 1 is within bicycle range. Site 1 is just 8km southwest of central Phonsavan, 2.3km west of the Muang Khoun road: turn at the signed junction in Ban Hay Hin. For Sites 2 and 3, turn west off the Muang Khoun road just past Km 8. Follow the unpaved road for 10km/14km to find the turnings for Sites 2/3, then follow muddy tracks for 1.5/1.8km, respectively.

Alternatively, sign up the night before to join one of several regular guided minibus tours. Most throw in a noodle-soup lunch at Site 3 and a quick stop to see the lumpy rusting remnant of an armoured vehicle in a roadside copse at Ban Nakho: its nickname, the 'Russian Tank', exaggerates its appeal.

Muang Khoun (Old Xieng Khuang)
ເມືອງຄູນ

POP 4000 / ☏ 061

The region's ancient capital, Muang Khoun was ravaged in the 19th century by Chinese and Vietnamese invaders, then so heavily bombarded during the Second Indochina War that by 1975 it was almost completely abandoned. However, a handful of aged monuments survived as ruins and the town slowly redeveloped, although it is very much a village in comparison to the new capital Phon-

PHAKEO TREK

Organised through Phonsavan agencies, the excellent two-day Phakeo trek combines many essential elements of the Xieng Khuang experience. On the long first day, hike across secondary forested mountain ridges to a three-part jar site with about 400 ancient jars and jar fragments, many moss-encrusted and shaded by foliage. The trek then descends into the roadless Hmong village of Ban Phakeo, whose shingle-roofed mud-floor homes huddle around a central rocky knoll. A purpose-built Hmong-style guest-shack provides a basic sleeping platform with space for eight hikers. There's no electricity. The next day, the hike descends into attractive semi-agricultural valleys then climbs up the cascades of a multi-terraced waterfall to arrive in the famous 'Bomb Village', which no longer has many bombs after extensive clearance work.

savan. It's certainly not a must-see but might be worth the detour for those staying a few days in the region.

A good asphalt road from Phonsavan (30km north) passes through some attractive rice-terrace villages, several sporting Phuan-style houses built of sturdy timbers. Buying the Muang Khoun Visitor's Ticket (10,000K; available at various sights in the area) supports ongoing maintenance efforts.

◉ Sights

The main historic sights are a trio of historic stupas, all walking distance from the Khoun Guesthouse. One is directly behind in the grounds of the colourfully rebuilt active monastery, **Wat Si Phoum**. The other two are on a facing ridge, accessed via the brick-and-mud lane that climbs opposite the guesthouse, petering out into a narrow footpath. The 1576 **That Foun** (also called That Chomsi) is around 25m tall and built in the Lan Xang/Lanna style. It now has a distinct lean to its spire and you can climb right through a hole that was made by 19th-century Chinese Haw marauders, who tunnelled in to loot the priceless Buddha relics enshrined within. A five-minute walk around the easy ridge track brings you to the stubbier remnants of the Cham-built 16th-century stupa **That Chom Phet**.

The main road continuing east swerves south just before Km 30 after **Wat Phia Wat**. Of Wat Phia Wat's original 1582 building just the base platform and a few brick columns survived a devastating 1966 bombing raid. But these columns photogenically frame an age-greyed, shell shocked Buddha with a whiplash smile.

The unpaved road continuing east passes the small, very degraded **Jar Site 16** after about 5km. This road becomes increasingly difficult and finally dead-ends some 12km beyond at **Ban Thalin**, an interesting village without any commercial facilities that's used as the starting point for the Phakeo trek.

🛏 Sleeping & Eating

Khoun Guesthouse & Restaurant
GUESTHOUSE $

(☑ 061-212464; Rte 10, Km 29; r 50,000-90,000K; ☎) Set in a garden, this is the town's sole accommodation option. The 50,000K rooms are cell-like at best but the 90,000K rooms are larger and include TV and hot water. The restaurant includes an English-language menu of Lao staples; some tour groups stop here for lunch.

ℹ Getting There & Away

Buses to Phonsavan (20,000K, 45 minutes) depart throughout the day. By motorbike it's possible to visit Muang Khoun plus the three main jar sites in one long day.

Sam Neua (Xam Neua)
ຊຳເໜືອ

POP 16,000 / ☑ 064

While Sam Neua (Xam Neua) is something of a nostalgic Soviet oddity, with its well-spaced concrete modernity, spartan communist monument and old boys with Muscovite hats, the real draw is the stunning countryside in which it sits. The town is a logical transit point for visiting nearby Vieng Xai or catching the daily bus to Vietnam, and remains one of Laos' least visited provincial capitals. Also it's at an altitude of roughly 1200m, some warm clothes are advisable in the dry winter period, at least by night and until the thick morning fog burns off. From April to October the lush landscapes are contrastingly warm and wet.

The eye-widening, photogenic produce markets here are worth visiting for the colourful ethnic diversity on display.

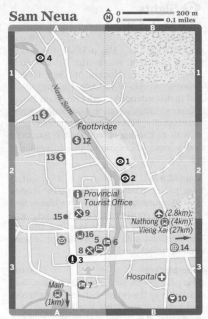

Sam Neua

Sam Neua

◎ Sights
1 Food Market B2
2 Main Market B2
3 Suan Keo Lak Meung Monument A3
4 Suspension Bridge A1

🛏 Sleeping
5 Bounhome Guest House A3
6 Phonchalern Hotel B3
7 Xayphasouk Hotel A3

✖ Eating
Chittavanh Restaurant .... (see 6)
8 Dan Nao Muang Xam Restaurant A3
Food Market .... (see 1)
9 Yuni Coffee A2

🍷 Drinking & Nightlife
10 Nang Nok Bar B3

ℹ Information
11 Agricultural Promotion Bank A1
12 BCEL A2
Foreign Exchange .... (see 2)
13 Lao Development Bank A2
14 Tam.com Internet Service B3

ℹ Transport
15 Motorcycle Shop A2
16 Tuk-Tuk Stand A3

◉ Sights

Suan Keo Lak Meung Monument
MONUMENT

(ສວນແກວຫຼັກເມືອງ; Map p75) At the town's central junction stands the bizarre Suan Keo Lak Meung Monument. Four hooked concrete pincers hold aloft a glittery disco ball that is intended to celebrate Sam Neua's folk-song image as an 'indestructible jewel'. However, the effect is unintentionally comic, with its backing of half-hearted fountains and a frieze full of communist triumphalist soldiers.

Main Market
MARKET

(Map p75; ☉ dawn-dusk) The main market is predominantly stocked with Chinese and Vietnamese consumer goods. However, some fabric stalls here stock regional textiles, and jewellers sell antique coins and silverware used for tribal headgear.

Food Market
MARKET

(Map p75; ☉ 6am-6pm) The fascinating food market is well stocked with fresh vegetables and meats, some rather startling. Field rats are displayed cut open to show the freshness of their entrails. Banana leaves might be stuffed with squirming insects. And there's plenty of dead furry wildlife that you'd probably prefer to see alive in the forests.

Suspension Bridge
BRIDGE

(Map p75) Enchanting river scenes are visible from this bike-and-pedestrian suspension bridge.

⊨ Sleeping

Phonchalern Hotel
HOTEL $

(Map p75; ☎ 064-312192; www.phonechalern hotel.com; r 80,000-110,000K; ✳🛜) This palatially sized hotel has a mix of rooms; some are dark and uninviting while those facing the river are full of light and have a communal balcony out front. Rooms have fridge, TV and clean en suite. Downstairs there's a lobby the size of a bowling alley. It's a sure bet for one night.

Bounhome Guest House
GUESTHOUSE $

(Map p75; ☎ 020-2348125, 064-312223; r with fan/air-con 80,000/100,000K; ✳🛜) Next to the bridge, this guesthouse has compact rooms with tiled floors, fans and low-set beds with fresh linen and blankets. You'll be glad to use their powerful hot showers.

Xayphasouk Hotel
HOTEL $$

(Map p75; ☎ 064-312033; xayphasoukhotel@ gmail.com; r 150,000-200,000K; ✳🛜) Currently the smartest hotel in Sam Neua. The huge lobby-restaurant is woefully underused, but the rooms are very comfortable for such a remote region of Laos. All include piping-hot showers, flat-screen TVs, tasteful furnishings and crisp linen. And there's free wi-fi, plus a cafe downstairs for breakfast.

✕ Eating & Drinking

★ Yuni Coffee
CAFE $

(Map p75; ☎ 020-52221515; www.yunicoffee. com; sandwiches US$2; ☉ 7.30am-7.30pm; ✳) A blessing for coffee snobs: if you're missing standard lattes your caffeine privations are over. With battleship-grey walls and a choice selection of refrigerated sandwiches, fresh-baked baguettes and brownies, as well as kick-ass locally grown coffee, Yuni is the only way to kick-start your day.

Dan Nao Muang Xam Restaurant
LAOTIAN $

(Map p75; mains 15,000-50,000K; ☉ 7am-9.30pm; 🖥) This hole-in-the-wall spot is hardly brimming with atmosphere, but it has the most foreigner-friendly menu in town in concise English. Breakfast includes cornflakes and a delicious fĕr. Dinner includes some excellent rice and soup combinations, plus a steak with al dente vegetables arranged starlike around the plate. It also serves decent portions of láhp, fried-rice variations and omelettes.

Chittavanh Restaurant
LAOTIAN $

(Map p75; mains 25,000-40,000K; ☉ 7am-9pm; 🖥) Savouring a delicious Chinese fried-tofu dish makes it worth braving the reverberant clatter of this cavernous hotel restaurant where vinyl tablecloths have been nailed into place. Locals like to eat here as well – always a good sign.

Food Market
MARKET $

(Map p75; ☉ 6am-6pm) For cheap fĕr (rice noodles), samosas, spring rolls and fried sweet potato, the food market is the place to go.

Nang Nok Bar
BAR

(Map p75; ☉ 6-10pm) Sam Neua is not going to win any awards for its nightlife, but Nang Nok might be one of the only contenders. It's a thatched pavilion on the edge of town where young locals come to down big bottles of Beerlao.

ℹ Information

INTERNET ACCESS

Many hotels and guesthouses have wi-fi these days. **Tam.com Internet Service** (Map p75; per min 150K; ⊗ 8am-10pm) is a relatively reliable internet cafe.

MONEY

Agricultural Promotion Bank (Map p75; ⊗ 8am-noon & 1.30-4pm Mon-Fri) Exchanges Thai baht and US dollars at fair rates.

BCEL (Map p75; ⊗ 8am-3.30pm Mon-Fri) Has a couple of ATMs dispensing kip, plus it can exchange most major currencies.

Foreign Exchange (Map p75; ⊗ 7am-6pm) Changing money is generally quickest through one of the fabric stalls in the main market: they exchange Vietnamese dong and are open at weekends.

Lao Development Bank (Map p75; ☑ 064-312171; ⊗ 8am-4pm Mon-Fri) On the main road 400m north of the bus station on the left; exchanges cash and travellers cheques.

POST

Post Office (Map p75; ⊗ 8am-4pm Mon-Fri) In a large building directly opposite the bus station. A telephone office at its rear offers international calls.

TOURIST INFORMATION

Provincial Tourist Office (Map p75; ☑ 064-312567; ⊗ 8am-noon & 1.30-4pm Mon-Fri) An excellent tourist office with English-speaking staff eager to help.

ℹ Getting There & Away

AIR

Sam Neua's little **Nathong Airport** is 3km east of the centre towards Vieng Xai. **Lao Skyway** (☑ 020-99755556, 064-314268; www.laoskyway.com; Nathong Airport; ⊗ 8am-4pm), which is based here, flies to Vientiane on Monday, Wednesday, Thursday, Friday and Saturday (US$62, 1½ hours). All too frequently the flights get cancelled just before departure. At the time of writing, there was no flight to Phonsavan.

BUS

Sam Neua has two bus stations. Schedules change frequently so double check and certainly don't rely on timetables printed on tourist maps and noticeboards.

Main Bus Station

The **main bus station** is on a hilltop 1.2km south of the central monument, just off the Vieng Thong road. From here buses leave to Vientiane (190,000K, 22 hours) via Phonsavan (80,000K, 10 hours) at 10am, 1pm, 3pm and 5pm. An additional 8.30am Vientiane bus (100,000K) goes via Vieng Thong (50,000K, six hours), Luang

---

GETTING TO VIETNAM: NAM SOI TO NA MEO

Getting to the Border

If going to the **Nam Soi (Laos)/Na Meo (Vietnam) border crossing** (Km 175; 7.30am to 11.30am and 1.30pm to 4.30pm), the easiest transport option is to take the daily direct bus (sometimes minibus) between Sam Neua and Thanh Hoa that passes close to Vieng Xai but doesn't enter town. It departs daily at 8am (180,000K, 11 hours). Pre-purchase your ticket at the main bus station to avoid overcharging. 'Through tickets' to Hanoi still go via Thanh Hoa with a change of bus.

It's quite possible to reach the border by the 8am Na Meo *sŏrngtăaou* (pick-up trucks fitted with benches in the back for passengers) from Sam Neua (three hours). However, organising onward transport from the Vietnamese side is complicated by unscrupulous operators who seem intent on overcharging.

At the Border

Westbound, note that the Lao border post (Nam Soi) isn't a town. There are a few simple restaurant shacks but no accommodation and no waiting transport apart from the 11.30am *sŏrngtăaou* to Sam Neua.

Laos visas are available on arrival at this border but Vietnamese visas are not, so plan ahead if heading east.

Moving On

Once in Thanh Hoa, there's a night train to Hanoi departing at 11.30pm and arriving very early (around 4am). Returning from Thanh Hoa (8am), tickets should cost US$14 but foreigners are often asked for significantly more.

Prabang (130,000K, 17 hours) and Vang Vieng. There are also daily minibuses to Luang Prabang (130,000K) at 7am, 7.30am and 3.30pm. Finally, there is a Vieng Thong bus at 7.20am.

Nathong Bus Station

The **Nathong bus station** is 1km beyond the airport on the Vieng Xai road at the easternmost edge of town (a taxi here costs 30,000K). *Sŏrngtăaou* to Vieng Xai (20,000K) leave at 8am, 10am, 11am, 2.30pm and 4pm. Other services include 'Nameo' (actually the Nam Soi border post) at 8am (30,000K, three hours) and Sam Tai (Xamtay) at 9.30am (50,000K, five hours).

🛈 Getting Around

There's a **tuk-tuk stand** (Map p75; town trips 15,000K) from where you can take trips around town. However, the easiest way to get around and to enjoy the stunning scenery en route to Vieng Xai is to hire a cheap scooter and do it yourself.

A central **motorcycle shop** (Map p75; manual/automatic scooter per day 100,000/ 120,000K; ☉7am-6pm) rents manual/automatic scooters.

For those wishing for a little more comfort when getting about locally or for reaching Vieng Xai there are a couple of **taxis** (☑020-95855513, 020-5627510; taxi rental to Vieng Xai caves one way/return 150,000/300,000K) in town.

Around Sam Neua

It doesn't take much effort to get into some timeless rural villages around Sam Neua. For random motorcycle trips you might try heading south from the hospital for a few kilometres or heading north up the unpaved lane directly to the right-hand side of Wat Phoxaysanalam. The latter winds its way after 11km to **Ban Tham**, just before which there's an inconsequential **Buddha cave** (to the left around 100m before the school and shop). But more appealing are rice-terrace valleys around 4km out of Sam Neua where two picturesque villages across the river each sport spindly, old, greying stupas. With a decent motorbike it is easy to make a day trip to Vieng Xai or a longer side trip to Hintang via Tat Saloei.

Vieng Xai   ອຽໄຊ

POP 10,000 / ☑064

The thought-provoking 'bomb-shelter caves' of Vieng Xai are set amid dramatic karst outcrops and offer a truly inspirational opportunity to learn about northern Laos' painful 20th-century history. Imagine Vang Vieng,

but with a compelling historical twist instead of happy tubing. Or think of it as Ho Chi Minh City's Cu Chi Tunnels cast in stone. The caves were shrouded in secrecy until they were opened to the world in 2007.

History

For centuries the minuscule hamlet of Long Ko sat peacefully here, lost amid deep ancient forests and towering karst outcrops. But in 1963, political repression and a spate of assassinations in Vientiane led the Pathet Lao leadership to retreat deep into the Hua Phan hinterland, eventually taking up residence in the area's caves. As the US Secret War gathered momentum, surrounding villages were mercilessly bombarded. Horrified and bemused, locals initially had no idea of who was attacking them, nor why. For safety, they retreated into the vastly expanded cave systems, more than 450 of which eventually came to shelter up to 23,000 people. As the war dragged on, cave sites came to host printing works, hospitals, markets and even a metalwork factory. After almost a decade in the caves, the 1973 ceasefire allowed the refugees to tentatively emerge and construct a small town here. Indeed, until December 1975, it was the de facto capital of the Pathet Lao's Liberated Territories. The town was named Vieng Xai as that had been the secret code name of future president Kaysone Phomvihane while in hiding here. Decades later, many of Vieng Xai's cave sites still retain visible signs of their wartime roles, making the complex one of the world's most complete revolutionary bases to have survived from the Cold War period.

👁 Sights

★ **Vieng Xai Caves**   CAVE

(ກ້ຳອຽໄຊ; ☑064-314321; entry incl audiotour 60,000K, bicycle rental per tour/day 15,000/ 30,000K; ☉9am-noon & 1-4pm) Joining a truly fascinating 18-point tour is the only way to see Vieng Xai's seven most important war-shelter cave complexes, set in beautiful gardens backed by fabulous karst scenery. A local guide unlocks each site while an audio guide gives a wealth of first-hand background information and historical context. The **Kaysone Phomvihane Cave** still has its air-circulation pump in working order and is the most memorable of the caves. Tours leave from the cave office.

Seeing all 18 sites in the three hours available is possible without feeling unduly rushed,

THAM NOK ANN

Tham Nok Ann (ถ้ำมิกแอน, Nok Ann Cave; entry 10,000K; twin kayak 30,000K; ⊘8am-5pm) is a newly opened cave complex that includes a gentle kayaking trip along an underwater stream that flows through the mountain. This is a mini Tham Kong Lo experience for those that don't have the time to explore central Laos and is well worth the detour. The caves are well-lit and include some huge jellyfish-like rock formations. The cave complex includes a Vietnamese military hospital. There are no life jackets included with the kayaks and you do need to stay alert for dangling stalactites.

Look for a signpost on the main road about 5km before Vieng Xai and follow the small track around to the right until it dead-ends at an entrance booth and small suspension bridge.

assuming you rent a bicycle (available from the caves office) and that you listen to the longer audio tracks while travelling between the sites rather than waiting to arrive before pressing play.

🛏 Sleeping & Eating

There isn't a great selection of eating establishments in Vieng Xai and many have run out of food by 8pm. By 9pm the town is in hibernation. Several *fěr* shops in the market serve rice and cheap noodle dishes until around 5pm.

Sabaidee Odisha INDIAN $
(mains 35,000K; ⊘7am-7pm; 🛜) Don't be fooled by the less than impressive exterior, cement floor and bare walls of this hole-in-the-wall joint, for the food is terrific. Prepared fresh and with care, it comes with a smile and the menu offers different levels of spiciness. It's in the northernmost corner of the Viengsai market, facing the main road.

As well as Indian, there are rice dishes and *láhp*. You'll be mopping your plate with their pillow-soft naan.

Thongnaxay Guesthouse GUESTHOUSE $
(📞030-99907206; r 60,000K; 🛜) Close to the caves, this new guesthouse has six super-fresh rooms with pink walls, private bathrooms, fans, clean linen and double beds. Oh, and rather nice views of the karsts.

Naxay Guesthouse GUESTHOUSE $
(📞020-55588060, 064-314330; r 80,000K) Opposite the cave office, these bamboo-accented bungalows are set around a manicured garden backed by an impressive split-toothed crag. Beds are comfy, hot water flows, lino floors are clean and fans keep you cool. They also have private verandahs and bathrooms, and if you're in luck the attached beach-style cafe occasionally serves up food. There's also a pétanque court.

Chitchareune Hotel HOTEL $$
(📞030-5150458; r 129,000-260,000K; ❄🛜) This newish white monolith sits immediately south of Viengsai market and has clean aircon rooms with above-average furniture and stylish en suites.

❶ Information

Vieng Xai Cave Tourist Office (📞064-314321; www.visit-viengxay.com; ⊘8-11.30am & 1-4pm) Around 1km south of the market, the cave office organises all cave visits, rents bicycles and has maps, a small book exchange and a useful information board. There's even a display case full of old Lenin busts and assorted socialist iconograpy.

❶ Getting There & Away

Sŏrngtǎaou to Sam Neua (20,000K, 50 minutes) leave at approximately 7am, 10am and 11am on the road parallel to the market (the bus station was closed for a rebuild at the time of writing). Buses between Sam Neua and Thanh Hoa (one bus daily to each, 25,000K) stop at this same spot. For Thanh Hoa catch the 8.30am, for Sam Neua the 5pm.

Visiting Vieng Xai by rented taxi from Sam Neua (including return) costs around 300,000K per vehicle.

Sam Neua to Vietnam

The scenic route via fascinating Vieng Xai is open to foreigners, Vietnamese visas permitting. It's narrow but paved and offers a feast of varied views. The best incorporate giant teeth of tree-dappled karst outcrops backing bucolic valleys layered with rice terraces. Several villages en route, including **Ban Piang Ban** (Km 144.5), specialise in basket-making and bamboo crafts. Across the river at Km 169 is a 'steel cave' where knives and agricultural tools were made on an almost-industrial scale during the Second Indochina War.

Turn south at Km 164 for the recently asphalted spur road to **Sam Tai** (Xamtay), famous for producing magnificent textiles. It has a couple of guesthouses should you feel like getting well off the beaten track to investigate. Public access to the remote **Nam Sam NPA** beyond is not currently permitted.

Sam Neua to Nong Khiaw

From Sam Neua, Rte 6 runs along winding mountain ridges passing **Hintang Archaeological Park** and meeting Phonsavan-bound Rte 1 at minuscule Phoulao (Ban Kho Hing), 92km west of Sam Neua, where kilometre markings reset. West of Phoulao the green mountains become much more heavily deforested until reaching the boundary of the **Nam Et/Phou Louey NPA**, which is best visited from Vieng Thong, and is a convenient place to break the journey. The long descent towards **Nong Khiaw** lasts many kilometres and offers some glimpses of superb scenery.

◉ Sights

Tat Saloei
WATERFALL

(Phonesai Waterfall) This impressive series of cascades forms a combined drop of almost 100m. It's briefly visible from eastbound Rte 6 roughly 1km after Km 55 (ie 36km from Sam Neua), but easy to miss westbound. There are some small local cafes and restaurants on the roadside here, plus what looks like a ticket booth, although no one was charging for entry at the time of writing.

Hintang Archaeological Park
ARCHAEOLOGICAL SITE

(ສວນຫີນ, Suan Hin) Almost as mysterious as Xieng Khuang's more famous jars, this unique, unfenced collection of standing stones is thought to be at least 1500 years old. Spindly stones up to 3m tall are interspersed with disks that formerly covered funerary sites. With some over a metre in diameter, these 'families' of stones do have a certain magic, and the place is now a Unesco World Heritage Site.

Chartered tuk-tuks from Sam Neua will ask around 500,000K return.

Access is up a rough, rutted track that cuts south from Rte 6 at Ban Phao (Km 35.3), 57km from Sam Neua. This track can be impractically muddy for vehicles after any rain. The main site is right beside the track after 6km, around 800m beyond the obvious

radio-mast summit. Some 2km back towards the main road, an orange sign points to the Keohintang Trail, which allows more intrepid visitors to seek out lesser-known megalith groups hidden along a partially marked two-hour hiking trail. Take the narrow rising path, not the bigger track that descends towards Ban Nakham. If you don't get lost, the trail should emerge back onto Rte 6 at Ban Tao Hin (Km 31.5), a tiny village without any facilities.

When driving between Sam Neua and either Phonsavan or Nong Khiaw, allow two hours extra for the very slow detour to the main site. Using public transport it is necessary to walk to and from Rte 6. Practicalities work out best if visiting between Sam Neua and Phonsavan: starting with the Vieng Thong–bound minibus, you'll have around six hours for the walk before the last Phonsavan/Vientiane–bound bus rumbles past.

Vieng Thong (Muang Hiam)
ວຽງທອງ

POP 4000 / ☐ 064

The original name of Vieng Thong was Muang Hiam, a Tai Daeng word meaning 'Watch Out'. Back when tigers roamed the surrounding forests it was relevant, but these days barely a dozen survive in the enormous Nam Et/Phou Louey NPA, on whose vast doorstep Vieng Thong sits. While the town is highly forgettable, the park is not and should be visited through the Nam Et/Phou Louey NPA office at Vieng Thong Visitor's Center.

Vieng Thong has a clutch of guesthouses and food stalls, and if you're travelling between Nong Khiaw and Sam Neua, stopping here for a night makes the 10-hour journey more palatable. The dazzling green rice fields around town are photogenic and short walks or bicycle rides can take you to pretty Tai Daeng, Hmong and Khamu villages.

🏃 Activities

★ Nam Nern Night Safari
SAFARI

(www.namet.org/namnern; night safaris per person in group of 4 1,200,000K) 🚲 Nam Nern Night Safari is a 24-hour, boat-based tour in the Nam Et/Phou Louey NPA. Highlights of the trip include a night-time boat-ride 'spotlighting' for tiger, gaur and white-cheeked gibbon. Seeing a tiger is unlikely but there's hope of spotting sambar and barking deer. Sleeping is at an ecolodge overlooking the

NAM ET/PHOU LOUEY NATIONAL PROTECTED AREA

In the vast Nam Et/Phou Louey NPA (ປ່າສະຫງວນແຫ່ງຊາດນ້ຳແອດພູເລີຍ) rare civets, Asian golden cats, river otters, white-cheeked crested gibbons and the utterly unique Laotian warty newt (*Paramesotriton laoensis*) share 4200 sq km of relatively pristine forests with around a dozen tigers. Approximately half is an inaccessible core zone. The remaining area includes 98 ethnic-minority hamlets. Two-day wildlife-watching excursions have been pioneered to the park's remote Nam Nern field station, a roadless former village site where a campsite and surrounding walking trails have been professionally cleared of unexploded ordnance (UXO).

Trips are organised by the Nam Et/Phou Louey NPA office in Vieng Thong, and contacting them well in advance is advisable since there's a limit of two departures per week. Night safaris cost 1,200,000K per person for a group of four, and include guides, cooks, food and camping equipment, with a significant proportion of your fee going into village development funds. The price also includes the 90-minute boat ride from Ban Sonkhua, around 50km east of Vieng Thong on Rte 1.

Nam Nern. The price includes a fireside dinner.

Book through the Nam Et/Phou Louey NPA office in Vieng Thong.

The Nests   WILDLIFE WATCHING
(www.namet.org/wp/en) 🌿 The Nam Et/Phou Louey NPA office offers the chance to go on The Nests, two- and three-day treks with accommodation in cosy spherical baskets hanging from trees. This also involves wildlife-viewing from an observation tower (under construction at the time of writing) at Poung Nied salt lick, which attracts animals such as the rare sambar deer.

🛏 Sleeping & Eating

**Dork Khoun Thong
Guesthouse**   GUESTHOUSE $
(📞 064-810017; r 50,000-80,000K; ❄) The most appealing of Vieng Thong's limited options, this guesthouse is located right in the centre of the small town. Very clean, decent-sized rooms have hot showers, netted windows and comfortable new beds with love-message sheets and teddy-bear towels. There's a pleasant 1st-floor sitting area and attractive views across riverside fields from the rear terrace.

Dokchampa Guesthouse   GUESTHOUSE $
(📞 064-810005; r with/without bathroom 50,000K/30,000; @🛜) This small guesthouse has basic rooms with mosquito nets, hot-water showers and squat toilets. The owners offer a few traveller-friendly services such as bicycles for rent (30,000K per day), free wi-fi and a small attached internet cafe (5000K per hour).

Tontavanh Restaurant   LAOTIAN $
(mains 10,000-20,000K; ⏰7am-8pm; 📶) This typical-looking local eatery serves unexpectedly appetising food and even has a menu in concise English.

ⓘ Information

Nam Et/Phou Louey NPA Office (📞064-810008; www.namet.org; ⏰8am-noon & 1-4.30pm Mon-Fri) The Nam Et/Phou Louey NPA office (in the Vieng Thong Visitors' Center, at the northwestern edge of Vieng Thong) organises award-winning Nam Nern Night Safaris to find the park's wildlife; you're taken by boat into the core zone of the protected area, incandescent eyes following you from towering jungle, followed by a picnic and homestay.

ⓘ Getting There & Away

Westbound buses arrive from Sam Neua around noon, continuing after lunch to Nong Khiaw (60,000K, five hours), Pak Mong and Luang Prabang (130,000K, nine hours). Eastbound, the best choice for Sam Neua is the 7am minibus (40,000K, six hours), as the two Sam Neua through-services (from Luang Prabang/Vientiane) both travel the road largely by night.

The bus station is 300m along Rte 6 from the market at the eastern edge of town.

MUANG NGOI DISTRICT

Tracts of green mountains are attractive wherever you go in northern Laos. But at Nong Khiaw and tiny Muang Ngoi Neua, the contours do something altogether more dramatic. At both places, vast karst peaks and towering cliffs rear dramatically out of the Nam Ou (Ou River), creating jaw-droppingly beautiful scenes. Both villages make convenient rural getaways from Luang Prabang and are accessible by riverboat from Muang Khua. Nong Khiaw also makes an excellent rural rest stop between Luang Prabang and Vieng Thong or Sam Neua.

Nong Khiaw   ໜອງຂ່ຽວ

POP 3500 / ☏ 071

Nong Khiaw is a traveller's haven in the truest sense, offering pampering, good food, decent accommodation and bags of activities with established adventure-tour operators. Nestled on the west bank of the Nam Ou (the river almost currentless since the building of the dam upstream), spanned by a vertiginous bridge and bookended by towering limestone crags, it's surely one of the most photogenic spots in Laos. On the river's scenic east bank (officially called Ban Sop Houn) is the lion's share of guesthouses and restaurants.

Be aware that Nong Khiaw is alternatively known as Muang Ngoi (the name of the surrounding district), creating obvious confusion with Muang Ngoi Neua, a 75-minute boat ride further north.

◉ Sights

At dusk a fabulous star show turns the indigo sky into a pointillist canvas subtly outlining the riverside massifs. Whether you're stationed at one of the town's two viewpoints, Pha Daeng Peak or Sleeping Woman, or just rubber-necking at these extraordinary karsts from ground level, you'll be manually shutting your jaw.

Tham Pha Thok   CAVE
(ຖ້ຳຜາທ໊ອກ; 10,000K; ⊙7.30am-6.30pm) Around 2km east along Rte 1C, Tham Pha Thok is a series of caves in a limestone cliff where villagers and Pathet Lao eluded bombing during the Second Indochina War. The first cave is around 30m high and accessed by wooden stairway. Continue to the second, somewhat-claustrophobic cave, 300m along a dark passage through the cliff.

Pha Daeng Peak Viewpoint   VIEWPOINT
(ຈຸດຊົມວິວຜາແດງ; Map p83; Pha Daeng Peak, Ban Sop Houn; 20,000K; ⊙6am-4pm) Reached by a testing though thoroughly doable 1½-hour walk (with a decent path) up Pha

Daeng mountain, directly above the town, this viewpoint offers an unforgettable panorama. Drink up the sunset view (but bring a strong torch for your descent) or head here at 6am to witness the valley below veiled in mist, with the mountain peaks painted gold.

Sleeping Woman Viewpoint   VIEWPOINT
(Map p83; Rte 1C, heading north from Nong Khiaw, roughly 1km out of town; 15,000K; ⊙6am-4pm) This recently opened viewpoint rivals that of Pha Daeng Peak Viewpoint for its widescreen drama of surging karsts and mountains, with the boats on the river far below like floating blue crayons. It's an hour's climb up a marked pathway, and while another route down is offered it's not sufficiently marked, so descend the same way you came up.

If you're here for sunset, on the way back down head for the newly relocated Hive Bar (p85) opposite the entrance.

🏃 Activities

Green Discovery   HIKING, CYCLING
(Map p83; ☏071-810081; www.greendiscovery laos.com; ⊙7.30am-10pm) Reliable Green Discovery has a range of trips, including a two-day trek to a Hmong village involving a homestay, with five hours' trekking per day (US$66 per person in a group of four). It also has challenging one-day cycling trips on forest dirt tracks covering 56km (US$39 per person in a group of four).

Tiger Trail   HIKING, CYCLING
(Map p83; ☏071-252655; www.laos-adventures. com; Delilah's Place; ⊙7.30am-11pm) 🏵 This ecoconscious outfit has treks and homestays around the local area, including memorable one-day trips to the '100 waterfalls', one-day trekking and boat rides, plus the new pursuit of paddleboarding on the now-becalmed Nam Ou. These trips, as with most of Tiger Trail's activities, cost US$31 per person in a group of four. The excellent office is run by amiable Harp.

Sabai Sabai   MASSAGE
(Map p83; ☏020-58686068; Ban Sop Houn; body massage 60,000K, oil massage 70,000K, steam bath 25,000K; ⊙9am-8pm) Set in a peaceful Zen-style garden, this wooden house is the perfect spot to restore the spirit and aching limbs with treatments like traditional Lao massage and herbal steam bath.

Nong Khiaw

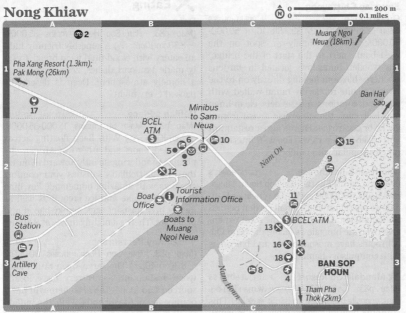

Nong Khiaw

🛏 Sleeping

★ Delilah's Place
HOSTEL $

(Map p83; ☎020-54395686, 030-9758048; www.delilahscafenongkhiaw.wordpress.com; Main St; dm 35,000K, d/r 55,000K; ☜) Delilah's Place has clean shared-bathroom rooms and cosy dorms with mozzie nets, super-thick matresses and safety lockers. Tiger Trail is also based here and there's a great cafe to 'carb-up' before activities, so one-stop-shop Delilah's is deservedly the main traveller hub in town. Thanks to the goodwill of eccentric owner Harp, it is also a great resource for info.

Sunrise Guesthouse
GUESTHOUSE $

(Map p83; ☎020-22478799; Rte 1C, Ban Sop Houn; bungalows 60,000-150,000K; ☀☜) Showing their age now, these tightly packed, termite-worn wooden bungalows are the polar opposite of luxury, but have stunning views of the river and bridge. There are four newer bungalows with relatively swish bathrooms, one of which has air-con. There's also a decent cafe with Western breakfasts and Lao fare.

Sengdao Chittavong Guesthouse
GUESTHOUSE $

(Map p83; ☑ 030-9237089; Rte 1C; r 50,000-90,000K; ☜) This family-run spot on the west bank (next to the start of the bridge) has wooden bungalows located in gardens of cherry blossom looking directly on to the river. En suite rooms are rattan-walled, with simple decorations, mozzie nets, clean linen and balconies, though expect a visit from a gecko or cockroach. There's also a restaurant with river-garden views. The wi-fi internet is patchy. Popular with families.

Namhoun Guesthouse
GUESTHOUSE $

(Map p83; ☑ 071-810039; Ban Sop Houn; bungalows 50,000-100,000K; ❋ ☜) The cheaper bungalows are set around a small garden behind the family house. Better are the most expensive riverside bungalows facing the Nam Ou. All rooms have mosquito nets and balconies with compulsory hammocks.

★ Mandala Ou Resort
BOUTIQUE HOTEL $$

(Map p83; ☑ 030-5377332; www.mandala-ou.com; opposite bus station; r US$65; ❋ ☜ ☒) This stunning boutique accommodation in vanilla-coloured chalets – four facing the river – has imaginative, quirky features like inlaid glass bottles in the walls that allow more light, contemporary bathrooms and swallow-you-up beds. The owners are friendly, there's a terrific Thai menu, the town's only swimming pool and a yoga deck used by Luang Prabang Yoga, which runs monthly retreats here.

★ Nong Kiau Riverside
GUESTHOUSE $$

(Map p83; ☑ 020-55705000; www.nongkiau.com; Ban Sop Houn; r incl breakfast US$53; @ ☜) ✍ Riverside's bungalows are romantically finished with ambient lighting, wooden floors, woven bedspreads and mosquito nets. Each includes an attractive bathroom and balcony for blissful river views of the looming karsts. There's an excellent restaurant serving Lao food with a mouthwatering breakfast buffet. It also has mountain bikes for hire.

Pha Xang Resort
HOTEL $$

(☑ 071-810014, 020-52220102; d US$60; ❋ ☜) About 1km out of town, Pha Xang is hardly a resort; it's instead a collection of comfy A-frame rattan bungalows with wood floors, white walls and en suites dotted around a manicured garden. The staff's English is limited, but the peace and sense of nature here is not – this is a serene spot to take in the karsts.

 Eating

Deen
INDIAN $

(Map p83; Ban Sop Houn; mains 35,000K; ◷ 8.30am-10pm; ☜) A superbly friendly Indian eatery with wood-fired naan bread, freshly made tandoori dishes, zesty curries and a homely atmosphere, Deen is deservedly packed every night.

Delilah's Place
INTERNATIONAL, LAOTIAN $

(Map p83; Main St; mains 15,000-35,000K; ◷ 7am-10pm; ☜) With Bach floating across the wood floors and a herd of African elephants thundering silently towards you on the mural, Delilah's satisfies your comfort cravings with amazing homemade key lime pies, lemon cake and ice cream; as well as hearty breakfasts of eggs, smoky bacon and pancakes. There's a nightly movie at 8.30pm.

Vongmany Restaurant
LAOTIAN $

(Map p83; Ban Sop Houn; mains 30,000K; ◷ 8.30am-10pm) This large, open rattan-and-wood restaurant serves very tasty locally sourced Lao food – the *láhp* here will put a bounce in your taste buds, while the buffalo steak is delicious, and the steamed fish and river shrimp are full of flavour.

CT Restaurant & Bakery
INTERNATIONAL, LAOTIAN $

(Map p83; Rte 1C, Ban Sop Houn; mains 35,000K; ◷ 7am-10pm) At the end of the bridge, this place has the best view in town. CT has a Western-friendly menu of pasta, pancakes, breakfasts, sandwiches and tasty staple Lao dishes. It also offers takeaway sandwiches for trekking.

Floating Restaurant
LAOTIAN $

(Map p83; ☑ 030-9546046; riverside lane, Ban Sop Houn; mains 30,000K; ◷ 8am-6pm) Set on pontoons, this peaceful, semi-alfresco Lao restaurant relies on the soothing river view as its wallpaper, and dishes up tasty noodle and rice dishes. There's a decked area from where you can go swimming in the gentle Nam Ou. Enquire about renting owner Thong's boat, which can be taken out on the river to have lunch on (rental including driver 100,000K).

★ Coco Home Bar & Restaurant
LAOTIAN, INTERNATIONAL $$

(Map p83; ☑ 020-58491741; Main St; mains 40,000-55,000K; ◷ 7.30am-10pm; ☜) Run by new owner Sebastien Chok, this recently refurbished impressive riverside oasis has a great menu, with dishes like papaya salad, mango sticky rice, chicken and cashew nuts, *mok phaa* (steamed fish in banana leaves) and duck in orange sauce. It's arguably the best place in town to delight your tastebuds. Eat in the lush garden or upstairs.

Drinking & Nightlife

Q Bar
BAR
(Map p83; ☎020-99918831; Rte 1C, Ban Sop Houn; ⊙7am-11.30pm; 🛜) Chilled Q sits on the main road with an ox-blood, rattan interior, a little roof terrace, good tunes and a friendly owner. In high season there's a nightly barbecue. Cocktails are 35,000K.

Hive Bar
BAR
(Map p83; Rte 1C; ⊙7.30am-11.30pm) Recently moved to a new location 1km outside of town (heading towards Pak Mong), Hive Bar is run by a friendly Lao, has a downstairs disco and karaoke for those inclined, plus a chilled terrace to sink a beer and watch the sunset explode in pinks and oranges behind the karsts. Great indy tunes; happy hour is from 7pm to 8pm.

❶ Information

INTERNET ACCESS
Wi-fi is now available pretty much everywhere, free of charge.

MONEY
BCEL (Map p83; ⊙24hr) has two 24-hour ATMs: one at the end of the bridge on the Ban Sop Houn side, and another 100m after the bridge on the road heading to Pak Mong.

POST
Post Office (Map p83; ⊙8.30am-5pm) The tiny post office exchanges baht and US dollars at slightly unfavourable rates.

TOURIST INFORMATION
Tourist Information Office (Map p83) Located above the boat landing, it's rarely open. Much better is reliable Harp at Delilah's Place (p83); a one-stop travel resource for bus and boat tickets, the home of Tiger Trail (p82) and also great budget digs.

❶ Getting There & Away

BOAT
Riverboat rides are a highlight of visiting Nong Khiaw; however, since the Nam Ou was dammed, the trip to Luang Prabang is currently no longer possible. **Boats to Muang Ngoi Neua** (Map p83; 25,000K, 1¼ hours) leave at 11am and 2pm (in high season extra departures are possible), taking you through some of the most dramatic karst country in Laos. The 11am boat

continues all the way to Muang Khua (120,000K, seven hours) for connections to Phongsali or Dien Bien Phu in Vietnam.

There needs to be a minimum of 10 people (on all the above journeys) before the boatman leaves, otherwise you will have to club together to make up the difference.

BUS & SÖRNGTÄAOU
The journey to Luang Prabang is possible in three hours but in reality usually takes at least four. Minivans or *sŏrngtăaou* (37,000K) run at 8.30am, 10am and 11am, while air-con minibuses leave from around 1.30pm. Tickets are sold at the **bus station** (Map p83) but the 11am service actually starts at the **boat office** (Map p83), filling up with folks arriving off the boat(s) from Muang Ngoi. When a boat arrives from Muang Khua there'll usually be additional Luang Prabang minivans departing at around 3pm from the boat office.

For Udomxai a direct minibus (45,000K, three hours) leaves at 9am and 11am. Alternatively, take any westbound transport and change at Pak Mong (40,000K, 50 minutes).

Originating in Luang Prabang, the **minibus to Sam Neua** (Map p83; 170,000K, 12 hours) via **Vieng Thong** (100,000K, five hours) makes a quick lunch stop in Nong Khiaw at around 11.30am, leaving at about noon. Another Sam Neua bus (arriving from Vientiane) passes through at 7pm. Both of these arrive at an unmarked bus stand on the Nong Khiaw side just before the start of the bridge. Try and get on the lunchtime bus as this is usually a larger vehicle compared to the cramped minibus in the evening. Plus there's the view you'll want to catch by daylight; one of the most beautiful mountain rides in Laos.

❶ Getting Around

Bicycle rental makes sense for exploring local villages or reaching the caves. Town bicycles cost 20,000K per day and mountain bikes cost 30,000K. Alternatively, hire a scooter (50,000/60,000K for a manual/automatic) from Delilah's Place (p83). *Sŏrngtăaou* to the nearby bus station cost 5000K.

Muang Ngoi Neua (Ban Ngoi Kao) ເມືອງງອຍເໜືອ

POP 1000 / ☎071

Muang Ngoi Neua is deliciously bucolic, a place to unwind and reset your soul. As the Nam Ou (Ou River) slides sedately beneath the shadow of sawtoothed karsts, cows wander the village's unpaved 500m-long road, while roosters strut past villagers mending fishing nets. Packed with cheap guesthouses and eateries, here there's enough competition to keep prices down. And while hammock-swinging on balconies is still de rigueur, there's plenty more to do if you have the energy: be it short, unaided hikes into timeless neighbouring villages, exploring caves, tubing and kayaking on the now pacified Nam Ou, or fishing and mountain-biking.

History

Muang Ngoi was once a regional centre but it was pulverised during the Second Indo-china War, with bombs destroying all three of its once-celebrated historic monasteries. Such was the devastation that a 'new' post-war Muang Ngoi (ie Nong Khiaw) took over as the district headquarters, a potential confusion that still sometimes causes mix-ups. The rebuilt village was 'discovered' by travellers in the late 1990s when its beauty and laissez-faire atmosphere gained it a major pre-Twitter-era buzz despite not featuring in any guidebooks. By 2002, virtually every guesthouse hosted dollar-a-night *falang* (Westerners), some of whom stayed for months in a chilled-out opiate haze, but Laos' clampdown on drugs changed the atmosphere radically. Most of the very cheapest guesthouses closed or improved their facilities to cater for a (slightly) more demanding new generation of travellers who still enjoy the enchanting boat journeys from Nong Khiaw but are now more interested in hiking, kayaking and simply enjoying the riverscape. If you want a super cheap homestay, that's still possible in nearby Huay Bo.

◉ Sights & Activities

Ensure you're by the river come sunset to enjoy one of the most photogenic views in Laos, as the sun falls like a mellow peach beyond the jagged black cliffs. A little after dawn it's also interesting to watch locals delivering alms to monks at the rebuilt monastery, **Wat Okadsayaram**.

Numerous freelance guides such as **Funny Guide** (☑020-97029526; khaomanychan@yahoo.com; Main St; ⊘6am-8pm) offer a range of walks to Lao, Hmong and Khamu villages and regional waterfalls. Prices are reasonable and some visits, such as to the That Mok falls, involve boat rides. Others are easy hikes that you could do perfectly well unguided. For a rough guide to the area, take a photo with your phone of the map outside **Lao**

Youth Travel (☑030-5140046; www.laoyouthtravel.com; ⊘7.30-10.30am & 1.30-6pm), located where the boat-landing path passes by the two-storey Rainbow Guest House.

Kayaking is a great way to appreciate the fabulous riverine scenery that stretches both ways along the Nam Ou. Lao Youth Travel has its own kayaks. The Ou now runs very gently after being dammed, making it safer for younger kids.

🛏 Sleeping

Lattanavongsa Guesthouse   GUESTHOUSE **$**
(☑020-23863640; touymoy.laos@gmail.com; r from 100,000K; ☎) Lattanavongsa offers a choice of bungalows at two locations: above the boat landing, and on the main drag in a pretty garden. Powder-blue rooms have choice art, mozzie nets, fresh linen and gas-fired showers; all have balconies. Book well ahead. Another boon is taking breakfast or dinner at its idyllically situated cafe (by the boat landing) with unbroken cliff views.

Nicksa's Place   GUESTHOUSE **$**
(☑020-3665957; r 60,000-100,000K) Overlooking the river from its pretty garden abuzz with butterflies, these seven house-proud cabanas are made of wood and stone and have fresh walls, en suites and mozzie nets. Each has a balcony and obligatory hammock to take in the impressive vista. Cold-water showers only.

Veranda   GUESTHOUSE **$**
(☑020-23862021; r 40,000K; ☎) The five bamboo-weave bungalows here form an arc around a panoramic river view. Recently refurbished, the great-value clean rooms have hammocks, good beds and solar-heated showers. There's also a restaurant attached. Lovely manager.

Aloune Mai Guesthouse   GUESTHOUSE **$**
(Main St; r 50,000K) This hidden gem, down a dirt track off the main drag and over a bridge, sits away from the riverside, with stunning views of the cliffs, 10 fresh rooms in a handsome rattan building and hammocks on the verandah. There's also a little restaurant serving pizza.

Rainbow Guest House   GUESTHOUSE **$**
(☑020-22957880; r 80,000K; ☎) Close to the boat ramp, this large house has clean, basic tiled-floor rooms with fresh linen and bathrooms, and a pleasant restaurant out front called the **Bamboo Bar**, with tasty Lao food, crêpes, curries and omelettes.

★ **Ning Ning Guest House**   GUESTHOUSE $$
(☑030-5140863, 020-23880122; ningning_guest
house@hotmail.com; r 200,000K; 🛜) Nestled
around a peaceful garden, Ning Ning offers
10 immaculate wooden bungalows with
mosquito nets, verandahs, en suites and
lily-white bed linen, with walls draped in
ethnic tapestries. There's also a great new
sister guesthouse nearby with a decidedly
more upscale look (nearing completion as of
the time of writing; rooms 250,000K). The
stylish riverfront restaurant with sumptuous
views is already finished.

The internet access does not extend from
the restaurant to the rooms.

PDV Riverview Guesthouse   GUESTHOUSE $$
(☑020-22148777;   pdvbungalows@gmail.com;
dm/r/f   40,000/100,000/150,000K,   bungalows
50,000-100,000K,   upstairs   r   150,000-200,000K;
❄🛜) Partly under construction at the time
of writing, this place halfway down Main St
promises to be fine riverside accommodation,
with fresh new rooms and a six-berth dorm
with stunning karst views. There's also a family room. The current bungalows are nothing
extraordinary but have great views and the
usual balcony and hammock.

✖️ Eating

★ **Gecko Bar & Shop**   LAOTIAN $
(☑020-58886295;   mains 20,000K;   ⏲7am-9pm;
🛜) Handmade woven gifts and tea are for
sale at this delightful, memorable little cafe
two-thirds of the way down the main drag on
your left heading south. There's a nice terrace
to sit and read on, the owners are charming
and the food, spanning noodles to soups, and
pancakes to curries, is among the most raved
about in the village.

★ **Riverside Restaurant**   LAOTIAN $
(☑030-5329920; meals 40,000K; ⏲7am-11pm; 🛜)
Since being damaged by a storm Riverside has
come back better than ever. In the evening its
Chinese lanterns sway in the breeze on the
decked terrace, beneath the sentinel arms of
an enormous light-festooned mango tree. Riverside has gorgeous cliff views, and its menu
encompasses noodles, fried dishes, *láhp* and
Indian fare. Pure magic.

**Phetdavanh Restaurant
& Street Buffet**   LAOTIAN $
(☑020-22148777;   vegie buffet 30,000K,   mains
30,000K; ⏲buffet 6.30-9pm, restaurant 7am-11pm;
🛜☑) This basic-looking restaurant runs a

nightly 'all you can eat' vegie buffet (high season only), as well as serving tortillas, bamboo
and duck, pancakes, soups, sandwiches and
shakshuka. Try the Lao Suzy (stew with po-
tato, carrot, eggplant and onion). It also has
rapid wi-fi, so you can eat and stream movies.
Great Swedish cook.

Find it on a corner on the main drag, at
the top of the stairs from the boat landing.

Vita Restaurant   LAOTIAN $
(☑020-52949488;   Main St;   mains 25,000K;
⏲8am-9pm; 🛜) Fairy-lit Vita sits three-
quarters of the way down the main drag on
the left-hand side as you walk south, and
dishes up decent *láhp*, sandwiches and curries. There are plenty of lounging cushions
for chilling and reading under a fan.

Meem Restaurant   LAOTIAN $
(Main St;   mains 30,000K;   ⏲7am-9.30pm;   🛜)
Halfway down Main St, welcoming Meem
has wood floors, plenty of lounging cushions,
and serves up flavoursome Lao and Indian
fare, including delicious chicken masala,
tomato curry, spring rolls and barbecued
chicken and duck. By night it's more enticing
than a bunch of melodic sirens, with claypot
candles and paper lanterns.

Pakphon Sabai   LAOTIAN $
(Main St; mains 30,000K; ⏲8am-9pm; 🛜) Serving up waffles, decent coffee, French toast,
Muang Ngoi sausage, noodles and fruit
shakes, this cafe-cum-bookshop is an unexpected boho treat with second-hand novels,
scatter cushions, original art and massage
(one hour 60,000K). It's halfway down Main
St on your right.

❶ Information

DANGERS & ANNOYANCES
Thefts from Muang Ngoi Neua's cheaper guesthouses tend to occur when over-relaxed guests
leave flimsy doors and shutters unsecured or
place valuables within easy reach of long-armed
pincers – most windows here have no glass.

INTERNET ACCESS
Muang Ngoi has internet access and wi-fi.

MONEY
There are no banks or ATMs here so bring plenty
of cash from either Muang Khua (upriver) or
Nong Khiaw (downriver). In an emergency you
could exchange US dollars at a few of the guesthouses but rates are unsurprisingly poor.

❶ Getting There & Away

Boats to Nong Khiaw (25,000K, one hour) leave around 9am, with tickets on sale from 8am at the boat office beside Ning Ning Guest House. At Nong Khiaw tuk-tuks will wait above the boat landing for your arrival to take you to the bus station.

Boats from Muang Khua pick up in Muang Ngoi Neua for Nong Khiaw around 1.30pm. Going to Muang Khua (100,000K, five hours), a boat leaves at 9.30am provided enough people sign up the day before on the list at the boat office. The first hour of the ride cuts through particularly spectacular karst scenery.

A new road running alongside the Nam Ou connecting Muang Ngoi Neua to Nong Khiaw has been created. However, it is still unsealed and passes through tributaries that have not yet been bridged; pretty useless for travellers unless you can hitch a lift with a boatman who happens to be there.

Around Muang Ngoi Neua

Muang Ngoi Neua is a great place for making short hikes through clouds of white and orange butterflies into beautiful karst-edged countryside. Reaching the three closest villages is easy without a guide or map. Start by heading east away from the river along the continuation of the boat-landing access track. Around 25 minutes' walk further is a small tollbooth that charges foreigners 10,000K to continue. Your toll also allows access to the adjacent **Tham Kang**, a modest limestone cave set between poinsettia bushes and trumpet lilies. Inside you might spot a few bats and there's the eerie sight of a stream emerging through what at first glance look like giant stone jaws. For refreshments, cross a little bamboo bridge over the crystal-clear Nam Ngoi (Ngoi River) to the simple little **Cave View Restaurant** (mains 20,000-30,000K; ☺8am-6pm).

Continuing for 15 minutes, cross a stream (wading is safer than risking the slippery stepping stones) and reach a large area of rice fields. Keep left just as you first enter the rice fields, then at the next junction (three minutes later) bear left for Huay Sen (45 minutes) or right for Ban Na (15 minutes) and Huay Bo (40 minutes). Sticking to the convoluted but well-worn main path is wise as there are little hand-painted signposts at each of the few possible confusion points. All three villages offer very basic, ultra cheap accommodation with shared outdoor squat toilets and associated restaurant shacks that are open if and when anyone happens to be around to cook.

For stilt-house architecture, **Huay Sen** has the most authentic vibe of the three villages. The sole **Huay Sen Guesthouse** (r 10,000K) is a sorry set of minuscule bamboo boxes, but the enthusiastic owner speaks some English, can rustle up a decent fried rice and stocks an unusually flavoursome bamboo-macerated *lòw-lów* (Lao whisky). He also offers guided two-hour walks to neighbouring Hmong villages.

The houses of **Ban Na** look less rustic but you can observe local weavers at work and both village guesthouses overlook a sea of rice fields with a jutting karst horizon. **OB Bungalows** (☑020-33863225; r 10,000K), at the furthest end of the village, has the better view and its new, relatively sizeable bamboo huts are particularly good value. **Chantanohm Guesthouse** (r 10,000K) has a pretty setting and features a *petang* (Lao version of pétanque) track and bomb casings.

The walk to **Huay Bo** is very attractive but requires fording one intermediate river. You'll pass a particularly sharp limestone spike and follow beneath a high ridge. The village comprises mostly stilt and bamboo-weave houses, albeit with a less serene atmosphere than in Huay Sen. Three simple side-by-side guesthouses all charge 10,000K.

PHONGSALI PROVINCE

No longer Laos, not yet China, Phongsali is a visual feast and is home to some of the nation's most traditional hill tribes. Trekkers might feel that they've walked onto the pages of *National Geographic*. For travellers, the province's most visited settlement is Muang Khua, a useful transit point linked by river to Nong Khiaw and by road to Dien Bien Phu in Vietnam. Further north the province is kept well off the standard tourist trail by arduous journeys on snaking roads that twist and turn endlessly. The only asphalt links Muang Khua to Udomxai, Phongsali and on to Mengla in China. Inconveniently, foreigners can't cross the Chinese border anywhere in the province. The road to Dien Bien Phu is now in great shape on the Lao side, but is not so great on the Vietnamese side.

Muang Khua ເມືອງຂວາ

POP 4000 / ☎ 088

Pretty little Muang Khua is an inevitable stop when transiting between Laos and Dien Bien Phu in Vietnam, or taking the brown Nam Ou (Ou River) by boat to Nong Khiaw. While not as scenically spectacular nor as developed for the traveller as the latter, Muang Khua, with its pastel-coloured houses, still has oodles of small-town charm, set amid starburst palms where the Nam Ou and Nam Phak (Phak River) meet. The heart of the place is its wet and dry market.

If arriving from Dien Bien Phu, please relax – unlike neighbouring Vietnam, hard bargaining here is neither required nor appropriate.

◉ Sights & Activities

The tourist office (p91) organises several trekking options, including a rewarding one-day trek to the Akha Pala village of Ban Bakha (450,000K per person in a group of two).

Luang Prabang–based Tiger Trail (p82) offers six-day Akha Village 'voluntourism' experiences costing US$399.

Independent guide **Mr Khamman** (☎ 020-99320743) runs one- to three-day treks (one day for a group of two costs 500,000K per person).

Suspension Bridge BRIDGE
(Map p90) For soaring mountain and river views head to this suspension bridge leading to the Khamu quarter. You'll need a head for heights and a good sense of balance on this safe but eminently wobbly construction.

Wat BUDDHIST TEMPLE
(Map p90) This peaceful temple is worth a visit given the limited sightseeing options in town.

🛏 Sleeping

Sensabai Guesthouse GUESTHOUSE $
(Map p90; ☎ 020-9998445; r 60,000K; 🛜) Overlooking the Nam Phak, new family-run Sensabai offers mint-coloured rooms with fragrant linen, flat-screen TV, fan and squat toilet. There's a pleasant lobby looking out over the river where you can read. It's on the main road, heading south out of town towards the bus station.

Chaleunsuk Guesthouse GUESTHOUSE $
(Map p90; ☎ 088-210847; r old block 70,000, new block 100,000-120,000K; ❄@🛜) Chaleunsuk is popular with travellers and has house-proud, generously sized rooms with large comfy beds and hot showers. Free tea is available in the ample communal sitting terrace. Next door there's a new block with shinier rooms and flat-screen TVs, although it's a little kitsch.

GETTING TO VIETNAM: PANG HOK TO TAY TRANG

Getting to the Border

Daily buses (60,000K, departing 6am in either direction) between Muang Khua and Dien Bien Phu cross the Laos–Vietnamese border at the **Pang Hok (Laos)/Tay Trang (Vietnam) border crossing** 26km east of Muang Mai. The road has been entirely rebuilt on the Lao side right up to the Pang Hok border post, but is still surprisingly rough in places on the Vietnamese side. It's a picturesque route, particularly down in the Dien Bien Phu valley, which is often a blanket of emerald rice paddies. Making the trip in hops is definitely not recommended, as it will cost far more than the bus fare and it's easy to end up stranded along the way.

At the Border

This remote crossing sees a handful of travellers. Laos visas are available on arrival for the usual price and you will be asked for a 4000K processing fee. Vietnamese visas, however, are definitely not available on arrival, so plan ahead to avoid getting stranded.

Moving On

There are no facilities or waiting vehicles at either of the border posts, which are separated by about 4km of no-man's land. From the Tay Trang side of the border it's about 31km to Dien Bien Phu.

Muang Khua

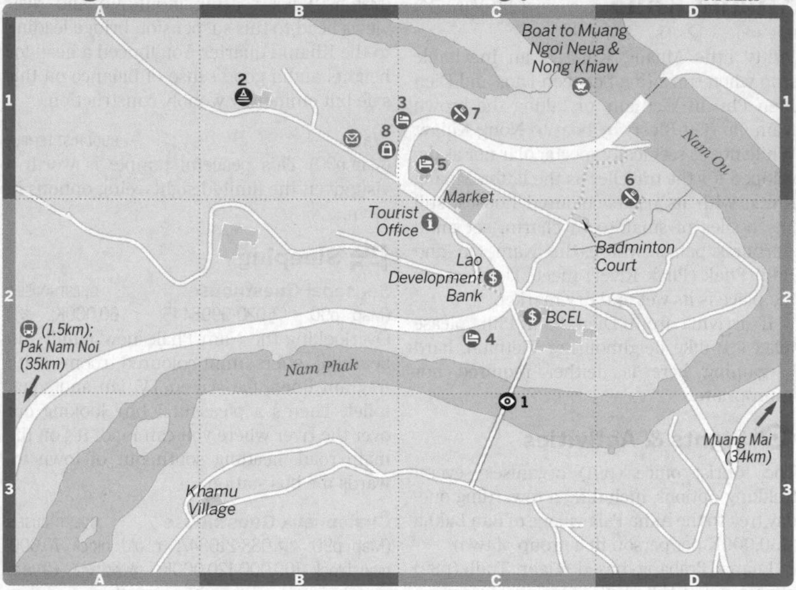

Muang Khua

Sights
1 Suspension Bridge C3
2 Wat B1

Sleeping
3 Chaleunsuk Guesthouse C1
4 Sensabai Guesthouse C2
5 Sernalli Hotel C1

Eating
6 Laosamai Restaurant D1
7 Sayfon C1

Shopping
8 Ethnic Handicrafts Shop B1

Sernalli Hotel HOTEL $$
(Map p90; ☎088-212445; r 200,000K; ❄📶) Muang Khua's top address, the Sernalli has a facade that suggests a certain neocolonial elegance and the often unlit, deserted small lobby is full of carved hardwood furniture. The rooms are clean and comfortable enough, if spartan, with wooden furnishings and slow-to-appear hot water. Extra touches include air-con and large flat-screen TVs. But really, this place is overpriced.

Eating

Sayfon LAOTIAN $
(Map p90; mains 30,000K; ⏰7am-9pm; 📶) Set high above the river with views through the palm trees, this basic joint offers a fan-cooled interior and a wide English-language menu with Western-friendly staples like omelettes and pancakes. Tasty *láhp*, noodle dishes and plenty of cool Beerlao. This spot is about as lively as it gets in Muang Khua come evening.

Laosamai Restaurant FUSION $
(Map p90; ☎088-210844; Nam Ou Guesthouse; mains 30,000K; ⏰7am-9pm) Perched on stilts overlooking the Nam Ou, this traveller-friendly restaurant is based at the **Nam Ou Guesthouse** and serves tasty, if wafer-thin, 'steak' and chips, plus a selection of stir-fries.

Shopping

Ethnic Handicrafts Shop ARTS & CRAFTS
(Map p90; ⏰9am-6pm) Based at the Chaleunsuk Guesthouse, this shop has hand-woven crafts and locally produced tea for sale.

ℹ Information

INTERNET ACCESS

Internet access is available at the **Chaleunsuk Guesthouse** (p89) for 10,000K per hour, including headphones and camera for Skype access.

MONEY

There are two ATMs in town. Both **BCEL** (Map p90; ☺ 8.30am-3.30pm Mon-Fri) and **Lao Development Bank** (Map p90; ☺ 8.30am-3.30pm Mon-Fri) can change major currencies such as US dollars (clean new notes only), euros, Vietnamese dong and Thai baht. Be aware that over the weekend banks are shut and ATMs may be empty, so if you're looking to catch a boat bring emergency cash.

POST

Post Office (Map p90; ☺ 8am-4pm Mon-Fri)

TOURIST INFORMATION

The helpful **tourist office** (Map p90; ☐ 020-22848020; ☺ 8.30-11.30am & 1.30-4.30pm Mon-Fri) opposite the Sernalli Hotel can answer questions and arrange treks. If you want to book a trek out of office hours, call Mr Keo to arrange a meeting, or try independent guide Mr Khamman (p89). Otherwise, check out www.muangkhua.com, which has some bookable treks and the lowdown on every last guesthouse in town.

ℹ Getting There & Away

The bus to Dien Bien Phu in Vietnam (60,000K) departs from outside the **BCEL bank** at 6am and

11am and takes about four hours, including the border crossing. However, it isn't guaranteed to leave daily if there aren't enough passengers.

Muang Khua's inconvenient **bus station** (Rte 2E, 900m past Km 97) is nearly 2km west of the river towards Udomxai. Very rare tuk-tuks (10,000K per person) head out there once full from outside BCEL. Buses to Udomxai (50,000K, three hours) depart at 8.30am, 11am and 3pm. For Phongsali take the 8am *sŏrngtǎaou* to Pak Nam Noi (20,000K, one hour) and await the Udomxai–Phongsali (100,000K) bus there. It usually arrives at around 10am.

You can no longer travel by river to Hat Sa since the damming of the Nam Ou. **Boats** (Map p90) run from here downriver to Muang Ngoi Neua (100,000K, five hours, 8.30am or when there are 10 people) and on to Nong Khiaw (120,000K, six hours) through stunning karst scenery.

Phongsali ພົງສາລີ

POP 15,000 / ☐ 088 / ELEVATION 1400M

As you approach Phongsali via a sinuous mountain road, the town rears up suddenly on a ridgetop plateau. Often wrapped in mist, its atmospheric wooden Yunnanese shophouses and other buildings, spanning biscuit-brown to powder-blue, shelter below the peak of Phu Fa (Sky Mountain; 1625m) rising majestically in the background. The location gives the town panoramic views and a refreshing climate that can swing from pleasantly warm to downright cold in a matter of hours – expect icicles in the cold

---

HILL-TRIBE TREKKING

Hill-tribe treks in Phongsali Province are among the most authentic and rewarding in all of Laos. Tours have a heavy emphasis on ecological and cultural sensitivity, with a sizeable chunk of fees going into development funds for the host villages. Carefully thought-out treks are offered through the well-organised tourist office. Most treks can be organised for next-day departure, especially if you phone ahead. A popular option is the **Jungle Trek** (two short days starting from Boun Neua), visiting an Akha Phixo village as well as crossing a rare surviving stand of primary forest. Various multiday treks include boat rides up the Nam Ou (Ou River) from Hat Sa and visiting unforgettable Akha Nuqui villages linked by high ridge-top paths. One-way treks like the three-day **Nam Lan Trek** to Boun Tai can include delivery of your backpack to the destination so that you don't have to backtrack. This trek passes through Yang, Laobit, Akha Djepia and Akha Nuqui villages. However, with more than 30 stream and river crossings, it should only be attempted later in the dry season. To organise guides, phone well ahead to Phongsali's tourist office (p94) or get in touch with Amazing Phongsali Travel (p93).

Prices per person per day range from around 350,000K as part of a larger group to about 500,000K if going it alone. This includes the guide's fee, food and ultra-basic homestays in real village homes. Add to this transport costs, which are widely variable depending on whether public transport or charter vehicles are used. 'Experience tours' allow you to spend more time with village folk including, perhaps, guided foraging trips to collect the ingredients for the family dinner.

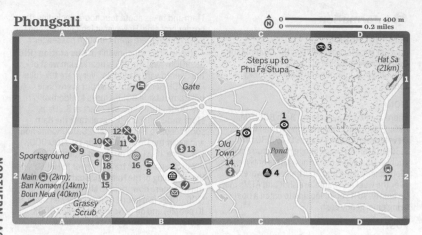

Phongsali

season and bring a jacket and waterproofs just in case, even in April.

The town's population is a mix of Phu Noi and Haw/Yunnanese, both long-term residents and more recent immigrants. That said, no one comes to Phongsali to experience the town, which can feel unfriendly and very untypically Lao; it's the trekking in the surrounding hill country and its vivid population of ethnic peoples that justifies the considerable effort to get here.

History

According to tradition the Phu Noi were originally a warlike tribe who had migrated from Burma to Luang Prabang. Seeing danger and opportunity in equal measure, the Lan Xang king granted them land in the far north of his domains, today's Phongsali, where they maintained the borderlands

against incursions from the Tai Lü kingdom of Sipsong Panna.

⊙ Sights

The town's modest but distinctive old-town area includes a three-block grid of rough, stone-flagged alleys and a winding street mostly lined with traditional **Yunnanese shophouses** FREE whose wooden frontages recall the architecture of old Kunming. Tiny, new and functional, the **Chinese Temple** overlooks a pond, behind which is **Wat Keo**, with its *petang*-playing monks.

Phu Fa   VIEWPOINT
(ພູຟ້າ; Sky Mountain) For great views across town climb to the stupa-topped peak of Phu Fa (1625m); it's a punishing, tree-shaded climb of more than 400 stone steps. A 4000K toll is payable on the last section of the

ascent. An alternative descent returns to the Hat Sa road near a tea factory 2km east of town.

Museum of Tribes
MUSEUM

(Map p92; 10,000K; ⊙8-11.30am & 1.30-4.30pm Mon-Fri) This museum gives you a chance to deepen your understanding of the ethnic peoples of Phongsali Province. It contains a wealth of cultural information on animism and customs, with photos and historical background, as well as displays of the vividly coloured costumes you're likely to see on your travels. If the door is locked, ask for the key from the post office across the road.

☞ Tours

Amazing Phongsali Travel
TREKKING

(Northern Travelling Center; Map p92; ☑088-210594, 020-55774354; www.explorephongsalylaos.com; ⊙8am-5pm or later) ⟡ In order to see a few of the 28 ethnicities in the province you need to penetrate deep jungle, and for this you'll require more than a guide who can take you to outlying villages along the road. Amazing Phongsali Travel is the main independent trekking operator in Phongsali, with a selection of treks that have brought rave reviews.

Check out the excellent website for information on the treks themselves. By the time you read this they may have moved office. They were also considering starting mountain-bike tours at the time of writing.

⌖ Sleeping

Phou Fa Hotel
HOTEL $

(Map p92; ☑088-210031; r 100,000-200,000K; ✳☎) Western toilets, room heaters and golden bed covers give the Phou Fa a marginal edge as Phongsali's best choice, but let's not get too excited. More expensive rooms are almost suites and include a carpet. This compound housed the Chinese consulate until 1975. There's also a rather drab restaurant here.

Sengsaly Guesthouse
GUESTHOUSE $

(Map p92; ☑088-210165; r 80,000-100,000K; ☎) The best of three cheapies on the main drag, the Sengsaly has uberbasic 80,000K rooms with clean bedding, bare walls, tiled floors and private bathroom. Better rooms are newly built and comfy, if overly colourful, and come with a hot shower and verandah. Expect indifferent service.

✗ Eating

Noodle Stands
NOODLES $

(Map p92; noodles 15,000K; ⊙6am-5pm) Head to the noodle stands at the rear of the wet market before you catch the 6.30am *sŏrngtăaou* to the bus station, or if you're headed out on a trek. Steaming deliciously fresh noodles and a slice of Yunnan-Lao culture await the early bird. Try the tasty *kòw sóy* (noodle soup with minced pork and tomato).

Laoper Restaurant
CHINESE $

(Map p92; mains 30,000K; ⊙5-10pm) Spot your dish in raw form behind the refrigerated glass counter: pork, intestines, buffalo steak and tofu, plus the day's fresh vegetables. Don't expect a menu, but point to what you want. Portions are huge so it's better to go as a couple or threesome. And be prepared for diners occasionally decongesting and spitting on the floor.

Laojerm Restaurant
LAOTIAN $

(Map p92; mains 30,000K; ⊙7am-10.30pm) At this family-run noodle house the well-prepared food comes in decent-sized portions and is served with a smile. The menu's approximate English includes inscrutable offerings such as 'High-handed Pig's liver' and 'Palace Protects the Meat Cubelets'.

Market
MARKET $

(Map p92; ⊙6am-5pm) Make a dawn visit to the earthy wet market (camera in hand) and thread through the labyrinthine collection of rickety stalls, with all manner of vegetables and fruit spread out on colourful display in the open area. It's a memorable experience, with its squawking Chinese vendors, exotic spices, brewing soup in forbidding cauldrons, ethnic visitors, and dogs optimistically attempting to procreate in the chaos.

☗ Drinking & Nightlife

The Phongsali region, especially in Ban Komaen, is famous for Chinese-style green tea. The tourist office sells samples (along with excellent local *lòw-lów*; whisky). The pale-green tint comes from having been passed over raspberry leaves after fermentation.

ⓘ Information

INTERNET ACCESS

Wang Electronics Shop (Map p92; ⊙7am-10pm) Internet access and a regular power supply.

TREKKING IN NORTHERN LAOS

Northern Laos has won prizes for its 'ecotrekking' system, pioneered in Luang Namtha and Nam Ha National Protected Area (NPA). Registered agencies pledge to return a significant (and stated) percentage of profits to the villages visited and to abide by sensible ecologically friendly guidelines. Visiting remote off-road villages without a guide is of dubious legality. Fortunately, guides and any necessary trekking permits can usually be arranged very quickly by local agencies, often the evening before departure. Costs excluding transport are typically around US$50 to US$75 per person per day if alone, falling to US$25 per person for a larger group. Agencies don't generally compete directly so comparing product is more relevant than comparing prices. Employing freelance guides might be cheaper but is discouraged as they'll rarely make contributions to village development funds. Visit the excellent website www.ecotourismlaos.com for more information. The following list is a generalised overview of what differentiates the various trekking centres.

Phongsali (p91) Nowhere is better for striking out into truly timeless villages where traditional costumes and arcane animist beliefs are still commonplace, particularly in the remote Akha communities. Many homes retain picture-book thatched roofs, at least for now. Virgin-forest treks are also possible near Boun Neua.

Luang Namtha (p103) Treks are very well organised and have numerous options, some combining trekking with other activities such as biking and kayaking. Forest hikes to Nam Ha NPA 'jungle camps' are especially popular. To reduce pressure on any single host village, most agents have unique routes. However, this inadvertently adds to the complexity of deciding just what you actually want to see and where you'll find it. Not all routes are equally inspiring. Ask how deep the trek goes into the forest to ensure you don't end up with a lightweight, peripheral experience.

Vieng Phukha (p108) A much less commercial starting point for Nam Ha forest treks.

Muang Sing (p109) Guided or DIY visits to colourful and relatively accessible Akha villages. The trekking scene has died off considerably, but there's still one very good operator here.

Udomxai (p97) A specialist agency makes Udomxai a popular centre for mountain biking, with some itineraries combined with treks.

Muang Khua (p89) Limited options include a one-day trek visiting an Akha Pala village (where some local women wear curiously gaudy semi-traditional costumes), with plenty of views en route but minimal forest.

Phonsavan (p68) One unique trek combines a mossy archaeological site, accommodation in a roadless Hmong village and an ascent of a multistage waterfall. It's a fascinating walk, but don't expect costumed tribesfolk in this area.

Muang Ngoi Neua (p85) Easy DIY day walks to pretty villages or very inexpensive group treks with freelance guides, some including scenic boat trips.

Nong Khiaw (p82) Try the '100 waterfalls' tour, a walk *in* a stream, following it upward through a series of cooling limestone cascades, to a summit.

MONEY

BCEL (Map p92; ⊗ 8.30am-3.30pm Mon-Fri) Includes an ATM across the road.

Lao Development Bank (Map p92; ⊗ 8.30am-3.30pm Mon-Fri) Can change multiple currencies to kip and cashes US-dollar travellers cheques without commission. Includes an ATM and represents Western Union.

POST

Post Office (Map p92; ⊗ 8am-noon & 1-4pm Mon-Fri)

TELEPHONE

Lao Telecom (Map p92; ⊗ 9am-5pm) International calls possible.

TOURIST INFORMATION

Tourist Office (Map p92; ☏ 088-210098; www.phongsaly.net; ⊗ 8-11.30am & 1.30-4pm

Mon-Fri) If you need emergency help or want to book a tour out of hours, call ☑ 020-22572373 or the mobile phone number of duty staff posted on the front door. Helpful maps and brochures are also available online (and are free from most guesthouses).

❶ Getting There & Away

Phongsali's airport is actually at Boun Neua, although at the time of writing neither of the country's airlines were running flights here.

Buses leave daily for Hat Sa (20,000K) at 8am and 1.30pm from the **Hat Sa Bus Station** (Map p92; Km 3), 10 minutes' walk east of town.

Phongsali's main bus station is at Km 3, west of town. A *sŏrngtǎaou* runs there from the market area (10,000K) at 6.30am but only very infrequently after that, so leave plenty of time. Route 1A has finally been sealed, allowing for safer, quicker and easier passage to and from Phongsali. The daily bus to Vientiane (230,000K, more than 20 hours) leaves at 8.30am and the VIP bus (250,000K) at 2pm, passing through Luang Prabang (140,000K). Buses to Udomxai (80,000K, seven hours) leave at 8am and 2pm. There's a 7.30am bus to Luang Namtha (60,000k), and a 7am bus to Dien Bien Phu (130,000K, five hours) on the Vietnamese side. As foreigners can't cross the Chinese border at Ban Pakha, the buses to Mengla, China (7am and 1.30pm) are only useful for reaching Boun Neua (50,000K).

There's a 7.30am bus to Muang Khua (80,000K, seven hours), from where you can catch the boat to Muang Ngoi Neua and Nong Khiaw (due to river damming, it is no longer possible to catch the boat upriver from Hat Sa). Note that you cannot get to Muang Ngoi Neua or Nong Khiaw in one day and will have to overnight at Muang Khua.

Amazing Phongsali Travel (p93) rents small motorbikes from 100,000K per day.

Around Phongsali

Ban Komaen ບ້ານກຳແມນ

Phongsali's famous tea village is a very attractive place commanding stupendous valley views. These sweep nearly 360 degrees when you stand on the promontory behind the school here. A fair percentage of authentic Phu Noi homes are set on stone-pile platforms. Arriving from Phongsali (15km away), the drive passes plenty of tea bushes, with those beside the main road through the village centre reputedly more than 400 years old and said to be the world's oldest.

Ban Komaen makes a very pleasant motorbike excursion. Take the Boun Neua road, turn left directly opposite the inspirationally named Km4 Nightclub (not the asphalt road just before) then curve steadily around on the main unpaved road, keeping left at most junctions but avoiding any turn that descends into the valley.

Rent a tuk-tuk from Phongsali (250,000K return) or hire a bike from the Phongsali tourist office for 50,000K per day. It's only a 15km ride between Phongsali and Ban Komaen, through stunning scenery.

Hat Sa ຫາດຊາ

Sadly, boats no longer make the journey from Hat Sa's little port downriver to Muang Khua since the Nam Ou (Ou River) was dammed, and as such there's slim pickings for even the most culturally fascinated traveller to get excited about, save a market on the 15th and 30th of each month that attracts hill-tribe folk.

It is possible to sleep in one of three unfurnished bamboo-walled crash pad rooms above **Wanna Ngyai Shop** (per person 40,000K). It is the first two-storey shack to the right above the boat landing. Mosquito nets and thin floor mats are available but it's preferable to bring your own sleeping bag. Wash in the river.

The only place to eat is **Boun Ma Restaurant** (mains 20,000K; ⊗7am-7pm). Basic Lao food is served here.

Given that the electricity in Hat Sa is turned off at 9pm, the town goes to sleep shortly thereafter.

Buses to Phongsali (20,000K) depart at around 9am and 2pm from the market, taking up to an hour westbound due to the steep climb.

Phu Den Din NPA ປ່າສະຫງວນແຫ່ງຊາດພູແດນດິນ

This vast area of partly unexplored, relatively pristine forest is layered across inaccessible mountains that climax at almost 2000m near the Vietnamese border. At present, the only legal way to get a glimpse of its grandeur is on irregular boating or kayaking trips down the Nam Ou (Ou River) between Ban Tha and Hat Sa. An army checkpoint currently prevents any access to the National Protected Area (NPA). Sneaking past it you risk being shot as a suspected poacher.

SENSITIVE TREKKING

When visiting tribal villages it is important to learn slightly different etiquette according to each local culture. The following notes focus particularly on the Akha, as Akha women's coin-encrusted indigo costumes make their villages popular trekking targets while their animist beliefs are also some of the most unexpected.

Shoes and feet Entering an ethnic Lao home it would be rude not to remove shoes, but in mud-floored dwellings of Hmong, Akha and some other tribal peoples, it is fine to keep them on. However, still avoid pointing feet at anyone.

Toilets If there's a village toilet, use it. When in the forest be sure to dump away from watercourses. But in remote villages with no toilets at all, check with the guide as to the local custom: although trekking etiquette usually dictates burying faeces, in some villages the deposit will be gobbled up greedily by the local pigs so shouldn't be wasted! Nonetheless, please do carry out used toilet paper, tampons etc, however unpleasant that might seem.

Photos While many hill-tribe boys are delighted to be photographed, most village women run squealing from a camera. Asking permission to snap a passing stranger often results in straight refusal, which should be respected. However, a great advantage of staying in a village homestay is that you become 'friends' with a family. Try snapping digital photos of babies and men, show those casually to your host ladies and eventually it's quite likely that they will want to see themselves on camera. Never force the issue, however, as a few really might believe the crusty old superstition that photographers are soul-stealers.

Gifts If you want to give gifts, consider fruit and vegetable seeds or saplings that continue to give after you've left. Always ask the guide first if it's appropriate to give anything and if so, only give directly to friends or to the village chief. Giving gifts to children can encourage begging, which undermines societies that have always been self-sufficient.

Beds In trekking villages it is common to sleep in the house of the village chief. In traditional Akha homes all the menfolk sleep on one raised, curtained platform, most of the women on another (which it is absolutely taboo to visit) and the daughter-in-law gets a curtained box-space poignantly befitting her almost slave-like status. To make space for visitors, most menfolk move out for the night to sleep in other houses, leaving the guide, trekkers and maybe a village elder or two to snuggle up in a line in the male section. Bringing a sleeping bag gives a greater semblance of privacy. Note that female trekkers count as 'honorary men'.

Spirits The spirit world is every bit as lively in hill-tribe cultures as it is in other Lao cultures and it would be exceedingly bad form for a visitor to touch a village totem (Tai Lü villages), a spirit gate (Akha) or any other taboo item. Ask the guide to explain and don't even think of dangling yourself on an Akha swing (hacheu).

Breasts and babies Akha women who display their bare breasts are neither being careless nor offering a sexual come-on; they're simply following a belief that young mothers who cover both breasts will attract harm to their newborn offspring. Eating stones while pregnant is an odder custom, while the Akha attitude that twins are unlucky is still common.

Boun Neua   ບຸນເໜືອ

A local transport hub 41km west of Phongsali, Boun Neua is a diffuse scattering of mostly newer concrete houses that has been tentatively proposed as the unlikely new provincial capital. Staying here might prove handy if connecting to Ou Tai or for those doing the Phongsali 'Jungle Trek'.

After Boun Neua (Km 41) the road to Phongsali climbs onto a ridge-top road surveying swaths of protected mountain forests. There's a signed viewpoint 500m past Km 31, with ridge-top panoramas continuing for the next 15km. Baka Luang (200m beyond Km 17) is the first noticeably Phu Noi village en route, where old women still wear distinctive Phu Noi leggings.

The bus station plus a few shops and basic eateries lie around the main junction where Rte 1A to Ou Tai turns north off the Phongsali road. Beside the bus station and market, convenient three-storey **Sivienkham** (r 50,000K) offers large and house-proud rooms with comfy beds, hot showers and sit-down toilets.

For Phongsali (20,000K, 1½ hours) use the through-buses from Mengla (China), Boun Tai, Udomxai or Vientiane, typically departing around 1pm and between 4pm and 6pm. The rickety bus from Boun Neua to Ou Tai (at least 4½ hours) departs at around 9.30am once the early bus from Phongsali arrives (if you're arriving from Vientiane you'll probably miss it).

NORTHWESTERN LAOS

Northern Udomxai and Luang Namtha provinces form a mountainous tapestry of rivers, forests and traditional villages that are home to almost 40 classified ethnicities. Luang Namtha is the most developed of several traveller-friendly towns ranged around the 2224-sq-km Nam Ha NPA, with hiking, biking, kayaking and boating adventures all easily organised at short notice. Udomxai is the regional transport hub, while Boten is the one China–Laos border open to international visitors.

❶ Getting There & Away

Head to the extreme north of this province and you'll be at the border with southern China. To the west is the Golden Triangle, where Laos meets Thailand and Myanmar (Burma). River trips due to damming have been curtailed somewhat but it's still possible to journey by boat some of the way between Luang Namtha and Huay Xai. In general the major roads are well maintained if you're travelling on a motorcycle.

Udomxai (Oudomsay, Muang Xai)   ຊຸດມໄຊ

Booming Udomxai (also known as Muang Xai) is a Laos–China trade centre and crossroads city, and with its cast of migrant truck drivers and Mandarin signage at every turn it certainly feels like it. The dusty, brash main street and lack of a traveller vibe puts off many short-term visitors, and you might think the highlight is the bus that spirits you out of here; however, it takes minimal effort to find the real Laos nearby. The well-organised tourist office – one of the best in the country – has many ideas to tempt you to stay longer, from cooking courses to treks, off-road motorcycling and cycling.

Around 25% of Udomxai's population is Chinese, with the Yunnanese dialect as common as Lao in some businesses and hotels.

◉ Sights

Phu That Stupa   BUDDHIST TEMPLE
(Map p98; ⊗dawn-dusk) Stairways lead up from the main road to pretty little Phu That Stupa, a historic structure that was totally rebuilt after wartime destruction. Religious ceremonies are held here on full-moon days.

Wat Phu That   BUDDHIST TEMPLE
(Map p98; ⊗dawn-dusk) This attractive hilltop temple is one of the best spots to head to for cooler air and fabulous sunset views of the valley below. The 15m-tall gold Buddha is equally impressive.

Museum   MUSEUM
(Map p98; 10,000K; ⊗8-11am & 2-4pm) **FREE** Stairways lead up from the main road to the town's new two-storey museum, featuring colonial-style shutters and oriental gables. Inside, much of it is dedicated to uninspiring communist propaganda; however, there are some interesting ethnic costumes and tools used in rural Lao life.

Banjeng Temple   BUDDHIST TEMPLE
(Wat Santiphab; Map p98; ⊗dawn-dusk) Udomxai's foremost monastery is Banjeng Temple, which is modest but very attractively set on a riverside knoll. The most notable feature here is an imaginative concrete 'tree of life'. Tinkling in the breeze, its metal leaves hide a menagerie of naively crafted animal and bird statues that illustrate a local Buddha myth.

PMC   ARTS CENTRE
(Productivity & Marketing Center of Oudomxay; Map p98; ☑081-212803; www.facebook.com/pmc. oudomxay; ⊗8am-noon & 2-5pm) **FREE** PMC is a small exhibition room and shop introducing local fibres such as jungle vine, and selling handmade paper products, bags and local essences. If you're wondering why it's part-funded by the UN Office on Drugs and Crime, that's because these crafts are an attempt to find non-narcotic-based commerce for former poppy-growing communities (hence its ironic nickname, the 'opium shop').

Udomxai

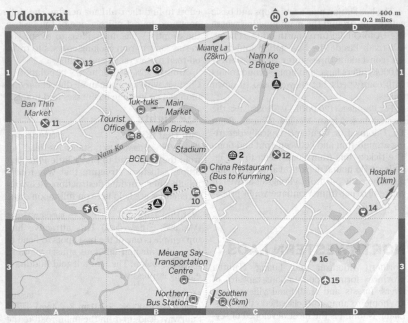

Udomxai

⊙ Sights
1 Banjeng Temple	C1
2 Museum	C2
3 Phu That Stupa	B2
4 PMC	B1
5 Wat Phu That	B2

⊕ Activities, Courses & Tours
6 Lao Red Cross	A2

🛏 Sleeping
7 Charming Lao Hotel	B1
8 Dansavanh Hotel	B2
9 Lithavixay Guesthouse	C2
10 Villa Keoseumsack	B2

✗ Eating
11 Ban Thin Market	A2
Cafe Sinouk	(see 7)
12 Meuang Neua Restaurant	C2
13 Souphailin Restaurant	A1

⊙ Drinking & Nightlife
14 Ming Khouan	D2

⊕ Transport
15 Airport	D3
16 Lao Airlines	D3
Lao Skyway	(see 15)

🏃 Activities

The tourist office (p100) offers one-day tours around Udomxai, a city walk, two- and three-day visits to the Chom Ong Caves, plus two possible trekking routes that include Khamu village homestays. To find potential fellow trekkers arrive at 4pm for a 'rendezvous meeting' the day before departure. It also has well-maintained dirt bikes taking you off-road on great local adventures.

Nam Kat Yorla Pa Adventure Park ADVENTURE SPORTS
(📞020-55564359, 081-212195; www.namkat yorlapa.com; Faen Village, Xay District) 🚲 Cycling, trekking, ziplining, rock climbing, abseiling, swimming, massage and shooting are all available at Oudomxay Province's newest forest resort 17km north of Udomxai by the picturesque Nam Kat (Kat River). Stunning accommodation in modern slick rooms starts at US$104. Alternatively, take the 'abseil, zipline and *via ferrata*' package, which also includes sleeping in a tree house for US$75.

Lao Red Cross
MASSAGE

(Map p98; ☎081-312391; steam bath 12,000K, massage per 30min 30,000K; ⊙3-7.30pm) On a hillock overlooking a beautiful river bend, the Lao Red Cross offers Lao Swedish-style massage and herbal steam baths in a modest bamboo-matted structure. All proceeds are recycled into first-aid training in local villages.

📖 Courses

The tourist office (p100) organises an interesting series of paper-making workshops (from 100,000K depending on group size) that include gathering the raw materials. Its cooking courses (from 100,000K per person with a minimum of four, 200,000K per person for a couple) include shopping for ingredients, but the teacher speaks better French than English.

🛏 Sleeping

Dansavanh Hotel
HOTEL $

(Map p98; ☎081-212698; Rte 1; r 150,000K; ❄@🖀🛜) Dansavanh was once Udomxai's top hotel and its dirty facade still retains an element of neocolonial grandeur, but the rooms, while large and properly equipped, lack any imagination. Facilities include a small spa, karaoke and an attractive riverside restaurant–beer garden. The De Syuen tea shop in the lobby is a must for tea aficionados.

Lithavixay Guesthouse
GUESTHOUSE $

(Map p98; ☎081-212175; Rte 1; r 70,000-150,000K; ❄🛜) A long-time traveller fave, with a large lobby and a cosy breakfast and internet cafe. Although some rooms look tired, they include TVs, couches and homely touches. Old showers suffer from slow drainage, and recently service has dropped a little. It's close to the old bus station and very central.

★Charming Lao Hotel
BOUTIQUE HOTEL $$

(Map p98; ☎081-212881, 020-23966333; www.charminglaohotel.com; r incl breakfast US$50-150; P❄@🛜) An unexpected treat for Udomxai, this hotel offers tastefully furnished rooms right in the centre of town. Extra touches include flat-screen TVs with cable, coffee-making facilities, safety deposit boxes and contemporary bathrooms. The complex includes a spa and a disappointing branch of Pakse's Cafe Sinouk. Staff are eager but speak little English.

Villa Keoseumsack
GUESTHOUSE $$

(Map p98; ☎081-312170; Rte 1; r 130,000-220,000K; ❄🛜) Udomxai's best guesthouse is set back from the road in a handsome Lao house with large, inviting rooms. They come with crisp linen, decent fittings, springy beds and varnished floors. Hmong bed runners, TV, free wi-fi and a communal reading balcony finish them off.

🍴 Eating

★Souphailin Restaurant
LAOTIAN $

(Map p98; mains 20,000-40,000K; ⊙7am-10pm) Don't be fooled by the modest bamboo exterior of this backstreet gem – easily the tastiest Lao food in the city is served here. Friendly Souphailin creates culinary magic with her *mok pa* (steamed fish in banana leaves), *láhp*, perfectly executed spring rolls, beef steak, fried noodles, and chicken and mushroom in banana leaf. Everything is fresh and seasonal.

Meuang Neua Restaurant
LAOTIAN $

(Map p98; mains 30,000-40,000K; ⊙7am-9pm) Festooned with lanterns and Che Guevara graffiti, this hole-in-the-wall is a 10-minute walk from the main drag. It's worth a visit for the fresh spring rolls, pancakes, juices, pad thai and noodle soup.

Ban Thin Market
MARKET $

(Map p98; ⊙6am-5pm) Among the noodles, vegetables and fruit expect a few appearances from songbirds, squirrels, tree frogs and rats. Cooked.

Cafe Sinouk
LAOTIAN, INTERNATIONAL $$

(Map p98; www.sinoukcafe.com; Charming Lao Hotel; mains 45,000-60,000K; ⊙7am-9pm; ❄🛜) Offering a level of aesthetic sophistication largely lacking in the city, Sinouk has a fusion menu of barbecued pork, steamed fish, papaya salad, pasta variations and breakfast. Staff, however, speak little English and international dishes can end up as curious hybrids – carbonara with carrots and hot dog was a first for us!

🍺 Drinking & Nightlife

Ming Khouan
BAR

(Map p98; ⊙11am-11pm) This is where it's at in Udomxai, a lively wooden and bamboo beer garden that draws a young crowd to quaff Beerlao by the crate. The central fountain is a bit of a diversion, but good Lao food is available, including barbecued skewers. It's near the airport.

ℹ Information

INTERNET ACCESS

Most guesthouses and hotels now offer free wi-fi to guests.

MONEY

BCEL (Map p98; ☎081-211260; Rte 1; ⊗8.30am-4.30pm Mon-Fri) Has an ATM, changes several major currencies and accepts some travellers cheques (2% commission).

TOURIST INFORMATION

Tourist Office (Provincial Tourism Department of Oudomxay; Map p98; ☎081-211797; www. oudomxay.info; ⊗8-11.30am & 2-5pm) Has masses of information about onward travel, accommodation and local sights. It has free town maps and sells GT-Rider Laos maps. There are 11 different tours on offer, including the two-day/one-night tour to an impressive local cave, and three-day/two-night treks and homestays with local ethnic villages.

ℹ Getting There & Away

AIR

Lao Airlines (Map p98; ☎081-312047; www. laoairlines.com) flies daily to/from Vientiane (US$79) to Udomxai's **airport** (Map p98), while **Lao Skyway** (Map p98; ☎020-23122219; www.laoskyway.com; Udomxai Airport; ⊗7am-5pm) flies to Vientiane as well (US$73) on Tuesday, Thursday and Saturday. Tickets are also available from Lithavixay Guesthouse (p99).

BUS & SŎRNGTĂAOU

There are two bus stations in Udomxai: the old **Northern Bus Station** (Map p98) in the centre of town, and the newer Long-distance Bus Station, aka **Southern Bus Terminal** (☎081-212218), 5km southwest from the centre. There is some crossover of routes as some of the same destinations are serviced by both minivans from the Northern Bus Station and buses from the Southern Bus Terminal.

Sŏrngtăaou (passenger trucks) to Muang La (20,000K) depart when full at around 8.30am and 11.30am from the **Meuang Say Transportation Centre** (Map p98).

BUSES FROM NORTHERN BUS STATION

DESTINATION	PRICE (K)	DURATION (HR)	DEPARTURES
Bokeo	85,000	8	9am, 1pm
Boten	50,000	4	8am
Dien Bien Phu (Vietnam)	95,000	5	8.30am
Luang Namtha	40,000	2	8.30am, 11.30am, 3.30pm
Muang Houn	30,000	2	noon, 2pm, 4pm
Muang Khua	35,000	3	8.30am, 11.30am, 3.30pm
Muang La	70,000	4	8am
Phongsali	75,000	9	9am

BUSES (LONG-DISTANCE) FROM SOUTHERN BUS TERMINAL

DESTINATION	PRICE (K)	DURATION (HR)	DEPARTURES
Luang Prabang	60,000	6	9am, noon, 3pm
Muang Hongsa	110,000	7	12.30pm
Nong Khiaw	45,000	4	10am
Pak Beng	40,000	4	8.30am, 10am
Pak Mong	30,000	3	1pm
Phonsavan	130,000	12	10am
Vientiane	170,000	14	11am, 2pm, 4pm, 6pm
Vientiane (sleeper)	190,000	14	8pm

To China

An 8am minibus to Mengla, China leaves from the Northern Bus Station. The Kunming-bound bed-bus from Luang Prabang bypasses this station but makes a short snack break at the **China Restaurant** (Map p98) at around 11.30am. Booking isn't possible but the bus takes extra passengers if space allows.

ℹ Getting Around

Lithavixay Guesthouse (p99) rents decent bicycles (per half-/full day 20,000/50,000K) and mountain bikes (per day US$10). The **tourist office** (p100) rents bicycles for 50,000K and motorbikes for 100,000K per day. Both can help arrange chauffeured minivans from US$100 per day.

Tuk-tuks (Map p98) cost 15,000K per person per hop within city limits, if you can find one.

Around Udomxai

Hop on a decent motorbike and head out in any direction and you'll quickly find attractive scenery and plenty of rural interest.

Nam Kat Waterfall, a picnic site 23km from Udomxai, is best reached on a decent motorbike. Turn right in Ban Fan, continue to the parking area then walk the last 30 minutes through protected forests (about 2km). Alternatively, hike 13.5km over 'red cliff' Phou Pha Daeng, which you'll need a guide for. The last 500m climb is the only testing section of the track and affords terrific views at the top. The falls themselves are 20m high and make for a chilled bucolic spot.

Chom Ong Caves ຖ້ຳຈອມອອງ

Udomxai's top tourist attraction, the extensive cave system of Chom Ong Caves burrows more than 15km beneath a forested karst ridge near the Khamu village Ban Chom Ong, 48km from Udomxai. Often as high as 40m within, it's a veritable cathedral of a place whose first 450m have been lit with solar-powered lamps. Over millions of years the time-worn stalactites have been coated with curious crusts of minerals and sometimes studded with gravel from later wash-throughs. To gain access you'll need to borrow the gate-key and engage a guide (40,000K) in **Ban Chom Ong**, from which the cave entrance is an hour's walk.

The village's simple, unmarked 'guesthouse' is a purpose-built local-style longhouse with roll-out bedding and the relative luxury of a tap and porcelain squat in the outside shared toilets. Note that the village has no electricity and that very little English is spoken. Udomxai is better for travellers to use as their base to return to.

As there are no restaurants or shops, organising food as well as the guide and key will require some spoken Lao, Khamu or plenty of gesticulation. We recommend arranging your trip through the tourist office in Udomxai, which involves a homestay.

The main problem with getting here is that the uncomfortable access 'roads' are almost entirely unpaved, impassably muddy after rain and improbably steep and rutted in places.

THE LEGEND OF THE PRA SINGKHAM BUDDHA

Inlaid with precious stones, the 200kg gold-and-bronze Pra Singkham Buddha statue (p102) has an interesting history. It is said to have been created in Sri Lanka, spending time in Ayodhya, India before arriving in Laos in AD 868. In 1355 it was reputedly one of five great Buddhist masterpieces sent out by Lan Xang founder Fa Ngum to inspire the faithful at the far reaches of his new kingdom.

However, the boat carrying the statue was sunk in a battle. Later found by a fisherman, Pra Singkham was dragged out of the water amid considerable tribulations and thereupon became the subject of a contest between residents of Muang La and Muang Khua regions. The sneaky folks from Muang Khua, downriver, suggested that the Buddha should choose for himself and set the statue on a raft to 'decide'. However, the seemingly hopeless contest went Muang La's way when the raft magically floated upstream against the current, 'proving' it belonged in La.

Kept initially in the Singkham Cave, by 1457 it had found a home in a specially built temple around which today's town of Muang La is now ranged. Like almost everything else in rural Laos, the temple was bombed to oblivion during the 20th-century Indochina wars. However, the statue had been rehidden in the Singkham Cave. By the time a new temple was consecrated in 1987, the Buddha had turned a black-green colour, apparently due to sadness at the destruction. But today he's once again a gleaming gold.

Two- and three-day tours, including meals, an English-speaking guide and ample time to observe typical village scenes can be organised through the tourist office in Udomxai, but transport is by excruciatingly uncomfortable jeep-*sŏrngtǎaou*. Two-day/one-night trips start from US$100 per person with a minimum of four people.

Muang La   ເມືອງຫລາ

♪ 021

Scenic Muang La, just 28km from Udomxai towards Phongsali, offers a charming rural alternative to the 'big city'. This Tai Lü village sits at the confluence of the Nam La (La River) and Nam Phak (Phak River), attractively awash with palm trees. Its central feature is a classically styled temple that hosts one of northern Laos' most revered Buddha statues, the Pra Singkham Buddha.

◎ Sights

Pra Singkham Buddha   BUDDHIST STATUE
(ພະເຈົ້າສິງຄຳ; ⊙8.30am-5pm) FREE Want to get rich? Afraid you might be infertile? Don't worry, just ask the Pra Singkham Buddha and your wish will be granted. Legend claims it was cast in Sri Lanka just a few generations after the historical Buddha's death, and reached Laos in AD 868 via Ayodhya in India. Kept initially in the Singkham Cave, by 1457 it had been housed in a specially built temple.

Singkham Cave   CAVE
(ຖ້ຳພະເຈົ້າສິງຄຳ) FREE The Singkham Cave where the famous Pra Singkham Buddha statue once rested is 3.7km west of Ban Samakisai, halfway between Udomxai and Muang La. In Samakisai ask 'Khor kajeh tham noy?' ('may I have the cave key please?') at the second hut south of the bridge. Then cross the bridge and take the second rough track west – just about passable by tuk-tuk or motorbike. This terminates at a collection of huts from which it's just three minutes' walk to the cave. Inside is a replica statue.

🛏 Sleeping

Lhakham Hotel   HOTEL $
(♪020-55555930; lhakhamhotel@gmail.com; r 100,000K) Nestled on a river bank, the Lhakham Hotel offers some of the best-value rooms in northern Laos. Furnishings are tasteful, the bathrooms include a rain shower and the river views are pretty, adding up to a steal. There's also a restaurant here. It's about 1km from the bus station.

Muang La Resort   BOUTIQUE HOTEL $$$
(♪020-22841264; www.muangla.com; 3-night package per person from US$691) The memorable Muang La Resort hides an elegant rustic refinement behind tall, whitewashed walls. It accepts neither walk-in guests nor visitors, so you'll need to prebook a package of two nights or more to enjoy the stylishly appointed half-timbered guestrooms, sauna

and creatively raised open-air hot tub, all set between palms and manicured lawns.

❶ Getting There & Away

Buses to Phongsali and Muang Khua pass through Muang La around an hour after departing Udomxai. The last bus returning to Udomxai usually rolls through at around 5pm. There's no bus station, just wave the bus down. Additional *sŏrngtăaou* to Udomxai (20,000K) depart at around 7am and 11am if there's sufficient custom.

Boten   ບໍ່ເຕນ

POP 500 / ☏ 086

Boten is the only Laos–China border open to foreigners and makes for an easy short excursion while en route from Udomxai to Luang Namtha. This frontier border outpost is a spectacular case of boom to bust and has become a ghost town since 2011 after China banned its citizens from gambling here, rendering Boten's hotels, casinos, malls and karaoke parlours redundant.

While there are places to stay, it's best to move on into real China or head south into Muang Sing or Luang Namtha. You'll find a few Chinese and Lao restaurants here, though most have closed down. Since the closure of the casinos most places in town have shut down and there is no nightlife at present.

At the top (north) end of the market on the main street the **Lao Development Bank** (⊙8.30am-3.30pm Mon-Fri) changes major currencies, but for effortless yuan–kip exchange at fair rates use the supermarket across the road.

Although Boten taxi drivers try to persuade travellers otherwise, there are regular buses to/from Luang Namtha (25,000K, two hours) plus assorted China–Laos through-buses. Chartered taxi-vans charge about 160,000K to Luang Namtha and around 80,000K to Ban Na Theuy.

Luang Namtha (Namtha)
ຫລວງນ້ຳທາ

POP 21,000 / ☏ 086

Welcoming travellers like no other town in northern Laos, Luang Namtha packs a powerful green punch with its selection of eco-minded tour companies catering for trekking to ethnically diverse villages, and cycling, kayaking and rafting in and around the stunning Nam Ha NPA.

NAM THA TRIPS

For some 35km south of Luang Namtha, the pea-green Nam Tha (Tha River) flows across a series of pretty rapids tumbling between high-sided banks that are attractively shaggy with bamboo-choked forests. Luang Namtha tour agencies can organise one-day supported kayaking trips here, possibly combined with Nam Ha jungle treks. By bicycle or motorbike, the passably well-graded dirt road that runs along the river's eastern bank offers a quiet if potentially dusty way to enjoy some pretty views and see some interesting minority villages without the need for hiking.

Locally there's bags to do before you set out into the boonies, such as exploring the exotic night market, or grabbing a rental bike and tootling around the gently undulating rice-bowl valleys to waterfalls and temples. In the golden glow of sunset distant mountain ridges form layered silhouettes, and while it's not the prettiest belle architecturally speaking, the friendly vibe of Luang Namtha will grow on you.

◉ Sights

Luang Nam Tha Museum   MUSEUM
(ພິພິດທະພັນຫຼວງນ້ຳທາ; Map p104; 10,000K; ⊙8.30-11.30am & 1.30-3.30pm Mon-Thu, 8.30-11.30am Fri) The Luang Nam Tha Museum contains a collection of local anthropological artefacts, such as ethnic clothing, Khamu bronze drums and ceramics. There are also a number of Buddha images and the usual display chronicling the Revolution.

Ban Nam Di   VILLAGE
(Nam Dy; parking fee bicycle/motorcycle/car 1000/2000/3000K) Although barely 3km out of Luang Namtha, this hamlet is populated by Lao Huay (Lenten) people whose womenfolk still wear traditional indigo tunics with purple sash-belts and silver-hoop necklaces. They specialise in turning bamboo pulp into rustic paper, using cotton screens that you'll spot along the scenic river banks.

At the eastern edge of the village, a three-minute stroll leads from a small carpark to a 6m-high **waterfall** (2000K). You'll find it's more of a picnic site than a scenic wonder but a visit helps put a little money into village coffers. Unless the water level is

Luang Namtha

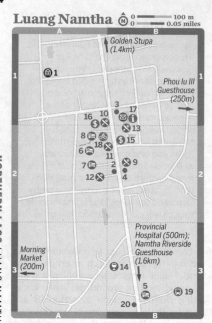

0 — 100 m
0 — 0.05 miles

Golden Stupa (1.4km)

Phou Iu III Guesthouse (250m)

Provincial Hospital (500m); Namtha Riverside Guesthouse (1.6km)

Morning Market (200m)

really high there's no need to struggle up and over the hillside steps so ignore that sign and walk along the pretty stream.

Golden Stupa   BUDDHIST TEMPLE
(5000K; ☉8am-5pm) By far Namtha's most striking landmark, this large golden stupa sits on a steep ridge directly northwest of town. It gleams majestically when viewed from afar. Up close, the effect is a bit more bling, but the views over town are impressive.

That Phum Phuk   BUDDHIST TEMPLE
(5000K; ☉8am-5pm) The red-gold stupa you see when first approaching the small and historic That Phum Phuk is a 2003 replica. Right beside it lies the brick and stucco rubble of an earlier version, blown over by the force of a US bombing raid during the Second Indochina War. Judging by the ferroconcrete protrusions, that wasn't the 1628 original either. The site is a hillock 3km northwest of the oddly isolated Phouvan Guesthouse.

Nam Ha NPA   NATIONAL PARK
(ປາສະຫງວນແຫງຊາດນ້ຳຫາ; www.namha-npa.org) ⚘ The 2224-sq-km Nam Ha NPA is one of Laos' most accessible natural preserves and home to clouded leopard and possibly a few unpoached tigers. Both around and within the mountainous park, woodlands have to compete with pressure from villages of various ethnicities, including Lao Huay, Akha and Khamu. Since 1999, an eco-touristic vision has tried to ensure tour operators and villagers work together to provide a genuine experience for trekkers while ensuring minimum impact on local communities and the environment.

Tours are limited to small groups, each agent has its own routes and, in principle, each village receives visitors no more than twice a week. Authorities don't dictate what villagers can and can't do, but by providing information on sustainable forestry and fishing practices it's hoped that forest protection will become a self-chosen priority for the communities.

☞ Tours

★ **Green Discovery** ECOTOUR
(Map p104; ☑ 086-211484; www.greendiscovery laos.com; Main St; ⊙ 8am-9pm) ✦ The grandaddy of ecotourism in Laos offers a combo of boat trips, mountain biking, kayaking, homestays and one- to three-day treks in Nam Ha NPA. Safety is a given and staff are helpful. At the time of writing, it had plans to move to a new office.

The Hiker TREKKING
(Map p104; ☑ 086-212343, 020-5924245; www. thehikerlaos.com; Main St) ✦ This new outfit is garnering some very glowing feedback. Cycling and kayaking trips are available but its main focus is on trekking, with one- to five-day options; the longest one is more hard core (seven hours' trekking per day) and promises to take you into untouched areas deep in the Nam Ha jungle, while one-day treks are much easier.

Forest Retreat Laos ECOTOUR
(Map p104; ☑ 020-55560007, 020-55680031; www.forestretreatlaos.com; Main St; ⊙ 7am-11.30pm) ✦ Based at the Minority Restaurant, this ecotourism outfit offers kayaking, trekking, homestays and mountain biking on one- to six-day multi-activity adventures, and recruits staff and guides from ethnic-minority backgrounds where possible. It also runs one-day cycle trips to Muang Sing and back. Another option here is to take a cooking class.

Discovering Laos KAYAKING, RAFTING
(Map p104; ☑ 086-212047, 020-22990344; www. discoveringlaos.com; ⊙ 8am-9pm) ✦ Specialises in kayaking and rafting trips through Khamu and Lenten villages as well as specialised cycling trips around Muang Sing. Also facilitates homestays and stays at its jungle camp on one-, two- and three-day treks.

🛏 Sleeping

🛏 Central

★ **Zuela Guesthouse** GUESTHOUSE $
(Map p104; ☑ 020-22391966; www.zuela-laos. com; r old block with fan/air-con 80,000/100,000K, new block with air-con without/with balcony US$25/38; ❄ 🛜) Located in a leafy courtyard, Zuela has an old block of spotless – though dim – rooms with exposed-brick walls and en suites. The newer block has better rooms with glazed rattan ceilings, lemon walls (some

NAM HA NPA TRIPS

Luang Namtha is a major starting point for trekking, rafting, mountain-biking and kayaking trips in the Nam Ha National Protected Area (NPA). Many of the tours stop for at least a night in a minority village. Most photogenic for their costumes are those of the Lao Huay and Akha peoples but all are fascinating for genuine glimpses of village life.

Treks all follow carefully considered sustainability guidelines but they vary in duration and difficulty. In the wet season leeches are a minor nuisance.

Namtha agents display boards listing their tour options and how many punters have already signed up, which is very helpful if you're trying to join a group to make things cheaper (maximum eight people). If you don't want others to join you, some agents will accept a 'private surcharge' of around US$50.

Around a dozen agencies operate, each with its own specialties.

with balcony), desks and vivid art. Located off the main drag down a quiet lane. Besides its great restaurant it also offers scooter rental.

Amandra GH GUESTHOUSE $
(Map p104; ☑ 030-9211319; Rte 3A, Ban Nong Bua Vieng; r from 100,000K; ❄) Set in a striking wooden building near the district bus station, Amandra has decent rattan-walled rooms with pretty lantern bedside lights, fan or air-con, satellite TV and hot water. The owner is helpful, and gives you his card so you can reach him if there's any hiccups. Rental bikes are available, too.

Thoulasith Guesthouse GUESTHOUSE $
(Map p104; ☑ 086-212166; www.thoulasith-guesthouse.com; Rte 3A; r with fan/air-con 80,000/120,000K; ❄🛜) This traveller-friendly place offers spotless rooms with bedside lamps, art on the walls, free coffee and wi-fi-enabled balconies. There's also a new block of swish rooms with baths. It's set back from the main strip so makes for a peaceful spot to wind down before or after a trek.

Manychan Guest House & Restaurant GUESTHOUSE $
(Map p104; ☑ 086-312209; dm 30,000K; r with fan/air-con 70,000/100,000K; 🛜) Manychan distinguishes itself not by its patchy rooms

but by the warm welcome of its eponymous owner. The restaurant has a coffee machine from Italy brewing lovely cappucinos, makes fresh bread and pastries for breakfast, and also has a new terrace for dinner (mains 30,000K). Rooms are bare-walled affairs with armoire, bathroom and hot-water shower, but little else.

★**Phou lu III Guesthouse** GUESTHOUSE **$$**
(☑ 030-5710422; www.luangnamtha-oasis-resort.com; r from US$25; ✸ ☎) Part of the same family as the Phou Iu II in Muang Sing, this place is cracking value and sits in pretty, flowering gardens. Bungalows are spacious and nicely fitted out with lumber-wood beds, brick floors, fireplaces and inviting terraces. It's well signposted from the centre of town.

Further Afield

Chaleunsuk Homestays HOMESTAY **$**
(☑ 020-55557768; Rte 3, 500m past Km 45; per person 80,000K) 🍴 Beside the main Rte 3 highway, 20km from central Luang Namtha, four rustic homes in Chaleunsuk village offer a real Khamu homestay experience without the need to trek. The fee includes breakfast, dinner and a contribution to the village development fund; a guided forest walk is an additional 20,000K. Ask at the Luang Namtha tourist office for more information. Limited English is spoken.

Namtha Riverside Guesthouse GUESTHOUSE **$$**
(☑ 086-212025; namthariverside@gmail.com; r 70,000-200,000K) With Noi and her friendly family, Namtha Riverside is more of a homestay than an impersonal guesthouse experience. It offers a tranquil setting with two spacious, riverfront bungalows that have solar-powered hot water. *Petang* is available and there are lounger-cushions on the balconies. It's 2km south of the centre. Good value, and you can use the bikes for free.

Boat Landing Guest House RESORT **$$**
(☑ 086-312398; www.theboatlanding.laopdr.com; Ban Kone; r incl breakfast US$47-60; ☎) 🍴 One of the country's original ecolodges, the Boat Landing has riverside acacia groves hugging tastefully finished wooden bungalows with solar-heated showers. The restaurant here produces some of the best Lao cuisine in the north, although cosy but weary rooms could do with a refresh. Located 6km south of the new town and about 150m off the main road.

✗ Eating & Drinking

Minority Restaurant LAOTIAN **$**
(Map p104; mains 35,000K; ☎ 7am-10.30pm; ☎) 🍴 This inviting, wood-beamed restaurant hidden down a little side alley offers the chance to sample typically ethnic dishes from the Khamu, Tai Dam and Akha tribes, as well as *láhp*, stir-fries, chicken curry and fried fish.

Manikong Bakery Cafe BAKERY, CAFE **$**
(Map p104; mains 10,000-50,000K; ☎ 6.30am-10.30pm; ☎) A hole-in-the-wall bakery/cafe serving tasty salads, bagels, panini, croissants, juices, sandwiches and homemade cakes. Sample shakes and coffees by day or cocktails by night; happy hour is from 5pm to 7pm.

Night Market MARKET **$**
(Map p104; Rte 3A; ☎ 7-11.30pm) Tightly thronged with tribeswomen and locals hawking freshly made broths, noodles and chicken on spits, with everything veiled in a stratosphere of smoke. Great for cheap quick eats. If you're feeling brave try the rhinoceros beetles, duck chicks in embryos, grilled intestines and bile soup!

Manychan Guesthouse & Restaurant LAOTIAN, INTERNATIONAL **$**
(Map p104; mains 30,000K; ☎ 6.30am-10.30pm; ☎) An inviting all-wood interior spilling out onto a fairy-lit street terrace keeps this place among the most popular *falang* (foreigner) venues in town. Wi-fi is free and the menu covers the gamut of possibilities. Beers arrive in coolers and the coffee has a kick.

Morning Market MARKET **$**
(noodles 10,000K; ☎ 7-10am) There are myriad noodle stands at the morning market, where you'll also be rewarded with a photogenic vista of fresh vegetables and fruit, buffalo skin, jungle meat, pig faces, live fish and even fried silkworms.

★**Bamboo Lounge** INTERNATIONAL **$$**
(Map p104; ☑ 020-22392931; mains/pizzas 50,000/75,000K; ☎ 7am-11.30pm, happy hour 5-7pm; ☻ ☎) 🍴 With its moss-green facade this place is the favourite in town for travellers, offering employment to young people from remote villages and donating over 2500 books to local schools. It's alluring by night with its winking fairy lights, thumping tunes and outdoor terrace piping delicious aromas from its wood-fired oven – there are myriad thin-crust pizza choices.

Boat Landing Restaurant LAOTIAN $$
(meals 35,000-160,000K; ⊙ 7am-8.30pm) The relaxing riverside setting complements some of the most authentic northern Lao cuisine on offer. From five-dish menus for two or three people to one-plate meals, the flavour combinations are divine. If you're baffled by the choice try snacking on a selection of *jqaou* used as dipping sauces for balls of sticky rice.

Chill Zone Beer Bar BAR
(Map p104; ☑ 020-98088878; ⊙ 7am-11pm; 🛜)
Overlooking a pond, paddy fields and the distant mountains, Chill Zone is a great new bar serving up beer, ice-blue cocktails, snacks and good tunes. By night it's attractive, whorled in ropes of glowing red lights.

❶ Orientation

Virtually flat, Namtha is in fact a 10km-long collection of villages coalescing in an administrative hub at the northern end. Dating from 1976, the administrative hub is a well-spaced grid containing a two-block traveller enclave dotted with guesthouses, internet cafes and tour agencies. A smaller, prettier second centre is 7km further south near the airport. This used to be Namtha's commercial heart before it was bombed to bits in the Second Indochina War. Today, it's a mostly residential area called Meuang Luang Namtha or simply Ban Luang. The new long-distance bus station is 3km further south on the Rte 3 bypass, 10km out of the main centre.

❶ Information

INTERNET ACCESS
There are several internet cafes on the main strip but most guesthouses and hotels offer free wi-fi these days.

MEDICAL SERVICES
Provincial Hospital (Rte 3A; ⊙ 24hr) Adequately equipped for X-rays, dealing with broken limbs and dishing out antibiotics. Ask for English-speaking Dr Veokham.

MONEY
BCEL (Map p104; ⊙ 8.30am-3.30pm Mon-Fri) Changes major currencies (commission-free), travellers cheques (2% commission, minimum US$3) and has a 24-hour ATM.

Lao Development Bank (Map p104; ⊙ 8.30am-noon & 2-3.30pm Mon-Fri) Exchanges US-dollar travellers cheques and cash.

POST
Post Office (Map p104; ⊙ 8am-noon & 1-4pm Mon-Fri)

TOURIST INFORMATION
Provincial Tourism Office (Map p104; ☑ 086-211534; ⊙ 8am-noon & 2-5pm) Helpful resource for things local, including trekking advice.

BUSES FROM LUANG NAMTHA

DESTINATION	COST (K)	DURATION (HR)	STATION	DEPARTURES
Boten	25,000	2	district	6 daily 8am-2pm
Dien Bien Phu (Vietnam)	130,000	10	long-distance	7.30am
Huay Xai ('Borkeo')	60,000	4	long-distance	9am, 12.30pm & 4pm
Jinghong (China)	90,000	6	long-distance	8am
Luang Prabang	100,000	8	long-distance	9am bus, 8am minibus
Mengla (China)	50,000	3½	long-distance	8am
Muang Long	60,000	4	district	8.30am
Muang Sing	25,000	2	district	6 daily 8am-3.30pm
Na Lae	40,000	3	district	9.30am, noon
Phonsavan	180,000K	12	long-distance	8am
Udomxai	40,000	4	long-distance	9am, noon, 2.30pm
Vieng Phukha	30,000	1½	long-distance	9.30am, 12.30pm
Vientiane	180,000-200,000	21-24	long-distance	8.30am, 2.30pm

WORTH A TRIP

KAO RAO CAVES

Well signed beside Rte 3, 1.5km east of Nam Eng village, is this extensive, accessible **cave system** (ຖ້ຳເກົາເລົ່າ; 10,000K), which has a 700m section open to visitors. The main limestone formations include old stalactites encrusted with crystal deposits.

Local guides accompany visitors through the cave, but speak no English and have feeble torches (flashlights). Extensive lighting is already wired up, but there are often power cuts, meaning your own torch is a handy accessory. Allow around 45 minutes for the visit.

Curious corrugations in the floor that now look like great old tree roots once formed the lips of carbonate pools like those at Turkey's Pamukkale.

❶ Getting There & Away

AIR

Lao Airlines (Map p104; ☑086-312180; www.laoairlines.com; ⊗9am-5pm) flies to Vientiane (US$75) daily, while **Lao Skyway** (☑020-99990011; Luang Namtha Airport; ⊗9am-5pm) flies there Monday, Wednesday, Friday and Sunday (US$61).

BOAT

You can now only take the boat as far as Ban Phaeng, where a dam was recently built. What was a two-day experience is now just a day, though you still have around eight hours of puttering downriver. Pick-up by car/van is at the **boat station** (☑086-312014), from where you will be driven to Na Lae. Contact Forest Retreat Laos (p105), which can organise a guide, transfers and prearrange your boat. The charter costs US$500 for two people (US$250 per person); it's cheaper per head the more of you go.

BUS & SŎRNGTĂAOU

There are two bus stations. The **district bus station** (Map p104) is walking distance from the traveller strip. The main long-distance bus station is 10km south of town. For buses at either station, prebooking a ticket doesn't guarantee a seat – you just have to arrive early and claim one in person.

For Nong Khiaw take a Vientiane or Luang Prabang bus and change at Pak Mong.

❶ Getting Around

Chartered tuk-tuks charge 15,000K per person between the long-distance bus station or airport and the town centre, more if you're travelling solo. Most agencies and guesthouses sell ticket packages for long-distance buses that include a transfer from the guesthouse and cost around 20,000K above the usual fare.

Cycling is the ideal way to explore the wats, waterfalls, villages and landscapes surrounding Luang Namtha. There are a couple of **bike shops** (Map p104; per day bicycle 10,000-25,000K; motorcycle 30,000-50,000K; ⊗9am-6.30pm) in front of the Zuela Guesthouse. Choose from a bicycle or motorcycle depending on how energetic you are feeling.

Around Luang Namtha

Vieng Phukha (Vieng Phoukha) ວຽງພູຄາ

Sleepy Vieng Phukha (also spelt 'Phoukha') is an alternative trekking base for visiting the western limits of the Nam Ha NPA, notably on three-day Akha trail hikes. Such trails see fewer visitors than many from Luang Namtha and the partly forested landscapes can be magnificent, though many hills in Vieng Phukha's direct vicinity have been completely deforested.

◉ Sights

Just 15 minutes' stroll south of Rte 3 near Km 85 but utterly hidden in thick secondary woodlands is the almost invisible site of the 1530 temple **Wat Mahapot**. What little had survived the centuries was mostly pillaged for building materials around 1977 when all the residents moved back after the war, so now all you'll see is the odd scattering of bricks poking out from a tree-choked muddy rise. Getting there involves walking along a steep V-shaped gully that once protected the **Khúu Wíeng** (Ramparts) of a short-lived 16th-century 'city'. Again there's nothing but muddy banks to see but a good guide (essential) can fill in sketchy historical details and explain the medicinal uses of plants you'll encounter on a 40-minute walking tour. There are no longer local tour guides operating here, but Mr Tong Mua at Tigerman Treks (p110) in Muang Sing can take you.

🏃 Activities

Nam Ha Hilltribe Ecotrek
HIKING

(☑020-99440084; www.trekviengphoukha.com; ⊙8am-noon & 1-6pm) Run by Somhack (an experienced Khmu hunter who hung up his gun to use his tracking skills as a guide), this great outfit has multiday treks (from moderately easy to challenging) from Vieng Phukha to explore the Nam Ha NPA.

Nam Ha Ecoguide Service
Vieng Phoukha
HIKING

(☑020-55985289; www.namha-npa.org; ⊙8am-noon & 1.30-5pm) One- to five-day treks with homestays in Nam Ha NPA.

🛌 Sleeping

Thongmyxai Guesthouse
GUESTHOUSE $

(☑020-22390351; r 50,000K) Just about the smartest accommodation in town is the Thongmyxai Guesthouse, set in an attractive garden with bungalows.

Phuet Mung Khun Guesthouse
GUESTHOUSE $

(☑020-55886089; r 60,000-70,000K; 🛜) Located on a riverbank, the friendly Phuet Mung Khun Guesthouse has neat little bungalows, plus a small restaurant. The owner speaks rudimentary English.

ℹ️ Getting There & Away

Sŏrngtăaou for Luang Namtha (40,000K, 1½ hours) depart at around 9am and 1pm from the middle of town. Or you can wave down a Huay Xai–Namtha through-service (three daily).

Muang Sing ເມືອງສິງ

POP 10,000 / ☑081

Bordering Myanmar and within grasp of the green hills of China, Muang Sing is a rural backwater in the heart of the Golden Triangle. Formerly on the once infamous opium trail, it's a sleepy town of wilting, Tai Lü–style houses where trekking has overtaken smuggling contraband. Hmong, Tai Lü, Akha and Tai Dam are all seen here in traditional dress at the old market (get there at dawn), giving the town a frontier feel.

Back in the late '90s, it was one of the must-visit destinations in Laos, but with the end of fast boat services and clampdown on the opium trade, it has dropped off the traveller radar. Recently, a growing Chinese population has settled here, replacing rice fields with banana and rubber plantations for

MYSTERIOUS TOM DOOLEY

Saint or shameless self-promoter? Humanitarian or CIA pawn? Fifty years after his early death, opinions are still divided over the 'jungle doctor' who set up his famous benevolent hospital in Muang Sing in 1958. Passionately Catholic yet dismissed from the US Navy for his sexual orientation, this complex character was cited by President Kennedy as an inspiration for the Peace Corps (founded in 1961, the year Dooley succumbed to cancer). However, his anti-communist books helped encourage the US political slide towards war in Indochina and rumours abound that the flights that brought in medical supplies to his Muang Sing base would return laden with opium. For much more read James Fisher's flawed but detailed Dooley biography *Dr America*.

consumption on the other side of the border. Regrettably, Western travellers have spoken of being turned away from restaurants and guesthouses by Chinese operators.

History

In the late 18th century, a dowager of the Chiang Khaen principality founded the square, grid-plan citadel of Wiang Fa Ya (today's Muang Sing) along with the That Xieng Tung stupa. In 1803, this area became vassal to Nan (now in Thailand) and was largely abandoned following the deportations of 1805 and 1813. But the Chiang Khaen princes returned, moving their capital here in 1884 from Xiang Khaeng on the Mekong. This kicked off a 20-year tug of war between France, Britain and Siam, causing the principality to be split in two, with the western sector, including Muang Sing, being absorbed into French Indochina. Muang Sing rapidly became the biggest opium market in the Golden Triangle, a function officially sanctioned by the French. In 1946, parts of town were devastated by Kuomintang troops who continued to operate here well into the 1950s after losing the Chinese civil war. In 1958, the famous American 'jungle doctor' Tom Dooley set up his hospital in Muang Sing, which became the setting for a series of international intrigues.

Muang Sing

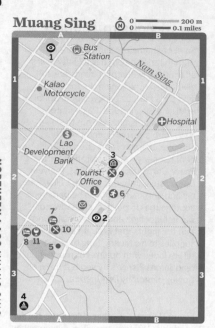

Muang Sing

◉ Sights
1 Morning Market A1
2 Old Market...A2
3 Tribal Museum.....................................B2
4 Wat Namkeo Luang............................A3

✪ Activities, Courses & Tours
5 Phou Iu Travel.....................................A3
6 Tigerman Treks B2

🛏 Sleeping
7 Phou Iu II Guesthouse.......................A2
8 Singduangdao Bungalows.................A3

✗ Eating
9 Thai Lü Restaurant.............................B2
10 Veranda Restaurant...........................A3

🍷 Drinking & Nightlife
11 Singsavanh Nightclub........................A3

◉ Sights

Sprinkled along the town's main street are a few classic Lao-French hybrid mansion-houses. These mostly 1920s structures have ground-floor walls of brick and stucco topped with a wooden upper storey featuring a wraparound roofed verandah. Classic examples house the tourist office and the Thai Lü Guesthouse.

The **old market** (Map p110; Main St), built in 1954, was under reconstruction at the time of writing as the roof had collapsed. The bustling new **market** (Map p110; ◔7am-10pm) is near the bus station and is very colourful first thing in the morning, though you'll be harder pressed to find ethnic women in tribal dress here.

Tribal Museum   MUSEUM
(Map p110; 5000K; ◔8.30am-4.30pm Mon-Fri, 8-11am Sat) The most distinctive of the old Lao-French buildings is now home to the two-room Tribal Museum, which boasts costume displays downstairs and six cases of cultural artefacts upstairs. Watching a 40-minute video on the Akha people costs 5000K extra.

That Xieng Tung   BUDDHIST TEMPLE
(ທາດຊຽງຕຶງ) Around 6km southeast of Muang Sing, That Xieng Tung sits on a grassy plateau dotted with sacred trees, 1km up a rough access track that branches south off the Luang Namtha road 200m after Km 52. This place really comes alive at festival time (full moon of the 12th lunar month, between late October and mid-November), with a carnival atmosphere, traditional dance performances and merit-makers offering candles and flowers around the base of the stupa.

Wat Namkeo Luang   BUDDHIST TEMPLE
(ວັດນໍ້າແກວຫລວງ; Map p110) Wat Namkeo Luang is one of most visually striking monastic buildings in Muang Sing. It features an entry porch with red-tongued golden *naga* (river serpent) and an unusually tall and ornate gilded stupa. Some villagers still draw water from *shaduf*-style lever wells in the slowly gentrifying *bâhn* (the general Lao word for house or village) opposite. Nearby you can also find a modest Lak Bâan spirit-totem, but touching it would cause offence.

🏃 Activities

Tigerman Treks   TREKKING
(Map p110; ☎020-55467833, 020-56783156, 030-5264881; tigermantrek@gmail.com; Main St; ◔7am-7pm) ✐ English-speaking teacher and nice guy Mr Tong Mua has long been a fixture of Muang Sing and with the slow death of the tourist office (located opposite), he's a safer bet for general information, decent treks and homestays in the Nam Ha NPA, as well as tuk-tuk tours and cycle/trek combos. He also rents bikes and motorcycles (50,000/100,000K).

TRIPS TO MINORITY VILLAGES

The main reason visitors come to Muang Sing is to venture into the minority villages that dot the valley of rice paddies and sugar-cane fields surrounding town. To do it yourself by bicycle or motorbike, start by purchasing Wolfgang Korn's helpful *Muang Sing Cultural Guide Book* from the tourist office. Its map shows major roads and labels the ethnicities of the valley's villages. To make the village-visiting experience somewhat less voyeuristic you can engage a guide for as little as 100,000K from one of Muang Sing's ecotour agencies, which also offer a gamut of longer treks and homestay experiences.

If you've got your own wheels, the dusty, unpaved but reasonably smooth Xieng Kok road leads through a predominantly Akha district where an unusually large proportion of women wear distinctive silver 'coin' headdresses and billowing indigo blouses.

Phou Iu Travel   ADVENTURE SPORTS
(Map p110; ☑ 081-400012; www.muangsingtravel. com; ☉ 7am-7pm) Run out of the Phou Iu II Guesthouse, this decent outfit offers well-organised treks around Muang Sing. It also offers treks to the more remote Xieng Khaeng district towards Burma; check www. adventure-trek-laos.com for details. Other options include one- and two-day cycling tours and minority-village homestays.

🛏 Sleeping

🛏 Central Muang Sing

Singduangdao Bungalows   GUESTHOUSE $
(Map p110; ☑ 020-22004565; i from 70,000K; 🛜) Set in a verdant garden, Singduangdao offers spartan bungalows hidden away behind the truck weighbridge. All have hot showers. English is spoken.

★Phou Iu II Guesthouse   GUESTHOUSE $$
(Map p110; ☑ 086-400012; www.muang singtravel.com; bungalow small/medium/large 100,000/200,000/400,000K) Set around an expansive garden, the biggest bungalows have fun, outdoor, rock-clad shower spaces. All rooms have comfortable beds, mosquito nets, fans and small verandahs (although rooms are cold at night during the cool season). There's an on-site herbal sauna (10,000K) and massage (50,000K per hour), plus the restaurant Veranda, probably the best place in town to eat.

🛏 Outside Muang Sing

Adima Guesthouse   GUESTHOUSE $
(☑ 020-22393398; r 100,000K; 🛜) Adima sits conveniently on the edge of an Akha village;

Nam Dath is only 700m up the trail. Many other minority villages are also within easy walking distance. Adima's sturdy brick-and-thatch bungalows have hot showers and bucket-flush toilets, though have faded considerably over recent years. The Veranda, their appealing rustic restaurant, overlooks fish ponds and is pleasant come sundown.

It's 8.5km from Muang Sing. From town take the Pang Hai road to the far edge of Ban Udomsin (500m after Km 7) and turn right; Adima is 600m south. A tuk-tuk from town costs about 30,000K.

🍴 Eating

Veranda Restaurant   ASIAN $
(Map p110; mains 30,000K; ☉ 6.30am-9pm) About the best Lao, Thai and Chinese food you can expect in town, this is a simple, cosy spot to eat Lao fare – think soups and noodle dishes – in a friendly atmosphere. It's based in the garden of the Phou Iu II Guesthouse.

Thai Lü Restaurant   LAOTIAN, THAI $
(Map p110; ☑ 086-400375; Hwy 17; mains 20,000K; ☉ 7am-9pm) Looking like a backdrop from an old Bruce Lee flick, this creaky wooden building has a certain charm and serves Laotian, Thai and Western dishes. The owner is friendly and produce is locally sourced and seasonal.

🍷 Drinking & Nightlife

Singsavanh Nightclub   CLUB
(Map p110; ☉ 7-11.30pm; 🛜) Most of Muang Sing is dead asleep by 9pm except at the Singsavanh, where the locals get down to live Lao and Chinese pop. It might look permanently closed down by day, but somehow it picks itself up at night.

ℹ Information

MONEY

Lao Development Bank (Map p110; ⊘8am-noon & 2-3.30pm Mon-Fri) Exchanges US dollars, Thai baht and Chinese yuan but at less-than-favourable rates.

POST

Post Office (Map p110; ⊘8am-4pm Mon-Fri) As tiny as the *petang* rectangle next to it.

TOURIST INFORMATION

Tourist Office (Map p110; ⊘8am-4pm Mon-Fri) Displays of fact scrolls are useful but the staff aren't likely to win any Lao National Tourism Authority employee of the month awards.

ℹ Getting There & Away

From the **bus station** (Map p110) in the northwest corner of town, *sŏrngtăaou* depart for Muang Long (30,000K, 1½ hours) at 9am and 11am. To Luang Namtha (25,000K, two hours) minibuses leave at 8am, 9am and 11am. The bus to Muang La (40,000K) leaves at 7.30am and 1pm.

ℹ Getting Around

Kalao Motorcycle (Map p110; per day 100,000K; ⊘8am-5pm), on the road to the morning market, rents motorbikes, but bring a good phrasebook as nobody here speaks English.

Bicycle rental (30,000K per day) is available from several main-street agencies and guesthouses.

Xieng Kok

Xieng Kok is a sleepy, riverine destination surveying a deep slice of Mekong Valley and the Burmese banks behind. Market days (the 14th and 28th of every month) attract hill-tribe folks and traders from the surrounding countries. Given that it's part of the Golden Triangle and on the drug-smuggling route, not surprisingly in 2012 Chinese supply boats were attacked by Burmese drug gangs, whose leader was caught and allegedly executed in China. Be warned that although it might appear soporific, things here are more mercurial than they might seem. In autumn, when river levels are high, Chinese barges call in at the river port; come April river levels are too low for boats to travel. Due to the Chinese pirates and Burmese drug traffickers attacking boats, speedboats no longer make the short journey downriver to Muang Mom, nor upriver to Muang Long.

Avoid wandering around by the river after dark as this is a major thoroughfare for drug smugglers.

Two roads converge where the minibus to Muang Long (20,000K, 35 minutes) leaves at 6am, 8am and 2pm from outside the town's little pharmacy. Finding any other vehicle can be hard here, even if you're prepared to charter.

THE MIDDLE MEKONG

For many tourists the region is seen merely in passing between Thailand and Luang Prabang – typically on the two-day slowboat route from Huay Xai via Pak Beng – but there's plenty to interest the more adventurous traveller. Bokeo, meaning 'Gem Mine', takes its name from the sapphire deposits in Huay Xai district, and the province harbours 34 ethnicities despite a particularly sparse population. Sainyabuli Province is synonymous with working elephants and the Elephant Conservation Center is just outside the eponymous capital. Other than in Huay Xai and Pak Beng you'll need a decent phrasebook wherever you go.

Western Sainyabuli remains particularly far off the traveller radar; places such as the dramatic Khop district are 'last frontiers' with a complex ethnic mix and reputedly high proportion of still-pristine forests.

Huay Xai   ຫ້ວຍຊາຍ

POP 20,000 / 🗗 084

Huay Xai was allegedly home to a US heroin-processing plant during the Secret War, but these days the only things trafficked through are travellers en route to Luang Prabang. Separated from Thailand by the mother river that is the Mekong, Huay Xai is for many their first impression of Laos: don't worry, it does get better. By night its central drag dons its fairy lights and roadside food vendors fire things up, and there are some welcoming traveller guesthouses and cafes serving tasty food. Huay Xai is also the HQ of the now-fabled Gibbon Experience, deservedly the most talked-about environmentally responsible jungle adventure in the country.

THE GIBBON EXPERIENCE

Adrenalin meets conservation in this ecofriendly adventure in the 1060 sq km of the Bokeo Nature Reserve wilderness, home to tigers, clouded leopards, black bears and the black-crested gibbon. The **Gibbon Experience** (☑ 030-5745866, 084-212021; www. gibbonexperience.org; 2-day Express US$190, 3-day Classic or Waterfall US$310; ☺ 7am-5pm) 🖋 is essentially a series of navigable 'ziplines' among pristine forest canopy.

Back in 1996 poaching was threatening the extinction of the black-crested gibbon, when Animo, a brilliantly inventive conservation-based tour group, convinced the hunters of Bokeo to become the forest's guardians. As guides they now earn more for their families than in their old predatory days.

The benchmark for sustainable monkey business, this two- to three-day experience is one of Laos' most unforgettable adventures, and your chance to play Tarzan; living two nights in soaring treehouses within thickly forested hills and swinging high across valleys on incredible ziplines, some more than 500m long. It's a heart-stopping, superhero experience. Should it rain, remember you need more time to slow down with your brake (a humble bit of bike tyre). The guides are helpful, though make sure you're personally vigilant with the knots in your harness. It's optional to wear a helmet, but we recommend asking for one – given the speed you travel along the cable you wouldn't want your head to come into contact with it. Also check that your karabiner actually closes.

There are three options: the two-day Express, during which there's little chance of seeing the gibbons, and the three-day Classic and Waterfall. While there's a good chance you'll hear the mellow ray-gun *whoop-whoop* of the gibbon's call at dawn, seeing a gibbon is less likely (though not unheard of). That said, the gibbons are flourishing and the treehouses for the Classic and Waterfall are built close to where these magnificent arboreal athletes live. All three trips involve a serious amount of trekking, particularly the Classic. And should you be here when it rains heavily, you may have to abandon Animo's vehicle and walk the slippery dirt roads to reach the park. We recommend you're in good shape for all three options.

Accommodation is located in unique thatched treehouses that are spaced sufficiently far from each other so that each feels entirely alone in the jungle. Often around 40m above the ground and set in natural amphitheatres with spectacular views, most of the treehouses sleep eight people with bedding laid out beneath large cloth nets, although some treehouses sleep just two people. Large spiders on the walls and rats rustling in the ceilings will be your companions too, but this is the jungle after all. Well-cooked meals consisting of rice and four accompaniments are ziplined in from one of three rustic kitchens, while coffee, tea, hot chocolate and various additional snacks are available in each treehouse. Keeping anything edible in the provided strong box is essential to avoid the forest rats being attracted.

Check in at the Huay Xai **Gibbon Experience Office** (Map p114; ☑ 084-212021; Th Saykhong; ☺ 8am-7pm) one day before departure. Gloves (essential for using the ziplines) are sold next door, as are spiked rubber jungle shoes (US$3). Other recommended items for your adventure include hiking boots, long socks, industrial-strength mozzie repellent, a torch (flashlight), water bottle and earplugs. Everything you bring must be carried on your back while hiking and ziplining (the rest of your luggage can be left in the office storeroom). There's no electricity so precharge all your batteries and devices. And book well ahead, before you leave home, as the Gibbon Experience gets jammed up in high season.

👁 Sights

Wat Thadsuvanna Phakham BUDDHIST TEMPLE
(ວັດຫາດສຸວັນນະພາຄໍາ; ☺ dawn-dusk) Commanding the rise directly above the speedboat landing, 3km south of the central area, Wat Thadsuvanna Phakham is a colourful new temple featuring a row of eight gilded Buddhas demonstrating the main meditation postures and disdaining Mekong views beneath floral foliage.

Huay Xai

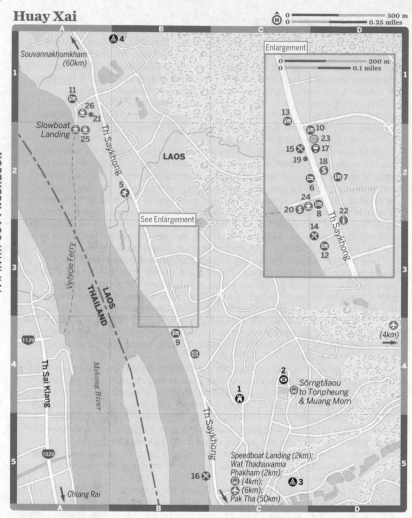

NORTHERN LAOS HUAY XAI

Wat Khonekeo Xaiyaram BUDDHIST TEMPLE
(ວັດໂຄນແກ້ວ; Map p114; ⊙dawn-dusk) Wat
Khonekeo Xaiyaram, in Ban Khonekeo, has
a lavish frontage with dazzling red, gold and
green pillars and doors.

**Wat Keophone
Savanthanaram** BUDDHIST TEMPLE
(Map p114; ⊙dawn-dusk) Wat Keophone Savanthanaram features murals of gruesome
torture scenes on the north wall of the *sĭm*
(ordination hall), while on the slope above a
long Buddha reclines behind chicken wire.

Fort Carnot FORT
(Map p114) The very dilapidated shell of
French-built Fort Carnot sits on the hilltop
behind the Bokeo Governor's Office. Two
towers are still standing, one straddling the
gateway, but the tiles are falling off the old
barrack room roofs and the whole sparse site
is hardly a highlight of Huay Xai.

Main Market MARKET
(Map p114; ⊙7am-12pm) Tucked in the valley behind Fort Carnot is Huay Xai's vibrant
main market.

Huay Xai

🏃 Activities

Most hill-tribe treks advertised by Huay Xai agencies actually start from Vieng Phukha so it's generally better to book them there. One-day tours to Souvannakhomkham, including a boat ride around the Golden Triangle, are also offered but there are rarely enough travellers signing up to make the prices viable. A DIY trip by motorbike is easier to arrange.

Lao Red Cross   MASSAGE
(Map p114; ☑084-211935; massage per hour from 35,000K, herbal sauna 15,000K; ⊙1.30-9pm Mon-Fri,10.30am-9pm Sat & Sun) Lao Red Cross offers Swedish-Lao massage and a traditional herbal sauna (from 4pm) in a stately old mansion beside the Mekong.

🛏 Sleeping

Daauw Homestay   HOMESTAY $
(Map p114; ☑030-9041296; www.projectkajsiab laos.org; r 100,000-140,000K) 🌶 Daauw Homestay is run by lovely Hmong folk, and your stay in a cosy bungalow near the heart of town enables you to contribute something to women's empowerment and minority rights, as this place is a grassroots initiative run by Project Kajsiab. Simple rooms come with sunset views, hammock, balcony and private bathroom.

BAP Guesthouse   GUESTHOUSE $
(Map p114; Th Saykhong; r 60,000-130,000K; ✴) Run by English-speaking Mrs Changpeng, trusty BAP has 16 rooms, some with fan or air-con and private bathroom. There are four newish ones that merit a mention for their colourful quilts, wood accents, TVs and sunset views over the Mekong, particularly rooms 108 and 109. The restaurant is also popular for its fried-rice dishes, pasta and hearty breakfasts.

Kaupjai Guesthouse   GUESTHOUSE $
(Map p114; ☑020-55683164; r with fan/air-con 100,000/120,000K; ✴🛜) Clean, simple rooms with private bathrooms in a relatively new guesthouse with a friendly owner. Fan rooms downstairs, air-con ones upstairs.

Oudomphone Guesthouse 2   GUESTHOUSE $
(Map p114; ☑020-55683134, 084-211308; r with fan/air-con 80,000/120,000K; ✴🛜) Clean and central, these digs have a pleasant breakfast cafe and spacious nondescript rooms with bathrooms. While nothing spectacular it's one of the slightly better options in town.

Gateway Villa Hotel   GUESTHOUSE $
(Map p114; ☑084-212180; gatewayconsult@ hotmail.com; Th Saykhong; r with air-con 140,000K; ✴🛜) Close to the boat landing, Gateway Villa has tastefully furnished rooms with hardwood floors, wicker chairs, TVs and contemporary-looking linen. Some rooms are more prettified than others. You'll get a good night's sleep, an OK breakfast, and the English-speaking owner is helpful.

Sabaydee Guest House   GUESTHOUSE $
(Map p114; ☑084-212252; Th Saykhong; r incl breakfast 90,000-130,000K; ✴@🛜) Sabaydee has unfailingly clean rooms with comfy beds, TVs, fans and en suites. Decked in bright colours and pleasant furnishings, some overlook the river. There's also a nice communal area with internet access.

Riverside Houayxay Hotel HOTEL $$
(Map p114; ☎084-1211064; riverside_houayxay_laos@hotmail.com; r incl breakfast from US$25; 📶) Located just off the main strip and overlooking the mighty Mekong, this is the most upmarket hotel in the centre of town. Rooms are spacious though bathrooms could do with a more thorough clean. Hot water is on tap, plus there's satellite TV and a minibar.

Phonevichith Guesthouse & Restaurant GUESTHOUSE $$
(Map p114; ☎084-211765; http://houayxairiverside.com; Ban Khonekeo; r US$45; ❄📶) Colourful fabrics, fans and kitschy lamps add a little character to the smart rooms, which come with piping-hot showers and air-con. A new wing offers the smartest beds in town, which are verging on the 'boutique hotel'. The main attractions are the Mekong perch and handy proximity to the slowboat landing. Some building was underway here at the time of writing.

Eating & Drinking

Daauw LAOTIAN $
(Map p114; www.projectkajsiablaos.org; mains 30,000-50,000K; ⏲6-10pm; 🌿) The friendliest vibe in town: soak up the sunset view on its chill-out terrace decked in low cushions and an open-pit fire, and choose from freshly prepared organic Hmong food, wood-fired pizza, plenty of vegetarian options, or whole barbecued Mekong fish or chicken. Linger for *laojitos* if there's a crowd – a mojito made with *lòw-lów*.

Tavendeng Restaurant LAOTIAN $$
(Map p114; mains 25,000-80,000K; ⏲7am-11pm) Predominantly aimed at Thai tourists, this large wooden dining complex features live music and exotic foods such as frog and fried crocodile.

Riverview Cafe LAOTIAN, INTERNATIONAL $$
(Map p114; Th Saykhong; meals 40,000K; ⏲6.30am-11pm; 📶) With its rattan ceiling dramatically on the verge of collapse and the thirsty walls peeling, Riverview Cafe (aka Muang Ner) might not look like much, but notice it's always full, and stand and catch the aromas from the kitchen, and in no time you'll be tucking into wood-fired pizzas, burgers, stir-fries, soup noodles and very zestful *láhp*.

It's next door to the Gibbon Experience Office; stock up on a sandwich to take with you to the jungle.

Riverside Restaurant LAOTIAN, THAI $$
(Map p114; Th Saykhong; mains 45,000K; ⏲7am-11pm; 📶) The Mekong terrace here offers a great vantage point from which to watch the boats shuttling to and from Thailand. The menu has a wide range of Thai and Lao food, including soups, stir-fries and curries, plus Western breakfasts.

Bar How BAR
(Map p114; Th Saykhong; ⏲6.30am-11pm; 📶) Decked in old muskets and rice-paddy hats, Bar How is darkly atmospheric. By night a row of sinister-looking homemade *lòw-lów* (rice wine), infused with everything from blueberry to lychee, catches the low light and resembles a Victorian apothecary. It also serves pasta, steak, *láhp* and spring rolls (mains 30,000K to 45,000K). However, the service is very slack – you may have to seek out staff.

Information

INTERNET ACCESS

Yon Computer Internet Cafe (Map p114; Th Saykhong; per hour 10,000K; ⏲9am-9pm) Decent connection with Skype. Also fixes laptops.

MONEY

BCEL (Map p114; Th Saykhong; ⏲8.30am-4.30pm Mon-Fri) Has a 24-hour ATM, exchange facility and Western Union.

Lao Development Bank Exchange Booth (Map p114; ⏲8am-5pm) Handy booth right beside the pedestrian immigration window. Most major currencies exchanged into kip. US-dollar bills must be dated 2006 or later.

POST

Post Office (Map p114; Th Saykhong; ⏲8am-noon & 1-4pm Mon-Fri) Also contains a telephone office (open from 8am to 10pm).

TOURIST INFORMATION

Tourist Information Office (Map p114; ☎084-211162; Th Saykhong; ⏲8am-4.30pm Mon-Fri) Has free tourist maps of the town and some suggestions for excursions around the province.

Getting There & Away

For years, streams of Luang Prabang–bound travellers have piled into Huay Xai and jumped straight onboard a boat for the memorable descent of the Mekong. Today, improving roads mean an ever-increasing proportion opt instead for the overnight bus. But while slightly cheaper than the slowboat, it's far less social, less attractive and, at around 15 hours of travel, leaves most travellers exhausted on arrival.

AIR

Huay Xai's airport is oddly perched on a hillside off the city bypass, 1.5km northwest of the bus station. Lao Skyway flies six days per week (except Thursday) to/from Vientiane for 759,000K.

BOAT

Slowboats to Pak Beng & Luang Prabang

Slowboats (Map p114) currently depart from Huay Xai at 11am daily. Purchase tickets at the **slowboat ticket booth** (Map p114; ✆084-211659) for Pak Beng (110,000K, one day) or Luang Prabang (220,000K not including accommodation, two days). Sales start at 8am on the day of travel. Avoid buying a ticket from a travel company – you'll get an overpriced tuk-tuk transfer to the pier and then have to sit around awaiting departure.

'Seats' are typically uncomfortable wooden benches for which you'll value the expenditure of 10,000K on a cushion (sold at many an agency in town). Some boats also have a number of more comfy airliner-style seats. If the boat operators try to cram on too many passengers (over 70 or so), a tactic that really works is for later arrivals to simply refuse to get aboard until a second boat is provided.

'Luxury' Slowboats

To do the two-day river journey to Luang Prabang in more comfort, a popular alternative is the stylish 40-seat **Luang Say Cruise** (Map p114; ✆071-252553, 020-55090718; www.luangsay. com; per person US$379-666, single supplement from US$67; ⊙8am-3pm). Packages include meals, guides, visits en route and a night's accommodation at the lovely Luang Say Lodge (p119) in Pak Beng. Departures are three or four times weekly in peak season, with prices varying according to season. There's no service at all in June or when the Mekong is too low.

Another, more affordable option is the newer **Shompoo Cruise** (Map p114; ✆020-59305555, 071-213189; www.shompoocruise. com; per person with/without accommodation from US$97/118). This is a tastefully upgraded boat that heads downstream Monday, Wednesday and Friday and upstream on Tuesday, Thursday and Sunday. It includes two lunches and a dinner in Pak Beng. It has accommodation but tickets can be sold without, leaving travellers free to select their own place to stay.

With some patience a small group could charter their own slowboat, starting from around US$750 (highly negotiable).

Speedboats & Longboats

The **speedboat landing** (✆084-211457; Rte 3, 200m beyond Km 202) is directly beneath Wat Thadsuvanna Phakham, 3km south of town. Six-passenger speedboats (*héua wái*) zip thrillingly but dangerously and with great physical discomfort to Pak Beng (190,000/1,140,000K per person/boat, three hours) and Luang Prabang (320,000/1,920,000K, seven hours including lunch stop), typically departing around 8am.

Due to a section of the Nam Tha (Tha River) being dammed it's no longer possible to catch a boat all the way up to Luang Namtha. From Ban Phaeng, you'll have eight hours of puttering upriver to Na Lae, where you'll be picked up and driven on to Luang Namtha. Contact Forest Retreat Laos (p105) in Luang Namtha, which organises guides, transfers and prearrange your boat. The charter costs US$500 for two (US$250 per person); it's cheaper per head the more of you go.

BUS & SŎRNGTĂAOU

Note that Huay Xai–bound buses are usually marked 'Borkeo'. The bus station is 5km east of town. Buses to Luang Prabang (120,000K,

---

GETTING TO THAILAND: HUAY XAI (HOKSAY) TO CHIANG KHONG

Getting to the Border

Since the completion of the Thai-Lao Friendship Bridge 4 at the **Huay Xai/Chiang Khong border crossing** in late 2013, the former ferry-boat crossing is for locals only.
Tuk-tuks cost about 80B per person to the immigration post.

At the Border

A bus (20B) crosses the bridge. A 15-day Thai visa waiver is automatically granted when entering Thailand. Arriving in Chiang Khong, pay the 30B port fee and catch a 30B tuk-tuk to take you to the bus station. The nearest ATM on the Thai side is 2km south.

Moving On

Many travellers leave Huay Xai bound for Chiang Rai (65B, 2½ hours), with buses typically departing from Chiang Khong's bus station every hour from 6am to 5pm. **Greenbus** (✆in Thailand 0066 5365 5732; www.greenbusthailand.com) has services to Chiang Mai at 6am, 9am and 11.40am. Several overnight buses for Bangkok (500B to 750B, 10 hours) leave at 3pm and 3.30pm.

14 to 17 hours) depart at 10am and 4pm; for Luang Namtha (60,000K) they leave at 9am and 12.30pm; for Udomxai (90,000K, nine hours) there is one at 9.30am. For Vientiane (230,000K, 25 hours) catch the 11.30am. There is also a bus to Mengla (120,000K) at 8.30am.

Travel-agency minibuses to Luang Namtha leave from central Huay Xai at around 9am (100,000K) but still arrive at Namtha's inconveniently out-of-town bus station.

Sŏrngtăaou (Map p114) to Tonpheung (40,000K) leave when full from beside the main market, very occasionally continuing to Muang Mom.

Around Huay Xai

Souvannakhomkham
ເມືອງເກົ່າສຸວັນນະໂຄມຄຳ

In a bend of the Mekong lie the scattered ruins of Souvannakhomkham, an ancient city site refounded in the 1560s by Lan Xang king Sai Setthathirat. Today, all you'll see are a few brick piles that were once stupas plus a couple of crumbling Buddha statues dotted about an expanse of fields. The greatest concentration of sites lies 900m off the lane between Ban Don That and Ban Hanjin. The setting amid towering flame trees is quietly magical.

Sadly, Souvannakhomkham's access roads are infuriatingly rutted, dusty when dry and appalling muddy when wet. Get here by heading 8km southwest from Tonpheung, turn right when you spot the '900' on an otherwise all-Lao script sign, then fork left just before arriving at the 7.2m-high seated brick Buddha, a very eroded figure that's the site's best-known icon.

Golden Triangle

Around 5km north of Tonpheung, small Rte 3 abruptly undergoes an astonishing transformation. Suddenly you're gliding along a two-coloured paved avenue, lined with palm trees and immaculately swept by teams of cleaners. Golden domes and pseudo-classical charioteers rear beside you. No, you haven't ingested a happy pizza. This is the Golden Triangle's very own Laos Vegas, a casino and entertainment project still a work in progress, but planned to eventually cover almost 100 sq km. After 2.5km this surreal strip turns left and dead-ends after 600m at the Mekong beside another Disneyesque fantasy dome and a mini Big Ben. The huge casino here is open to all, but most of the games are aimed at Chinese or Thai gamblers and may not be familiar. Electronic roulette tables are the most accessible of the games on offer.

This area of riverfront is part of the famous Golden Triangle, where Thailand and Laos face off, with Myanmar sticking a long-nosed sand bank between the two. Boat cruises potter past from the Thai side. On the Lao bank speedboats await but foreigners can't cross the border without prearranged authorisation.

Pak Beng
ປາກແບ່ງ

POP 20,000 / ✆ 084

The best time to enjoy Pak Beng is late afternoon from on high at one of the restaurant balconies clinging to its vertiginous slope, watching the Mekong slide indolently by in a churn of gingery eddies, dramatically framed by giant boulders and sharp jungle banks.

Pak Beng

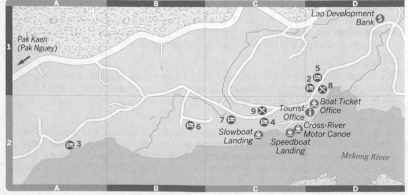

A halfway riverine stop between Luang Prabang and Huay Xai (lunch for speedy longtails, overnight for slowboats), this one-street town is short on architectural charm, but there are some good places to stay and nice spots to eat, including bakeries and Western-friendly cafes.

◉ Sights & Activities

The tourist office offers treks to a Hmong village (400,000K per person for a group of four) or cooking classes (100,000K per person for a group of four), and can suggest a typical selection of local caves and waterfalls in the district to explore if you can find a motorbike for rent (try asking at your guesthouse; individuals around the market ask a steep 40,000K per hour).

A pleasant excursion is to cross the river by **motor canoe** (5000K) then walk for about 10 minutes diagonally right away from the river to a tiny, authentic Hmong hamlet.

Wat Sin Jong Jaeng   BUDDHIST TEMPLE
(ວັດສິນຈົງແຈງ) Overlooking the Mekong, archaic little Wat Sin Jong Jaeng dates back to the early colonial period. Although its eaves have been entirely repainted, an old, very faded mural remains on the eastern exterior of the *sim*. Look carefully and you'll spot a moustached figure with hat, umbrella and big nose, presumably representing an early European visitor.

⊨ Sleeping

Villa Santisouk   GUESTHOUSE $
(☏020-55781797; r US$5-15; ✻🛜) This uber-friendly place is a welcoming joint to stay in. The new building includes rooms

with stylishly presented towels, comfy new beds and sash curtains. In contrast, rooms in the old building are basic, with hard beds and hard-board ceilings. A simple terrace restaurant allows guests to contemplate the Mekong.

Monsavan Guesthouse   GUESTHOUSE $
(☏084-212619, 020-55771935; r from 130,000K; ✻🛜) This decent guesthouse on the main strip has a hammer-and-sickle flag out front and polished wood doors. Bamboo-walled rooms are clean affairs with TV, bathroom and tasteful fittings. Better still is the river-view bakery just across the street (open from 6.30am to 10pm) for fresh *pain au chocolat* (chocolate croissants), muffins, croissants, sandwiches and delicious shakes and coffee.

★**Luang Say Lodge**   LODGE $$
(☏084-212296; www.luangsay.com; r US$73) Principally for the use of passengers aboard the Luang Say Cruise (p117), this traditional hardwood-and-rattan lodge has stylish bungalows in a pretty garden, overlooking a dramatic stretch of river, with fans and hot-water showers. A terrace restaurant overlooks the Mekong, for breakfast and dinner. Be warned: it's a steep and sometimes slippery climb from the jetty to the hotel.

★**D.P Guesthouse**   GUESTHOUSE $$
(☏081-212624; operation@duangpasert.com; Main St; s/d US$40/45; ✻🛜) Run by a friendly Lao guy, this fresh new guesthouse outstrips the competition with mint-green and orange walls and above-average rooms with nice touches like bedrunners, air-con and cool tile floors and bathrooms. Just the shot in

Pak Beng

NORTHERN LAOS PAK BENG

ELEPHANT CONSERVATION CENTER

Set on the shores of the stunning Nam Tien lake, the **Elephant Conservation Center** (ECC; ☑ 020-23025210; www.elephantconservationcenter.com; 1-day visit US$60, 3-day experience US$205, 6-day eco-experience US$495) ✎ has placed Sainyabuli firmly on the visitor map. Established in partnership with elephant NGO ElefantAsia (www.elefantasia.org), the centre offers visitors a unique insight into the lives of these majestic creatures in a natural setting. Life as an elephant in Laos – be it one of the remaining 400-odd left in the wild, forever on the run from ivory poachers, or one of the 450 captive elephants working in logging or elephant tourism – is not much fun. It's hard to say which is worse, giving 20 rides a day overladen with people on your back (the spine of an elephant is jagged and unsuitable to carry loads on anywhere but its neck) or trying to extract trees on dangerously steep mountain slopes. For every 10 elephants born in Laos, only two survive.

Given these depressing statistics the work of the ECC is evermore vital, paying mahouts the equivalent of three years' salary to come and live at the centre and give their females the chance to breed, and care for their baby – something the average elephant owner could not even consider as their workhorses must be constantly earning to pay for their care (US$250 per week to feed). Aside from their conservation work here, vets are busy throughout Laos helping keep its domesticated elephants as well as possible. The complex includes a mahouts' training centre, an elephant hospital with qualified international vets, an information centre, a restaurant and some traditional bungalows and dormitory rooms for overnight guests.

Arriving at the centre is a memorable experience in itself, as a small wooden boat glides through the green weeds that carpet the water. It's straight out of *Apocalypse Now* and as the boat approaches the centre, visitors may see some of the resident elephants enjoying their morning bath. A one-day visit includes a guided tour of the centre to learn more about the conservation work done here, including the on-site hospital, which works to safeguard the health of the resident elephants and some of the other 360 registered elephants working in Sainyabuli Province. Mobile teams head out for regular check-ups on the health of elephants around the province and beyond.

the arm the midrange sector needed. There's also a terrific restaurant to hang in.

★ Mekong Riverside

Lodge   BOUTIQUE HOTEL **$$**
(Map p118; ☑ 020-55171068; www.mekongriver sidelodge.com; r from US$45; 🛜) Widescreen views of the river from romantically finished private-balcony bungalows, with stylish bathrooms, lacquered rattan walls, wood floors, fresh linen, mozzie nets and swan towel origami. Some rooms can be combined for families with an adjoining door. Breakfast is included at Khopchaideu opposite. Good value for what's on offer and lovely management.

Sanctuary Pakbeng

Lodge   BOUTIQUE HOTEL **$$$**
(Map p118; ☑ 084-212304; www.sanctuaryhotel sandresorts.com/english/main/pakbeng; r US$120; ❄🛜) ✎ Sanctuary Pakbeng Lodge has elegantly presented rooms with pretty interiors, Western-style bathrooms and minibars, all offering panoramic views. The bar-restaurant is a stylish spot for a sundown drink or a meal, and traditional Lao massage is also available. Part of the profits go towards funding a health-care initiative called Les Medicins du Pakbeng.

✘ Eating

★ Khopchaideu   INDIAN **$**

(Map p118; ☑ 020-55171068; mains 30,000K; ⏰7am-10pm; 🍴) Based at the Mekong Riverside Lodge, this place may serve some of the best Indian food you'll find in northern Laos. You can expect all the usual curries, as well as dishes like buffalo masala, executed with flair and sufficiently zesty spice. The English-speaking staff are charming and the view superb. They also dish up Lao and Western food.

D.P Bakery   BAKERY **$**

(Map p118; mains 30,000K; ⏰6.30am-8.30pm; 🛜) Fresh and bursting with doughy aromas, D.P is a great new spot for Western or healthy fruit breakfasts. And as well as mouthwatering pastries (get here early before they go),

On another part of the lakeshore is the elephant nursery, where young elephants are safely reared in isolation from possible threats to their health. Witness the elephants enjoying a hearty breakfast and taking a bath in the lake.

If time allows, it's rewarding to immerse yourself in the work of the centre with a three-day stay. This includes the chance to observe the elephants from morning until evening, as they bathe, are fed (you get to feed them), and let loose in the socialisation area (you are able to watch unseen from a treehouse high above). You'll also get the chance to watch one of the vets at the hospital giving a check-up to a pachyderm in the 'medical crush', a humane wooden structure that allows the carer to examine its feet and body without getting trodden on.

For those with a jumbo-sized interest in elephants, it is possible to volunteer for six days or more, offering an even greater insight into the lives of the elephants and their mahouts, as well as the work of the centre. Those on the longer volunteer stay live in the dormitory accommodation and take meals with the project staff, offering a fascinating insight into the Lao lifestyle.

Accommodation at the centre is in basic thatched bungalows that include some electricity after dark to power LED lights for reading. They include a mosquito net and a small verandah to relax on during the heat of the day. Bathroom facilities are shared but scrupulously clean.

All meals and transport from and to Sainyabuli are included in all packages. The ECC has also teamed up with **Sakura Tour** (☑ 074-212112) to run minibuses from Luang Prabang to Sainyabuli. Meals are enjoyed at the welcoming restaurant, which offers a panoramic view of the lake and centre. The food is tasty Laotian cuisine and a range of snacks and drinks are available on demand. However, this is a long way from Vientiane, so should you be craving something special or have special dietary requirements, then plan ahead.

The ECC is not your typical tourist elephant camp. It is run by people with a passion for the animals and the proceeds generated from your visit go towards funding the centre and other elephant conservation projects around the country. The only hope for Laos' dwindling elephant population, they are a bright light in a very grim storm.

it makes good coffee, fruit shakes and ice cream. Spotlessly clean. You'll find it – surprise, surprise – in the same location as D.P Guesthouse.

Hashan   INDIAN $
(Map p118; mains 30,000K; ⊘ 7am-10pm; ☑)
By night, its paper lanterns like glowing pupas hanging from the ceiling, this trusty old place pulls you in with its delicious aromas drifting out on to the street. Terrific Indian food – try the melt-in-your-mouth roti. Grab a table overlooking the river.

❶ Information

INTERNET ACCESS
Most guesthouses offer free wi-fi as part of their packages.

MONEY
Guesthouses change money at unimpressive rates. Thai baht are also widely used here.
Lao Development Bank (Map p118; ⊘ 24hr) Has an ATM in town near the market. It's been known to run out of money at busy times.

TOURIST INFORMATION
Tourist Office (Map p118; www.oudomxay. info; ⊘ 7am-noon & 2-9pm) Can arrange guides and has maps of the town.

❶ Getting There & Away

The tiny bus station is at the northernmost edge of town, with departures to Udomxai (40,000K, four hours) at 9am and 12.30pm. Once the new bridge is completed to the north of Pak Beng, there will also be daily transport to Muang Ngeun and the Thai border, plus Hongsa.

The downriver **slowboat** (Map p118) to Luang Prabang departs between 9am and 10am (110,000K, around eight hours) with request stops possible at Pak Tha and Tha Suang (for Hongsa). The slowboat for Huay Xai (110,000K, around nine hours) departs 8.30am.

Speedboats (Map p118) take around three hours to either Luang Prabang or Huay Xai, costing 180,000K per person assuming a crushed-full quota of six passengers (dangerous and highly uncomfortable, but cheaper than a 1,300,000K charter). Arriving by speedboat, local boys will generally offer to carry your bags for about 5000K (after some bargaining). If your

LAND OF A MILLION ELEPHANTS

Laos was originally known as Lan Xang, the Land of a Million Elephants, yet curiously no recent statistics accurately record how many remain. Especially in Sainyabuli Province, working elephants have long been a mainstay of the logging industry, allowing tree trunks to be dragged out selectively without the clear-felling required for tractor access. Elephants are trained and worked by a mahout (handler) whose relationship with the animal is akin to a marriage and can last a lifetime. Elephants are generally owned by a consortium of villagers who share profits, costs and risks. To ensure a profit, owners need their animals to keep working but as a result, few working elephants have the energy for romance nor the time for a two-year maternity leave. With Lao elephants dying more often than they're born, the domestic elephant is likely to be extinct within 50 years, according to **ElefantAsia** (www.elefantasia.org), a partner in the highly impressive Elephant Conservation Center (p120) outside town. It also helped to found the popular Elephant Festival (p123), held in Sainyabuli in mid-February. Meanwhile, numerous retired or 'unemployed' elephants have found alternative employment in tourism, notably around Luang Prabang and Pak Beng. However, this is not an altogether happy alternative as many are overworked, having to do as many as 20 treks a day with humans on their back, particularly uncomfortable for their stickleback spine, in blistering heat, with no socialisation time and largely unvaried diets. ElefantAsia's website offers various 'Read before you ride' tips to help tourists choose well-managed elephant camps, as not all are equal.

In 2015, a caravan of 12 elephants organised by the Center walked 440km to educate Laotians about their natural heritage and draw attention to the plight of the country's highly vulnerable elephant population. Their destination? Luang Prabang, for its 20th anniversary as a World Heritage Site. The arrival and parade of the elephants was its highlight.

bags are unwieldy this can prove money well spent, as when river levels are low you'll need to cross two planks and climb a steep sandbank to reach the road into town. Get tickets at the **boat ticket office** (Map p118).

Hongsa   ທົງສາ

POP 10,000 / 📞 074

Hongsa, famous for elephants, is also the site of a massive new power station constructed by Thai investors and this is a major blight on the horizon. Still, it has been good for employment in the town and there is a mini-boom going on here. Hongsa is a logical break between Luang Prabang and Nan (Thailand, via Muang Ngeun). Its centre is a grid of newer constructions but the town's stream-ribboned edges (away from the power station) are backed by beautiful layered rice fields.

The most characterful of Hongsa's several monasteries is **Wat Simungkhun** (ວັດສີມົງຄຸນ, Wat Nya; ☉ dawn-dusk). Its *hang song pa* (initiation pavilion) is fashioned in attractive naive style while the archaic, murralled *sĭm* (ordination hall) sits on an oddly raised stone platform covering a large hole that is said to lead to the end of the world. It's 1km west of

the centre towards Muang Ngeun, then 100m north after the first river bridge.

Located behind the market, **China Si Chuan Restaurant** (📞 074-2666009; mains 30,000K; ☉ 7am-10pm) is a clean Chinese restaurant that packs them in with rice dishes, *kung pao* chicken and some interesting options such as 'smell chicken slices' and 'couples lung'.

The **ticket office** (📞 020-5558711) beside the market opens at around 7.30am, with vehicles departing for Sainyabuli (70,000K, three hours) and Muang Ngeun (25,000K, 1¼ hours) as soon as a decent quota of guests has piled aboard (usually before 9am).

Sainyabuli (Sayaboury)
ໄຊຍະບູລີ

POP 28,000 / 📞 074

One of Laos' 'elephant capitals', Sainyabuli (variously spelt Sayaboury, Sayabouri, Sayabouli, Xaignabouri and Xayaboury) is a prosperous town backed to the east by an attractive range of high forested ridges. Making a self-conscious attempt to look urban, central Sainyabuli consists of overspaced avenues and showy new administrative buildings that are surprising for their scale but hardly attractions. Starting around the tourist office and continuing south you'll find an increasing proportion of attractive wooden or part-timber structures, some with languid settings among arching palm trees. Overall, it's a friendly and entirely un-touristed place, but numbers are unlikely to increase dramatically with new roads, as most visitors will be heading directly to the Elephant Conservation Center (p120).

◉ Sights

Wat Sibounheuang　　BUDDHIST TEMPLE
(ວັດສີບຸນເຮືອງ; Map p123) Wat Sibounheuang, the town's most evocative monastery, sports a lopsided gilded stupa and reclining Buddha in a delightful garden setting where the bare-brick ruins of the tiny original *sĭm* are reckoned to be from the early 14th century. The 'new' *sĭm* is covered in murals, including anti-adultery scenes in a style reminiscent of Matisse.

This building covers a mysterious 'hole' traditionally associated with *singkhone* spirit-ghosts who are placated in the Phaveth Festival (the 13th to the 15th day of the third Lao month) leading up to the February full moon.

Nam Tien　　LAKE
(ນ້ຳຕຽນ) To fully appreciate the charm of Sainyabuli's setting, drive 9km southwest to the Nam Tien reservoir-lake, access point for the Elephant Conservation Center. A restaurant here is perched above the dam, offering views across emerald rice paddies and wooded slopes towards a western horizon where the Pak Kimin and Pak Xang ridges overlap.

Wat Sisavangvong　　BUDDHIST TEMPLE
(Map p123) More central than the other wats in Sainyabuli, Wat Sisavangvong was reportedly built by King Sisavang Vong on an older temple site.

🎏 Festivals & Events

Elephant Festival　　CULTURAL
(http://festival.elefantasia.org; ⊙mid-Feb) The popular Elephant Festival is a vast two-day jamboree featuring music, theatre and many a beer tent as well as elephant parades and skills demonstrations. In past years the venue has rotated annually between Pak Lai and Ban Viengkeo (near Hongsa), but it has finally settled in Sainyabuli.

Sainyabuli (Sayaboury)

🛏 Sleeping

Santiphap Guesthouse　　GUESTHOUSE $
(Map p123; 13 Northern Rd; r with fan/air-con 60,000/100,000K; ❄) Fresh rooms with en suite, armoire and desk, in these house-proud digs on the main drag. The manager is especially friendly and speaks good English.

Alooncheer Hotel　　GUESTHOUSE $
(Map p123; ☎074-213136; r with fan 50,000-70,000K, with air-con 80,000-120,000K; ❄) This sizeable Hmong-owned complex is quiet yet central. Its polished wood-panelled lobby is decorated with traditional instruments and most rooms have high ceilings, twee lamps

and minibars. It's good value, but beware that the very cheapest rooms are a significant step down in quality.

✗ Eating & Drinking

Night Market   MARKET $
(☉6-10pm) This night market near the central roundabout has food stalls for noodle soup, Lao grills, fresh fruits and khànŏm (traditional sweets).

Nam Tiene Restaurant   LAOTIAN $
(mains 25,000-60,000K, fish by weight; ☉6.30am-11pm) Well-made, professionally presented food along with lovely reservoir views amply reward the excursion out here to the Nam Tien dam. Locals descend here at weekends and rent kooky avian-inspired pedalos.

Sainamhoung Restaurant   LAOTIAN $$
(Map p123; ☑074-211171; mains 25,000-70,000K; ☉7am-10pm; ☎) Contemplate the bamboo-banked river and the looming Pak Kimin massif as you dine on tasty Lao food. Dishes include delectable steamed fish, grilled meats and varied exotica such as fried crickets and wasps, and bamboo worms.

Beer Gardens   BEER GARDEN
(Map p123; 6-11pm) There is some life beyond the dodgy and dark nightclubs in Sainyabuli and it comes in the form of a pair of lively beer gardens on the banks of the Nam Heung (Heung River). They draw a young crowd with a thirst for Beerlao.

❶ Information

MONEY
BCEL (Map p123; ☉8.30am-3.30pm Mon-Fri) Changes money and has an ATM.

POST
Post Office (Map p123; ☉8-11am & 1-5pm Mon-Fri)

TOURIST INFORMATION
Tourist Office (Map p123; ☑030-5180095; Sayaboury_ptd@tourismlaos.org; ☉8.30-11am & 2-4pm Mon-Fri) Good free city maps, English-speaking staff and rental of bikes and motorcycles.

❶ Getting There & Around

The airport is beside the main Pak Lai road, around 3km south of the centre. Lao Skyway used to fly to/from Vientiane, however, these flights were not operational at the time of writing.

From the **main bus station** 2.5km north of the centre, an 11am sŏrngtăaou runs to Hongsa (60,000K, three hours), continuing some days to Muang Ngeun (80,000K).

Vientiane is served via Luang Prabang and Pak Lai, both buses costing 120,000K. Services via Luang Prabang depart at 1pm and 4pm. The Pak Lai service (80,000K, four hours) departs at 9.30am and in the dry season only. Given the appallingly dusty road, this bus is a much better way to reach Pak Lai than taking sŏrngtăaou, which depart around 9am and noon from the **southern bus station**, a tiny stand 4km southwest of the airport.

GETTING TO THAILAND: MUANG NGEUN TO HUAY KON

Getting to the Border
The **Muang Ngeun (Laos)/Huay Kon (Thailand) border crossing** (8am to 5pm) is around 2.5km west of Muang Ngeun junction. Several sŏrngtăaou (passenger truck) make the run from Hongsa (45,000K, 1½ hours) to Muang Ngeun. Once the new bridge north of Pak Beng is open, there will also be a bus service.

Coming from Thailand, there's no restaurant nor any waiting transport on the Lao side, but if you can persuade the immigration officer to call for you, the afternoon sŏrngtăaou to Hongsa should be prepared to collect you for a small fee.

At the Border
Lao visas are available on arrival at this border, payable in US dollars or Thai baht, albeit at a bad exchange rate. Most nationalities crossing into Thailand do not require a visa.

Moving On
From the Thai side, if you don't want to walk your bags across the 1km of no-man's land you can pay 100B for a motorbike with a luggage-carrying sidecar. The Thai border post, Huay Kon, is not quite a village but does have simple noodle shops. The only public transport is a luxurious minibus (☑083-0243675) to Phrae (170B, five hours) via Nan (110B, three hours) departing from the border post at 11.45am. Northbound it leaves the bus stations in Phrae at 6am, and Nan at 8am.

GETTING TO THAILAND: KAEN THAO TO THA LI

Getting to the Border

The quiet, rural **Kaen Thao (Laos)/Tha Li (Thailand) border crossing** (8am to 6pm) is the home of yet another (small) Friendship Bridge, this time over the Nam Heuang. From Pak Lai, there are *sŏrngtăaou* (passenger truck) to the border post at Kaen Thao at around 10am and noon (40,000K, 1¾ hours).

At the Border

Lao visas are available on arrival at this border – one passport-sized photo is required. Most nationalities crossing into Thailand do not require a visa.

Moving On

After walking across the bridge you'll have to take a short *sŏrngtăaou* ride (30B) 8km to Tha Li before transferring to another *sŏrngtăaou* (40B) for the remaining 46km to Loei, from where there are regular connections to Bangkok and elsewhere.

The new Tha Deua bridge over the Mekong River is now open and this slashes journey times to Luang Prabang to just two to three hours by minibus or private vehicle. Slower buses (60,000K, three hours) depart at 9am and 2pm. **Sakura Tour** (p59) has teamed up with the **Elephant Conservation Center** (p120) to run a daily shuttle bus between Sainyabuli and Luang Prabang (100,000K, 2½ hours), departing at 8.30am in both directions. Contact Sakura or the Elephant Conservation Center for more details on this service.

Tuk-tuks to the bus stations (Map p123) (main/southern 15,000/20,000K per person) depart from the main market.

Pak Lai ປາກລາຍ

POP 12,000 / ☎ 074

The bustling Mekong river port of Pak Lai is an almost unavoidable stop on the offbeat route between Sainyabuli and Loei in Thailand. The town follows a 5km curl of Rte 4, paralleled a block further east by a shorter riverside road that's sparsely dotted with historic structures in both Lao and French-colonial style. Exploring north to south, start at Wat Sisavang. Within the next 500m you'll pass the main guesthouses and river port before crossing a little old wooden bridge into an attractive village-like area of local homes beyond a small market.

⊙ Sights

Wat Sisavang   BUDDHIST TEMPLE
(Wat Sisavangvong) Wat Sisavang sports some older monks' quarters as well as a gaudily ornate new bell tower and gateway.

🛏 Sleeping

Sengchaleurn Guesthouse   GUESTHOUSE $
(☎ 020-22068888; r 120,000K; ❋🛜) Sengchaleurn Guesthouse has tidy rooms with air-con, bathroom and cool tile floors.

Jenny Guesthouse   GUESTHOUSE $
(☎ 020-22365971; r with fan/air-con 70,000/ 110,000K; ❋) Jenny's is clean with decent Mekong views, protective mozzie netting over windows and built-on bathroom blocks for each room. There's TV, blankets and comfortable beds. Sadly there's no cafe here.

🍴 Eating

Saykhong   LAOTIAN $
(mains 20,000-40,000K; ⊙7am-10.30pm) With a great terrace and simple menu, Saykhong also pulls in the lion's share of the nightlife.

Kemkhong Restaurant   LAOTIAN $
(mains 20,000-40,000K; ⊙6am-10.30pm) Passable Lao grub from pork *láhp* to stir-fried food. The best thing is the river view; park yourself with a beer and watch the light turn a burnt peach.

ℹ Information

MONEY
BCEL (⊙8.30am-3.30pm Mon-Fri) An ATM and currency exchange are available.

ℹ Getting There & Away

Bring a face mask and disposable clothes if you attempt the Pak Lai–Sainyabuli journey by *sŏrngtăaou* (80,000K, four hours). These depart in both directions between 7.30am and 9.30am and once again around noon. Mud-crusted victims arrive at Pak Lai's little Sainyabuli bus station, 3km north of the centre. From there, tuk-tuks charge 10,000K per person to the guesthouses or 15,000K to the southern bus terminal. This terminal has a 9am bus to Vientiane (100,000K, six hours).

Vientiane, Vang Vieng & Around

Best Places to Eat

➡ Doi Ka Noi (p150)

➡ Lao Kitchen (p148)

➡ Le Silapa (p147)

➡ Makphet Restaurant (p146)

➡ Senglao Cafe (p150)

Best Places to Sleep

➡ Ansara Hôtel (p144)

➡ Hotel Khamvongsa (p142)

➡ LV City Riverine Hotel (p142)

➡ Mandala Boutique Hotel (p145)

➡ Mixay Paradise Guesthouse (p144)

Why Go?

Vientiane is one of the smallest capital cities in Southeast Asia, but what it lacks in size it more than makes up for in character. Set on the banks of the mighty Mekong River, there is a palpable French influence, and it's the perfect place to recharge the batteries on an overland journey through Laos.

The urbane sophistication of Vientiane is a world away from the poetic beauty of the karst mountains of Vang Vieng and the dense jungles of Phu Khao Khuay National Protected Area (NPA).

Vang Vieng, one of Southeast Asia's leading adventure centres, is also one of the most beautiful spots in Laos. Rising up across the Nam Song (Song River), the limestone karst is a throwback to the Jurassic-era and is peppered with caves.

Throw in homestays and jungle treks around Phu Khao Khuay, the most accessible protected area in the country, and prepare to encounter some remarkable contrasts on your travels.

When to Go
Vientiane

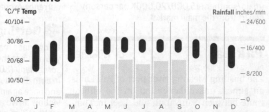

Nov–Feb A great time to visit, with the magical Bun Pha That Luang (Full Moon Festival) in November.

Mar–May Temperatures and humidity levels climbs, but hotel prices fall.

Jun–Nov The monsoon brings fresh air and river festivals like Bun Awk Phansa and Bun Nam.

VIENTIANE ວຽງຈັນ

POP 700,000 / ♪ 021

From its sleepy tuk-tuk drivers to its cafe society and affordable spas, this former French trading post is languid to say the least. Eminently walkable, the historic old quarter of Vientiane beguiles with glittering temples, lunging *naga* (river serpent) statues, wandering Buddhist monks, and boulevards lined with frangipani and tamarind.

Meanwhile, with most of its old French villas now stylishly reincarnated into restaurants and small hotels, Vientiane is achieving an unprecedented level of panache with a distinctly Gallic flavour. For the well-heeled traveller and backpacker the city acquits itself equally well, be it with low-cost digs and street markets, or upscale boutique accommodation and gastronomic eateries.

Whether you spend your time in Vientiane lounging over a novel in an old-fashioned bakery, shopping in silk shops or swigging Beerlao while drinking up the fiery sunset over the Mekong, once you leave you'll miss this place more than you expected.

History

Set on a bend in the Mekong River, Vientiane was first settled around the 9th century AD and formed part of one of the early Lao valley *meuang* (city-states) that were consolidated around the 10th century under the control of the Khmer empire. The Lao who settled here did so because the surrounding alluvial plains were so fertile, and initially the Vientiane *meuang* prospered and enjoyed a fragile sovereignty following the decline of Angkor.

In the ensuing centuries, Vientiane's fortunes have been mixed. At various times it has been a major regional centre; at other times it has been controlled by the Vietnamese, Burmese and Siamese.

The height of Vientiane's success was probably in the years after it became the Lan Xang capital in the mid-16th century, after King Setthathirat moved the capital from Luang Prabang. Several of Vientiane's wats were built following this shift and the city became a major centre of Buddhist learning.

It didn't last. Periodic invasions by the Burmese, Siamese and Chinese, and the eventual division of the Lan Xang kingdom took their toll on the city.

It wasn't until the Siamese installed Chao Anou, a Lao prince who had been educated in Bangkok, on the throne in 1805 that the city received an overdue makeover. Chao Anou's public works included Wat Si Saket, built between 1819 and 1824.

Unfortunately, Chao Anou's attempts to assert Lao independence over the Siamese resulted in the most violent and destructive episode in Vientiane's history. In 1828 the Siamese defeated Chao Anou's armies and

---

VIENTIANE IN...

Two Days

Start with a coffee and croissant at **Le Banneton** (p146) before embarking on the Monument to **Mekong cycling tour** (p140), taking you through most of Vientiane's main sights, including **Wat Si Saket** (p130), **Haw Pha Kaeo** (p130) and **Talat Sao** (p153). Top off your day with riverside cocktails at **Spirit House** (p150). On day two consider getting some motorised wheels and leaving the city centre to visit the concrete Buddhas and Hindu deities at **Xieng Khuan** (p134). On the way back stop at **Pha That Luang** (p134) for great afternoon photos. Enjoy a fine French dinner at **Le Silapa** (p147).

Four Days

Depending on what time you crawl out of bed on day three, make **PVO** (p148) your lunch destination. It's then a short walk to the **COPE Visitor Centre** (p130), where you could easily spend a couple hours checking out the excellent exhibits and powerful documentaries. After a light Lao dinner at **Khambang Lao Food Restaurant** (p149), head to nearby **Herbal Sauna** (p137) for a healthy Lao-style sweat. Rehydrate with draught Beerlao at **Bor Pen Yang** (p150).

Day four can be spent at a Lao cooking course at **Villa Lao** (p138), handicraft and textile shopping along **Thanon Nokèokoummane**, rummaging for communist wristwatches and glass Buddhas at **Indochina Handicrafts** (p152), or sniffing and waxing lyrical about the handmade soaps and oils at **T'Shop Lai Gallery** (p152).

Vientiane, Vang Vieng & Around Highlights

① Vang Vieng
(p163) Tubing, climbing, kayaking, cycling, motorbiking or walking through the rivers and stunning karst terrain.

② Lao cuisine
(p145) Indulging in a culinary journey through Vientiane by sampling mod Lao, Gallic gastronomy and a fusion of other flavours.

③ Pha That Luang
(p134) Seeking out the spiritual side of Laos with a visit to one of the principal Buddhist wats in Vientiane.

④ Nightlife
(p150) Bar-hopping in Vientiane along Th Fa Ngoum and Th Setthathirath to discover another side to the sometimes sleepy Lao capital.

⑤ Phu Khao Khuay NPA (p160) Getting off the grid with a trip to this national protected area, with its diverse landscape, pretty waterfalls and authentic homestays.

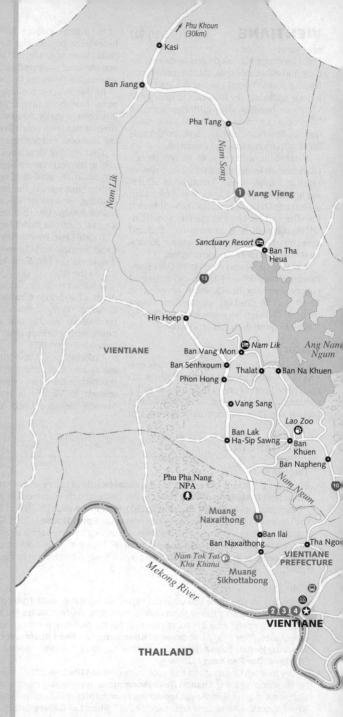

wasted no time in razing the city and carting off much of the population. Wat Si Saket, the base for the Thai invaders, was the only major building to survive, and the city was abandoned.

In 1867 French explorers arrived but it wasn't until late in the century, after Vientiane had been made capital of the French protectorate, that serious reconstruction began. A simple grid plan was laid out for the city and a sprinkling of colonial-style mansions and administrative buildings emerged. However, Vientiane was always low in the French order of Indochinese priorities, as the modest building program testifies.

In 1928 the 'city' was home to just 9000 inhabitants – many of them Vietnamese administrators brought in by the French – and it wasn't until the end of WWII that Vientiane's population began to grow with any vigour. It was a growth fed primarily by Cold War dollars, with first French and later American advisors arriving in a variety of guises.

After a couple of coups d'état in the politically fluid 1960s, Vientiane had by the early '70s become a city where almost anything went. Its few bars were peopled by an almost surreal mix of spooks and correspondents, and the women who served them.

Not surprisingly, things changed with the arrival of the Pathet Lao (PL) in 1975. Nightclubs filled with spies were the first to go and Vientiane settled into a slumber punctuated by occasional unenthusiastic concessions to communism, including low-level collectivisation and an initial crackdown on Buddhism. These days the most noticeable leftovers from the period are some less-than-inspired Soviet-style buildings.

Things picked up in the 1990s and in recent years Vientiane has seen a relative explosion of construction, road redevelopment and vehicular traffic, much of it financed by China, the country that will likely have the most significant influence on Vientiane's future.

◉ Sights

The bulk of sights are concentrated in a small area in the centre of the city. With the exception of Xieng Khuan (Buddha Park), all sights are easily reached by bicycle and, in most cases, on foot. If you're interested in visiting the city's minor temples, consider tackling our bicycle tour (p140). Most wats welcome visitors after the monks have collected alms in the morning until about 6pm.

★ **COPE Visitor Centre** CULTURAL CENTRE
(ສູນພື້ນຟູຄົນພິການແຫ່ງຊາດ; Map p132; ☑021-218427; www.copelaos.org; Th Khu Vieng; donations welcome; ⊙9am-6pm) FREE COPE (Cooperative Orthotic & Prosthetic Enterprise) is the main source of artificial limbs, walking aids and wheelchairs in Laos. Its excellent Visitor Centre, part of the organisation's National Rehabilitation Centre, offers myriad interesting and informative multimedia exhibits about prosthetics and the unexploded ordnance (UXO) that make them necessary.

Wat Si Saket BUDDHIST TEMPLE
(ວັດສີສະເກດ; Map p136; cnr Th Lan Xang & Th Setthathirath; 5000K; ⊙8am-noon & 1-4pm, closed public holidays) Built between 1819 and 1824 by Chao Anou, Wat Si Saket is believed to be Vientiane's oldest surviving wat. And it is starting to show, as this beautiful temple is in need of a facelift. Along the western side of the cloister is a pile of Buddhas that were damaged during the 1828 Siamese-Lao war.

Haw Pha Kaeo MUSEUM
(ຫໍພະແກ້ວ; Map p136; Th Setthathirath; 5000K; ⊙8am-noon & 1-4pm) Once a royal temple built specifically to house the famed Emerald Buddha, Haw Pha Kaeo is today a national museum of religious art. It is about 100m southeast of Wat Si Saket. The main hall contains a mix of Khmer carvings, Laotian Buddhas and relics from temples around town.

★ **Patuxai** MONUMENT
(ປະຕູໄຊ, Victory Monument; Map p132; Th Lan Xang; 3000K; ⊙8am-5pm) Vientiane's Arc de Triomphe replica is a slightly incongruous sight, dominating the commercial district around Th Lan Xang. Officially called 'Victory Monument' *and* commemorating the Lao who died in prerevolutionary wars, it was built in 1969 with cement donated by the USA intended for the construction of a new airport. Climb to the summit for panoramic views over Vientiane.

Lao National Museum MUSEUM
(ພິພິດທະພັນປະຫວັດສາດແຫ່ງຊາດລາວ; Map p136; ☑021-212461; Th Samsènethai; 10,000K; ⊙8am-noon & 1-4pm) Unfortunately, this charming French-era building, flanked by cherry blossom and magnolia trees, is due to be knocked down and moved to newer premises. It was formerly known as the Lao Revolutionary Museum, and much of its collection retains an unshakeable revolutionary zeal.

VIENTIANE, VANG VIENG & AROUND VIENTIANE

Wat Si Muang
BUDDHIST TEMPLE

(ວັດສີເມືອງ; Map p132; cnr Th Setthathirath, Th Samsènethai & Th Tha Deua; ⊙6am-7pm, special days to 10pm) **FREE** The most frequently used grounds in Vientiane are those of Wat Si Muang, the site of the *lák méuang* (city pillar), which is considered the home of the guardian spirit of Vientiane. The large *sĭm* (ordination hall; destroyed in 1828 and rebuilt in 1915) was constructed around the *lák méuang*, and consists of two halls.

The large entry hall features a copy of the Pha Kaeo (Emerald Buddha), and a much smaller, rather melted-looking seated stone Buddha that allegedly survived the 1828 inferno. Locals believe it has the power to grant wishes or answer troubling questions, and the practice is to lift it off the pillow three times while mentally phrasing a question or request. If your request is granted, then you are supposed to return later with an offering of bananas, green coconuts, flowers, incense and candles (usually two of each).

The pillar itself is located in the rear hall, and is believed to date from the Khmer period, indicating the site has been used for religious purposes for more than 1000 years. Today it is wrapped in sacred cloth, and in front of it is a carved wooden stele with a seated Buddha in relief.

Behind the *sĭm* is a crumbling laterite *jĕh-dii* (stupa), almost certainly of Khmer origin. Devotees deposit broken deity images and pottery around the stupa's base so the spirits of the stupa will 'heal' the bad luck created by the breaking of these items. In front of the *sĭm* is a little public park with a statue of King Sisavang Vong (1904–59).

Kaysone Phomivan Memorial
MUSEUM

(ທ່ພິພິດທະພັນແລະອະນຸສາວລີໄກສອນພົມວິຫານ; Km 6, Silivay Village; 5000K; ⊙8am-noon & 1-4pm Tue-Sun) In contrast to the huge Kaysone Phomvihane Museum, Kaysone's house is a remarkably modest affair, yet fascinating both because of its history and that it remains virtually untouched since the great man died in 1992. A Lao People's Revolutionary Party (LPRP) guide will show you through the house, making for a good-value experience.

The house is inside the former USAID/CIA compound, a self-contained headquarters known as 'Six Klicks City' because of its location 6km from central Vientiane. It once featured bars, restaurants, tennis courts, swimming pools, a commissary and assorted offices from where the Secret War was orchestrated. During the 1975 takeover of Vientiane, Pathet Lao forces ejected the Americans and occupied the compound. Kaysone lived here until his death.

The house includes Kaysone's half-empty bottles of scotch, tacky souvenirs from the Eastern bloc, white running shoes, notepads and original Kelvinator air-conditioners. Even the winter coats he wore on visits to Moscow remain neatly hanging in the wardrobe.

Kaysone's house can be tricky to find, so it's easiest to backtrack from the nearby **Kaysone Phomvihane Museum** (ທ່ພິພິດທະພັນແລະອະນຸສາວລີໄກສອນພົມວິຫານ; Km 6, Rte 13 South; 5000K; ⊙museum 8am-noon & 1-4pm Tue-Sun). Head back towards the city centre and turn right at the first set of traffic lights, continuing about 1km until you see the sign on your right that says 'Mémorial du Président Kaysone Phomvihane'. Alternatively, a tuk-tuk will cost around 40,000K from the centre.

THE LEGEND OF WAT SI MUANG

Legend has it that a group of sages selected the site for Wat Si Muang in 1563, when King Setthathirat moved his capital to Vientiane. Once the spot was chosen, a large hole was dug to receive the heavy stone pillar (probably taken from an ancient Khmer site nearby) that would become the *lák méuang* (city pillar). When the pillar arrived it was suspended over the hole with ropes. Drums and gongs were sounded to summon the townspeople to the area and everyone waited for a volunteer to jump into the hole as a sacrifice to the spirit.

Depending on who's relating it, the legend has several conclusions. What is common to all of them is that a pregnant woman named Sao Si leaped in and the ropes were released, killing her and in the process establishing the town guardianship. Variations include her leaping in upon a horse, and/or with a diminutive monk.

However, Lao scholars think that if there is any truth to this story it is likely to have occurred much earlier than Setthathirat's time, in the pre-Buddhist Mon or Khmer periods when human sacrifice was ritually practised...and that Sao Si's legendary leap might not have been her choice at all.

Vientiane

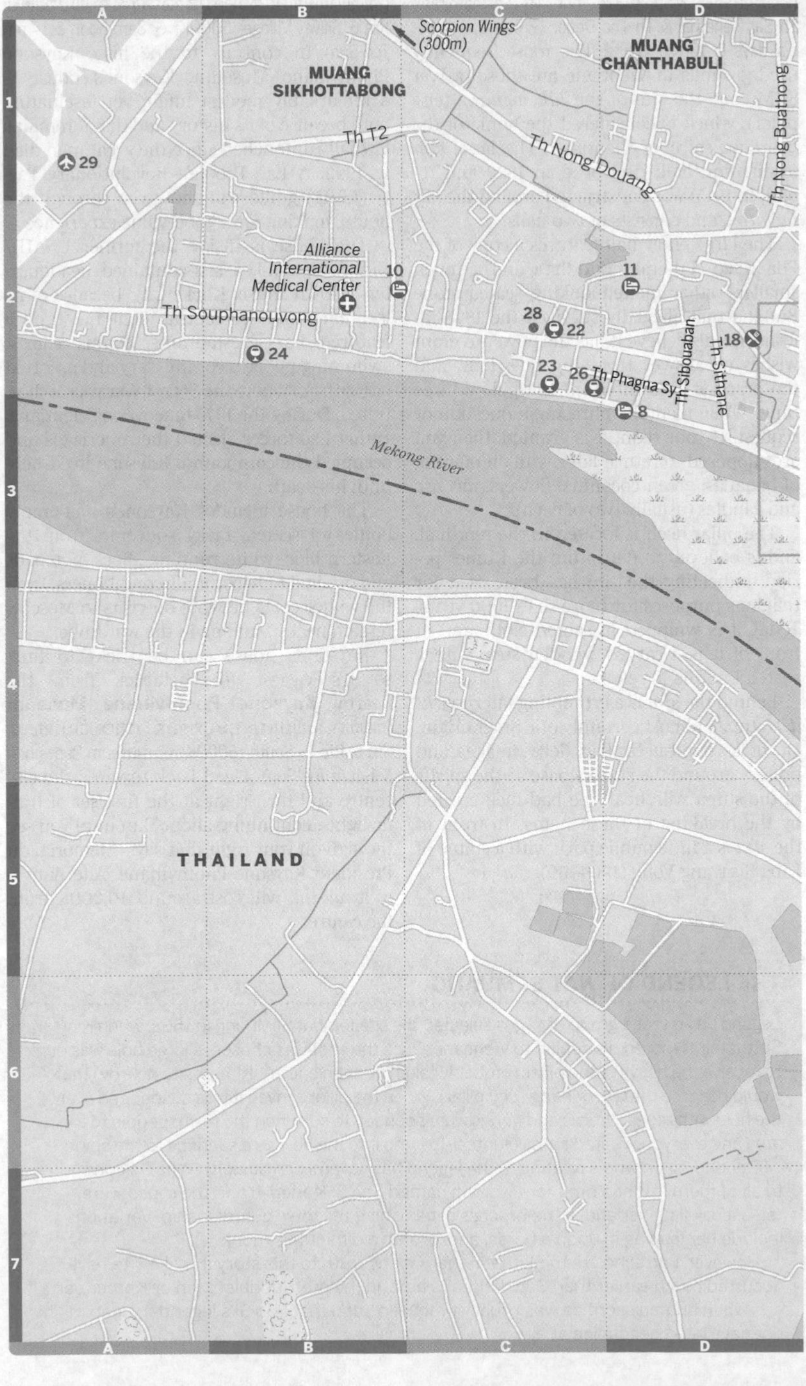

Scorpion Wings
(300m)

**MUANG
SIKHOTTABONG**

**MUANG
CHANTHABULI**

Th Nong Buathong

Th T2

Th Nong Douang

Alliance
International
Medical Center

10

11

Th Souphanouvong

28

22

24

23

26 Th Phagna Sy

Th Sibouaban

18

Th Sithane

8

Mekong River

THAILAND

29

VIENTIANE, VANG VIENG & AROUND VIENTIANE

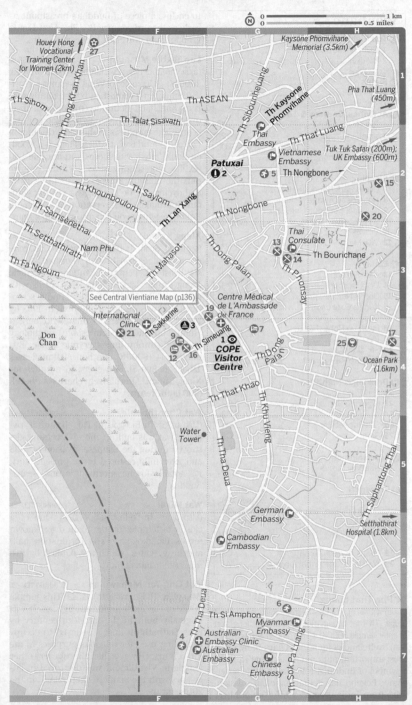

N 0 ——————— 1 km
0 ——————— 0.5 miles

Houey Hong Vocational Training Center for Women (2km) 27

Kaysone Phomvihane Memorial (3.5km)

Th Sihom

Th Thong Khan Kham

Th ASEAN

Th Subounheuang

Th Kaysone Phomvihane

Th Talat Sisavath

Thai Embassy

Th That Luang

Pha That Luang (450m)

Tuk Tuk Safari (200m); UK Embassy (600m)

Patuxai 2

Vietnamese Embassy 5

Th Nongbone

15

Th Khounboulom

Th Saylom

Th Lan Xang

Th Nongbone

20

Th Samsenethai

Th Setthathirath

Nam Phu

Th Mahasot

Th Dong Palan

Thai Consulate

13

14 — Th Bourichane

Th Phonsay

Th Fa Ngoum

See Central Vientiane Map (p136)

Centre Médical de L'Ambassade de France

19

International Clinic 21

Th Sakkarine

3

Th Simeuang

1 COPE Visitor Centre

7

25 17

Ocean Park (1.6km)

Don Chan

9 12 16

Th Dong Palan

Th That Khao

Th Khu Vieng

Water Tower

Th Tha Deua

German Embassy

Th Saphantong Thai

Setthathirat Hospital (1.8km)

Cambodian Embassy

Th Tha Deua

Th Si Amphon

6

Myanmar Embassy

4

Australian Embassy Clinic
Australian Embassy

Chinese Embassy

Th Sok Pa Luang

★**Pha That Luang**　BUDDHIST STUPA

(ພະທາດຫລວງ, Great Sacred Reliquary, Great Stupa; Th That Luang; 5000K, rental of long skirt to enter temple 5000K; ⊙8am-noon & 1-4pm Tue-Sun) Svelte and golden Pha That Luang is the most important national monument in Laos; a symbol of Buddhist religion and Lao sovereignty. Legend has it that Ashokan missionaries from India erected a *tâht* (stupa) here to enclose a piece of Buddha's breastbone as early as the 3rd century BC. Pha That Luang is about 4km northeast of the city centre.

Lao Textile Museum　MUSEUM

(ພິພິດຕະພັນຜ້າໄໝບູຮານລາວ; ☎030-5727423; 30,000K; ⊙10am-4pm) What began as a private museum, established by the family that runs Kanchana Boutique (p153), has subsequently become something of a Lao cultural centre. The emphasis at this leafy traditional Lao compound is on textiles. There is a wooden house filled with looms and antique Lao textiles representing several ethnic groups, plus the museum offers courses in weaving and dyeing. We do not suggest visiting without first making a reservation at Kanchana Boutique, where you can also pick up a map.

Xieng Khuan　MUSEUM

(ຊຽງຄວນ, Suan Phut, Buddha Park; 5000K, camera 3000K; ⊙8am-4.30pm) Located 25km southeast of central Vientiane, eccentric Xieng Khuan, aka Buddha Park, thrills with other-worldly Buddhist and Hindu sculptures, and was designed and built in 1958 by Luang Pu, a yogi-priest-shaman who merged Hindu and Buddhist philosophy, mythology and iconography into a cryptic whole. Bus number 14 (8000K, one hour, 24km) leaves Talat Sao Bus Station every 15 minutes for Xieng Khuan. Alternatively, charter a tuk-tuk (200,000K return).

Wat Chanthabuli　BUDDHIST TEMPLE

(Map p136; Th Fa Ngoum) This beautiful riverside wat was built in the 16th century, destroyed during the Siamese invasion of 1828 and later fully restored to its present glory. It's notable for its enormous bronze seated Buddha.

Wat Mixai　BUDDHIST TEMPLE

(Map p136; Th Setthathirath) FREE One of a cluster of temples on the main drag, known for its Bangkok-style *sĭm* (ordination hall) and heavy gates, which are flanked by two *nyak* (guardian giants).

Wat Ong Teu Mahawihan　BUDDHIST TEMPLE

(Map p136; Th Setthathirath) FREE This temple is one of the most important in Laos. It was originally built in the mid-16th century by King Setthathirat and is believed to occupy a site first used for religious purposes in the 3rd century. However, like almost every other temple in Vientiane it was destroyed in later wars with the Siamese, then rebuilt in the 20th century.

VIEWING PHA THAT LUANG

Each level of Pha That Luang has different architectural features in which Buddhist doctrine is encoded; visitors are supposed to contemplate the meaning of these features as they walk around. The first level is an approximately square base measuring 68m by 69m that supports 323 *sĕe máh* (ordination stones). It represents the material world, and also features four arched *hŏr wái* (prayer halls), one on each side, with short stairways leading to them and beyond to the second level.

The second level is 48m by 48m and is surrounded by 120 lotus petals. There are 288 *sĕe máh* on this level, as well as 30 small stupas symbolising the 30 Buddhist perfections *(báhlamée săhm-síp tat)*, beginning with alms-giving and ending with equanimity.

Arched gates again lead to the next level, a 30m by 30m square. The tall central stupa, which has a brick core that has been stuccoed over, is supported here by a bowl-shaped base reminiscent of India's first Buddhist stupa at Sanchi. At the top of this mound the superstructure, surrounded by lotus petals, begins.

The curvilinear, four-sided spire resembles an elongated lotus bud and is said to symbolise the growth of a lotus from a seed in a muddy lake bottom to a bloom over the lake's surface, a metaphor for human advancement from ignorance to enlightenment in Buddhism. The entire *tâht* was regilded in 1995 to celebrate the 20th anniversary of the Lao People's Democratic Republic (PDR), and is crowned by a stylised banana flower and parasol. From ground to pinnacle, Pha That Luang is 45m tall.

That Dam
MONUMENT

(Black Stupa; Map p136; Th Bartholomie) That Dam sits on a quiet roundabout near the centre of Vientiane. Legend has it that this stupa was once coated in a layer of gold. The gold is said to have been carted off by the Siamese during their pillaging of 1828, after which the stupa took the 'black' sobriquet in memory of the dastardly act.

🏃 Activities

Nakarath Travel
ADVENTURE SPORTS

(www.nakarathtravel.com) Upscale destination management company based in Vientiane that arranges guided cultural immersions around the country.

Sinouk Coffee Pavilion
COFFEE

(☑ 030-2000654; www.sinouk-cafe.com; Km 9, Th Tha Deua; ☺ 8am-5pm) Located at the headquarters of Sinouk Coffee, one of Laos's best-known coffee producers, this is an education in the bean. Learn more about the art of coffee production at the coffee gallery and mini-museum paying homage to caffeine, and in roasting and cupping rooms, where you might be lucky enough to see the production process underway.

Regular cupping sessions are held on Saturdays, but check on its Facebook page (sinoukcoffeeofficial) for details. This is like wine tasting for coffee connoisseurs and costs about 60,000K for a two-hour session.

Ocean Park
WATER PARK

(☑ 030-2819014; ITECC Vientiane; adult/child 50,000/25,000K; ☺ 11am-7pm) Shiver me timbers me hearties! This new water park has a pirate theme and includes a good range of slides, tubes, lazy river riding and more. A good option for families on a hot day.

Lao Bowling Centre
BOWLING

(Map p136; ☑ 021-218661; Th Khounboulom; per game with shoe hire 16,000K; ☺ 9am-midnight) Bright lights, Beerlao and boisterous bowlers are what you'll find here. While the equipment is in bad shape, it's still a fun place to come in the evening for a Lao-style night out. It sometimes stays open into the wee hours.

Health & Fitness

Vientiane Yoga Studio
YOGA

(Map p132; ☑ 020-78510490; www.vientianeyoga studio.weebly.com; 90min class 80,000K; ☺ 9am & 6pm Mon-Fri, 8.30am, 1.30pm, 3.30pm & 5.30pm Sat) Hatha, vinyasa, yin and advanced (upside-down) yoga, as well as pilates, are available at this location in a quiet garden down a secluded street. Instructor Nanci has 10 years' experience.

Bee Bee Fitness
HEALTH & FITNESS

(Map p132; ☑ 021-315877; 1-day membership 45,000K; ☺ 6am-9pm Mon-Fri, 7am-9pm Sat & Sun) This terrific gym overlooks the Mekong so you can run on a treadmill and watch passing boats. There's loads of room to enjoy its decent equipment: rowing machines, spinning

Central Vientiane

bikes and weightlifting apparatus. Regular Zumba and pilates classes are available. It's located opposite the Australian embassy.

Massage & Spa

★Oasis

MASSAGE

(Map p136; Th François Ngin; ⊗9am-9pm) Cool, clean and professional, Oasis is an excellent central place to enjoy a foot massage (50,000K), a Lao-style body massage (60,000K) or a peppermint body scrub (200,000K), to name a few. Probably the best-value spa in the city.

Tangerine Garden Spa

SPA

(Map p136; ☑021-251452; off Th Fa Ngoum; ⊗9am-9pm) Arguably the most upscale spa in Vientiane, Tangerine Garden is located opposite the beautiful Ansara Hôtel and complements its colonial-era look. The Sino-Lao lobby sets the tone for a relaxing journey that includes foot massage (80,000K), aroma massage (180,000K) and the 'office syndrome' massage (100,000K) that focuses on the neck, shoulders and back.

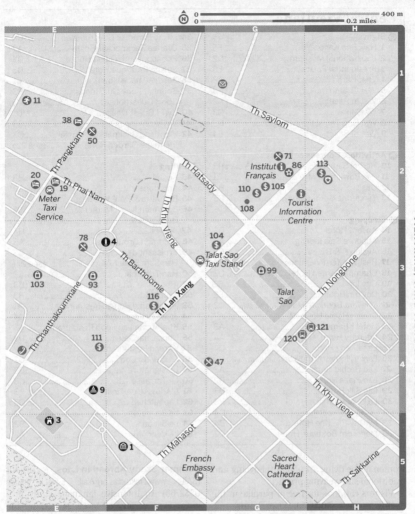

Herbal Sauna

MASSAGE

(Map p136; ☑020-55044655; off Th Chao Anou; ⊙1-9pm) Located near the river, this no-frills outfit offers Lao-style herbal saunas (15,000K) in separate rooms for men and women. In addition to the sauna, it also offers a variety of massage, including Lao (per hour 40,000K), oil (per hour 80,000K) and foot (per hour 40,000K).

Wat Si Amphon

SPA

(Map p132; Th Si Amphon; ⊙7am-5pm) Wat Si Amphon does herbal saunas and is one of the only temples to offer this experience after the demise of the Wat Sok Pa Luang herbal sauna in a 2013 fire.

📚 Courses

Houey Hong Vocational Training Center for Women

WEAVING

(☑021-560006; www.houeyhongcentre.com; Ban Houey Hong; ⊙8.30am-4.30pm Mon-Sat) You can learn how to dye textiles using natural pigments and then weave them on a traditional loom at this NGO centre, run by a Lao-Japanese woman. It was established north of Vientiane to train disadvantaged rural

Central Vientiane

women in the dying art of natural dyeing and traditional silk-weaving practices.

Visitors can look for free or partake in the dyeing process (100,000K, two hours, one scarf) or weaving (250,000K, whole day). You keep the fruits of your labour. Transport to and from the centre is provided for an additional 50,000K from True Colour (p153), the centre's retail location in town.

Villa Lao   COOKING

(Map p132; ☎ 020-22217588; www.villalaos. com; off Th Nong Douang; half-day class per person US$25) Villa Lao offers cooking courses at 9am and 1pm by appointment, and involve a trip to the market, preparation of three dishes of your choice and sampling your creations. It's a very peaceful setting for classes, like a slice of country life in the city.

Summer Study Abroad in Laos   LANGUAGE

(SAIL; www.laostudies.org/sail; 5-week course US$2760) An intensive language study program at a variety of levels hosted by the Lao-American College in Vientiane.

⌦ Tours

★ Tuk Tuk Safari   CULTURAL

(☎ 020-54333089; www.tuktuksafari.com; adult/ child under 12 US$70/40; ⊗ 8am-5pm) This community-conscious tour company gets under the skin of Vientiane in a tuk-tuk. Tour guide Ere spirits you to a Lao market; a silversmith's workshop; behind the scenes at a restaurant helping street kids learn to become chefs (before sampling their delicious food!); and finally, the inspiring COPE Visitor Centre for UXO victims.

VIENTIANE, VANG VIENG & AROUND VIENTIANE

**Lao Disabled Women's
Development Centre**   CULTURAL
(☑ 021-812282; http://laodisabledwomen.com; 100 Th Tha Deua; tours 50,000-100,000K; ⊙ 8.30am-4.30pm Mon-Fri, weekends by appointment) 🖉 Run by a collective of Lao disabled women, this centre challenges the prejudices that the disabled community in Laos sometimes faces. Concentrating on abilities, the centre offers training and education to empower disabled women. It is open to drop-in visitors for free, or you can sign up for a tour to learn about recycled-paper handicrafts.

Backstreet Academy   TOURS
(☑ 020-58199216;   www.backstreetacademy.com) For some original local encounters, contact Backstreet Academy, a peer-to-peer travel website that specialises in connecting travellers to cultural experiences with local hosts.

Choose from a *muay Lao* (kickboxing) class, a traditional dance lesson, a Lao cooking class in a private home, a painting class, zen meditation and a whole lot more.

🎉 Festivals & Events

Pi Mai   CULTURAL
Lao New Year is celebrated in mid-April with a mass water fight and tourists are considered fair game. Be warned, drunk driving and theft are rampant at these times so remain vigilant with your driver and wallet!

Bun Nam   SPORTS
(Bun Suang Héua; ⊙ Oct) A huge annual event at the end of *pansăh* (the Buddhist rains retreat) in October, during which boat races are held on the Mekong River. Rowing teams from all over the country, as well as from Thailand, China and Myanmar (Burma), compete;

the river bank is lined with food stalls, temporary discos, carnival games and beer gardens for three days and nights.

Bun Pha That Luang
CULTURAL

(That Luang Festival; ☉Nov) Bun Pha That Luang, usually held in early November, is the largest temple fair in Laos. Festivities begin with a *wéean téean* (circumambulation) around Wat Si Muang, followed by a procession to Pha That Luang, which is illuminated all night for a week.

The festival climaxes on the morning of the full moon with the *đák bàht* ceremony, in which thousands of monks from across Laos receive alms. Fireworks cap off the evening and everyone makes merit or merry until dawn. Look out for devotees carrying *ĥạhsàht* (miniature temples made from banana stems and decorated with flowers and other offerings).

🛏 Sleeping

🛏 Thanon Setthathirath & Nam Phu

Dream Home Hostel 2
HOSTEL **$**

(Map p136; ☎020-95591102; dreamhomehostel2@gmail.com; Th Sihom; dm 50,000K; r US$25; ❄️ 🛜) A classic backpacker crash pad, this is one of the most popular hostels in the city. Reception introduces the party atmosphere with some cranked-up tunes and a pool table, and murals deck the upper walls. The rooms are actually pretty good value given the size and features like flat-screen TV – almost flashpacker territory.

Vientiane Backpackers Hostel
HOSTEL **$**

(Map p136; ☎020-97484277; www.vientianebackpackershostel.com; Th Nokèokoummane; dm incl breakfast 40,000K; ❄️@🛜) This fresh hostel has three mixed dorms for 12, 16 and 20 people. There's a cafe selling burgers and shakes, laundry services, free wi-fi, and bicycle/motorbike hire (10,000/70,000K). Bathrooms and showers are modern and clean, but there's no self-catering. Free ticketing and visa services round things off.

Orange Backpacker Hostel
HOSTEL **$**

(Map p136; ☎020-22455588; vonglatsamy24@gmail.com; Th Sihom; dm 45,000K; r 70,000-120,000K; ❄️@🛜) A popular backpacker hostel in the emerging Th Sihom strip, Orange has cheap dorms for those on a budget, especially when you consider the rate includes

🏃 Cycling Tour
Monument to Vientiane

START LE BANNETON
END CHOKDEE CAFE
LENGTH 5KM; FOUR TO SIX HOURS

Vientiane is a great city to explore on bicycle. We suggest starting in the cool hours of the morning and including breakfast and lunch stops; if you're doing the tour later you could regard these as lunch and dinner stops. Some attractions, such as Talat Khua Din, are best visited early in the day.

Begin your day with coffee and a crispy croissant at one of Th Nokèokoummane's excellent French bakeries such as ❶ **Le Banneton** (p146). There's a bike-rental place virtually next door, and a few more on adjacent Th François Ngin; most open at 7am and charge about 10,000K per day.

Hop on your bike, turn on to one-way Th Setthathirath, and passing ❷ **Nam Phu**, Vientiane's underwhelming fountain, continue about 1km to the stoplight. On your right is the ❸ **Presidential Palace** (Map p136), a vast beaux-arts-style chateau built to house the French colonial governor.

Directly opposite is ❹ **Wat Si Saket** (p130), with its thousands of Buddha figures, and just up the road, ❺ **Haw Pha Kaeo** (p130), the national museum for religious objects. By arriving in the morning you'll beat most of the crowds.

Continuing on along Th Setthathirath, cross Th Mahasot and turn left down Th Gallieni. You'll know you're in the right place by the white walls of the ❻ **French Embassy** on your left and the towering ❼ **Sacred Heart Cathedral** (Map p136) on your right. Continue northwest along this street until you reach the T-intersection; on the opposite side is the barely noticeable entrance to ❽ **Talat Khua Din**, one of Vientiane's largest fresh-food markets.

Continuing northwest along Th Khu Vieng, turn right onto Th Lan Xang, a street sometimes (very) generously described as the 'Champs-Elysées of the East'. At this point you're directly in front of Vientiane's biggest market, ❾ **Talat Sao** (p153), a great place for textiles.

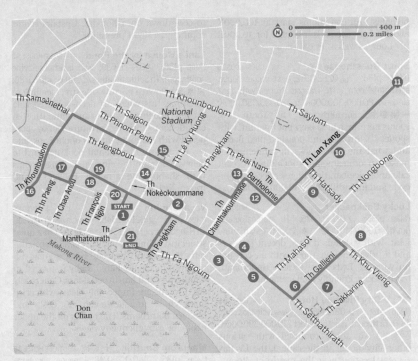

Continuing northeast along Th Lan Xang, you'll pass by the 10 **Tourist Information Centre** (p155). At this point you're also only 500m from 11 **Patuxai** (p130), which is worth climbing for unbeatable views of the city.

Circle around Patuxai and go back southwest along Th Lan Xang. Turn right into quiet Th Bartholomie. Pass the site of the 12 **former US Embassy** and continue to 13 **That Dam** (p135). The gold that covered this stupa was allegedly carted off by the Siamese during their pillaging of 1828. If you can pass here without being swallowed by the giant *naga* (river serpent) that allegedly lurks beneath, continue southwest and turn right onto Th Samsènethai.

Continue two blocks until, on your left-hand side you see the gaudy Chinese-funded 14 **Lao National Culture Hall** (p151). Directly opposite this is the 15 **Lao National Museum** (p130), worth a stop to gain some insight into ancient and modern Laos.

Continue another 500m along one-way Th Samsènethai until you reach the stoplight. Turn left and head southwest along Th Khounboulom. Continue until you reach 16 **Khambang Lao Food Restaurant** (p149). This family-run place is central Vientiane's best Lao restaurant and your lunch destination.

Backtrack a block northeast along Th Khounboulom until you reach 17 **Wat In Paeng** (Map p136), famed for the artistry displayed in the stucco relief of the *sĭm* (ordination hall). Weaving to Th Setthathirath via Th Chao Anou, park your bike at 18 **Wat Ong Teu Mahawihan** (p134) and visit the temple's namesake, a 16th-century bronze Buddha measuring 5.8m tall and weighing several tonnes. The *sĭm* that houses the Buddha is famous for the wooden facade over its front terrace, a masterpiece of Lao carving. Take a break at shady and little-visited 19 **Wat Haysoke** (Map p136) before your final temple stop, 20 **Wat Mixai** (p134), with its Bangkok-style *sĭm* and heavy gates, flanked by two *nyak* (guardian giants).

Continue east on Th Setthathirath until you reach the Nam Phu fountain again and turn right down Th Pangkham, then right again on Th Fa Ngoum where you will find the 21 **Chokdee Cafe** (p150), a homely little spot with an incredible number of Belgian beers to slake your well-earned thirst.

breakfast. Air-con rooms start at 100,000K and internet access is available for 10,000K per hour, as well as free wi-fi.

Sport Guesthouse
GUESTHOUSE $

(Map p136; 021-241352; sportguesthouse. sg@hotmail.com; Th François Ngin; with fan/ air-con r 80,000/100,000K, tr 120,000/150,000K;) Formerly the Lao Youth Inn; rooms here are a little boxy but fragrant, with spotless bathrooms and polished tiled floors, and what the place lacks in refinement it makes up for in amenities, including a decent cafe and juice bar, ticketing services, and bicycle and motorbike hire (10,000/60,000K).

Lucky Backpacker
HOSTEL $

(Map p136; 021-255636; Th Manthatourath; dm/d 40,000/140,000K;) A clean new joint, with spacious dorms, decent showers and a private double room with air-con but no window. Beds have lockers underneath but no locks. Friendly management.

★ LV City Riverine Hotel
HOTEL $$

(Map p136; 021-214643; www.lvcitylaos.com; 48 Th Fa Ngoum; r incl breakfast 220,000-390,000K;) Not to be confused with various other 'city' hotels in the capital, the LV has a great location near the riverfront. Rooms are spacious and well appointed, although it is worth the ego-massage of VIP just for the four-poster bed and extra space. Rooms include laundry, so will be even better value if you are returning from a jungle trek.

★ Hotel Khamvongsa
HOTEL $$

(Map p136; 021-218415; www.hotelkhamvongsa. com; Th Khounboulom; s/d/tr incl breakfast US$40/60/80;) Lovely French-era building lovingly reincarnated as a welcoming boutique hotel; think belle époque touches like glass tear lightshades, chess-tiled floors, and softly lit simple rooms with two-poster beds, wood floors and Indo-chic decor. Rooms on the 3rd and 4th floors have masterful views. There's also a restful courtyard and restaurant. Breakfast is a treat.

Vientiane Garden Hotel
HOTEL $$

(Map p136; 021-241964; http://vientianegarden hotel.com; 56 Th Sihom; r incl breakfast US$40-80;) Something of a flashpacker hotel amid an emerging strip of backpacker hostels, this is a little oasis that's not immediately apparent from the understated entrance. Venture inside to find a hidden courtyard pool and leafy garden that are perfect places

to cool down on a hot day. Upstairs rooms command a slight premium.

Lani's House by the Pond
GUESTHOUSE $$

(Map p136; 021-215639; www.lanishouse-bythe ponds.com; Th Setthathirath; s/d/ste US$45/65/80;) Down a narrow side street leading to a temple, this white art deco–accented villa evokes Indochina with its authentic Parisien chandeliers, antique furniture, lobby peppered with stunning images of old Laos, and coy carp in an ornamental pool. It's hard to believe you're in the city centre. Huge rooms with shabby-chic armoire, cable TV and fridge. Tasteful.

Vayakorn Inn
HOTEL $$

(Map p136; 021-215348; www.vayakorn.biz; 19 Th Hèngbounnoy; r US$35;) On a quiet street just off increasingly hectic Th Setthathirath, this tasteful, peaceful hotel is great value given its chandeliered lobby festooned in handicrafts and hardwood floors. Generously sized rooms are impeccably clean, with crisp linen, choice art, flat-screen TVs, desks and modern bathrooms. The rooms on the upper floors have excellent city views.

Manorom Boutique Hotel
BOUTIQUE HOTEL $$

(Map p136; 021-250748; manoromboutique hotel@hotmail.com; Th Hèngbounnoy; r US$35-45;) Looming large over a small *soi* (lane) in the centre of town, this hotel offers exceptional value. The stylish lobby sets the tone for a well-presented Lao hospitality experience including polished wood floors, silk runners and tasteful handicrafts. This is verging on the budget boutique.

Phonepaseuth Guest House
GUESTHOUSE $$

(Map p136; 021-212263; 97 Th Pangkham; r from US$28;) This old, trusty place near Nam Phu is still going strong thanks to cool, spacious rooms, clean en suites, cable TV, wi-fi and fresh walls and linen. Opt for rooms facing the road if you want your own little balcony. Some nice interior touches include Hmong bed runners and wall-mounted shell lampshades.

Souphaphone Guesthouse
GUESTHOUSE $$

(Map p136; 021-261468; www.souphaphone. net; off Th François Ngin; r 170,000-200,000K;) A very tidy and house-proud guesthouse with 22 rooms, some with windows but all with fresh linen, cool tiled floors and pristine walls. Rooms also include attached bathroom, fridge, wi-fi and TV. Understandably, given the price point, it's often full.

Salana Boutique Hotel   BOUTIQUE HOTEL **$$$**
(Map p136; ☎021-254254; www.salanaboutique.
com; Th Chao Anou; standard/deluxe r US$135/145,
ste from US$200; ☯❊☍) Highly polished,
wood-flavoured Salana fuses Lao and contem-
porary styles to add a sleek dimension to Vien-
tiane's accommodation scene. Rooms have
wood floors, ethnically inspired bed runners,
soft lighting, flat-screen TVs, safety deposit
boxes, rain showers and nice little touches in-
cluding frangipani flowers scattered around.
Some rooms have fantastic temple views.

Dhavara Boutique Hotel   BOUTIQUE HOTEL **$$$**
(Map p136; ☎021-222238; www.dhavarahotel.
com; 25 Th Manthatourath; r US$180-600;
☯❊@☍) An opulent neoclassical hotel, the
Dhavara offers some of the smartest rooms
in the capital. Features include marble-clad
bathrooms and parquet floors, as well as
more predictable touches such as free wi-fi
and a well-stocked minibar.

Le Luxe Boutique Hotel   BOUTIQUE HOTEL **$$$**
(Map p136; ☎021-255777; www.leluxehotel.com;
Th Fa Ngoum; r US$68-148; ☯❊☍) Le Luxe Bou-
tique does what it says on the tin and com-
bines a boutique hotel with some affordable
luxe. With just 15 rooms, it is an intimate
place to stay and the attention to detail is evi-
dent in every aspect. Good location in a quiet
backstreet near the river.

🏨 Thanon Samsenthai &
Around

Syri 1 Guest House   GUESTHOUSE **$**
(Map p136; ☎021-212682; Th Saigon; r 50,000-
150,000K; ❊@☍) Syri sits on a quiet street
and has been a traveller fave for many years,
and with good reason: generously sized
rooms (with air-con or fan, en suite or shared
bathroom), recesses to chill, a DVD lounge,
bikes for rent, and tailored bike tours of the
city. And 100% friendly.

Avalon B & B   B&B **$**
(Map p136; ☎030-5828801; avalonbed@gmail.
com; Th Phanompenh; dm 50,000-70,000K, r
200,000-240,000K, all incl breakfast; ☯❊☍) A
popular little guesthouse on the backstreets
near the national stadium, with 10-bed dorms
available, including female-only options. The
rooms are spacious and well appointed and
all rates include a basic breakfast downstairs.
Part of a growing Avalon empire that in-
cludes hotels in Vientiane and Savannakhet.

Champa Garden Hotel   BOUTIQUE HOTEL **$$**
(Map p136; ☎020-91585858; http://champa
gardenhotel.com; off Th François Ngin; r US$50-60;
☯❊☍☎) Tucked away just off popular Th
François Ngin, this is a delightful all-wooden
boutique hotel set around a courtyard
swimming pool. Despite its central location
in the capital, it is very peaceful and feels
more like a Luang Prabang–style hideaway.
Rooms include flat-screen TV and a safety
deposit box.

Day Inn Hotel   HOTEL **$$**
(Map p136; ☎021-222985; dayinn@laopdr.com;
59/3 Th Pangkham; s/d/tr incl breakfast
500,000/600,000/900,000K; ☯❊@☍) This
hotel is something of a business-traveller's
choice, and from its vanilla exterior to its
restaurant serving up Asian fusion cuisine,
it's easy to understand why. It has 32 rooms,
although some are starting to show their age,
with large beds, bureau, flat-screen TVs, air-
con and no-nonsense international-style de-
cor. There's also free airport pick-up.

City Inn   HOTEL **$$**
(Map p136; ☎021-281333; www.cityinnvientiane.
com; Th Pangkham; r incl breakfast 600,000-
1,000,000K; ☯❊@☍) As well as offering long-
term apartment stays, this place is one of the
smarter midrange biz-boutique hotels in town.
The contemporary lobby sets the tone for a
smooth stay with the rooms exhibiting some
artsy flourishes, as well as amenities galore.

★Settha Palace Hotel   HOTEL **$$$**
(Map p136; ☎021-217581; www.setthapalace.com;
6 Th Pangkham; r standard/deluxe US$157/185, ste
US$330; ☯❊@☍☎) This stately building, set
in grounds ablaze with flowers, is as graceful
as it is relaxing. Fans whirr over marble floors
so polished you can see your champagne glass
in them, while service is impeccable. Rooms,
particularly the larger deluxe ones, are also
enchanting, with four-poster beds, desks and
wood floors.

Lao Plaza Hotel   HOTEL **$$$**
(Map p136; ☎021-218800; www.laoplazahotel.
com; 63 Th Samsènethai; s/d US$190/215, ste
US$380, all incl breakfast; ☯❊☍☎) A strong
choice for business travellers, this bland-
ly designed marbled edifice boasts a vast
international-style lobby and comfy rooms.
Expect wi-fi, fridges, cable TV, bath-tubs and
silk bedheads. There's also a great pool here
(120,000K for nonguests) that's perfect for
sun basking and escaping the heat.

Mekong Riverfront & Around

★ Mixay Paradise Guesthouse
GUESTHOUSE $

(Map p136; ☎021-254223; laomixayparadise@yahoo.com; Th François Ngin; s/d with fan & shared bathroom 90,000/100,000K, r with air-con & bathroom 130,000-150,000K; ❄❋☎) Mixay Paradise has 50 rooms with pastel-coloured walls, some of which have balconies, bathrooms and air-con. Spotless floors, a lovely lobby cafe with lime-green walls and a lift. One of the best, most hygienic budget options in the city. Safety deposit lockers cost 50,000K.

Villa Manoly
GUESTHOUSE $$

(Map p132; ☎021-218907; www.villa-manoly.com; off Th Fa Ngoum; r incl breakfast US$35-45; ❄❋☎☼) This beautifully antiquated house, in a garden swimming in mature plants and frangipani flowers, feels like the sort of place John le Carré might ensconce himself in to write a novel, especially given its collection of vintage telephones and typewriters. Nicely furnished rooms with wood floors, air-con, en suites and bedside lamps look on to a delightful pool. It's like a boutique homestay.

Auberge Sala Inpeng
GUESTHOUSE $$

(Map p136; ☎021-242021; www.salalao.com; Th In Paeng; r incl breakfast US$25-50; ❄❋☎) Unlike anything else in the city, this vernal oasis of wood cabanas and a handsome traditional Laotian house is set in gardens spilling with tamarind and *champa* flowers. The grander rooms display rustic chic with bathrooms and air-con. And although the cheaper cabanas are small, they don't lack atmosphere.

Best Western Vientiane
HOTEL $$

(Map p136; ☎021-216909; www.bestwestern vientiane.com; 2-12 Th François Ngin; s/d incl breakfast US$75/85; ❄❋@☎☼) This gleaming hotel is a welcoming spot if you're looking for a cool, plush lobby, calm garden with pool, gym and a general sense of upscale style. Rooms, of which there are 44, are equally swanky with wood floors, snow-white linen and quality fittings.

Lao Silk Hotel
GUESTHOUSE $$

(Map p136; ☎021-213976; www.laosilkhotel.com; Th François Ngin; r 189,000-328,000K; ❄❋☎) All 20 rooms in this sleek hotel are fragrantly fresh and well attired in stylish decor and bijou en suites. While rooms might be a little small for a professional wrestler, the wi-fi, cable TV, air-con and general plushness make this one a winner. Downstairs is a relaxing cafe-bar to work or read in.

Hotel Beau Rivage Mekong
GUESTHOUSE $$

(Map p132; ☎021-243375; www.hbrm.com; Th Fa Ngoum; r incl breakfast US$47-59; ❄❋☎) A little less romantic from the outside since the dirt track running parallel with the river was paved and denuded of trees, this pink boutique hotel still packs a punch, with superb rooms decked in bamboo screens, waffled bedspreads, high ceilings and a pleasant garden out back. All rooms are named after Lao provinces.

Intercity Hotel
HOTEL $$

(Map p136; ☎021-242843; 24-25 Th Fa Ngoum; s/d/ste incl breakfast US$40/60/80; ❋@☎) While unprepossessing and dust-ridden from its river-facing exterior, within its wine-dark walls, however, is a world of mosaic floors and 46 rooms boasting traditional art and fine handicrafts. The deluxe rooms are *far* superior with romantic Mekong views while the standards in comparison are forgettable.

Lao Orchid Hotel
HOTEL $$

(Map p136; ☎021-264134; www.lao-orchid-hotel.com; Th Chao Anou; d/ste incl breakfast 615,000/945,000K; ❋☎) An attractive, modern hotel with a swish lobby and chilled verandah cafe with a great view of the road. There are 32 welcoming rooms here with varnished wood floors, mint-fresh linen, desks, balconies, fridges and Indochinese-style furniture. Ask for a room at the front to take in the Mekong views. Good value.

★ Ansara Hôtel
BOUTIQUE HOTEL $$$

(Map p136; ☎021-213514; www.ansarahotel.com; off Th Fa Ngoum; r US$125-160, ste US$190-330, all incl breakfast; ❄❋@☎) Achingly beautiful Ansara is housed in a pair of colonial-chic French villas with a heavy whiff of old Indochina. There are 28 rooms set across the property, including four suites, and all are lovely, offering wooden floor, balcony, TV, bath and refined decorations. Its alfresco dining terrace is as refined as its Gallic cuisine.

★ S Park Design Hotel
BOUTIQUE HOTEL $$$

(Map p132; ☎021-256339; www.sparkdesignhotel.com; 40 Th Dongnasok; r US$70-120; ❄❋@☎☼) This place has some serious style on the inside. The reception will get you hooked, with a chopped-up classic Mercedes for a front desk and a vintage Vespa. It features 64 rooms, all with separated toilet.

Around Vientiane

Villa Lao
GUESTHOUSE $$
(Map p132; ☎020-22217588; www.villalaos.com; off Th Nong Douang; r US$20-80; ☀❀@🛜) A garden oasis about 1km west of town, Villa Lao sprawls with ferns and palms, and has 23 delightful, rustic rooms bursting with character: think wood stilts, white walls, mosquito nets and a charming communal balcony and lounge. The cheapest rooms are bare, fan-cooled and have shared bathrooms; however, all rooms are large.

★Mandala Boutique Hotel
BOUTIQUE HOTEL $$$
(Map p132; ☎021-214493; www.mandalahotel. asia; off Th Fa Ngoum; r incl breakfast US$75-100; ☀❀@🛜) This super chic boutique hotel offers the city's brightest, coolest accommodation (we're talking *Wallpaper* rather than the Fonz). An old French villa built in the 1960s is its setting, and flashes of vivid colour and chichi flourishes such as lacquered granite floors, flat-screen TVs and dark-wood furniture blend perfectly with the aesthetic of its art-deco lines.

Green Park Boutique Hotel
BOUTIQUE HOTEL $$$
(Map p132; ☎021-264097; www.greenpark vientiane.com; 248 Th Khu Vieng; r incl breakfast US$150-450; ☀❀@🛜≋) A real urban oasis, this boutique hotel exudes calm and escapism from the moment you enter its dark-wood lobby and step into its lush garden abuzz with flowers and a sparkling pool. Rooms are super stylish and feature hardwood floors, capacious bathrooms, couches, safety deposit boxes and step-in mosquito nets.

✗ Eating

For such a small capital city, Vientiane boasts a range of culinary options. The city has a wide range of global cuisine, including everything from falafel at an authentic Turkish restaurant to upscale Japanese and Korean barbecue. The streets that radiate off Th Setthathirath are vivid with smells and steam as old-school restaurants serve up fine Italian and French fare in the choicest of surroundings.

Lao food has in recent years enjoyed a real contemporary makeover with well-executed traditional dishes given a modern twist in 21st-century-style restaurants. If it's comfort food you seek, look no further than the bakeries left by the French footprint, for the city is famous for its fresh-baked baguettes and crispy croissants, with full-bodied coffee that could make the Seine glow green with envy.

For all its Gallic refinement Vientiane is equally informal; cheap food on the hop can be grabbed from street vendors dotted around the old quarter, and the impromptu braziers that fire up grilled chicken and Mekong fish on skewers. And don't miss the chance to wander through the redolent witch's broth that is Chinatown on Th Hengboun.

✗ Thanon Setthathirath & Nam Phu

★Naked Espresso
CAFE $
(Map p136; ☎020-56222269; Th Manthatourath; dishes 15,000-40,000K; ☺7am-5pm; ❀🛜) One of the best-loved coffee shops in Vientiane, Naked specialises in home-grown Lao coffee and selected gourmet imports from places as diverse as Ethiopia and Indonesia. Light meals are also available, including salads and wraps, plus some impressive homemade cakes.

JoMa Bakery Café
BAKERY $
(Map p136; Th Setthathirath; mains 20,000-50,000K; ☺7am-9pm Mon-Sat; ❀🛜) Vientiane's most contemporary bakery has a friendly, air-con-chilled atmosphere and a cornucopia of lush salads (30,000K) and bespoke subs and bagels – choose from salami, ham, salmon, chicken, cheese and salad fillings. It also serves brownies, cake and delicious yoghurt. Comfy couches, free wi-fi, unfailing cleanliness and superb staff.

Little Hanoi
VIETNAMESE $
(Map p136; Th Fa Ngoum; mains 30,000-60,000K; ☺9am-11.30pm; ❀🛜) This mercifully chilled restaurant on the waterfront is peaceful and shadowy, with wall-mounted antique drums and soft lighting that transports you to the artist quarter of its eponymous city. The menu is varied and includes Hanoi *pho* (noodle soup), spring rolls, papaya salad and fried squid in celery.

Pricco Cafe
CAFE $
(Map p136; ☎021-215889; Th Nokèokoummane; mains 25,000-50,000K; ☺8am-8pm; ❀🛜) A popular cafe not far from the Mekong River, Pricco offers reliable comfort food, including toasted baguettes, warm ciabatta creations and open sandwiches with little treats like goat's cheese and walnuts or smoked salmon and cream cheese. Indulgent desserts, fresh fruit shakes and creative coffees complete the picture.

VIENTIANE, VANG VIENG & AROUND VIENTIANE

Croissant d'Or

BAKERY $

(Map p136; ☑ 021-223741; 96/1 Th Nokèokoummane; salads 20,000-40,000K; ☺6.30am-9pm; ❄️📶) This simple bakery has a modest interior of umbrella-shaded lights and a cold counter of ham, salami, cheeses and salads. Its coffee packs a punch and the baguettes are fluffy.

Taj Mahal Restaurant

INDIAN $

(Map p136; off Th Setthathirath; meals 25,000-60,000K; ☺10am-10.30pm Mon-Sat, 4-10.30pm Sun; ❄️📶📄) Hidden down a side-street opposite the back of the Lao National Culture Hall, this unpretentious earthy joint dishes up fresh and lively curries (tasty chicken masala) and melt-in-your mouth naan. Portions are generous and you can sit semi alfresco. There's a good vegie selection, too (20 dishes).

iPho

VIETNAMESE $

(Map p136; ☑ 030-9581163; off Th Setthathirath; mains 20,000-40,000K; ☺7am-9pm; ❄️📶) This hole-in-the-wall Vietnamese eatery specialises in the eponymous *pho*, with various meat offerings. Other dishes include regional Vietnamese specialties like *bo bun Hue* (spicy beef noodle soup) and broken-rice dishes.

Phimphone Market

MARKET $

(Map p136; 94/6 Th Setthathirath; ☺7am-9pm Mon-Sat; ❄️📶) This self-catering oasis stocks everything from gleaming fresh veg, to ice cream, imported salami, bread, biscuits and chocolate, as well as Western toiletries and magazines. It also stocks Hobo maps of the city. It's located in the same building as Benoni Café.

★Le Banneton

BAKERY $$

(Map p136; Th Nokèokoummane; breakfast 45,000K; ☺7am-9pm; ❄️📶) Get here early before the country's best croissants run out. The simple interior makes for a nice place to read a paper over a tart, salad, panini or omelette, or you can sit outside on the small terrace. Tasty breakfasts and home-made marmalade and jam.

★Makphet Restaurant

LAOTIAN $$

(Map p136; ☑ 021-260587; makphet-restaurant.org; Th In Paeng; mains 40,000-82,000K; ☺11am-10.30pm; ❄️📶📄) 🖋 Makphet, managed by Friends International (www.friends-international.org), helps disadvantaged kids build a future as chefs and waiters. The stunning villa sits in lush gardens, lit with fairy-lights at night. The interior is no less inviting, the service a cut above average, and the cuisine superb, with

Lao fare like green papaya salad with aquatic beetle or buffalo *láhp*. It's a romantic spot.

Acqua

ITALIAN $$

(Map p136; ☑ 021-255466; www.acqua.la; 78 Th François Ngin; mains 40,000-200,000K, lunch buffet 98,000K; ☺11am-10pm; ❄️📶) Considered by many residents to be the finest Italian restaurant in the city. The 98,000K lunch buffet is justifiably popular and includes a choice of entrées. Indulgent mains include sockeye-salmon ravioli and some sumptuous imported cuts from land and sea. The owner also runs Vinoteca, a leading wine importer, so the Italian wine list is top notch.

Khop Chai Deu

ASIAN, FUSION $$

(Map p136; ☑ 021-251564; 54 Th Setthathirath; mains 25,000-90,000K; ☺8am-midnight; ❄️📶📄) In a remodelled colonial-era villa near Nam Phu, Khop Chai Deu has been a travellers' favourite for years because of its range of well-prepared Lao, Thai, Indian and assorted European fare. Upstairs is a new low-lit bar with slick urban swagger.

Benoni Café

ASIAN, FUSION $$

(Map p136; ☑ 021-213334; Th Setthathirath; mains 40,000-60,000K; ☺10am-6pm Mon-Sat; ❄️📶) A stylish place on Th Setthathirath, Benoni is only open till early evening, which seems to be making it even *more* popular. Come lunchtime its contemporary interior is packed with NGO and Lao urbanites. The menu is Asian-fusion-meets-Italian, and includes super-fresh snacks, salads and pasta dishes.

Amphone

LAOTIAN $$

(Map p136; 10/3 Th Wat Xieng Nyean; mains 35,000-100,000K, set menu 80,000K; ☺11am-10pm; ❄️📶) Featured on celebrity chef Anthony Bourdain's Discovery TV series, this upscale oasis of wood floors and salmon-coloured walls is refined and cool. Aside from an encyclopedic wine list, Amphone's menu replicates traditional Laotian dishes based on owner Mook's grandmother's creations. 'Luang Prabang sausage' and 'fish citronella' are but a couple.

Le Vendôme

FRENCH $$

(Map p136; 39 Th In Paeng; mains 40,000-90,000K; ☺5-10pm Tue-Sun; ❄️) Located behind a cascade of ivy, it's almost as if this vintage French restaurant is in hiding. The menu comprises very reasonably priced soufflés, pâtés, salads, wood-fired pizzas, terrines and steaks. The candlelit interior, peppered with vintage bull-fighting posters, is perfect for a romantic escape.

OODLES OF NOODLES

Noodles of all kinds are popular in Laos, and Vientiane has the country's greatest variety. The most popular noodle of all is undoubtedly *fĕr*, the local version of Vietnamese *pho*, served with beef or pork and accompanied, Lao-style, by a huge plate of fresh herbs and vegetables and a ridiculous amount of condiments. Also popular are *kòw ʉ̀ûn*, the thin rice noodles known as *kànŏm jeen* in Thailand, taken in Laos with a spicy curry-like broth or sometimes in a clear pork broth (*kòw ʉ̀ûn nâm jąaou*). There's also *kòw ʉ̀ęak sèn*, thick rice- and tapioca-flour noodles served in a slightly viscous broth with crispy deep-fried pork belly or chicken.

Other popular noodles include *mii* (traditional Chinese egg noodle), particularly prevalent in the unofficial Chinatown area bounded by Th Hengboun, Th Chao Anou, Th Khounboulom and the western end of Th Samsènethai, and *băn kŭan* (Lao for *bánh cuôn*), a freshly steamed rice noodle filled with minced pork, mushrooms and carrots, a Vietnamese speciality that is popular in Laos. Look for it in the mornings near the intersection of Th Chao Anou and Th Hengboun.

La Terrasse FRENCH $$
(Map p136; Th Nokèokoummane; mains 40,000-100,000K; ⊙11am-2pm & 6-10pm Mon-Sat; ❄🛜)
With its old-fashioned French ambience of white-topped tables and custard-cream interior, this is a good spot for well-executed Gallic cuisine. There's plenty of choice, including *steak au frites, steak Provencal,* boeuf bourguignon, pan-fried fish, quiche, soup and thin-crust pizza.

Osaka JAPANESE $$
(Map p136; ☏021-213352; Th Nokèokoummane; mains 30,000-80,000K; ⊙8am-10pm; ❄🛜) A lively hole-in-the-wall, with slatted chairs on a plant-filled verandah, cosy Osaka tempts you inside with its lipstick-red booths. Oodles of noodle variations, sashimi, vegie dishes, sushi and tempura.

Sputnik Burger BURGERS $$
(Map p136; ☏020-56386386; www.facebook.com/SputnikBurger; Th Setthathirath; mains 45,000-75,000K; ⊙11am-10pm; ❄🛜) A contemporary burger joint featuring great beef burgers with Swiss cheese, bacon, eggplant and many other additions and sauces. Salads and milkshakes, too. Exposed-brick walls, low lighting and a bisected VW bug outside – which serves as two little booths – make this a fun spot.

★**L'Adresse de Tinay** FRENCH $$$
(Map p136; ☏020-56913434; Wat Ongteu; mains 80,000-200,000K; ⊙5-10.30pm; ❄🛜) Alchemising an eclectic gastronomic landscape of snails and scrambled eggs, sea-bream fillet, beef tenderloin, rack of lamb and rosemary, plus to-die-for crème brûlée perfumed with Madagascan vanilla, Chef Tinay is one of the city's top chefs. Happy hour on bubbles and wine is from 5pm to 7pm daily. It's located behind the temple.

★**Pimentón** SPANISH $$$
(Map p136; ☏021-215506; www.pimentonrestaurant-vte.com; Th Nokèokoummane; mains 60,000-200,000K; set lunch 75,000K; ⊙11am-2.30pm & 5-10pm Mon-Sat; ❄🛜) Pimentón, with its high ceilings and sleek bar, is widely considered to be the best steak restaurant in the capital. Only the choicest cuts of sirloin, chateaubriand and rib-eye make it to its open grill. At lunch there's tapas: think imported *jamón ibérico* (a type of cured ham), *calamares* (squid) and charcuterie of cured meats.

★**Le Silapa** FRENCH $$$
(Map p136; ☏021-219689; 88 Th Setthathirath; mains 80,000-250,000K; set lunches 65,000-120,000K; ⊙11am-11pm; ❄🛜) Recently relocated Le Silapa is beautiful in its chichi whiteness complemented by the wood floors, raftered ceiling and birdcage lights. A contender for Vientiane's finest Gallic restaurant, it features favourites from foie gras to salads, and steaks to veal brains casserole. It's upstairs at the excellent iBeam bar. *Magnifique*, especially the excellent-value set lunches.

🍴 Thanon Samsènethai & Around

★**Kung's Cafe Lao** LAOTIAN $
(Map p132; ☏021-219101; near Ministry of Health, Phiawat Village; mains 12,000-20,000K; ⊙7am-4pm) Approaching cult status with Vientiane residents in the know, Kung's Cafe is hard to find, but well worth the extra effort. Affable Kung has decorated the local diner with

hanging gourds and has a simple and effective menu that is superb value. Try the sticky rice pancake or *phat Lao* and wash it down with a signature coffee and coconut.

Vieng Sawan
VIETNAMESE $

(Map p136; ☑ 021-213990; Th Hengboun; mains 20,000-50,000K; ⊗11am-10pm; 🐾) In the middle of Chinatown, Vieng Sawan is a bustling open-sided restaurant that offers a fun eating experience. It specialises in *năem néuang* (Vietnamese barbecued pork meatballs) and many varieties of *yáw* (spring rolls), usually sold in 'sets' *(sut)* with *khào pûn*, fresh lettuce leaves, mint, basil, various sauces for dipping, sliced carambola (starfruit) and green banana.

Han Ton Phai
LAOTIAN $

(Map p136; ☑ 021-252542; Th Pangkham; mains 10,000-20,000K; ⊗9am-10pm) An escape from carb-heavy bakeries, this Lao mainstay is earthy and authentic, its menu spanning pork *láhp* (spicy Lao-style salad) to *kôy pqa*, a chunky salad of freshwater fish and fresh herbs (10,000K to 20,000K). There's no English-language sign, so keep an eye open for the billboard that says 'traditional food'.

PVO
VIETNAMESE $

(Map p132; ☑ 021-454663; off Th Simeuang; mains 15,000-25,000K; ⊗6am-7pm Mon-Sat, to 2pm Sun; 🐾🖉) This fresh, no-frills Vietnamese-run eatery is one of the better places in town to grab lunch, and in addition to several tasty spring-roll-based Vietnamese dishes, PVO does some of the best *khào jĩi pá-tê* (baguettes with liver pâté, veg and cream cheese, dripping with sweet chilli sauce) in town.

That Dam Noodle
LAOTIAN $

(Map p136; ☑ 021-214441; mains 15,000-30,000K; ⊗8.30am-2pm) Hidden away down a side street near That Dam, this place is run by an affable Lao chef who is clearly proud of his noodle-soup creations. Duck is a speciality, but chicken, pork and fish variations are also available. Look out for the larger-than-life sign of the owner with a steaming bowl of soup.

Jamil Zahid Punjab Restaurant
PAKISTANI $

(Map p136; ☑ 020-58871133; Ban Haysoke; mains 25,000-50,000K; ⊗10am-10pm; 🐾🖉) Run by the irrepressible Jamil, who likes to take photographs of all his customers to post on Facebook (although there's is no offence taken if you decline the opportunity to be immortalised). The predominantly Pakistani

and North Indian menu is excellent and good value, but the place is a little hard to find as it's tucked away down an alley.

Noy's Fruit Heaven
CAFE $

(Map p136; Th Hengboun; mains 20,000-30,000K; ⊗7am-9pm; 🐾🖾) Noy's is a homely, colourful juice bar with Chinese paper lanterns hanging from the ceiling. Stop in to pick up a few of your 'five a day' or decimate your hangover with one of its dragonfruit, coconut, mango, or tomato-juice shakes (10,000K). It also turns out super fresh fruit salads and burgers, and rents bikes (10,000K).

Temple View Cafe
CAFE $

(Map p136; ☑ 021-262359; mains 19,000-89,000K; ⊗10am-5pm; 🐾🖾) A popular bolthole for those in the know, this cafe offers a temple view of Wat Haysoke. The menu is very affordable and includes a mix of light Lao bites and general cafe fare of salads and wraps. It's a funky little spot with the added bonus of air-con on a hot day.

Baguette & Pâté Vendor
STREET FOOD $

(Map p136; Th Samsènethai; half/whole baguette 11,000/22,000K; ⊗6am-8pm) Serves great *khào jĩi pá-tê*. There's no English-language sign here, but the stall is directly on the corner of Th Pangkham and Th Samsènethai.

Once Upon a Time
CAFE $

(Map p132; ☑ 030-5809988; Th Dong Palan; mains 20,000-40,000K; ⊗7am-6pm; 🐾🖾) Feed your inner princess with a trip to this fairy-tale-themed cafe in the Phonthan part of town. The owner-barista here has won multiple awards in Thailand and the coffee will definitely deliver a caffeine fix. The breakfasts are a cut above the guesthouse and budget-hotel offerings.

★ Lao Kitchen
LAOTIAN $$

(Map p136; ☑ 021-254332; www.lao-kitchen.com; Th Hengboun; mains 40,000-70,000K; ⊗11am-10pm; 🐾🖾🖉) This superb contemporary Lao restaurant is unfailingly creative in its execution of trad-Lao dishes. Colourful walls, alt tunes and decent service complement a menu spanning stews, Luang Prabang sausage, *láhp* variations, stir-fried morning glory (water spinach), spring rolls, Mekong fish soup and palate-friendly sorbets. Choose the level of spice with chilli gradings of one to three.

La Cag du Coq
FRENCH $$

(Map p136; ☑ 020-54676065; off Th Hengboun; mains 40,000-100,000K; ⊗11am-11pm; 🐾) Named after the fighting-cock cages that ornately decorate the garden, this is a classic French restaurant offering duck confit, buffalo fillet and *coquilles* San-Jacques (angel-hair-encrusted scallops in this case). Popular weekend brunch, plus the owner is known for his penchant for big-screen rugby.

Korean Restaurant
KOREAN $$

(Map p136; ☑020-22087080; Th Hengboun; mains 30,000-180,000K; ☺9am-11pm; ❄️🛜) Lacklustre name aside, this Korean-run place is great for sampling what is currently the most popular foreign cuisine in Southeast Asia. Most locals go directly for the Korean barbecue (80,000K), but we liked the kimchi stew (30,000K), served Korean-style with heaps of side dishes.

Xayoh
STEAK $$

(Map p136; ☑021-261777; www.inthira.com; mains 40,000-800,000K; ☺7am-10pm; ❄️🛜) One of the more popular steakhouses thanks to its hugely tasty Japanese Kobe steak: soaked in beer it's massaged daily for 30 days before it arrives impossibly tenderised on your plate. At US$100 it's not cheap but for a special occasion, it may be the best steak you ever taste.

Pizza Da Roby (PDR)
ITALIAN $$

(Map p132; ☑020-59989926; mains 30,000-90,000K; ☺11am-2.30pm & 5.30-10.30pm; 🛜) Paying homage to its location in Laos People's Democratic Republic (PDR), Pizza Da Roby turns out some of the best oven-baked pizzas in the country. Choose from a greatest-hits combination of toppings, pizza by the slice or a luscious lasagne, and follow up with a caffeine kick from the homemade tiramisu.

Otafuku
JAPANESE $$

(Map p136; ☑020-55518561; Th Phanompenh; mains 25,000-75,000K; ☺10am-9.30pm; ❄️🛜🖊️) This Japanese restaurant supports the work of international NGO IV-Japan in educating the underprivileged children of Laos, so dining here is for a good cause. It's also good for your wallet, as this is some of the best-value Japanese food in Laos.

Suntara Restaurant
INTERNATIONAL $$

(Map p132; ☑021-261165; Vientiane New World; mains 30,000-90,000K; ☺7am-midnight; ❄️🛜) Part of the expansive Inthira group, this was one of the first restaurants to open in the new Vientiane New World shophouse development on the Mekong River. Occupying a grand corner building, it offers a panoramic menu of world food, including traditional Lao dishes, popular international favourites and barbecued meats.

Bistrot 22
FRENCH $$$

(Map p136; ☑020-55527286; Th Samsènethai; mains 65,000-250,000K; ☺11.30am-2pm & 6-10pm; ❄️🛜) Moved a little further out of the centre to a less bubbly locale, Bistrot 22 is nonetheless enjoying great reviews for Chef Philippe's lustrous cuisine, with dishes like pear salad, deep-fried apple and camembert salad, tender steaks and cauliflower soup.

✖️ Mekong Riverfront & Around

Khambang Lao Food Restaurant
LAOTIAN $

(Map p136; ☑021-217198; 97/2 Th Khounboulom; mains 10,000-70,000K; ☺10.30am-3pm & 5-9pm; 🛜) The Lao food in this powder-blue joint, located a little up from the river, is worth the wait. Expect fresh grub so spicy it leaves a zingy footprint on your palate. Delicious *láhp*, roasted Mekong fish, fried frogs' legs; *âw lám,* described on the menu as 'spicy beef stew', and tasty Luang Prabang–style sausage.

Common Ground Café
MEXICAN $

(Map p136; ☑020-78727183; Th Chao Anou; mains 25,000-40,000K; ☺7am-8pm Mon-Sat; ❄️🛜🖊️🧒) It's air-con cool in this family-friendly Mexican cafe. Sofas to read on, a cold-selection counter boasting wraps, quesadillas, falafel, salads and homemade cookies. Best of all though, if you've got kids, is the enclosed shaded play area out back with a slide and climbing frame.

Han Sam Euay Nong
LAOTIAN $

(Map p136; Th Chao Anou; mains 8000-20,000K; ☺8am-7pm) Cheap and tidy, this busy family-run restaurant features tasty must-have dishes like *năem khào* (crispy balls of deep-fried rice and sour pork sausage shredded into a salad-like dish) and the delicious *khào pûn nâm jqew* (thin rice noodles served in a pork broth with pork, bamboo and herbs). The restaurant is unmarked and is located directly adjacent to the Lao Orchid Hotel.

La Signature
FRENCH $$

(Map p136; ☑021-213523; www.ansarahotel. com; Ansara Hôtel; set menu 95,000K; ☺11.30am-2.30pm & 5.30-10.30pm; ❄️🛜) With jazz drifting onto the fan-cooled terrace of glass-topped wicker tables (and upstairs in the ochre-hued restaurant), La Signature is perfect for throwing on your smart clothes and taking a romantic supper. Pan-fried salmon with blue cheese, lobster, roast lamb and thyme – these are just a few of the delights awaiting you in this beautiful French villa.

Istanbul
TURKISH $$

(Map p136; ☑020-77978190; Th François Ngin; mains 40,000-100,000K; ☺9.30am-10.30pm; ❋🛜) An authentic slice of Istanbul, this welcoming place has doner and shish kebabs, meatballs, hummus and falafel. Try the Iskender kebab: grilled beef with pepper sauce, yoghurt and green chilli. All meats are fully marinated and the supercharged Turkish coffee will put a spring in your step.

✕ Around Vientiane

★ Doi Ka Noi
LAOTIAN $

(Map p132; ☑020-55898959; 424 Th Sisavangvong; mains 25,000-50,000K; ☺7am-2.30pm; 🛜) An authentic Lao restaurant near That Luang, this is the place to spice up your life. The menu changes almost daily and focuses on home recipes and seasonal ingredients. Sample dishes include fish curry with hummingbird-tree flowers and bamboo curry with mushrooms.

Cafe Nomad
CAFE $

(Map p132; Th Phonsay; mains 25,000-50,000K; ☺8am-7pm Mon-Fri, to 6pm Sat & Sun; ❋🛜) Right near the Thai consulate, this little gem has original artwork on the mustard-coloured walls, whirring fans, various delicious panini and perhaps the best brownies in town. Flavoursome coffee and friendly staff.

Paradice
FRENCH $

(Map p136; ☑021-312836; Th Lan Xang; mains 35,000-50,000K; ☺11am-7pm Mon-Sat; 🛜) On the grounds of the Institut Français, this airy, comfortable cafe is a real oasis in which to sit and read with a coffee (and quick wi-fi). There's French news on the tube and a range of sandwiches and cakes to keep you quiet. Don't miss the delicious homemade ice creams and chocolates.

Ban Anou Night Market
LAOTIAN $

(Map p136; meals 10,000-20,000K; ☺5-10pm) Setting up on a small street off the north end of Th Chao Anou every evening, this atmospheric open-air market dishes up Lao cuisine, from grilled meats to chilli-based dips with vegetables and sticky rice.

★ Senglao Cafe
FUSION $$

(Map p132; ☑030-5880588; mains 30,000-300,000K; ☺11am-10pm Mon-Sat; ❋🛜) Named after a now-defunct cinema in the centre of town, this contemporary restaurant has a cinematic theme and restored leather chairs from the old movie hall. The fusion menu is ambitious but executed with some panache and includes everything from fusion squid-ink pasta with scallops to stone-baked pizzas. Films are shown in the garden at weekends.

Delhi Durbar
INDIAN $$

(Map p132; ☑021-410013; www.delhidurbarlaos.com; Th Phonsay; mains 25,000-90,000K; ☺11am-2.30pm & 6-10.30pm; ❋🛜✎) One of the smarter Indian restauarants in town, with a menu that includes chicken, mutton and seafood classics, plus a generous selection of vegetarian dishes. A full spread with a main, side, rice and breads will set you back about 100,000K.

🍺 Drinking & Nightlife

Vientiane is no longer the illicit pleasure palace it once was. Nowadays, brothels are strictly prohibited and Beerlao has replaced opium as the nightly drug of choice. Most of the bars, restaurants and discos close by 11.30pm or midnight, apart from a few late-night stragglers.

DJs have only recently caught on in Vientiane. Karaoke is popular, as are live-music performances of international songs or Thai classics.

★ Spirit House
COCKTAIL BAR

(Map p132; ☑021-262530; Th Fa Ngoum; cocktails 40,000-60,000K; ☺7am-11pm; 🛜) This traditional Lao house facing the Mekong has a well-stocked bar with enough cocktails on the menu to keep a roué rolling along. A chilled soundtrack complements the dark woods and comfy couches of its stylish interior. Hit the happy hours from 5pm to 7pm.

★ Bor Pen Yang
BAR

(Map p136; ☑020-27873965; Th Fa Ngoum; ☺10am-midnight; 🛜) Overlooking mother Mekong, a cast of locals, expats, bar girls and travellers assembles at this tin-roofed, wood-raftered watering hole to gaze at the sunset over nearby Thailand. Western tunes, pool tables and a huge bar to drape yourself over, as well as international football and rugby on large flat-screen TVs.

Chokdee Cafe
BAR

(Map p136; ☑021-263847; www.chokdeecafe.com; Th Fa Ngoum; ☺7am-11pm; 🛜) A Belgian bar and restaurant on the riverfront, Chokdee offers one of the best selections of Belgian brews in Asia with around 70 varieties to sample. Keep the flag flying with a bucket of *moules* (mussels) and *frites* (French fries), with 20 original sauces available to douse them in.

Khop Chai Deu
BAR

(Map p136; ☑ 021-223022; www.inthira.com; Th Setthathirath; ☉ 7am-midnight) KCD boasts low-lit interiors and a sophisticated drinks list, plus activities like speed dating and women's arm wrestling. On the 3rd floor there's a super-slick bar with great views. A popular place for draught Beerlao, and there's plenty of good food to go with it.

Sea Sunset Bar
COCKTAIL BAR

(Map p132; ☑ 021-264193; Th Dong Palan; ☉ 10.30am-11.30pm; ☎) Set in the suburbs of popular Dong Palan, Sea Sunset Bar offers one of the most extensive cocktail menus in this neck of the woods. It also offers decent food, including popular burgers and a 65,000K buffet on Monday and Tuesday. Cocktails are 50% off during a generous happy hour on Saturdays.

@ Home
CLUB

(Map p132; ☑ 020-55444555; Th Souphanouvong; ☉ 9pm-1am) There are a few clubs on the road to the airport and the best known of the bunch is the heavy-duty techno club @ Home. Don't come expecting conversation as the volume is permanently set to 11, but the drinks flow and a young crowd dances until the DJ stops.

CCC Bar
BAR

(Map p136; ☑ 020-55448686; Th Souphanouvong; ☉ 7pm-late) The most popular gay bar in town, this place draws a convivial crowd to its small bar. It pushes it up a gear at weekends with a cabaret show and draws a mixed crowd from 1am as one of the only late, late places in the capital.

Le Trio
CAFE

(Map p136; ☑ 020-22553552; Th Setthathirath; ☉ 8am-4pm; ☎) Le Trio roasts its own coffee and is one of the top hang-outs for caffeine cravers in Vientiane. As well as original coffees, it also offers fragrant herbal teas, juices and blends, plus some creative cocktails and desserts.

Scorpion Wings
BAR

(☑ 030-5945367; Th Dongnasok; ☉ 5-11pm; ☎) A self-proclaimed dive bar run by a long-term American resident, this is the place for cheap drinks far from the madding crowd. Craft beers are available, but the signature dish is the scorpion wings – barbecued chicken wings that get progressively hotter until the sting kicks in.

TRADITIONAL MUSIC & DANCING

Six types of traditional Lao dance can be seen nightly from 7.30pm to 11pm in the **Lane Xang Hotel** (Map p136; ☑ 021-214100; www.lanexanghotel.com.la). The **Lao National Culture Hall** (Map p136; Th Samsènethai) also hosts similar performances on occasions, but with no publicly available schedule of events you'll need to keep a close eye on the *Vientiane Times* for announcements.

Highland Bar
BAR

(Map p132; ☑ 021-251206; Th Fa Ngoum; ☉ 11am-11pm; ☎) Located on a breezy stretch of the Mekong River to the west of the city centre, this bar is a great spot to catch your favourite sporting action, from rugby union to Aussie rules and everything in between. There is a solid bar menu and the drinks are usually flowing early evenings and all weekend.

Kong View
BAR

(Map p132; ☑ 021-520522; off Th Luang Prabang; ☉ 11am-midnight) The stylish balcony here, suspended over a quiet section of the Mekong, functions equally well as a beer garden or dinner destination (dishes 25,000K to 200,000K), and is a great spot for a sundowner on the way to or from the airport.

Jazzy Brick
BAR

(Map p136; ☑ 021-212489; Th Setthathirath; ☉ 7pm-late; ☎) With its stylish, exposed-brick interior adorned in old jazz posters, and Coltrane sliding through the low-lit atmosphere, this place is perfect for an upscale evening on the tiles. Occasional live Latin and bossa nova, and enough cocktails on the menu to keep a connoisseur on their toes.

☆ Entertainment

Cinema

Centre Culturel et de Coopération Linguistique
CINEMA

(French Cultural Centre; Map p136; ☑ 021-215764; www.ambafrance-laos.org; Th Lan Xang; entry free, cinema 10,000K; ☉ 9.30am-6.30pm Mon-Fri, to noon Sat) Dance, art exhibitions, literary discussions and live music all take place in this Gallic hive of cultural activity. As well as cult French films – shown weekends at 3pm (kids) and 6.30pm (adults) – the centre also offers French and Lao language lessons.

Live Music

Wind West
LIVE MUSIC

(Map p136; ☑021-265777; ⊙6pm-1am) A road-house-style bar and restaurant, Wind West has live Lao and Western rock music most nights. The music usually starts about 9pm and finishes around 1pm. Depending on the night it can be heaving, or completely dead, but the interior, hung with 10-gallon hats, antlers and wooden Native American statues, lends the place a folksy atmosphere.

Anou Cabaret
LIVE MUSIC

(Map p136; ☑021-213630; cnr Th Hengboun & Th Chao Anou; ⊙8pm-midnight) On the ground floor of the Anou Paradise Hotel, the cabaret has been swinging along here for years. It's a funny place, with old crooners and a palpable 1960s feel.

Performing Arts

Lao National Opera Theatre
THEATRE

(Map p136; ☑021-26000; Th Khounboulom; ⊙7-8.30pm Tue, Thu & Sat) This state-sponsored performance venue features a smorgasbord of Lao entertainment ranging from self-proclaimed 'Lao oldies' to Lao boxing and traditional performances of *Pha Lak Pha Lam,* the Lao version of the Indian epic the Ramayana.

National Circus
PERFORMING ARTS

(Hong Kanyasin; Map p132; Th Thong Khan Kham; ✈) The old 'Russian Circus' established in the 1980s is now known as Hong Kanyasin. It performs from time to time in this National Circus venue, in the north of town. It has mainly acrobatic performances plus clowns. Check for dates in the *Vientiane Times.*

🔒 Shopping

⭐ **T'Shop Lai Gallery** COSMETICS, HOMEWARES

(Map p136; ☑021-223178; www.laococo.com/tshoplai.htm; off Th In Paeng; ⊙8am-8pm Mon-Sat, 10am-6pm Sun) 🌿 Vientiane's finest shop. Imagine a melange of aromas: coconut, aloe vera, honey, frangipani and magnolia, all of them emanating from body oils, soaps, sprays, perfumes and lip balms, plus bangles, prints, fountain pens and more. These wonderful products are made with sustainable, locally sourced products by disadvantaged women who make up the Les Artisans Lao cooperative.

Carol Cassidy Lao Textiles
ARTS & CRAFTS

(Map p136; ☑021-212123; www.laotextiles.com; 84-86 Th Nokèokoummane; ⊙8am-noon & 2-5pm

TEXTILES & CLOTHING

Downtown Vientiane is littered with stores selling textiles. Th Nokèokoummane is the epicentre, but the city's main market, Talat Sao, is also a good place to buy fabrics. You'll find antiques as well as modern fabrics, plus utilitarian items such as shoulder bags (some artfully constructed around squares of antique fabric), cushions and pillows.

To see Lao weaving in action, seek out the weaving district of Ban Nong Buathong, northeast of the town centre in Muang Chanthabuli. About 20 families (many originally from Sam Neua in Hua Phan Province) live and work here, including a couple of households that sell textiles directly to the public.

Mon-Fri, 8am-noon Sat, or by appointment) Lao Textiles sells high-end contemporary, original-design fabrics inspired by generations-old Lao weaving patterns, motifs and techniques. The American designer, Carol Cassidy, employs Lao weavers who work out the back of the attractive old French-Lao house.

Night Market
MARKET

(Map p136; Th Fa Ngoum; ⊙6-10.30pm) Vientiane's night market lights up the riverfront with a selection of stalls hawking handicrafts and T-shirts. It's not quite the atmosphere of Luang Prabang's, but nonetheless a good place to browse and hone your haggling skills.

Dee Traditional Antique Textiles
ARTS & CRAFTS

(Map p136; ☑020-55519908; khamtanh44@hotmail.com; Th Setthathirath; ⊙8am-9pm) It might not look much from the outside but within this chilled shop, stuffed from floor to ceiling with an array of fine silk scarves and Akha tapestries, there are great bargains to be found. The best-value quality scarves on the block.

Indochina Handicrafts
ARTS & CRAFTS

(Map p136; ☑021-223528; Th Setthathirath; ⊙10am-7pm) Vientiane's version of the Old Curiosity Shop, this enchanting den of Buddha statuary sells antique Ho Chi Minh and Mao busts, Russian wristwatches, communist memorabilia, Matchbox cars, medals, snuff boxes and vintage serving trays. It's a visit that shouldn't be missed.

Oriental Bookshop
BOOKS

(Map p136; ☑021-215352; 121 Th Chao Anou; ⊘10am-8pm) Mr Ngo stocks a decent selection of second-hand novels, postcards and stamps, and also a comprehensive range of books on Lao ethnicity. Coffee and internet (5000K per hour) are also available.

Treasures of Asia
ART

(Map p136; ☑021-222236; 86/7 Th Setthathirath; ⊘noon-7pm Mon-Fri) This tiny gallery holds the original works of established Lao artists, many of whom are featured in the book *Lao Contemporary Art*, also available here.

Vins de France
WINE

(Map p136; ☑021-217700; 354 Th Samsènethai; ⊘8am-8pm) Vins de France (the sign says 'Baràvin') is one of the better French wine cellars in Southeast Asia. Even if you don't like wine, it's worth popping in for a look at a place so completely out of character with its surrounds. If you do like wine, the US$3 degustation might be a wise investment.

True Colour
ARTS & CRAFTS

(Map p136; ☑021-214410; Th Setthathirath; ⊘9am-8pm Mon-Sat) 🍃 This store sells a wide spectrum of hand-spun silk shawls and wall hangings, as well as vividly coloured Hmong handbags and pincushions. All products are made in the affiliated Houcy Hong Vocational Training Center for Women (p137), which offers daily weaving courses.

Talat Sao
MARKET

(Morning Market; Map p136; Th Lan Xang; ⊘7am-5pm) A once-memorable shopping experience has sadly undergone a facelift; two-thirds of its world of stalls selling opium pipes, jewellery and traditional antiques have been ripped down and replaced with a eunuch of a modern mall. The remaining building's fabric merchants are hanging by a thread.

Monument Books
BOOKS

(Map p136; 124 Th Nokèokoummane; ⊘9am-8pm Mon-Fri, to 6pm Sat & Sun) A great one-stop shop for glossy magazines and a tasteful range of modern classic novels, plus travel guides, thrillers and lush pictorials on Laos.

Satri Lao
GIFTS & SOUVENIRS

(Map p136; ☑021-244384; Th Setthathirath; ⊘9am-8pm Mon-Sat, 10am-7pm Sun) Set across three fragrant floors, this Aladdin's cave of an emporium hawks high-quality jewellery, Hmong handbags, pillowcases, chemises, Tintin lacquer paintings, Buddha statuary and a whole lot more. It's expensive, but perfect for some last-minute shopping.

Kanchana Boutique
ARTS & CRAFTS

(Map p136; ☑021-213467; 102 Th Chanthakoummane; ⊘8am-9pm Mon-Sat) This shop carries what is possibly the most upscale selection of Lao silk in town (the most expensive designs, some of which sell for several thousand US dollars, are kept in an adjacent room). The friendly owners can arrange a visit to their Lao Textile Museum (p134), as well as lessons in weaving and dyeing.

❶ Orientation

Vientiane curves along the Mekong River following a meandering northwest–southeast axis, with the central district of Muang Chanthabuli at the centre of the bend. Most of the government offices, hotels, restaurants and historic temples are located in Chanthabuli, near the river. Some old French colonial buildings and Vietnamese-Chinese shophouses remain, set alongside newer structures built according to the rather boxy social realist school of architecture.

Wattay International Airport is around 4km northwest of the centre. The Northern Bus Station, where long-distance services to points north begin and end, is about 2km northwest of the airport. The Southern Bus Station deals with most services heading south and is 9km northeast of the centre on Rte 13. The border with Thailand at the Thai-Lao Friendship Bridge is 19km southeast of the city.

Street signs are limited to major roads and the central, more touristy part of town. Where they do exist, the English and French designations vary (eg route, *rue*, road and avenue) but the Lao script always reads Thanon (Th). Therefore, when asking directions it's always best to just use Thanon.

The parallel Th Setthathirath (which is home to several famous temples) and Th Samsènethai are the main streets in central Vientiane. Heading northwest they both eventually lead to Th Luang Prabang and Rte 13 north. In the other direction they run perpendicular to and eventually cross Th Lan Xang, a major boulevard leading from the presidential palace past Talat Sao (Morning Market) to Patuxai (Victory Gate) and, after turning into Th Phon Kheng, to Rte 13 south and the Southern Bus Station.

The *meuang* of Vientiane are broken up into *bâan* (Ban), which are neighbourhoods or villages associated with local wats. Wattay International Airport, for example, is in Ban Wat Tai, the area in which Wat Tai is located.

ℹ️ Information

COURSES

The **Institut Français** (Map p136; ☎ 021-215764; www.centredelangue.org; Th Lan Xang; ⊙ 8.15am-6.15pm Mon-Fri, 9.30am-4.30pm Sat; 🛜) has French and Lao language classes (as well as a busy schedule of movies, musical and theatrical performances).

DANGERS & ANNOYANCES

By international standards Vientiane has a very low crime rate, but there's a small risk of getting mugged. Be especially careful around the BCEL Bank on the riverfront where bag-snatchers, usually a two-man team with a motorbike, have been known to strike; common sense should be an adequate defence. Violent crime against visitors is extremely rare, but watch out for commando ladyboys on Th Setthathirath close to midnight, as locals suggest they are very experienced at helping drunks part with their wallets.

Also stay off the city's roads during festivals, particularly Pi Mai (p139), when drunk-driving-related accidents skyrocket. Pick-pocketing also occurs more frequently then.

Call the **Tourist Police** (Map p136; ☎ 021-251128; Th Lan Xang) if you need to talk to an English-speaking police officer.

GAY & LESBIAN TRAVELLERS

While Lao culture is very tolerant of homosexuality, it's a pretty low-key scene compared to neighbouring Thailand. Vientiane is the most liberal city in the country, but it's also the political capital, and there are only a handful of gay venues in the city. Visit www.utopia-asia.com/laosvien.htm for Vientiane services and venues.

INTERNET ACCESS

Wi-fi is now available at most of Vientiane's guesthouses, hotels, cafes and restaurants.

There's a row of **internet cafes** (Map p136; per hour 6000K; ⊙ 9am-11pm) on the north side of Th Setthathirath between Nam Phu (the fountain) and Th Manthatourath. The **Oriental Bookshop** (Map p136; ☎ 021-215352; 121 Th Chao Anou; per hour 5000K; ⊙ 10am-8pm) offers several computers with internet access.

MAPS

Hobo Maps (www.hobomaps.com) has probably the best generally available map of the city. Pick up a copy at bookshops or Phimphone Market.

Midnight Mapper (☎ 020-58656994; esprit demer@hotmail.com) It might sound like an old Stones song but the Midnight Mapper, aka Don Duvall, has tirelessly mapped Laos over the last 10 years to produce the most in-depth, accurate GPS map available. This is a blessing for motorcyclists and cyclists alike who might otherwise get lost if heading off the beaten track (also see box, p160).

MEDIA

Laos' only English-language newspaper is the government-run *Vientiane Times*. Although state censored, it does, however, feature stories on Laos' commercial relations with China and other foreign countries, detailing mining and hydroelectric-power developments.

French-speakers should look for *Le Rénovateur*.

MEDICAL SERVICES

Vientiane's medical facilities can leave a lot to be desired, so for anything serious make a break for the border and the much more sophisticated hospitals in Thailand. **Aek Udon International Hospital** in Thailand can dispatch an ambulance to take you to Udon Thani. Less serious ailments can be dealt with in Vientiane.

Alliance International Medical Center (Map p132; ☎ 021-513095; www.aimclao.com; Th Luang Prabang) This hospital is fresh and clean, and treats basic ailments like broken bones and dispenses antibiotics.

Australian Embassy Clinic (Map p132; ☎ 021-353840; Th Tha Deua; ⊙ 8.30am-5pm Mon-Fri) For nationals of Australia, Britain, Canada, Papua New Guinea and New Zealand only. This clinic's Australian doctor treats minor problems by appointment; it doesn't have emergency facilities. Accepts cash or credit cards.

Centre Médical de L'Ambassade de France (French Embassy Medical Center; Map p132; ☎ 021-214150; cnr Th Khu Vieng & Th Simeuang; ⊙ 8.30am-noon & 4.30-7pm Mon, Tue, Thu & Fri, 1.30-5pm Wed, 9am-noon Sat) Open to all, but visits outside regular hours by appointment only.

International Clinic (Map p132; ☎ 021-214021; Th Fa Ngoum; ⊙ 24hr) Part of the Mahasot Hospital; probably the best place for not-too-complex emergencies. Some English-speaking doctors. Take ID and cash.

Poppy's Pharmacy & Beauty (Map p136; ☎ 030-9810108; Th Hengboun; ⊙ 8am-10pm) Bright and clean, this modern, well-stocked pharmacy is great for toiletries, cosmetics, sun cream, malaria pills (not Larium), and sleeping tablets for long bus journeys.

Setthathirat Hospital (☎ 021-351156) Thanks to a recent overhaul by the Japanese, this hospital northeast of the city is another option for minor ailments.

MONEY

There are plenty of banks and licensed money-changers in the capital.

Banks

Banks listed here change cash and travellers cheques and issue cash advances (mostly in kip, but occasionally in US dollars and Thai baht) against Visa and/or MasterCard. Many now have ATMs that work with foreign cards, but it's often cheaper to get a cash advance manually.

ANZ (Map p136; ☑ 021-222700; 33 Th Lan Xang; ⊙ 8.30am-3.30pm Mon-Fri) Main branch has two ATMs and can provide cash advances on Visa or MasterCard for a flat fee of 45,000K. Additional ATMs can be found on Th Setthathirath and Th Fa Ngoum.

Bank of Ayudhya (Map p136; ☑ 021-214575; 79/6 Th Lan Xang; ⊙ 8.30am-3.30pm Mon-Fri) Cash advances on Visa cards here carry a 1.5% commission.

Banque pour le Commerce Extérieur Lao (BCEL; Map p136; cnr Th Pangkham & Th Fa Ngoum; ⊙ 8.30am-7pm Mon-Fri, to 3pm Sat & Sun) Best rates; longest hours. Exchange booth on Th Fa Ngoum and three ATMs attached to the main building.

Joint Development Bank (Map p136; 75/1-5 Th Lan Xang; ⊙ 8.30am-3.30pm Mon-Fri) Usually charges the lowest commission on cash advances. Also has an ATM.

Krung Thai Bank (Map p136; ☑ 021-213480; Th Lan Xang; ⊙ 8.30am-3.30pm Mon-Fri) Also has an **exchange booth** (Map p136; Th Fa Ngoum) on Th Fa Ngoum.

Lao-Viet Bank (Map p136; ☑ 021-214377; Th Lan Xang; ⊙ 8.30am-3.30pm Mon-Fri) Has an ATM and money exchange.

Siam Commercial Bank (Map p136; 117 Th Lan Xang; ⊙ 8.30am-3.30pm Mon-Fri) ATM and cash advances on Visa.

Thai Military Bank (Map p136; ☑ 021-216486; cnr Th Samsènethai & Th Khounbou-lom; ⊙ 8.30am-3.30pm Mon-Fri) Cash advance on Visa only for 200B.

Changing Money

Licensed money-changing booths can be found in much of central Vientiane, particularly along Th Setthathirath between Th François Ngin and Th Pangkham. You can also change cash at various shops, hotels or markets for no commission but at poor rates.

POST

Main Post Office (Map p136; ☑ 020-22206362; Th Saylom; ⊙ 8am-5pm Mon-Fri, to noon Sat & Sun) Come here for post restante, stamps, wiring money and courier service.

TELEPHONE

International calls can be made from most internet cafes, although it's better to use Skype or WhatsApp via a wi-fi link if you have your own mobile device. Local calls can be made from any hotel lobby, often for free.

For cheaper local calls have your mobile unlocked and buy a pay-as-you-go SIM card. Tigo and M-Phone top-up cards are widely available.

Lao Telecom Namphu Centre (Map p136; Th Setthathirath; ⊙ 9am-7pm) has international faxing, and domestic and international calls.

TOURIST INFORMATION

Tourist Information Centre (NTAL; Map p136; ☑ 021-212248; www.ecotourismlaos. com; Th Lan Xang; ⊙ 8.30am-noon & 1.30-4pm) A worthwhile tourist information centre with easy-to-use descriptions of each province, helpful staff who speak decent English, as well as brochures and regional maps.

TRAVEL AGENCIES

Central Vientiane has plenty of agencies that can book air and Thai train tickets and organise visas for Myanmar and Vietnam.

Green Discovery (Map p136; ☑ 021-264528; www.greendiscoverylaos.com; Th Setthathirath; ⊙ 9am-9pm)

Lin Travel Service (Map p136; ☑ 021-218707; 239 Th Hanoi/Phnom Penh; ⊙ 8.30am-9pm)

TRAVEL WITH CHILDREN

Small by the standards of Asian megacities, Vientiane is not such a daunting prospect for families. Many midrange hotels now have swimming pools and there is even the Ocean Park (p135) water park in town. Vientiane's sights are not particularly noteworthy for children, but they should appreciate the surreal sculptures of Xieng Khuan (Buddha Park; p134) and clambering around the larger monuments.

TRAVELLERS WITH DISABILITIES

While Vientiane is the most disabled-friendly city in Laos, rarely do hotels, restaurants and other public buildings feature ramps or other access points for wheelchairs. For wheelchair users, any trip to Vientiane will require a good deal of advance planning.

VISAS

Getting an extension on a tourist visa is easy. Go to the **Immigration Office** (Map p136; ☑ 021-212250; Th Hatsady; ⊙ 8am-4.30pm Mon-Fri), in the Ministry of Public Security building opposite Talat Sao, fill out a form, supply your passport, a photo and pay US$2 per day for the extra time you want. The whole process can be completed in one hour.

🛈 Getting There & Away

AIR

Departures from Vientiane's **Wattay International Airport** (Map p132; ☑ 021-512165; www. vientianeairport.com) are very straightforward. The domestic terminal is in the older, white building east of the more impressive international terminal. There is an (often unstaffed) information counter in the arrivals hall, and food can be found upstairs in the international terminal.

Air Asia (Map p132; www.airasia.com; Wattay Airport International Terminal) Vientiane to Bangkok and Kuala Lumpur daily.

VIENTIANE, VANG VIENG & AROUND VIENTIANE

GETTING TO THAILAND: THA NE LONG TO NONG KHAI

Getting to the Border

At the **Tha Na Leng (Laos)/Nong Khai (Thailand) border crossing** (6am to 10pm), the Thai-Lao Friendship Bridge (Saphan Mittaphap Thai-Lao) spans the Mekong River. The Laos border is approximately 20km from Vientiane, and the easiest and cheapest way to the bridge is to cross on the Thai-Lao International Bus. It conducts daily departures for the Thai cities of Khon Kaen, Nakhon Ratchasima, Nong Khai and Udon Thani. Alternative means of transport between Vientiane and the bridge include taxi (300B), tuk-tuk (shared/charter 5000K/250B), jumbo (250B to 300B) or the number 14 Tha Deua bus from Talat Sao Bus Station (15,000K) between 6am and 5.30pm.

To cross from Thailand, tuk-tuks are available from Nong Khai's train station (20B) and bus station (55B) to the Thai border post at the bridge. You can also hop on the Thai-Lao International Bus from Nong Khai bus station (55B, 1½ hours) or Udon Thani bus station (80B, two hours), both of which terminate at Vientiane's Talat Sao Bus Station. If flying into Udon Thani, a tuk-tuk from the airport to the city's bus station should cost about 120B.

It's also possible to cross the brige by train, as tracks have been extended from Nong Khai's train station 3.5km into Laos, terminating at Dongphasy Station, about 13km from central Vientiane. From Nong Khai there are two daily departures (9.30am and 4pm, fan/air-con 20/50B, 15 minutes) and border formalities are taken care of at the respective train stations. But in reality, unless you are a trainspotter, it is much more convenient to use the international bus or other road transport.

At the Border

Travellers from most countries enjoy 30-day, visa-free access to Thailand. Lao visas (30 days) are available for US$20 to US$42, depending on your nationality. If you don't have a photo you'll be charged an extra US$1, and be aware that an additional US$1 'overtime fee' is charged from 6am to 8am and 6pm to 10pm on weekdays, as well as on weekends and holidays. Don't be tempted to use a tuk-tuk driver to get your Lao visa, no matter what they tell you, as it will take far longer than doing it yourself, and you'll have to pay for the 'service'. Insist they take you straight to the bridge.

Moving On

Sleeper trains from Nong Khai to Bangkok leave at 6.20pm and 7.10pm and cost 1217/778B for a 1st/2nd-class sleeper ticket. Tickets on the 7am day train cost 498/388B for air-con/fan seating.

Bangkok Airways (Map p136; www. bangkokair.com; Lao Plaza Hotel, 63 Th Samsènethai; ⊗8am-5pm Mon-Fri, to noon Sat) Daily flights between Bangkok and both Vientiane and Luang Prabang.

China Eastern Airlines (Map p132; www. ce-air.com; Th Luang Prabang; ⊗8am-5pm Mon-Fri, to noon Sat) Flies daily to Kunming and Nanning.

Korean Air (www.koreanair.com) Daily connections between Vientiane and Seoul.

Lao Airlines (Map p132; ☑021-512028; Wattay Airport International Terminal; ⊗6am-6pm) Domestic flights to Savannakhet, Pakse, Luang Prabang, Phonsavan (Xieng Khuang) and Luang Namtha; plus international flights to Siem Reap, Phnom Penh, Seoul, Singapore, Bangkok, Chiang Mai, Hanoi, Ho Chi Minh, Kunming and Guangzhou.

Lao Skyway (Map p132; ☑021-513022; www. laoskyway.com; Domestic Terminal, Wattay International Airport; ⊗8am-8pm) Local airline with flights from Vientiane to Luang Prabang, Luang Namtha, Udomxai and Huay Xai.

Thai Airways International (Map p132; www. thaiairways.com; Th Luang Prabang ⊗8.30am-5pm Mon-Fri, to noon Sat) Vientiane to Bangkok twice daily.

Vietnam Airlines (Map p136; www.vietnam airlines.com; Lao Plaza Hotel, 63 Th Samsènethai, Vientiane; ⊗9am-5pm Mon-Fri, to noon Sat) Connects Vientiane with Hanoi, Ho Chi Minh City and Phnom Penh.

BOAT

Passenger-boat services between Vientiane and Luang Prabang are almost extinct as most people now take the bus, which is both faster and cheaper.

BUS

In Laos roads are poor and buses break down, so times can take longer than advertised. Buses use three different stations in Vientiane, all with some English-speaking staff, and food and drink stands. The **Northern Bus Station** (Th Asiane), about 2km northwest of the airport, serves all points north of Vang Vieng, including China. Destinations and the latest ticket prices are listed in English.

The **Southern Bus Station** (Rte 13 South), commonly known as Dong Dok Bus Station or just *khíw lot lák káo* (Km 9 Bus Station), is 9km out of town and serves everywhere to the south. Buses to Vietnam depart from here.

The final departure point is the **Talat Sao Bus Station** (Map p136; ☎ 021-216507; Th Khu Vieng), from where desperately slow local buses run to destinations within Vientiane Province, including Vang Vieng, and some more distant destinations, though for the latter you're better going to the Northern or Southern Bus Stations. The **Thai-Lao International Bus** (Map p136) also uses this station for its trips to Khon Kaen, Nakhon Ratchasima, Nong Khai and Udon Thani.

For sleeper buses to Kunming, China (US$95, 38 hours, departing 2pm), contact the **Tong Li Bus Company** (☎ 021-242657) at the Northern Bus Station. For Vietnam, buses leave the Southern Bus Station daily at 7pm for Hanoi (220,000K, 24 hours) via Vinh (180,000K, 16 hours), and also for Danang (230,000K, 22 hours) via Hue (200,000K, 19 hours), except for Monday, Thursday and Sunday when they leave at 6pm. For Ho Chi Minh City change at Danang; contact **SDT** (☎ 021-720175) for details.

TRAIN

In 2009 tracks were extended from Nong Khai's train station across the Thai-Lao Friendship Bridge to Dongphasy in Laos, effectively forming Laos' first railway line. There are plans to extend the tracks an additional 9km, part of a greater plan that will see the commencement of a national railway grid in the coming years, but for now Laos boasts a grand total of 3.5km of rolling track, making connections with Nong Khai in Thailand very inconvenient when compared with the Thai-Lao International Bus.

ℹ Getting Around

Central Vientiane is entirely accessible on foot. For exploring neighbouring districts, however, you'll need transport.

TO/FROM THE AIRPORT

Wattay International Airport Taxis to the centre cost US$7 and minivans are available for US$8. Only official taxis can pick up at the airport.

If you're on a budget and don't have a lot of luggage, simply walk 500m to the airport gate and cross Th Souphanouvong and hail a shared jumbo (p157; 20,000K per person). Prices on shared transport will rise if you're going further than the centre.

Bus number 49 (Nong Taeng) from Talat Sao Bus Station makes the journey out to the airport for 6000K.

BICYCLE

Cycling is a cheap, easy and recommended way of getting around mostly flat Vientiane. Loads of guesthouses and several shops hire out bikes for 10,000K to 20,000K per day. Mountain bikes are available but are more expensive at 30,000K to 40,000K; try **Lao Bike** (Map p136; ☎ 020-55090471; Th Setthathirath; ⊗ 9am-6pm).

BUS

There is a city bus system, but it's oriented more towards the distant suburbs than the central Chanthabuli district. Most buses leave from Talat Sao Bus Station, which is currently undergoing a massive renovation. The number 14 Tha Deua bus to the Thai-Lao Friendship Bridge and Xieng

---

A BEGINNER'S GUIDE TO TUK-TUKS & JUMBOS

Tourist tuk-tuks You'll find these loitering in queues outside popular tourist spots, such as at Nam Phu. In theory, chartering a tuk-tuk should be no more than 20,000K for distances of 1km or so, but these guys will usually show you a laminated card with a list of fares that are at least double what a Lao person would pay. Bargaining is essentially fruitless because there is an agreement within the queue that tuk-tuks won't budge from the agreed tariff.

Wandering tuk-tuks These tuk-tuks will pick you up anywhere and negotiate a fare to anywhere. Prices are lower than tourist tuk-tuks and rise as you head further away from main roads. If you're going somewhere within the centre of town, you can probably get away with handing the driver 15,000K to 20,000K and telling him where you want to go.

Fixed-route share jumbos The cheapest tuk-tuks are more like buses, starting at tuk-tuk stations and operating along set routes for fixed fares. The biggest station is near Talat Sao and one very useful route runs to the Friendship Bridge (5000K, compared with about 200B for a charter). Just turn up and tell them where you want to go.

Khuan (Buddha Park) runs every two hours from 6am to 5.30pm and costs 15,000K. Bus number 49 runs past the airport (6000K) regularly. Bus number 8 runs to the Northern Bus Station (5000K) and number 29 to the Southern Bus Station (3000K).

CAR & MOTORCYCLE

There are several international car-hire companies with representation in Vientiane, including **Avis** (Map p136; ☏ 021-223867; www.avis.la; Th Setthathirath; ⊗ 8.30am-6.30pm Mon-Fri, to 1pm Sat & Sun) and **Sixt** (Map p132; ☏ 021-513228; www.sixtlao.com; Wattay International Airport; ⊗ 7am-7pm).

Scooters are a popular means of getting around Vientiane and can be hired throughout the centre of town. Recommended hire places include **First-One Motorbike Rental** (Map p136; ☏ 020-55528299; Th François Ngin; scooters per day 70,000K; ⊗ 8.30am-6pm) and **Mixay Bike 2** (Map p136; ☏ 020-77882510; Th Chau Anou; scooter per 24hr 60,000-80,000K; ⊗ 8am-8pm).

BUSES FROM VIENTIANE

DESTINATION	DEPARTURE POINT	PRICE (K)
Attapeu (fan)	Southern Bus Station	140,000
Attapeu (VIP)	Southern Bus Station	200,000
Don Khong (fan)	Southern Bus Station	150,000
Huay Xai	Northern Bus Station	230,000-250,000
Khon Kaen (air-con)	Talat Sao Bus Station	50,000
Lak Sao (fan)	Southern Bus Station	85,000
Luang Namtha	Northern Bus Station	200,000
Luang Prabang	Northern Bus Station	110,000
Luang Prabang (VIP)	Northern Bus Station	130,000-150,000
Nakhon Ratchasima (air-con)	Talat Sao Bus Station	149,000
Nong Khai (air-con)	Talat Sao Bus Station	17,000
Nong Khiang (fan)	Southern Bus Station	130,000
Paksan	Southern Bus Station	40,000-50,000
Pakse (fan)	Southern Bus Station	140,000
Pakse (VIP)	Southern Bus Station	170,000
Phongsali	Northern Bus Station	210,000-230,000
Phonsavan	Northern Bus Station	110,000
Phonsavan (sleeper)	Northern Bus Station	150,000
Sainyabuli	Northern Bus Station	110,000-130,000
Salavan (air-con)	Southern Bus Station	160,000
Salavan (fan)	Southern Bus Station	130,000
Salavan (VIP)	Southern Bus Station	190,000
Sam Neua	Northern Bus Station	170,000-190,000
Sam Neua (sleeper)	Northern Bus Station	210,000
Savannakhet	Southern Bus Station	75,000
Savannakhet (VIP)	Southern Bus Station	120,000
Tha Khaek	Southern Bus Station	60,000
Tha Khaek (VIP)	Southern Bus Station	80,000
Udomxai	Northern Bus Station	150,000-170,000
Udomxai (VIP)	Northern Bus Station	190,000
Udon Thani (air-con)	Talat Sao Bus Station	22,000
Vang Vieng (fan)	Talat Sao Bus Station	30,000

JUMBO & TUK-TUK

Drivers of jumbos and tuk-tuks will take passengers on journeys as short as 500m or as far as 20km. Understanding the various types of tuk-tuk is important if you don't want to be overcharged (and can save you arguments in addition to money). Tourist tuk-tuks are the most expensive, while share jumbos that run regular routes around town (eg Th Luang Prabang to Th Setthathirath or Th Lan Xang to That Luang) are much cheaper, usually less than 5000K per person.

TAXI

Car taxis of varying shapes, sizes and vintages can often be found stationed in front of the larger hotels or at the airport. Bargaining is the general rule, although there are a couple of meter-taxi companies operating now, including the following:

Meter Taxi Service (Map p136; ☎021-454168) Drivers from this company often wait for fares on Th Pangkham, just across from the Day Inn Hotel.

DISTANCE (KM)	DURATION (HR)	DEPARTURES
812	22-24	9.30am, 5pm
812	14-16	8.30pm
788	16-19	10.30am
869	24	10am, 5.30pm
197	4	8.15am, 2.45pm
334	6-8	5am, 6am, 7am, 8.30pm
676	24	8.30am, 5pm
384	10-11	6.30am, 7.30am, 8.30am, 11am, 1.30pm, 4pm, 6pm, 7.30pm (air-con)
384	9-12	8am, 9am, 7.30pm, 8pm
387	7	5pm
25	1½	7.30am, 9.30am, 12.40pm, 2.30pm, 3.30pm, 6pm
818	16-20	11am
143	3-4	7am-3pm (tuk-tuk); take any bus going south
677	16-18	regular from 7am to 8pm
677	8-10	8.30pm
811	25-28	7.15am (fan), 6pm (sleeper)
374	10-11	6.30am, 7.30am, 9.30am, 4pm, 6.40pm
374	10-11	8pm
485	14-16	9am, 4pm, 6.30pm
774	16	7.30pm
774	15-20	4.30pm, 7.30pm
774	13	8.30pm
612	22-24	7am, 9.30am, noon (fan), 5pm
612	22-24	2pm
457	8-11	half-hourly 5.30-9am, or any bus to Pakse
457	8-10	8.30pm
332	6	4am, 5am, 6am, noon, or any bus to Savannakhet or Pakse
332	5	noon, 1pm
578	16-19	6.45am, 1.45pm, 5pm
578	15-17	4pm
82	2½	8am, 10.30am, 11.30am, 2pm, 4pm, 6pm
157	3-4	7am, 9.30am, 1pm, 3pm

MOTORBIKE TOURING FROM VIENTIANE

Motorbike activities have been growing in popularity for several years now. It's now possible to travel on sturdy, well-maintained motocross bikes, connected by Laos' competent mobile-phone service for backup with base, and handheld GPS devices to always keep you on track. And with drop-off and luggage-forwarding facilities to your destination available, you're now able to tackle a slice of your holiday on two wheels (an alternative to duking it out on soggy, overcrowded buses). Rent by the week and take in the north via the mountains of Vang Vieng, continuing on to Luang Prabang and the rest of the north before leaving your bike in Luang Prabang. Or head south to explore the karst limestone mountains around Tha Khaek and eventually leave the motorbike in Pakse.

Recommended operators that hire dirt bikes or touring bikes and offer pick-up services at the end of your trip:

Drivenbyadventure (📱020-58656994; www.hochiminhtrail.org; rental per day US$38-95, tours per day US$160-200) Offers the most professionally maintained dirt bikes in Laos, including Honda CRF250s (US$38 per day), Honda XR400s (US$50) and KTM XCW450s (US$95).

Fuark Motorcycle Hire (📱021-261970; fuarkmotorcross@yahoo.com) A leading locally owned and operated motorbike-hire place that offers a range of well-maintained dirt bikes (from US$30 per day) and drop-offs at key cities around the country.

Drivenbyadventure owner Don Duvall also masquerades as mysteriously monikered Midnight Mapper (p154), spending the last 10 years tirelessly mapping Laos, and you can buy his satellite map off his website and plug it into your GPS gadget. It costs US$50, and he mails you the SIM card, or can rent you a Garmin handheld GPS device for US$7 per day and plug in your coordinates so you never get lost.

Taxi Vientiane Capital Lao Group (📱021-454168; ⊘24hr) Another useful metered-taxi option in the capital.

Tourist Taxi (📱1420; to airport around 50,000K; ⊘24hr) This new metered service just for tourists gives you a chance to keep an eye on your fare.

A car and driver costs about US$50 per day as long as the vehicle doesn't leave town. If you want to go further afield, such as to Ang Nam Ngum or Vang Vieng, expect to pay more.

At the **Talat Sao taxi stand** (Map p136; cnr Th Lan Xang & Th Khu Vieng; ⊘7am-6pm), across from Talat Sao, you'll find taxis to the Thai-Lao Friendship Bridge (300B).

AROUND VIENTIANE

There are several places worth seeing that are an easy trip from Vientiane; some make good day trips while others could detain you for much longer. Popular places include the jungle and homestays of Phu Khao Khuay NPA and the islands and bays of Ang Nam Ngum.

Phu Khao Khuay NPA
ປ່າສະຫງວນແຫ່ງຊາດພູເຂົາຄວາຍ

Covering more than 2000 sq km of mountains and rivers to the east of Vientiane, the underrated Phu Khao Khuay NPA is the most accessible protected area in Laos. Treks ranging in duration from a couple of hours to three days have been developed in partnership with Ban Na and Ban Hat Khai villages on the edge of the NPA.

Phu Khao Khuay (*poo cow kwai*) means 'Buffalo Horn Mountain', a name derived from local legend, and is home to three major rivers that flow off a sandstone mountain range. It boasts an extraordinary array of endangered wildlife, including wild elephant, gibbon, Asiatic black bear, clouded leopard, Siamese fireback pheasant and green peafowl. Depending on elevation, visitors may encounter dry evergreen dipterocarp (a Southeast Asian tree with two-winged fruit), mixed deciduous forest, conifer forest or grassy uplands. Several impressive waterfalls are accessible as day trips from Vientiane.

❶ Getting There & Away

Buses from Vientiane's Southern Bus Station leave regularly for Ban Tha Bok and Paksan. For Wat Pha Baht Phonsan and Ban Na get off at Tha Pha Bat (25,000K) near the Km 81 stone; the shrine is right on Rte 13 and Ban Na is about 1.5km north and well signposted.

For Ban Hat Khai, keep on the bus until a turn-off left (north) at Km 92, just before Ban Tha Bok (30,000K). If you have your own transport, continue 8km along the smooth laterite road until you cross the new bridge. Turn right at the Y-intersection and it's 1km to Ban Hat Khai. Alternatively, villagers in Ban Hat Khai can arrange motorcyle pick-up from Ban Tha Bok for 25,000K one way if you call ahead.

Note that as you come from Vientiane there are three signed entrances to Phu Khao Khuay – the second leads to Ban Na and the third to Ban Hat Khai and the waterfalls.

Ban Na   ບ້ານນາ

Village guides lead one-, two- and three-day treks from Ban Na to **Keng Khani** (three to four hours one way) and through deep forest to the waterfall of **Tat Fa** (four to five hours). There is also a one-hour trek to the old elephant observation tower, passing by plantations and through the skirts of the jungle itself. The tower overlooks a salt lick, which the elephants used to visit regularly. Trekkers sleep in the tower (100,000K per person) beneath a mosquito net on a mattress, and guides cook a tasty local dinner. Even without the elephants it still makes for a fun adventure.

Ban Na offers 10 homestays in simple wooden houses (24-hour electricity and mosquito nets with bedding are provided). Vegetarian meals are possible. For bookings contact **Mr Bounathom/Mr Khampak** (☑ 020-22208262), or find a Lao speaker to call ahead for you.

Ban Hat Khai   ບ້ານຫາດໄຊ

Ban Hat Khai is a pretty riverside village offering 11 homestays in traditional Lao houses, including 24-hour electricity and mosquito nets. Vegetarian meals are available on request. To book a stay in Ban Hat Khai contact **Mr Khammuan** (☑ 020-2224 0303) or find a Lao speaker to call ahead for you.

Destinations accessible from Ban Hat Khai include the huge cliff, views and beautiful landscape of **Pha Luang** (three to four hours one way), and the forested areas around **Huay Khi Ling** (two to three hours one way). A trek taking in both these areas takes two or three days, depending on the season, and involves sleeping in the forest.

Tat Xai, Pha Xai & Tat Leuk

Tat Leuk **FREE** is a small waterfall, but is a beautiful place to camp for the night. You can swim above the falls if the water isn't flowing too fast, and the visitor centre has some information about the area, including a detailed guide to the 1.5km-long Huay Bon Nature Trail.

The guy who looks after the visitor centre can arrange local treks for 160,000K, and rents quality four-person tents for 30,000K, plus hammocks, mattresses, mosquito nets and sleeping bags for 10,000K each. There's a very basic restaurant (best supplemented with food you bring), a small library of wildlife books and a pair of binoculars.

From the junction to Ban Hat Khai village, turn left and continue another 6km until you see a rough 4km road on the left, which leads to Tat Leuk.

Tat Xai (ຕາດໄຊ) **FREE** cascades down seven steps, and 800m downstream **Pha Xai** (ຜາໄຊ) plunges over a 40m-high cataract. There's a pool that's good for swimming, though it can get dangerous during the wet season. Both waterfalls are accessed from Rte 13, just before Ban Tha Bok. From the junction to Ban Hat Khai, it's 9km to Tat Xai and Pha Xai.

Ang Nam Ngum & Around

Located midway between Vientiane and Vang Vieng, Ang Nam Ngum is a vast artificial lake created when the Nam Ngum (Ngum River) was dammed in 1971. The highest peaks of the former river valley became forested islands after the inundation and, following the 1975 PL conquest of Vientiane, an estimated 3000 prostitutes, petty criminals and drug addicts were rounded up from the capital and banished to two of these islands; one each for men and women. Today, the Nam Ngum hydroelectric plant generates most of the electricity used in the Vientiane area. Potential stops around the lake include Nam Tok Tat Khu Khana, the Vang Sang Buddhas and Nam Lik Eco-Village.

◉ Sights & Activities

Ang Nam Ngum is dotted with picturesque little islands and it is well worth arranging a boat cruise (150,000/300,000K for a half-/full day) from Ban Na Khuen or Ban Tha Heua, where several attractive resorts dot the lakeshore.

Vang Sang Buddhas   BUDDHIST SITE
FREE At Vang Sang, 65km north of Vientiane via Rte 13, sits a cluster of 10 high-relief Buddha sculptures on cliffs thought to date from the 16th century. Two of the Buddhas

ENDANGERED ELEPHANTS

The lowland farming village of Ban Na, 82km northeast of Vientiane, is home to about 600 people. The village is typical Lao, with women weaving baskets from bamboo and men tending the fields. But it was the local herd of elephants that was historically of most interest to visitors.

The farmers of Ban Na grow rice and vegetables, but several years ago they began planting sugar cane. What they didn't count on was the collective sweet tooth of the elephants in the nearby mountains. It wasn't long before these jumbos sniffed out the delights in the field below and were happily eating the sugar cane, pineapples and bananas planted around Ban Na. Not surprisingly, the farmers weren't happy. They decided the only way to get rid of the elephants was to rip up the sugar cane and go back to planting boring (and less lucrative) vegetables.

It was hoped the 30-odd elephants would take the hint and return to the mountains. Instead, they made the lowland forests, bamboo belt and fields around Ban Na their home, causing significant destruction to the environment and finances of Ban Na. The only way the villagers could continue to live with the elephants (ie not shoot them) was by making them pay their way. The result was elephant ecotourism.

The truth is that today the elephants have vanished. In 2007 there was an estimated 25-strong herd in Phu Khao Khuay National Protected Area (NPA). In 2009 five were killed – stripped of their tusks and hind legs, which suggests that they were murdered by poachers rather than local villagers. In 2010 a further two were recorded dead; according to the Lao Army, they had been electrocuted by lightning. Villagers say they have not sighted elephants for several years, so it is likely they have been killed or have fled north into more remote areas of the NPA.

are more than 3m tall. The name means 'Elephant Palace', a reference to an elephant graveyard once found nearby.

To reach Vang Sang, follow the sign to the Vang Xang Resort, near the Km 62 marker, then take the laterite road around a small lake, up the hill and right until you reach the shaded forest at the end.

Nam Tok Tat Khu Khana WATERFALL

FREE It's a bit of a mouthful, but the Nam Tok Tat Khu Khana (Tat Khu Khana Waterfall, also called Hin Khana) is one of the easier waterfalls to reach from Vientiane. Follow a 10km dirt road, which leads west from Rte 13 near the village of Ban Naxaithong, near Km 17.

Sleeping & Eating

Ban Na Khuen and Ban Tha Heua are villages near the lakeshore that are home to a number of nice resorts. These can be a good alternative to the hustle and bustle of downtown Vang Vieng if you want a relaxing escape.

★**Sanctuary Resort** BOUTIQUE HOTEL $$

(☎020-55320612; www.sanctuaryhotelsandresorts.com; Ban Tha Heua; r from US$38-50; ❄📶🏊) Sanctuary Resort has impressive new bungalow villas on the shores of the Ang Nam Ngum. They're lovingly appointed with contemporary fixtures; there are also larger deluxe villas with an outdoor jacuzzi that can double up as a two-bedroom family villa. There is also a floating swimming pool in the lake, quite a novelty.

Nam Lik Eco-Village BUNGALOW $$

(☎020-55508719; http://namlik.org/eco; s/d US$30/40) 🍃 Nam Lik Eco-Village is a riverside resort located on the west bank of the Nam Lik (Lik River) and makes a good base for outdoor activities such as orchid walks, kayaking in the river or mountain biking on fixed trails. It's located 7km east of the Ban Senhxoum, itself just past the Km 80 marker.

Nirvana Archipel Resort BUNGALOW $$

(☎020-54894272; www.nirvana-archipel-resort.com; Ban Tha Heua; camping 25,000K, bungalows 100,000-200,000K, f US$40-130; ❄📶) 🍃 Overlooking Ang Nam Ngum, this quirky eco-resort is made from reclaimed timber and petrified wood from the reservoir. Accommodation includes twin bungalows (cheaper ones with shared bathroom), and some impressive family houses and bungalows with two rooms that can sleep up to eight or more. There is an on-site wildlife rescue centre, with proceeds going towards helping the animals.

Nam Ngeum LAOTIAN $

(☎ 020-55513521; Ban Na Khuen; mains 20,000-60,000K; ⊘ 9am-9pm) One of a handful of restaurants at Ban Na Khuen, Nam Ngeum gets good reviews for its tasty *gôy Ɓạh* (tart and spicy fish salad), *gạang Ɓạh* (fish soup) and *neung Ɓạh* (steamed fish with fresh herbs).

❶ Getting There & Away

It's easier to access most places around Ang Nam Ngum with your own transport. Public transport is convenient for the resorts near Ban Tha Heua, but not so straightforward for other destinations.

Getting to Ban Tha Heua is easy as it's on the main road between Vientiane and Vang Vieng. Heading north you'll probably have to pay the full fare to Vang Vieng. Heading south from Vang Vieng, you may be able to get away with a lower *sŏrngtăaou* fare of around 10,000K.

For Ban Na Kheun, buses depart Vientiane's Talat Sao Bus Station for Thalat (15,000K, 2½ hours, 87km), the nearest town, every hour from 6.30am to 5.30pm; you'll then need to arrange a *sŏrngtăaou* (passenger trucks) to Ban Na Kheun (costing about 15,000K).

Nam Lik Eco-Village can provide transport with advance bookings. Otherwise, take a bus to Vang Vieng and get off at Ban Senhxoum (25,000K, three hours) and seek local transport for the remaining 7km.

Vang Vieng   ວັງວຽງ

POP 35,000 / ☎ 023

Like a rural scene from an old Asian silk painting, Vang Vieng crouches low over the Nam Song (Song River) with a backdrop of serene cliffs and a tapestry of vivid green paddy fields. Thanks to the Lao government closing the river rave bars in 2012, the increasingly toxic party scene has been driven to the fringes and the community is rebooting itself as an adrenaline fuelled adventure destination with some impressive accommodation options on tap. While the town itself is no gem, as concrete hotels build ever higher in search of the quintessential view, across the Nam Song lies a rural idyll.

Spend a few days here – rent a scooter, take a motorcycle tour, go tubing or trekking – and soak up one of Laos' most stunningly picturesque spots. But explore with care and enjoy it sober, as the river and mountains around Vang Vieng have claimed too many travellers' lives already.

◉ Sights & Activities

Vang Vieng has evolved into Laos' number-one adventure destination, with tubing, kayaking, rafting, mountain biking and world-class rock climbing all available. You can also explore the many caves that pepper the karst limestone peaks, while ziplining is also very popular, with several zipline adventures combining some cave exploration with a river splashdown.

Caves

Of the most accessible *tàm* (caves), most are signed in English as well as Lao, and an admission fee is collected at the entrance to each cave. The caves around Vang Vieng are spectacular, but caves come with certain hazards: they're dark, slippery and disorienting. A guide (often a young village boy) will lead you through a cave for a small fee; bring water and a torch (flashlight), and be *sure* your batteries aren't about to die. In fact, bearing in mind some of the 'lost in the darkness' horror stories that circulate, it's vital to have a spare torch.

For more extensive multicave tours, most guesthouses can arrange a guide. Trips including river tubing and cave tours cost around US$15/25 for a half-/full day.

Tham Nam   CAVE

(5000K) Tham Nam is the highlight of the cluster of caves near Vang Vieng. The cave is about 500m long and a tributary of the Nam Song flows out of its low entrance. It's about 400m south of Tham Hoi, along a path.

Tham Jang   CAVE

(ຖ້ຳຈັງ; entry incl footbridge fee 17,000K) The most famous of the caves around Vang Vieng, Tham Jang was used as a bunker to defend against marauding *jeen hór* (Yunnanese Chinese) in the early 19th century (*jang* means 'steadfast'). Stairs lead up to the main cavern entrance.

Tham Hoi   CAVE

(combined entry 10,000K) The entrance to Tham Ho is guarded by a large Buddha figure; reportedly the cave continues about 3km into the limestone and an underground lake. The combined entry fee covers all the caves in the Tham Sang area (p166).

It's reached via a signed path from Tham Sang that takes you 1km northwest through rice fields.

Vang Vieng

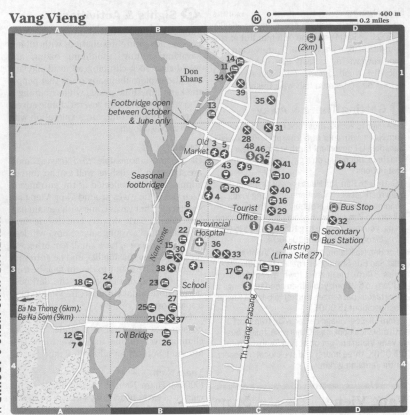

Tham Phu Kham
CAVE

(ຖ້ຳພູຄຳ, Blue Lagoon; 10,000K) The vast Tham Phu Kham is considered sacred by Lao and is popular largely due to the lagoon in the cave. The beautiful green-blue waters are perfect for a dip after the stiff climb. The main cave chamber contains a Thai bronze reclining Buddha, and from here deeper galleries branch off into the mountain.

Tham Loup
CAVE

(combined entry 10,000K) Tham Loup is a large and delightfully untouched cavern with some impressive stalactites. The combined entry fee covers all the caves in the Tham Sang area.

The entrances to the cave are reached from Tham Sang via a signed path that takes you 1km northwest through rice fields.

Tubing

Virtually every younger traveller who comes to Vang Vieng goes tubing down the Nam Song in an inflated tractor-tyre tube. The tubing drop-off point is 3.5km north of town, and depending on the speed and level of the river it can be a soporific crawl beneath the jungle-vined karsts, or a speedy glide downstream back to Vang Vieng. Since the river bars shut in 2012 there's less chance of getting plastered and losing your balance in dangerous currents, but always wear a life jacket when the river runs fast (even if you're not floating in an alternative universe). The many stories of travellers who have drowned in this seemingly peaceful river don't make for pleasant reading. Whether tubing or kayaking down the Nam Song, rivers can be dangerous, and in times of high water, rapids along the Nam Song can be quite daunting. When tubing, it's worth asking how long the trip should take (durations vary depending on the time of year) so you can allow plenty of time to get back to Vang Vieng before dark, as it's pitch black by about 6pm in winter. Finally, don't forget that while tubing the Nam

Vang Vieng

Song might be more fun when you're stoned, it's also more dangerous.

The **tubing operators** (⊗8.30am-7pm) have formed a cartel so all tubing is organised from a small building across from where the old market once was. It costs 55,000K to rent a tube and there's a 60,000K refundable deposit. Life jackets are available and you can rent a dry bag for 20,000K. The fee includes transport to the tubing drop-off point, but keep in mind that you must return the tube before 6pm, otherwise you'll have to pay a 20,000K late fee. If you lose your tube, you will forfeit the 60,000K deposit.

The other thing you should remember is to take something – a sarong, perhaps – to put on when you finish the trip and have to walk through town. The locals don't appreciate people walking around in bikinis or Speedos.

Kayaking

Kayaking is almost as popular as tubing, and trips are typically combined with other activities such as visits to caves and villages, optional climbing, cycling, and the traverse of a few rapids (the danger of which depends on the speed of the water). There are loads of operators and prices are about US$15 per person per day. Kayaking trips to Vientiane along the Nam Lik (Lik River) are conducted by the excellent **Green Discovery** (☑023-511230; www.greendiscoverylaos.com; Th Luang Prabang; 1-day cycling tour per person US$25-35, half-/full-day rock climbing US$27/36) 🏊, which also runs kayaking adventures on the Nam Song, and involve a lot of paddling. These are only possible post-monsoon, when the water is sufficiently high. Another useful tour operator for kayaking is the well-established VLT.

Rock Climbing

In just a few years the limestone walls around Vang Vieng have gained a reputation for some of the best climbing in Southeast Asia. More than 200 routes have been identified and most have been bolted. The routes are rated between 4a and 8b, with the majority being in or near a cave. The most popular climbing spots are at **Tham Non** (Sleeping Cave), with more than 20 routes, and the tougher **Sleeping Wall** nearby, where some routes have difficult overhangs.

THE THAM SANG TRIANGLE

A popular half-day trip that's easy to do on your own takes in **Tham Sang** plus **Tham Hoi**, **Tham Loup** and **Tham Nam**, all within a short walk. Begin this caving odyssey by riding a motorcycle or taking a jumbo 13km north along Rte 13, turning left a few hundred metres beyond the barely readable Km 169 stone.

A rough road leads to the river, where you cross a toll bridge (5000K), or during the wet season, a boatman will ferry you across to Ban Tham Sang (20,000K return). Tham Sang itself is right here, as is a small restaurant.

Tham Sang, meaning 'Elephant Cave', is a small cavern containing a few Buddha images and a Buddha 'footprint', plus the (vaguely) elephant-shaped stalactite that gives the cave its name. It's best visited in the morning when light enters the cave.

From Tham Sang a path takes you about 1km northwest through rice fields to the entrances of Tham Hoi and Tham Loup. The path isn't entirely clear, but the local kids are happy to show you the way for a small fee. The entrance to Tham Hoi is guarded by a large Buddha figure; reportedly the cave continues about 3km into the limestone and an underground lake. Tham Loup is a large and delightfully untouched cavern with some impressive stalactites.

About 400m south of Tham Hoi, along a well-used path, is the highlight of this trip, Tham Nam. The cave is about 500m long, and a tributary of the Nam Song (Song River) flows out of its low entrance. In the dry season you can wade into the cave, but when the water is higher you need to take a tube from the friendly woman near the entrance; the tube and headlamp are included in the entrance fee. Dragging yourself through the tunnel on the fixed rope is fun.

If you've still got the energy, a path leads about 2km south from Tham Nam along a stream to **Tham Pha Thao**, a cave said to be a couple of kilometres long with a pool in the middle. Otherwise, it's an easy 1km walk back to Ban Tham Sang. This loop is usually included in the kayaking/trekking/tubing combo trip run by most Vang Vieng tour operators.

The climbing season usually runs between October and May, with most routes too wet at other times. However, there are some rock-shaded overhangs on Phadeng Mountain that have recently been bolted down (23 routes), and can still be used in the wet season.

Adam's Rock Climbing School (☎020-56564499; www.laos-climbing.com; opposite the hospital; half-/full-day climbing 180,000/260,000K, 2-day course US$100, private climbing guide 320,000K) offers fully outfitted courses ranging in skill from beginner to advanced. Adam himself is one of the most experienced climbers in the area, his multilingual guides get good reports and equipment rental is also available (350,000K).

Green Discovery conducts climbing courses, and when available, can provide a handy climbing guide to the area.

Ziplining

It's all about air and cable these days, with the jungles around Vang Vieng criss-crossed with adrenaline-inducing ziplines. The following tour outfits combine a trek, kayak, abseil or tubing session with zipping:

Nam Thip Tours (☎020-23333616, 023-511318; ◷9am-7pm)

TCK (☎023-511691; tckamazingtour@gmail.com; ◷9am-8pm)

Vang Vieng Adventure Tours (AK Home Ziplining; ☎020-55033665; http://vangviengadventure.wixsite.com/home; opposite Vansana Hotel; half-/full day US$25/35)

Vang Vieng Challenge (☎023-511230; www.greendiscoverylaos.com; Th Luang Prabang)

Wonderful Tours (☎023-511566; www.wonderfultourslaos.la; Th Khann Muang)

Other Activities

★ **Hot Air Ballooning**   BALLOONING
(www.vangviengtour.com/balloon-over-vangvieng; flight US$95) A hot air balloon is a lovely way to see the cliffs, tapestry of paddy fields and snaking river below. The flights are at 6.30am, 4pm and 4.30pm every day, and last 40 minutes. To book contact Mr Vone at VLT.

Blue Lagoon 3   SWIMMING
Forget the circus that is the original Blue Lagoon and head 14km further west to the Blue Lagoon 3, part of the West Vang Vieng Loop.

The azure waters are fed by a natural spring that emerges from a nearby karst limestone peak and it is still relatively quiet compared with its more infamous namesake.

Pony Trekking Vang Vieng HORSE RIDING
(☑ 030-5074524; reservations@silvernaga.com; ⊕) Pony trekking is now available amid the karsts of Vang Vieng. Short led rides are available for smaller children without experience, and longer rides out to rice fields, farms and caves are also possible.

Yoga in Vang Vieng YOGA
(Silver Naga; per session US$10, for 2 sessions US$15; ☺ 7.30-9am & 5-6.30pm) ✐ Daily yoga sessions are available at the Silver Naga hotel with an experienced international yoga instructor.

VLT OUTDOORS
(☑ 023-511369; www.vangviengtour.com) Run by Vonc, VLT is well established and charges US$13 to US$35 for one day's kayaking, US$25 for one-day mountain-bike trips, and US$20 for one-day treks to local caves, including lunch.

Vang Vieng Jeep Tour SCENIC DRIVE
(☑ 020-54435747; noedouine@yahoo.fr; minimum group of 4, per person 180,000K) Based at Chez Mango guesthouse, VV Jeep Tour takes in the best of the countryside in friendly Noé's jeep; first he'll take you to a nearby mountain that you'll gently ascend for an amazing view, then for a walk in the paddy fields followed by a swim in the Blue Lagoon at Tham Phu Kham, before taking a closer look at the cave.

🛏 Sleeping

🛏 Vang Vieng Town

★Champa Lao GUESTHOUSE $
(☑ 020-58234612; www.facebook.com/champalao bungalows; r without bathroom 70,000K, tr with bathroom 150,000K, cabanas with bathroom 120,000K, without 60,000K; P⊕❄@☎) With new Thai owners, this stilted Lao house has basic fan rooms with mozzie nets. The garden, choked with plants, is a delight and you can swing on a hammock while taking in the sunset and karst from its aerial balcony. There are also bungalows down by the river bank.

★Pan's Place GUESTHOUSE $
(☑ 023-511484; Th Luang Prabang; dm 30,000K, s/d with bathroom 70,000/88,000K, without bathroom 50,000/64,000K; ⊕@☎) Radiating a welcoming vibe, Pan's is a VV backpacking

institution, with its basic but cosy fan rooms with tiled floors and en suites. Out back are cabanas in a leafy garden, plus a communal chilling area. There's also a little cafe and a cinema room upstairs with hundreds of DVDs to choose from.

Central Backpacker's Hostel HOSTEL $
(☑ 020-56770677; www.vangviengbackpackers.com; dm 40,000K, r with fan/air-con 100,000/150,000K, tr 200,000K; ⊕❄☎) This hostel, with wedding-cake-style architecture, boasts private rooms with fan or air-con and private balcony and TV, as well as comfy well-spaced dorms, and communal balconies to drink up the view of the cliffs. There's a huge lobby with a cafe and DVD bar, and safety lockers too (BYO lock). Not much atmosphere but decent value.

Vinutda Guesthouse GUESTHOUSE $
(☑ 020-22244638; r 120,000-180,000K; ⊕❄☎) Located at the southern end of the riverside road, this family-run guesthouse has a good range of new rooms with sparkling bathrooms and ample beds.

Khamphone Guest House GUESTHOUSE $
(☑ 023-511062; r 80,000-120,000K; ⊕❄☎) Peach-coloured Khamphone's three buildings are on the southern edge of town, and offer good-value en suite rooms; the 120,000K options with TV, air-con and fridge are best. Check out the newer building as its rooms are the most spacious.

Domon Guesthouse GUESTHOUSE $
(☑ 020-99898678; domonvangvieng@hotmail.com; r with/without air-con 200,000/120,000K; ⊕❄☎) With fine views of the karsts this old-timer has characterful blue and green rooms with bags of charm, private bathrooms, balconies and art on the walls. There's a breezy verandah cafe-bar and money exchange.

Easy Go Hostel HOSTEL $
(☑ 020-55366679; www.easygohostel.com; dm 25,000K, r with/without air-con 90,000/60,000K, tr with air-con 120,000K; ⊕❄☎) Crafted from bamboo and rattan, and run by a lively team, Easy Go offers eight-berth and four-berth dorms and eight private rooms. The ace card is its laid-back lounge with comfy cushions, pool table and flat-screen TV, with even wider-screen views of the cliffs.

Elephant Crossing HOTEL $$
(☑ 023-511232; www.theelephantcrossinghotel. com; r US$40-60; ⊕❄@☎) Set in leafy gardens peppered with swing chairs and with an attractive verandah to take breakfast by

the river, Elephant Crossing has 36 tasteful rooms with glass-panel walls and spotless en suites. Hmong bed runners, wood floors, aircon, TV and fridge complete the picture. It's often booked out by Contiki Travel though, so reservations are hard to score.

Thavonsouk Resort HOTEL $$
(☎023-511096; www.thavonsouk.com; r incl breakfast US$40-65; P✳@☎) One of Vang Vieng's original hotels, Thavonsouk offers beautiful wood-accented rooms bursting with light and enjoying full-frontal views of the karsts and lush gardens. Waffle quilts, antique beds, the scent of freshly applied beeswax and a good range of amenities make this a winner.

Vang Vieng Eco-Lodge BUNGALOW $$
(☎030-5517705; r 200,000K; ☻☎) We don't vouch for its green credentials, but this delightful accommodation, opposite Tham Jang, sits in a peaceful spot by the river. The only sounds you're likely to hear are the babbling water and the odd rooster. Under new Thai management, with bungalows that are cool and traditional with wood floors, four-posters and desks.

Silver Naga HOTEL $$
(☎023-511822; www.silvernaga.com; r US$65-180; ☻✳@☎✲) A major new hotel on the east-bank riverfront, from the owners of Elephant Crossing. The new rooms here features contemporary decoration and lots of nice touches like private balcony, flat-screen TV and rain shower. There is a 2nd-floor pool with a killer karst view that is open to nonguests for 50,000K.

Villa Nam Song GUESTHOUSE $$
(☎023-511015; www.villanamsong.com; r US$42-70; ☻✳☎) With serene views of the cliffs, this fine hotel sits in grounds choking on mango, palm, orchid and bougainvillea. The pink adobe bungalows are fragrant and parquet-floored, with cream walls and high-end furniture. There's also a semi-alfresco restaurant featuring Asian favourites.

Inthira Hotel BOUTIQUE HOTEL $$
(☎023-511070; www.inthirahotel.com; Th Luang Prabang; standard/superior/deluxe r incl breakfast US$32/43/54; ☻✳@☎) While it is located on the main drag and not by the river, the Inthira is still a fine place to stay, with ox-blood rooms enjoying views of the karsts and the old CIA runway (Lima Site 27). Expect hardwood floors, elegant furniture and spotless bathrooms. Avoid the downstairs rooms simply because they lack natural light.

Motorcycling
West Vang Vieng Loop

START MAYLYN GUEST HOUSE
END MAYLYN GUEST HOUSE
LENGTH 26KM; SIX HOURS

To get right into the heart of the limestone karsts rising out of the rice paddies opposite Vang Vieng, consider this loop by motorbike or mountain bike. We reckon it's best approached as a day trip, with stops at the various caves, viewpoints and swimming holes. It's ideally done on a trail bike, although possible on smaller motos or mountain bikes. The best guide to the area is the Hobo Maps *Vang Vieng* (www.hobomaps.com; US$2) map, which includes heaps of helpful details including handy references to the numbered power poles that run along part of the road.

Heading west from ❶**Maylyn Guest House** you'll see hand-painted signs to various caves along the first couple of kilometres of the path, only some of which are visit-worthy, and all of which charge 10,000K for admission and/or guiding. Worth considering is ❷**Tham Pha Daeng**, the turn-off to which is located after pole 16. There's a cave pool and the area is the best place to watch the bats stream from their caves every evening. The 2km walk to ❸**Tham Khan**, approached via a 1.5km side road after pole 24, is probably more worthwhile than the long but claustrophobic cave.

At the Hmong village of Ban Phone Ngeun about 3km from Maylyn Guest House, turn right just after pole 42, opposite two basic shops. A flagged road leads past the local school to a desk where the local kids will collect a fee of 10,000K to take you on the steep 45-minute hike to the top of ❹**Pha Ngeun**, a rocky cliff where the locals have built a few basic observation decks. These offer arguably the most dramatic views of the area for those that don't fancy leaving terra firma with the hot air balloon or ultralight flights on offer in town.

Returning to the main road, keep right at the next intersection where you'll pass through the Lao Loum village of Ban Na Thong. After 2km you'll come to another fork and a sign pointing right to ❺**Tham**

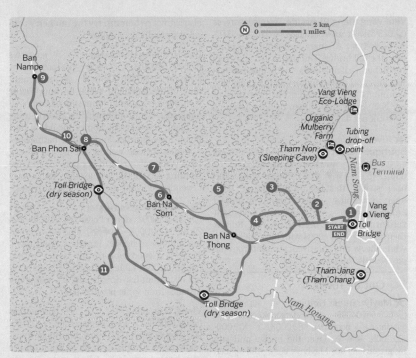

Phu Kham (p164), about 700m along a track. Don't confuse this with nearby Tham Phu Thong, as both are referred to by locals as the Blue Lagoon, but Tham Phu Thong is more like a muddy pond. The natural pool at Tham Phu Kham used to be a great place to stop for a refreshing swim, but it has now been overrun with development, including slides, rope swings and more. It can be quiet during the week, but it's packed at the weekend. It's may be better to skip it and head on to Blue Lagoon 3.

Back on the main track, continue west and you'll soon be in ⑥ **Ban Na Som**, a village of Hmong who have been resettled here. Around here the vegetation on the karsts is scarred by slash-and-burn farming. Just beyond Na Som are signs to ⑦ **Golden Flower Cave**. Reaching it involves walking through rice fields, climbing a fence and following two white arrows for a few minutes. The cave is about 50m up the hill: look into the undergrowth for the vague stairs, but it's barely worth the effort.

Continuing west a beautiful stretch of track hugs the edge of the karsts and crosses a couple of streams and eventually comes to ⑧ **Ban Phon Sai**. Here the track joins with

a better dirt road, but first you need to cross the Nam Houang (Houang River), which might be tricky in the wet season.

You have a choice now: continue 5km west through more dramatic scenery to ⑨ **Ban Nampe**, a pretty village but nothing more, or soon start heading back east along the southern route. Either way, don't miss the nearby ⑩ **Blue Lagoon 3** (p166), one of the most beautiful swimming spots in the Vang Vieng area and not the organised chaos that is the original Blue Lagoon. About 6km southeast of Ban Phon Sai, over another couple of creeks, signs point across a small bridge to a track to ⑪ **Python Cave**, about 800m away. Once you've seen this, it's plain sailing back to Vang Vieng. Keep along the road, then go left at the junction (follow the power poles), immediately cross a stream and soon you'll be back on the main track, loop complete.

Villa Vang Vieng Riverside   BOUTIQUE HOTEL **$$**
(📞 023-511460; www.villavangvieng.com; r US$60-76; 🔁❄🛜❄) A smart new boutique hotel near the toll bridge. The rooms are relatively small but well-appointed with tasteful furnishings and contemporary bathrooms. The swimming pool is located on the banks of the Nam Song and is open to nonguests for 30,000K per day.

★**Riverside
Boutique Resort**   BOUTIQUE HOTEL **$$$**
(📞 021-511726; www.riversidevangvieng.com; r US$123-150; 🔁❄@🛜❄) Sugar-white and uber stylish, this beautiful boutique belle offers generously spaced rooms wrapped around a citrus-green pool and a verdant garden looking out onto the karsts. Rooms themselves are gorgeous with balconies, crisp white sheets, and chic decor straight from the pages of *Wallpaper*.

🛏 Out of Town

★**Maylyn Guest House**   GUESTHOUSE **$**
(📞 020-55604095; www.facebook.com/maylyn guesthouse; bungalows 80,000K, r 100,000-120,000K; 🔁❄🛜) Over the bridge and run by gregarious Jo, Maylyn's cosy, well-spaced cabanas afford dramatic views of the karsts. There's also a number of immaculate rooms including a newer wing of en suite doubles with tasteful decor and private balcony overlooking the river and cliffs. The lush garden is a wonderland for kids and there is a pair of family rooms for 200,000K.

Chez Mango   GUESTHOUSE **$**
(📞 020-54435747; www.chezmango.com; r with/without bathroom 80,000/60,000K; 🛜) Located over the bridge, Mango is friendly, scrupulously clean and has seven basic but colourful cabanas (some with bathrooms) with private balconies in its flowery gardens. Shaded by trees, there's also a *sala* (open-sided shelter) to read in. Run by Noé, who also runs the excellent Vang Vieng Jeep Tour (p167) from here, this is a soporific and restful spot.

Vang Vieng Organic Farm   GUESTHOUSE **$**
(📞 023-511220; www.laofarm.org; dm 35,000-50,000K, r 150,000-250,000K; 🔁❄🛜) 📍 Located by the Nam Song in an idyllically quiet spot a few kilometres out of town, this organic farm has clean bungalows with mosquito nets, bedside lamps, en suites and verandahs looking out onto the soaring cliffs. Up the hill are three fan-cooled, eight-bed dorms. There's

also a great restaurant: try the mulberry pancakes or mulberry mojitos!

Ban Naduang Homestay   HOMESTAY **$**
(📞 020-55200013; douang_pcl@hotmail.com; homestay 25,000-100,000K; 🔁) 📍 As an antidote to the late-night scene in Vang Vieng, consider a traditional homestay in Ban Naduang, just 4km from town, but a world away in many respects. All homes include a bed, linen, mosquito net and shared bathrooms. Activities include visiting the nearby Kaeng Nyui Waterfall (30,000K per person) and tree planting (100,000K per group). Rates vary depending on your meal plan and activities.

Real Backpackers Hostel   HOSTEL **$**
(📞 030-5259002; dm incl breakfast 55,000K, tr/q 200,000/250,000K; 🔁❄🛜) One of a growing number of budget hostels around town. There is a good vibe to this hostel, with a pool table and table football in the communal restaurant-bar downstairs. It's stumbling distance from some popular bars.

Vieng Tara Villa   BOUTIQUE HOTEL **$$**
(📞 030-5023102; www.viengtara.com; r US$50-90; 🔁❄@🛜❄) This new boutique resort really takes advantage of its location on the west-bank riverside to deliver some incredible views of the looming karst. Choose one of the villa paddy-view rooms, which are set on stilts in the middle of lush rice fields and accessible via a wooden walkway. River-view rooms are cheaper in this instance, as they look towards town. In a word, stylish.

🍴 Eating

★**Living Room**   ASIAN **$**
(📞 020-54919169; mains 30,000-50,000K; ⏰3-11pm; 🛜) Classy custard-coloured cafe with unbroken views of the cliffs from its hilltop eyrie, and a romantic place to eat with its low-lit and exposed-brick and bamboo interior. Gazpacho, homemade bread, NZ lamb, spicy beef goulash – this Lao-Austrian affair is in every sense a fusion cafe. And the best spot in town for a sunset Bloody Mary.

Amigos Vang Vieng   MEXICAN **$**
(📞 020-58780574; mains 30,000-60,000K; ⏰9am-1pm & 5-10pm; 🛜📍) It may come as something of a surprise to find an authentic Mexican restaurant in the backstreets of Vang Vieng, but the tacos, burritos, fajitas and nachos here are some of the best we've tried in all of Laos. Swing by early evening to sample the margaritas and get the evening going with a buzz. It's also open for brunch.

The Kitchen INTERNATIONAL $
(www.inthira.com; Th Luang Prabang; mains 30,000-90,000K; ☺7am-10pm; ✳🖥📶) This smart roadside restaurant at the Inthira Hotel is stylishly informal with an open-range kitchen and decent service. Feast on the spring rolls, pork and lemongrass skewers, pad thai, spare ribs and steamed fish. The menu is similar to Khop Chai Deu (p146) in Vientiane if you need a reference point.

Cafe Eh Eh CAFE $
(☑030-5074369; breakfast 20,000-40,000K; ☺7.30am-7pm; ✳🖥) Cafe Eh Eh offers a chilled (we are talking air-con here) retreat from the downtown heat of Vang Vieng, offering a tempting selection of freshly made cakes and gourmet coffee. Breakfast is available, including a trio of pastries for 10,000K, and a limited selection of sandwiches and salads.

Sabaidee Burger BURGERS $
(☑020-98648691; mains 30,000-55,000K; ☺11am-3pm & 5-11pm; 🖥) This Belgian burger bar turns out the tastiest burgers in Vang Vieng, with a good range of meat, fish, salmon and vegie options. Beyond burgers, there are salads, wraps, kebabs and 'la mitraillette' – the Belgian answer to a footlong Subway. A Belgian beer selection rounds things off.

Veggie Tables VEGETARIAN $
(Th Luang Prabang; mains 30,000-40,000K; ☺8am-10pm; 🖥📶) It's vegie heaven at this simple hole-in-the-wall delight. Think colourful check tables, Lao life murals, and a wealth of salads, soups, spring rolls, spaghetti dishes and tofu variations.

Sababa Organic Restaurant JEWISH $
(mains 15,000-40,000K; ☺7am-10pm; 🖥📶) Sababa ('Cool' in Hebrew), allegedly run by a Lao Jew, boasts a Hebrew-language menu and, not surprisingly, is the best place in town to find your inner falafel. The chicken schnitzel also gets good reviews, as do the tofu, salads and steak.

★**Il Tavolo** ITALIAN $$
(☑023-511768; Rte 13; mains 38,000-80,000K; ☺5-11pm Thu-Tue; ✳🖥) The most authentic Italian restaurant in town, 'The Table' is run by a father-and-son team. The menu includes 19 varieties of oven-baked Neapolitan pizzas, a wide selection of pasta, gnocchi and risotto dishes, plus some generous entrées. Wash down your meal with a botttle of Prosecco.

★**Restaurant du Crabe d'Or** INTERNATIONAL $$
(☑023-511726; www.riversidevangvieng.com; mains 50,000-150,000K; ☺7-10am & noon-10pm; ✳🖥📶) Set on the tasteful grounds of the Riverside Boutique Resort, this fine restaurant exudes high-end decor with a Lao flavour, and affords amazing views of the cliffs. The menu will please most palates with grilled salmon steak, pork cutlet with honey and lime sauce, as well as a raft of trad-Asian dishes.

Pizza Luka PIZZA $$
(☑020-98190831; mains 60,000K; ☺6-11pm; 🖥) Pizza Luka is based in a pretty wooden Lao house. Dine in the mint-green interior or alfresco in the garden where homemade pizza is baked in a wood-fired oven. Flavoured with sausage, goat cheese, bacon and many more ingredients, the pizzas are decked in sauces made from locally grown vegetables.

Le Café De Paris FRENCH $$
(mains 50,000-80,000K; ☺6-11pm; 🖥) The best spot in town for Gallic grub like duck breast, Tournedos Rossini, and goat-cheese salad. Add to this a cosy interior of vintage film posters and a low-lit atmosphere and you have the recipe for a decent dinner.

Mitthaphap Fusion KOREAN $$
(☑020-22254515; Th Luang Prabang; set barbecue 50,000K; ☺5-10pm; 🖥) Popular Mitthaphap Fusion serves *seen dàat*, do-it-yourself Korean-style barbeque and a Lao interpretation of hotpot, and is busy with a local crowd most evenings.

Drinking & Nightlife

★**Gary's Irish Bar** IRISH PUB
(☑020-58255774; www.irishbar.weebly.com; ☺9am-11.30pm; 🖥) Still the best bar in town thanks to its friendly, unpretentious atmosphere, indie tunes, free pool and great grub like homemade pies, burgers and Lao fare (mains 40,000K to 60,000K). When there's live rugby or footy you'll find it on the flatscreen TV. And watch out for live music!

Jungle Project CLUB
(☺10pm-6am Fri, 9pm-3am Sun) If you want to recapture the hedonistic spirit of Va Va Vang Vieng before the clampdown, the Jungle Project parties are the easiest way to get your flashback. Friday night is the big all-nighter and Sunday night sees the occasional foam party, both at the decrepit Vang Vieng Mai Resort, about 2km north of town.

PARADISE LOST? PARADISE POSTPONED

Back in 1999, Vang Vieng was a little-known, bucolic affair where travellers came to float on tractor inner tubes down the river, cycle through its stunning karst country and maybe smoke the odd spliff between exploring its fantastical caves. Then the word got out – Vang Vieng was Southeast Asia's next hedonistic mecca and ravers were marking it on their party itinerary like a sort of Thailand's Ko Pha Ngan in the mountains. As Lao locals were quick to erect guesthouses to serve the increased traffic, the drugs got heavier, the party darker.

By 2009 makeshift rave platforms had established themselves along the tubing route. Forget the natural scenery and outdoor activities like climbing, biking, kayaking and trekking; gap-year kids were here to get wasted on reefer, Red Bull and shots, methamphetamine and opium cocktails. Ugly, but great business – some bars were making US$2500 per day (a fortune in Laos). Drug busts were frequent, as were half-naked travellers, wandering around town like lost extras from *The Beach*.

But behind the revelry was a darker truth: by 2011 at least 25 Western kids (mainly Aussies and Brits) had variously died from heart attacks, drownings and broken necks, having ridden the 'deathslide' (a hastily erected zipline over a seasonally perilously low river). Under pressure from the Australian government after more deaths in 2012, the Laos government moved to close down the rave bars in August. Vang Vieng's river-bar owners were called to a meeting by the Ministry of Tourism and Culture and those without licences (most of them) were ordered to shut down within 10 days.

With drugs generally off the menu, the town has been repositioning itself from a soiled party venue to the rural paradise it once was. And while local doctors in Vang Vieng's diminutive emergency ward are less overworked, guesthouse owners are looking for ways to fill their rooms with an influx of South Korean tourists and family visitors.

For the first time in years mainstream visitors are heading to Vang Vieng, many en route to fabled Luang Prabang, stopping to kayak the Nam Song, go caving and climb the karsts. Relief pretty much describes the current feeling of Vang Vieng's more conservative inhabitants. Locals are glad that Vang Vieng is now untroubled by thumping music, disrespectful teens and the misconception that anything goes.

Kangaroo Sunset Bar
BAR

(☏ 020-55578477; ◷ 9am-midnight;) Long-running Kangaroo Sunset Bar no longer has the sunset view as it has relocated to the centre of town, but it still offers a friendly venue for an evening session, including cocktails, shots and regular promos. It holds regular *baci* (*bạasǐi*; sacred string-tying) ceremonies for visitors and, in contrast, regular party nights.

Heartbeat
CLUB

(☏ 020-55113366; Nathom Village; ◷ 6pm-late;) For something completely different with more of a Lao flavour, head to this big beer garden and nightclub about 2km north of town. This is where the visiting weekenders from Vientiane end up for fun and frolics and it often hosts live bands from the capital.

Sakura Bar
BAR

(☏ 020-78008555; Rte 13; ◷ 6pm-late) At the time of writing, Sakura, one of the most popular late-night bars in Vang Vieng, had just opened a new spot in an old beer garden and nightclub on Rte 13. Expect a raucous crowd, shot promotions and a loud, late night.

Earth
BAR

(◷ 5-11.30pm;) Made from driftwood and clay, this hip hillside bar-restaurant pipes out fine tunes to match the ambience. Check out the sumptuous view of the cliffs from the candlelit garden, between snacking on toasties, waffles, sandwiches and curries.

ℹ Information

A useful website detailing up-to-date events is www.vangvieng.biz.

DANGERS & ANNOYANCES

Most visitors leave Vang Vieng with nothing more serious than a hangover, but this tranquil setting is also the most dangerous place in Laos for travellers. Visitors die every year from river accidents and while caving. Theft can also be a problem, with fellow travellers often the culprits. Take the usual precautions and don't leave valuables outside caves.

INTERNET ACCESS

Most hostels, guesthouses, hotels, cafes and bars now offer free wi-fi. There are a few internet cafes on the main drags, usually charging around 10,000K per hour.

MEDICAL SERVICES

Provincial Hospital (📞023-511604) This modest hospital has X-ray facilities and is fine for broken bones, cuts and malaria. When we visited, the doctor spoke reasonable English. However, if it is more serious, you will need to get to Vientiane or Thailand.

MONEY

Agricultural Promotion Bank (Th Luang Prabang; ⊘8.30am-3.30pm) Exchanges cash, plus has an ATM.

Banque pour le Commerce Extérieur Lao (⊘8.30am-3.30pm) Money exchange, cash advances and has a 24-hour ATM.

BCEL (📞023-511434; Th Luang Prabang; ⊘8.30am-3.30pm) Exchanges cash and travellers cheques, and handles cash advances on Visa, MasterCard and JCB. Has two ATMs in town including at its other **branch** (⊘8.30am-3.30pm) by the old market.

POST

Post Office (📞023-511009; ⊘8am-5pm Mon-Sat, to noon Sun) Right next to the old market.

TOURIST INFORMATION

Tourist Office (📞023-511707; Th Luang Prabang; ⊘8am-noon & 2-4pm) The staff's English might be lamentable, but this is a useful port of call to pick up various leaflets on things to do in the area.

ℹ Getting There & Away

Buses, minibuses and *sŏrngtăaou* depart from the **main bus station** (Rte 13) about 2km north of town, although if you're coming in from Vientiane you'll most likely be dropped off at or near the **bus stop** (Rte 13) near the former runway, a short walk from the centre of town. When leaving Vang Vieng, be aware that, even if you purchased your tickets at the bus station, the more expensive minibuses and air-con buses often cater predominantly to *falang* (Westerners) and will circle town, picking up people at their guesthouses, adding as much as an additional hour to the departure time. They then stop at the **secondary bus station** (📞023-511657; Rte 13) to ensure they are full before departure.

Heading north, buses for Luang Prabang stop at the bus stop for about five minutes en route from Vientiane about every hour between 11am and 8pm. These services also stop at Kasi and Phu Khoun (for Phonsavan). However, do be aware that there have been occasional attacks on night buses heading north through the edge of Saisomboun Province in the district of Kasi.

Heading south, there are several bus options to Vientiane. Alternatively, *sŏrngtăaou* (30,000K, three to four hours) leave about every 20 minutes from 5.30am until 4.30pm and, as they're often not full, the ride can be quite enjoyable.

ℹ Getting Around

Vang Vieng is easily negotiated on foot. Renting a bicycle (per day 10,000K) or mountain bike (per day 30,000K) is also popular; they're available almost everywhere. Most of the same places also rent motorcycles from about 50,000K per day (automatics cost 80,000K). For cave sites out of town you can charter *sŏrngtăaou* near the old market site: expect to pay around US$10 per trip up to 20km north or south of town.

Vang Vieng towards Luang Prabang

The road between Vang Vieng and Luang Prabang winds its way up over some stunning mountains and back down to the Mekong at Luang Prabang. If you suffer from motion sickness, take precautions before you begin.

Roughly 20km north of Vang Vieng, **Ban Pha Tang** is a pretty riverside village named after Pha Tang, a towering limestone cliff. The town's bridge offers a very photogenic view of its namesake.

In the middle of a fertile valley filled with rice fields, **Kasi**, 56km north of Vang Vieng, is a lunch stop for bus passengers and truck drivers travelling on this route. The surrounding area is full of interesting minority villages, and there are allegedly a few big caves in the area, but few people bother to stop as there isn't much tourist infrastructure.

Uncle Tom's Trail Bike Tours (📞020-29958903; uncletomslaos@gmail.com; Rte 13, Kasi; 2 lessons & overnight stay for 1/2 people US$120/208) in Kasi is a reputable operator with decent 125cc hybrid motocross bikes on which to learn to ride off-road (an essential skill for motorcycle travel in Laos).

If you've got trailblazing on your mind, you can base yourself at **Somchit Guesthouse** (📞020-22208212; Rte 13, Kasi; r 80,000-170,000K; ⊛❄🖤), an expansive and tidy hotel about 1km north of the city. Another option is to book a basic room at **Vanphisith Guest House** (📞023-700084; Rte 13, Kasi; r 60,000K).

While Kasi isn't memorable, the road on towards Luang Prabang is, despite the ravages of slash-and-burn agriculture. For around 50km to Phu Khoun, you'll ascend through some of the most spectacular limestone mountains to be found anywhere in Laos.

Central Laos

Best Places to Eat

➡ Savannakhet Plaza Food Market (p193)

➡ Sala Vann (p193)

➡ Khop Chai Deu (p187)

➡ Lin's Café (p193)

Best Places to Sleep

➡ Inthira Hotel (p186)

➡ Spring River Resort (p181)

➡ Thakhek Travel Lodge (p186)

➡ Vivanouk Homestay (p191)

Why Go?

Ever since Tha Khaek opened its French-colonial shutters to travellers and the dramatic 7km-long underworld of Tham Kong Lor became a must-see fixture on itineraries, central Laos has been enticing visitors. Thanks to its honeycomb of caves and dragon-green jungle, activities on offer run from world-class rock climbing to trekking in Dong Phu Vieng NPA where you can sleep with the spirits in a Katang village. Cave exploration is an obvious headline attraction, but kayaking trips are also a big draw thanks to the myriad rivers that course like veins around and, often, through the karst mountains.

This part of the country claims the most forest cover and highest concentrations of wildlife, including some species that have disappeared elsewhere in Southeast Asia. With its rugged, intrepid travel, and stylish pockets of comfort in Savannakhet and Tha Khaek, central Laos makes for a great place to combine your inner Indiana Jones with a Bloody Mary.

When to Go
Savannakhet

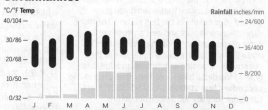

Nov–Feb The best time to visit: temperatures are balmy, paddy fields green and roads passable.

Mar–May Leading up to the monsoon, fields are bone dry and the humidity ratchets up. Avoid the oven that is the south.

Jun–Nov Despite pockets of intense rain, sealed roads are still passable, the landscape vividly green and air cool.

Climate

The Mekong River valley is always pretty warm and from March to May Savannakhet is positively steaming. It gets cooler as you head east towards the Annamite Chain and Lak Sao, and the villages along Rte 8B can be close to freezing during winter nights. The southwestern monsoon brings bucketloads of rain from June to October. Far-eastern areas around the Nakai-Nam Theun National Biodiversity Conservation Area (NBCA) also receive rain from the South China Sea that lasts longer, thus supplying enough water to maintain the thicker vegetation.

National Protected Areas

Central Laos is the best-preserved part of the country with six National Protected Areas (NPAs) accounting for vast swaths of the region. Access to Nakai-Nam Theun NBCA, Hin Namno NPA and Se Ban Nuan NPA is limited to those with decent Lao language skills and plenty of time and money, but others are easy to get to.

In Khammuan Province the labyrinth of limestone karsts, caves and rivers in Phu Hin Bun NPA is accessible either on your own or on a community-based or commercial trek. Similar treks lead to the sacred forests and animist villages of Dong Phu Vieng in Savannakhet Province.

❶ Getting There & Away

Central Laos is well connected to the rest of the country by road and there are regular bus services connecting the region with towns and cities of the north. Flight connections are more limited via Savannakhet, but Nakhon Phanom Airport in Thailand offers some affordable budget flights to Bangkok and beyond.

Rte 13 is sealed, and thanks to its vital status as a Chinese trade route, it's particularly well maintained. Other decent roads include Rte 9 from Savannakhet to the Vietnamese border at Lao Bao; Rte 8 between Rte 13 and the Vietnamese border at Nam Phao; Rte 12 between Tha Khaek and the Vietnamese border; and the road to Tham Kong Lor.

BOLIKHAMSAI & KHAMMUAN PROVINCES

Bolikhamsai and Khammuan straddle the narrow, central 'waist' of the country. Physically the land climbs steadily from the Mekong River valley towards the north and east, eventually reaching the Annamite Chain bordering Vietnam, via an area of moderately high but often spectacular mountains. Laid-back Tha Khaek is the logical base.

Lowland Lao dominate the population and, along with smaller groups of tribal Thais, are the people you'll mostly meet. In remoter areas the Mon-Khmer-speaking Makong people (commonly known as Bru) make up more than 10% of the population of Khammuan.

Much of the region is relatively sparsely populated and six large tracts of forest have been declared NPAs. These areas have become a major battleground between those wishing to exploit Laos' hydroelectricity capacity and those wishing to preserve some of the most pristine wilderness areas in Asia. For now, the developers have the upper hand.

❶ Getting There & Away

These twin provinces are well connected to the rest of Laos with bus links and good surfaced roads connecting Tha Kheak with Vientiane to the north; Savannakhet and Pakse to the south; Thailand (via the Mekong to the west); and Vietnam to the east.

Paksan ປາກຊັນ

POP 45,000 / ☎054

Located at the confluence of the Nam San (San River) and the Mekong River, Paksan (Pakxan or Pakxanh) is the capital of Bolikhamsai Province. Although it's not the most exciting place in Laos, it has a few guesthouses and restaurants and is a possible stop if you're pedalling between Vientiane and Tha Khaek or Kong Lor. It's possible to cross into Thailand via the Mekong River, but hardly anyone travels this way.

🛏 Sleeping & Eating

BK Guest House GUESTHOUSE $
(☎054-212638; r 70,000-80,000K; ❋🛜) Set in a leafy garden dripping in frangipani flowers, this house-proud guesthouse has eight rooms, all immaculately clean with en suites and fresh linen, and the friendly owner speaks English.

Paksan Hotel HOTEL $
(☎054-791444; Rte 13; r 120,000-200,000K; ➦❋🛜) This huge Vietnamese-run, temple-roofed colossus has 32 well-sized rooms with TV, fridge, verandah and armoire. 'VIP' rooms are available, but only if your idea of VIP is faux-leather sofas.

Central Laos Highlights

1 Tham Kong Lor (p179) Going underground to experience a boat trip through this incredible 7km-long limestone underworld.

2 Phu Hin Bun NPA (p185) Trekking amid gothic limestone karsts, subterranean caves and meandering rivers.

3 The Loop (p182) Riding and journeying on winding roads through flooded valleys, dense jungle and jagged mountain peaks.

4 Savannakhet (p190) Soaking up the old-world atmosphere of the colonial-era architecture.

5 Dong Phu Vieng NPA (p197) Staying in the remote villages and experiencing life in the spirit forests.

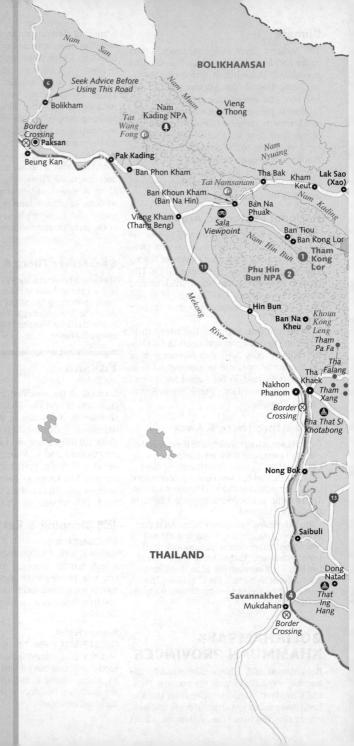

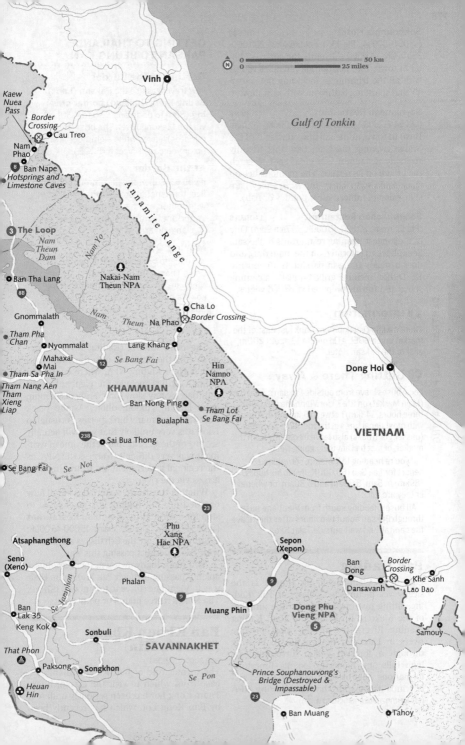

Sokbounma Hotel HOTEL $$
(☑054-790994; Rte 13; r incl breakfast 200,000-350,000K; ⊜❄🛜) Currently the smartest hotel in town, the Sokbounma offers 34 rooms with all the trimmings, including flat-screen TV and sparkling bathroom with rain shower.

Saynamsan Restaurant LAOTIAN $
(☑054-212608; mains 15,000-90,000K; ⊘7am-11pm) In town, at the northwestern end of the bridge crossing the Nam San, this friendly riverside restaurant is a great spot to catch the breeze on its terrace. The menu dishes up spicy squid soup, curry and *láhp* (spicy Lao-style salad of minced meat poultry or fish).

Sengphachan Restaurant LAOTIAN $
(Rte 13; mains 20,000-40,000K; ⊘7am-9pm) One of the longest-running restaurants in Paksan, Sengphachan is located on the main drag and does a steady trade in passing traffic on Rte 13. Dishes include grilled meats, steaming soups and freshly prepared stir-fried vegies.

❶ Information

There's a Lao Development Bank just east of the market and a BCEL ATM on Rte 13 about 200m east of the Paksan Hotel.

❶ Getting There & Away

Local buses leave from outside Paksan's Talat Sao (Main Market) on Rte 13 for Vientiane (30,000K, three hours, 143km) between 6am and 4.30pm, with most departures in the morning. *Sŏrngtǎaou* (passenger trucks) also leave frequently from the market, or just hail anything going west.

If you're heading to Vietnam, *sŏrngtǎaou* depart for Lak Sao (60,000K, five to six hours, 189km) at 5am, 5.30am and 6.30am, or whenever they are full.

All buses heading south from Vientiane pass through Paksan about two hours after they leave the capital: just wait outside Talat Sao.

Pak Kading

East from Vientiane along Rte 13 is the sleepy yet picturesque village of Pak Kading, sitting just upstream from the junction of the Mekong River and the Nam Kading (Kading River), one of the most pristine rivers in Laos (for now, at least). Flowing through a forested valley surrounded by high hills and menacing-looking limestone formations, this broad, turquoise-tinted river winds its way into the **Nam Kading NPA** (ປ່າສະຫງວນແຫ່ງຊາດນ້ຳກະດິງ) ☂.

GETTING TO THAILAND: PAKSAN TO BEUNG KAN

Getting to the Border
Few travellers use the **Paksan (Laos)/ Beung Kan (Thailand) border crossing** (8am to noon and 1.30 to 4.30pm) via the Mekong River. The boat (60B, 20 minutes) leaves when eight people show up or you can charter it (500B).

At the Border
If you turn up at the Lao immigration office, they should process the paperwork without too much fuss, though it is very important to note that Lao visas are not available on arrival.

Moving On
In Thailand buses leave Beung Kan for Udon Thani (245B, four hours), where there are onward connections to Bangkok via budget airlines or long-distance bus.

The Nam Kading (Kading River) is undoubtedly the best way into the wilderness that is Nam Kading NPA, where confirmed animal rarities include the elephant, giant muntjac, pygmy slow loris, François' langur, douc langur, gibbon, dhole, Asiatic black bear, tiger and many bird species. As usual in Laos, it is very unlikely that you will actually see any of these. Note that at the time of writing it was very difficult to access the NPA, as the regional government are restricting boat access via the river.

Whether the nearby waterfall is in full flow or dried up, Pak Kading is a good place to stop for a meal at the **Bounxou Restaurant** (☑055-320046; Rte 13; mains 15,000-45,000K; ⊘8am-9pm), where the fish dishes are famous with Lao itinerants passing this way.

As a main highway town, there are buses aplenty passing through Pak Kading on their way to Vientiane (three to four hours, 187km), Tha Khaek (three hours) or points east.

Ban Khoun Kham (Ban Na Hin)

POP 3000 / ☑054
The former role of Ban Khoun Kham as a base from which to visit the extraordinary Tham Kong Lor has been seriously undercut by Ban Kong Lor, which has recently been

acquitting itself to cater for tourists headed to the nearby cave, and as such there's a little tumbleweed blowing through town. However, there is an attractive waterfall near town and some great viewpoints across the jagged karst landscape if you do decide to stay here.

◉ Sights

Tat Namsanam   WATERFALL
(ຕາດນ້ຳສະບາມ) The main local attraction is the impressive twin-cataract of Tat Namsanam, 3km north of town, although in the dry season, it's, well, dry. The falls are in a striking location surrounded by karst and the upper tier is quite high.

Unfortunately, the path and signs leading to the falls aren't entirely clear, and more than one foreign visitor has got lost here. Proceed with caution, or better yet, hire a guide through the excellent Tourist Information Centre, just south of the Tat Namsanam entrance, which runs community-based treks from here into the Phu Hin Bun NPA.

Stone Forest Viewpoint   VIEWPOINT
As you approach Ban Khoun Kham from Rte 13, there is a *sala* (open-sided shelter) viewpoint between Km 32 and Km 33. Do not, whatever you do, miss the spectacularly dramatic scenery below; somewhere between a dream and a nightmare, the landscape rears raggedly with black rock formations.

Tha Bak Bomb Boats   HISTORIC SITE
About 18km east of Ban Khoun Kham, Tha Bak sits near the confluence of the Nam Kading and Nam Theun. The reason to stop here is to either take photos of the river or get out on the incredible bomb boats, which are made out of huge missile-shaped drop tanks that carried fuel for jets operating overhead during the war. If you fancy a spin on one, just head down to the riverbank at the eastern end of the bridge and negotiate a price.

⌷ Sleeping

Sanhak Guesthouse   GUESTHOUSE $
(☑020-22334691; sanhak.guesthouse@gmail.com; dm 25,000K; r 50,000-80,000K; ❂❈☎) One of the most popular guesthouses in Ban Khoun Kham thanks to advertising in the motorbike-rental shops along Tha Khaek, this is a friendly backstreet place to stay. Cheap-as-chips dorms and comfortable rooms with hot water are available. There's also a small restaurant here.

Inthapaya Guesthouse   GUESTHOUSE $
(☑020-22336534; r with fan/air-con 60,000/90,000K; ❂❈@☎) Fresh-smelling powder-blue rooms with tiled floors, clean en suites and optional fan or air-con. There's also a little courtyard cafe. It's northeast of the main street. The owner speaks excellent English.

★Sainamhai Resort   RESORT $$
(☑020-22331683; www.sainamhairesort.com; r 150,000-240,000K; ❂❈☎) By far the dreamiest and most cosy accommodation in town – except it's not in town. Thankfully Sainamhai sits by the Nam Hai (Hai River) a little out of the village. There's a handsome longhouse restaurant, a fertile garden and well-maintained rattan-walled cabanas with private balconies, en suites and clean linen. Add to this warm service and cool air-con.

It's 3km east of Rte 8 via a turn-off a few kilometres down the road that leads to Tham Kong Lor. Staff will pick you up for free at the *sŏrngtăaou* station if you call ahead.

ℹ Information

Tourist Information Centre (☑020-55598412; Rte 8; ◷8am-4pm) Just south of the Tat Namsanam entrance, this efficiently run centre operates community-based treks from here into the Phu Hin Bun NPA. Ask to speak to Thoum.

ℹ Getting There & Away

There are two morning departures from Tha Khaek to Ban Khoun Kham (50,000K, three hours, 143km) at 8am and 9am. Alternatively, from Tha Khaek or Vientiane, simply hop on any north- or southbound bus and get off at Vieng Kham (also known as Thang Beng), at the junction of Rtes 13 and 8, and continue by *sŏrngtăaou* (25,000K, one hour, 7am to 7pm) to Ban Khoun Kham. It's easier to take a Vientiane–Lak Sao bus and ask to get off in Ban Khoun Kham (75,000K).

Later in the day you'll need to take any of the semi-regular *sŏrngtăaou* to Vieng Kham (30,000K, 7am to 5pm) or, if you're bound for the Vietnam border, Lak Sao (25,000K, 7am to 5pm) and change there. Both are about one hour from Ban Khoun Kham. To Tham Kong Lor, *sŏrngtăaou* leave at 10am, 12.30pm and 3pm (25,000K, one hour).

Tham Kong Lor   ຖ້ຳລອດກອງລໍ

Tham Kong Lor is one of central Laos', if not the country's, most vivid highlights. A journey into this preternatural underworld is like a voyage into the afterworld itself, with a 7.5km river passing through the cathedral-high limestone cave.

Ban Kong Lor (Kong Lor Village) is the most convenient base for visiting the cave and has seen an explosion of guesthouses and small resorts in the last few years.

 Activities

★**Tham Kong Lor** CAVING, BOATING
(cave entrance 5000K, parking fee 5000K, boat trip 1/2/3 persons 110,000/120,000/130,000K) A boat trip through the other-worldly Tham Kong Lor is an absolute must. Situated in the 1580-sq-km wilderness of Phu Hin Bun NPA, the 7.5km river cave runs beneath an immense limestone mountain. Your imagination will be in overdrive as the boat takes you further into the bat-black darkness and the fear dial will ratchet up as if on some natural Gothic ghost ride. The experience is unforgettable.

A section of Kong Lor has now been atmospherically lit, allowing you a greater glimpse of this epic spectacle; your longtail docks in a rocky inlet to allow you to explore a stalactite wood of haunting pillars and sprouting stalagmites like an abandoned *Star Trek* set.

Boat trips through Tham Kong Lor take up to an hour each way, and in dry season when the river is low, you'll have to get out while the boatman and point man haul the wooden craft up rapids. At the other end of the cave, a brief five minutes upstream takes you to a refreshment stop. Catch your breath and then head back in for more adrenaline-fuelled excitement.

Life jackets are provided. Be sure to bring a torch (flashlight) as the ones for rent are inadequate, and wear rubber sandals; the gravel in the riverbed is sharp and it's often necessary to disembark and wade at several shallow points.

Tham Nam None CAVING
(per person 120,000K) Tham Kong Lor is not the only major cave in the area. Tham Nam None is a 'new' cave that has been more recently discovered, but not yet fully explored. At 15km, it is one of the longest river caves in Laos, and it's possible to trek into the cave in the dry season. Don't venture into this cave alone; contact Spring River Resort to set up a trip and take plenty of torches and batteries.

👉 **Tours**

Khammuan Province's Tourist Information Centre (p188) offers day trips to Tham Kong Lor (per person for a group of one/two/five 1,500,000/850,000/550,000K); speak to the ever-proficient Mr Somkiad. Green Discovery (p186) also runs one-day trips to Tham Kong Lor from US$70 per person and overnight trips from US$155 per person.

TREKKING IN CENTRAL LAOS

Underrated central Laos is a great place to combine a cultural and environmental experience. Most treks in central Laos are run by either the state-run eco-guide units in Tha Khaek and Savannakhet or the private company Green Discovery (p186), and range in cost from approximately US$40 to US$500 per person (prices drop significantly the greater the number of people in the group). Listed below are some particularly recommended trekking destinations in the region:

Phu Hin Bun NPA (p185) From Tha Khaek. For beauty, it's hard to beat these trekking and boating trips through the monolithic limestone karsts. Two- and three-day options are available at Tha Khaek's Tourist Information Centre, and four-day trips with Green Discovery.

Tham Lot Se Bang Fai/Hin Namno NPA (p189) From Tha Khaek. Although trekking here is still in its infancy, and mostly revolves around the Nam Lot cave, it is also possible to combine a homestay with walks in the spectacular Hin Namno NPA. Enquire at Green Discovery; the Tha Khaek Tourist Information Centre is not currently offering trips here.

Dong Natad (p197) From Savannakhet. One- and two-day trips to the provincial protected area near Savannakhet are cheap and popular for their homestays and explanations of how villagers use the sacred forest to exist. Contact Savannakhet's **eco-guide unit** (Map p192; ☑ 041-214203; Th Latsaphanith; ⊗ 8am-noon & 1-4.30pm Mon-Fri; 🛜) for details.

Dong Phu Vieng NPA (p197) From Savannakhet. This three-day trek (with a fair bit of road time at either end) takes you to two Katang villages where animist beliefs come with a host of taboos. It's a real head-bending cultural experience, but the transport makes prices a bit steep. Organised by Savannakhet's eco-guide unit.

🛏 Sleeping & Eating

Say the word 'homestay' and you'll be hooked up with a family somewhere in the village. **Homestay accommodation** (Ban Kong Lor; per person incl dinner & breakfast 50,000K) is also available at the opposite end of the cave, in Ban Na Tan and the prettier Ban Phon Kham, but you'll get charged a second time when you return through the cave.

Both villages are within walking distance of the drink stalls where the boats terminate; Ban Na Tan is a 2km walk along the left fork, and Ban Phon Kham is the second village you'll come to after about 1km along the right fork. The drink vendors are more than happy to point you in the right direction.

Kong Lor Eco Lodge   GUESTHOUSE $
(✔030-9062772; Ban Kong Lor; r 50,000K; 🕾) Kong Lor Eco Lodge has 12 spartan but clean rooms set back from the road. The small restaurant here is one of the most popular in town and draws a steady crowd of travellers.

Chantha House   GUESTHOUSE $
(✔020-22100002; Ban Kong Lor; dm 40,000K, r 70,000-150,000K; ❈🕾) This Swiss-style accommodation on the main road to Kong Lor, at the start of the village, has 15 cool, well-kept rooms plus a dorm. The owners are friendly and, best of all, there are magnificent views of the cliffs. There's also a DVD lounge, a small cafe and bicycles for rent.

★ **Spring River Resort**   BUNGALOW $$
(✔020-59636111; www.springriverresort.com; Ban Tiou; bungalows US$15-50, tr US$40-50; ❈🕾) Formerly Sala Kong Lor, these stilted bungalows range from basic to superior and sit by the beautiful Nam Hin Bun. En suite triple rooms include mozzie nets and private balconies to enjoy the lush river view, and breakfast is included with the more expensive room.

Kong Lo View Hotel & Resort   BUNGALOW $$
(✔030-9143544; www.kongloview.com; d/tw/ VIP US$35/$50/$150, all incl breakfast; ❂❈🕾) Boasting the closest location to Tham Kong Lor, this attractive cluster of traditional wooden bungalows features a range of options including a vast VIP room. The restaurant features a terrace with views of the karst.

Auberges Sala Hinboun   GUESTHOUSE $$
(✔041-212445; www.salalao.com; r incl breakfast US$23-29; 🕾) On the banks of the Nam Hin Bun, Auberges Sala Hinboun has 12 homely, guacamole-green wood cabanas on stilts. Rooms have gypsy-chic curtains, rattan floors, balconies and comfy beds. The ones facing the river are the largest, but the smaller ones are decent too.

Mithuna Restaurant   LAOTIAN $
(Ban Kong Lor; mains 20,000-40,000K; ⊙7am-8pm) Close to the entrance to Tham Kong Lor, this semi-alfresco, fan-cooled restaurant serves up noodles, fried rice and pork *láhp,* as well as Western breakfasts. It's good for a refuel before or after a trip into the depths of the cave.

❶ Getting There & Away

The 50km road from Ban Khoun Kham to Ban Kong Lor winds through a beautiful valley of rice fields, hemmed in on either side by towering karst cliffs. It's an easy one-hour motorbike or *sŏrngtăaou* ride. From Ban Kong Lor, *sŏrngtăaou* to Ban Khoun Kham (25,000K) depart at 6.30am, 8am and 11am. There's also now a direct daily bus between Vientiane and Ban Kong Lor (80,000K, seven hours), which departs from Kong Lor Eco Lodge at 7am or from the Southern Bus Station in the capital at 10am.

Lak Sao   ຫລັກຊາວ

POP 33,000 / ✔054

Essentially a dusty two-street affair in the eastern reaches of Bolikhamsai Province, Lak Sao is humming with trucks passing through to Vietnam (only 36km away), and has made its name as a logging town. It's surrounded by beautiful sawtoothed cliffs that, come dusk, are evocatively etched a burnt charcoal.

There's plenty of uninspiring guesthouses, a maze of a market, 24-hour ATMs, plus a couple of places to eat. Not the prettiest place thanks to the eternal screen of dust that hangs in the air, but it's a useful pit stop to stock up on cash, fuel up and eat a reliable Lao lunch if you're on 'the Loop' (p182).

🛏 Sleeping & Eating

Phoutthavong Guest House   GUESTHOUSE $
(✔054-341074; Rte 1E; r 80,000K; ❂❈🕾) Sitting back from busy Rte 8, this pleasant guesthouse has large rooms with mahogany beds and furniture, basic en suite and TV. A talking mynah bird will keep you company.

Souriya Hotel   HOTEL $
(✔054-341111; Rte 1E; r 50,000-80,000K; ❂❈🕾) All rooms here have fan or air-con, and although some are smaller than others, they are fresh with firm beds and en suite with very hot water. There is also cable TV and motorbike parking.

Only One Restaurant   LAOTIAN **$**
(☑054-341034; Rte 1E; mains 20,000-60,000K; ⏰7am-10pm) Although it's no longer quite the 'only one' in town, it remains one of the best. The cavernous restaurant has a great terrace out back which makes a good place to eat your *láhp*, barbecued pork, stir-fries and fried morning glory (water spinach).

ⓘ Information

Lao Development Bank (Rte 1E) Located near the market, this bank changes Thai baht, US dollars, UK pounds and Vietnamese dong.

Post Office (cnr Rtes 8 & 1E)

ⓘ Getting There & Away

Buses leave from east of the market for Vientiane (85,000K, seven to eight hours, 334km) daily at 5.30am, 6.30am, 8am and 8pm. These buses stop at Vieng Kham (Thang Beng; 35,000K, two hours, 100km), where you can change for regular buses heading south, or get off at Paksan (50,000K, five to six hours, 189km). Other buses and *sǒrngtǎaou* head along Rte 8 to Vieng Kham/Thang Beng (between 8am and 5pm) and one bus goes to Tha Khaek (60,000K, five to six hours, 202km) at 7.30am.

Tha Khaek   ທ່າແຂກ

POP 80,000 / ☑051

This ex-Indochinese trading post is a delightful melange of crumbling French villas and warped Chinese merchant's shopfronts, with an easy riverside charm which, despite the new bridge over to nearby Thailand, shows few signs of change. An evocative place to stop for a day and night, you begin the Loop from here, and can also use Tha Khaek as a base from which to make organised day trips to Tham Kong Lor. There are also loads of caves, some with swimmable lagoons, nearby that can be accessed by scooter or tuk-tuk.

While you shouldn't expect Luang Prabang levels of sophistication from Tha Khaek, you will find a historically appealing old town and slice of authentic Lao life. The epicentre (if you can call it that) of the old town is the modest Fountain Sq at the western end of Th Kuvoravong near the river.

History

Tha Khaek traces its present-day roots to French-colonial construction in 1911 and 1912. Evidence of this period can be found in the slowly decaying buildings around Fountain Sq. The town served as a port, border post and administrative centre during the French period.

🏃 Motorcycle Tour
'The Loop'

START THA KHAEK
END THA KHAEK
DURATION THREE DAYS

'The Loop; an off-the-beaten-track circuit through some of the more remote parts of Khammuan and Bolikhamsai Provinces, has achieved mythic status with intrepid travellers and it's best done on a motorbike. Thankfully, there are now several companies in Tha Khaek renting out decent dirt bikes and smaller scooters. Make sure you spend a day practising your riding skills if you are a relative novice. Visiting the caves around Tha Khaek as a day trip is a good warm-up to tackling the Loop. Fuel is available in most villages along the way.

Begin in ❶ **Tha Khaek** (p189). Its Tourist Information Centre can provide advice on the circuit. It's also a good idea to sit down with a cold Beerlao and the ever-expanding logbook at **Thakhek Travel Lodge** (p186) before you head off.

Once you've got your wheels, and assuming you have already spent one day heading east on Rte 12 from Tha Khaek, visiting the caves and swimming spots on the way, then set out early enough to allow plenty of stops along the way. The 20km stretch north of ❷ **Mahaxai Mai**, about 40km from Tha Khaek, has a few accommodation options if you're running late, but they are all pretty forgettable places aimed at travelling dam workers. Just north of Km 55 is the Rte 12 turn-off to Vietnam and the expansive Nam Theun 2 Main Camp, across from which is **Phothavong Guest House** (☑020-56635555), one of the better places to stay along this stretch of the Loop. However, we would recommend continuing to Ban Tha Lang for the night.

Continuing past Gnommalath, an additional 5km north of the Rte 12 intersection, where there's petrol and basic food, you'll reach Nam Theun 2 Power Station. This is also the location of the educational **Nam Theun 2 Visitors Centre** (☑020-22213855), set in a traditional Luang Prabang–style house, which looks a touch out of place in the middle of nowhere. At the top of the hill the road splits at a busy village called Ban Oudomsouk; keep straight for 3km to ❸ **Nakai**, where fuel is available.

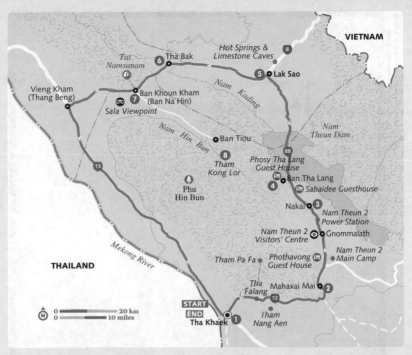

The next 23km is a disturbing corridor of pristine jungle on your left and the environmental disaster zone created by the flooding of the Nam Theun 2 dam on the right. You'll also start to see successive *bâan jat sàn*, tidy villages created for those displaced by the flooding. Just before the road crosses the Nam Theun (Theun River) via a new bridge, you'll arrive in tiny **4 Ban Tha Lang**, where the **Phosy Tha Lang Guesthouse** (☑ 020-58804711) offers respite in clean, basic turquoise cabanas with fresh sheets, en suites and balconies with hammocks. The view is pretty good, with the ghostly stumps of trees poking out of the recently flooded reservoir. More lively these days is **Sabaidee Guesthouse** (p185), the most popular place on the Loop thanks to the convivial owner and inviting restaurant. Rooms are set in bungalows in a spacious garden and firepits are lit nightly during the peak season. From Mahaxai Mai to Ban Tha Lang takes about two hours.

Continuing over the bridge at Ban Tha Long it's about 50km to Lak Sao. This stretch is stunning as you drive through the corridor between the Nakai-Nam Theun NBCA and **Phu Hin Bun NPA** (p185). But drive carefully; although the road is now surfaced, there are lots of tight switchbacks. Take it slowly and

drink up the view as you weave through an other-worldly flooded valley, with its eternity of oddly angled dead trees sticking out of the water and not a soul in sight. After 17km keep straight at the junction (the left fork will take you to the Nam Theun 2 dam site).

When you finally hit the frontier-feel town of **5 Lak Sao** (p181), there is plenty of accommodation and food, and it's also a good place if you need bike repairs. We recommend a pit stop for lunch and continuing on to Ban Khoun Kham (Ban Na Hin) or Tham Kong Lor for the overnight. Riding the 56km of smooth Rte 8 between Lak Sao and Ban Khoun Kham is like stepping into a video game: the road runs between walls of impregnable karst on one side, into winding hills of deep forest, and crosses the wide Nam Theun at **6 Tha Bak**, where it's worth stopping for a look at the **bomb boats** (p179).

7 Ban Khoun Kham (p178) has a petrol station and heaps of accommodation and is one base for trips into **8 Tham Kong Lor** (p179). However, over the last few years, accommodation has now sprung up in Kong Lor village itself and is more convenient for seeing the cave first thing in the morning. From Ban Khoun Kham, it's about 145km back to Tha Khaek if you want to get to there quickly.

Tha Khaek

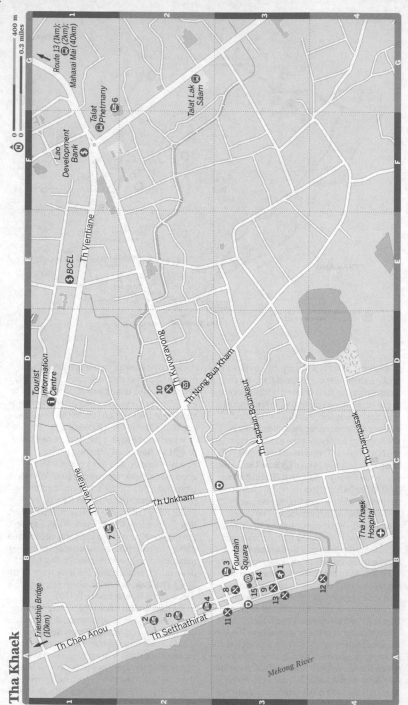

0   400 m
0   0.2 miles

Route 13 (1km);
Mahaxai Mai (40km)

Lao Development Bank

Talat Phetmany

Talat Lak Sàam

BCEL

Th Vientiane

Th Kuvoravong

Tourist Information Centre

Th Nong Bua Kham

Th Captain Bounkeut

Th Unkham

Th Vientiane

Th Champasak

Tha Khaek Hospital

Friendship Bridge (10km)

Th Chao Anou

Th Setthathirat

Fountain Square

Mekong River

Tha Khaek

Sights

Phu Hin Bun NPA
NATIONAL PARK

(ປາສະຫງວນແຫງຊາດພູຫີນບູນ) Phu Hin Bun NPA is a huge (1580 sq km) wilderness area of turquoise streams, monsoon forests and striking karst topography across central Khammuan. It was made a protected area in 1993 and it's no overstatement to say this is some of the most breathtaking country in the region.

Passing through on foot or by boat, it's hard not to feel awestruck by the very scale of the limestone cliffs that rise almost vertically for hundreds of metres into the sky. Although much of the NPA is inaccessible by road, local people have reduced the numbers of key forest-dependent species through hunting and logging. Despite this, the area remains home to the endangered douc langur, François' langur and several other primate species, as well as elephants, tigers and a variety of rare species of deer.

A trip out to Tham Kong Lor will give you a taste of what the NPA has to offer, but there are two more immersive ways to go deeper into this area of almost mythical gothic peaks and snaking streams.

Khammuan Province runs five different community-based treks of varying lengths. From Tha Khaek, the popular two-day trip (1,700,000K for one person, 950,000K each for two, 650,000K for five or more) into the Phu Hin Bun NPA is especially good. The route includes plenty of karst scenery, a walk through Tham Pa Chan and overnight accommodation in an ethnic village. Bookings can be made through the Tourist Information Centre (p188) in Tha Khaek.

Green Discovery offers similar treks including a very tempting two-day kayaking and cycling trip between spectacularly sheer cliffs, as the Nam Hin Bun (Hin Bun River) follows a large anticlockwise arc towards the Mekong.

Tham Pa Seuam
CAVE

(ຖ້ຳປາເຊືອມ) The recently discovered river cave of Tham Pa Seuam runs for 3km. A much smaller version of Tham Kong Lor, it features include impressive stalactites and stalagmites and is conveniently only 15km from Tha Khaek. A day trip to multiple caves, including Tham Pa Seuam, with the Tourist Information Centre (p188) costs from 350,000K per person and includes a 400m kayak paddle into the main chamber.

Activities

Most of the activities take place in the karst countryside around Tha Khaek, including clambering the karst at Green Climbers Home or exploring the many caves that pepper the jagged mountains.

When it comes to Tha Khaek town, other than wandering the streets and soaking up the atmosphere, there's not a lot to keep you occupied. If you're looking for something (slightly) more active, then head to **Namfon Petang Field** (Map p184; ☎020-55619331; ⊙4-10.30pm) for a game of boule and a Beerlao.

Green Climbers Home
CLIMBING

(☎020-56105622; www.greenclimbershome.com; Ban Kouanphavang; courses per person 140,000-500,000K, depending on duration & size of group; ⊙Oct-May) This efficiently run training school set in a valley in soaring karst country 18km from Tha Khaek is hugely popular and often booked up thanks to its cosy cabanas, great food and excellent courses. It also boasts one of the easiest overhangs in the world to learn on and has beginner-, intermediate- and expert-level climbs, with more than 250 routes from class 4 to 8B.

Green Discovery ADVENTURE SPORTS
(Map p184; ☑ 051-251390; www.greendiscovery laos.com; Inthira Hotel, Th Chao Annou; ⊘ 8am-9pm) Green Discovery is the country's most experienced ecotourism outfit and runs a number of interesting trips around central Laos. A range of treks and kayaking excursions in the lush Phu Hin Bun NPA are available, including Tham Kong Lor (from US$70 for a day trip to US$155 for an overnight trip). Also arranges cycling and climbing.

⎋ Tours

The Tourist Information Centre (p188) runs tours in the area. Trek prices vary depending on group size, so it's worth calling reliable Mr Somkiad who runs the centre to coordinate with other travellers. As an example, a two-day trek in the Phu Hin Bun NPA for a group of four will cost a reasonable 650,000K per person. These treks typically involve a homestay. Also ask about day trips to multiple caves, including Tham Pa Seuam.

⎙ Sleeping

★**Thakhek Travel Lodge** GUESTHOUSE $
(Map p184; ☑ 051-212931; thakhektravellodge@gmail.com; Rte 13; dm 30,000K, r 60,000-130,000K; ⊜✳@✨) It might be an inconvenient five minutes out of town by tuk-tuk, but this place has a great vibe thanks to its nightly garden fire pit, drawing travellers together. Rooms vary from basic fan options to expansive air-con bungalows, and a cafe serves *láhp*, salads and juices. Check out the logbook for updated news from the Loop.

Mekong Hotel HOTEL $
(Map p184; ☑ 051-250777; mekonghotel@yahoo.com; Th Setthathirat; r 100,000-250,000K; ⊜✳✨) Thanks to a bit of tender, loving care, this blue, Soviet-inspired monolith is somewhat improved, with house-proud, decent rooms that have cable TV, air-con and fresh en suites. There's also a Mekong-facing restaurant.

Sooksomboon Hotel GUESTHOUSE $
(Map p184; ☑ 051-212225; Th Setthathirat; r 100,000-150,000K; ⊜✳✨) Set in a colonial-era police station right on the Mekong, the rooms here are clean and have high ceilings, scrolled mahogany bedsteads, TV and en suite. Bag a room in this atmospheric main building, as the rooms in the motel-like annexe are bland with a capital B.

★**Inthira Hotel** BOUTIQUE HOTEL $$
(Map p184; ☑ 051-251237; www.inthirahotel.com; Th Chao Anou; r incl breakfast US$29-49; ⊜✳@✨) Set in an old French villa with a pretty facade, Inthira offers the most romantic, stylish digs in town. Its restaurant fronts the old fountain, and its chic wine-hued rooms, with exposed-brick walls, rain showers, cable TV, dark wood furniture, air-con and safety deposit boxes, are a delight for weary travellers. The best rooms face the street and have balconies.

Xayluedy Hotel HOTEL $$
(Map p184; ☑ 051-214299; Th Vientiane; r 130,000-250,000K; ⊜✳✨) This smart new hotel in the middle of town has a good range of clean rooms with wall-mounted TVs and hot-water rain showers. All rooms come with air-con and there are even some VIP options for that inner celebrity.

Hotel Riveria HOTEL $$
(Map p184; ☑ 051-250000; www.hotelrivieriathakhek.com; Th Setthathirat; r 330,000-960,000K; ⊜✳@✨) Hotel Riveria has terrific views of Thailand on one side and even more dramatic vistas of the jagged karsts on the other. But this is very much a business person's choice. Large rooms have king-sized beds, TV, fridge, bath and international-style furniture. Downstairs, there's a decent restaurant with a generous buffet breakfast and egg station. Professional but somewhat soulless.

⎙ Eating

There are several outdoor grilled-meat **restaurants** (Map p184; Th Setthathirat; mains 10,000-20,000K; ⊘11am-11pm) specialising in duck (Ms Noy, Ms Kay and Ms Mo) on the waterfront strip directly south of the night market.

La Parisian Cafe CAFE $
(Map p184; ☑ 020-96244999; Th Kuvoravong; mains 10,000-35,000K; ⊘7am-9pm; ✳✨) Our French friends will have to excuse the spelling, but this is a delightful little cafe opposite the post office. Mains are limited to salads and sandwiches, but the real draw is the delectable dessert, which includes elaborate fruit concoctions and designer French toast.

Sabaidee Restaurant LAOTIAN $
(Map p184; Th Setthathirat; mains 20,000-40,000K; ⊘8am-midnight; ✨) Catching whatever breeze is going, this joint sits on the

riverfront and serves rice dishes, *láhp* variations, soup and some heaped portions of international favourites like fish and chips. Nice place for a sundowner and draws a steady crowd of travellers trading tales from 'the Loop' (p182).

Local Food Place
LAOTIAN $
(Map p184; Th Setthathirath; mains 10,000-20,000K; ⏰7am-7pm) Head to this busy local food place alongside the river if you fancy tasty Lao favourites such as *pîng kai* (grilled chicken) and sticky rice for next to no money.

DD Bistro & Cafe
INTERNATIONAL $
(Map p184; ☏051-212355; Fountain Sq; mains 20,000-80,000K; ⏰7am-10pm; ❄️📶) This new glass-fronted cafe overlooking Fountain Sq offers a fusion menu of Lao, Thai and international dishes in a cool atmosphere, both figuratively and literally, thanks to the powerful air-con. Twinings teas, coffees and fresh juices are also available.

★ Khop Chai Deu
FUSION $$
(Map p184; Inthira Hotel, Th Chao Anou; mains 30,000-90,000K; ⏰7am-10pm; ❄️📶♿) Classy and low-lit, this fine restaurant is as sophisticated as sleepy Tha Khaek gets. Based in a pretty French colonial-era building, the open-range kitchen, visible but behind glass, dishes up tasty Lao salad, burgers, substantial tenderised steak and decent cocktails from the sleek glass bar.

Smile Barge Restaurant
LAOTIAN $$
(Map p184; Th Setthathirat; meals 25,000-100,000K; ⏰noon-11.30pm; 📶) Riverside Smile is atmospheric with lanterns hung from the walls, and decked verandahs under the shade of trees where you can coolly work your way through a menu of steak, soup, salad, fried fish and vegie dishes. Aptly enough, it also includes a floating barge on the river to complement the sprawling restaurant on land.

ℹ Information

INTERNET ACCESS
There are a couple of places on Th Chao Anou, north of Fountain Sq, that offer decent internet connections. They are open approximately 10am to 10pm and charge 6000K per hour.

Wangwang Internet (Map p184; Fountain Sq; per hr 7000K; ⏰7.30am-9.30pm) Offers internet on a few laptops, as well as **scooter rental** (Map p184; ☏020-56978535; Fountain Sq; per day 50,000-220,000K; ⏰8am-9pm).

MEDICAL SERVICES
Tha Khaek Hospital (Map p184; cnr Th Chao Anou & Th Champasak) Fine for minor ailments. Seek out English-speaking Dr Bounthavi.

MONEY
BCEL (Map p184; Th Vientiane) Changes major currencies and travellers cheques, and offers cash advances on debit or credit card.

Lao Development Bank (Map p184; Th Vientiane) Cash exchange only, plus an ATM.

GETTING TO VIETNAM: THA KHAEK TO DONG HOI

Getting to the Border
Despite the fact that Rte 12 is now fully paved, for *falang* (Westerners) the **Na Phao (Laos)/Cha Lo (Vietnam) border crossing** (7am to 4pm) remains one of the least used and most inconvenient of all Laos' borders. This is partly because transport on both sides is slow and infrequent, though there's a daily *sŏrngtăaou* (passenger trucks) from Tha Khaek (50,000K, 3½ to four hours, 142km) at 8am bound for Lang Khang, 18km short of the border. If you're determined to cross here, take the early departure as there's no accommodation in the area and you'll almost certainly have to wait a while for transport all the way to the border.

At the Border
The Lao border offers 30-day tourist visas on arrival. Some nationalities require a Vietnam visa in advance, so check with the **Vietnamese consulate** (Map p192; ☏041-212418; Th Sisavangvong, Savannakhet) in Savannakhet. Most regional visitors and Scandinavian, British, French, German, Italian and Spanish visitors do not need a visa.

Moving On
On the Vietnam side, the nearest sizeable city is Dong Hoi. A bus does run directly between Tha Khaek and Dong Hoi (90,000K, 10 to 14 hours), leaving Tha Khaek at 7pm on Monday, Wednesday, Friday and Sunday, making this the most logical way to cross this border.

POLICE

Police (Map p184; cnr Th Kuvoravong & Th Unkham)

Tourist Police (Map p184; ☎250610; Fountain Sq) The police here know how to write insurance reports, if you can track down an officer.

POST

Post Office (Map p184; Th Kuvoravong) Offers expensive international phone calls.

TOURIST INFORMATION

Tourist Information Centre (Map p184; ☎020-55711797, 030-5300503; www. khammouanetourism.com; Th Vientiane; ⊗8.30am-5pm) This excellent tourist office offers exciting one- and two-day treks in Phu Hin Boun NPA, including a homestay in a local village. There are also treks to the waterfall by Ban Khoun Kham and Tham Kong Lor (800,000K). Offers advice on journeying the Loop as well.

❶ Getting There & Away

BUS

Tha Khaek's **bus station** (Rte 13) is about 3.5km from the town centre and has a sizeable market and basic guesthouses to complement the regular services going north and south. Buses for Vientiane (60,000K, six hours, 332km) depart at 4am, 5.30am, 7am, 8.30am and 9am, as well as a VIP service at 9.15am (80,000K) and a sleeper VIP at 1am (90,000K). From 9am to midnight, buses stop en route from Pakse and Savannakhet every hour or so. Any bus going north stops at Vieng Kham (Thang Beng; 30,000K, 1½ hours, 102km), Pak Kading (40,000K, three hours, 149km) or Paksan (50,000K, four hours, 193km).

Heading south, buses for Savannakhet (30,000K, two to three hours, 125km) depart every half-hour, and there's an air-con departure for Pakse (70,000K, six to seven hours, 368km) at 9am and regular local buses every hour during the day (60,000K). There are two daily departures to Attapeu (90,000K, about 10 hours) at 3.30pm and 11pm. Buses originating in Vientiane leave at around 5.30pm for Don Khong (150,000K, about 15 hours, 452km) and around 5.30pm for Non Nok Khiene (90,000K, about 16 hours, 482km), on the Cambodian border. They stop at Tha Khaek between 5pm and 6pm, but you'd need to be in a hurry.

If you're heading to Vietnam, a bus for Hué (120,000K) leaves every Monday, Tuesday, Wednesday, Saturday and Sunday at 8pm. There are also departures for Danang (120,000K) at 8pm every Monday and Friday; for Dong Hoi (90,000K, 10 to 14 hours) at 7am on Monday, Wednesday, Friday and Saturday; and for Hanoi (160,000K) at 8pm on Tuesday and Saturday.

SŎRNGTĂAOU

Sŏrngtăaou (passenger trucks) regularly depart when full from **Talat Phetmany** (Map p184; Th Kuvoravong) to Mahaxai Mai (20,000K, one hour, 50km). A direct service goes to Ban Kong Lor (60,000K, four hours) at 7.30am.

Talat Lak Săam (Sook Som Boon Bus Terminal; Map p184) serves buses into the Khammuan Province interior. There's a daily departure at 8am for Lang Khang (40,000K), and one at 8pm for Na Phao (60,000K, 3½ hours, 142km), 18km short of the Vietnam border.

❶ Getting Around

It should cost about 20,000K to hire a jumbo (motorised three-wheeled taxi) to the bus terminal, though you'll need to negotiate. From the bus terminal, jumbos don't budge unless they're full or you're willing to fork out 30,000K or more to charter the entire vehicle. Rides around town can cost around 15,000K per person.

GETTING TO THAILAND: THA KHAEK TO NAKHON PHANOM

Getting to the Border

Crossing the Mekong at the **Tha Khaek (Laos)/Nakhon Phanom (Thailand) border** is now only possible for locals. Travellers can catch an international bus (18,000K/70B, around 1½ hour) to Nakhon Phanom via the Friendship Bridge from the main bus station in Tha Khaek. Buses run every 30 minutes from 7am to 4.30pm. If crossing the border after 4pm you'll have to pay an overtime fee.

At the Border

In Tha Khaek, Lao immigration issues 30-day tourist visas on arrival and there's a BCEL money exchange service and 24-hour ATM at the immigration office. In Thailand, travellers are given visa-free, 30-day entry.

Moving On

Once in Nakhon Phanom, buses depart for Udon Thani (regular) and Bangkok (at 7.30am and from 7pm to 8pm). Faster and almost as cheap are the budget flights to Bangkok offered by Air Asia and Nok Air with several flights per day.

CAR & MOTORCYCLE

A handful of places around town offer motorbike hire.

Mad Monkey Motorbike (Map p184; ☑ 020-59939909; www.madmonkey-thakek. com; Fountain Sq; per day scooters 60,000-100,000K, 250cc dirt bikes 250,000K; ☺9am-8pm) The best place to hire a tough, reliable motocross bike to tackle the Loop and other adventures. Mad Monkey has a couple of Honda 250cc dirt bikes and some perky 150cc Kawasaki Fox dirt bikes, plus the usual automatic and semi-automatic scooters. The owners are also a great source of information on the Loop.

Wangwang (p187) Offers the biggest range of motorbikes in town, including dirt bikes, scooters and more.

Mr Ku's Motorbike Rental (Map p184; ☑ 020-22205070; per day 60,000-100,000K; ☺7.30am-4.30pm) Located at Thakhek Travel Lodge. Mr Ku has reliable scooters for tackling the Loop and getting around town or to the closer caves.

Around Tha Khaek

👁 North & South of Tha Khaek

Pha That Sikhottabong   BUDDHIST TEMPLE
(ພະທາດສິໂຄດຕະບອງ) About 6km south of town is the much-venerated Pha That Sikhottabong, which stands in the grounds of a 19th-century monastery of the same name. Considered one of the most important *tâht* (stupa) in Laos, Sikhottabong was first renovated by King Setthathirat in the 16th century, when it assumed its current general form.

Tham Pa Fa   CAVE
(Buddha Cave; 5000K; ☺8am-noon & 1-4pm) When Mr Bun Nong used a vine to scramble up a sheer 200m-high cliff in 2004, he discovered a narrow cave mouth and was greeted by 229 bronze Buddha images. The Buddhas, ranging from 15cm to about 1m tall, were sitting as they had been for centuries facing the entrance of a cave of impressive limestone formations.

No photographs are allowed inside the cave, but it is an atmospheric spot tended by local ascetics. It's 14km from Tha Khaek; a tuk-tuk costs 100,000K.

Khoun Kong Leng   LAKE
(ຂຸນກອງແລງ; 5000K) Nestled amid the limestone karsts of the Phu Hin Bun NPA is the stunningly beautiful Evening Gong Lake. The luminescent green waters spring from a subterranean river that filters through the limestone, making the water crystal clear. It's only about 30km northeast of Tha Khaek.

You must ask at the village before swimming in the lake. Once you get approval, only swim in the stream that flows from the lake, near the wooden footbridge, and not in the lake itself. Fishing is banned.

To get here, head north along Rte 13 and turn right (east) at Km 29 onto a dirt road. After 2km, turn right (south) again, and bump up over hills and through villages for 16km until you reach Ban Na Kheu. It's another 1km to the lake.

👁 East on Route 12

The first 22km east of Tha Khaek on Rte 12 is an area with several caves, an abandoned railway line and a couple of swimming spots and can be visited as a day trip or as part of the Loop. This is part of the vast Khammuan Limestone area, which stretches roughly between Rtes 12 and 8 and east towards Rte 8B. There are thousands of caves, sheer cliffs and jagged karst peaks. All these places can be reached by tuk-tuk, bicycle or motorcycle.

Tham Lot Se Bang Fai   CAVE
(ຖ້ຳລອດເຊບັ້ງໄຟ) The most impressive, and yet least visited, cave in Khammuan is the amazing Tham Lot Se Bang Fai. Located in Hin Namno NPA, the cave results from the Se Bang Fai river plunging 6.5km through a limestone mountain, leaving an underground trail of immense caverns, impressive rock formations, rapids and waterfalls that have been seen by only a handful of visitors.

The cave wasn't professionally mapped until 2006, and the Canadian-American that led the expedition concluded that Tham Lot Se Bang Fai is among the largest river caves in the world. Traversing the entire cave involves eight portages and is only possible during the dry season, from January to March. Local wooden canoes can only go as far as the first portage, about 1km into the cave, making inflatable rafts or kayaks the only practical option for traversing the entire length of the cave.

The base for visiting the cave is Ban Nong Ping, a mixed Lao Loum/Salang village about 2km downstream from the cave entrance. Homestays are available as part of an organised tour with ecotourism operator Green Discovery (p186). With a week or so advance notice, you can organise a trip here, starting from about US$265 for a larger group of six or more to as much as US$550 per person for a couple.

Tham Xang
CAVE

(ຖ້ຳຊ້າງ, Elephant Cave; 5000K) Famous for its stalagmite 'elephant head', which is found along a small passage behind the large golden Buddha, this is one of the closest caves to Tha Khaek (it's about 4km away). Bring a torch (flashlight).

Tham Xieng Liap
CAVE

(ຖ້ຳຊຽງລຽບ) **FREE** Turning off Rte 12 at Km 14 (before a major bridge) you'll come across a sign pointing to this cave. Follow the dirt track south for about 400m near the village of Ban Songkhone (about 10.5km from Rte 13), to the stunning limestone cave Tham Xieng Liap, the entrance of which is at the base of a dramatic 300m-high cliff.

The cave is about 200m long and, in the dry season, you can walk/wade through and swim in the picturesque valley on the far side. *Paa faa* (soft-shelled turtles) live in the cave, while the cliffs outside are said to be home to the recently discovered *kan yoo* (Laotian rock rat). In the wet season you'll need to rent a boat (30,000K) from the Xieng Liap bridge.

Tham Nang Aen
CAVE

(ຖ້ຳນາງແອນ; 20,000K; ⊙8am-5pm) The last cave along this stretch of Rte 12 is the touristy Tham Nang Aen, about 18km from Tha Khaek. It's well lit inside, but a little kitsch in terms of the colour scheme. It is also possible to take a small boat deeper into the cave via an underground river.

The turn-off to the cave is indicated by a clear sign just past a left-hand bend 16km from the junction with Rte 13. The 700m-long track should be passable at all but the wettest times.

Tham Pha Chan
CAVE

(ຖ້ຳພະຈັນ, Sandalwood Buddha Cave) **FREE** Tham Pha Chan has an entrance 60m high and about 100m wide. A stream runs about 600m through a limestone karst and in the dry season it's possible to walk to the far side. At its western end there is a sandalwood Buddha image about 15m above the ground, hence the cave's name. To get here, head north towards Tham Pha Fa at around the Km 14 sign on Rte 12. When the road forks, head northwest for 9km to reach this cave.

Not far from Tham Pha Chan is the **Nam Don Resurgence** (ຂຸນນ້ຳໂດນ), a cave where the Nam Don (Don River) emerges from the ground. It's quite a physical marvel to see the water coming up and out from the cave, and the lagoon that sits at the bottom of the tall limestone karst is a beautiful swimming spot.

Unfortunately, both are accessed via a rough road that runs 9km north from about 10km east of the junction with Rte 13. Go by motorbike, tuk-tuk or arrange an English-speaking guide through Tha Khaek's Tourist Information Centre (p188).

SAVANNAKHET PROVINCE

Savannakhet is the country's most populous province and is home to about 15% of all Lao citizens. Stretching between the Mekong and Thailand in the west and the Annamite mountains and Vietnam in the east, it has become an important trade corridor between these two bigger neighbours. With the smooth surface of Rte 9 complemented by yet another Thai-Lao Friendship Bridge, the province is witnessing even more traffic.

The population of around one million includes Lowland Lao, Tai Dam, several small Mon-Khmer groups and communities of Vietnamese and Chinese.

There are three NPAs here: Dong Phu Vieng to the south of Rte 9; remote Phu Xang Hae to the north; and Se Ban Nuan straddling the border with Salavan Province. Eastern Savannakhet is a good place to see remnants of the Ho Chi Minh Trail, the primary supply route to South Vietnam for the North Vietnamese Army during the Second Indochina War.

Savannakhet ສະຫວັນນະເຂດ

POP 140,000 / ☏041

Languid, time-trapped and somnolent during the sweltering days that batter the old city's plasterwork, Savannakhet is an attractive blend of past and present Laos. The highlight is the historic quarter with its staggering – and that might just be the right adjective – display of decaying early 20th-century architecture. Leprous and listing, these grand old villas of Indochina's heyday now lie unwanted like aged dames crying out for a makeover. There's little to do in town but wander the riverfront and cool off in one of a clutch of stylish restaurants and bijou cafes that are steadily growing in number.

That said, there's plenty to do nearby and Savannakhet has a very dedicated **Tourist Information Centre** (Map p192; ☏041-212755; Th Si Muang; ⊙8am-noon & 1-4pm Mon-Fri) and eco-guide unit, which offers myriad intrepid trips into the nearby NPAs.

⊙ Sights

Much of the charm of Savannakhet is in simply wandering through the quiet streets in the town centre, between the old and new buildings, the laughing children and the slow-moving, *petang*-playing old men. The Tourist Information Centre's *Savannakhet Downtown* brochure features a self-guided tour of the city's most interesting buildings. The centre also offers guided tours of the historic downtown district.

Musée Des Dinosaures   MUSEUM
(ຫໍພິພິດທະພັນໄດໂນເສົາ, Dinosaur Museum; Map p192; ☑041-212597; Th Khanthabuli; 10,000K; ☺8am-noon & 1-4pm) In 1930 a major dig in a nearby village unearthed 200-million-year-old dinosaur fossils. The enthusiastically run Dinosaur Museum is an interesting place to see three different dinosaurs. Savannakhet Province is home to five dinosaur sites.

Wat Sainyaphum   BUDDHIST TEMPLE
(ວັດໄຊຍະພູມ; Map p192; Th Tha He) **FREE** The oldest and largest monastery in southern Laos. The large grounds include some centuries-old trees and a workshop near the river entrance that's a veritable golden Buddha production line.

Wat Rattanalangsi   BUDDHIST TEMPLE
(ວັດລັດຕະນະລັງສີ; Map p192; Th Phagnapui) **FREE** Wat Rattanalangsi was built in 1951 and houses a monks' primary school. The *sĭm* (ordination hall) is unique in that it has glass windows (most windows in Lao temples are unglazed). Other structures include a rather gaudy Brahma shrine, a modern *sǎhláh lóng tám* (sermon hall) and a shelter containing a 15m reclining Buddha backed by Jataka paintings.

Savannakhet Provincial Museum   MUSEUM
(ພິພິດທະພັນແຂວງຊະຫວັນນະເຂດ; Map p192; Th Khanthabuli; admission 10,000K; ☺8-11.30am & 1-4pm Mon-Sat) The Savannakhet Provincial Museum is a good place to see war relics, artillery pieces and inactive examples of the deadly unexploded ordnance (UXO) that has claimed the lives of more than 20,000 Lao since the end of the Secret War.

🛏 Sleeping

Pilgrim's Inn   B&B $
(Map p192; ☑020-22133733; www.facebook.com/pilgrimskitchenandinn; 106 Th Lhatphanith; r US$20-25; ❄🛜) Pilgrim's Inn is a small B&B-style place attached to the popular Pilgrim's

Kitchen (p193). Guacamole-green rooms feature ample beds, air-con and attached bathrooms with hot water. The current five rooms are set to expand to seven rooms and include some larger family-friendly options.

Fundee Guesthouse   GUESTHOUSE $
(Map p192; ☑030-4841873; Th Santisouk; r 120,000K; ❄❄🛜) A new guesthouse tucked down a side *soi* (lane) off Th Santisouk, Fundee offers great value for money thanks to its smart new rooms with all the trimmings. Ten rooms are already open and another 10 rooms are being added to ensure it can cater to its growing reputation.

Souannavong Guest House   GUESTHOUSE $
(Map p192; ☑041-212600; Th Saenna; r with/without air-con 120,000/70,000K; ❄❄🛜) This little guesthouse down a quiet street abloom in bougainvillea has clean en suite rooms and is unfailingly fresh. A welcoming place to stay thanks to the English-speaking owners. Bicycles and motorbikes are available to rent.

★Vivanouk Homestay   HOMESTAY $$
(Map p192; ☑020-91606030; www.vivanouk.com; Th Khantabouly; r without bathroom US$30-45; ❄❄🛜) This funky little place is akin to a boutique homestay and is a great new addition to the Savan scene. There are just three rooms sharing two bathrooms – one with an alfresco outdoor shower – and are delightfully decorated in a contemporary-colonial-era fusion style. Breakfast is available downstairs in an artsy venue that doubles as a bar by night.

Avalon Residence   HOTEL $$
(☑041-252770; www.hotel.avalonbooking.com; Th Sisavangvong; r US$20-32; ❄❄@🛜) Avalon Residence offers smart midrange rooms at an affordable price and is pretty convenient for a stroll to the bus station. The rooms are spacious and have glistening bathrooms, Lao silks and flat-screen TVs. Downstairs is a small air-conditioned cafe.

Phonepaseud Hotel   HOTEL $$
(Map p192; ☑041-212158; Th Santisouk; r 200,000-280,000K; ❄❄🛜❄) Phonepaseud has a friendly English-speaking owner, a clean lobby and imaginatively tile-floored, French-wallpapered rooms with air-con, TV, fridge and en suite plus much larger VIP rooms. Outside there's a fountain guarded by a *naga* (river serpent), mature trees, plenty of plants and a tennis court.

Savannakhet

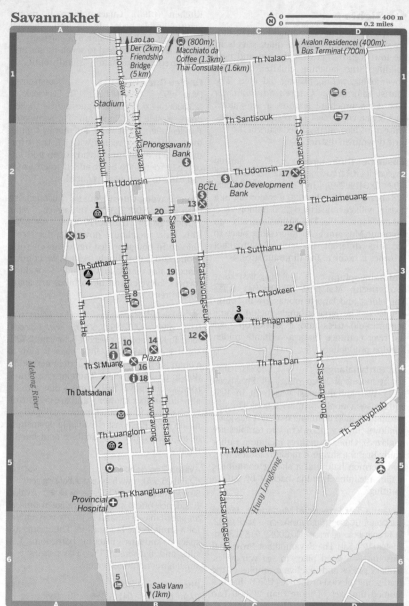

CENTRAL LAOS SAVANNAKHET

Daosavanh Resort & Spa Hotel HOTEL $$$
(Map p192; ☎041-252188; www.dansavanh.com;
Th Tha He; r incl breakfast US$51-107; ❀✲@☎✖) This ostentatious hotel overlooking the Mekong offers a slice of international comfort, and its kidney-shaped pool is very welcome on sweltering days, of which there are many in Savan. Rooms are large and immaculate, and prices include free airport transfers.

Savannakhet

✖ Eating

⭐ Savannakhet Plaza Food Market
MARKET, LAOTIAN $

(Map p192; Savannakhet Plaza; meals 10,000-30,000K; ☾5-10pm) An excellent new addition to the Savan dining scene, this nightly food market brings 20 or more stalls to the Savannakhet Plaza area in the heart of the old town. This is street-food surfing at its best, with a choice of freshly barbecued skewers, steaming noodle soups, dim-sum-sushi-tapas confusion and more.

⭐ Sala Vann
LAOTIAN $

(☎020-55645111; Ban Phonsavan; mains 10,000-90,000K; ☾10am-10pm; 🛜) Stunningly set on the Mekong about 500m south of the old hospital, this lovely Laotian restaurant is housed in a traditional wooden *sala*. The menu is enticingly affordable and draws a mixed crowd come sunset and beyond, when there is sometimes live music. As well as Lao and Thai favourites, there are even steaks and pasta.

⭐ Lin's Café
INTERNATIONAL $

(Map p192; ☎030-5332188; Th Phetsalat; mains 30,000-60,000K; ☾8am-10pm; ❄🛜✎) Savannakhet's original travellers cafe, this delightful spot has outgrown its former home and relocated to a new open-plan house near St Theresa's Cathedral. It's popular for its easy vibe, friendly staff, reservoir of local information, retro eclectic interior and gallery upstairs. But best of all are the cappuccinos, Thai green curry, tasty burgers, fruit salad and fresh pastries.

Pilgrim's Kitchen
INTERNATIONAL $

(Map p192; ☎020-22133733; www.facebook.com/pilgrimskitchenandinn; 106 Th Lhatphanith; mains 30,000-60,000K; ☾7am-10pm Mon-Sat; ❄❄🛜) This international cafe has an eclectic menu of Tex-Mex, Americana, Indian and more. It's a delightful air-conditioned retreat on a hot day and offers its own concoctions such as an iced espresso bomb, where an iced espresso melts into a glass of fresh milk. Top Indian food, good burgers and some vegetarian options too. Five rooms (p191) are available upstairs.

Cafe Chai Dee
JAPANESE, INTERNATIONAL $

(Map p192; ☎030-5003336; www.cafechaidee.com; Th Ratsavongsouk; mains 20,000-50,000K; ☾9am-3pm & 5-9.30pm Mon-Sat; ❄🛜✎) This spotless Japanese-owned cafe has rattan mats to lounge on, a book exchange and a wide menu of Japanese classics like ramen and tonkatsu (pork coated in breadcrumbs and fried), plus samosas, homemade yoghurt, Thai food and healthy shakes. Great breakfasts, too. Expect super fresh, well-presented food, fast wi-fi and warm service.

Khao Piak Nang Noy
LAOTIAN $

(Map p192; ☎020-77744248; Th Ratsavongseuk; soups 10,000K; ☾8am-8pm) Nang Noy sells what is probably the most popular, and almost certainly the richest, *khào pìak sèn* (thick noodles served in a slightly viscous broth with crispy deep-fried pork belly or chicken) in Savannakhet. There's no English-language sign, so look for the busy stall under the Pepsi awning.

Riverside Snack & Drink Vendors STREET FOOD $

(Map p192; ⊘5-10pm) The riverside snack and drink vendors are a great place for sundowners, serving cheap big bottles of Beerlao (10,000K) and *sìn daat* (Lao hotpot barbecue) sizzling away on charcoal grills.

Macchiato da Coffee CAFE $$

(☑020-99111298; 999 Rte 9 West; mains 35,000-200,000K; ⊘7am-11pm; ✳️🛜) This cavernous contemporary coffee shop on the road to the Friendship Bridge is a bit bling for Savannakhet. With a London Underground theme and a Savannakhet tube sign, this is all about designer, barista-brewed coffees and jam-jar juices. The food menu is impressive, but a little on the pricey side for Savan – 800,000K for Wagyu beef!

White House Restaurant INTERNATIONAL $$

(Map p192; ☑030-9775588; Th Udomsin; mains 45,000-245,000K; ⊘7am-9pm; ✳️🛜) Brace yourselves, you may not have expected this in Savannakhet. A huge colonial-style compound is home to one of the city's most upscale restaurants and a charming little cafe. The menu is an around-the-world tour, including Lao, Thai and Chinese favourites, plus New Zealand lamb and Australian tenderloin. Steaming noodle soup is an affordable breakfast option.

Lao Lao Der LAOTIAN $$

(☑041-212270; mains 30,000-90,000K; ⊘10am-11pm) This riverside restaurant, 2km north of the old stadium, is one of the only places in town to offer great Mekong views. The hefty menu spans Lao, Thai and Chinese dishes, but Lao Lao Der functions equally well as a bar. It was undergoing a major renovation during our last visit.

Café Chez Boune FRENCH $$

(Map p192; www.cafechezboune.com; Th Ratsavongseuk; mains 15,000-150,000K; ⊘7am-10pm; ✳️🛜) Glacially cool, orange-walled and hung with Parisian oils, Chez Boune has a French-speaking owner and is deservedly popular with expats. This must have something to do with the decent service and tasty steaks, pasta dishes, pork chops and filet mignon, all of which are executed with élan.

Dao Savanh FRENCH $$$

(Map p192; ☑041-260888; Th Si Muang; mains 100,000-150,000K, 3-course cafe lunch 65,000K; ⊘7am-10pm; ✳️🛜) With its elegant colonial-era facade, this cool, square-facing restaurant is still one of the city's finest, despite increased competition. Fans whir and wine glasses clink as you tuck into a French-accented menu of soups, grilled entrecôte and lamp chop Provençal. The upstairs restaurant is the classy sister (evenings only), while downstairs the all-day cafe has salads, sandwiches and *croque-monsieur*.

🍷 Drinking & Nightlife

★**Sook Savan** BAR

(Map p192; Th Si Muang; ⊘4pm-midnight; 🛜) The atmospheric Sook Savan occupies a strategic corner overlooking Savannakhet Sq and draws a lively crowd from about 7pm onwards. Beer is the main ingredient on the menu here, but it also offers traditional Laotian food with a spicy kick to help wash it down. Live music on weekend nights and a bit of a party atmosphere.

Savanlaty Nightclub CLUB

(⊘7pm-late) One of a cluster of out-of-town nightclubs in this area, Savanlaty Nightclub is one of the most rockin' with a live band belting out Thai rock anthems and international tunes. Open late if you have the legs for it.

ℹ️ Information

INTERNET ACCESS

There are several internet cafes along the western side of Th Ratsavongseuk, between Th Sutthanu and Th Chaokeen; most are open from about 8am to 10pm and charge 6000K per hour.

MEDICAL SERVICES

Provincial Hospital (Map p192; ☑041-212717; Th Khanthabuli) Ask for English-speaking Dr Outhon.

MONEY

BCEL (Map p192; Th Ratsavongseuk; ⊘8.30am-4pm) and **Lao Development Bank** (Map p192; Th Udomsin; ⊘8.30-11.30am & 1.30-3.30pm) both have cash exchange, credit-card advances and an ATM. **Phongsavanh Bank** (Map p192; ☑041-300888; Th Ratsavongseuk; ⊘8.30am-4pm Mon-Fri, to 11.30am Sat) services are limited to cash exchange and an ATM.

POLICE

Tourist Police (Map p192; ☑041-260173)

POST

Post Office (Map p192; ☑041-212205; Th Khanthabuli) International calls here are overpriced; make calls via an internet connection instead.

TOURIST INFORMATION

Tourist information in Savannakhet is plentiful and professional.

Eco-Guide Unit (Map p192; ☑ 041-214203; Th Latsaphanith; ⊗ 8am-noon & 1-4.30pm Mon-Fri) The industrious eco-guide unit provides a range of services, from bookings for treks to Dong Natad PPA and Dong Phu Vieng NPA, to bus times, accommodation and tips on where to get a decent massage or hire a motorbike (not both at the same time!).

Savanbanhao Tourism Co (Map p192; ☑ 041-212944; Savanbanhao Hotel, Th Saenna; ⊗ 9am-5pm Mon-Sat) Tours to Sepon and the Ho Chi Minh Trail and Heuan Hin can be arranged here. Bus tickets to Vietnam are also available.

SK Travel & Tour (Map p192; ☑ 041-300177; Th Chaimeuang; ⊗ 8am-4pm) Air tickets can be arranged here.

Tourist Information Centre (p190) A useful stop for a selection of well-produced brochures on Savannakhet and its surrounds.

❶ Getting There & Away

Most travellers arrive and depart Savannakhet by road, with convenient bus links to all points in Laos and international destinations in Thailand and Vietnam. The airport offers limited flight connections to Vientiane, Pakse and Bangkok.

AIR

Savannakhet's **airport** (Map p192; ☑ 041-212140; Th Kaysone Phomvihane) is served solely by Lao Airlines, with domestic connections to Vientiane (490,000K–895,000K, 55 minutes, four weekly), Pakse (320,000K–520,000K, 30 minutes, four weekly) and Bangkok (US$105–US$150, 80 minutes, four weekly). Tickets can be purchased at the **Lao Airlines office** (Map p192; ☑ 041-212140; Savannakhet Airport; ⊗ 8.30am-4.30pm) at the airport or travel agents in town.

The airport is located at the southeastern edge of town; jumbos make the trip downtown for 30,000K, although they may start higher when fresh off the plane on arrival.

An alternative option for those wanting to save money on the Bangkok route is to cross the Friendship Bridge and connect with the Fly-Drive services offered with Air Asia or Nok Air via Nakhon Phanom Airport; tickets are available from less than 1000B.

BUS

Savannakhet's **bus terminal** (☑ 041-212143), usually called the *khíw lot*, is near the Talat Savan Xai at the northern edge of town. Buses leave here for Vientiane (75,000K, eight to 11 hours, 457km) roughly every half-hour from 6am to 11.30am. From 1.30pm to 10pm you'll have to hop on a bus passing through from Pakse, which stop at Tha Khaek (30,000K, 2½ to four hours, 125km). Hourly *sŏrngtǎaou* and minivans also

---

GETTING TO THAILAND: SAVANNAKHET TO MUKDAHAN

Since the construction of the second Thai-Lao Friendship Bridge back in 2006, non-Thai and non-Lao citizens are not allowed to cross between Mukdahan and Savannakhet by boat.

Getting to the Border

The Thai-Lao International Bus crosses the **Savannakhet (Laos)/Mukdahan (Thailand) border crossing** (6am to 10pm) in both directions. From Savannakhet's bus terminal, the Thai-Lao International Bus (15,000K, 45 minutes) departs approximately every hour from 8am to 7pm. It leaves Mukdahan's bus station (50B, 45 minutes) roughly every hour from 7.30am to 7pm and also stops at the border crossing to pick up passengers.

At the Border

Be sure not to board the Savan Vegas Casino staff bus at the border, as this also stops at the international bus stop but heads out of town to the eponymous casino resort.

The Lao border offers 30-day tourist visas on arrival. If you don't have a photo you'll be charged the equivalent of US$1. An additional US$1 'overtime fee' is charged from 6am to 8am and 6pm to 10pm on weekdays, as well as on weekends and holidays. Most nationalities do not require a visa to cross into Thailand; check with the Vietnamese consulate (p187) in Savannakhet.

Moving On

Onward from Mukdahan, there are at least five daily buses bound for Bangkok. Alternatively, to save time, consider a fly-drive option with Air Asia or Nok Air, including an express minivan to Nakhon Phanom Airport and a budget flight to Bangkok.

GETTING TO VIETNAM: SAVANNAKHET TO DONG HA

Getting to the Border

Crossing the **Dansavanh (Laos)/Lao Bao (Vietnam) border** (7am to 7.30pm) is a relative pleasure. From Savannakhet's bus terminal, buses leave for Dansavanh (60,000K, five to six hours, 236km) at 7am, 8.30am and 11am. Alternatively, consider breaking the journey for a night in Sepon as a base for seeing the Ho Chi Minh Trail.

The bus station in Dansavanh is about 1km short of the border; Vietnamese teenagers on motorbikes are more than happy to take you the rest of the way for about 10,000K.

At the Border

The Lao border offers 30-day tourist visas on arrival and has an exchange booth. Some nationalities require a Vietnam visa in advance, so check with the Vietnamese consulate (p187) in Savannakhet. Most regional visitors, Scandinavian visitors, and British, French, German, Italian and Spanish visitors do not need a visa.

Moving On

Once through, take a motorbike (40,000d or US$2) 2km to the Lao Bao bus terminal and transport to Dong Ha (70,000d, two hours, 80km) on Vietnam's main north–south highway and railway. Entering Laos, there are buses to Savannakhet (60,000K, five to six hours) at 7.30am, 9.30am, 10am and noon, as well as regular *sŏrngtăaou* (passenger trucks) to Sepon (30,000K, one hour) from 7am to 5pm. Simple accommodation is available on both sides of the border.

If you're in a hurry, an alternative is to take one of the various direct buses from Savannakhet bound for the Vietnamese cities of Dong Ha, Hué and Danang.

head to Tha Khaek (30,000K) from 8am to 4pm. A VIP sleeper bus (120,000K, six to eight hours) to Vientiane leaves at 9.30pm, or you could try to pick up a seat on one of the VIP buses coming through from Pakse.

Ten daily buses to Pakse (45,000K, five to six hours, 230km) originate in Savannakhet; the first is at 7am and the last at 10pm. Otherwise, jump on one of the regular buses passing through from Vientiane. There's also a daily bus to Don Khong (80,000K, six to eight hours, 367km) at 7pm, and two daily buses to Attapeu (80,000K, eight to 10 hours, 410km) at 9am and 7pm.

Buses leave for the Laos–Vietnam border at Dansavanh (60,000K, five to six hours, 236km) at 7am, 8.30am and 11am, stopping at Sepon (50,000K, four to five hours).

To Vietnam, there's a bus to Dong Ha (80,000K, about seven hours, 350km), departing at 8am on even-numbered dates. For Hué, there's a local bus (90,000K, about 13 hours, 409km) daily at 10pm and a VIP bus (110,000K, about eight hours) at 10.30am from Monday to Friday. There's also a bus to Danang (110,000K, about 10 hours, 508km) at 10pm on Tuesday, Thursday and Saturday; the same bus continues to Hanoi (200,000K, about 24 hours, 650km), but we reckon you'd have to be a masochist to consider this journey.

ℹ️ Getting Around

Savannakhet is just big enough that you might occasionally need a jumbo. A charter around town costs around 15,000K and more like 20,000K to the bus station.

Motorcycles can be hired at Souannavong Guest House (p191) for 70,000K to 80,000K per day. The eco-guide unit (p180) provides a comprehensive list of places that hire out motorbikes. There are also a few places to rent bicycles; most are along Th Ratsavongseuk and charge about 10,000K per day.

Around Savannakhet

◉ Sights

That Ing Hang　　　　　　　　　　TEMPLE
(ທາດອິງຮັງ; 5000K; ⊙7am-6pm) Thought to have been built in the mid-16th century, this well-proportioned, 9m-high *thâat* is the second-holiest religious edifice in southern Laos after Wat Phu Champasak. It's located about 11.5km northeast of Savannakhet via Rte 9, then 3km east and the turn-off is clearly signposted. Going by bicycle or motorbike is the easiest option.

The Buddha is believed to have stopped here when he was sick during his wanderings back in ancient times. He rested by leaning (ing) on a hang tree (thus Ing Hang).

Not including the Mon-inspired cubical base, That Ing Hang was substantially rebuilt during the reign of King Setthathirat (1548–71) and now features three terraced bases topped by a traditional Lao stupa and a gold umbrella weighing 40 baht (450g). A hollow chamber in the lower section contains a fairly undistinguished collection of Buddha images; by religious custom, women are not permitted to enter the chamber. The French restored That Ing Hang in 1930. The That Ing Hang Festival is held on the full moon of the first lunar month.

Any northbound bus can stop here, or you could haggle with a *sakai-làap* (jumbo) driver to take you here (you'll do well to knock him down below 100,000K return).

Dong Natad WILDLIFE RESERVE

(ດົງນາຕາດ) Dong Natad is a sacred, semi-evergreen forest within a provincial protected area 15km from Savannakhet. It's home to two villages that have been coexisting with the forest for about 400 years, with villagers gathering forest products such as mushrooms, fruit, oils, honey, resins and insects. It's possible to visit Dong Natad by bicycle, motorbike or tuk-tuk from Savannakhet. Travelling alone to Dong Natad will be something of a 'forest-lite' experience, however. It's better to engage one of Savannakhet's English-speaking guides through the eco-guide unit (p180).

The unit offers various programs, ranging from multiday homestays to one-day cycling trips, and ranging in price from 1,000,000K to 2,000,000K for one person in a group of two (prices drop substantially the more people there are). These community-based trips have had plenty of positive feedback and the combination of English-speaking guide and village guide proves a great source of information about how the local people live. If you visit, there's a good chance you'll encounter villagers collecting red ants, cicadas or some other critter, depending on the season; all are important parts of their diet and economy. Make arrangements at least a day ahead.

Heuan Hin RUINS

(ເຮືອນຫິນ, Stone House) On the Mekong River about 90km south of Savannakhet is this set of Cham or Khmer ruins, built between AD 553 and 700. Apart from a few walls, most of the stones of this pre-Angkorian site now lie in piles of rubble. *Sŏrngtăaou* (30,000K, two to three hours, 78km) leave Talat Savan Xai when full (usually mid-morning).

No carvings remain, with the only known lintel having been carted off to Paris. It's a long haul by public transport and you'd need to be a truly dedicated temple enthusiast to make the trip here. With your own transport, head south along Rte 13 and turn west at Ban Nong Nokhian, near Km 490, from where it's a dusty 17km to the site. Guided tours are also available from Savannakhet.

Dong Phu Vieng NPA
ປ່າສະຫງວນແຫ່ງຊາດດົງພູວຽງ

One of the most fascinating treks in Laos is to Dong Phu Vieng NPA, which offers a rare chance to step into a rapidly disappearing world. The park, south of Muang Phin in the centre of Savannakhet Province, is home to a number of Katang villages, where you can stay if you observe local customs.

SLEEPING WITH SPIRITS

The Katang villagers of Dong Phu Vieng National Protected Area (NPA) believe in the myriad spirits that surround them in the forest. One of the most important is the house spirit, which is believed to live in the home of every village family. Over the centuries a series of taboos have been developed in an effort to avoid disturbing this spirit, and as a visitor in a Katang home, it is vitally important you don't break them.

➡ You should never enter the owner's bedroom or touch the spirit place.

➡ Do not sleep beside a person of the opposite sex, even if that person is your spouse. If you really can't be separated tell the eco-guide unit and they can bring a tent for you.

➡ Sleep with your head pointed towards the nearest outside wall; never point your feet at the outside wall or, spirits forbid, another person's head.

It goes without saying that these villages are extremely sensitive to outside influence, which is why you can only visit them as part of the organised trek through the eco-guide unit (p180) in Savannakhet.

HO CHI MINH TRAIL

The infamous Ho Chi Minh Trail is actually a complex network of dirt paths and gravel roads running parallel to the Laos–Vietnam border from Khammuan Province in the north to Cambodia in the south. The trail's heaviest use occurred between 1966 and 1971 when more than 600,000 North Vietnamese Army (NVA) troops – along with masses of provisions and 500,000 tonnes of trucks, tanks, weapons and ordnance – passed along the route in direct violation of the 1962 Geneva Accords. At any one time around 30,000 NVA troops guarded the trail, which was honeycombed with underground barracks, fuel and vehicle repair depots, hospitals and rest camps, as well as ever-more-sophisticated anti-aircraft emplacements.

The North Vietnamese denied the existence of the trail throughout most of the war. And the US denied bombing it. In spite of 1.1 million tonnes of saturation bombing (begun in 1965 and reaching up to 900 sorties per day by 1969, including outings by B-52 behemoths), traffic along the route was never interrupted for more than a few days. Like a column of ants parted with a stick, the Vietnamese soldiers and supplies poured southward with only an estimated 15% to 20% of the cargo affected by the bombardment. One estimate says 300 bombs were dropped for every NVA casualty.

Contrary to popular understanding, the trail was neither a single route nor a tiny footpath. Several NVA engineering battalions worked on building roads, bridges and defence installations, and methods to hide the trails from the air were simple but ingenious. Bridges were built just below the water level and branches were tied together to hide what had become wide roads.

Today, the most accessible points are at Ban Dong, east of Sepon, and the village of Pa-am in Attapeu Province, which sits almost right on the main thoroughfare. Here you can see a couple of tanks and a surface-to-air missile. Elsewhere you'll need to get way out into the sticks and get locals to guide you.

Drivenbyadventure (p160) runs all-inclusive history-infused motorbike trips on the trail. Check out some amazing photographs to whet your appetite for adventure at www. laosgpsmap.com/ho-chi-minh-trail-laos.

The trek involves a fair bit of walking through a mix of forests ranging from dense woodlands to bamboo forests and rocky areas with little cover, or paths only accessible during the dry season (November to May). There's a boat trip on the third day. A village guide leads trekkers through a sacred forest where you'll see *lak la'puep* (clan posts placed in the jungle by village families). Animals regularly seen include the rare silver langur, the leaf monkey and the hornbill.

Phu Xang Hae NPA

ປ່າສະຫງວນແຫ່ງຊາດຊ້າງແຫ

Named after Wild Elephant Mountain, Phu Xang Hae NPA is a long expanse of forest stretching east–west across the remote north of Savannakhet Province, and its hills are the source of several smaller rivers. The eco-guide unit (p180) in Savannakhet previously ran a five-day community-based trek here, but this is currently not operating due to a lack of demand.

The Phu Thai people who live here, like the Katang of Dong Phu Vieng NPA, observe a series of taboos. Unfortunately, the diabolical state of the roads means getting into Phu Xang Hae is very difficult.

Sepon (Xepon) & the Ho Chi Minh Trail

POP 40,000 / ☎ 041

Like so many other towns that needed to be rebuilt following the Second Indochina War, Sepon (often spelt Xepon) is today fairly unremarkable. The main reason for coming here is to see parts of the Ho Chi Minh Trail and what's left of the old district capital, Sepon Kao, 6km to the east.

◉ Sights

Sepon was once an important hub on the Ho Chi Minh Trail and there are several key war-related sites in the area. Savannakhet's Tourist Information Centre (p190) publishes a map-based guide of the area, which is useful when exploring the area.

War Museum
MUSEUM

(☑ 020-99919709; Ban Dong; 10,000K; ☉ 8am-11.30am & 1.30-4pm Mon-Sun) Twenty kilometres east of Sepon, Ban Dong (Dong Village) was on one of the major thoroughfares of the Ho Chi Minh Trail and is the easiest place to see what little material is left from the war. Most of what was previously scattered around the area has been gathered into the gated front lawn of the newly opened War Museum.

These include two American-built tanks used during Operation Lam Son 719, a disastrous Army of the Republic of Vietnam (ARVN) assault on the Ho Chi Minh Trail in February 1971. Despite support from US combat aircraft, the ARVN troops retreated across the border at Lao Bao after being routed by seasoned North Vietnamese Army (NVA) troops at Ban Dong. To see the tanks, part of a plane, guns and other scrap, the museum is at the eastern edge of Ban Dong and is bordered by a baby-blue-and-pink fence.

Muang Phin
HISTORIC SITE

(ເມືອງພິນ) FREE An imposing Vietnamese-built monument to Lao-Vietnamese co-operation during the Indochina wars stands in Muang Phin, 155km east of Savannakhet and 34km west of Sepon. Done in the stark 'Heroes of Socialism' style, the monument depicts North Vietnamese Army (NVA) and Pathet Lao (PL) soldiers waving an AK-47 and Lao flag aloft.

🛏 Sleeping

Vieng Xay Guesthouse
GUESTHOUSE $

(☑ 041-214895; Rte 9; s/d from 70,000/80,000K; 🗱) The Vieng Xay is hands down the town's best digs, with 30 mostly large rooms with TV, air-con and hot water. There's also a decent cafe serving Lao fare. A stairway bordered by bomb casings leads to more rooms out the back.

Khamvieng Tienmalay Guesthouse
GUESTHOUSE $

(☑ 020-2246519; r 80,000-100,000K) This guesthouse just west of the market has 10 basic rooms with fans and en suite bathrooms but little else in the way of comforts.

❶ Getting There & Away

Sŏrngtǎaou and the occasional bus leave from outside Sepon's market for Savannakhet (35,000K, four to five hours, 196km) between about 8am and 3pm; otherwise, flag down any bus heading west for the same price. There are also relatively frequent *sŏrngtǎaou* to Ban Dong (10,000K) and the border at Dansavanh (20,000K, one hour) during the same times, or you could hop on any bus going in that direction.

Southern Laos

Includes ➡

Best Places to Eat

➡ Four Thousand Sunsets (p242)

➡ Rahn Naem Khao Mae Fuean (p205)

➡ King Kong Resort (p241)

Best Places to Sleep

➡ Kingfisher Ecolodge (p218)

➡ Captain Hook Coffee Break (p222)

➡ Residence Sisouk (p203)

➡ Sala Done Khone (p241)

Why Go?

Near the Cambodian border, the Mekong awakes from its slumber, slams into Si Phan Don (Four Thousand Islands) and disintegrates into a series of churning rapids. Downstream, a dwindling pod of rare Irrawaddy dolphins seek solace in a deep river pool. In between, an expanding pod of travellers find their own solace in the hammock-strewn bungalows of Don Det and Don Khon.

Kayaking or bicycling around these bucolic islands is the signature southern Laos experience, but the rest of this incredibly diverse region – home to Angkorian temples, highland cultures, waterfalls, prime trekking, and raw off-the-beaten-track experiences – remained off the radar until recently.

No longer just the realm of backpackers, southern Laos now has a scattering of upscale rural lodges and boutique hotels. New highways and dams are changing the landscape forever, so hurry up and get here.

When to Go
Pakse

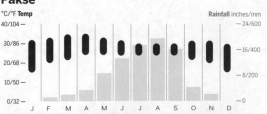

Oct–Nov Ideal time for bike touring, as rains trickle and dust remains manageable.

Dec–Feb Sunny and cooler – make that downright cold – on the Bolaven Plateau.

Apr It's terribly hot, but the three-day Pi Mai (New Year) means water fights and Beerlao parties.

Southern Laos Highlights

1 Don Khon (p236)
Ogling fierce cascades and spotting rare dolphins while touring the island by bicycle or kayak.

2 Kiet Ngong (p218)
Taking a trek and a boat trip in the jungle around the region's premier ecotourism area.

3 Wat Phu Champasak (p215) Exploring this ancient Khmer temple complex.

4 Bolaven Plateau (p219) Gazing in awe at 100m-high waterfalls, sipping fair-trade coffee and soaking in the cool climate on a motorcycle trip around this plateau.

5 Si Phan Don (p232)
Watching the sun set over the Mekong from the horizontal perspective of your hammock at this tropical island paradise in the Mekong River.

6 Tat Lo (p221) Waterfall-hopping and village visiting around this backpacker magnet with a laid-back vibe.

PAKSE ປາກເຊ

POP 75,000 / ☎ 031

Pakse, the capital of Champasak Province and the gateway to southern Laos, sits at the confluence of the Mekong and the Se Don (Don River). Most travellers don't linger long because there's not much to do. The city lacks the sort of Mekong River–town lethargy found in Savannakhet and Tha Khaek further north and fewer colonial-era buildings remain.

Pakse serves mostly as a launching pad for forays to surrounding attractions such as the Bolaven Plateau (p219) and Wat Phu Champasak (p215), and the many good restaurants, stylish hotels and clued-in tour companies make it a comfortable and convenient one.

◉ Sights

Talat Dao Heuang MARKET
(ຕະຫຼາດດາວເຮືອງ, New Market; Map p204; ⊙5am-6pm) This vast market near the Lao-Japanese Bridge is one of the biggest in the country. It's at its most chaotic in the food zones, but just about anything a person might need – from medicinal herbs to mobile phones – is sold here. It's worth a wander.

Wat Phou Salao VIEWPOINT
(ວັດພູສະເຫຼົ້າ; Rte 16) The centrepiece of this hilltop temple across the Mekong from Pakse is the giant Buddha statue looking out over the city. The views from his perch are as fantastic as you'd expect, especially at sunset. To enjoy them, take the first left after the bridge and either climb up the long staircase or take the 4.5km road route up the back.

Sacred Heart Cathedral CHURCH
(ມະຫາວິຫານທີ່ສັກສິດຫົວໃຈ; Map p204; Th 10; ⊙5.30am-8pm) This modest, tin-roofed building isn't much to look at from the outside, but the one-of-a-kind paintings inside are worth the trip. They show Jesus in various spots around southern Laos, including Wat Phu Champasak and Khon Phapheng Falls, meeting with various tribal peoples wearing traditional dress.

Wat Luang BUDDHIST TEMPLE
(ວັດຫຼວງ; Map p204; Th 11) There are about 20 wats in Pakse, among which the riverside Wat Luang is one of the largest. The old monastic school, built in 1935, features a commanding tiled roof and ornate concrete pillars while two newer buildings have modern murals telling the Buddha's life story and other tales.

Champasak Historical Heritage Museum MUSEUM
(ພິພິດທະພັນມໍລະດົກປະຫວັດສາດຈຳປາສັກ; Map p204; Rte 13; 10,000K; ⊙8.30-11.30am & 2-4pm Mon-Fri) Though the labelling certainly could be better, this is a museum worth visiting. Highlights include ancient Dong Son bronze drums, unusual stone carvings unearthed up on the Bolaven Plateau in Bachieng District, stelae in Tham script dating from the 15th to 18th centuries, Khmer stone carvings, musical instruments, and some American Unexploded Ordnance (UXO). Also of interest is the textile and jewellery collection from ethnic minorities such as the Nyaheun, Suay and Laven, with large iron ankle bracelets and ivory ear plugs.

🏃 Activities

Vat Phou Cruises CRUISE
(Map p204; ☎031-251446; www.vatphou.com; just off Th 11; ⊙office 8am-5pm Mon-Sat, no cruises in Jun) Operates three-day luxury Mekong cruises between Pakse and Si Phan Don, including visits to Wat Phu Champasak (p215) and Khon Phapheng (p237) waterfall.

Dok Champa Massage MASSAGE
(Map p204; ☎020-54188778; Th 5; massages 50,000-100,000K; ⊙9am-10pm) Again and again Dok Champa comes out on top as the favourite Pakse spa, thanks to its friendly and professional staff offering you exactly the level of robust or soft pampering your weary muscles require. Reservations are recommended.

Clinic Keo Ou Don MASSAGE
(Traditional Medicine Hospice; ☎031-251895, 020-5431115; massage 45,000-120,000K, sauna 20,000K; ⊙9am-9pm, sauna 3-9pm) Professional and popular, this centre has an air-conditioned massage room and herbal sauna segregated by gender. To get here, head out of town on Rte 38 and turn right towards Pakse Golf, 1km east of Champasak Grand Hotel.

👉 Tours

Most people organise their southern Laos tours and treks in Pakse. Pretty much all hotels and travel agencies sell a standard selection of day trips to the Bolaven Plateau, Wat Phu Champasak, and Kiet Ngong. The cheapest tours are simply transportation; admission fees and meals are not included and there is no guide. For many people this is fine, but for others it's a disappointing surprise. Be sure you know what you are getting before you agree to go.

Green Discovery
ADVENTURE

(Map p204; ☑ 031-252908; www.greendiscovery
laos.com; Th 10; 2-day Tree Top Explorer tour
2-/4-person group per person US$308/240; ☺ 8am-
8pm) Green Discovery is a solid all-around
tour company offering private and small
group tours. It goes places and does things
no other company does. Its signature trip
is the Tree Top Explorer adventure in Dong
Hua Sao NPA (p220) near Paksong on the
Bolaven Plateau. It consists of two or three
days' ziplining, canopy walking and jungle
trekking around waterfalls beyond any roads.

🛏 Sleeping

The tourist centre is on Rte 13 between the
Souphanouvong Bridge (formerly the French
Bridge) and Th 24. Stay here if you want easy
access to travel agencies, motorbike rentals,
money changers and touristy restaurants.
Around the corner you'll find more hotels
and restaurants in the commercial district,
which is centred around the Champasak
Shopping Centre (p206). If you're staying
anywhere else, rent a motorbike or bicycle to
get around.

★ Alisa Guesthouse
HOTEL $

(Map p204; ☑ 031-251555; www.alisa-guesthouse.
com; Rte 13; r 120,000-150,000K, f 200,000K;
☻❋@☎) Perhaps the best value lodging in
Pakse, Alisa has sparkling rooms, tiled floors,
solid wood beds, armoires, working satellite
TV and a fridge. Service is good too. The only
significant knock is that some rooms barely
catch a wi-fi signal. No surprise, it's often full.

Nang Noi Guesthouse
GUESTHOUSE $

(Map p204; ☑ 030-9562544; bounthong1978@
hotmail.com; Th 5; dm 40,000K, r 60,000-110,000K,
f 200,000K; ❋☎) Around the corner from the
tourist strip, but seemingly far away, this popular (ie often full) spot has quiet, spiffy rooms
and English-speaking owners. Note the 11pm
curfew.

Sabaidy 2 Guesthouse
GUESTHOUSE $

(Map p204; ☑ 031-212992; www.sabaidy2tour.
com; Th 24; dm 35,000K, d with fan/air-con
100,000/125,000K, s/d without bathroom 50,000/
70,000K; ❋☎) Though not the great place it
used to be, Sabaidy 2 still has an easy, relaxed
vibe and is the most communal spot in town.
Rooms are split between the older wooden
building, which is basic but clean, and a much
better new building in back: think wood-
en balcony, beneath which coy carp swim;
rustic-chic interiors; desks and air-con.

★ Athena Hotel
HOTEL $$

(Map p204; ☑ 031-214888; www.athenahotelpakse.
com; Rte 13; r incl breakfast US$70-100; ☻❋☎☎)
Easily the most modern and slick hotel in
Pakse, Athena's subdued style features a lot of
wood. The beds are marshmallowy delights,
and dimming inlaid ceiling lights let you illu-
minate them in many ways.

★ Residence Sisouk
BOUTIQUE HOTEL $$

(Map p204; ☑ 031-214716; www.residence-sisouk.
com; cnr Th 9 & Th 11; r US$50-100; ☻❋@☎)
This exquisite boutique hotel occupies a lovely old house and evokes a bit of old France.
The rooms enjoy polished hardwood floors,
flat-screen TVs, verandahs, Hmong bed runners, stunning photography and fresh flowers everywhere. Breakfast is in the penthouse
cafe with great views. Paying extra gets you a
bigger, brighter room with a balcony in front;
standard rooms are at the back.

Pakse Hotel
HOTEL $$

(Map p204; ☑ 031-212131; www.paksehotel.com;
Th 5; s 200,000-500,000K, d 250,000-550,000K,
ste 700,000-950,000K, all incl breakfast; ❋@☎)
This traditional-luxe hotel towering over
central Pakse has a welcoming lobby and cor-
ridors festooned with indigenous sculptures
and textiles. The economy rooms are dark
and the standard rooms are cramped, so con-
sider an upgrade to at least a superior (from
350,000K), which includes Mekong views.

Mekong Paradise Resort
HOTEL $$

(☑ 031-212120; r US$38-85; ☻❋☎) A riverside
spot just 3km southeast of central Pakse that
makes for a wonderful escape from the city.
Most rooms have unbeatable Mekong sunset
views. The superior rooms (US$55) with their
private balconies are almost romantic, but
the views are actually better from the US$45
Mekong Paradise rooms. The Garden View
rooms (US$38) defeat the point of staying
out here.

Champasak Palace Hotel
HOTEL $$

(Map p204; ☑ 031-212263; www.champasak-
palacehotel.com; Rte 13; s 200,000-350,000K,
d 250,000-400,000K, ste 550,000-2,000,000K;
❋☎) You can't miss this vast, wedding-cake-
style building originally built as a palace for
Chao Boun Oum, the last prince of Cham-
pasak and Lao prime minister between 1960
and 1962. The standard rooms are well-kept
with comfortable beds, while the restaurant
and common areas turn heads with wood
columns, louvred windows and random flair
such as the rooftop lounge's ceiling.

Pakse

0 400 m
0 0.2 miles

2km (500m);
International Art
Museum (5km);
Southern (7km);
Paksong (49km);
Si Phan Don (135km)

Rte 16W

Talat Dao
Heuang

Champasak (30km);
Vang Tao (43km)

Clinic Keo Ou Done (1.2km);
Mekong Paradise Resort (2km);
Pakse Golf (4km)

Se Don

Russian
Bridge

Souphanouvong
Bridge

(2.5km);
Northern (7km);
Ban Saphai (13km)

King of
Bus
Terminal

Mekong River

Th 21
Th 14
Th 5
Th 13
Th 11
Th 9
Th 8
Th 10
Th 24
Th 34
Th 35
Th 36
Th 42
Th 38
Th 11
Th 46
Rte 13
Th 1

1
2
3
4
5
6
7
8
9
10
11
12
13
14
15
16
17
18
19
20
21
22
23
24
25
26
27
28
29
30
31
32
33
34
35
36
37
38

Pakse

Eating

Two good morning spots for delicious *fĕr* (rice noodles) are the **Noodle Shop Mengky** (Map p204; Rte 13; noodles 15,000K; ◷6am-1pm) and the more tourist-friendly **Lankham Noodle Shop** (Map p204; Rte 13; noodles 15,000-25,000K; ◷6am-2pm; 🛜) across the road. The later also does baguette sandwiches.

Self-caterers can head to the centrally located **Friendship Minimart** (Map p204; Rte 13; ◷8am-8pm) or the larger, but distant **Friendship Super Mart** (Rte 13; ◷9am-9pm) inside the Friendship Mall. Several fruit vendors open early to late next to Champasak Shopping Centre (p206).

★ Pon Sai
LAOTIAN **$**
(Map p204) For a wonderful local morning experience, head to Pon Sai at the junction of Th 34 and Th 46, which bustles with small shops and street vendors selling *fĕr*, baguette sandwiches, *kòw nĕeo bîng* (grilled, egg-dipped sticky rice patties) and many doughy delights. Though it's best in the morning, some shops stay open through the day and into the night.

★ Rahn Naem Khao Mae Fuean
LAOTIAN, THAI **$**
(Map p204; Th 11; mains 25,000-40,000K; ◷9am-10.30pm; 🛜🛜) This local joint offers a rare combination: real-deal Lao food and an English-language menu. Well, something close to English anyway…the 'fried chicken power' is really stir-fried holy basil with chicken. It's well-known for *pan mîiang baa* (a sort of make-your-own fish sandwich) and also serves *láhp* (spicy Lao-style salad of minced meat poultry or fish) and Mekong River algae soup. The deck on the Se Don is a big bonus.

La Terrasse
LAOTIAN, INTERNATIONAL **$**
(Map p204; Th 24; mains 20,000-65,000K; ◷7.30am-11pm; 🛜) A block off the main road on the edge of the tourist strip, the clientele are a mix of travellers and expats. The menu is half Lao-Thai and half Western, though the stars are the giant wood-fired pizzas (evenings only) and over-stuffed baguette sandwiches. It also brews its own special fruity *lòw-lów* (rice whisky).

Daolin Restaurant
LAOTIAN, INTERNATIONAL $

(Map p204; Rte 13; mains 15,000-50,000K; ⏱6am-10pm; 🛜🍴) Despite the incessant traffic noise, this restaurant is usually filled with backpackers due to good food and service. It has a range of pastas and some of the best Thai food in town. It's the perfect spot for vegetarians to try Lao food that is usually meat-based, such as pumpkin *om* curry and mushroom *gôy*.

Champady
THAI, LAOTIAN $

(Map p204; Th 13; mains 13,000-40,000K; ⏱7am-8pm; 🛜🍴) One of Pakse's best choices for Thai food, Champady has a fairly extensive menu from glass-noodle salad to southern sour curry, plus a good selection of coffees and juices, all served on a small patio. We recommend the hearty *tôm yam*.

Sinouk Coffee Shop
CAFE $

(Map p204; cnr Th 9 & Th 11; mains 30,000-45,000K; ⏱6.30am-9pm; ❄🛜) Stylish Sinouk has glass-topped tables inlaid with coffee beans as that's what it's all about – delicious Arabica coffee grown on its plantation in the Bolavan Plateau. If you're after more, then get started on the panini sandwiches, salads, pastas and the usual Thai-Lao mix of dishes. It's one of the priciest spots in the city, but the quality is high.

Jasmine Restaurant
INDIAN $

(Map p204; Rte 13; mains 10,000-30,000K; ⏱7am-11pm; 🍴) It's the location as much as the masala that keeps this old-timer bulging with happy customers. The menu mixes both Indian and Malay food and there are many vegie choices.

Dok Mai Trattoria Italiana
ITALIAN $$

(Map p204; Th 24; mains 25,000-60,000K; ⏱11am-11pm Wed-Mon; 🛜) Italian-owned, this little gem aims for culinary authenticity (there's no garlic bread, for example) with perfectly prepared pasta and eggplant parmigiana, plus a big selection of salads. And it all comes with a fantastic rock and roll soundtrack and garden seating in back.

Banlao
THAI, LAOTIAN $$

(Map p204; Th 11; mains 20,000-80,000K; ⏱10am-10pm) One of several floating restaurants in Pakse, Banlao has a reliable menu of expected favourites but also many dishes you might not have encountered before, such as the seasonal ant egg *gôy* (*gôy kài mót sòm* – *gôy* is similar to *láhp* but with added blood) and a whole page of sticky rice dipping sauces (*jaew*) including eggplant and cricket. For the less adventurous there's central-Thai papaya salad and grilled fish with herbs.

Le Panorama
LAOTIAN, INTERNATIONAL $$

(Map p204; Th 5; mains 30,000-85,000K; ⏱4.30-10pm; 🛜🍴) The rooftop restaurant of the Pakse Hotel serves up delicious Franco-Asian cuisine and unbeatable 360-degree city views. The menu includes duck breast, pizza and a succulent *bah neung het hörm* (stuffed fish steamed in banana leaves). It's a shame the service is downright dreadful.

🛍 Shopping

Coffee from the Bolaven Plateau is the traditional souvenir from the region; pick up a bag at any cafe. Several shops in **Champasak Shopping Centre** (Champasak Plaza; Map p204; ⏱8am-7pm) and Talat Dao Heuang (p202) sell typical Lao skirts.

Pakse Souvenirs
ARTS & CRAFTS

(Map p204; Th 5; ⏱8am-6pm) The quality textiles and woven bamboo products here come mostly from northern Laos, but there is some southern stuff too. Unique to this shop are the owners' modern designs incorporating older textiles into bags, table runners and the like.

Dream Weaver
ARTS & CRAFTS

(Map p204; Th 11; ⏱8am-8pm) 🖋 This small NGO-supported shop stocks, as the name suggests, mostly woven fabrics, but there are other souvenirs as well. Most of the products are made by trafficking victims and their families.

Monument Books
BOOKS

(Map p204; Th 5; ⏱9am-8pm Mon-Sat, to 6pm Sun) This upmarket bookshop is your best stop for maps of Laos and her neighbours, plus postcards and a superb range of regional historical and cultural books.

ℹ Information

INTERNET ACCESS

Miss Noy (Map p204; 📞020-22272278; noy7days@hotmail.com; Rte 13; internet per hour 8000K; ⏱8am-8pm) and **SL Travel** (Map p204; Th 24; internet per hour 10,000K, bicycle 20,000K; ⏱6.30am-9pm) have internet with good connections.

MEDICAL SERVICES

International Hitech Polyclinic (VIP Clinic; Map p204; 📞031-214712; ihpc_lao@yahoo.com; cnr Th 1 & Th 10; ⏱24hr) Adjacent to the

public hospital (Map p204; ☑ 031-252928; Th 10; ⊘24hr), it has English-speaking staff and much higher standards of care, service and facilities, plus a pharmacy.

MONEY

Banks, such as the conveniently located **BCEL** (Map p204; Th 11; ⊘8.30am-3.30pm Mon-Fri) and **Lao Development Bank** (Map p204; Rte 13; ⊘8am-4pm Mon-Fri, to 3pm Sat & Sun), have the best currency-exchange rates, though the exchange counter at the **Lankham Hotel** (Map p204; ⊘7am-7pm) is good too. All three give cash advances (3% commission) on credit cards. LDB also has Western Union and can exchange US dollar travellers cheques (1%).

ATMs are plentiful in the city centre.

POST

Main Post Office (Map p204; Th 8; ⊘8am-noon & 1-5pm Mon-Fri) A short walk from the tourist strip.

TELEPHONE

Unitel (Map p204; Rte 13; ⊘8am-4pm Mon-Fri, to noon Sat) Makes a convenient stop for a local SIM card if you are just arriving in Laos. Staff can set your smartphone up with 3G internet.

TOURIST INFORMATION

Provincial Tourism Office (Map p204; ☑ 031-212021; Th 11; ⊘8am-4pm Mon-Fri) Mostly exists to hand out maps and brochures, but some staff can answer questions or help you make bookings for homestays and activities at Kiet Ngong, Don Kho and Don Daeng.
Miss Noy The gang here are clued in to the region, especially the Bolaven Plateau.

VISAS

Pakse's **immigration bureau** (Map p204; Th 10; ⊘8-11am & 2-4pm Mon-Fri) is at the main police station, in the tallest building. To extend your stay, bring a photocopy of your passport name page and visa, two photos, and 30,000K plus 20,000K per day. A minimum of three days and a maximum of 30 should be ready the next afternoon.

❶ Getting There & Away

AIR

The **Pakse International Airport** (Rte 13) is 2.5km northwest of the Souphanouvong Bridge. A tuk-tuk to/from the airport will cost about 40,000K.

Lao Airlines (☑ 031-212252; www.laoairlines.com; Pakse Airport; ⊘8.30am-5pm Mon-Fri, 8am-5pm Sat, 8am-7pm Sun) has direct flights to the following cities in Asia:
Vientiane 750,000K, two daily
Luang Prabang 890,000K, three weekly

Savannakhet 320,000K, four weekly
Attapeu 520,000K, three weekly
Siem Reap US$105, four weekly
Ho Chi Minh City US$110, two weekly
Bangkok US$125, four weekly
A cheaper way to fly to Bangkok is to travel overland to Ubon Ratchathani and catch a budget flight from there.

BOAT

A tourist boat motors from Pakse to Champasak (one way per person 70,000K) at 8.30am, provided there are enough punters – in the low season there usually aren't. The return trip from Champasak is at 1.30pm. It's two hours downstream to Champasak, and a bit longer on the return. Book through any travel agent or call **Mr Khamlao** (☑ 020-22705955; per boat US$80, per person for 10 people US$8).

BUS & SŎRNGTĂAOU

Pakse, frustratingly, has many bus and sŏrngtăaou (passenger truck) stations. The vast majority of tourists simply book bus journeys through their guesthouse or a travel agency, and since these are either special tourist buses that pick you up in the centre or include a free transfer to the relevant departure point, the prices are usually reasonable.

Note that on long-distance routes (Cambodia, Vietnam and Vientiane) you'll want to be careful which company you use: choosing the wrong one could cost you several hours and cause a lot of pain. Buy your ticket from a travel agency that actually knows the details of the route, rather than a guesthouse, which probably does not.

There are six main stations.
Southern Bus Terminal (Rte 13) Pakse's main bus station with departures to most places. Also known as khíw lot lák pąet (8km bus terminal) because it's 8km out of town on Rte 13.
Northern Bus Terminal (Rte 13) This is usually called khíw lot lák jét (7km bus terminal); it's – you guessed it – 7km north of town. Only for northern destinations. The English-language signs on departures are frequently wrong.
Talat Dao Heuang (Morning Market; Map p204) Vans and sŏrngtăaou to nearby destinations, such as the Thai border, depart from a chaotic lot in the southeast corner of the market and also from Th 38 in front of the market.
2km Bus Station (Sengchalern Bus Station; ☑ 031-212428; Rte 13) Also known as Sengchalern station after the company that owns it, the office is in the lobby of SL Hotel.
King of Bus Terminal (Map p204; 020-5501 2299; Th 11) Only serves night buses to Vientiane and towns along the way.
Kiang Kai Bus Station (off Th 38) This small, hard-to-find station, in a red-and-yellow building set back well off Th 38, is 1.5km past the

Japanese bridge. It's used by buses to/from Thailand, though these also use the Southern Bus Terminal.

Vientiane & Points North

Most travellers prefer the comfortable 'VIP' night sleeper buses to Vientiane (170,000K, 10 hours). You can book these through your guesthouse or head to the King of Bus Terminal (p207), from where there are several nightly departures, all leaving at 8.30pm; or the 2km Bus Station (p207), with one departure at 8pm. It's possible to take these buses to Tha Khaek (130,000K, 4½ hours) and Seno (for Savannakhet; 120,000K, three hours).

If you prefer day travel, slower-moving ordinary air-con buses (110,000K, 12 to 14 hours) depart throughout the day from the Southern Bus Terminal (p207), stopping to pick up more passengers at the 2km and Northern (p207) stations.

These buses also go to Tha Khaek (40,000K, five hours) and Seno (60,000K, seven hours).

Bolaven Plateau & Points East

Transport to the Bolaven Plateau and points east consists of air-con buses from the Southern Bus Terminal (p207) and ordinary fan buses from the 2km Bus Station (p207). The last departures to all cities are at 4pm, except for Sekong from the Southern Terminal, which is at 2.30pm. Buses to Salavan (fan/air-con 30,000/40,000K, three hours) can drop you at Tat Lo. Buses to Attapeu (fan/air-con 45,000/50,000K, 3½ to five hours) pass through Paksong (fan/air-con 15,000/20,000K, 90 minutes) and about half use the long route via Sekong (fan/air-con 35,000/40,000K, 3½ hours).

Champasak & Si Phan Don

Regular sŏrngtǎaou leave Talat Dao Heuang (p207) for Champasak (20,000K, one hour) until noon or so – sometimes even as late as

---

GETTING TO THAILAND: VANG TAO TO CHONG MEK

Getting to the Border

Other than finding the right counters to use at immigration, crossing at the **Vang Tao (Laos)/Chong Mek (Thailand) border** (open 6am to 8pm) is straightforward.

The easiest way to get there is on the Thai-Lao International Bus (50,000K, 2½ to three hours, 8.30am and 3pm) between Pakse's Southern Bus Terminal (p207) and Ubon Ratchathani's bus station. It picks up more passengers at the little Kiang Kai Bus Station (p207) on the way. If you're travelling to Pakse (departures from Ubon at 9.30am and 3pm) note that this bus does wait long enough for people to get Lao visas.

There are also frequent minivans from Pakse to Vang Tao (25,000K, 45 minutes) departing from the street in front of Talat Dao Heuang market (p207) and also sŏrngtǎaou (passenger trucks) leaving from inside the market until about 4pm. Vans to Vang Tao also depart hourly from the Southern Bus Terminal. You'll be dropped off in a dusty/muddy parking area about 500m from the Lao immigration office.

If you are headed to Bangkok (225,000K, 14 hours), a direct service (that sometimes involves changing buses at Ubon) departs the Southern Bus Terminal daily at 4pm. Pakse travel agents also offer a combination bus/sleeper train ticket to the Thai capital with prices starting at 290,000K for 2nd-class fan carriages and going much higher for better service.

At the Border

Laos issues visas on arrival (around US$35, depending on which passport you hold), while on the Thai side most nationalities are issued 15-day visa waivers free of charge; residents of the G7 countries get 30 days. You walk between the two countries using a pointless underground tunnel for part of the way.

Although it seems like a scam, there is a legitimate overtime fee on the Laos side after 4pm weekdays and all day on weekends and holidays. The real scam is that the officials demand 100B even though the actual price is 10,000K. Just tell them you want a receipt and you'll pay the correct price.

Moving On

Minivans head to Ubon (100B, 1¼ hours, every 30 minutes) from Chong Mek's bus terminal, which is 600m (20B by motorcycle taxi) up the main road. Alternatively, informal taxi drivers hang around immigration and charge 1000B to anywhere in Ubon Ratchathani city.

2pm. There's also a morning tourist bus-boat combo to Champasak (55,000K, 1½ hours) offered by most travel agencies. Be sure your ticket includes the boat crossing from Ban Muang. The regular price for the boat is 10,000K per person or 30,000K if you're alone.

For Si Phan Don, tourist buses and mini-vans – including pick-ups in town and boat transfer to Don Khong (70,000K, 2½ hours), Don Det (70,000K, three hours) and Don Khon (75,000K, 3¼ hours) – are most comfortable and convenient. Book these through any guest-house or travel agent. All departures are in the morning around 8am. Note that prices fluctuate considerably on these trips over time, and also sometimes even on the north- and southbound journeys due to attempts at price fixing.

If you want to leave later in the day, take a *sörngtǎaou* from the Southern Bus Terminal (p207) to Ban Nakasang (for Don Det and Don Khon; 40,000K, 3½ hours). These depart hourly until 5pm and go via Hat Xai Khun (for Don Khong).

One *sörngtǎaou* services Kiet Ngong (30,000K, two hours), leaving at 11am.

Neighbouring Countries

Travelling to Cambodia (p245) is a guaranteed hassle, while entering Thailand is a breeze. Travelling to Vietnam falls in between.

The most comfortable way to Hue (200,000K, 12 hours) and Danang (220,000K, 14 hours) in Vietnam is to catch a morning sleeper bus from the Southern Bus Terminal (p207), which for legal reasons use the long route through the Lao Bao border east of Savannakhet. Note that these do not go every day – sometimes a regular bus goes instead and sometimes there is simply no bus. Up to three hours faster for the same price are the modern, comfortable minibuses that go via Salavan and use the Lalay border (p224), through the drivers tend to be reckless. Then there are the slower and truly crappy cargo buses that only save a few of their seats for passengers. These make for a very uncomfortable and much longer journey. If there is no large bus, some unscrupulous travel agencies will book passengers on these buses without telling them, so be sure you know what vehicle your ticket is really for. For Kom Tun or Ho Chi Minh City you travel via the Bo Y border (p135). Some travel agencies sell direct buses to Ho Chi Minh City (450,000K, 15 hours), but these go via the southern route so you need to buy a Cambodian visa. It takes several hours longer, but is actually much cheaper to travel to Kom Tum and take a connecting bus (240,000d) from there.

ℹ Getting Around

BICYCLE

Cycling around to the city's few sites can make for a pleasant few hours. SL Travel (p206) and Miss Noy (p206) hire bikes (15,000K to 20,000K).

CAR & MOTORCYCLE

Several shops and guesthouses in the tourist belt along Rte 13 rent motorbikes from 50,000K per day for 100cc bikes, rising to 100,000K for an automatic Honda Scoopy. Safe bets are Miss Noy (p206), which has a nightly planning meeting for those heading to the Bolaven Plateau, and **Pakse Travel** (Map p204; ☑ 020-22277277; Rte 13; ⊘ 7.30am-8.30pm).

Talk to any travel agency or hotel about hiring a car with driver, which should cost about 400,000K (plus fuel) depending on where you want to go. **Avis** (Map p204; ☑ 031-214946; www.avis.la; Th 10; per day from US$58; ⊘ 8.30am-6pm Mon-Fri, 9am-1pm Sat & Sun) rents out vehicles – from compacts to SUVs – with or without drivers and can provide paperwork to allow the cars to go to neighbouring countries.

LOCAL TRANSPORT

Local transport in Pakse is expensive by regional standards. Figure on about 10,000K for a short *sǎhm-lór* (three-wheels) trip (including between Talat Dao Heuang and the city centre) if you're one person – more if you're in a group or use a tuk-tuk. A ride to the Northern or Southern Bus Terminal costs 15,000K per person shared and 50,000K for a whole tuk-tuk.

AROUND PAKSE

Don Kho & Ban Saphai

The Mekong-hugging Ban Saphai (Saphai Village) and adjacent island of Don Kho just north of Pakse are famous for their weaving. Women work on large looms underneath their homes producing silk (both real and artificial) and cotton dresses and other products, and are happy to show you how. While this is a well-known destination, it's not over-run. The rarely visited Ban Don Khoh (Don Khoh Village), not far away, does stone carving. These three destinations combine for a good half-day trip out of Pakse and cultural explorers can dig deeper with a night at Don Kho's homestay.

Don Kho   ດອນໂຄ

There are no cars and hardly any motorcycles on this 450m-wide island and, despite the advent of electricity, it's easy to feel like you're stepping back to a simpler time. The 350 residents live along both shores on the island's northern half and farm rice in the centre. There are no traditional tourist sites on the island, though the women weaving silk under their homes welcome drop-in visitors.

Wat Silattana Satsadalam (aka Wat Don Kho) has a manuscript hall mixing Lao and French style and a giant tree that locals dubiously claim is 500 years old. For about half the year you can walk out to some beaches and for 50,000K boatmen will take you out for a fishing trip. The 'traditional twin roof house' shown on the map at the landing is gone and it will take some bushwhacking to find the traces of the old village and the cemetery in the mostly forested southern half of the island; and if you do find them, the payoff is very small.

Though it's small enough to walk, there are bikes (20,000K per day) for hire. Turn left from the landing and ask at the little administration centre where you can also arrange a village **homestay** (per person 30,000K, per meal 20,000K).

Believe it or not, Don Kho was briefly the capital of southern Laos following the French arrival in the 1890s. It served as a mooring point for boats steaming the Mekong River between Don Det and Savannakhet.

Ban Saphai   ບ້ານສະພາຍ

First stop in this weaving village should be the **Ban Saphai Handicraft Centre** (⊙6am-7pm) next to the boat pier. Several weavers have their looms here and locally woven textiles and other crafts are on sale. Also, you aren't just welcomed, you're openly encouraged to visit women weaving at their homes elsewhere in the village. A map posted outside the Handicraft Centre leads you on a short walking tour to some weaving houses, an old school building at the temple, and the local market.

Ban Don Khoh   ບ້ານດອນເຂາະ

Not to be confused with single-'H' Don Kho island to the north, little-known Ban Don Khoh (rhymes with 'law') is home to dozens of stone-carvers who mostly make Buddha images. Some basic work is done with power tools, but most of the carving is still done with hammer and chisel. They work all day every day, except when there's a ceremony at the temple or a big *muay thai* fight on TV.

The workshops are in front of Wat Chompet, which has a 30m-tall Buddha image on its grounds. Ban Don Khoh proper is bit to the west along the Mekong River; so this carving community is also known as Ban Chomphet.

❶ Information

Some people at the Ban Saphai Handicraft Centre can speak some English. They will call to arrange your homestay and/or activities on Don Kho.

The Provincial Tourism Office (p207) in Pakse can do the same.

❶ Getting There & Away

Ban Saphai is 16km north of Pakse's Souphanouvong Bridge and the turn-off is clearly signed. *Sŏrngtǎaou* from Pakse to Ban Saphai (20,000K, 45 minutes) leave fairly regularly from the street in front of the Talat Dao Heung (p207) gate.

From Ban Saphai to Don Kho, longtail boats cost 40,000K round trip and can hold up to five people. Set a time for pick-up, or take the boatman's phone number and call when you want to return.

Ban Don Khoh is between Pakse and Ban Saphai, 9km from the Souphanouvong Bridge. The turn is unmarked, but it's the paved road going west just before the bus station.

Phou Xieng Thong NPA

ປ່າສະຫງວນແຫ່ງຊາດພູຊຽງທອງ

Spread over 1200 sq km in Champasak and Salavan Provinces, Phu Xieng Thong NPA is most accessible about 50km upriver from Pakse. The area has a sometimes other-worldly beauty with oddly eroded outcroppings and exposed sandstone ridges, some of which contain prehistoric paintings. Most of the big wildlife has been eradicated by hunting, but there are still lots of birds, including significant concentrations of green peafowl, and a diversity of wild orchids.

The typical trip, available December to June, through Green Discovery (p203) for US$132 per person (in a group of four or more), begins in the Mekong River village of Ban Mai Singsamphan, where you will do a homestay between two days of moderately challenging trekking. A highlight is the sunset view from the top of Phu Khong (Khong Mountain). The return trip to Pakse includes a boat trip on the Mekong.

Independent travellers are pretty much out of luck since Pakse's Provincial Tourism Office no longer arranges trips here and none of the local guides speak much English. If you get yourself to Ban Mai Singsamphan you can make it happen.

CHAMPASAK ຈຳປາສັກ

POP 14,000 / ☎ 030

It's hard to imagine Champasak as a seat of royalty, but from 1713 until until 1946 it was just that. These days the town is a somnolent place, the fountain circle (that no longer hosts a fountain) in the middle of the main street alluding to a grandeur long since departed, along with the former royal family. Scattered French colonial-era buildings share space with traditional Lao wooden stilt houses, and the few vehicles that venture down the narrow main street share it with chickens and cows.

With a surprisingly good range of accommodation and several attractions in the vicinity – most notably the Angkor-period ruins of Wat Phu Champasak (p215) – it's easy to see why many visitors to the region prefer staying in Champasak over bustling Pakse.

Just about everything in Champasak is spread along the riverside road, both sides of the fountain circle.

👁 Sights & Activities

★ Shadow Puppet Theatre & Cinéma Tuktuk   THEATRE
(Map p211; www.cinema-tuktuk.org; 50,000K; ⏰ 8.30-10pm Oct to Apr, shadow puppets Tue & Fri, movie Wed & Sat) Run by Frenchman Yves Bernard, this magical theatre next to the tourist office tells the story of the epic Ramayana using the ancient art of shadow puppets. On Wednesday and Saturday nights it screens the enchanting, Academy Award–nominated silent film *Chang* (1927), filmed over 18 months in the jungles of northeast Thailand by the writer and director of Hollywood's original *King Kong*. What makes it so great is the presence of live musicians providing the soundtrack.

Wat Muang Kang   BUDDHIST TEMPLE
(ວັດເມືອງກາງ, Wat Phuthawanaram; Map p214) About 5km south of town along the Mekong stands the oldest active temple in Champasak, and arguably the most interesting in southern Laos. The soaring Thai-style *ubosot* (ordination hall), with its red-tiled roof and

Champasak

ring of pillars, will be the first thing to catch your eye, but up close the star is the *hăw taị* (Tripitaka library), which combines elements of Lao, Chinese, Vietnamese and French-colonial architecture.

The damaged, but still beautiful, tower supposedly holds Buddha images and, if you ask some locals, it has another magical purpose: in the middle of the night, a mystic light beam comes from across the river, bounces through a *kâew* (crystal) and alights atop Sri Lingaparvata, the holy mountain above Wat Phu Champasak.

It's easy enough to reach Wat Muang Kang: head out of Champasak on the riverside road and continue south on the dirt road where the main road turns towards Wat Phu. Coming back, if you're on a bike or motorcycle, you can follow the pleasant narrow path directly on the riverfront for part of the way.

SOUTHERN LAOS PHOU XIENG THONG NPA

FORMER PALACES

The two standout white buildings 300m south of the fountain circle are Champasak's most enduring reminders of its distant glory. The large 1952 building was the **palace of Chao Boun Oum** (the king's younger brother; Map p214) while one street over is **Chao Ratsadanai's residence** (Map p214), a faded 1926 French Colonial palace for his father. Distant relatives of the king still own them today.

Champasak Spa   SPA
(Map p214; ☑020-56499739; www.champasak-spa.com; massages 90,000-160,000K; ⊙10am-noon & 1-7pm, closed Mon Apr-Oct, all of Jun) 🏊 Run by Nathalie, this is a fragrant oasis of free tea and sensitively executed treatments using locally grown and sourced organic bio products. And it creates jobs for local women. The spa also offers yoga and free morning meditation sessions (you must book ahead). A full-day spa package (reservations required) comprising facial, body scrub, hair spa, massage and lunch costs 550,000K.

🛌 Sleeping

Dokchampa Guesthouse   GUESTHOUSE $
(Map p211; ☑020-55350910; r with fan/air-con 50,000/200,000K; ❄️🛜) Porches in front of all rooms, a well-placed restaurant along the river, a helpful English-speaking owner and a good mellow vibe make this one of Champasak's best choices. The fan rooms are typical, though we have no clue what they were thinking when building glass-walled bathrooms in the recently renovated air-con rooms. There are big discounts in the low season.

Saythong Guesthouse   GUESTHOUSE $
(Map p211; ☑020-22206215; bobbychampa@yahoo.com; r with fan/air-con 50,000/120,000K; ❄️🛜) One of the first guesthouses in town, this friendly place has received a remodel and is now very good value. The restaurant occupies a pleasant perch over the Mekong.

Anouxa Guesthouse   GUESTHOUSE $
(Map p214; ☑031-511006; r with fan 60,000K, with air-con 100,000-200,000K; ❄️🛜) Set amid tall trees (some of them holding hammocks) and trilling birdsong a bit north of the action, Anouxa has ageing but good rooms with private bathroom, mosquito nets, Hmong tapestries and balconies. The air-con rooms have

porches looking out to the river and the best room is perched out almost directly over the water. There's also a good riverside restaurant, and bike and motorcycle hire.

★**Inthira**
Champasak Hotel   BOUTIQUE HOTEL $$
(Map p214; ☑031-511011; www.inthira.com; r incl breakfast US$44-71; ⊙❄️🛜) The belle of the river, Inthira's 14 rooms are a mix of old and new, but all ooze charm and induce relaxation. And all have little touches of luxury – wooden floors, ambient lighting, flat-screen TVs, safes and rain showers – that set them apart from the in-town competition.

★**River Resort**   RESORT $$$
(Map p214; ☑020-56850198; www.theriver resortlaos.com; garden villas US$120-130, riverview villas US$160-170; ⊙❄️🛜🏊) The 15 duplex villas (12 riverfront and three set back along a pond and rice paddies) are outfitted with gargantuan beds, indigenous wall hangings, indoor-outdoor showers, and big balconies with five-star views. It has a pair of pools, Thai and Lao massage, a beautiful restaurant, and runs upscale excursions by boat (the sunset trip is fantastic) and other means.

ℹ️ Information

INTERNET ACCESS
Internet & Copy (Map p214; per min 250K; ⊙7am-6pm) About 150m south of the Inthira Hotel.

MONEY
Lao Development Bank (Map p211; ⊙8.30am-3.30pm Mon-Fri) Has an ATM, changes cash and does Western Union.

TOURIST INFORMATION
Champasak District Visitor Information Centre (Map p211; ☑020-97404986; ⊙8am-noon & 2-4.30pm Mon-Fri, also open weekends Sep-Apr) Can arrange boats to, and accommodation on, Don Daeng. Local guides, some of whom speak English, lead day walks around Wat Phu and can accompany you to Uo Moung. You can also arrange boats to Uo Moung here (400,000K), taking in Don Daeng and Wat Muang Kang.

ℹ️ Getting There & Away

Champasak is 30km from Pakse along a beautiful, almost empty sealed road running along the west bank of the Mekong. *Sŏrngtǎaou* to Pakse (20,000K, one hour) depart only in the morning, up to around 8am. There are also the tourist buses and boats direct to/from Pakse, but they don't run often due to lack of demand.

The regular morning tourist buses from Pakse to Champasak (55,000, 1½ hours) are actually the buses heading to Si Phan Don and these drop you at Ban Muang on the eastern bank of the Mekong where a small ferry (10,000K per person, 20,000K for motorbikes) crosses to the village of Ban Phaphin just north of Champasak. Be sure you know whether your ticket includes the ferry or not. (The ferrymen won't rip you off over this, but some of the ticket agents in Pakse have been known to.) None of the tickets include the final 2km into Champasak, so you'll probably need to walk it.

To reach Si Phan Don, you can also use the Ban Muang ferry route, take a direct morning minibus (70,000K, three hours) if there are enough passengers, or travel by boat. The later costs US$200 private, but the Champasak District Visitor Information Centre (p212) will know if others are interested in sharing the cost.

ⓘ Getting Around

All guesthouses rent bicycles (10,000K to 20,000K per day) and a few, including **Vong Paseud** (Map p214; ☑ 031-920038; r with fan 30,000-50,000K, air-con 100,000K; ✴ 🛜) and **Khamphouy** (Map p211; ☑ 030-9995866; r with fan 50,000-60,000K, with air-con 120,000K; ✴ 🛜), also have motorbikes (from 70,000K).

AROUND CHAMPASAK

Don Daeng   ດອນແດງ

Stretched out like an old croc sunning itself in the middle of the Mekong, Don Daeng is a little like an island that time forgot. It's classic middle Mekong, with eight villages scattered around its edge and rice fields in the middle. The small and mostly shaded tracks that run along the edge and across the heart of the 8km-long island are mercifully free of cars – bicycles, *dok dok* (mini tractor) and a few motorcycles are all the transport that's required.

About the only thing that qualifies as a sight is a ruined ancient brick stupa, presumed to be from the days of Wat Phu Champasak, at the forest temple in the middle of

> #### MUANG KAO
>
> Under the palm trees and rice paddies 3km east of Champasak town are the remains of a city that was, about 1500 years ago, the capital of the Mon-Khmer Chenla kingdom. The site is known today as **Muang Kao** (Old City; ເມືອງເກົ່າ; Map p214) , but scholars believe it was called Shrestapura.
>
> Aerial photographs show the remains of a rectangular city measuring 2.3km by 1.8km, surrounded by double earthen walls on three sides and protected on the east by the Mekong River. Other traces of the old city include small *baray* (a Khmer word meaning 'artificial body of water'), the foundations for circular brick monuments, evidence of an advanced system of irrigation, various Hindu statuary and stone carvings, stone implements and ceramics. The sum of all this is an extremely rare example of an ancient urban settlement in Southeast Asia, one whose design reveals how important religious belief was in the workings of everyday life.
>
> The origin of the city remained a mystery until Southeast Asia's oldest Sanskrit inscription was discovered here. The 5th-century stele stated the city was founded by King Devanika and was then called Kuruksetra and also mentions the auspicious Sri Lingaparvata nearby, a clear reference to the mountain near Wat Phu Champasak. 'Honoured since antiquity', the mountain was believed to be the residence or the manifestation of the Hindu god Shiva, and even today local people honour the mountain as the place of Phi Intha (the soul or protecting spirit of the mountain).
>
> By the end of the 5th century the city was thriving. It continued as a major regional centre until at least the 7th century, as shown by two Nandi (Shiva's bull mount) pedestal sculptures discovered in 1994–95 bearing inscriptions by King Citrasena-Mahendravarman, the 'conqueror' who later shifted the kingdom's capital to Sambor Prei Kuk in central Cambodia. Archaeological material suggests the city was inhabited until the 16th century.
>
> Ongoing research by Dr Patrizia Zolese and her team has revealed that a second city was built near Wat Phu after the 9th century. She believes the **Hong Nang Sida** (ໂຮງນາງສິດາ; Map p214; ☺8am-4.30pm) FREE was at the centre of this city, which was probably Lingapura, a place mentioned in many ancient inscriptions but which has not been categorically identified by modern scholars.

Around Champasak

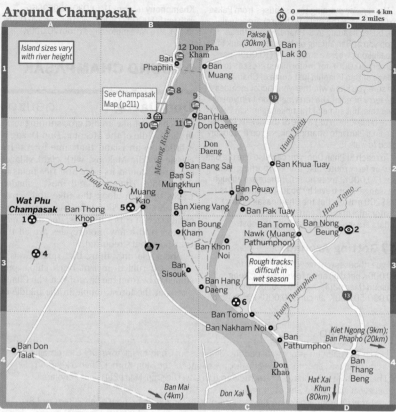

N 0 _____ 4 km
   0 _____ 2 miles

Island sizes vary with river height

Pakse (30km)

Ban Lak 30

12 Don Pha Kham

Ban Phaphin

Ban Muang

See Champasak Map (p211)

8

9

3

10 11

Ban Hua Don Daeng

Don Daeng

Ban Bang Sai

Ban Si Mungkhun

Ban Khua Tuay

Ban Peuay Lao

Wat Phu Champasak

Ban Thong Khop

5 Muang Kao

Ban Xieng Vang

Ban Pak Tuay

1

4

Ban Boung Kham

7

Ban Khon Noi

Ban Tomo Nawk (Muang Pathumphon)

Ban Nong Beung 2

Rough tracks; difficult in wet season

Ban Sisouk

Ban Hang Daeng

6

Ban Tomo

Ban Nakham Noi

Ban Pathumphon

Kiet Ngong (9km); Ban Phapho (20km)

Ban Thang Beng

Ban Don Talat

Ban Mai (4km)

Don Xai

Don Khao

Hat Xai Khun (80km)

13

Huay Tuay

Huay Tomo

Huay Thumphon

Huay Sawa

Mekong River

13

SOUTHERN LAOS DON DAENG

Around Champasak

◎ Top Sights
1 Wat Phu Champasak A3

◎ Sights
2 Ban Nong Beung D3
3 Chao Boun Oum's Palace B1
  Chao Ratsadanai's Residence .... (see 3)
4 Hong Nang Sida A3
5 Muang Kao B2
6 Uo Moung C3
7 Wat Muang Kang B3

✪ Activities, Courses & Tours
  Champasak Spa .... (see 8)

⌂ Sleeping
8 Anouxa Guesthouse B1
9 Hua Don Daeng Village Lodge B1
10 Inthira Champasak Hotel B2
11 La Folie Lodge B2
12 River Resort B1
  Vong Paseud Guesthouse .... (see 10)

✖ Eating
  Inthira Hotel Restaurant .... (see 10)
  Nakorn Restaurant .... (see 10)

ⓘ Information
  Internet & Copy .... (see 10)

the island. There are plenty of beaches for swimming (only if you are a strong swimmer, the current can be deceptive) but women should wear sarongs and shirts when they bathe, not bikinis.

🛏 Sleeping

Hua Don Daeng Village Lodge
GUESTHOUSE $

(Map p214; ☎ 020-55275277; per person 30,000K) Hua Don Daeng village, at the island's northern tip, has a small, simple community lodge with two mattress-on-the-floor rooms and also offers genuine homestays. For both options, local meals (20,000K to 30,000K) are prepared by the villagers who also hire bikes (20,000K). Either call to book or arrange a stay through the visitor centre in Champasak.

★**La Folie Lodge** RESORT $$$
(Map p214; ☑030-5347603; www.lafolie-laos.com; d/villas incl breakfast low season US$90/$500, high season US$170/$600; ⊝❄@🕸☲) 🏊 Set on the riverbank facing Wat Phu, La Folie makes the most of the views. The gorgeous wooden bungalows have lots of attention to detail (except for the thin walls), including Lao textiles, colonial motifs and polished wood floors, while the atmospheric poolside restaurant includes a wide selection of Lao and international dishes. Boat transfer and use of bikes is included in the price.

La Folie supports community projects on Don Daeng, including renovation of the village health centre.

❶ Getting There & Away

To get to Don Daeng from Champasak, hire a boat (ostensibly fixed at 50,000K one way, but a return journey could be cheaper) through your guesthouse or the visitor information centre. If you can communicate what you want, you can do it for cheaper (perhaps 30,000K one way with negotiation) from Muang Kao, south of Champasak (the landing is just north of the bridge), or Ban Muang on the Mekong's east bank.

❶ Getting Around

Both of the lodges on Don Daeng have bikes, but if you're not spending the night it's best to bring your own from Champasak since there are few.

Wat Phu World Heritage Area

A visit to the ancient Khmer religious complex of Wat Phu is one of the highlights of any trip to Laos. Stretching 1400m up the slopes of Phu Pasak (also known more colloquially as Phu Khuai or Mt Penis), Wat Phu is small compared with the monumental Angkor-era sites near Siem Reap in Cambodia. The tumbledown pavilions, ornate Shiva-lingam sanctuary, enigmatic crocodile stone and tall trees that shroud much of the walkway in soothing shade give Wat Phu an almost mystical atmosphere. These, and a layout that is unique in Khmer architecture, led to Unesco declaring the Wat Phu complex a World Heritage Site in 2001.

An electric cart shuttles guests from the ticket office area past the *baray* (ceremonial pond; năwng sá in Lao). After that, you must walk.

History

Sanskrit inscriptions and Chinese sources confirm the site has been a place of worship since the mid-5th century. The temple complex was designed as a worldly imitation of heaven and fitted into a larger plan that evolved to include a network of roads, cities, settlements and other temples. What you see today is the product of centuries of building, rebuilding, alteration and addition, with the most recent structures dating from the late-Angkorian period.

At its height, the temple and nearby city formed the most important economic and political centre in the region, though there is still much to uncover, both figuratively and literally, about the way the ancients lived. Years of work by the Italian Archaeological Mission and the inimitable Dr Patrizia Zolese – the leading expert on Wat Phu, who has been working at the site since 1990 – have documented sites spread over a 400-sq-km region around the 84-hectare main site.

◉ Sights

Wat Phu is situated at the junction of the Mekong plain and Phu Phasak, a mountain that was sacred to the Austro-Asiatic tribes living in this area centuries before the construction of any of the ruins now visible.

South of Wat Phu are three small Angkor-era sites in poor condition that will mainly interest die-hard fans of Khmer architecture. Each stands beside the ancient road to Angkor Wat in Cambodia. On the opposite bank of the Mekong, Uo Moung (p217) is also thought to be related to Wat Phu and is encompassed by the Wat Phu Unesco World Heritage Site.

★**Wat Phu Champasak** RUINS
(ວັດພູຈໍາປາສັກ; Map p214; 50,000K; ◉ site 8am-6pm, museum to 4.30pm) Bucolic Wat Phu sits in graceful decrepitude, and while it lacks the arresting enormity of Angkor in Cambodia, given its few visitors and more dramatic natural setting, these small Khmer ruins evoke a more soulful response. While some buildings are more than 1000 years old, most date from the 11th to 13th centuries. The site is divided into six terraces on three levels joined by a frangipani-bordered stairway

Wat Phu Champasak

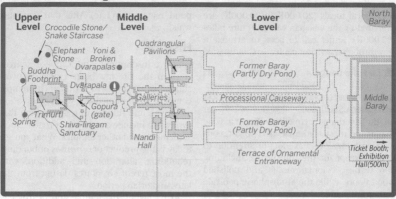

Upper Level — Crocodile Stone/Snake Staircase — Elephant Stone — Yoni & Broken Dvarapalas — Quadrangular Pavilions — Buddha Footprint — Dvarapala — Trimurti — Gopura (gate) — Spring — Shiva-lingam Sanctuary — Middle Level — Galleries — Nandi Hall — Lower Level — Former Baray (Partly Dry Pond) — Processional Causeway — Former Baray (Partly Dry Pond) — Terrace of Ornamental Entranceway — North Baray — Middle Baray — Ticket Booth; Exhibition Hall (500m)

ascending the mountain to the main shrine at the top.

Visit in the early morning for cooler temperatures and to capture the ruins in the best light.

➔ Lower Level

The electric cart takes you past the great baray (ceremonial pond; *nǎwng sá* in Lao) and delivers you to the large sandstone base of the ancient main entrance to Wat Phu. Here begins a causeway-style ceremonial promenade lined by stone lotus buds and flanked by two much smaller *baray* that still fill with water, lotus flowers and the odd buffalo during the wet season.

➔ Middle Level

Wat Pu's middle section features two exquisitely carved **quadrangular pavilions** built of sandstone and laterite. Believed to date from the mid-10th or early 11th century, the style resembles Koh Ker in Cambodia. The buildings consist of four galleries and a central open courtyard. Wat Phu was converted into a Buddhist site in later centuries but much of the original Hindu sculpture remains in the lintels, which feature various forms of Vishnu and Shiva.

Next to the southern pavilion stands the much smaller **Nandi Hall** (dedicated to Shiva's mount). It was from here that an ancient royal road once led over 200km to Angkor Wat in Cambodia. In front is a smaller version of the initial causeway, this one flanked by two collapsed galleries, leading to a pair of steep staircases.

At the base of a second stairway is an impressive and now very holy **dvarapala** (sentinel figure) standing ramrod straight with sword held at the ready. Most Thai and Lao visitors make an offering to his spirit before continuing up the mountain. If you step down off the walkway and onto the grassy area just north of here you'll come to the remains of a yoni pedestal, the cosmic vagina-womb symbol associated with Shaivism, and two unusually large, headless and armless **dvarapala statues** half-buried in the grass. These are the largest *dvarapala* found anywhere in the former Angkorian kingdom.

After the *dvarapala* a rough sandstone path ascends quickly to another steep stairway, atop which is a small terrace holding six ruined brick shrines – only one retains some of its original form. From here two final staircases, the second marked by crouching guardians also sans heads and arms, take you to the top, passing through the large terraces you saw clearly from the bottom of the mountain.

➔ Upper Level

On the uppermost level of Wat Phu is the **sanctuary** itself. It has many carvings, notably two guardians and two *apsara* (celestial dancers), and it once enclosed a Shiva lingam that was bathed, via a system of sandstone pipes, with waters from the **sacred spring** that still flows behind the complex. The sanctuary now contains a set of very old, distinctive Buddha images on an altar. The brick rear section, which might have been built in the 9th century, is a *cella* (cell), where the holy linga was kept.

Sculpted into a large boulder behind the sanctuary is a Khmer-style **Trimurti**, the Hindu holy trinity of Shiva, Vishnu and Brahma. Further back, beyond some terracing to the south of the Trimurti, is the cave from which the holy spring flowed into the sanctuary. Up a rough path to the north of the Trimurti, a **Buddha footprint** and an elephant are carved into a rock wall.

Just north of the Shiva linga sanctuary, amid a mess of rocks and rubble, look around for two unique stone carvings known as the **elephant stone** and the **crocodile stone**. Crocodiles were semi-divine figures in Khmer culture, but despite much speculation that the stone was used for human sacrifices, its function – if there was one – remains unknown. The crocodile is believed to date from the Angkor period, while the elephant is thought to date from the 16th century. Also look out for an interesting chunk of a staircase framed by two snakes and some small caves that were probably used for meditation in ancient days.

When you've seen everything here, just sitting and soaking up the wide-angle view of the *baray*, the plains and the Mekong is fantastic.

Wat Phu Exhibition Hall   MUSEUM
(ຫໍພິພິດຂະພັນວັດພູ; admission with Wat Phu ticket; ☉8am-4.30pm) The Exhibition Hall near the ticket office showcases dozens of lintels, *naga* (mythical water serpents), Buddhas and other stone work from Wat Phu and its associated sites. Detailed descriptions are in English, plus the building includes clean bathrooms.

✨ Festivals & Events

Bun Wat Phu Champasak   BUDDHIST
(Wat Phu Champasak Festival) The highlight of the year in Wat Phu Champasak is this three-day festival, held as part of Magha Puja (Makha Busa) during the full moon of the third lunar month, usually in February. The central ceremonies performed are Buddhist, culminating on the full-moon day with an early-morning parade of monks receiving alms from the faithful, followed that evening by a candlelit *wéean téean* (circumambulation) of the lower shrines.

Throughout the three days of the festival Lao visitors climb around the hillside, stopping to pray and leave offerings of flowers and incense. The festival is more commercial than it once was, and for much of the time has an atmosphere somewhere between a kids' carnival and music festival. Events include kick-boxing matches, cockfights, comedy shows and plenty of music and dancing. After dark, the beer and *lòw-lów* (Lao whisky) flow freely and the atmosphere gets pretty rowdy.

ℹ Getting There & Away

Wat Phu Champasak is 43km from Pakse and 10km from Champasak. It's a flat, easy bike ride from Champasak, though there's not a lot of shade. A tuk-tuk from Champasak will cost around 100,000K return.

Uo Moung (Tomo Temple)
ອູໂມງ (ວັດໂຕະໂມຍ)

The Khmer temple ruin of **Uo Moung** (Map p214; 10,000K; ☉8am-4pm), beside a small tributary of the Mekong, is believed to have been built late in the 9th century during the reign of the Khmer King Yasovarman I. Its exact function is unknown, though its orientation towards the holy mountain Phu Pasak suggests its location was somehow related to Wat Phu Champasak (p215), and thus it's included as part of the Wat Phu World Heritage Site, even though it sits on the east side of the river. It's not worth a trip for everyone, but the forest and excessive moss do give it a 'lost' feeling.

The ruins include an entranceway bordered by lotus-bud carvings, like those found at Wat Phu, and two crumbling *gopura* (ornate entranceways), one still partially standing. Several lintels and other sandstone carvings are displayed on rocks beneath towering dipterocarp trees, but the best art from this site is in the Wat Phu Exhibition Hall, including an unusual lingam-style stone post on which two faces have been carved. It's unusual because *mukhalinga* usually have four *mukha* (faces), while most ordinary linga have no face at all. The white building at the heart of the site houses a bronze Sukhothai-style Buddha.

ℹ Getting There & Away

Uo Moung is 45km from Pakse. The signed turn-off along Rte 13 is just past the Huay Tomo bridge next to a market where you can look for *săhm-lór* or tuk-tuk if you are travelling by public transport and don't want to walk the 4.5km to the site.

You can also visit Uo Moung by boat from Don Daeng or Champasak on the opposite bank of the Mekong. From Champasak, you're looking at about 400,000K return to charter a boat, including waiting time of an hour or so, to the nearby village of Ban Tomo. The price will be about 60,000K or so return from Ban Sisouk at the south end of Don Daeng; although keep in mind that there is a small possibility that no boats will be available.

A good full-day option is to rent a bicycle in Champasak and take a boat first to Don Daeng, then to Ban Tomo, then cross the river back to the western shore (also about 60,000K) and ride back to Champasak.

Kiet Ngong ບ້ານກຽດໂງ້ງ

☑030

The Lao Loum villagers of Kiet Ngong, near the Se Pian NPA, run southern Laos' most successful community-based ecotourism project. Started in the mid-2000s with help from the Asian Development Bank, Kiet Ngong is functioning on its own now.

Kiet Ngong sits at the edge of a bird-rich wetland about 9km from Rte 13. Working elephants and an unusually large herd of buffalo give the wetland a safari feel. It's best to sleep here for at least a night, but it also works as a day trip from Pakse or Champasak.

Visitors heading to Kiet Ngong must pay a 25,000K entry fee for Se Pian NPA at the little white building 2km east of Rte 13 that you pass on your way there.

◉ Sights

Ban Nong Beung   VILLAGE

(ບ້ານໜອງບຶງ; Map p214) On your way to or from Kiet Ngong, you may want to stop at this woodcarving village populated by ethnic Tahoy families who migrated here from Salavan Province over a century ago. They make a lot of modern, marketable products, but also still carve masks and other traditional designs, most of which are carefully burned to turn the wood black. Be sure to have a look at the old-style community meeting house.

☝ Activities

The community-run Visitor Information Centre organises homestays, **trekking**, **birdwatching** and other activities. It's best to contact them in advance, although you can usually just show up and arrange things on the spot.

Elephant riding is what Kiet Ngong is famous for, but forest walks and traditional canoe rides (July to March only) in the swamp are the real highlights. Trips into the jungle of the Se Pian NPA can range from half-day nature walks to extended overnight treks. Camping gear is available for hire. The wetland, Bueng Kiet Ngong, covers 13.8 sq km and was designated a Ramsar Site (a wetland of international importance) in 2010. It's emerging as a birdwatching destination, with the rare white-winged duck a possible tick.

Guides cost 100,000K per day with additional costs depending on the particular activity. Things can be arranged either at the Visitor Information Centre or Kingfisher Ecolodge, although mountain biking (per person 430,000K with two people) is only available from the lodge.

🛏 Sleeping

In addition to the excellent Kingfisher Ecolodge, the Kiet Ngong community offers two types of accommodation, both booked through the Visitor Information Centre. Choose from a homestay with a local family or the community guesthouse with dorm-style sleeping in bungalows in a great spot overlooking the wetland. Some, but not all, homestay homes have hot-water showers. Both options cost 40,000K per person, plus 30,000K for meals.

Bounhome Homestay   HOMESTAY $

(☑030-5346293; per bed 50,000K) In Ban Phapho (Phapho Village), 10km east of Kiet Ngong, this homestay has four small, ultra simple rooms in the family's wooden house. The bathroom is shared and there's no hot water, but Mr Bounhome and his family speak some English and French and have been welcoming travellers for well over 20 years.

★Kingfisher Ecolodge   LODGE $$

(☑020-55726315; www.kingfisherecolodge.com; eco/comfort r high season 250,000/750,000K, low season 210,000/650,000K; ⊘closed May & Jun; ❄@🛜) 🌿 Run by a Lao-Italian family, the Kingfisher Ecolodge is set on 7 hectares at the edge of the wetland, about 700m past Kiet Ngong village. It's a beautiful spot. Sitting on your balcony at dawn and watching birds flit across the wetland is a memorable experience and the two-tiered restaurant-bar could easily be in an East African safari lodge.

The six comfortable bungalows ooze Italian panache, with huge wooden countertops in the bathrooms, polished hardwood pillars and floors, lovely beds and – the coup de grâce – huge balconies with large bamboo hammocks. The economy rooms have more modest balconies and share a spotless bathroom.

Most activities offered by the Visitor Information Centre are also offered here with the addition of full-day guided mountain-bike tours (per person 430,000K with two people) into Se Pian NPA. And it lives up to the 'eco' in its name by supporting the local school, using solar power and promoting conservation within Se Pian NPA.

ℹ Information

Visitor Information Centre (☑ 030-9552120; toui_ps@hotmail.com; ⊙ 8am-4pm) This community-run centre in the middle of Kiet Ngong arranges activities, accommodation and transport from Rte 13. Placards on the walls have useful information about the various options and also the ecology, history and culture of the area. A few of the guides speak some English. All activities can also be arranged through the excellent Kingfisher Ecolodge.

ℹ Getting There & Away

Kiet Ngong is 56km from central Pakse. Most visitors come here as part of a tour, but travelling independently is fairly easy. One van or *sŏrngtăaou* (30,000K, two to 2½ hours) leaves Kiet Ngong for Lak 8 bus station in Pakse at about 8am and heads back at 11am. Kiet Ngong is often mispronounced so ask instead for 'Phu Asa'. Alternatively, board anything going south on Rte 13, get off at Ban Thang Beng and call the Visitor Information Centre for a pick-up by motorcycle (per person 25,000K) for the last 9km to the village.

Se Pian NPA
ປ່າສະຫງວນແຫ່ງຊາດເຊປຽນ

Se Pian NPA (www.xepian.org) is one of the most important protected areas in Laos. The 2400-sq-km park boasts small populations of Asiatic black bears, yellow-cheeked crested gibbons and Siamese crocodiles, and is home to many birds, including the rare sarus crane, vultures and hornbills. Banteng, Asian elephants, gaur and tigers once roamed here, but sightings of these creatures have been rare to nonexistent in recent years.

Stretching from Rte 13 in the west into Attapeu Province in the east, and to the Cambodian border in the south, it is fed by three major rivers: the Se Pian (Pian River), Se Khampho (Khampho River) and Se Kong (Kong River).

It's almost impossible to visit the park under your own steam, but you can get into the park for either tough multi-day jungle treks or short nature walks, bike trips and boat rides through Kiet Ngong village or Green Discovery (p203) tour company in Pakse. Though almost nobody does it, Se Pian can also be accessed from Attapeu. If you're feeling really frisky and adventurous, you could try to charter a boat down the Sekong from Sanamsay, on Rte 18A about 35km west of Attapeu. This trip towards the Cambodian border would get you deep into a scenic section of Se Pian NPA.

BOLAVEN PLATEAU REGION ພູພຽງບໍລະເວນ

Spreading across parts of all four southern provinces, the fertile Bolaven Plateau (known in Lao as Phu Phieng Bolaven) is famous for its cool climate, dramatic waterfalls and high-grade coffee.

The French started planting coffee, rubber and bananas in the early 20th century, but many left following independence in the 1950s and the rest followed when US bombardment began in the late '60s. Controlling the Bolaven Plateau was considered strategically vital to both the Americans and North Vietnamese, as evidenced by the staggering amount of unexploded ordnance (UXO) still lying around. But where it has been cleared, both local farmers and large companies are busy cultivating coffee. Other local products include fruit, cardamom and rattan.

The largest ethnic group on the plateau is the Laven (Bolaven means 'Home of the Laven'). Several other Mon-Khmer ethnic groups, including the Alak, Katu, Tahoy and Suay, also live on the plateau and its escarpment.

Paksong Area

Paksong, Laos' coffee capital, is not much to look at, most of it having been obliterated in a storm of bombs during the Second Indochina War. Other than doing a coffee tour or buying a fresh cuppa, you probably won't want to stop here. But, many of the waterfalls near the town definitely should be part of your Bolaven itinerary.

⊙ Sights

Tat Fan   WATERFALL
(ຕາດຟານ; Rte 16, Km 38; admission 5000K, motorcycle/car 3000/5000K) Tat Fan is one of the most spectacular waterfalls in Laos. Twin streams plunge out of dense forest and tumble down more than 120m to form the Huay Bang Lieng. Early morning and late afternoon have the best sunlight, but the falls are often shrouded by fog. The viewing point is at **Tad Fane Resort** (☑ 020-55531400; www.tadfaneresort.com; Rte 16, Km 38; r US$28-42; ⊛), a jungle lodge atop the cliff opposite the falls, and it's a near-mandatory stop for anyone in the area.

One way to beat the crowds is to take a half-day trek to the top or bottom. The price is US$15 per person with a minimum cost of

US$40 and this includes the national-park entrance fee. To arrange this, ask at the resort for Arui.

The access road to the falls is 12km from Paksong.

Tat Gneuang
WATERFALL

(ຕາດເຍື້ອງ; Rte 16, Km 40; admission 10,000K, motorcycle/car 10,000K; ⊙ticket booth 8am-5pm, falls to 6.30pm) Tat Yuang, as some signs spell it, is impressive, with its twin torrents falling about 40m and flowing into lush jungle. It's hugely popular with day trippers from Pakse and tour buses from Thailand, so getting there early or lingering late is a good idea. An easy set of steps leads down to the main viewing area and to a little bridge that takes you to the top of the waterfall.

It is 10km to the access road from Paksong, then 1.2km from the highway to the park. A guesthouse near the entrance should be open in 2017.

Tat E-Tu
WATERFALL

(ຕາດອີຕູ້; Rt 16, Km 35; admission 5000K, motorcycle/car 3000/5000K) Tat E-Tu, 1km north of the main road (Rte 16), is the first large waterfall you reach on the drive up from Pakse. Though this 40m drop is pretty impressive, it doesn't get nearly as many visitors as the more famous waterfalls nearby. It's just a short, easy walk to the viewpoint from the Baan E-Tu Waterfall Resort parking area.

Dong Hua Sao NPA
NATIONAL PARK

(ປ່າສະຫງວນແຫ່ງຊາດດົງຫົວສາວ) The 1100-sq-km Dong Hua Sao NPA, south of Paksong, is home to large tracts of pristine jungle where you might spot monkeys, large butterflies and rare hornbills. Poaching is a problem, as is illegal logging to plant coffee. Adventure specialist Green Discovery (p203) runs its Tree Top Explorer trips here, which are an excellent way to experience the park, though bookings must be must be made in Pakse. Treks run by Tad Fane Resort (p219) also get you into the park.

★Tayicseua
WATERFALL

(ຕາດຕາຍັກເສືອ; admission 5000K, parking 5000K) There are seven significant waterfalls (none of them named Tayicseua) and several smaller ones at this remote, but easily accessible private nature reserve. Some sit right near the restaurant-parking area while others, such as postcard-worthy Tat Halang (aka Tat Alang) are down in the forest along a good set of trails, which you can walk without a guide. It's in the early stages of growing into a proper resort but, for now, crowds remain rare.

Due to the size of the area and the serene setting, the best way to visit is to spend the night at a guesthouse.

Tayicseua sits off the main paved road 43km from Paksong. Coming from the east it's 4km from the paved road to the signed entrance. For the most part, this dirt road is fine, but there are some steep, rough spots that require care on a motorcycle, especially in the rainy season. The longer dirt road from the west is much smoother.

Tat Champee
WATERFALL

(ຕາດຈຳປີ; Rte 16, Km 38; admission 5000K, motorcycle/car 3000/5000K) Not to be confused with the far inferior waterfall of the same name along Rte 20 on the way to Tad Lo, this is the smallest of the four waterfalls west of Paksong, but it's the most fun to visit. A good set of concrete steps leads down to an up-close viewpoint, then a sketchy wooden staircase or a longer footpath takes you down to the river, where you can swim and even go behind the waterfall.

The 2km road leading to it (which begins directly across from the road to Tat Fan) is a bit rough, so it's the only waterfall around Paksong that doesn't get crowded. The access road is 12km from Paksong.

Tat Katamtok
WATERFALL

(ຕາດກະຕາມຕົກ) Running off the Bolaven Plateau, the Huay Katam drops more than 100m out of thick forest at Tat Katamtok. These beautiful falls are made even more impressive by their relative isolation – there are no concessions or other facilities here. While on the one hand this isolation is appealing, it has facilitated some violent robberies. Ask motorcycle-hire companies in Pakse if the situation has changed before you visit.

🏃 Activities

Rafting and kayaking trips are possible on Huay Bang Lieng, the river that feeds Tat Fan, during the wet season from July to November. For details speak to Green Discovery (p203) in Pakse.

👉 Tours

Jhai Coffee Farmers Co-operative Tours
TOURS

(☎020-97672424; www.jhaicoffeehouse.com; Rte 16; tour per person 150,000K) Part of the philanthropic Jhai Coffee House, these half-day tours run from 9am to noon and go out to a local farmer's home and plantation for a 'bean to cup' lesson on the coffee business. They are only offered between October and January (the picking season), but a 45-minute tour (50,000K per person) around the coffee shop is available at any time.

Koffie's Coffee Tours   TOURS
(☑ 020-22760439; www.paksong.info; coffee tour per person 50,000K, coffee tour with roasting workshop per person 180,000K) 'Mr Koffie', an expat Dutch coffee connoisseur, has been leading coffee tours around Paksong for nearly a decade. On the regular two-hour tour you'll get a look at growing, harvesting and processing coffee, and also sample some local brews. Add the afternoon roasting workshop and you'll finish the day with a cup you brewed yourself and a bag of beans to take home. Tours start at 10am at Won Coffee.

🛏 Sleeping

★ Tayicseua Guesthouse   GUESTHOUSE $
(☑ 020-29878926; www.tayicseua.com; dm 60,000K; 🛜) This friendly spot surrounded by seven large waterfalls deserves its rave reviews. You'll fall asleep to tumbling water and wake up to birdsong from under mosquito nets in rustic bamboo huts (or your own tent) and share the hot-water showers. A communal lodge overlooks the distant mists of Tat Jariem deep in the valley below.

Mystic Mountain Coffee   HOMESTAY $
(☑ 020-99661333; www.mysticmountain.coffee; r per person 50,000K) Friendly Mr Khamsone has built a bamboo and wood room with two beds at his remote coffee plantation. Though facilities are super simple, you'll be well cared for by his family. He's also a tour guide, so most of his guests include his homestay as part of a bigger trip around the area in his classic Jeep. It's about 12km north of Paksong on the rough road to Lao Ngam. Reservations required. Meals are 20,000 to 25,000K.

Sinouk Coffee Resort   BOUTIQUE HOTEL $$
(☑ 030-9558960; www.sinoukcoffeeresort.com; r US$40-90; ⊜❄@🛜) Set beside a babbling brook on a working coffee plantation 32km northeast of Paksong on the road to Tha Taeng, there's a hill-station feel here. Like its sister lodge, Pakse's Residence Sisouk (p203), it's loaded with indigenous textiles, period furniture and framed old-world photos. It's also worth stopping in for a meal (mains 25,000K to 75,000K) amidst the manicured gardens if you're passing by.

Baan E-Tu Waterfall Resort   RESORT $$
(☑ 020-28347766, Thailand 0066 81 9177264; www. baanetuwaterfallresort.com; Rte 16, Km 35; r incl breakfast 276,000-391,000K; 🛜) Set on a former coffee and tea plantation 15km west of Paksong, the smart bungalows at this sprawling resort have polished wooden floors, ultrasoft beds and – in the priciest rooms – large balconies within earshot of Tat E-Tu. New management seems to have improved the old service. Wi-fi is only available in the lobby and restaurant.

🍷 Drinking & Nightlife

Jhai Coffee House   COFFEE
(www.jhaicoffeehouse.com; Rte 16; coffee from 10,000K; ⏰ 8.30am-5.30pm; 🛜) Billing itself as the world's first completely philanthropic coffee roaster and cafe located at the source, Jhai buys its beans at fair-trade prices from the Jhai Coffee Farmer Cooperative and puts 100% of profits back into local water and hygiene projects. It's a surprising little oasis with perfect coffee, plus a limited food menu during the high season. It's in the centre of Paksong town.

Won Coffee   COFFEE
(Rte 16; coffee from 10,000K; ⏰ 7am-5.30pm; 🛜) Though run in part by 'Mr Koffie', this is very much a local spot. Besides regular organic coffees, he produces his own civet-excreted *kopi luwak* (30,000K per cup or 250,000K per 100g) and leads coffee tours. It's in the centre of town. Look for the mushroom-shaped tables and chairs and a white sign with blue and red letters reading 'Fresh roasted coffe'.

❶ Getting There & Away

Travel by hired motorcycle is best, but all buses heading east from Pakse can drop you in Paksong (fan/air-con 15,000/20,000K, 90 minutes) or near any of the waterfalls to the west of town. For Tayicseua, take an Attapeu bus, but make sure it's one using the direct route rather than going via Sekong.

Tat Lo   ຕາດເລາະ
☑ 030

Tat Lo (pronounced dàat láw) has taken a place on the backpacker trail thanks to an attractive setting, cheap accommodation and some beautiful waterfalls. It lacks the party scene of Don Det and Vang Vieng, and locals are set on it staying this way. Thankfully, several Westerners who have settled here and opened businesses are in full agreement. The result is a serenity that sees many visitors stay longer than they planned.

The availability of day treks, along with widespread use of English, makes Tat Lo the best base for getting to know the Bolaven Plateau, even though it actually sits against the foot of it, rather than up on top of it. The real name of Tat Lo village is Ban Saen Vang, but these days everybody just calls it Tat Lo.

⊙ Sights

There are actually three waterfalls on this stretch of river: Tat Lo, Tat Hang and Tat Soung. Tat Lo, ironically, is the least impressive. In fact, all three are much less beautiful than they once were due to a new dam built upstream.

Note that dam authorities upstream release water in the evening and being in its path could be fatal. Check with locals about the release time before you visit the falls.

★ Tat Soung   WATERFALL
(ຕາດສູງ; parking 5000K) Tat Soung is a 50m drop over the edge of the Bolaven Plateau, and though the dam has damaged these falls more than the others – slowing them to a trickle for most of the year – you can walk around the rocky top of the falls from where the views are fantastic. During heavy August to October rains, when they reach their full width, the falls themselves are quite spectacular too.

Tat Soung is 8km south of Tat Lo town, uphill almost the entire way. Along the way, 3.5km out of Tat Lo town, you'll pass a sign for the bottom of the falls at Ban Kiang Tat Soung (Kiang Tat Soung Village). (Note that the sign inside the village saying 'top' is a mistake.) It's a fun walk and a beautiful destination, and young guides will offer to walk you there for a small tip. It's about 1.5km round trip. Definitely don't leave anything in your motorcycle basket; chances are it won't be there when you get back.

Tat Lo   WATERFALL
(ຕາດເລາະ) **FREE** Tat Lo, about 500m upriver from Tat Hang, is a little bigger than its neighbour, but probably won't knock your socks off. To get here, walk past Saise Resort's bungalows and follow the road to the end, then you need to scramble over some rocks. To reach the top of the falls, it's 1km up the eastern road from the village's junction to the signed turn-off.

Tat Hang   WATERFALL
(ຕາດຮັງ) **FREE** Tat Hang is the waterfall you see from the bridge in town and some guesthouses. It's about 6m tall and wide, with several steps making it quite beautiful even in low flow. You can swim here; often along with hordes of locals.

Ban Houay Houn   VILLAGE
(ບານຫວຍຫຸນ) You'll know you've arrived in this village, 24km from Tat Lo, by the 'Katu Weavers' sign or the tourists gathered around the traditional community meeting hall. The women here weave cotton textiles using backstrap looms held taut with their feet. Bold patterns are added with white beads. While red and black are the Katu tribe's traditional colours, they now weave from the whole rainbow to match tourist demand.

✦ Activities

The Tat Lo Guides Association, operated out of the Tat Lo Tourism Information Centre, offers highly recommended walks (half-/full day 80,000/160,000K per person) combining all three waterfalls – Tat Hang, Tat Lo and Tat Soung – with Katu, Tahoy and/or Suay ethnic-minority villages.

For something more adventurous they can also lead you to some more distant waterfalls and cultural stops, such as a cave with ancient stone caskets. Or, consider the two-day excursion to **Phou Tak Khao** mountain, with an overnight in an ethnic Suay village. This costs US$100/60 per person for a group of two/four people with local guides; English-speaking guides cost extra.

🛏 Sleeping & Eating

★ Captain Hook Coffee Break   HOMESTAY $
(☎020-98930406; www.facebook.com/hook.laos; homestay incl breakfast & dinner per person 50,000K) Mr Hook (who, not surprisingly, has acquired the nickname 'Captain Hook' from foreigners) runs an excellent organic coffee farm and homestay 15km from Tat Lo. He's full of stories, and the unvarnished look at Katu village life you get will be quite enlightening; often shocking. His village is Ban Khokphung Tai, halfway between Ban Beng and Tha Taeng.

★ Mr Vieng Coffee & Homestay   HOMESTAY $
(☎020-99837206; per person 20,000K, per meal 15,000K) This is a fun and friendly homestay on a coffee plantation in Ban Houay Houn, right along Rte 20, 19km southwest of Tat Lo. Rooms are simple, but quite good for the

price, and the ethnic Katu couple who run it give plantation tours (15,000K per person), and make and sell weavings.

Green Garden
GUESTHOUSE $

(📞 020-96163699; tadlogarden@hotmail.com; r/ste 35,000/60,000K) There are five rooms here under a big roof in a small patch of forest along the road heading north of town, plus one separate private-bath bungalow. Though ultra simple, they're great value. Long-time resident Em, an Austrian, uses this as his base for teaching how to wok-roast coffee beans.

Fandee
GUESTHOUSE $

(www.fandee-guesthouse.com; r 50,000-60,000K; 🛜) Fandee means 'Sweet Dreams' in Lao, and the warm welcome from the French hosts helps make that a reality. There are four solid wooden bungalows with private porches and thatched roofs behind an attractive and re-laxing terraced restaurant, which serves good toasted sandwiches.

Mama Pap
GUESTHOUSE $

(dm 20,000K) It doesn't get cheaper or more basic than this popular backpacker crash pad smack in the centre of town. It's just mat-tresses with mozzie nets on a floor in a big second-floor room. Mama Pap promises 'big food for small kip' in the ground-floor restau-rant and delivers with obscenely large plates. If Mama Pap is full, some of her neighbours have followed her example.

Tadlo Lodge
RESORT $$

(📞 031-218889; souriyavincent@yahoo.com; r/ ste incl breakfast from US$50/100; ❄🛜) Situat-ed above Tat Hang, about 1km from Tat Lo village, this is the only semi-fancy lodging around. The main building exudes some clas-sic Lao style, with parquet floors and Buddha statuary, while rooms are stylish and com-fortable with decks out front. Only the suite has air-conditioning. Animal lovers should note that the hotel keeps trekking elephants chained up most of the day.

Saise Resort
LAOTIAN, THAI $

(mains 20,000-60,000K; ⏲7am-8pm; 🛜) With good food (mostly Thai) served on a great deck with an awesome view of Tat Hang wa-terfall, it's worth making one trip out here during your stay.

❶ Information

INTERNET ACCESS
Internet access is available at **Tim Guesthouse** (📞 034-211885; per min 200K).

MONEY
The only financial resource in this area is an ATM up at the highway, though guesthouses change money at terrible rates.

TOURIST INFORMATION
Tat Lo Tourism Information Centre (📞 020-5445590/; kouka222@hotmail.com; ⏲8-11.30am & 1.30-4.30pm Mon-Fri, daily Nov-Feb) This helpful centre runs the Tat Lo Guides Association. It should be your first stop if you need a guide or info on local excursions, or plan to venture deeper into Salavan Province and beyond. It can also help you with public trans-port options around the Bolaven Plateau. Maps and brochures on the region are available. Kouka speaks English and is worth contacting in advance to book an English-speaking guide.

❶ Getting There & Away

Just say 'Tat Lo' at Pakse's Southern Bus Terminal and you'll be pointed to one of the nine daily bus-es to Salavan that stop on Rte 20 at Ban Khoua Set (30,000K, two hours), from where it's a 1.5km walk or moto-taxi ride (10,000K) to Tat Lo.

For Sekong (20,000K, one hour) or Attapeu (40,000K, three hours), your best bet is the morning bus that passes through Ban Beng, which is a 15,000K moto-taxi ride away from Tat Lo. In Ban Beng you can also catch some mini-buses and *sŏrngtăaou* to Sekong and passing buses to Paksong (20,000K, one hour). The Tat Lo Tourism Information Centre can call to have buses to Vietnam stop and pick you up at Ban Khoua Set.

❶ Getting Around

Sabai Sabai (📞 020-98556831), between the Tat Lo Tourism Information Centre and the bridge, has a few motorcycles for hire for 80,000K per day.

Salavan
ສາລະວັນ

POP 25,000 / 📞 034

Even though Salavan (also spelt Saravan and Saravane) is just 30km from popular Tat Lo, foreign visitors are very rare. And though the town is no longer quite the backwater it used to be, thanks to development that's come on the heels of newly paved roads, it's still nota-ble more for its remoteness than any tradi-tional tourism draws. The best thing visitors can do here is get out and explore the ethnic diversity of the countryside.

While more than half of the population of Salavan Province is ethnically Lao (Loum and Soung), few are native to this area. The remainder of the 350,000 inhabitants belong to various Mon-Khmer groups, including the

Tahoy, Lavai, Alak, Laven, Ngai, Tong, Pako, Kanay, Katu, Kado and Katang, the latter being expert weavers.

History

Once a Champasak kingdom outpost known as Muang Mam, the town was renamed Salavan (Sarawan in Thai) by the Siamese in 1828. It later became a French administrative centre and was all but destroyed in the Indochina War, when it bounced back and forth between Royal Lao Army and Pathet Lao occupation. It also suffered extensive bombing by American troops trying to disrupt the several branches of the Ho Chi Minh Trail that cut through Salavan Province.

◉ Sights

The most appealing of Salavan's meagre attractions is its market, but anyone with an interest in Buddhist art will also enjoy a quick jaunt around town. The folks at the tourism office told us that a provincial museum is planned, but had no clue as to when.

Better than anything in town, and reason enough to come up here, are the ruined Prince Souphanouvong's Bridge and the weaving villages around Toumlan.

Salavan Market   MARKET
(ตะหาดสาລະວัน; ⊘ 6am-6.30pm) Many women come in to this market from the surrounding villages to sell foods they've collected or caught in the forest, such as mushrooms, bamboo shoots, ant eggs and monitor lizards.

Wat Kang Salavan   BUDDHIST TEMPLE
(ວັດກາງສາລະວັນ, Wat Simongkhoun) Salavan's most important temple, founded over two centuries ago, has a very large *hŏr đại* – monastery building dedicated to the storage of the Tripitaka (Buddhist scriptures) – in a pond, to prevent termites from eating the holy manuscripts stored inside. It is supported by 57 pillars and is slowly being renovated. Much of the temple was destroyed in 1972 and brick remains of the former *ubosot* and stupa are hidden by brush across the road.

🛏 Sleeping & Eating

Most lodging is on Rte 15 west of the centre and there are some more choices on the way into town from the south. The owners of **Phoufa Hotel** (☑ 030-5370799; Rte 20; r 60,000-150,000K; ❄) have a new hotel in the works and it should be the best in town when finished.

Jindavone Guesthouse   GUESTHOUSE $
(☑ 034-211065; r with fan/air-con 70,000/100,000K; ❄) This eye-catching blue building just off the southeast corner of the market is cheap and central. Rooms on the second floor can catch a bit of a breeze. The friendly family who run it speak a little English.

Phonexay Hotel   HOTEL $
(☑ 034-211093; Rte 15; r with fan 70,000-80,000K, air-con 120,000-200,000K; ❄ 🛜) By virtue of the fact that the main building is fairly youngish and that the rooms have wi-fi, this mostly clean place 1.5km west of the market is the best lodging choice in town. But that's not a tough competition to win.

GETTING TO VIETNAM: LA LAY TO LALAY

Getting to the Border

Most people travelling from Pakse to Hué and Danang use sleeper buses, which go through the Lao Bao border crossing east of Savannakhet. The faster, but more dangerous, minibuses, on the other hand, go via Salavan and cross at La Lay (Laos)/Lalay (Vietnam) – border open from 6am to 7pm – as do the slow and thoroughly uncomfortable cargo buses, which only save a few seats for passengers. If you're in Salavan, you don't need to backtrack to Pakse. There are usually seats available when the buses from Pakse pass through. There isn't much traffic on this route, so doing the trip in stages is not recommended, but if you're set on it, start with the 7.30am minibus to Samouy (35,000K, 3½ hours) which is very near the border.

Moving On

For those going in stages, most of the traffic here is trucks, so you should be able to buy an onward ride, though be sure you know whether the driver will be taking a right at the junction to Hué and Danang or turning left to Dong Ha.

Sabaidee Salavan LAOTIAN, THAI **$**
(mains 15,000-50,000K; ☺7am-9pm) One of the few dining options in town with an English menu, Sabaidee has all the standard Lao and Thai dishes, but also offers sukiyaki.

ⓘ Information

DANGERS & ANNOYANCES
Unexploded ordnance (UXO) remain a serious problem in rural areas, so exercise caution if you go out exploring the province beyond main roads: stick to established tracks and trails.

MONEY
There are several banks and ATMs in town, including some around the market.

TOURIST INFORMATION
Salavan Tourism Centre (034-211528; ☺8am-4pm Mon-Fri) Staff are eager to help and some are knowledgable about tourism in the area. It's south of the market, next to the large, glass-fronted Phongsavanh Bank building.

ⓘ Getting There & Away

Salavan's bus terminal is 2km west of the town centre, where Rte 20 meets Rte 15. There are nine daily buses to Pakse (fan/air-con 30,000/40,000K, three hours), with three (8.30am, 4pm, 4.30pm) continuing on to Vientiane (regular/sleeper 130,000/190,000K, 12 to 14 hours), and one bus to Attapeu (50,000K, 4½ hours).

No buses to Vietnam originate here, but you can hope one passing through from Pakse has empty seats.

Around Salavan

Toumlan ບ້ານຕຸມລານ

Toumlan, 50km north of Salavan, is a slapped-together boomtown with some small shops and restaurants and several oversized, out-of-place government buildings. The surrounding Katang villages comprise one of Laos' most important **weaving** regions. Women here weave a variety of silk and cotton styles, including some *mat-mee* (ikat or tie-dye), using large wooden floor looms instead of the back-strap looms typical in the Bolaven region.

Although virtually no English or Thai is spoken, if you see someone weaving you will almost certainly be welcome to stop and watch, as long as you're polite and friendly – this includes not turning your visit into a photo shoot. The best place to look is along the highway east of Toumlan proper where seemingly every house has a loom under it.

The famous Lapup buffalo sacrifice festival is usually held in late February.

There's no public transport up here, but Rte 15A is paved and in good condition, or you can take the adventurous way using Rte 23 past Prince Souphanouvong's Bridge.

Prince Souphanouvong's Bridge

Named after its builder, the 'Red Prince' Souphanouvong (who was a trained engineer), this 150m-long bridge over the Se Don was blown up by American bombers in 1968 due to its position on a supply branch of the Ho Chi Minh Trail. Today, most of the massive concrete supports and a part of the steel span remain standing. The contrast between heavy war damage and the peaceful, beautiful setting makes it quite interesting.

You can take a ferry (10,000K) to visit the other side; in dry months you can just walk across the river.

It is along Rte 23, 10km west of Salavan and then 10km north. If you're travelling by motorcycle, you can continue on to Toumlan, though there are lots of missing small bridges, so enquire in Salavan before attempting this route in the rainy season. Other than the bridge issue, the road is in good shape the entire way and it's a beautiful drive following the mountains of the Se Ban Nuan NPA.

Ta-Oy ບ້ານຕາໂອຍ

Though it's hard to justify a trip all the way to Ta-Oy on its own, it makes a good add-on if you'd like to turn a half-day trip to Toumlan into a full-day journey. The route here crosses a remote mountainous area with few villages, and – though most of the area has been logged – there are still some beautiful moments. Ta-Oy was once an important marker on the Ho Chi Minh Trail and two major branches split off here.

This is a centre for the Tahoy ethnic group, who number around 30,000 spread across the eastern areas of Salavan and Sekong Provinces. Other groups in this region include Katang, Pako, Kado and Kanay. The Tahoy live in forested mountain valleys and, like many Mon-Khmer groups in southern Laos, they practise a combination of animism and shamanism; during village ceremonies, the Tahoy put up diamond patterned bamboo totems to warn outsiders not to enter. Keep your eyes peeled for some of their enormous longhouses in and around town. You'll see some in a village just before crossing the large bridge into Ta-Oy. Down below the town, upstream from the bridge, are beautiful **rapids** that can be easily reached by a short footpath.

Ta-Oy is 80km from Salavan on a good paved road, and you could double the distance and continue to Samouy near the Vietnamese border. Both are small but developed towns with a few guesthouses as well as places to eat and fuel up.

Sekong   ເຊກອງ

POP 15,000 / ☑ 038

This sleepy city on its namesake river was built from scratch in 1984, the year Sekong Province was created. It's not a destination as much as a place intrepid travellers visit just because it's there.

This may change in the next few years when a new bridge shortens the route from Ubon Ratchathani, Thailand, to the Vietnamese port of Danang, facilitating access to gold and other mines on the Dak Cheung Plateau. A border crossing open to foreigners should also be part of the equation.

By population Sekong is the smallest of Laos' provinces and also the most ethnically diverse: almost all of its 90,000 inhabitants are from one of 14 different Mon-Khmer tribal groups, with the Alak, Katu, Talieng, Yai and Nge the largest. These diverse groups are not Buddhists, so you won't see temples. Rather, their belief systems mix animism and ancestor worship. Sekong is also one of the country's poorest provinces.

◉ Sights

Sekong Provincial Historical Museum   MUSEUM

(ຫໍພິພິດຫະພັນປະຫວັດສາດແຂວງເຊກອງ; Rte 16; ⊙8-11.30am & 1.30-4pm Mon-Fri) **FREE** The first floor has just a few old stones, UXO and photos from the war years. But the tribal displays of textiles and household tools (don't miss the bamboo forge for making knives) upstairs are well presented with labels in English. The focus is Katu, but Alak, Yai, Talieng, Suay and many more are covered, too.

Sekong Market   MARKET

(ຕະຫຼາດເຊກອງ; ⊙5am-6pm) Fresh food offerings in this market include mushrooms, squirrels, herbs and other forest products. It's best in the late afternoon.

⌑ Sleeping

Sakda Guesthouse   GUESTHOUSE $

(☑030-9921992; r 80,000K; ❀🛜) Sakda's small but fairly modern rooms are both better value and quality than many of the pricier places in town. It's 100m north of the market's west side, past the UXO office. There is no English sign, so look for a white building with a green roof.

Tat Faek Waterfall Guesthouse   GUESTHOUSE $

(☑030-5238353; r 50,000K) There are some very simple thatch huts up above Tat Faek waterfall. After 5pm it's just you, a security guard, and a bonfire if you wish. Some people enjoy the all-alone feeling at night, while others find it eerie.

✗ Eating

Thida Hotel Restaurant   LAOTIAN, THAI $

(mains 20,000-50,000K; ⊙6am-10pm; 🛜) Although its perch high above the river with good mountain views would be enough reason to dine here, the kitchen holds up its end of the bargain with good Thai food including the obligatory *tom yam gung* and stir-fried holy basil.

Khamting Restaurant   LAOTIAN, THAI $

(mains 15,000-50,000K; ⊙7am-9pm; 🗎) Ask a local to recommend a place to eat and this is probably the only name you'll hear. It serves good stir-fries, noodle soups and Thai standards. The forest animals on the menu are rarely available, but even if they are you should avoid them as some, like pangolin, are endangered species and others are poached illegally. Note that the menu has English but no prices.

It's 600m southwest of the market on the road closest to the river, opposite the Sekong Hotel.

ⓘ Information

MONEY

Banks and ATMs are spread around town. The **Lao Development Bank** (⊙8am-3.30pm Mon-Fri), 200m southwest of the market on the central road, changes Thai baht, euros, US dollars and more, and has a Western Union branch.

POST

The **post office** (⊙8-11.30am & 1-4.30pm Mon-Fri) is 350m southwest of Lao Development Bank.

SOUTHERN LAOS SEKONG

VISITING PROTECTED AREAS

Though much of the province is still covered by natural forest, visiting the protected areas is really tough since they have nearly no tourist infrastructure. The tourism office (p225) in Salavan had recently organised a survey of an overnight trek to a sunrise viewpoint (16km round trip) in the Se Xap National Protected Area (NPA) in the far east; guides will be available through the office when this is up and running. Truthfully, though, you'd probably have better luck arranging it through the Tat Lo Tourism Information Centre (p223).

TOURIST INFORMATION

The **Sekong Provincial Tourism Office** (☑ 038-211361; 2nd fl; ⊙ 8-11.30am &1-4.30pm Mon-Fri) is 700m west of the market on the central road. Don't expect much help here. Requests for guides are supposed to be submitted in writing two days before you wish to travel, though if you just show up they should be able to sort things out.

Around Sekong

South of Sekong, Rte 16 morphs into Rte 11 and the waterfalls along this road have more appeal than anything actually in the town.

For a bit of easy adventure, take a relaxed ride on the new highway to Dak Cheung. It's a beautiful and still relatively remote region, especially once you hit the mountains. Until the new bridge is completed, cross the Se Kong on the rickety ferry (5000K) southwest of the market and follow the dirt road for 2.5km to reach the pavement.

◉ Sights

Tat Faek　　　　　　　　　　WATERFALL
(ຕາດແຝກ; admission 5000K) Sixteen kilometres south of Sekong, and well-signed off Rte 11, is this wide, beautiful 5m-high waterfall where you can swim in the pool atop the falls. Do heed the red and white 'Watch Out For Biting Fish' signs around the lower pools as a diabolical puffer fish called *pa pao* lurks there. Stories of their fondness for attacking men's penises are only legend – told with glee by local women – but they really can take a chunk of flesh out of unlucky swimmers with their razor-sharp teeth.

Tat Hua Khon　　　　　　　　WATERFALL
(ຕາດຫົວຄົນ; 5000K) Three kilometres south of the Tat Faek turn-off (just past the market), this waterfall is 7m tall and an impressive 100m wide. The name translates as 'Waterfall of the Heads', owing to a WWII episode in which Japanese soldiers decapitated a number of Lao soldiers and tossed their heads into the falls. Facilities, including good trails and boardwalks through the forest, kayaks (80,000K) and a restaurant, are part of the little P&S Garden resort. This is a busy place on holidays and weekends.

🛌 Sleeping

P&S Garden　　　　　　　　　RESORT $
(☑ 020-98836555; 1-/2-person tents 40,000/50,000K; @ 🛜) This lovely and orderly resort near Tat Hua Kon is a welcome surprise. Though it started out with just tents, which are pitched on a stilted and thatched-roof platform, actual guestrooms are in the works. The restaurant serves coffee and juice and a small menu (mains 15,000K to 80,000K) of Lao food including 'bugs' (roasted crickets) and spicy papaya salad.

Attapeu　　　　　　ອັດຕະປື

POP 19,200 / ☑ 036

The capital of Attapeu Province, set where the Se Kong (Kong River) and the smaller Se Kaman (Kaman River) meet, is an unexciting, but not unpleasant place. Around Laos, Attapeu is known as the 'garden village' for its abundant trees and shrubbery.

This reputation is deserved, though quite ironic given that Attapeu actually means 'buffalo shit'. In the old local Mon-Khmer dialect, this area was called *itkapu* (*ait krapeau* in contemporary Khmer) because of the many wild buffalo living in the area. With some subsequent adjustment in pronunciation by the French, the town became Attapeu.

Despite any hope inspired by the greenery, the town itself is short on attractions, though the nearby temples at Saisettha and war junk in Pa-Am are interesting.

A Vietnamese phrasebook will be just as useful as a Lao dictionary since about half the population is Vietnamese.

◉ Sights

Attapeu's standard attractions are pretty ho-hum, but the sunsets down by the river can be fantastic. Indeed, the city's most interesting sights are not in Attapeu at all: a visit to

Attapeu (Samakhi Xai)

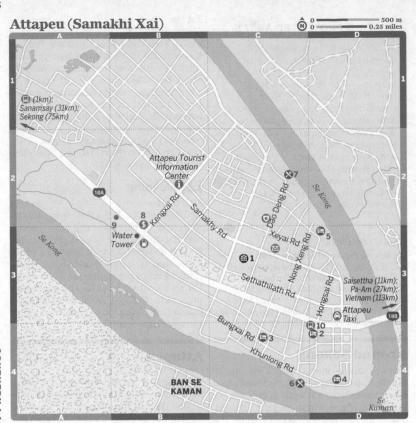

the villages of Saisettha and Pa-Am (p230) makes a great half-day trip, while the beautiful volcanic crater lake Nong Fa (Sky Blue Lake) in Dong Amphan NPA (p232) is more challenging to reach, but worth it.

Attapeu Provincial Museum   MUSEUM
(ຫໍພິພິດທະພັນແຂວງອັດຕະປື; Map p228; Samakhy Rd; ⊙8.30-11.30am & 1.30-4pm Mon-Fri) **FREE** This large, elegant building holds a small humdrum collection with a few old rocks, weapons and UXO, plus countless photos of local dignitaries. The only things that make it worth a quick visit, other than the price, are the tribal displays. Too bad nobody bothered to give them better labels.

🛏 Sleeping

Sokpaserd Riverside   GUESTHOUSE $
(Map p228; ✆036-210088; Khunlong Rd; r 100,000K; ❋🐾) Good-quality rooms (with newer ones under construction) at a fair price. Though it's across the street from, rath-er than on, the Se Kong, you can see the river through the trees from some of the rooms and a second-floor patio.

Soukdaoxay Guesthouse   GUESTHOUSE $
(Map p228; ✆020-22900054; r/f 100,000/200,000K; ❋🐾) The rooms in this eye-catching pink building on the Se Kong river north of the centre are relatively new and good value. Three of the second-floor rooms in back have nice river views.

🍴 Eating

Huean Phae Nang Gulap   LAOTIAN, THAI $
(Map p228; Khunlong Rd; mains 20,000-70,000K; ⊙9am-11pm; 🐾) Down on the river with beautiful views, 'Ms. Rose's Raft' is great for a sun-downer. The food is good, though only a tiny section of the menu is in English. Just order any common Lao or Thai dish and they can probably make it. The spicy *tom sap* with fish (labelled as 'a sweet and sour soup') is a good, safe Lao choice.

Attapeu (Samakhi Xai)

◎ Sights
1 Attapeu Provincial Museum................C3

⊜ Sleeping
2 Dúc Lôc Hotel................................D4
3 Phoutthavong Guesthouse................C4
4 Sokpaserd Riverside.........................D4
5 Soukdaoxay Guesthouse...................D3

⊗ Eating
6 Huean Phae Nang Gulap....................C4
7 Sabaidee Attapeu...............................C2
Thi Thi Restaurant.......................(see 2)

ⓘ Information
8 BCEL...B2
Thi Thi Money Exchange............(see 10)

ⓘ Transport
9 Lao Airlines......................................B2
10 Mai Linh Express................................D4

Sabaidee Attapeu   LAOTIAN $
(Map p228; mains 25,000-70,000K; ⊙8am-8.30pm; ❉❂) It's all about the setting here, in a converted wooden house with a broad deck overlooking the Se Kong and the distant mountains. The menu features grilled and fried meats galore, but also lighter dishes such as a delicious spicy papaya salad.

Thi Thi Restaurant   VIETNAMESE $
(Map p228; Rte 18A; mains 15,000-35,000K; ⊙6am-9pm; ❂) The Dúc Lôc Hotel's restaurant serves some of the best Vietnamese food in town. Fish dishes and soups, plus fried rice and *fĕr* (rice noodles) grace the menu.

ⓘ Information

MONEY
Banks, including the full-service **BCEL** (Map p228; Rte 18A; ⊙8.30am-3.30pm Mon-Fri), line Rte 18A, but there are no ATMs in the city centre. More convenient than the banks is **Thi Thi Money Exchange** (Map p228; Rte 18A; ⊙6am-8pm).

POST
Post Office (Map p228; Samakhy Rd; ⊙8-11.30am & 1-4.30pm Mon-Fri)

TOURIST INFORMATION
There is an official **Attapeu Tourist Information Center** (Map p228; ☑020-98976475; Kengxai Rd; ⊙8-11.30am & 1.30-4pm Mon-Fri), but if you really want to do some exploring stop by the Dokchampa Hotel instead. It doesn't promote much, due to the lack of tourists, but staff can arrange guides and vehicles.

ⓘ Getting There & Away

AIR
Attapeu now has an airport (25km outside the city) and **Lao Airlines** (Map p228; ☑036-210195; Rte 18A; ⊙8am-5pm Mon-Fri) offers a biweekly Vientiane–Pakse–Attapeu–Vientiane flight (Vientiane to/from Attapeu is 820,000K), though this is highly subject to change.

BUS
Buses to/from Pakse (fan/air-con 45,000/50,000K, 3½ to five hours) run hourly, with about half using the direct Paksong (35,000–40,000K, 2½ hours) route and half passing through Sekong (20,000K, two hours). Five of them go all the way to Vientiane (regular 140,000–170,000K, sleeper 220,000K, 16 to 18 hours). There's also a morning bus to Salavan (50,000, 4½ hours). All buses leave from the **station** (Rte 11).

Mai Linh Express (Map p228; ☑020-98302222; Rte 18A), at the Dúc Lôc Hotel, also has morning minibuses to Kon Tum (60,000K, five hours), Danang (150,000K, nine hours) and Hué (140,000K, 12 hours).

ⓘ Getting Around
Attapeu Taxi (Map p228; ☑030-9393939; ⊙24hr) charges 8000K for the first kilometre and 7000K per kilometre after this up to 20km. Negotiate prices for any longer trip.

Tuk-tuks from the bus station to the city centre cost 10,000K per person, or 20,000K if you're alone. **Phoutthavong Guesthouse** (Map p228; ☑020-5551 7870; r with fan/air-con 60,000/90,000K; ❉) hires bicycles for 20,000K per day.

There's a **petrol station** (Map p228) near the centre of town.

Around Attapeu

Saisettha   ໄຊເຊດຖາ

Saisettha, 11km east of Attapeu on Rte 18B, is a sizeable village on the north bank of the Se Kaman (Kaman River). It used to be a quiet village with a good vibe, but it's mostly outgrown that; however, art lovers will appreciate some of the temples here.

Just past the Houay Phateun Bridge, turn right to the peaceful riverfront **Wat Siliawat That Inping** (aka Wat Fang Daeng), which has a large octagonal stupa. Inside the adjacent hall is a rather complete set of paintings telling the Wetsandon Jataka (the Buddha's penultimate birth) tale.

Just over a kilometre to the east, at the end of the road, the *sala* (open-sided shelter) of

Wat Ban Xai has more adroit mural paintings, focusing mostly on the Buddha's life story. The old *ubosot* (ordination hall) has some original floral stucco work on the front.

From Wat Ban Xai, go back to the highway and continue east. Take a sharp right at the first large road after crossing the Se Kaman bridge and continue to the second temple you meet (6.5km total) in Muang Kao (Old City). This is **Wat Luang**, famous because the Lan Xang King Setthathirat, for whom the district is named, is buried here. The temple was supposedly founded in 1571, the year of his death, and the stupa in which he is interred was erected soon after, though it has been rebuilt since then. There's also a crumbling old *wihǎhn* (temple hall) with a large Buddha inside and some original woodcarving on the front gable and door. The little *ubosot* in front is in better shape.

Pa-Am   ພະອໍ

The area east of Attapeu was an integral part of the Ho Chi Minh Trail – two main branches, the Sihanouk Trail continuing south into Cambodia and the Ho Chi Minh Trail veering east towards Vietnam, split here – and as such was heavily bombed during the war. One of the few visible reminders of this time is a Russian-made surface-to-air missile (SAM), complete with Russian and Vietnamese stencilling, that was set up in the village of Pa-Am (aka Ban Sombun) by the North Vietnamese in 1974 to defend against aerial attack.

It has survived the scrap hunters and, by government order, is now on display, surrounded by a barbed-wire fence held up, in part, by cluster-bomb casings.

Next to the missile is a small handicraft shop with textiles and baskets woven by local Talieng women. If you drive around the village you might get lucky and see some women weaving.

Pa-Am is 16km past Saisettha (follow the signs for San Xai off Rte 18B) and the two villages make a great half-day trip from Attapeu if you have your own wheels. There is no public transport to Pa-Am.

North of Pa-Am the road quickly turns rocky and continues on to Chaleun Xai, 38km north, then northwest to Sekong. This route has recently been improved somewhat, but it's still rough and recommended for dry-season travel only.

🏃 Motorcycle Tour
The Southern Swing

START PAKSE
FINISH PAKSE
LENGTH 480KM; FIVE DAYS

The Southern Swing starts in Pakse and circles up, down and around the Bolaven Plateau. The route we've laid out here will take most people five days, but this is only a guide – you could easily take your time and spend many more days. Head out of ❶ **Pakse** (p202) on Rte 13 and continue straight to Rte 16 at the traffic circle. You'll pass stretches of roadside basket, fruit, and knife vendors (you can stop and watch the latter make their wares) and then turn north onto Rte 20 just after the huge Dao Coffee Factory.

After 13km you'll see a signed turn-off for the beautiful, U-shaped ❷ **Tat Phasuam** (entrance 10,000K, motorcycle/car 2000/5000K, ☺ 8am-6pm), which is 2km from the highway within the Utayan Bajiang Nature Resort. Besides the waterfall, the bus loads of Thai tourists flock to the ethnic model village where families from a variety of the region's ethnic minorities wear traditional clothes and sell crafts from their particular style of house. It makes for some great photos, but it's hard to shake the feeling of being in a human zoo.

From here it's about 27km to Ban Houay Houn (Houay Houn Village), known for its Katu weavers and for ❸ **Mr Vieng Coffee & Homestay** (p222), both of which warrant a visit. Then get your camera out for some snaps of the vista before you drop down to backpacker-friendly ❹ **Tat Lo** (p221), 19km after Ban Houay Houn.

It's easy to spend a few nights in Tat Lo visiting villages and waterfalls. When you're ready to leave, head 5.5km up Rte 20 to Ban Beng and either take a left off the beaten path to ❺ **Salavan** (p223) or turn right and reascend the Bolaven Plateau to Tha Taeng, passing many Katu and Alak villages. One that is worth stopping at is Ban Khokphung Tai, home to the fantastic ❻ **Captain Hook Coffee Break** (p222).

At Tha Taeng you meet Rte 16 again. The 'small loop' takes you south directly to Paksong (37km) while the 'big loop' continues due east to Sekong (47km).

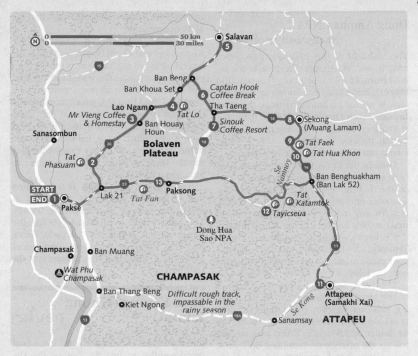

Regardless of which loop you choose, it's worth having lunch or a drink in the garden at **7 Sinouk Coffee Resort** (p221), 6km south of Tha Taeng.

8 Sekong (p226) can be a useful lunch or overnight stop, though few rate it highly as a tourist destination. Some 16km and 19km south of Sekong respectively are the short but beautiful **9 Tat Faek** and **10 Tat Hua Khon** waterfalls. Accommodation is available at both for those who want to bypass Sekong.

At Ban Benghuakham, 6km south of Hua Khon waterfall, is the road to Paksong, but skip it for now and continue another 49km south to **11 Attapeu** (p227), a boring, but not unpleasant town with fantastic sunsets. Plus, there are old temples and impressive war junk to be found in nearby villages.

Banish the urge to go rogue by following Rte 18A to the south of the Bolaven Plateau back to Champasak Province. This road, if you can still call it that, remains impassable to regular traffic and shouldn't be attempted without first reading trip reports on www.gt-rider.com and then making an honest assessment of your motorcycling skills. There are several river crossings that lack ferries, and the rough road forks frequently

From Attapeu head back to Ban Beng-huakham (better known simply as Ban Lak 52) and head west. Until recently this stretch was a rugged ride with little or no traffic that passed through pristine jungle; but alas, the jungle is pristine no more. There is still, however, some beautiful scenery as you quickly climb through a valley up the plateau.

After 16.5km you pass the spectacular Tat Katamtok, but don't visit without getting an update on the current safety situation in Pakse first. It's another 8km, partly on a dirt road with some rough spots (if you're driving a car, not a motorcycle, you'll have to go the long way around), to the almost Edenic **12 Tayicseua** (p220), one of the Bolaven's most relaxing spots.

Once you're ready to head back to civilisa-tion, it's 44km to **13 Paksong** (p219), the Bolaven's charmless coffee capital. After Pak-song, you will pass four impressive waterfalls – Tat Gneuang, Tat Fan, Tat Champee and Tat E-Tu – before you end up back in Pakse.

Dong Amphan NPA
ປ່າສະຫງວນແຫ່ງຊາດດົງອຳພານ

The highlight of this 1975-sq-km protected area in eastern Attapeu Province is the fabled **Nong Fa** (Sky Blue Lake). This beautiful volcanic crater lake, also known as Nong Kai Ork, is similar to, but larger than, the more heralded Yeak Lom in Cambodia's Ratanakiri Province. Sitting at an elevation of about 1500m, the view looking back away from the lake is just as beautiful as the lake itself.

Used by the North Vietnamese as an R&R (rest and recuperation) spot for soldiers hurt on the Ho Chi Minh Trail, this beautiful lake was once only able to be reached via a difficult five-day trek. New roads mean you can make it there and back from Attapeu in a day if you have a 4x4 or an enduro motorcycle. Typically, it's visited on a two-day trip, with your guide arranging an informal homestay near the lake.

The park itself was, until recently, one of the most intact ecosystems in the country. However, logging, gold mining, wildlife poaching and hydroelectric projects on the Se Kaman and Se Su (Su River) have taken a toll on the pristine environment. Still, gaur, tiger, elephant and some 280 bird species, including the beautiful crested argus, inhabit the forests of Dong Amphan NPA.

The 65km of dirt track off Rte 18B from Attapeu to the park has steep hills, lots of rock, and some streams to cross, making it tough in the dry season and impossible for much of the rainy season. Theoretically you could get here on your own, but it's a very remote route and you risk being turned back by officials before you reach your goal.

SI PHAN DON ສີ່ພັນດອນ
⏲ 031

Si Phan Don is where Laos becomes the land of the lotus-eaters, an archipelago of islands where the pendulum of time swings slowly and postcard-worthy views are the rule rather than the exception. Many a traveller has washed ashore here, succumbed to its charms and stayed longer than expected.

Down here the Mekong bulges to a breadth of 14km – the river's widest reach along its 4350km journey from the Tibetan Plateau to the South China Sea – and if you count every islet and sandbar that emerges in the dry months the name, which literally means 'Four Thousand Islands', isn't that big of an exaggeration.

Travellers hone in on three islands: Khong, Det and Khon. Don Khong, by far the largest island in Si Phan Don, is the sleepiest of the three and sees the fewest tourists, and this is its appeal. There's much more to do on Don Khon and Don Det, which have become de rigueur stops on the Southeast Asia backpacking circuit. Activities include cycling, tubing, kayaking, waterfall-watching and dolphin-spotting, although many travellers forsake these and pass the days getting catatonic in a hammock.

The villages of Si Phan Don are often named for their position at the upriver or downriver ends of their respective islands. The upriver end is called *hŭa* (head); the downriver end is called *hăang* (tail). Hence Ban Hua Khong is at the northern end of Don Khong, while Ban Hang Khong is at the southern end.

Don Khong (Khong Island) ດອນໂຂງ
POP 60,000 / ⏲ 031

Life moves slowly on Don Khong, like a boat being paddled against the flow on the Mekong. It's a pleasant place to spend a day or two, wandering past fishing nets drying in the sun, taking a sunset boat ride, pedalling about on a bicycle or just chilling and reading by the river.

Don Khong measures 18km long by 8km at its widest point. Most of the roughly 60,000 islanders live on the perimeter and there are only two proper towns: lethargic Muang Khong on the eastern shore and the charmless market town of Muang Saen on the west; an 8km road links the two.

Khamtay Siphandone The, the postman who went on to serve as president of Laos from 1998 to 2006, was born in Ban Hua Khong at the north end of Don Khong in 1924.

⊙ Sights & Activities

Don Khong is a pretty island with rice fields and low hills in the centre and simple-life villages around the perimeter, and a bike trip around the island makes for a fantastic day for cultural travellers. The road around the island is paved, though heavily potholed, the whole way. The temples in Ban Hin Siew (Hin Siew Village) and Ban Hang Khong (Hang Khong Village) on the southern end of the island have old buildings that are worth a quick peek if you happen to be passing by.

A new bridge in Ban Hua Khong Lem makes it easy to extend your exploration from Don Khong to sparsely populated and rarely visited Don San. A frequently rough dirt track follows the east side 6km to the very tip of the island where, when the river is low, a beach emerges. This is Si Phan Don's northernmost point.

Ban Hin Siew Tai Palm Sugar Trees FARM
(Map p234) Although sugar palms can be seen across the island, Ban Hin Siew Tai is southern Laos' sugar capital. Many farmers here climb the trees twice a day to collect the juice and then boil it down to sugar, and if you see them working you are welcome to pop in for a visit. The sugar season is from November to February and early morning is the best time to go.

◉ Muang Khong & Around

Don Khong History Museum MUSEUM
(ພິພິດທະພັນປະຫວັດສາດດອນໂຂງ; Map p234; Muang Khong; 5000K; ⊘8.30-11.30am & 1-4pm Mon-Fri) When the local governor built this two-story French colonial-style home in 1935, he was so proud of himself that he christened it Sathanavoudthi, which means 'Garden of Eden' in an old Lao dialect. Level-headed locals just called it 'The Brick House'. In 2010 it was restored and now houses one of Laos' smallest museums. But the musical instruments, animal traps and photos of the Don Khon railway are worth a few minutes of your time.

Wat Jom Thong BUDDHIST TEMPLE
(ວັດຈອມທອງ; Map p234; Muang Khong) At the northern end of Muang Khong is Wat Jom Thong, the oldest temple on the island, dating from the Chao Anou period (1805-28). The *wihǎhn* (temple hall) features a cruciform floor plan, a unique triple-gated entrance, carved wooden doors and shutters, and a bevy of mythical Hindu-Buddhist creatures adorning the roof and gables.

Tham Phu Khiaw CAVE
(ຖ້ຳພູຂຽວ; Map p234) Two kilometres north of Muang Khong a trail leads to Green Mountain Cave, a small, shallow shelter in the middle of the forest. It holds some fairly crude Buddha images and bits of broken pottery and is the object of an annual pilgrimage, usually in June. It's definitely more about the journey than the destination.

It's only a 15-minute walk, mostly uphill. Follow what is clearly the main trail to the second rocky opening in the forest and then veer south (left) to the little cliff. The trailhead is marked by a blue sign. If you wish to continue past the cave to the viewpoint or even all the way across the island, you'll need a guide.

◉ Muang Saen & Around

Wat Phu Khao Kaew BUDDHIST TEMPLE
(ວັດພູເຂົາແກວ, Glass Hill Monastery; Map p234) About 6.5km northeast of Muang Saen, Wat Phu Khao Kaew was built on the site of some presumed pre-Khmer ruins, making it a holy spot for locals. Nothing of that era is visible; now there is a bright red and gold modern stupa and a large reclining Buddha in the arm-down, 'Entering Nirvana' posture. It sits atop some exposed bedrock and the beautiful Mekong-side perch is more of a reason to stop than any of the structures.

🏃 Activities

Sabaldee Don Khong VOLUNTEERING
(☑020-59692777; www.facebook.com/laoschool volunteer) Teach English in the after-school program here in exchange for basic but friendly homestay accommodation. A one-week commitment is preferred.

✯✯ Festivals & Events

Bun Suang Heua BOAT RACING
(Bun Nam) A boat-racing festival is held on Don Khong in early December or late November around National Day. Four days of carnival-like activity include longboat races opposite Muang Khong, much closer to the shore than in larger towns.

🛏 Sleeping

★ Khong View Guesthouse GUESTHOUSE $
(Map p234; ☑020-22446449; Muang Khong; r with fan/air-con 80,000/100,000K; ✹🛜) It's hard to beat the location of this place. It's near, but serenely separate from, the tourist strip and the big, breezy second-floor deck provides the best Mekong views in town. The friendly owners give it a homestay feel. There's no restaurant, but sometimes they will cook food for guests.

Ratana Riverside Guesthouse GUESTHOUSE $
(Map p234; ☑020-55533550; vongdonekhong@ hotmail.com; Muang Khong; r 100,000K; ✹🛜) The four comfortable river-facing rooms

Si Phan Don

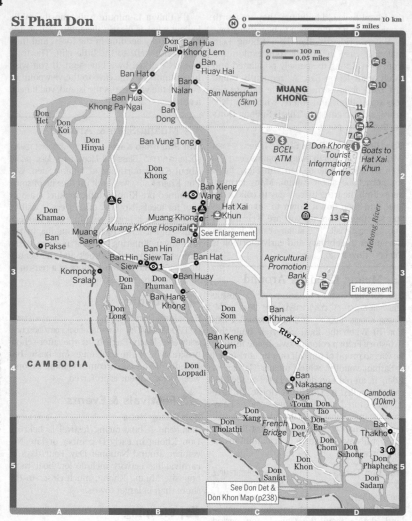

here enjoy balconies, Siberian air-con and handsome furnishings. Ground-floor rooms have enormous windows close to the road, so get one upstairs where you'll have an obstructed view of the river across the road and won't feel like you're in a fish bowl.

Done Khong Guesthouse GUESTHOUSE **$**
(Map p234; ☎020-98789994; kham_bkk1987@yahoo.com; Muang Khong; r with fan/air-con 70,000/100,00K; ☀☎) The first place you'll see when you get off the boat, Done Khong has dark rooms with tiled floors and homely furnishings in an old house run by a French-

and English-speaking lady. Try to bag a second-floor room with a river-facing balcony. The riverside restaurant, with a mostly Lao menu, is a good place to chill and the staff are a good source of island info.

Pon's Riverside Guesthouse GUESTHOUSE **$**
(Map p234; ☎020-55406798; www.ponarenahotel.com; Muang Khong; r 100,000K; ☀☎) The most popular spot in town for sleeping and eating, Pon's has pleasant lemon-hued rooms with tiled floor, cable TV and a relaxed atmosphere. There's a riverside restaurant deck across the road. Good value.

Si Phan Don

◎ Sights

🛌 Sleeping

★**Pon Arena Hotel** BOUTIQUE HOTEL **$$**
(Map p234; ☑020-22270037, 031-515018; www.
ponarenahotel.com; Muang Khong; r US$50-85;
❄🗙🛜🛁) This upscale hotel has one building
that sits right on the river and boasts large
rooms with neat wood trim, flat-screen TVs
and a small swimming pool that is so close
to the river it actually sticks out over it. The
original building with the cheaper rooms sits
across the road but still scores style points
and has the same soft beds.

Mekong Inn HOTEL **$$**
(Map p234; ☑031-213668; www.gomekong
inn.com; Muang Khong; r incl breakfast US$30;
❄🗙🛜🛁) Rooms at this spot a bit south of
the centre are more upmarket than a typical guesthouse, but when the Lao-Canadian
owners are around (they spend some low-
season months in Canada), it's just as welcoming. Breakfast includes pancakes with
maple syrup and Tim Horton's coffee. Rooms
are in two buildings, one of which fronts the
pool, and wi-fi only reaches a few of them.

Senesothxeune Hotel HOTEL **$$**
(Map p234; ☑031-515021; www.ssx-hotel.com;
Muang Khong; r US$50-60, ste US$80; ❄@🛜)
This modern hotel a short ways away from
the tourist strip has comfortable rooms and
a pleasant restaurant with a view of the river
through its blossoming garden. The pricier
rooms have balconies, hardwood floors and
river views. It's been around a while, but the
French-Lao owners keep it shipshape. A pool
is in the works.

ℹ Information

INTERNET ACCESS

Senesothxeune Hotel is the only option for
public internet access (200K per minute).

MEDICAL SERVICES

Muang Khong Hospital (Map p234; ⊙24hr)
Right on the south edge of town. There are
some English-speaking staff.

MONEY

Agricultural Promotion Bank (Map p234;
Muang Khong; ⊙8.30am-4pm Mon-Fri) Ex-
changes major currencies, does Western Union
and has an ATM out front.

BCEL ATM (Map p234; Muang Khong) Below
the Lao Telecom tower.

POLICE

Police Station (Map p234) A block back from
the river in Muang Khong.

POST

Post Office (Map p234; ⊙8-11.30am &
1-4.30pm Mon-Fri) In Muang Khong town.

TOURIST INFORMATION

Don Khong Tourist Information Centre (Map
p234; ☑029-250303; panhjuki@yahoo.com;
Muang Khong; ⊙8.30am-4.30pm Mon-Fri)
Near the boat landing, this office is manned by
helpful Mr Phan. There's information for the
whole Si Phan Don region and he can set you up
with a local guide for 60,000K per day.

ℹ Getting There & Away

BOAT

The Don Khong boatmen's association runs a
boat most days to Don Det and Don Khon (one
way/return per person 40,000/60,000K) at
8.30am and departing Don Det at 3pm. It's 1½
hours downstream and two hours back. The
price rises if there are fewer than six people,
although everything is negotiable and you might
be able to hire a boat to go for around 200,000K.
You can book this through any guesthouse.

BUS

The vast majority of travellers ride the tourist
bus, which always includes getting dropped off
on Rte 13 with a connecting leg to the island.
Sometimes you will get dropped off at the road
to the bridge and head to Muang Khong by tuk-
tuk. Other times you will be dropped off at Hat
Xai Khun on the mainland (1km from the high-
way) and then squeezed into a small **ferry** (Map
p234) boat. If you need the **boat** (Map p234)
or tuk-tuk on your own, the price is 15,000K per
head with a 30,000K minimum.

For leaving the island, tourist transport heading south to Don Det (60,000K) and Don Khon (70,000K including boat transfer, two hours) passes by about 10am while pick-up for going north to Pakse (60,000K, two hours) is about 11.30am.

There is also a 9am non-air-conditioned bus (60,000K, three hours) from Muang Khong to Pakse's Southern Bus Terminal (p207). At other times, you can go to Rte 13 and wait for the hourly Pakse–Nakasang *sŏrngtăaou*.

CYCLING

If you're up for some adventure, you can walk, cycle or motorbike 15km across Don Som down to Don Det with a **ferry** (Map p234) ride (10,000K per person) at each end. In the rainy season this trip ranges from tough to impossible due to mud. People in Muang Khong will have only a rough idea what the conditions are at any particular time, but the ferryman will know everything for certain.

❶ Getting Around

Motorbikes (from 50,000K to 60,000K per day) that are real clunkers and newish bicycles (10,000K) can be hired at several places on the tourist strip in Muang Khong.

Don Det & Don Khon
ດອນເດດ/ດອນຄອນ

The vast majority of travellers to Si Phan Don end up on these twin islands. Don Det is defined by its hippyesque party scene, though it's really quite mild and there's nothing stronger than grass in the 'happy' snacks sold openly at some bars.

Of course there's much more to these two islands. Heading south from Ban Hua Det (Hua Det Village), the guesthouses thin out

and the icons of rural island life – fishermen, rice farmers, weavers, buffalo, sugar palms – are on full display. Chill in a hammock, wander aimlessly around the islands or languidly drift downstream in an inner tube in the turquoise arms of the Mekong.

The serenity continues across the French bridge on Don Khon, but down here there are also some gorgeous waterfalls to visit, sandy beaches to lounge on, dolphins to spot and even a little patch of wilderness to explore.

◉ Sights

These twin islands are famous for soaking up low-key village life rather than ticking off a list of attractions, but the dolphins and waterfalls on Don Khon are genuinely wonderful destinations.

When you cross the French bridge to Don Khon, you will be asked to pay a 35,000K tourism tax at the little blue shack. This is good for the whole day and covers the entrance fee to Tat Somphamit. If you are sleeping on Don Khon and you want to go north, you don't need to pay it. Just check in before you cross to Don Det and hope they remember you when you return.

★ **Khon Pa Soi Falls**   WATERFALL
(ຕາດຄອນປາສອຍ; Map p238; Don Khon) FREE
Although it's not the largest waterfall in the islands, Khon Pa Soi Falls is still pretty impressive, and it never gets crowded due to its isolated location. From the little restaurant (sometimes only serving cold drinks) cross the big, fun (or scary, depending on the person) wooden suspension bridge to Don Po Soi island and follow the roar 200m to the main waterfall.

DOLPHIN-WATCHING

A pod of severely endangered Irrawaddy dolphins lives along the southern shore of Don Khon and spotting these rare creatures in the wild is a highlight of any trip to southern Laos. The population has dropped to just five as some have died and others have gone south. Though nothing in nature is guaranteed, sightings here are virtually certain.

Boats are chartered (70,000K, maximum four people) from the old French landing pier in Ban Hang Khon. Where you go depends on where the dolphins are. In the hot season they stay close to village, but when the river runs high they can travel further away. You may be able to see them from your boat, or you may need to disembark in Cambodia and walk to a spot that overlooks the conservation zone. This will require a 20,000K payment to the officials there. Try to go in the early morning or early evening to avoid the heat.

The boat trips from Bang Hang Khon can combine dolphin-watching with Khon Phapheng Falls (250,000K) or little Nook Xume (100,000K) waterfalls.

CYCLING THE DON KHON LOOP

A bike trip around Don Khon is a pure delight. Begin in Ban Khon (Khon Village) and take the paved path to Ban Don Khon Neua temple, then follow the twisting little paths through the rice paddies until you reach the riverbank.

Head south and you'll soon see large portions of the concrete **diversion walls** the French built to direct logs. Usually sent down from forests in Sainyabuli Province, west of Vientiane, the logs were lashed together into rafts of three. To prevent them going off course, a Lao 'pilot' would board the raft and steer it through the maze of islands. When they reached the critical area at the north end of Don Khon, the pilots were required to guide the raft onto a reinforced concrete wedge, thus splitting the binds and sending the logs into the correct channel. The pilot would jump for his life moments before impact.

Turn at the sign for Khon Pa Soi Falls, which is reached by a big wooden suspension bridge that would be worth a visit even if there was no waterfall here. South of the falls the path enters a thick forest full of birds, crosses three wonky bridges made of old railroad track, passes a tiny village and deposits you at the ruins of the large **French port** in the dolphin-watching Ban Hang Khon (Hang Khon Village), at the southern tip of the island.

The village also has a hilltop **viewpoint** (Map p238; Ban Hang Khon), a decrepit old French colonial-era **steam locomotive** (Map p238), several restaurants and a real village homestay (p240).

The road taking you back north follows the old rail bed 5km across the island. Next to the **French Bridge** sits another, better-preserved French **steam locomotive** (Map p238). From there, head southwest, taking either the road around or through historic Wat Khon Tai (p238) to finish your trip at the impressive Tat Somphamit (p237) waterfall.

★ **Tat Somphamit** WATERFALL
(ຕາດສົມພາມິດ, Li Phi Falls; Map p238; Don Khon; 35,000K.; ☺ticket booth 8am-5pm) Located on Don Khon, 1.5km downriver from the French Bridge, vast Tat Somphamit is a gorgeous set of raging rapids. Its other name, Li Phi, means 'Spirit Trap' and locals believe the falls act as just that, a trap for bad spirits as they wash down the river. Local fishermen risk their skin edging out onto rocks in the violent flow of the cascades to empty bamboo traps. Don't try this stunt yourself – travellers have died slipping off the rocks beyond the barrier.

At the back end of the park, below the falls, is little **Li Phi Beach** (under water in the rainy season) A fundamental fear of ghosts means you'll never see locals swimming here. But even rationalists need to be wary as the current runs fast. Xai Kong Nyai Beach, a kilometre downriver, is a safer, year-round swimming option.

Khon Phapheng Falls WATERFALL
(ຕາດຄອນພະເພັ່ງ; Map p234; 55,000K; ☺8am-5pm) The largest, and by far the most awesome waterfall anywhere along the Mekong, Khon Phapheng is pure, unrestrained aggression as millions of litres of water crash over the rocks every second. That said, you'll have to decide whether or not it's worth the jacked-up price since you can see the smaller but similar Tat Somphamit for a lower price and without the tour-bus crowds.

Like all the waterfalls in this area, there's a shaky network of bamboo scaffolds on the rocks next to the falls used by daring fishermen. A free shuttle runs continuously between both ends of the park – a 500m trip.

Khon Phapheng is at the eastern shore of the Mekong near Ban Thakho. From Ban Nakasang it's 3km out to Rte 13, then 8.5km southeast to the turn-off and another 1.5km to the falls. A *săhm-lór* from Nakasang costs about 50,000K return with an hour wait time. You can also easily motorcycle down from Don Khong. The falls are included in kayak tours out of Don Det and Don Khon. Since amateurs can't kayak anywhere near these falls, you'll be taken there by vehicle as your kayaks are driven up to Ban Nakasang.

Xai Kong Nyai Beach BEACH
(Tha Sanam; Map p238; Don Khon) If a beach towel is more your style than a hammock, then this little stretch of sand will satisfy. Swimming is possible year-round, but you need to be careful of fast currents away from the shore. There are two simple restaurants with cold drinks, and fishermen here will take you out to see waterfalls, dolphins or the sunset in their small longtail boats. They have no sunshades, life jackets or fixed prices.

SOUTHERN LAOS DON DET & DON KHON

Don Det & Don Khon

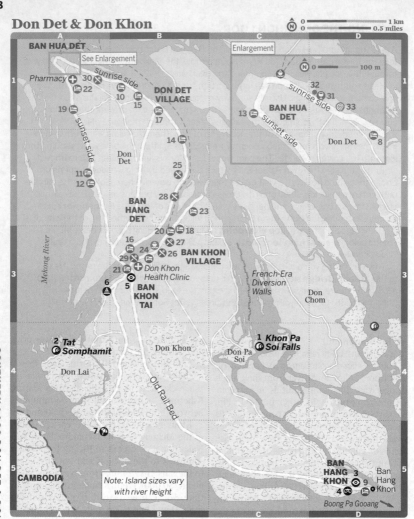

Wat Khon Tai   BUDDHIST TEMPLE
(ວັດຄອນໃຕ້; Map p238; Don Khon) Don Khon's main Buddhist temple was built on the site of an ancient Khmer shrine. Hidden behind the old ordination hall, which is itself tucked away behind a modern building, is an old, beautifully decrepit stupa and a Khmer-era shiva linga. Other ancient stone blocks lie scattered around the grounds. Also take a look at the long racing boats stored nearby.

🏃 Activities

Kayaking around the islands is very popular, and for good reason considering the sublime beauty of the Mekong in these parts. Full-day trips (180,000K per person) paddle to Khon Pa Soi Falls and then down to the dolphin pool – unlike the regular dolphin-watching trips, seeing them while on a kayak tour is hit or miss – before you visit Khon Phapheng Falls by vehicle. Prices are sometimes negotiable – mostly in the low season – or in lieu of a discount, some guesthouses will give you free breakfast the morning of the tour if you book it through them.

Due to the potential dangers, businesses are unwilling to just rent out kayaks. **Tubing** (10,000K), however, is a big thing here.

Don Det & Don Khon

⊙ Top Sights
1 Khon Pa Soi Falls C4
2 Tat Somphamit A4

⊙ Sights
3 Ban Hang Khon Steam Locomotive D5
4 Ban Hang Khon Viewpoint D5
5 Ban Khon Steam Locomotive B3
6 Wat Khon Tai A3
7 Xai Kong Nyai Beach A5

⊜ Sleeping
8 Baba Guesthouse D2
9 Ban Hang Khon Homestay D5
10 Crazy Gecko B1
11 Easy Go Backpackers Hostel A2
12 Last Resort A2
13 Little Eden.. C1
14 Mama Leuah Guesthouse.................... B2
15 Mama Piang.. B1
16 Mekong Dream Guesthouse B3
17 Mr Tho's Bungalows B1
18 Pa Kha Guesthouse B3

19 Peace Love Guesthouse A1
20 Sala Done Khone B3
21 Seng Ahloune Resort B3
22 Seng Thavan 1 Guesthouse.................. A1
23 Souksan Guesthouse........................... B2
24 Xaymountry Guesthouse B3

⊗ Eating
25 Boathouse B2
26 Chanthoumma's Restaurant B3
Four Thousand Sunsets ....(see 20)
27 Garden B3
28 King Kong Resort.................................. B2
Little Eden Restaurant ....(see 13)
29 Pizza Don Khon.................................... B3
30 Street View Restaurant A1

⊖ Drinking & Nightlife
31 Adam's Bar... D1

⊕ Information
32 Green Paradise Travel D1
33 Mr Khieo Internet D1

But don't float past the French bridge or you'll hit the fast currents that feed into the lethal falls. You could also have a boat take you upstream so you float back to Don Det. December to July is the best season, but you can go any time.

A relaxing alternative to the kayak tours are the afternoon BBQ **boat tours** (55,000K per person or 30,000K just for transport), such as that offered by **Souksan Guesthouse** (Map p238; ☑020-22337722). All guesthouses can also arrange other sorts of boat tours: sunset cruises, full-day island hops, morning bird-watching trips, fishing – you name it.

⌁ Sleeping

The common wisdom is to stay on Don Det to party, and Don Khon to get away from it all. But this is not how things really work. The party is confined to the northern tip of Don Det, at the busy village where the ferry from Ban Nakasang alights. In fact, the quietest and most isolated guesthouses in all of Si Phan Don are actually on the southern portion of Don Det. Many places offer low-season discounts; sometimes it's automatic and sometimes you need to ask.

⌁ Don Det

Don Det's best accommodations – and highest prices – are on the sunrise side, though

there are still plenty of good budget beds here too. Flimsy bamboo bungalows predominate on the sunset side. The drawback here is that late in the day rooms become furnace-like after baking in the afternoon sun. On the other hand, there's less boat traffic (ie noise) here.

On both sides of the island, walk far enough (on the sunrise side this means going past the old French Port in Don Det village) and the modest party scene of Ban Hua Det feels light years away. The sunset side gets downright rural after a kilometre.

⌁ Sunset Strip

Last Resort GUESTHOUSE $
(Map p238; mrwatkinsonlives@googlemail.com; sunset side, Don Det; r 60,000K) This tepee 'resort' in a field about a 20-minute walk south of Ban Hua Det embraces the natural life, with the expat owner growing vegies and baking bread. Made with bamboo and thatch, the tepees are in the shade of mature trees and share a bathroom. There are often communal meals and alfresco movies in the evening.

Seng Thavan 1 Guesthouse GUESTHOUSE $
(Map p238; ☑020-56132696; sunset side, Don Det; r 100,000K; ☜) Probably the best the sunset side has to offer in the budget range, Seng Thavan's four ensuite rooms are old but fastidiously clean. They're off the river, but you get the great views from its low-key cafe.

Peace Love Guesthouse GUESTHOUSE $
(Map p238; ☎020-56763298; sunset side, Don Det; r 50,000K) These ageing split-bamboo bungalows perched over the river hark back to Don Det's old days of US$1 rooms. Though things are bare bones, and the cold-water facilities are across the road, there are great views, it's in a very local area and the family who runs it is very nice. It's got a hard-to-find sign, so look for the 'Take It Easy' restaurant.

Little Eden HOTEL $$
(Map p238; ☎020-77739045; www.littleedendon det.com; sunset side, Ban Hua Det; r from US$41-50; ☀❄🌐🏊) Don Det's most luxurious complex is set on a large plot on its northern tip. Fragrant rooms tempt with contemporary dark-wood furniture and polished wood floors, plus plenty of mod cons. Also, the hotel has a beautiful free 18m-long swimming pool, a bar and a sunset-perfect restaurant. You will feel like you have escaped Ban Hua Det.

🛏 Sunrise Strip

★Crazy Gecko GUESTHOUSE $
(Map p238; ☎020-97193565; www.crazygecko.ch; sunrise side, Don Det; r 80,000-100,000K; 🌐) In a stilted structure made of solid wood, Crazy Gecko's four tidy rooms surround a balcony that's equal parts funky and functional. Festooned with hammocks and random decoration, it's a superior place to relax. There's a pool table and board games down below and across the road is a little restaurant on a deck over the water.

Mama Piang GUESTHOUSE $
(Map p238; ☎020-91816479; sunrise side, Don Det; r 50,000K) If there is a more fun and friendly host in Si Phan Don than Mama Piang – who proudly calls herself 'crazy' – we didn't meet her. There are six cold-water fan rooms across the road from her riverfront restaurant.

Mama Leuah Guesthouse GUESTHOUSE $
(Map p238; ☎020-59078792; www.mamaleuah-dondet.com; sunrise side, Don Det; r with/without bathroom 100,000/80,000K; 🌐) The rooms are super basic, but it's quiet and beautiful up here and you can hang out at the restaurant, where ambient music plays and excellent Thai cuisine is served, along with Swiss surprises such as *Zürcher geschnetzeltes* (pork with creamy mushroom sauce).

Mr Tho's Bungalows GUESTHOUSE $
(Map p238; ☎020-55928598; mrthobungalow@gmail.com; sunrise side, Don Det; bungalows 10,000, new r fan/air-con 120,000/160,000K; ☀🌐) Just south of Don Det village, Mr Tho's has long been popular for the relaxed atmosphere fostered by the helpful, English-speaking family and the location, which is where the sunrise side starts to feel more like a village than a holiday resort. The old cold-water bungalows are right on the water and the block across the road has taken them into the flashpacker market.

Baba Guesthouse GUESTHOUSE $$
(Map p238; ☎020-98893943; www.dondet.net; sunrise side, Ban Hua Det; r 350,000K; ☀🌐) This beautiful guesthouse looks out on the Mekong on one side, and emerald paddy fields on the other. The price is well above average for this area, but you really do get more for your money here. Rooms are sleekly white and almost luxurious, with private balcony, tasteful decor and spotless bathroom.

🛏 South

★Mekong Dream Guesthouse GUESTHOUSE $
(Map p238; ☎020-55275728; Don Det; r 50,000K; 🌐) At the south of Don Det, facing the strip on Don Khon, Mekong Dream is one of the homiest, best-value guesthouses on the islands. The 12 rooms, all with private bathrooms and comfortable king-size beds, are the antidote to claustrophobic rooms elsewhere (except for the three inferior concrete rooms downstairs) and share a roomy balcony/hammock lounge.

🛏 Don Khon

Ban Hang Khon Homestay HOMESTAY $
(Map p238; ☎020-98893204; Don Khon; per person 36,000K, per meal 20,000K) The small village of Ban Hang Khon at the southern tip of Don Khon – where the dolphin-watching trips start – offers an unadulterated local experience. Little English is spoken, but the seven families who take in guests are impeccable hosts. It's best to call ahead.

Xaymountry Guesthouse GUESTHOUSE $
(Map p238; ☎020-96516513; Don Khon; r with/without bathroom 80,000/50,000K; 🌐) No place on Don Khon has more character than this giant stilted wood house. It was the first lodging on the island and the massive front porch is a nice place to unwind, despite the lack of a river view.

Pa Kha Guesthouse GUESTHOUSE $
(Map p238; 055-847522; Don Khon; r with fan/
air-con 80,000/120,000K; ❄ 🛜) Great-value
digs with welcoming, clean rooms, good service and a quiet location. The cheapest rooms
are on the river and the newer air-con rooms
are across the road, as is the restaurant.

★ **Sala Done Khone** BOUTIQUE HOTEL $$
(Map p238; 031-260940; www.salalaoboutique.
com; Don Khon; r US$60-80; ❄❄❄❄) 🍴 Five
hotels in one, Sala Done Khone has both
the classiest and the most original rooms in
Si Phan Don. Its signature unit, the French
Residence, is a renovated 1921 timber trading
headquarters with tiled floors and louvred
blinds, while out on the river the Sala Phae
wing features floating cottages with bio-safe
toilets and private decks.

Seng Ahloune Resort RESORT $$
(Map p238; 031-260934; www.sengahloune
resort.com; Don Khon; r/f incl breakfast
300,000/450,000K; ❄🛜) The busy location
next to the bridge doesn't seem ideal until
you see the sunsets. The cosy and solid-
ly built bungalows have wicker walls and
wooden floors. Its huge riverfront restaurant
(mains 20,000K to 100,000K) fills up with
tour groups at lunch, but it's more relaxing
at dinner.

✕ Eating

Most guesthouses serve a range of Lao, Thai
and Western favourites from virtually identical menus. Stand-alone restaurants are usually a step above the guesthouses and the extra
5,000 to 10,000K per dish that they charge is
worth it. Generally the best dining is on Don
Khon and the southeast shore of Don Det.

✕ Don Det

★ **King Kong Resort** INTERNATIONAL $$
(Map p238; Don Det; mains 25,000-120,000K;
☻6am-11pm; 🛜) This Brit-run establishment
on a peaceful slice of the Mekong in south
Don Det is a cut above the competition with
a range of pastas, pizzas, burgers, fish and
chips, Thai curries, Sunday roasts (60,000K)
and – we hear – the tastiest and happiest
shakes on the island. The guitars and chess
sets scattered around fit the vibe. Has added
a few new bungalows (40,000K) across the
road.

Street View Restaurant PIZZA $$
(Map p238; sunrise side, Don Det; mains from
25,000-65,000K; ☻8am-11pm; 🛜) This attractive
wooden riverside haunt has decks for chilling
on; a long, well-stocked bar; and a good reputation. Tuck into mouth-watering wood-fired
pizza, barbecued chicken, Mekong fish, beef
chops, burgers, salads and healthy breakfasts.
Prices are high, but worth it.

Boathouse SEAFOOD $$
(Map p238; Don Det; mains 20,000-65,000K;
☻7am-11pm) Run by a German former fisher-
man married to a local gal, the emphasis here
is on freshly made fish dishes. Try the catfish
mók (steamed in banana leaf) or the fish bar-
becue, which needs to be ordered in advance.
It's in a sturdy raised structure off the river in
the south of Don Det.

Little Eden
Restaurant LAOTIAN, INTERNATIONAL $$
(Map p238; sunset side, Ban Hua Det; mains 30,000-
140,000K; ❄🛜) Catching the breeze from the
tip of the island, Little Eden's perfectly placed
new restaurant is one of the best spots to eat
upmarket Lao and Western cuisine. Think
tender *duck à l'orange*, spaghetti bolognese
and fish *láhp* using Mekong catfish.

✕ Don Khon

Garden LAOTIAN, THAI $
(Map p238; Don Khon; mains 20,000-65,000K;
☻7am-10pm; 🌿) Taking freshness seriously,
this thatched-roof, open-kitchen restaurant
is a good place for the uninitiated to sample
Laotian foods, such as spicy papaya salad and
grilled Mekong River fish. It also serves all the
usual traveller comfort foods and the cook's
personal version of lemongrass chicken.

Chanthoumma's Restaurant LAOTIAN $
(Map p238; Don Khon; mains 20,000-70,000K;
☻6.30am-9pm; 🌿) This friendly family has
been serving good food, including spring
rolls, papaya salads and vegie options, from
in front of their tumbledown home for many
years.

Pizza Don Khon LAOTIOAN, INTERNATIONAL $
(Map p238; Don Khon; small pizzas 40,000K;
☻7.30am-10pm) A focus on quality, fresh ingredients results in a top-notch pizza. There's
a full menu including English breakfasts
and daily specials such as *mók* (fish and egg
steamed inside banana leaves).

★ **Four Thousand Sunsets** FUSION $$
(Map p238; Don Khon; mains 25,000-80,000K; ⏰7am-11pm; 🐾📶) Aptly named, this high-class floating restaurant lowers your pulse with the metronomic flow. The menu is a big break from the usual with many dishes you won't find elsewhere in the islands such as northern Thai *hinlay* curry and a chicken *láhp* burger. There's also steamed and grilled fresh river fish, Lao 'smoking' herbal sausages and many stir-fries.

Drinking & Nightlife

Ban Hua Det is where the action is. There's a semi-solid midnight curfew when the bars wind down and the action moves to the 'beach' (under water in the rainy season), where bonfires and midnight dips are not unheard of.

Adam's Bar BAR
(Map p238; sunrise side, Ban Hua Det) Staff are upfront about their special 'secret' ingredients, so if that's your kind of scene then this is your kind of place. Has a full menu of Lao and Western food and helpful advice about the islands, too.

❶ Information

INTERNET ACCESS
Computers for public internet access have largely vanished, but **Mr Khieo Internet** (Map p238; sunrise side, Ban Hua Det; per min 200K; ⏰7am-10pm) on Don Det is still in the game. Wi-fi is now available in just about all guesthouses and hotels.

MEDICAL SERVICES
Don Khon has a simple **health clinic** (Map p238; Don Khon) while Don Det has just a small **pharmacy** (Map p238; sunset side, Ban Hua Det). These can also be found in Ban Nakasang on the mainland. The nearest proper health facility is on Don Khong, but for anything serious you should head straight to Pakse.

MONEY
There are no banks on the islands. Cash can be exchanged, at generally poor rates, at most guesthouses and some, including Baba (p240), do cash advances on credit cards for a 6% commission. There's an Agricultural Promotion Bank and a BCEL with ATMs on the main drag in Ban Nakasang. Kayaking tours budget enough time at the end of the trip for people to make an ATM stop.

TOURIST INFORMATION
There is no tourism office on these islands, so you're left with guesthouses and travel agencies. The Baba Guesthouse (p240) website (www.dondet.net) has lots of helpful information.

❶ Getting There & Away

BOAT
Boat prices between **Ban Nakasang** (Map p234) and the islands are fixed by a local boat association, and there are very few running each day on a shared basis. Expect to pay 15,000K per person (or 30,000K if travelling on your own) to Don Det, and 20,000K per person (or 60,000K if travelling alone) to Don Khon (Map p238).

For Pakse, most travellers book tickets on the island, which includes the local boat and an 11am bus or minibus (60,000K, three hours). If you want to leave at another time there are hourly *sŏrngtǎaou* from Ban Nakasang to the Southern Bus Terminal (p207) in Pakse (40,000K, 3½ hours). One shared boat always leaves the islands in time for the 8am *sŏrngtǎaou*. These all stop in Hat Xai Khun (for Don Khong).

Even in the best of circumstances, travel to Cambodia (p245) from the islands by public transport is a hassle. Kayak-boat trips from Don Det to Stung Treng run by **Xplore-Asia** (Map p204; ☎ 031-251983; www.xplore-laos.com; Th 14; ⏰7.30am-6.30pm) are a great alternative.

River travel to Don Khong (200,000K) and Champasak (US$200) is only available by chartered boat, but very often there are other people willing to join together to share the cost. For Don Khong you could also call Done Khong Guesthouse (p234) or Pon's Riverside Guesthouse (p234) on that island to see if a boat is coming from there in the morning. If so, you can probably buy a seat (40,000K) for the return journey.

❶ Getting Around

With virtually no traffic and only a few small hills, Don Det and Don Khon are ideally explored by bicycle (hired from just about any guesthouse for 10,000K per day) though they are small enough that everything is also walkable.

There are some *sǎhm-lór* available in Ban Hua Det and Ban Khon. It's 100,000K for a trip to both Ban Hua Det to see the dolphins and Tat Somphamit, including sufficient waiting time, and 40,000K just to travel between Ban Hua Det and Ban Khon.

Understand Laos

Laos Today

Laos sits on one of the world's major geo-political crossroads, where Southeast Asia meets China, and this is a huge challenge for such a small country. Hemmed in by the Asian tigers of China, Vietnam and Thailand, Laos often looks like vulnerable prey. Traditionally, Vietnam has held political sway, China wields financial clout and Thailand has a dominant cultural influence. While the government tries to parry these competing influences, the Lao people are ever more plugged into a global world and this contributes to domestic tension.

Best on Film

The Rocket (2013) The story of a young Lao boy blamed for bringing bad luck to his family. To win back the trust of the family he builds a giant firework to enter the annual Rocket Festival.

Bomb Harvest (2007) Powerful documentary about the impact of unexploded ordnance (UXO) on communities in Laos today and the work the Mines Advisory Group (MAG) is doing to clear the legacy of war. For some, the war goes on.

Best in Print

The Coroner's Lunch (Colin Cotterill; 2004) Delve into the delightful world of Dr Siri, full-time national coroner in the 1970s and part-time super sleuth. The first instalment in a 10-part Siri series.

Ant Egg Soup (Natacha Du Pont de Bie; 2004) Subtitled *The Adventures of a Food Tourist in Laos,* the author samples some local delicacies (including some that aren't suitable for a delicate stomach).

One Foot in Laos (Dervla Murphy; 2001) Renowned Irish travel writer explores Laos back in the early days of the 1990s and discovers a country undergoing profound change.

Political Snapshot

Officially Laos remains a one-party communist state controlled by the ruling Lao People's Revolutionary Party (LPRP). However, the 'communist' government long ago ditched the Marxist baggage in favour of capitalist couture. The LPRP is not the unified monolith it might appear and contains several factions. Trying to keep all these elements happy is a challenge. New President Bounnhang Vorachith and Prime Minister Thongloun Sisoulith both came to power in 2016 and early populist moves included a total ban on logging in Laos. But it remains to be seen if there is actually the political will to enforce this on the ground.

Economy & Infrastructure

The Lao economy has seen 7% to 8% growth from 2010 to 2015, one of the best performances in the world. However, the World Bank still rates Laos as one of the least developed countries in East Asia, with more than 75% of people living on less than US$2 a day.

Major exports are timber products, garments, electricity and coffee. In recent years, tourism has become one of the main generators of foreign income, much of which flows directly into the pockets of those who need it most.

Foreign aid remains a crutch for the Laos economy, with Western governments and their NGOs picking up much of the development tab. China is a political role model as well as a major source of funding, and Chinese spending comes without reform targets, unlike assistance from the West.

Infrastructure is the buzz word in Laos, as aid and investment is channelled towards hydroelectricity, roads and bridges. China is funding a new high-speed railway that will eventually connect Kunming with Bangkok via Luang Prabang and Vientiane. Other mega-projects include the Xayaburi Dam on the lower Mekong, which is causing much consternation for downstream neighbours Cambodia and Vietnam, who rely on the river for irrigation and fish stocks.

Corruption

Corruption remains a major problem, and Transparency International ranked Laos 139 out of 168 countries in its Corruption Perceptions Index 2015, level with Bangladesh and Guinea. Increased investment has brought increased exports and increased revenue for the government, but much of this new wealth has not been effectively accounted for in the national budget. Widespread corruption is a source of great frustration to the average Laotian, and contributes to a widening gap between rural and urban living standards.

We the People

And where do the Lao people fit into all this? While they may be politically disenfranchised, they are more economically empowered than in the past. They also have greater access to basics such as electricity and running water – a major improvement on the bad old days of collectivisation. Access to technology has also improved, with the number of Lao people using the internet more than doubling in the past five years.

However, ethnic minorities, who make up a large proportion of the population, are not sharing the economic bonanza with their lowland cousins who dominate the cities. And while use of social media continues to spread, laws curtail freedom of speech: a 2014 decree prohibits criticism of the government online (an offence that got three Lao citizens arrested in 2016), and the vast majority of media outlets are state run. Laos is a conservative country, but there are increasing numbers of the younger generation who have spent time abroad working in Thailand or with foreigners in the tourism sector who feel disconnected from their ageing leadership.

POPULATION: **6.9 MILLION**

AREA: **236,800 SQ KM**

OFFICIAL LANGUAGE: **LAO**

INFLATION: **1.3%**

GDP PER CAPITA: **US$1660**

BORDER COUNTRIES:
CAMBODIA, CHINA, MYANMAR (BURMA), THAILAND, VIETNAM

if Laos were 100 people

55 would be Lao
11 would be Khmu (Mon-Khmer)
8 would be Hmong
3 would be Chinese
3 would be Vietnamese
20 would be Ethnic Minorities

belief systems
(% of population)

50 Buddhist

45 Animist

2 Christian

3 Other

population per sq km

LAOS   UK   THAILAND

≈25 people

History

Laos first emerged in the region as Lan Xang, or the 'Kingdom of a Million Elephants', in the 14th century. Despite some bursts of independence, the kingdom generally found itself paying tribute to more powerful neighbours, including the Siamese and Vietnamese. Geography ensured Laos was sucked into the Vietnam War and a lengthy civil war culminated in a communist takeover in 1975. After many years of isolation, Laos began to experiment with economic reforms in the 1990s but political reform remains a distant dream for most.

Martin Stuart-Fox is Emeritus Professor of History at the University of Queensland, Australia. He has written multiple books and dozens of articles and book chapters on the politics and history of Laos.

Prehistory & Tai-Lao Migration

The first modern humans *(Homo sapiens)* arrived in Southeast Asia around 50,000 years ago. Their stone-age technology remained little changed until a Neolithic culture evolved about 10,000 years ago. These hunter-gatherers spread throughout much of Southeast Asia, including Laos. Their descendants produced the first pottery in the region, and later bronze metallurgy. In time they adopted rice cultivation, introduced down the Mekong River valley from southern China. These people were the ancestors of the present-day upland minorities, collectively known as the Lao Thoeng (Upland Lao), the largest group of which are the Khamu of northern Laos.

The earliest kingdom in southern Laos was identified in Chinese texts as Chenla, dating from the 5th century. One of its capitals was close to Champasak, near the later Khmer temple of Wat Phu. A little later Mon people (speaking another Austro-Asiatic language) established kingdoms on the middle Mekong: Sri Gotapura (Sikhottabong in Lao) with its capital near Tha Khaek, and Chanthaburi in the vicinity of Viang Chan (Vientiane).

Tai peoples probably began migrating out of southern China in about the 8th century. They included the Tai-Lao of Laos, the Tai-Syam and Tai-Yuan of central and northern Thailand, and the Tai-Shan of northeast Burma. They are called Tai to distinguish them from the citizens (Thai) of modern Thailand, although the word is the same. All spoke closely related

The Lao believe most *ngeuk* (snake deities) have been converted to become serpent protectors of Buddhism, called *naga* (in Lao *nak*). They still require propitiation, however, and annual boat races are held for their amusement. Many Buddhist temples (wat) have protective *naga* balustrades.

TIMELINE	500	1181	1256
	The early Mon-Khmer Chenla capital of Shrestapura is a thriving city based around the ancient temple of Wat Phu Champasak.	King Jayavarman VII vanquishes the Chams from Angkor and becomes the most powerful ruler of the Khmer empire, extending its boundaries to include most of modern-day Laos.	Kublai Khan sacks the Tai state of Nan Chao, part of the Xishuangbanna region of modern-day Yunnan in China. This sparks a southern exodus of the Tai people.

Tai languages, practised wet-rice cultivation along river valleys, and organised themselves into small principalities, known as *meuang,* each presided over by a hereditary ruler, or *jow meuang* (lord of the *meuang*). The Tai-Lao, or Lao for short, moved slowly down the rivers of northern Laos, like the Nam Ou and the Nam Khan, running roughly from northeast to southwest, until they arrived at the Mekong, the Great River.

The Kingdom of Lan Xang

The first extended Lao kingdom dates from the mid-14th century. It was established in the context of a century of unprecedented political and social change in mainland Southeast Asia. At the beginning of the 13th century, the great Khmer king Jayavarman VII, who had re-established Cambodian power and built the city of Angkor Thom, sent his armies north to extend the Khmer empire to include all of the middle Mekong region and north-central Thailand. But the empire was overstretched, and by the mid-13th century the Khmer were in retreat. At the same time, the Mongol Yuan dynasty in China abandoned plans for further conquest in Southeast Asia.

This left a political vacuum in central Thailand, into which stepped Ramkhamhaeng, founder of the Tai-Syam kingdom of Sukhothai. To his north, his ally Mangray founded the Tai-Yuan kingdom of Lanna (meaning 'A Million Rice Fields'), with his capital at Chiang Mai. Other smaller Tai kingdoms were established at Phayao and Xiang Dong Xiang Thong (Luang Prabang). In southern Laos and eastern Thailand, however, the Khmer still held on to power.

The Cambodian court looked around for an ally, and found one in the form of a young Lao prince, Fa Ngum, who was being educated at Angkor. Fa Ngum's princely father had been forced to flee Xiang Dong Xiang Thong after he seduced one of his own father's concubines. So Fa Ngum was in direct line for the throne.

The Khmer gave Fa Ngum a Khmer princess and an army, and sent him north to wrest the middle Mekong from the control of Sukhothai, and so divert and weaken the Tai-Syam kingdom. He was successful and Fa Ngum was pronounced king in Xiang Dong Xiang Thong, before forcibly bringing Viang Chan into his growing empire. He named his new kingdom Lan Xang Hom Khao, which means 'a million elephants and the white parasol'. Fa Ngum built a fine capital at Xiang Dong Xiang Thong and set about organising his court and kingdom.

Fa Ngum performed sacrifices to the *pĕe* (traditional spirits) of the kingdom. But he also acquiesced to his wife's request to introduce Khmer Theravada Buddhism to Lan Xang. Fa Ngum began to seduce the wives and daughters of his court nobles, who decided to replace him, and he was sent into exile in Nan (now in Thailand), where he died within five

By naming his kingdom Lan Xang Hom Khao, Fa Ngum was making a statement about power and kingship. Elephants were the battle tanks of Southeast Asian warfare, so to claim to be the 'Kingdom of a Million Elephants' was to issue a warning to surrounding kingdoms: 'Don't mess with the Lao!' A white parasol was the traditional symbol of kingship.

1353	1421	1479	1501
Fa Ngum establishes the Lao kingdom of Lan Xang and builds a capital at Xiang Dong Xiang Thong.	King Fa Ngum's son and successor Samsenthai dies and Lan Xang implodes into warring factions for the next century.	The Vietnamese emperor Le Thanh Tong invades Lan Xang, sending a large force including many war elephants.	King Visoun comes to the throne and rebuilds the Lao kingdom, marking a cultural renaissance for Lan Xang. He installs the Pha Bang Buddha image in Luang Prabang.

years. His legacy, however, stood the test of time. The kingdom of Lan Xang remained a power in mainland Southeast Asia until early in the 18th century, able to match the power of Siam, Vietnam and Burma.

Fa Ngum was succeeded by his son Un Heuan, who married princesses from the principal Tai kingdoms (Lanna and Ayutthaya, which had replaced Sukhothai), consolidated the kingdom and developed trade. With his wealth he built temples and beautified his capital.

Following Un Heuan's (throne name Samsenthai) long and stable reign of 42 years, Lan Xang was shaken by succession disputes, a problem faced by all Southeast Asian *mandala* (circles of power). The throne eventually passed to Samsenthai's youngest son, who took the throne name Xainya Chakkaphat (Universal Ruler). It was an arrogant claim, but he ruled wisely and well.

Tragedy struck at the end of his reign, when Lan Xang suffered its first major invasion. After a bitter battle, the Vietnamese captured and sacked Xiang Dong Xiang Thong. Xainya Chakkaphat fled and the Lao mounted a guerrilla campaign. Eventually the Vietnamese were forced to withdraw, their forces decimated by malaria and starvation. So great were their losses that the Vietnamese vowed never to invade Lan Xang again.

Consolidation of the Kingdom

The Lao kingdom recovered under one of its greatest rulers, who came to the throne in 1501. This was King Visoun, who had previously been governor of Viang Chan. There he had been an ardent worshipper of the Pha Bang Buddha image, which he brought with him to Xiang Dong Xiang Thong to become the palladium of the kingdom. For it he built the magnificent temple known as Wat Wisunarat (Wat Visoun), which, though damaged and repaired over the years, still stands in Luang Prabang.

A new power had arisen in mainland Southeast Asia, the kingdom of Burma. It was the threat of Burma that convinced King Setthathirat in 1560 to move his capital to Viang Chan. Before he did so, he built the most beautiful Buddhist temple surviving in Laos, Wat Xieng Thong. He also left behind the Pha Bang, and changed the name of Xiang Dong Xiang Thong to Luang Prabang in its honour. With him he took what he believed to be an even more powerful Buddha image, the Pha Kaew, or Emerald Buddha, now in Bangkok.

Setthathirat was the greatest builder in Lao history. Not only did he construct or refurbish several monasteries in Luang Prabang, besides Wat Xieng Thong, but he also did the same in Viang Chan. His most important building projects, apart from a new palace on the banks of the Mekong, were the great That Luang stupa, a temple for the Emerald Buddha (Wat Pha Kaeo) and endowment of a number of royal temples in the vicinity of the palace.

Southeast Asian kingdoms were not states in the modern sense, with fixed frontiers, but varied in extent depending on the power of the centre. Outlying *meuang* (principalities) might transfer their allegiance elsewhere when the centre was weak. That is why scholars prefer the term *mandala*, a Sanskrit word meaning 'circle of power' (in Lao *monthon*).

1560	1638	1641–42	1694
King Setthathirat, grandson of King Visoun, moves the capital to Viang Chan because of the threat from Burma, a rising power in the region.	The great Lao king Suriya Vongsa begins a 57-year reign known as the 'Golden Age' of the kingdom of Lan Xang.	The first Europeans to write accounts of Lan Xang arrive in Viang Chan providing information about trade and culture, descriptions of King Setthathirat's royal palace and details of the king's power.	King Suriya Vongsa dies and Lan Xang once again fractures into competing kingdoms.

ALTERNATE ORIGINS

The early Lao text known as the Nithan (story of) Khun Borom recounts the myth of creation of the Lao peoples, their interaction and the establishment of the first Lao kingdom in the vicinity of Luang Prabang. The creation myth tells how two great gourds grew at Meuang Thaeng (Dien Bien Phu, now in Vietnam) from inside which sounds could be heard. Divine rulers, known as *khun*, pierced one of the gourds with a hot poker, and out of the charred hole poured the dark-skinned Lao Thoeng. The *khun* used a knife to cut a hole in the other gourd, through which escaped the lighter-skinned Tai-Lao (or Lao Loum, Lowland Lao). The gods then sent Khun Borom to rule over both Lao Loum and Lao Thoeng. He had seven sons, whom he sent out to found seven new kingdoms in the regions where Tai peoples settled (in the Tai highlands of Vietnam, the Xishuangbanna of southern China, Shan state in Burma, and in Thailand and Laos). While the youngest son founded the kingdom of Xieng Khuang on the Plain of Jars, the oldest son, Khun Lo, descended the Nam Ou (Ou River), seized the principality of Meuang Sua from its Lao Thoeng ruler, and named it Xiang Dong Xiang Thong (later renamed Luang Prabang).

It was more than 60 years before another great Lao king came to the throne, a period of division, succession disputes and intermittent Burmese domination. In 1638 Suriya Vongsa was crowned king. He would rule for 57 years, the longest reign in Lao history and a 'golden age' for the kingdom of Lan Xang. During this time, Lan Xang was a powerful kingdom and Viang Chan was a great centre of Buddhist learning, attracting monks from all over mainland Southeast Asia.

The Kingdom Divided

King Suriya Vongsa must have been stern and unbending in his old age, because he refused to intervene when his son and heir was found guilty of adultery and condemned to death. As a result, when he died in 1695 another succession dispute wracked the kingdom. This time the result was the division of Lan Xang. First the ruler of Luang Prabang declared independence from Viang Chan, followed a few years later by Champasak in the south.

The once-great kingdom of Lan Xang was thus fatally weakened. In its place were three (four with Xieng Khuang) weak regional kingdoms, none of which was able to withstand the growing power of the Tai-Syam kingdom of Ayutthaya. The Siamese were distracted, however, over the next half century by renewed threats from Burma. In the end Ayutthaya was sacked by a Burmese army. Chiang Mai was already a tributary to Burma, and Luang Prabang also paid tribute.

Naga Cities of Mekong (2006), by Martin Stuart-Fox, provides a narrative account of the founding legends and history of Luang Prabang, Vientiane and Champasak, and a guide to their temples.

1707–13	1769	1778	1826–28
Lan Xang is divided into three smaller and weaker kingdoms: Viang Chan, Luang Prabang and Champasak.	Burmese armies overrun northern Laos and annex the kingdom of Luang Prabang.	Thai forces invade southern Laos and conquer the kingdom of Champasak.	Chao Anou succeeds his two older brothers on the throne of Viang Chan and wages war against Siam for Lao independence. He is captured and Viang Chan is sacked by the Siamese armies.

However, it did not take the Siamese long to recover. The inspiring leadership of a young military commander called Taksin, son of a Chinese father and a Siamese mother, rallied the Siamese and drove the Burmese out. After organising his kingdom and building a new capital, Taksin sought new fields of conquest. The Lao kingdoms were obvious targets. By 1779 all three had surrendered to Siamese armies and accepted the suzerainty of Siam. The Emerald Buddha was carried off by the Siamese and all Lao kings had to present regular tribute to Bangkok.

When Chao Anou succeeded his two older brothers on the throne of Viang Chan, he was determined to assert Lao independence. First he made merit by endowing Buddhist monasteries and building his own temple (Wat Si Saket). Then in 1826 he made his move, sending three armies down the Mekong and across the Khorat plateau. The Siamese were taken by surprise, but quickly rallied. Siamese armies drove the Lao back and seized Viang Chan. Chao Anou fled, but was captured when he tried to retake the city a year later. This time the Siamese were ruthless. Viang Chan was thoroughly sacked and its population resettled east of the Mekong. Only Wat Si Saket was spared. Chao Anou died a caged prisoner in Bangkok.

For the next 60 years the Lao *meuang,* from Champasak to Luang Prabang, were tributary to Siam. At first these two remaining small kingdoms retained a degree of independence, but increasingly they were brought under closer Siamese supervision. One reason for this was that Siam itself was threatened by a new power in the region and felt it had to consolidate its empire. The new power was France, which had declared a protectorate over most of Cambodia in 1863.

Four years later a French expedition sent to explore and map the Mekong River arrived in Luang Prabang, then the largest settlement upstream from Phnom Penh. In the 1880s the town became caught up in a

FIRST CONTACT

The first European to have left an account of the Lao kingdom arrived in Viang Chan (Vientiane) in 1641. He was a merchant by the name of Gerrit van Wuysthoff, an employee of the Dutch East India Company, who wanted to open a trade route down the Mekong. He and his small party were royally accommodated and entertained during their eight-week stay in the Lao capital. Van Wuysthoff had more to say about the prices of trade goods than about Lao culture or religion, but he was followed a year later by a visitor who can offer us more insight into 17th-century Viang Chan. This was the Jesuit missionary Giovanni-Maria Leria, who stayed in Viang Chan for five years. During that time he had singularly little success in converting anyone to Christianity and eventually gave up in disgust. But he liked the Lao people (if not the monks) and has left a wonderful description of the royal palace and the houses of the nobility.

1867	1885	1893	1904
Members of the French Mekong expedition reach Luang Prabang. Over the next 20 years the town is caught up in a struggle which sees the king offered protection by France.	Following centuries of successive invasions by neighbouring powers, the former Lan Xang is broken up into a series of states under Siamese control.	A French warship reaches Bangkok, guns trained on the palace. This forces the Siamese to give France sovereignty over all Lao territories east of the Mekong.	King Sisavang Vong founds the modern royal family.

struggle that pitted Siamese, French and roving bands of Chinese brigands (known as Haw) against each other. In 1887 Luang Prabang was looted and burned by a mixed force of Upland Tai and Haw. Only Wat Xieng Thong was spared. The king escaped downstream. With him was a French explorer named Auguste Pavie, who offered him the protection of France.

French Rule

In the end French rule was imposed through gunboat diplomacy. In 1893 a French warship forced its way up the Chao Phraya River to Bangkok and trained its guns on the palace. Under duress, the Siamese agreed to transfer all territory east of the Mekong to France. So Laos became a French colony, with the kingdom of Luang Prabang as a protectorate and the rest of the country directly administered.

In 1900 Viang Chan (Vientiane) was re-established as the administrative capital of Laos, although real power was exercised from Hanoi, the capital of French Indochina. In 1907 a further treaty was signed with Siam adding two territories west of the Mekong to Laos (Sainyabuli Province and part of Champasak). Siem Reap and Battambang provinces were regained by Cambodia as part of the deal.

Over the next few years the French put into place the apparatus of colonial control, but Laos remained a backwater. Despite French plans for economic exploitation, Laos was always a drain on the budget of Indochina. Corvée labour was introduced, particularly to build roads, and taxes were heavy, but the colony never paid its own way. Some timber was floated down the Mekong, and tin was discovered in central Laos, but returns were meagre. Coffee was grown in southern Laos, and opium in the north, most of it smuggled into China.

In the interwar years the French cast around for ways to make Laos economically productive. One plan was to connect the Lao Mekong towns to coastal Vietnam by constructing a railway across the mountains separating the two colonies. The idea was to encourage the migration of industrious Vietnamese peasants into Laos to replace what the French saw as the indolent and easy-going Lao. Eventually Vietnamese would outnumber Lao and produce an economic surplus. The railway was surveyed and construction begun from the Vietnamese side, but the Great Depression intervened, money dried up and the Vietnamisation of Laos never happened.

Nationalism & Independence

The independence movement was slow to develop in Laos. The French justified their colonial rule as protection of the Lao from aggressive neighbours, particularly the Siamese. Most of the small Lao elite, aware of their own weakness, found this interpretation convincing, even though they resented the presence of so many Vietnamese. The Indochinese Communist

The first Frenchman to arrive in Laos was Henri Mouhot, an explorer and naturalist who died of malaria in 1861 near Luang Prabang (where his tomb can still be seen).

1907	1935	1942	1945
The present borders of Laos are established by international treaty. Vientiane (the French spelling of Viang Chan) becomes the administrative capital.	The first two Lao members join the Indochinese Communist Party (ICP), founded by Ho Chi Minh in 1930.	As WWII spills over into Asia, the Japanese invade and occupy Laos with the cooperation of pro-Vichy French colonial authorities.	The Japanese occupy Laos then force the king to declare independence; a nationalist resistance movement, the Lao Issara, takes shape and forms an interim government.

Party (ICP), founded by Ho Chi Minh in 1930, did not espouse separate independence for Vietnam, Laos and Cambodia. It only managed to recruit its first two Lao members in 1935.

It took the outbreak of war in Europe to weaken the French position in Indochina. A new aggressively nationalist government in Bangkok took advantage of this French weakness to try to regain territory 'lost' 50 years before. It renamed Siam Thailand, and opened hostilities. A Japanese-brokered peace agreement deprived Laos of its territories west of the Mekong, much to Lao anger.

To counter pan-Tai propaganda from Bangkok, the French encouraged Lao nationalism. Under an agreement between Japan and the Vichy French administration in Indochina, French rule continued, although Japanese forces had freedom of movement. The Japanese were in place, therefore, when in early 1945 they began to suspect the French of shifting their allegiance to the Allies. On 9 March the Japanese struck in a lightning coup de force throughout Indochina, interning all French military and civilian personnel. Only in Laos did a few French soldiers manage to slip into the jungle to maintain some resistance, along with their Lao allies.

Paths to Conflagration: Fifty Years of Diplomacy and Warfare in Laos, Thailand and Vietnam, 1778–1828 (1998), by Mayoury Ngaosyvathn and Pheuiphanh Ngaosyvathn, provides the best account of the Lao revolt against Bangkok, from a Lao perspective.

The Japanese ruled Laos for just six months before the atomic bombing of Hiroshima and Nagasaki brought WWII to an end. During this time they forced King Sisavang Vong to declare Lao independence, and a nationalist resistance movement took shape, known as the Lao Issara (Free Lao). When the Japanese surrendered on 15 August, the Lao Issara formed an interim government, under the direction of Prince Phetsarat, a cousin of the king. For the first time since the early 18th century, the country was unified. The king, however, thereupon repudiated his declaration of independence in the belief that Laos still needed French protection. The king dismissed Phetsarat as prime minister, so the provisional National Assembly of 45 prominent nationalists passed a motion deposing the king.

Behind these tensions were the French, who were determined to regain their Indochinese empire. In March 1946, while a truce was held in Vietnam between the Viet Minh and the French, French forces struck north to seize control of Laos. The Lao Issara government was forced to flee to exile in Bangkok, leaving the French to sign a modus vivendi with the king reaffirming the unity of Laos and extending the king's rule from Luang Prabang to all of Laos. West Bank territories seized by Thailand in 1940 were returned to Laos.

By 1949 something of a stalemate had developed between the French and the Viet Minh in the main theatre of war in Vietnam. In order to shore up their position in Laos, the French granted the Lao a greater measure of independence. A promise of amnesty for Issara leaders attracted most back to take part in the political process in Laos. Among the returnees was

1946	1949	1950	1953
The French reoccupy Laos, sending the Lao Issara government into exile.	France grants Laos partial independence within the Indochinese Federation and some of the Lao Issara leaders return to work for complete Lao independence from France.	Lao communists (the Pathet Lao) form a 'Resistance Government'. Souphanouvong becomes the public face of the Resistance Government and president of the Free Laos Front.	The Franco–Lao Treaty of Amity and Association grants full independence to Laos and a Lao delegation attends a conference in Geneva where a regroupment area is set aside for Pathet Lao Forces.

Souvanna Phouma, a younger brother of Phetsarat, who remained in Thailand. Meanwhile, Souphanouvong, a half-brother of the two princes, led his followers to join the Viet Minh and keep up the anticolonial struggle.

Rise of the Pathet Lao

The decisions of the three princes to go their separate ways divided the Lao Issara. Those members who returned to Laos continued to work for complete Lao independence from France, but within the legal framework. Those who joined the Viet Minh did so in pursuit of an altogether different political goal – expulsion of the French and formation of a Marxist regime. Their movement became known as the Pathet Lao (Land of the Lao), after the title of the Resistance Government of Pathet Lao, set up with Viet Minh support in August 1950.

The architect of the Lao Issara–Viet Minh alliance was Prince Souphanouvong. In August 1950, Souphanouvong became the public face of the Resistance Government and president of the Free Laos Front (Naeo Lao Issara), successor to the disbanded Lao Issara. Real power lay, however, with two other men, both of whom were members (as Souphanouvong then was not) of the Indochinese Communist Party (ICP). They were Kaysone Phomvihane, in charge of defence, and Nouhak Phoumsavan, with the portfolio of economy and finance.

By this time the whole complexion of the First Indochina War had changed with the 1949 victory of communism in China. As Chinese weapons flowed to the Viet Minh, the war widened and the French were forced onto the defensive. The siege of Dien Bien Phu, close to the Lao border in Northern Vietnam, emerged as the decisive battle of the First Indochina War. The isolated French garrison was surrounded by Viet Minh forces, which pounded the base with artillery hidden in the hills. Supplied only from the air, the French held out for over two months before surrendering on 7 May. The following day a conference opened in Geneva that eventually brought the curtain down on the French colonial period in Indochina.

Division & Unity

At the Geneva Conference it was agreed to temporarily divide Vietnam into north and south, Cambodia was left undivided, and in Laos two northeastern provinces (Hua Phan and Phongsali) were set aside as regroupment areas for Pathet Lao forces. There the Pathet Lao consolidated their political and military organisation, while negotiating with the Royal Lao Government (RLG) to reintegrate the two provinces into a unified Lao state.

The first thing Pathet Lao leaders did was to establish the Marxist-leaning Lao People's Party (LPP) in 1955 (later renamed the Lao People's Revolutionary Party; LPRP). Today, it remains the ruling party of the Lao People's Democratic Republic (Lao PDR). The LPP established a broad

Kaysone Phomvihane was born in central Laos. As his father was Vietnamese and his mother Lao, he had a Vietnamese surname. He personally adopted the name Phomvihane, which is Lao for Brahmavihara, a series of four divine states – an interesting choice for a committed Marxist.

1955	1957	1958	1960
Pathet Lao leaders form the Lao People's Party (later the Lao People's Revolutionary Party) with a broad political front called the Lao Patriotic Front (LPF).	The First Coalition Government of National Union is formed and collapses after a financial and political crisis.	The government falls and comes under the control of the right-wing, US-backed Committee for the Defence of National Interests (CDNI).	Guerrilla warfare covers large areas. A neutralist coup d'état is followed by the battle for Vientiane.

THE 'SECRET ARMY' & THE HMONG

After Laos gained independence in 1953, the US trained and supplied the Royal Lao Army as part of its strategy to combat communism in Southeast Asia. In 1961 Central Intelligence Agency (CIA) agents made contact with the Hmong minority living on and around the Plain of Jars. They spread a simple message – 'Beware of the Vietnamese; they will take your land' – handed out weapons and gave basic training. There were also some vague promises of Hmong autonomy. To protect more vulnerable communities, several thousand Hmong decided to relocate to mountain bases to the south of the plain. Their leader was a young Hmong army officer named Vang Pao.

In October 1961 President John F Kennedy gave the order to recruit a force of 11,000 Hmong under the command of Vang Pao. They were trained by several hundred US and Thai Special Forces advisors and parachuted arms and food supplies by Air America, all under the supervision of the CIA.

With the neutralisation of Laos and formation of the second coalition government in 1962, US military personnel were officially withdrawn. Even as it signed the 1962 Geneva Agreements, however, the US continued its covert operations, in particular the supply and training of the 'secret army' for guerrilla warfare. The CIA's secret headquarters was at Long Cheng, but the largest Hmong settlement, with a population of several thousand, was at Sam Thong.

Over the next 12 years the Hmong 'secret army' fought a continuous guerrilla campaign against heavily armed North Vietnamese regular army troops occupying the Plain of Jars. They were supported throughout by the US, an operation kept secret from the American public until 1970. So, while American forces fought in Vietnam, a 'Secret War' was also being fought in Laos. The Hmong fought because of their distrust of the communists, and in the hope that the US would support Hmong autonomy.

As the war dragged on, so many Hmong were killed that it became difficult to find recruits. Boys as young as 12 were sent to war. The 'secret army' was bolstered by recruits from other minority groups, including Yao (Mien) and Khamu, and by whole battalions of Thai volunteers. By the early 1970s it had grown to more than 30,000 men, about a third of them Thai.

When a ceasefire was signed in 1973, prior to formation of the third coalition government, the 'secret army' was officially disbanded. Thai volunteers returned home and Hmong units were absorbed into the Royal Lao Army. Hmong casualty figures have been put at 12,000 dead and 30,000 more wounded, but may well have been higher.

Years of warfare had bred deep distrust, however, and as many as 120,000 Hmong out of a population of some 300,000 fled Laos after 1975, rather than live under the Lao communist regime. Most were resettled in the US. Among the Hmong who sided with the Pathet Lao, several now hold senior positions in the Lao People's Revolutionary Party (LPRP) and in government.

1961	1962	1964	1964–73
Orders given to the Central Intelligence Agency (CIA) to form a 'secret army' in northern Laos with links to the American war in Vietnam.	The Geneva Agreement on Laos establishes the second coalition government that balances Pathet Lao and rightist representation with neutralist voting powers.	The US begins air war against ground targets in Laos, mostly against communist positions on the Plain of Jars.	The Second Indochina War spills over into Laos. Both the North Vietnamese and US presence increases dramatically and bombing extends along the length of Laos.

political front, called the Lao Patriotic Front (LPF), with Souphanou-vong as its president and Kaysone secretary-general. Together with other members of the 'team' they led the Lao revolution throughout its '30-year struggle' (1945 to 1975) for power.

The first priority for the RLG was to reunify the country with a political solution palatable to the Pathet Lao. In its remote base areas, the Pathet Lao was entirely dependent for weapons and most other kinds of assistance on the North Vietnamese, whose own agenda was the reunification of Vietnam under communist rule. Meanwhile, the RLG became increasingly dependent on the US, which soon took over from France as its principal aid donor. Thus Laos became the cockpit for Cold War enmity.

The Lao politician with the task of finding a way through both ideological differences and foreign interference was Souvanna Phouma. As prime minister of the RLG, he negotiated a deal with his half-brother Souphanouvong which saw two Pathet Lao ministers and two deputy ministers included in a coalition government. The Pathet Lao provinces were returned to the royal administration. Elections were held, in which the LPF did surprisingly well. And the US was furious.

Between 1955 and 1958, the US gave Laos US$120 million, or four times what France had provided over the previous eight years. Laos was almost entirely dependent, therefore, on American largesse to survive. When that aid was withheld, as it was in August 1958 in response to the inclusion of Pathet Lao ministers in the government, Laos was plunged into a financial and political crisis. As a result, the first coalition government collapsed after just eight months.

As guerrilla warfare resumed over large areas, moral objections were raised against Lao killing Lao. On 9 August 1960, the diminutive commanding officer of the elite Second Paratroop Batallion of the Royal Lao Army seized power in Vientiane while almost the entire Lao government was in Luang Prabang making arrangements for the funeral of King Sisavang Vong. Captain Kong Le announced to the world that Laos was returning to a policy of neutrality, and demanded that Souvanna Phouma be reinstated as prime minister. King Sisavang Vatthana acquiesced, but General Phoumi refused to take part, and flew to central Laos where he instigated opposition to the new government.

In this, he had the support of the Thai government and the US Central Intelligence Agency (CIA), which supplied him with cash and weapons. The neutralist government still claimed to be the legitimate government of Laos, and as such received arms, via Vietnam, from the Soviet Union. Most of these found their way to the Pathet Lao, however. Throughout the country large areas fell under the control of communist forces. The US sent troops to Thailand, in case communist forces should attempt to cross

1968	1974	1975	1979
The Tet Offensive by the Viet Cong in neighbouring Vietnam turns public opinion in the US against the Second Indochina War.	Finally a 1973 ceasefire in Vietnam means an end to fighting in Laos and the formation of the third coalition government.	Communists seize power and declare the Lao People's Democratic Republic (LPDR). This ends 650 years of the Lao monarchy.	Agricultural cooperatives are abandoned and first economic reforms introduced.

the Mekong, and it looked for a while as if the major commitment of US troops in Southeast Asia would be to Laos rather than Vietnam.

The Second Indochina War

At this point the new US administration of President John F Kennedy had second thoughts about fighting a war in Laos. In an about-face it decided instead to back Lao neutrality. In May 1961 a new conference on Laos was convened in Geneva.

Delegates of the 14 participating countries reassembled in Geneva in July 1962 to sign the international agreement guaranteeing Lao neutrality and forbidding the presence of all foreign military personnel. In Laos the new coalition government took office buoyed by popular goodwill and hope.

Within months, however, cracks began to appear in the facade of the coalition. The problem was the war in Vietnam. Both the North Vietnamese and the Americans were jockeying for strategic advantage, and neither was going to let Lao neutrality get in the way. Despite the terms of the Geneva Agreements, both continued to provide their respective clients with arms and supplies. But no outside power did the same for the neutralists, who found themselves increasingly squeezed between left and right.

By the end of 1963, as each side denounced the other for violating the Geneva Agreements, the second coalition government had irrevocably broken down. It was in the interests of all powers, however, to preserve the facade of Lao neutrality, and international diplomatic support was brought to bear for Souvanna Phouma to prevent rightist generals from seizing power in coups mounted in 1964 and 1965.

In 1964 the US began its air war over Laos, with strafing and bombing of communist positions on the Plain of Jars. As North Vietnamese infiltration picked up along the Ho Chi Minh Trail, bombing was extended across all of Laos. According to official figures, the US dropped 2,093,100 tons of bombs on 580,944 sorties. The total cost was US$7.2 billion, or US$2 million a day for nine years. No one knows how many people died, but one-third of the population of 2.1 million became internal refugees.

During the 1960s both the North Vietnamese and the US presence increased exponentially. By 1968 an estimated 40,000 North Vietnamese regular army troops were based in Laos to keep the Ho Chi Minh Trail open and support some 35,000 Pathet Lao forces. The Royal Lao Army then numbered 60,000 (entirely paid for and equipped by the US), Vang Pao's forces (see box, p254) were half that number (still under the direction of the CIA) and Kong Le's neutralists numbered 10,000. Lao forces on both sides were entirely funded by their foreign backers. For five more years this proxy war dragged on, until the ceasefire of 1973.

The turning point for the war in Vietnam was the 1968 Tet Offensive, which brought home to the American people the realisation that the war

1986	1987	1991	1995
The 'New Economic Mechanism' opens the way for a market economy and foreign investment.	A three-month border war breaks out between Laos and Thailand, ending in a truce in February 1988.	The constitution of the Lao PDR is proclaimed. General Khamtay Siphandone becomes state president.	Luang Prabang is World Heritage–listed. Wat Phu, the ancient Khmer temple near Champasak, is listed shortly after.

was unwinnable by military means, and convinced them of the need for a political solution. The effect in Laos, however, was to intensify both the air war and fighting on the Plain of Jars. When bombing was suspended over North Vietnam, the US Air Force concentrated all its efforts on Laos. The Pathet Lao leadership was forced underground, into the caves of Vieng Xai.

By mid-1972, when serious peace moves were underway, some four-fifths of the country was under communist control. In peace as in war, what happened in Laos depended on what happened in Vietnam. Not until a ceasefire came into effect in Vietnam in January 1973 could the fighting end in Laos. Then the political wrangling began. Not until September was an agreement reached on the composition of the third coalition government and how it would operate.

Revolution & Reform

In April 1975, first Phnom Penh and then Saigon fell to communist forces. Immediately the Pathet Lao brought political pressure to bear on the right in Laos. Escalating street demonstrations forced leading rightist politicians and generals to flee the country. Throughout the country, town after town was peacefully 'liberated' by Pathet Lao forces, culminating with Vientiane in August.

Souvanna Phouma, who could see the writing on the wall, cooperated with the Pathet Lao in order to prevent further bloodshed. Hundreds of senior military officers and civil servants voluntarily flew off to remote camps for 'political re-education', in the belief that they would be there only months at most, but hundreds of these inmates remained in re-education camps for several years.

In November an extraordinary meeting of what was left of the third coalition government bowed to the inevitable and demanded formation of a 'popular democratic regime'. Under pressure, the king agreed to abdicate, and on 2 December a National Congress of People's Representatives assembled by the party proclaimed the end of the 650-year-old Lao monarchy and the establishment of the Lao PDR. Kaysone Phomvihane, who in addition to leading the LPRP became prime minister in the new Marxist-Leninist government. Souphanouvong was named state president.

The new regime was organised in accordance with Soviet and North Vietnamese models. The government and bureaucracy were under the strict direction of the Party and its seven-member politburo. Immediately the Party moved to restrict liberal freedoms of speech and assembly, and to nationalise the economy. As inflation soared, price controls were introduced. In response, around 10% of the population, including virtually all the educated class, fled across the Mekong to Thailand as refugees, setting Lao development back at least a generation.

The Politics of Ritual and Remembrance: Laos Since 1975 (1998), by Grant Evans, provides a penetrating study of Lao political culture, including attitudes to Buddhism and the 'cult' of communist leader Kaysone.

1997	1998–2000	2000	2001
Laos joins the Association of Southeast Asian Nations (ASEAN).	The Asian economic crisis seriously impacts on the Lao economy. China and Vietnam come to the country's aid with loans and advice.	The economic crisis sparks some political unrest. Anti-government Lao rebels attack a customs post on the Thai border. Five are killed.	A series of small bomb explosions worries the regime, which responds by increasing security.

The Hmong insurgency dragged on for another 30 years. In 1977, fearing the king might escape his virtual house arrest to lead resistance, the authorities arrested him and his family and sent them to Vieng Xai, the old Pathet Lao wartime headquarters. There they were forced to labour in the fields. The king, queen and crown prince all eventually died, probably of malaria and malnutrition, although no official explanation of their deaths has ever been offered.

By 1979 it was clear that policies had to change. Kaysone announced that people could leave cooperatives and farm their own land, and that private enterprise would be permitted. Reforms were insufficient to improve the Lao economy. Over the next few years a struggle took place within the Party about what to do. By the advent of Mikhail Gorbachev in 1985, the Soviet Union was getting tired of propping up the Lao regime, and was embarking on its own momentous reforms. Meanwhile, Vietnam had Cambodia to worry about. Eventually Kaysone convinced the party to follow the Chinese example and open the economy up to market forces while retaining a tight monopoly on political power. The economic reforms were known as the 'new economic mechanism', and were enacted in November 1986.

Post-War Laos: The Politics of Culture, History and Identity (2006), by Vatthana Pholsena, expertly examines how ethnicity, history and identity intersect in Laos.

Economic improvement was slow in coming, partly because relations with Thailand remained strained. In August 1987 the two countries fought a brief border war over disputed territory, which left 1000 people dead. The following year, relations with both Thailand and China were patched up. The first elections for a national assembly were held, and a constitution at last promulgated. Slowly a legal framework was put into place, and by the early 1990s, foreign direct investment was picking up and the economy was on the mend.

Modern Laos

In 1992 Kaysone Phomvihane died. He had been the leading figure in Lao communism for more than a quarter of a century. The LPRP managed the transition to a new leadership with smooth efficiency, much to the disappointment of expatriate Lao communities abroad. General Khamtay Siphandone became both president of the LPRP and prime minister. Later he relinquished the latter to become state president. His rise signalled control of the Party by the revolutionary generation of military leaders. When Khamtay stepped down in 2006, he was succeeded by his close comrade, General Chummaly Sayasone.

The economic prosperity of the mid-1990s rested on increased investment and foreign aid, on which Laos remained very dependent. The Lao PDR enjoyed friendly relations with all its neighbours. Relations with Vietnam remained particularly close, but were balanced by much-improved relations with China. Relations with Bangkok were bumpy at times, but

2004	2006	2009	2010
Security is still tight when Laos hosts the 10th ASEAN summit in Vientiane, the largest gathering of world leaders ever assembled in Laos.	The Eighth Congress of the Lao People's Revolutionary Party and National Assembly elections endorse a new political leadership.	Laos hosts the 25th Southeast Asia Games. Four thousand Hmong refugees are forcibly repatriated from Thailand.	The Nam Theun II hydropower dam, the largest in mainland Southeast Asia, begins production.

Thailand was a principal source of foreign direct investment. In 1997, Laos joined the Association of Southeast Asian Nations (ASEAN).

The good times came to an end with the Asian economic crisis of the late 1990s. The collapse of the Thai baht led to inflation of the Lao kip, to which it was largely tied through trading relations. The Lao regime took two lessons from this crisis: one was about the dangers of market capitalism, the other was that its real friends were China and Vietnam, both of which came to its aid with loans and advice.

The economic crisis sparked some political unrest. A small student demonstration calling for an end to the monopoly of political power by the LPRP was ruthlessly crushed and its leaders given long prison sentences.

In 2003 Western journalists for the first time made contact with Hmong insurgents. Their reports revealed an insurgency on the point of collapse. Renewed military pressure forced some Hmong to surrender, while others made their way to refuge in Thailand. However, the Thai classified the Hmong as illegal immigrants; negotiations for resettlement in third countries stalled, and in December 2009, despite widespread international condemnation, some 4000 Hmong were forcibly repatriated to Laos.

Political & Economic Inspiration

In the decade to 2010, China greatly increased investment in Laos to equal that of Thailand. Japan remained the largest aid donor. However, Chinese companies invested in major projects in mining, hydropower and plantation agriculture and timber. Meanwhile, cross-border trade grew apace. Increased economic power brought political influence at the expense of Vietnam, though Lao-Vietnamese relations remained close and warm. Senior Lao Party cadres still take courses in Marxism-Leninism in Vietnam, although their economic inspiration is more likely from the mighty northern neighbour, China.

In April 2016 former Vice President Bounnhang Vorachith became president of the Lao PDR, establishing himself as a force against corruption. Calling for a halt on logging, making a pledge to reforest 70% of Laos by 2020 and (allegedly) sacking many of his minsters and replacing them with people he could trust, he set the stage for the August gathering of ASEAN, held in Laos and attended by former US President Barack Obama. This followed high-profile visits from Hillary Clinton in 2010 and John Kerry in 2015. America seemed keen to signal to China it intended to take an interest in Laos' future as the Asian superpower pushed on with funding dams and high-speed rail lines through Laos, placing the diminutive country ever more in its debt, as a key conduit to Southeast Asia in its 'new Silk Road' trade strategy.

Bamboo Palace: Discovering the Lost Dynasty of Laos (2003) by Christopher Kremmer builds on his personal travelogue told in *Stalking the Elephant Kings* (1997) to try to discover the fate of the Lao royal family.

2012	2013	2016	2016
Internationally acclaimed community-development worker Sombath Somphone disappears. The Lao Government deny responsibility for his disappearance.	Work begins on the Xayaboury Dam, the first dam to be built on the Mekong River in Laos. Cambodia and Vietnam raise objections.	Vice President of Laos Bounnhang Vorachith becomes Laos' new supreme leader.	US President Barack Obama becomes the first sitting president to visit Laos, pledging US$90m over the next three years for UXO clean-up.

People & Culture

It's hard to think of any other country with a population as laid-back as Laos – bor ben nyăng (no problem) could be the national motto. On the surface at least, nothing seems to faze the Lao people, whose national character is a complex combination of culture, environment and religion.

The National Psyche

To a large degree 'Lao-ness' is defined by Buddhism, specifically Theravada Buddhism, which emphasises the cooling of human passions. Thus strong emotions are a taboo in Lao society. *Kamma* (karma), more than devotion, prayer or hard work, is believed to determine one's lot in life, so the Lao tend not to get too worked up over the future. It's a trait often perceived by outsiders as a lack of ambition.

Lao commonly express the notion that 'too much work is bad for your brain' and they often say they feel sorry for people who 'think too much'. Education in general isn't highly valued, although this attitude is changing with modernisation and greater access to opportunities beyond the country's borders. Avoiding any undue psychological stress, however, remains a cultural norm. From the typical Lao perspective, unless an activity – whether work or play – contains an element of *móoan* (fun), it will probably lead to stress.

The contrast between the Lao and the Vietnamese is an example of how the Annamite Chain has served as a cultural fault line dividing Indo-Asia and Sino-Asia, as well as a geographic divide. The French summed it up as: 'The Vietnamese plant the rice, the Cambodians tend the rice and the Lao listen to it grow'. And while this saying wasn't meant as a compliment, a good number of French colonialists found the Lao way too seductive to resist, and stayed on.

The Lao have always been quite receptive to outside assistance and foreign investment, since it promotes a certain degree of economic development without demanding a corresponding increase in productivity. The Lao government wants all the trappings of modern technology – the skyscrapers seen on socialist propaganda billboards – without having to give up Lao traditions, including the *móoan* philosophy. The challenge for Laos is to find a balance between cultural preservation and the development of new attitudes that will lead the country towards a measure of self-sufficiency.

Laos: Culture and Society (2000), by Grant Evans (ed), brings together a dozen essays on Lao culture, among them a profile of a self-exiled Lao family that eventually returned to Laos, and two well-researched studies of the modernisation and politicalisation of the Lao language.

Lifestyle

Maybe it's because everything closes early, even in the capital, that just about everyone in Laos gets up before 6am. Their day might begin with a quick breakfast, at home or from a local noodle seller, before work. In Lao Loum (Lowland Lao) and other Buddhist areas, the morning also sees monks collecting alms, usually from women who hand out rice and vegetables outside their homes in return for a blessing.

School-age children will walk to a packed classroom housed in a basic building with one or two teachers. Secondary students often board during the week because there are fewer secondary schools and it can be too far to commute. Almost any family who can afford it pays for their kids to learn English, which is seen as a near-guarantee of future employment.

Given that most Lao people live in rural communities, work is usually some form of manual labour. Depending on the season, and the person's location and gender (women and men have clearly defined tasks when it comes to farming), work might be planting or harvesting rice or other crops. Unlike neighbouring Vietnam, the Lao usually only harvest one crop of rice each year, meaning there are a couple of busy periods followed by plenty of time when life can seem very laid-back.

During these quiet periods, men will fish, hunt and repair the house, while women might gather flora and fauna from the forest, weave fabrics and collect firewood. At these times there's something wonderfully social and uncorrupted about arriving in a village mid-afternoon, sitting in the front of the local 'store' and sharing a *lòw-lów* (rice whisky) or two with the locals, without feeling like you're stealing their time.

Where vices are concerned, *lòw-lów* is the drug of choice for most Lao, particularly in rural areas where average incomes are so low that Beerlao is beyond most budgets. Opium is the most high profile of the other drugs traditionally used – and tolerated – in Laos, though recent crop-clearing has made it less available. In cities, *yaba* (methamphethamine), in particular, has become popular among young people.

Because average incomes are low in Laos (US$111 per month), despite the minimum wage being increased by 44% in 2015, the Lao typically socialise as families, pooling their resources to enjoy a *bun wat* (temple festival) or picnic at the local waterfall together. The Lao tend to live in extended families, with three or more generations sharing one house or compound, and dine together sitting on mats on the floor with rice and dishes shared by all.

Most Lao don some portion of the traditional garb during ceremonies and celebrations: the men a *pàh bęeang* (shoulder sash), the women a similar sash, tight-fitting blouse and *pàh nung* (sarong). In everyday life men wear neat but unremarkable shirt-and-trousers combinations. However, it's still normal for women to wear the *pàh nung* or *sin* (sarong). Other ethnicities living in Laos, particularly Chinese and Vietnamese women, will wear the *pàh nung* when they visit a government office, or risk having any civic requests denied.

Population

Laos has one of the lowest population densities in Asia, but the number of people has more than doubled in the last 30 years, and continues to grow quickly. One-third of the country's seven million inhabitants live in cities in the Mekong River valley, chiefly Vientiane, Luang Prabang, Savannakhet and Pakse. Another one-third live along other major rivers.

This rapid population growth comes despite the fact that about 10% of the population fled the country after the 1975 communist takeover. Vientiane and Luang Prabang lost the most inhabitants, with approximately a quarter of the population of Luang Prabang going abroad. During the last couple of decades this emigration trend has been reversed so that the influx of immigrants (mostly repatriated Lao, but also Chinese, Vietnamese and other nationalities) now exceeds the number of émigrés.

Most expatriate Westerners living in Laos are temporary employees of multilateral and bilateral aid organisations. A smaller number are employed by foreign companies involved in mining, petroleum, hydropower and the tourism industry.

The Laos Cultural Profile (www.culturalprofiles.net/laos) was established by Visiting Arts and the Ministry of Information & Culture of Laos. It covers a broad range of cultural aspects, from architecture to music, and is an easy entry point into Lao culture.

PEOPLE & CULTURE POPULATION

Ethnic Groups

Laos is often described as less a nation state than a conglomeration of tribes and languages. And depending on who you talk with, that conglomeration consists of between 49 and 134 different ethnic groups. The lower figure is officially used by the government.

While the tribal groups are many and varied, the Lao traditionally divide themselves into four categories: Lao Loum, Lao Tai, Lao Thoeng and Lao Soung. These classifications loosely reflect the altitudes at which the groups live, and, by implication (it's not always accurate), their cultural proclivities. To address some of these inaccuracies, the Lao government recently reclassified ethnic groups into three major language families: Austro-Tai, Austro-Asiatic and Sino-Tibetan. However, many people do not know which language family they come from, so here we'll stick with the more commonly understood breakdown.

Just over half the population are ethnic Lao or Lao Loum (Lowland Lao), and these are clearly the most dominant group. Of the rest, 10% to 20% are tribal Tai; 20% to 30% are Lao Thoeng ('Upland Lao' or lower-mountain dwellers, mostly of proto-Malay or Mon-Khmer descent); and 10% to 20% are Lao Soung ('Highland Lao', mainly Hmong or Mien tribes who live higher up).

The Lao government has an alternative three-way split, in which the Lao Tai are condensed into the Lao Loum group. This triumvirate is represented on the back of every 1000 kip bill, in national costume, from left to right: Lao Soung, Lao Loum and Lao Thoeng.

Small Tibeto-Burman hill-tribe groups in Laos include the Lisu, Lahu, Lolo, Akha and Phu Noi. They are sometimes classified as Lao Thoeng, but like the Lao Soung they live in the mountains of northern Laos.

Lao Loum

Due to Laos' ethnic diversity, 'Lao culture' only exists among the Lao Loum (Lowland Lao), who represent about half the population. Lao Loum culture predominates in the cities, towns and villages of the Mekong River valley.

The dominant ethnic group is the Lao Loum, who live in the fertile plains of the Mekong River valley or lower tributaries of the Mekong. Thanks to their superior numbers and living conditions, they have dominated the smaller ethnic groups for centuries. Their language is the national language; their religion, Buddhism, is the national religion; and many of their customs, including the eating of sticky rice and the *baqsii* (sacred string-tying ceremonies), are interpreted as those of the Lao nation, even though they play no part in the lives of many other ethnic groups.

Lao Loum culture has traditionally consisted of a sedentary, subsistence lifestyle based on wet-rice cultivation. The people live in raised homes and, like most Austro-Tais, are Theravada Buddhists who retain strong elements of animist spirit worship.

The distinction between 'Lao' and 'Thai' is a rather recent historical phenomenon, especially considering that 80% of all those who speak a language recognised as 'Lao' reside in northeastern Thailand. Even Lao living in Laos refer idiomatically to different Lao Loum groups as 'Tai' or 'Thai', such as Thai Luang Phabang (Lao from Luang Prabang).

Lao Tai

Although they're closely related to the Lao, these Tai (or sometimes Thai) subgroups have resisted absorption into mainstream Lao culture and tend to subdivide themselves according to smaller tribal distinctions. Like the Lao Loum, they live along river valleys, but the Lao Tai have chosen to reside in upland valleys rather than in the lowlands of the Mekong floodplains.

Depending on their location, they cultivate dry (mountain) rice as well as wet (irrigated) rice. The Lao Tai also mix Theravada Buddhism and animism, but tend to place more importance on spirit worship than do the Lao Loum.

Generally speaking, the various Lao Tai groups are distinguished from one another by the predominant colour of their clothing, or by the general area of habitation; for example, Tai Dam (Black Tai), Tai Khao (White Tai), Tai Pa (Forest Tai), Tai Neua (Northern Tai) and so on.

Lao Thoeng

The Lao Thoeng are a loose affiliation of mostly Austro-Asiatic peoples who live on mid-altitude mountain slopes in northern and southern Laos. The largest group is the Khamu, followed by the Htin, Lamet and smaller numbers of Laven, Katu, Katang, Alak and other Mon-Khmer groups in the south. The Lao Thoeng are also known by the pejorative term *khàa,* which means 'slave' or 'servant'. This is because they were used as indentured labour by migrating Austro-Thai peoples in earlier centuries and more recently by the Lao monarchy. They still often work as labourers for the Lao Soung.

The Lao Thoeng have a much lower standard of living than any of the three other groups. Most trade between the Lao Thoeng and other Lao is carried out by barter.

The Htin (also called Lawa) and Khamu languages are closely related, and both groups are thought to have been in Laos long before the arrival of the Lowland Lao, tribal Tai or Lao Soung. During the Lao New Year celebrations in Luang Prabang the Lowland Lao offer a symbolic tribute to the Khamu as their historical predecessors and as 'guardians of the land'.

Lao Soung

The Lao Soung include the hill tribes who live at the highest altitudes. Of all the peoples of Laos, they are the most recent immigrants, having come from Myanmar (Burma), southern China and Tibet within the last 150 years.

The largest group is the Hmong, also called Miao or Meo, who number more than 300,000 in four main subgroups: the White Hmong, Striped Hmong, Red Hmong and Black Hmong. The colours refer to certain clothing details and these groups are found in the nine provinces of the north, plus Bolikhamsai in central Laos.

The agricultural staples of the Hmong are dry rice and corn raised by the slash-and-burn method. The Hmong also breed cattle, pigs, water buffalo and chickens, traditionally for barter rather than sale. For years their only cash crop was opium, and they grew and manufactured more than any other group in Laos. However, an aggressive eradication program run by the government, with support from the US, has eliminated most of the crop. The resulting loss of a tradeable commodity has hit many Hmong communities very hard. The Hmong are most numerous in Hua Phan, Xieng Khuang, Luang Prabang and northern Vientiane Provinces.

The second-largest group are the Mien (also called Iu Mien, Yao and Man), who live mainly in Luang Nam Tha, Luang Prabang, Bokeo, Udomxai and Phongsali. The Mien, like the Hmong, have traditionally cultivated opium poppies. Replacement crops, including coffee, are taking time to bed in and generate income.

The Mien and Hmong have many ethnic and linguistic similarities, and both groups are predominantly animist. The Hmong are considered more aggressive and warlike than the Mien, however, and as such were perfect for the CIA-trained special Royal Lao Government forces in the 1960s and early 1970s. Large numbers of Hmong–Mien left Laos and fled abroad after 1975.

Other Asians

As elsewhere in Southeast Asia, the Chinese have been migrating to Laos for centuries to work as merchants and traders. Most come directly from

Yunnan but more recently many have also arrived from Vietnam. Estimates of their numbers vary from 2% to 5% of the total population. At least half of all permanent Chinese residents in Laos are said to live in Vientiane and Savannakhet. There are also thousands of Chinese migrant workers in the far north.

Substantial numbers of Vietnamese live in all the provinces bordering Vietnam and in the cities of Vientiane, Savannakhet and Pakse. For the most part, Vietnamese residents in Laos work as traders and own small businesses, although there continues to be a small Vietnamese military presence in Xieng Khuang and Hua Phan Provinces. Small numbers of Cambodians live in southern Laos.

Religion
Buddhism

About 60% of the people of Laos are Theravada Buddhists, the majority being Lowland Lao, with a sprinkling of tribal Tais. Theravada Buddhism was apparently introduced to Luang Prabang (then known as Muang Sawa) in the late 13th or early 14th centuries, although there may have been contact with Mahayana Buddhism during the 8th to 10th centuries and with Tantric Buddhism even earlier.

King Visoun, a successor of the first monarch of Lan Xang, King Fa Ngum, declared Buddhism the state religion after accepting the Pha Bang

POST-REVOLUTION BUDDHISM

During the 1964–73 war years, both sides sought to use Buddhism to legitimise their cause. By the early 1970s, the Lao Patriotic Front (LPF) was winning this propaganda war as more and more monks threw their support behind the communists.

Despite this, major changes were in store for the Sangha (monastic order) following the 1975 takeover. Initially, Buddhism was banned as a primary-school subject and people were forbidden to make merit by giving food to monks. Monks were also forced to till the land and raise animals in direct violation of their monastic vows.

Mass dissatisfaction among the faithful prompted the government to rescind the ban on the feeding of monks in 1976. By the end of that year, the government was not only allowing traditional giving of alms, it was offering a daily ration of rice directly to the Sangha.

In 1992, in what was perhaps its biggest endorsement of Buddhism since the Revolution, the government replaced the hammer-and-sickle emblem that crowned Laos' national seal with a drawing of Pha That Luang, the country's holiest Buddhist symbol.

Today, the Department of Religious Affairs (DRA) controls the Sangha and ensures that Buddhism is taught in accordance with Marxist principles. All monks must undergo political indoctrination as part of their monastic training, and all canonical and extracanonical Buddhist texts have been subject to 'editing' by the DRA. Monks are also forbidden to promote *pěe* (earth spirit) worship, which has been officially banned in Laos along with *săinyasąht* (magic). The cult of *khwăn* (the 32 guardian spirits attached to mental/physical functions), however, has not been tampered with.

One major change in Lao Buddhism was the abolition of the Thammayut sect. Formerly, the Sangha in Laos was divided into two sects, the Mahanikai and the Thammayut (as in Thailand). The Thammayut is a minority sect that was begun by Thailand's King Mongkut. The Pathet Lao saw it as a tool of the Thai monarchy (and hence US imperialism) for infiltrating Lao political culture.

For several years all Buddhist literature written in Thai was also banned, severely curtailing the teaching of Buddhism in Laos. This ban has since been lifted and Lao monks are even allowed to study at Buddhist universities throughout Thailand. However, the Thammayut ban remains and has resulted in a much weaker emphasis on meditation, considered the spiritual heart of Buddhist practice in most Theravada countries. Overall, monastic discipline in Laos is far more relaxed than it was before 1975.

Buddha image from his Khmer sponsors. Today the Pha Bang is kept at the Royal Palace in Luang Prabang. Buddhism was fairly slow to spread throughout Laos, even among the lowland peoples, who were reluctant to accept the faith instead of, or even alongside, *pĕe* (earth spirit) worship.

Theravada Buddhism is an earlier and, according to its followers, less corrupted school of Buddhism than the Mahayana schools found in east Asia and the Himalayas. It's sometimes referred to as the 'southern' school since it took the southern route from India through Sri Lanka and Southeast Asia.

Theravada doctrine stresses the three principal aspects of existence: *dukkha* (suffering, unsatisfactoriness, disease), *anicca* (impermanence, transience of all things) and *anatta* (nonsubstantiality or nonessentiality of reality; no permanent 'soul'). Comprehension of *anicca* reveals that no experience, state of mind or physical object lasts. Trying to hold onto experience, states of mind and physical objects that are constantly changing creates *dukkha*. *Anatta* is the understanding that there is no part of the changing world we can point to and say 'This is me' or 'This is God' or 'This is the soul'.

The ultimate goal of Theravada Buddhism is *nibbana* (nirvana in Sanskrit), which literally means the 'blowing-out' or 'extinction' of all causes of *dukkha*. Effectively it means an end to all corporeal or even heavenly existence, which is forever subject to suffering and which is conditioned from moment to moment by *kamma* (karma, 'intentional action'). In reality, most Lao Buddhists aim for rebirth in a 'better' existence rather than the goal of *nibbana*. By feeding monks, giving donations to temples and performing regular worship at the local wat, Lao Buddhists acquire enough 'merit' (Lao *bun*) for their future lives. And it's in the pursuit of merit that you're most likely to see Lao Buddhism 'in action'. Watching monks walking through their neighbourhoods at dawn to collect offerings of food from people who are kneeling in front of their homes is a memorable experience.

Lao Buddhists don't visit the wat on a set day. Most often they'll visit on a *wan Sĭn* (ວັນສິນ), meaning 'Precept Day' (or rule day), which occur with every full, new and quarter moon (roughly every seven days). On such a visit, typical activities include the offering of lotus buds, incense and candles at various altars and bone reliquaries, offering food to the monks, meditating, and attending a *táirt* (*dhamma* talk) by the abbot.

Monks & Nuns

Unlike other religions in which priests or nuns make a lifelong commitment to their religious vocation, being a Buddhist monk or nun can be a much more transient experience. Socially, every Lao Buddhist male is expected to become a *kóo-bạh* (monk) for at least a short period in his life, optimally between the time he finishes school and starts a career or marries. Men or boys under 20 years of age may enter the Sangha (monastic order) as *náirn* (novices) and this is not unusual since a family earns merit when one of its sons takes robe and bowl. Traditionally the length of time spent in the wat is three months, during the *pansăh* (Buddhist lent), which coincides with the rainy season. However, nowadays men may spend as little as a week or 15 days to accrue merit as monks or novices. There are, of course, some monks who do devote all or most of their lives to the wat.

Spirit Cults

No matter where you are in Laos the practice of *pĕe* (spirit) worship, sometimes called animism, won't be far away. *Pĕe* worship predates Buddhism and despite being officially banned it remains the dominant non-Buddhist belief system. But for most Lao it is not a matter of Buddhism *or* spirit

Article 9 of the current Lao constitution forbids all religious proselytising, and the distribution of religious materials outside churches, temples or mosques is illegal. Foreigners caught distributing religious materials may be arrested and expelled from the country.

worship. Instead, established Buddhist beliefs coexist peacefully with respect for the *pěe* that are believed to inhabit natural objects.

An obvious example of this coexistence is the 'spirit houses', which are found in or outside almost every home. Spirit houses are often ornately decorated miniature temples, built as a home for the local spirit. Residents must share their space with the spirit and go to great lengths to keep it happy, offering enough incense and food that the spirit won't make trouble for them.

In Vientiane, Buddhism and spirit worship flourish side by side at Wat Si Muang. The central image at the temple is not a Buddha figure but the *lák méuang* (city pillar from the time of the Khmer empire), in which the guardian spirit for the city is believed to reside. Many local residents make daily offerings before the pillar, while at the same time praying to a Buddha figure. A form of *pěe* worship visitors can partake in is the *bąasǐi* ceremony.

Outside the Mekong River valley, the *pěe* cult is particularly strong among the tribal Tai, especially the Tai Dam, who pay special attention to a class of *pěe* called *then*. The *then* are earth spirits that preside not only over the plants and soil, but over entire districts as well. The Tai Dam also believe in the 32 *khwăn* (guardian spirits). *Mŏr* (master/shaman), who are specially trained in the propitiation and exorcism of spirits, preside at important Tai Dam festivals and ceremonies. It is possible to see some of the spiritual beliefs and taboos in action by staying in a Katang village during a trek into the forests of Dong Phu Vieng National Protected Area (NPA).

The Hmong–Mien tribes also practise animism, plus ancestral worship. Some Hmong groups recognise a pre-eminent spirit that presides over all earth spirits; others do not. The Akha, Lisu and other Tibeto-Burman groups mix animism and ancestor cults.

Lao Buddha: The Image and Its History (2000), by Somkiart Lopetcharat, is a large coffee-table book containing a wealth of information on the Lao interpretation of the Buddha figure.

Other Religions

A small number of Lao, mostly those of the remaining French-educated elite, are Christians. An even smaller number of Muslims live in Vientiane, mostly Arab and Indian merchants whose ancestry as Laos residents dates as far back as the 17th century. Vientiane also harbours a small community of Chams, Cambodian Muslims who fled Pol Pot's Kampuchea in the 1970s. In northern Laos there are pockets of Muslim Yunnanese, known among the Lao as *jęen hór*.

Women in Laos

For the women of Laos, roles and status vary significantly depending on their ethnicity, but it's fair to say that whatever group they come from they are seen as secondary to men. As you travel around Laos the evidence is overwhelming. While men's work is undoubtedly hard, women always seem to be working harder, for longer and with far less time for relaxing and socialising.

Lao Loum women gain limited benefits from bilateral inheritance patterns, whereby both women and men can inherit land and business ownership. This derives from a matrilocal tradition, where a husband joins the wife's family on marriage. Often the youngest daughter and her husband will live with and care for her parents until they die, when they inherit at least some of their land and business. However, even if a Lao Loum woman inherits her father's farmland, she will have only limited control over how it is used. Instead, her husband will have the final say on most major decisions, while she will be responsible for saving enough money to see the family through any crisis.

This fits with the cultural beliefs associated with Lao Buddhism, which commonly teaches that women must be reborn as men before they can attain nirvana, hence a woman's spiritual status is generally less than that of a man. Still, Lao Loum women enjoy a higher status than women from other ethnic groups, who become part of their husband's clan on marriage and rarely inherit anything.

Women in Laos face several other hurdles: fewer girls go to school than boys; women are relatively poorly represented in government and other senior positions; and although they make up more than half the workforce, pay is often lower than male equivalents. If a Lao woman divorces, no matter how fair her reasons, it's very difficult for her to find another husband unless he is older or foreign.

In the cities, however, things are changing as fast as wealth, education and exposure to foreign ideas allows, and in general women in cities are more confident and willing to engage with foreigners than their rural counterparts. Women are gradually pushing into more responsible positions, like Pany Yathortou, a Hmong woman chosen as President of the National Assembly.

Arts

The focus of most traditional art in Lao culture has been religious, specifically Buddhist. Yet, unlike the visual arts of Thailand, Myanmar and Cambodia, Lao art never encompassed a broad range of styles and periods, mainly because Laos has a much more modest history in terms of power and because it has only existed as a political entity for a short period. Furthermore, since Laos was intermittently dominated by its neighbours, much of the art that was produced was either destroyed or, as in the case of the Emerald Buddha, carted off by conquering armies.

Laos' relatively small and poor population, combined with a turbulent recent history, also goes some way towards explaining the absence of any strong tradition of contemporary art. This is slowly changing, and in Vientiane and Luang Prabang modern art in a variety of media is finding its way into galleries and stores.

Weaving is the one art form that is found almost everywhere and has distinct styles that vary by place and tribal group. It's also the single most accessible art the traveller can buy, often directly from the artist.

Literature & Film

Pha Lak Pha Lam, the Lao version of the Indian epic the Ramayana, is the most pervasive and influential of all classical Lao literature. The Indian source first came to Laos with the Hindu Khmer as stone reliefs at Wat Phu Champasak and other Angkor-period temples. Oral and written versions may also have been available; later the Lao developed their own version of the epic, which differs greatly both from the original and from Cambodia's *Reamker.*

Of the 547 Jataka tales in the *Pali Tipitaka,* each chronicling a different past life of the Buddha, most appear in Laos almost word for word as they were first inscribed in Sri Lanka. A group of 50 'extra' or apocryphal stories, based on Lao-Thai folk tales of the time, were added by Pali scholars in Luang Prabang between 300 and 400 years ago.

Contemporary literature has been hampered by decades of war and communist rule. The first Lao-language novel was printed in 1944, and only in 1999 was the first collection of contemporary Lao fiction, Ounthine Bounyavong's *Mother's Beloved: Stories from Laos,* published in a bilingual Lao and English edition. Since then, a growing number of Lao novels and short stories have been translated into Thai, but very few have seen English-language translations. One of the most popular was 2009's *When the Sky Turns Upside Down: Memories of Laos,* a translation of short stories, some of which date back 60 years, by prominent Lao authors Dara Viravongs Kanlaya and Douangdeuane Bounyavong.

Feature-film-making resumed in Laos in 1997 with the release of *Than Heng Phongphai* (The Charming Forest) directed by Vithoun Sundara. This was followed in 2001 by *Falang Phon* (Clear Skies After Rain), and in 2004 by *Leum Teua* (Wrongfulness), also directed by Sundara.

Not surprisingly, Laos has one of the quietest film industries in Southeast Asia, and 2008's *Good Morning, Luang Prabang* is only one of a handful of feature films produced in the country since 1975. Starring Lao-Australian heart-throb Ananda Everingham and led by Thai director Sakchai Deenan, the film features a predictably 'safe' love-based plot that nonetheless required the close attention of the Lao authorities during filming.

The Betrayal – Nerakhoon (2008) is a documentary directed by American Ellen Kuras, with the help of the film's main subject, Thavisouk Phrasavath. Shot over a 23-year period, the film documents the Phrasavath family's experience emigrating from Laos to New York City after the communist revolution.

In 2013, *The Rocket,* the story of a young Lao boy who builds a rocket to regain his family's trust, was released.

The year 2015 saw the release of *Banana Pancakes and The Children of Sticky Rice,* a gentle and touching story of two cultures colliding with the meeting of a Lao boy and Western girl in northern Laos.

Finally, 2016's *Dearest Sister* is a disturbing and well-wrought horror set in Laos, directed and written by Laos' first female film director Mattie Do, and tells the story of a rural girl looking after her cousin in Vientiane who goes blind but gains the ability to talk to the dead.

Music & Dance

Lao classical music was originally developed as court music for royal ceremonies and classical dance-drama during the 19th-century reign of Vientiane's Chao Anou, who had been educated in the Siamese court in Bangkok. The standard ensemble for this genre is the *sep nyai* and consists of *kôrng wóng* (a set of tuned gongs), the *ranyâht* (a xylophone-like instrument), the *kooi* (bamboo flute) and the *bee* (a double-reed wind instrument similar to the oboe).

Traditional Music of the Lao (1985), by Terry Miller, although mainly focused on northeast Thailand, is the only book-length work yet to appear on Lao music, and is very informative.

The practice of classical Lao music and drama has been in decline for some time, as 40 years of intermittent war and revolution simply made this kind of entertainment a low priority among most Lao. Generally, the only time you'll hear this type of music is during the occasional public performance of the *Pha Lak Pha Lam,* a dance-drama based on the Hindu Ramayana epic.

Not so with Lao folk and pop, which have always stayed close to the people. The principal instrument in folk, and to a lesser extent in pop, is the *káan* (common French spelling: *khene*), a wind instrument that is made of a double row of bamboo-like reeds fitted into a hardwood soundbox and made airtight with beeswax. The rows can be as few as four or as many as eight courses (for a total of 16 pipes), and the instrument can vary in length from around 80cm to about 2m. An adept player can produce a churning, calliope-like dance music.

When the *káan* is playing locals dance the *lám wóng* (circle performance), easily the most popular folk dance in Laos. Put simply, in the *lám wóng* couples dance circles around one another until there are three circles in all: a circle danced by the individual, a circle danced by the couple, and one danced by the whole crowd.

Măw Lám

The Lao folk idiom also has its own musical theatre, based on the *mŏr lám* tradition. *Mŏr lám* is difficult to translate but roughly means 'master of verse'. Led by one or more vocalists, performances always feature a witty, topical combination of talking and singing that ranges across themes as diverse as politics and sex. Very colloquial, even bawdy, language is employed. This is one art form that has always bypassed government censors and it continues to provide an important outlet for grass-roots expression.

There are several different types of *mŏr lám*, depending on the number of singers and the region the style hails from. *Mŏr lám koo* (couple *mŏr lám*) features a man and woman who engage in flirtation and verbal repartee. *Mŏr lám jót* (duelling *mŏr lám*) has two performers of the same gender who 'duel' by answering questions or finishing an incomplete story issued as a challenge, similar to freestyle rap.

Northern Lao *kàan*-based folk music is usually referred to as *káp* rather than *lám*. Authentic live *mŏr lám* can be heard at temple fairs and on Lao radio. Born-and-bred American artist Jonny Olsen (also known as Jonny Khaen) has become a celebrity in Laos for his *kàan*-based music.

Lao Pop

Up until 2003 performing 'modern' music was virtually outlawed in Laos. The government had decided it just wasn't the Lao thing, and bands such as local heavy-metal outfit Sapphire, who chose to play anyway, were effectively shut down. Instead, the youth listened to pirated Thai and Western music, while Lao-language pop was limited to the *look tûng,* syrupy arrangements combining cha-cha and bolero rhythms with Lao-Thai melodies.

Then the government decided that if Lao youth were going to listen to modern pop, it might as well be home-grown. The first 'star' was Thidavanh Bounxouay, a Lao-Bulgarian singer more popularly known as Alexandra. Her brand of pop wasn't exactly radical, but it was decidedly upbeat compared with what went before. In the last couple of years other groups have followed including girl band Princess and pop-rock group Awake.

In recent years, slightly edgier rock bands such as Crocodile and Leprozy have emerged, the latter of which have even played relatively high-profile gigs in Thailand. The hard-rock band Cells is another example of a Lao band for whom success has been much more rewarding in Thailand, where they've played big and relatively lucrative gigs in Bangkok.

There's also a tiny but burgeoning school of Lao-language hip hop that until recently was almost exclusively associated with Los Angeles and that city's Lao diaspora. However, in recent years a domestic scene has developed around home-grown acts such as Hip Hop Ban Na and L.O.G., the latter of which scored a chart-topping hit in Thailand.

In Vientiane, recordings by many if not all of the artists mentioned above are available at the open-air market near Pha That Luang and at Talat Sao mall. Some can also be caught live at venues in Vientiane, though you're more likely to see them at outdoor gigs to celebrate major holidays.

Architecture

As with all other artistic endeavours, for centuries the best architects in the land have focused their attention on Buddhist temples. The results are most impressive in Luang Prabang.

However, it's not only in temples that Laos has its own peculiar architectural traditions. The *that* (stupas) found in Laos are different to those found anywhere else in the Buddhist world. Stupas are essentially monuments built on top of a reliquary which itself was built to hold a relic of the Buddha, commonly a hair or fragment of bone. Across Asia they come in varying shapes and sizes, ranging from the multilevel tiered pagodas found in Vietnam to the buxom brick monoliths of Sri Lanka. Laos has its own unique style combining hard edges and comely curves. The most famous of all Lao stupas is the golden Pha That Luang in Vientiane, which doubles as the national symbol.

Traditional housing in Laos, whether in the river valleys or in the mountains, consists of simple wooden or bamboo-thatch structures with leaf or grass roofing. Among Lowland Lao, houses are raised on stilts to avoid flooding during the monsoons and allow room to store rice underneath,

Traditional Khamu houses often have the skulls of domestic animals hanging on a wall with an altar beneath. The skulls are from animals the family has sacrificed to their ancestors, and it is strictly taboo to touch them.

while the highlanders typically build directly on the ground. The most attractive Lowland Lao houses often have a starburst pattern in the architraves, though these are increasingly difficult to find.

Colonial architecture in urban Laos combined the classic French provincial style – thick-walled buildings with shuttered windows and pitched tile roofs – with balconies and ventilation to promote air circulation in the stifling Southeast Asian climate. Although many of these structures were torn down or allowed to decay following independence from France, today they are much in demand, especially by foreigners. Luang Prabang and Vientiane both boast several lovingly restored buildings from this era. By contrast, in the Mekong River towns of Tha Khaek, Savannakhet and Pakse, French-era buildings are decaying at a disturbing rate.

Buildings erected in post-Revolution Laos followed the socialist realism school that was enforced in the Soviet Union, Vietnam and China. Straight lines, sharp angles and an almost total lack of ornamentation were the norm. More recently, a trend towards integrating classic Lao architectural motifs with modern functions has taken hold. Prime examples of this include Vientiane's National Assembly and the Luang Prabang airport, both of which were designed by Havana- and Moscow-trained architect Hongkad Souvannavong. Other design characteristics, such as those represented by the Siam Commercial Bank on Th Lan Xang in Vientiane, seek to gracefully reincorporate French colonial-era features ignored for the last half-century.

Sculpture

Perhaps most impressive of all the traditional Lao arts is the Buddhist sculpture of the period from the 16th to 18th centuries, the heyday of

TEMPLE ARCHITECTURE: A TALE OF THREE CITIES

The *sĭm* (ordination hall) is usually the most important structure in any Theravada Buddhist wat. The high-peaked roofs are layered to represent several levels (usually three, five, seven or occasionally nine), which correspond to various Buddhist doctrines. The edges of the roofs almost always feature a repeated flame motif, with long, fingerlike hooks at the corners called *chôr fâh* (sky clusters). Umbrella-like spires along the central roof-ridge of a *sĭm,* called *nyôrt chôr fâh* (topmost *chôr fâh*) sometimes bear small pavilions (*naga*s – mythical water serpents) in a double-stepped arrangement representing Mt Meru, the mythical centre of the Hindu-Buddhist cosmos.

There are basically three architectural styles for such buildings: the Vientiane, Luang Prabang and Xieng Khuang styles.

The front of a *sĭm* in the Vientiane style usually features a large verandah with heavy columns supporting an ornamented overhanging roof. Some will also have a less ornamented rear verandah, while those that have a surrounding terrace are Bangkok-influenced.

In Luang Prabang, the temple style is akin to that of the northern Siamese (Lanna) style, hardly surprising as for several centuries Laos and northern Thailand were part of the same kingdoms. Luang Prabang temple roofs sweep very low, almost reaching the ground in some instances. The overall effect is quite dramatic, as if the *sĭm* were about to take flight. The Lao are fond of saying that the roof line resembles the wings of a mother hen guarding her chicks.

Little remains of the Xieng Khuang style of *sĭm* architecture because the province was so heavily bombed during the Second Indochina War. Pretty much the only surviving examples are in Luang Prabang and to look at them you see aspects of both Vientiane and Luang Prabang styles. The *sĭm* raised on a multilevel platform is reminiscent of Vientiane temples, while wide sweeping roofs that reach especially low are similar to the Luang Prabang style, though they're not usually tiered. Cantilevered roof supports play a much more prominent role in the building's overall aesthetic, giving the *sĭm*'s front profile a pentagonal shape.

the kingdom of Lan Xang. Sculptural media usually included bronze, stone or wood, and the subject was invariably the Lord Buddha or figures associated with the Jataka (*sáh-dók;* stories of the Buddha's past lives). Like other Buddhist sculptors, the Lao artisans emphasised the features thought to be peculiar to the historical Buddha, including a beak-like nose, extended earlobes and tightly curled hair.

Two types of standing Buddha image are distinctive to Laos. The first is the 'Calling for Rain' posture, which depicts the Buddha standing with hands held rigidly at his side, fingers pointing towards the ground. This posture is rarely seen in other Southeast Asian Buddhist art traditions. The slightly rounded, 'boneless' look of the image recalls Thailand's Suk-hothai style, and the way the lower robe is sculpted over the hips looks vaguely Khmer. But the flat, slablike earlobes, arched eyebrows and aquiline nose are uniquely Lao. The bottom of the figure's robe curls upward on both sides in a perfectly symmetrical fashion that is also unique and innovative.

The other original Lao image type is the 'Contemplating the Bodhi Tree' Buddha. The Bodhi tree (Tree of Enlightenment) refers to the large banyan tree that the historical Buddha purportedly was sitting beneath when he attained enlightenment in Bodhgaya, India, in the 6th century BC. In this image the Buddha is standing in much the same way as in the 'Calling for Rain' pose, except that his hands are crossed at the wrists in front of his body.

The finest examples of Lao sculpture are found in Vientiane's Haw Pha Kaeo and Wat Si Saket, and in Luang Prabang's Royal Palace Museum.

Handicrafts

Mats and baskets woven of various kinds of straw, rattan and reed are common and are becoming a small but important export. Minority groups still wear these baskets, affirming that until recently most Lao handicrafts were useful as well as ornamental. In villages it's possible to buy direct from the weaver. Among the best baskets and mats are those woven by the Htin (Lao Thoeng).

Among the Hmong and Mien hill tribes, silversmithing plays an important role in 'portable wealth' and inheritances. In years past, the main source of silver was French coins, which were either melted down or fitted straight into the jewellery of choice. In northern villages it's not unusual to see newer coins worn in elaborate head dresses.

The Lowland Lao also have a long tradition of silversmithing and gold-smithing. While these arts have been in decline for quite a while now, there are still plenty of jewellers working over flames in markets around the country.

Paper handcrafted from *sǎh* (the bark of a mulberry tree) is common in northwestern Laos, and is available in Vientiane and Luang Prabang. Environmentally friendly *sǎa* is a renewable paper resource that needs little processing compared with wood pulp.

Textiles

Silk and cotton fabrics are woven in many different styles according to the geographic provenance and ethnicity of the weavers. Although Lao textiles do have similarities with other Southeast Asian textiles, Lao weaving techniques are unique in both loom design and weaving styles, generating fabrics that are very recognisably Lao.

Southern weavers, who often use foot looms rather than frame looms, are known for the best silk weaving and for intricate *mat-mii* (ikat or tie-dye) designs that include Khmer-influenced temple and elephant motifs. The result is a soft, spotted pattern similar to Indonesian *ikat*. *Mat-mii* cloth can be used for different types of clothing or wall hangings. In

Lao Textiles and Traditions (1997), by Mary F Connors, is useful to visitors interested in Lao weaving; it's the best overall introduction to the subject.

Sekong and Attapeu Provinces some fabrics mix beadwork with weaving and embroidery. One-piece *pàh nung* are more common than those sewn from separate pieces.

In central Laos, typical weavings include indigo-dyed cotton *mat-mii* and minimal weft brocade (*jók* and *kìt*), along with mixed techniques brought by migrants to Vientiane.

Generally speaking, the fabrics of the north feature a mix of solid colours with complex geometric patterns – stripes, diamonds, zigzags, animal and plant shapes – usually in the form of a *pàh nung* or *sìn* (a women's wrap-around skirt). Sometimes gold or silver thread is woven in along the borders. Another form the cloth takes is the *pàh bęeang,* a narrow Lao-Thai shawl that men and women wear singly or in pairs over the shoulders during weddings and festivals.

Gold and silver brocade is typical of traditional Luang Prabang patterns, along with intricate patterns and imported Tai Lü designs. Northerners generally use frame looms; the waist, body and narrow *sìn* (bottom border) of a *pàh nung* are often sewn together from separately woven pieces.

In northeastern Laos, tribal Tai produce *yìap ko* (weft brocade) using raw silk, cotton yarn and natural dyes, sometimes with the addition of *mat-mii* techniques. Large diamond patterns are common.

Among the Hmong and Mien tribes, square pieces of cloth are embroidered and quilted to produce strikingly colourful fabrics in apparently abstract patterns that contain ritual meanings. In Hmong these are called *pandau* (flowercloth). Some larger quilts feature scenes that represent village life, including both animal and human figures.

Many tribes among the Lao Soung and Lao Thoeng groups produce woven shoulder bags in the Austro-Thai and Tibetan-Burmese traditions, such as those seen all across the mountains of South Asia and Southeast Asia. In Laos, these are called *nyahm*. Among the most popular *nyaam* nowadays are those made with older pieces of fabric from 'antique' *pàh nung* or from pieces of hill-tribe clothing. Vientiane's Talat Sao is one of the best places to shop for this kind of accessory.

Natural sources for Lao dyes include ebony (both seeds and wood), tamarind (seeds and wood), red lacquer extracted from the *Coccus iacca* (a tree-boring insect), turmeric (from a root) and indigo. A basic palette of five natural colours – black, orange, red, yellow and blue – can be combined to create an endless variety of other colours. Other unblended, but more subtle, hues include khaki (from the bark of the Indian trumpet tree), pink (sappanwood) and gold (jackfruit and breadfruit woods).

Sport

Laos has a few traditional sports and these are often as much an excuse for betting as they are a means of exercise. *Gá-đôr* and *móoay láo* (Lao boxing) certainly do involve exercise, and these are taken increasingly seriously as international competition raises their profiles.

In ethnic Tai areas you might find the more off-beat 'sport' of beetle fighting. These bouts involve notoriously fractious rhinoceros beetles squaring off while a crowd, usually more vociferous after liberal helpings of *lôw-lôw*, bets on the result. The beetles hiss and attack, lifting each other with their horns, until one decides it no longer wants to be part of this 'entertainment' and runs. If you bet on the runner, you lose. Beetle bouts are limited to the wet season.

Kids in Laos are likely to be seen chasing around a soccer ball (football). Opportunities for pursuing football professionally are few, limited by an almost complete lack of quality coaching, pitches and youth leagues where players can get experience of proper competition. Interprovincial matches at the National Stadium in Vientiane or in modest stadium in provincial capitals draw relatively large crowds.

Environment

Laos' environment has up until now been largely threatened by legal and illegal logging, and while this may have been given temporary respite with the recent ban on logging, increased mining and agriculture and the widespread construction of hydroelectric dams is exerting considerable stress on the land. Tourism is recognised as a lucrative natural resource and may be the key to preserving Laos' remaining natural areas, but currently commerce seems to be winning against conservation.

The Land

Covering an area slightly larger than Great Britain, landlocked Laos shares borders with China, Myanmar (Burma), Thailand, Cambodia and Vietnam. Rivers and mountains dominate, folding the country into a series of often-spectacular ridges and valleys, rivers and mountain passes, extending westward from the Laos–Vietnam border.

Mountains and plateaus cover more than 70% of the country. Running about half the length of Laos, parallel to the course of the Mekong River, is the Annamite Chain, a rugged mountain range with peaks averaging between 1500m and 2500m in height. Roughly in the centre of the range is the Khammuan Plateau, a world of dramatic limestone grottoes and gorges where vertical walls rise hundreds of metres from jungle-clad valleys. At the southern end of the Annamite Chain, covering 10,000 sq km, the Bolaven Plateau is an important area for the cultivation of high-yield mountain rice, coffee, tea and other crops that flourish in the cooler climes found at these higher altitudes.

The larger, northern half of Laos is made up almost entirely of mountain ranges. The highest mountains are found in Xieng Khuang Province, including Phu Bia, the country's highest peak at 2820m, though this remains off limits to travellers for now. Just north of Phu Bia stands the Xieng Khuang plateau, the country's largest mountain plateau, which rises 1200m above sea level. The most famous part of the plateau is the Plain of Jars, an area somewhat reminiscent of the rolling hills of Ireland, except for the thousands of bomb craters. It's named for the huge prehistoric stone jars that dot the area, as if the local giants had pub-crawled across this neighbourhood and left their empty beer mugs behind.

Much of the rest of Laos is covered by forest, most of which is mixed deciduous forest. This forest enjoys a complex relationship with the Mekong and its tributaries, acting as a sponge for the monsoon rains and then slowly releasing the water into both streams and the atmosphere during the long dry season.

The Mekong River is known as Lancang Jiang (Turbulent River) in China; Mae Nam Khong (the Mother of Water) in Thailand, Myanmar (Burma) and Laos; Tonle Thom (Great Water) in Cambodia; and Cuu Long (Nine Dragons) in Vietnam.

The Mekong & Other Rivers

Springing forth nearly 5000km from the sea, high up on the Tibetan Plateau, the Mekong River so dominates Lao topography that, to a large extent, the entire country parallels its course. Although half of the Mekong's length runs through China, more of the river's volume courses through Laos than through any other Southeast Asian country. At its widest, near Si Phan Don in the south, the river can expand to 14km across during the rainy season, spreading around thousands of islands and islets on its inevitable course south.

The Mekong's middle reach is navigable year-round, from Heuan Hin (north of the Khemmarat Rapids in Savannakhet Province) to Kok Phong in Luang Prabang. However, these rapids, and the brutal falls at Khon Phapheng in Si Phan Don, have prevented the Mekong from becoming the sort of regional highway other great rivers have.

The fertile Mekong River flood plain, running from Sainyabuli to Champasak, forms the flattest and most tropical part of Laos. Virtually all of the domestic rice consumed in Laos is grown here, and if our experience seeing rice packaged up as 'Produce of Thailand' is any indication, then a fair bit is exported via Thailand too. Most other large-scale farming takes place here as well. The Mekong and, just as importantly, its tributaries are also an important source of fish, a vital part of the diet for most people living in Laos. The Mekong valley is at its largest around Vientiane and Savannakhet, which, not surprisingly, are two of the major population centres.

Major tributaries of the great river include the Nam Ou (Ou River) and the Nam Tha (Tha River), both of which flow through deep, narrow limestone valleys from the north, and the Nam Ngum (Ngum River), which flows into the Mekong across a broad plain in Vientiane Province. The Nam Ngum is the site of one of Laos' oldest hydroelectric plants, which provides power for Vientiane-area towns and Thailand. The Se Kong (Kong River) flows through much of southern Laos before eventually reaching the Mekong in Cambodia, and the Nam Kading (Kading River) and Nam Theun (Theun River) are equally important in central Laos.

All the rivers and tributaries west of the Annamite Chain drain into the Mekong, while waterways east of the Annamites (in Hua Phan and Xieng Khuang Provinces only) flow into the Gulf of Tonkin off the coast of Vietnam.

> Marco Polo was probably the first European to cross the Mekong, in the 13th century, and was followed by a group of Portuguese emissaries in the 16th century. Dutch merchant Gerrit van Wuysthoff arrived by boat in the 17th century.

Wildlife

Laos still boats one of the least disturbed ecosystems in Asia due to its overall lack of development and low population density. Least disturbed, however, does not mean undisturbed, and for many species like the tiger and Asian elephant the future looks very dark indeed.

Animals

The mountains, forests and river networks of Laos are home to a range of animals both endemic to the country and shared with its Southeast Asian neighbours. Nearly half of the animal species native to Thailand are shared by Laos, with the higher forest cover and fewer hunters meaning that numbers are often greater in Laos. Almost all wild animals, however, are threatened to some extent by hunting and habitat loss.

In spite of this Laos has seen several new species discovered in recent years, such as the bent-toed gecko and long-toothed pipistrelle bat, while others thought to be extinct have turned up in remote forests. Given their rarity, these newly discovered species are on the endangered list.

As in Cambodia, Vietnam, Myanmar and much of Thailand, most of the fauna in Laos belong to the Indochinese zoogeographic realm (as opposed to the Sundaic domain found south of the Isthmus of Kra in southern Thailand or the Palaearctic to the north in China).

Notable mammals endemic to Laos include the lesser panda, raccoon dog, Lao marmoset rat, Owston's civet and the pygmy slow loris. Other important exotic species found elsewhere in the region include the Malayan and Chinese pangolins, 10 species of civet, marbled cat, Javan and crab-eating mongoose, the serow (sometimes called Asian mountain goat) and goral (another type of goat-antelope), and cat species including the leopard cat and Asian golden cat.

> The Mekong: Turbulent Past, Uncertain Future (2000), by Milton Osborne, is a fascinating cultural history of the Mekong that spans 2000 years of exploration, mapping and war.

RESPONSIBLE TRAVEL & WILDLIFE

While subsistence hunting is permitted by the Lao government for local rural villagers, the sale and purchase of *any* wildlife is illegal in Laos. Here are a few pointers to make sure you're not contributing to the downfall of endangered species:

➡ Never buy a wild animal – dead or alive – at a market.

➡ Though they are available on some menus, avoid eating endangered species or prey of endangered species, such as soft-shelled turtles, rat snakes, mouse deer, sambar deer, squirrels, bamboo rats, muntjac deer and pangolins.

➡ No matter the macabre value, avoid buying necklaces made from animal teeth; stuffed animals; spiders in glass frames; and witchy bottles of alcohol with snakes, birds or insects inside.

➡ Keep an eye out for products with a label stating they are certified by the Convention on International Trade in Endangered Species of Wild Fauna and Flora (CITES). These are legal to buy in Laos and take home.

For more information visit the **Wildlife Conservation Society** (www.wcs.org/international/Asia/laos) website.

Among the most notable of Laos' wildlife are the primates. Several smaller species are known, including Phayre's leaf monkey, François' langur, the Douc langur and several macaques. Two other primates that are endemic to Laos are the concolour gibbon and snub-nosed langur. It's the five species of gibbon that attract most attention. Sadly, the black-cheeked crested gibbon is endangered, being hunted both for its meat and to be sold as pets in Thailand. Several projects are underway to educate local communities to set aside safe areas for the gibbons.

Elephants

It's a sad statistic that for every 10 elephants born in Laos, according to the Elephant Conservation Centre in Sainyabuli, only two survive. Veterinary care and the ability to give their working female elephant three to four years to gestate, birth, lactate and rear her calf is more time than the average mahout can afford. About four years too much. So no wonder the population is withering.

Laos might once have been known as the Land of a Million Elephants, but these days only about 800 remain in total. Exact figures are hard to come by, but it's generally believed that there are about 300 to 400 wild elephants, roaming in open-canopy forest areas predominantly in Sainyabuli Province west of Vientiane, Bolikhamsai Province in the Phu Khao Khuay NPA, and along the Nakai Plateau in central eastern Laos.

Hunting and habitat loss are their main threats. In areas such as the Nakai Plateau, Vietnamese poachers kill elephants for their meat and hides, while the Nam Theun 2 hydropower project in Khammuan Province has swallowed up a large chunk of habitat. The **Wildlife Conservation Society** (WCS; www.wcs.org) has an ongoing project in this area, with a long-term aim of establishing a 'demonstration site that will serve as a model for reducing human-elephant conflict nationwide'.

Working, domesticated elephants are also found in a number of provinces. Logging elephants are currently put in extreme danger on the sides of mountains trying to access the last available hardwood. In 2016 the new president of Laos outlawed logging indefinitely. Since then many mahouts and their elephants have been out of a job. Given the considerable funds needed to feed an elephant (about US$250 per week), their only alternative is finding income through tourism, where ex-logging pachyderms give rides to tourists with a howdah (chair) strapped on their backs.

The World Conservation Union believes wildlife in Laos has a much better chance of surviving than in neighbouring Vietnam. Lending weight to this is the Vietnam warty pig *(Sus bucclentus)*, a species found in Laos but last recorded in Vietnam in 1892 and until recently considered extinct.

Given that the spine of an elephant is jagged and convex this is extremely painful. Most travellers are also unaware that to subjugate a young elephant to the point they can be trusted to carry travelers, it must first be subjected to the 'crush', a cage where it is broken down and starved, with regular beatings by a bull-hook. It is this fear of the bull-hook as an adult that makes them do as they are told. Elephant Village is the only camp we're aware of that is howdah and bull-hook free; tourists do still ride the elephants, though on the animal's neck rather than the back.

A further concern is that many of these logging elephants in search of a job are males and because of musthing, during which a huge release of testosterone occurs, their tempers can be mercurial to put it lightly, and are dangerous to ride on. The mahout cannot argue with his employer who runs the camp if he insists on working the elephant through this lethal period. And fatal events do occur, such as in Thailand in 2015 when a musthing elephant killed his mahout and a Scottish man and his daughter.

There are positive ways to encounter elephants in Laos. The impressive **Elephant Conservation Center** (ECC; ☏020-23025210; www.elephant conservationcenter.com; 1-day visit US$60, 3-day experience US$205, 6-day eco-experience US$495) ✐ near Sainyabuli offers an immersive elephant experience for visitors which focuses on observing them in a natural area, and the yearly elephant festival held here is growing in popularity as a tourist event. In 2015 some 12 elephants and their mahouts walked 440km from the Elephant Conservation Center in Xayaboury Province to Luang Prabang (coinciding with the city's 20th anniversary as a World Heritage Site), stopping at schools and villages to reacquaint Laotians with their natural heritage and headline the plight of the nation's rapidly shrinking elephant population.

Odd-shaped rocks are venerated across Laos. Even in what appears to be the middle of nowhere, you'll see saffron robes draped over rocks that look vaguely like turtles, fishing baskets or stupas. Local legends explain how the rocks came to be, and some are famous around the country.

Endangered Species

All wild animals in Laos are endangered due to widespread hunting and gradual but persistent habitat loss. Laos ratified the UN Convention on International Trade in Endangered Species of Wild Fauna and Flora (CITES) in 2004, which, combined with other legal measures, has made it easier to prosecute people trading species endangered as a direct result of international trade. But in reality you won't need 20/20 vision to pick out the endangered species, both dead and alive, on sale in markets around the country. Border markets, in particular, tend to attract the most valuable species, with Thais buying species such as gibbons as pets, and Chinese and Vietnamese shopping for exotic food and medicines.

Of the hundreds of species of mammals known in Laos, several dozen are endangered according to the **IUCN Red List** (www.iucnredlist.org). These range from bears, including the Asiatic black bear and Malayan sun bear, through the less glamorous wild cattle such as the gaur and banteng, to high-profile cats like the tiger, leopard and clouded leopard. Exactly how endangered they are is difficult to say. Camera-trapping projects (setting up cameras in the forest to take photos of anything that wanders past) are being carried out by various NGOs and, in the Nakai-Nam Theun NPA, by the Nam Theun 2 dam operators themselves.

In the Nam Et-Phou Louey NPA, there are said to be nine tigers remaining, perhaps the last in Laos. The WCS employs 150 staff composed of foresters, military officers, locals and biologists, as well as setting up a successful ecotourism community outreach program (Nam Nern Night Safari; p80) to maintain this most delicate of populations. The WCS is also focusing its conservation activities on species including the Asian elephant, Siamese crocodile, western black-crested gibbon and Eld's deer.

Some endangered species are so rare they were unknown until very recently. Among these is the spindlehorn (*Pseudoryx nghethingensis*; known as the *saola* in Vietnam, *nyang* in Laos), a horned mammal found in the Annamite Chain along the Laos–Vietnam border in 1992. The spindlehorn, which was described in 14th-century Chinese journals, was long thought not to exist, and when discovered it became one of only three land mammals to earn its own genus in the 20th century. Unfortunately, horns taken from spindlehorn are a favoured trophy among certain groups on both sides of the border.

In 2005 WCS scientists visiting a local market in Khammuan Province discovered a 'Laotian rock rat' laid out for sale. But what was being sold as meat turned out to be a genetically distinct species named the *Laonastes aenigmamus*. Further research revealed the species to be the sole survivor of a prehistoric group of rodents that died out about 11 million years ago. If you're very lucky you might see one on the cliffs near the caves off Rte 12 in Khammuan Province.

Among the most seriously endangered of all mammals is the Irrawaddy dolphin, found in increasingly small pockets of the Mekong River near the Cambodian border. The construction of the Don Sahang dam, only 3.2km from where they feed, will involve the use of dynamite to blast away rocks.

Birds

Those new to Laos often ask: 'Why don't I see more birds?' The short answer is 'cheap protein'. If you can get far enough away from people, you'll find the forests and mountains of Laos do in fact harbour a rich selection of resident and migrating bird species. Surveys carried out by a British team of ornithologists in the 1990s recorded 437 species, including eight globally threatened and 21 globally near-threatened species. Some other counts rise as high as 650 species.

Notable among these are the Siamese fireback pheasant, green peafowl, red-collared woodpecker, brown hornbill, tawny fish-owl, Sarus crane, giant ibis and the Asian golden weaver. Hunting keeps urban bird populations noticeably thin. In 2008, scientists from the WCS and the University of Melbourne conducting research in central Laos discovered a new bird species, the bare-faced bulbul, the first bald songbird to be spotted in mainland Asia, and the first new bulbul to have been discovered in the last century.

Plants

According to the UN Food and Agriculture Organization, in 2005 forest covered more than 69% of Laos. Current figures linger at around 45%. Of these woodlands, about 11% can be classified as primary forest.

Most indigenous vegetation in Laos is associated with monsoon forests, a common trait in areas of tropical mainland Southeast Asia that experience dry seasons lasting three months or longer. In such mixed deciduous forests many trees shed their leaves during the dry season to conserve water. Rainforests, which are typically evergreen, don't exist in Laos, although nonindigenous rainforest species such as the coconut palm are commonly seen in the lower Mekong River valley. There are undoubtedly some big trees in Laos, but don't expect the sort of towering forests found in some other parts of Southeast Asia. The conditions do not, and never have, allowed these sorts of giants to grow here.

Instead the monsoon forests of Laos typically grow in three canopies. Dipterocarps – tall, pale-barked, single-trunked trees that can grow beyond 30m high – dominate the top canopy of the forest, while a middle canopy consists of an ever-dwindling population of prized hardwoods, including teak, padauk (sometimes called 'Asian rosewood') and mahogany. Underneath there's a variety of smaller trees, shrubs, grasses and, along

ENVIRONMENT WILDLIFE

The Mekong giant catfish may grow up to 3m long and weigh as much as 300kg. Due to Chinese blasting of shoals in the Upper Mekong and the building of dams, it now faces extinction in Laos.

Wildlife Trade in Laos: The End of the Game (2001), by Hanneke Nooren and Gordon Claridge, is a frightening description of animal poaching in Laos.

river habitats, bamboo. In certain plateau areas of the south, there are dry dipterocarp forests in which the forest canopies are more open, with less of a middle layer and more of a grass-and-bamboo undergrowth. Parts of the Annamite Chain that receive rain from both the southwestern monsoon as well as the South China Sea are covered by tropical montane evergreen forest, while tropical pine forests can be found on the Nakai Plateau and Sekong area to the south.

In addition to the glamour hardwoods, the country's flora includes a toothsome array of fruit trees, bamboo (more species than any country outside Thailand and China) and an abundance of flowering species such as the orchid. However, in some parts of the country orchids are being stripped out of forests (often in protected areas) for sale to Thai tourists; look for the markets near the waterfalls of the Bolaven Plateau to see them. In the high plateaus of the Annamite Chain, extensive grasslands or savannahs are common.

> Around 85% of Laos is mountainous terrain and less than 4% is considered arable.

National Protected Areas (NPAs)

Laos boasts one of the youngest and most comprehensive protected-area systems in the world. In 1993 the government set up 18 National Biodiversity Conservation Areas, comprising a total of 24,600 sq km, or just over 10% of the country's land mass. Most significantly, it did this following sound scientific consultation rather than creating areas on an ad hoc basis (as most other countries have done). Two more were added in 1995, for a total of 20 protected areas covering 14% of Laos. A further 4% of Laos is reserved as Provincial Protected Areas, making Laos one of the most protected countries on earth.

The areas were renamed National Protected Areas (NPAs) a few years ago. And while the naming semantics might seem trivial, they do reflect some important differences. The main one is that an NPA has local communities living within its boundaries, unlike a national park, where only rangers and those working in the park are allowed to live and where traditional activities such as hunting and logging are banned. Indeed, forests in NPAs are divided into production forests for timber, protection forests for watershed and conservation forests for pure conservation.

The largest protected areas are in southern Laos, which, contrary to popular myth, bears a higher percentage of natural forest cover than the north. Nakai-Nam Theun, the largest of the NPAs, covers 3710 sq km and is home to the recently discovered spindlehorn, as well as several other species unknown to the scientific world until not that long ago.

While several NPAs remain difficult to access without mounting a full-scale expedition, several others have become much easier to reach in recent years. The best way in is usually by foot.

> For more information on all of Laos' National Protected Areas (NPAs), see the comprehensive website www. ecotourismlaos. com.

The wildlife in these areas, from rare birds to wild elephants, is relatively abundant. The best time to view wildlife in most of the country is just after the monsoon in November. However, even at these times you'll be lucky to see very much. There are several reasons for this, the most important of which is that ongoing hunting means numbers of wild animals are reduced and those living are instinctively scared of humans. It's also difficult to see animals in forest cover at the best of times, and many animals are nocturnal. Teaming up with a recommended outfit will increase your chances of seeing wildlife.

Environmental Issues

Flying over Laos it's easy to think that much of the country is blanketed with untouched wilderness. But first impressions can be deceiving. What that lumpy carpet of green conceals is an environment facing several interrelated threats.

For the most part they're issues of the bottom line. Hunting endangers all sorts of creatures of the forest but it persists because the hunters can't afford to buy meat from the market. Forests are logged at unsustainable rates because the timber found in Laos is hugely valuable and loggers see more profit in cutting than not. And hydropower projects affect river systems and their dependent ecologies, including the forests, because Laos needs the money hydroelectricity can bring, and it's relatively cheap and easy for energy companies to develop in Laos.

Laws do exist to protect wildlife and plenty of Laos is protected as NPAs. But most Laotians are completely unaware of global conservation issues and there is little will and less money to pay for conservation projects, such as organised park rangers, or to prosecute offenders. Lack of communication between national and local governments and poor definitions of authority in conservation areas just add to the issues.

One of the biggest obstacles facing environmental protection in Laos is corruption (Laos being ranked 139 out of 168 nations in the Transparency International Corruption Perceptions Index 2015). Fortunately, with the support of several dedicated individuals and NGOs, ecotourism is growing to the point where some local communities are beginning to understand – and buying into – the idea that an intact environment can be worth more money than an exhausted one.

One long-standing environmental problem has been the unexploded ordnance (UXO) contaminating parts of eastern Laos where the Ho Chi Minh Trail ran during the Second Indochina War. Bombs are being found and defused at a painstakingly slow rate; however, on his 2016 visit former US President Obama pledged US$90m over a three-year period to speed up the process.

The major challenges facing Laos' environment are, therefore, the internal pressures of economic growth as well as external pressures from the country's more populated and affluent neighbours, particularly China, Vietnam and Thailand, who all benefit from Laos' abundant resources.

Damming the Mekong for Hydroelectric Power

For millenniums the Mekong River has been the lifeblood of Laos and the wider Mekong region. It's the region's primary artery, and about 60 million people depend on the rich fisheries and other resources provided by the river and its tributaries. The Mekong is the world's 12th-longest river and 10th largest in terms of volume. But unlike other major rivers, a series of rapids have prevented it from developing into a major transport and cargo thoroughfare, or as a base for large industrial cities.

When the Nam Theun 2 dam in Khammuan Province was approved by the World Bank in 2005, it was the equivalent of opening hydropower's Pandora's box. Since then hydropower has become an important contributor to Laos' economic growth. Six big dams are already in operation, seven are currently under construction, at least 12 more are planned, and development deals ready to go on another 35.

According to a BBC report, the $3.5 billion Xayaburi dam (funded by Thailand) will block critical fish-migration routes for between 23 and 100 species, among them the Mekong giant catfish. Meanwhile in southern Laos, work has begun near Si Phan Don (Four Thousand Islands) on the Malaysian-financed $300 million Don Sahong dam, despite massive protest from Cambodian fishermen and the WWF, who argue it will devastate the small population of Irrawaddy dolphin that resides in a deep-water pool close by.

The negative impacts associated with these dams have so far included forced displacement of local communities and the uprooting of their traditional riverine culture, flooding upstream areas, reduced sediment flows, and increased erosion downstream with resulting issues for fish stocks and those who work the rivers. Less immediately visible, but with a potentially much greater influence in the long term, are the changes these dams will have on the Mekong's flood pulse, especially the Tonlé Sap Lake in Cambodia, which is critical to the fish spawning cycle, and thus the food source of millions of people.

However, hydropower is a relatively clean source of energy and to a certain extent dams in Laos are inevitable. Hydropower dams have also become a major contributor to Laos' economic growth, so it's no great surprise that there's a push for more to be built across the country.

More information can be found online, including through the **Mekong River Commission** (www.mrcmekong.org), which oversees the dam developments; Save the **Mekong Coalition** (www.savethemekong.org); and the **WWF** (www.panda.org).

Deforestation

In 2016 the new president of Laos banned the export of timber and logs, throwing long-established illegal smuggling operations into panic. Since the ban, truckloads of hardwood have been seized from forest hideouts and sawmills across the country. In 2015 Radio Free Asia exposed a Lao politburo member's son as a smuggling kingpin of hardwood trees across the border into China via Móhān, and it's widely alleged that illegal logging has been clandestinely run by elements of the Lao Army, such as in Khammuan Province and remote areas of the country's far south.

The national electricity-generating company also profits from the timber sales each time it links a Lao town or village with the national power grid, as it clear-cuts along Lao highways. Large-scale plantations and mining, as well as swidden (slash-and-burn) methods of cultivation, are also leading to habitat loss. This can have a knock-on effect in rural communities: in some rural areas 70% of non-rice foods come from the forest.

Hunting & Overfishing

The majority of Lao citizens derive most of their protein from food culled from nature, not from farms or ranches. How threatening traditional hunting habits are to species survival in Laos is debatable given the nation's extremely sparse population. But, combined with habitat loss, hunting for food is placing increasing pressure on wildlife numbers.

The cross-border trade in wildlife is also potentially serious. Much of the poaching that takes place in Laos' NPAs is allegedly carried out by Vietnamese hunters who have crossed into central Laos illegally to round up species such as pangolins, civets, barking deer, goral and raccoon dogs to sell back home. These animals are highly valued for both food and medicinal purposes in Vietnam, Thailand and China, and as the demand in those countries grows in line with increasing wealth, so too do the prices buyers are prepared to pay.

Foreign NGOs run grass-roots education campaigns across Laos in an effort to raise awareness of endangered species and the effects of hunting on local ecosystems. But, as usual, money is the key to breaking the cycle.

In more densely populated areas such as Savannakhet and Champasak Provinces, the overfishing of lakes and rivers poses a danger to certain fish species. Projects to educate fishermen about exactly where their catch comes from, and how to protect that source, have been successful in changing some unsustainable practices. One area given particular attention is fishing using explosives. This practice, whereby fishermen throw explosives into the water and wait for the dead fish to float to the surface, is incredibly destructive. Most fishermen don't realise that for every dead fish they collect from the surface, another two or three lie dead on the riverbed. The practice is illegal in Laos, and anecdotal evidence suggests education and the law have reduced the problem.

While opium has been cultivated and used in Laos for centuries, the country didn't become a major producer until the passing of the 1971 Anti-Narcotics Law. Having almost been eradicated, opium is allegedly being grown again in remote parts of northern Laos.

Conservation Websites

➡ ElefantAsia (www.elefantasia.org)

➡ Traffic East Asia (www.traffic.org)

➡ Wildlife Conservation Society (www.wcs.org)

➡ World Conservation Union (www.iucn.org/lao)

➡ World Wildlife Fund (www.panda.org)

Survival Guide

Directory A–Z

Accommodation

It's worth booking in advance in popular destinations like Luang Prabang and Vientiane during peak-season months of November to February and around Lao New Year in April.

Room Rates

Paying in the requested currency is usually cheaper than letting the hotel or guesthouse convert the price into another currency. If the price is quoted in kip, pay in kip; if priced in dollars, pay in dollars.

It's worth remembering that rates are pretty reasonable by international standards before trying to bargain the price down, particularly at the budget end where competition is fierce and margins are small. Generally speaking, the Lao people are happy to bargain a little, but they are not keen on protracted negotiations or arguments over price.

Room rates may continue to rise, as inflation and cost of living are real issues for the everyday Lao population.

Guesthouses

The distinction between 'guesthouse', 'hotel' and 'resort' often exists in name only, but legally speaking a guesthouse in Laos has fewer than 16 rooms. In places such as Don Det in southern Laos or Muang Ngoi Neua in northern Laos there are guesthouses consisting of simple bamboo-thatch huts with shared facilities, costing just US$3 a night.

Facilities are improving across the country, but the most inexpensive places might still have cold-water showers or simple Lao-style bathing. Hot water is hardly a necessity in lowland Laos, but it is very welcome in the mountains.

The price of simple rooms in most towns averages between US$5 and US$10 per night with shared bathrooms. For an attached bathroom and hot shower expect to pay about US$10 to US$20; anything above this will usually also have air-conditioning and a TV, with some English channels. Some guesthouses, especially in Luang Prabang, have stepped up the style and offer upscale rooms from US$20 to US$50.

Homestays

Staying in a village home is becoming increasingly popular in rural areas, cost little (about US$5 for a bed and US$10 for full board) and provide a chance for travellers to experience local life, Lao style.

Villages are small, dusty/ muddy depending on the season, and full of kids. You'll be billeted with a family, usually with a maximum of two travellers per family. Toilets will be the squat variety, with scoop flush, in a dark hut at the corner of the block. You'll bathe before dinner, either in a nearby stream or river, or by using a scoop to pour water over yourself from a well, 44-gallon drum or concrete reservoir in your family's yard. Bathing is usually a public event, so don't forget a sarong. Don't expect a mirror.

Food will be simple fare, usually two dishes and sticky rice. In our experience it's almost always been delicious, but prepare yourself for a sticky-rice extravaganza. Even if the food doesn't appeal, you should eat something or your host will lose face. Dinner is usually served on mats on the floor, so prepare to sit lotus-style or with legs tucked under. Don't sit on pillows as that's bad form, and always take off your shoes before entering the house.

Your meal will most likely be followed by a communal drinking session. If you're lucky this will mean cold bottles of Beerlao, but more likely it will revolve around homemade rice alcohol served from a communal cup. The stuff can be pretty harsh, but if you can stomach it, it's a great icebreaker, and some of our best nights in Laos have been spent this way.

Sleeping will probably be under a mosquito net on a mattress on the floor, and might change to 'waking' once the cocks start crowing outside your window.

It might not be luxurious, but a homestay is very much the 'real Laos' and is a thoroughly worthwhile and enjoyable experience. Just remember that for most villagers, dealing with *falang* (foreigner) tourists is pretty new and they are sensitive to your reactions. Their enthusiasm will remain as long as their guests engage with them and accept them, and their lifestyle, without undue criticism. To get the most out of it, take a phrasebook and photos of your family, and, most importantly, a torch, flip-flops, a sarong and toilet paper.

Hotels

Hotel rooms in Vientiane, Luang Prabang, Vang Vieng, Savannakhet and Pakse offer private bathrooms and fans as standard features for between about US$10 and US$20 per night.

Small and medium-size hotels oriented towards Asian business and leisure travellers and tour groups exist in the larger cities. Prices at these hotels run from about US$40 to US$100 for rooms with air-con, hot water, TVs and refrigerators.

Then there are the few top-end hotels with better decor, more facilities and personalised service. These typically cost between US$80 and US$200, occasionally more in Luang Prabang.

While the price is undoubtedly right, the trade-off, however, is in the service. Few hotels in Laos have managed to hone their service to Western standards, and English

levels are often quite weak, even in the more expensive hotels.

Resorts

The term 'resort' in the Lao context may be used for any accommodation situated outside towns or cities. It does not imply, as it usually does in many other countries, the availability of sports activities, a spa and other similar features.

Lao resorts typically cost about the same as a midrange hotel, from about US$25 to US$75 a night. A few, such as those outside Luang Prabang, come closer to the international idea of a resort, with prices to match.

Bargaining

Bargaining in most places in Laos is not nearly as tough as in other parts of Southeast Asia. Lao-style bargaining is generally a friendly transaction where two people try to agree on a price that is fair to both of them. Good bargaining is one way to cut costs.

Most things bought in a market can be bargained for, but in shops prices are mostly fixed. The first rule to bargaining is to have a general idea of the price. Ask around at a few vendors to get a ballpark figure. Once you're ready to buy, it's generally a good strategy to start at 50% of the asking price and work up from there. In general, keeping a friendly, flexible demeanour throughout the transaction will almost always work in your favour. Don't get angry or upset over a few thousand kip. The locals, who invariably

have less money than foreign visitors, never do this.

Climate

The annual monsoon cycles that affect all of mainland Southeast Asia produce a dry and wet monsoon climate, with three basic seasons for most of Laos. The southwest monsoon arrives in Laos between May and July and lasts into November.

The monsoon is followed by a dry period (from November to May), beginning with lower relative temperatures and cool breezes created by Asia's northeast monsoon (which bypasses most of Laos) and lasting until mid-February. Exceptions to this general pattern include Xieng Khuang, Hua Phan and Phongsali Provinces, which may receive rainfall coming from Vietnam and China during the months of April and May.

Temperatures also vary according to altitude. In the humid, low-lying Mekong River valley, temperatures range from 15°C to 38°C, while in the mountains of the far north they can drop to 0°C at night.

Customs Regulations

Customs inspections at ports of entry are lax, as long as you're not bringing in more than a moderate amount of luggage. You're not supposed to enter the country with more than 500 cigarettes or 1L of distilled spirits. All the usual prohibitions on drugs, weapons and pornography apply.

Electricity

Type A
230V/50Hz

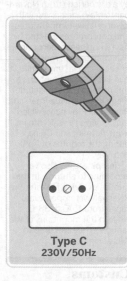

Type C
230V/50Hz

Embassies & Consulates

There are about 25 embassies and consulates in Vientiane. Many nationalities are served by their embassies in Bangkok, Hanoi or Beijing.

Australian Embassy (Map p132; 021-353800; www. laos.embassy.gov.au; Th Tha Deua, Ban Wat Nak, Vientiane; 8.30am-5pm Mon-Fri) Also represents nationals of Canada and New Zealand.

Cambodian Embassy (Map p132; 021-314952; Th Tha Deua, Km 3, Ban That Khao, Vientiane; 8.30am-3.30pm Mon-Fri) Issues visas for US$30.

Chinese Embassy (Map p132; 021-315105; http://la.china-embassy.org/eng; Th Wat Nak Nyai, Ban Wat Nak, Vientiane; 8-11.30am Mon-Fri) Issues visas in four working days.

French Embassy (Map p136; 021-215258; www.amba france-laos.org; Th Setthathirath, Ban Si Saket, Vientiane; 9am-12.30pm & 2-5.30pm Mon-Fri)

German Embassy (Map p132; 021-312110; www.vientiane. diplo.de; Th Sok Pa Luang, Vientiane; 9am-noon Mon-Fri)

Myanmar Embassy (Map p132; 021-314910; Th Sok Pa Luang, Vientiane; 8.30am-3.30pm Mon-Fri) Issues tourist visas in three days for US$20.

Thai Embassy (Map p132; 021-214581; www.thai embassy.org/vientiane; Th Kaysone Phomvihane, Vientiane; 8.30am-noon & 1-3.30pm Mon-Fri) For visa renewals and extensions, head to the consulates in Vientiane (Map p132; 021-214581; 15 Th Bourichane, Vientiane; 8am-noon & 1-4.30pm) or Savannakhet (041-212373; Rte 9 West, Savannakhet; 8.30am-4.30pm Mon-Fri), which issues same-day tourist and non-immigrant visas (1000B).

UK Embassy (030-7700000; www.gov.uk; Th J Nehru, Ban Saysettha, Vientiane; 8.30-11.30am Mon-Fri)

US Embassy (021-487000; http://laos.usembassy.gov; Th Tha Deua, Ban Somvang Thai, Km 9, Hatsayfong District, Vientiane; 8.30am-5pm Mon-Fri) Based in a new building to the south of the city.

Vietnamese Embassy (Map p132; 021-413400; www. mofa.gov.vn/vnemb.la; Th That Luang, Vientiane; 8.30am-5.30pm Mon-Fri) Issues tourist visas in three working days for US$45, or in one day for US$60. The Luang Prabang consulate (Map p38; www.vietnam consulate-luangprabang.org; Th Naviengkham, Luang Prabang; 8-11.30am & 1.30-5.30pm Mon-Fri) issues tourist visas for US$60 in a few minutes, or US$45 if you wait a few days. At the consulates in Pakse (Map p204; 031-214199; www. vietnamconsulate-pakse.org; Th 21; 7.30-11.30am & 2-4.30pm Mon-Fri) and Savannakhet (Map p192; 041-212418; Th Sisavangvong, Savannakhet), visas cost US$60.

Etiquette

The Lao people are generally very gracious hosts, but there are some important spiritual and social conventions to observe.

➡ **Buddhism** When visiting temples, cover up to the knees and elbows, and remove your shoes and any head covering when entering temple buildings. Sit with your feet tucked behind you to avoid pointing them at Buddha images. Women should never touch a monk or his belongings; step out of the way and don't sit next to them on public transport.

➡ **Local greeting** Called the nop, the local greeting in Laos involves putting your hands together in a prayer-like manner. Use this when being introduced to new Lao friends.

➡ **Modesty** Avoid wearing swimsuits or scanty clothing when walking around towns in Laos, particularly after tubing in Vang Vieng. Wear a sarong or similar to cover up.

➡ **Saving face** Never get into an argument with a Lao person. It's better to smile through any conflict.

Food & Drink

While Lao food may not have the variety and depth of the more famous cuisines of neighbouring China, Thailand and Vietnam, you can still have a culinary adventure in Laos if you take the time to learn a little about the cuisine. Experimentation goes a long way to appreciating the cuisine and can be very rewarding.

It's little surprise that Lao food is similar to Thai cuisine given the long interwoven history of the two countries, but there are some dishes in the cuisine that are unmistakably Lao.

The Basics

Laos has a great range of dining options in the cities, but the choice dries up quickly in remote areas. Booking ahead may occasionally be necessary at popular places in Luang Prabang or Vientiane during peak season or at weekends.

➡ **Cafes** A legacy of the French, Laos has a sophisticated coffee culture. The best cafes are found in Luang Prabang and Vientiane, but most larger towns offer some sort of caffeine fix.

➡ **Beer gardens** A lot of larger restaurants in provincial Laos double as beer gardens by night, serving copious amounts of Beerlao to a local crowd.

➡ **Restaurants** These range from local hole-in-the-wall spots and street markets to sophisticated international bistros. Most cuisines are covered in Vientiane and Luang Prabang, but it's mainly Lao, Thai, Chinese and Vietnamese elsewhere.

Typical Dishes

The standard Lao breakfast is *fĕr* (rice noodles), usually served floating in a broth with vegetables and a meat of your choice. The trick is

in the seasoning, and Lao people will stir in some fish sauce, lime juice, dried chillies, mint leaves, basil, or one of the wonderful speciality hot chilli sauces that many noodle shops make, testing it along the way.

Láhp is the most distinctively Lao dish, a delicious spicy salad made from minced beef, pork, duck, fish or chicken, mixed with fish sauce, small shallots, mint leaves, lime juice, roasted ground rice and lots and lots of chillies. Another famous Lao speciality is *đạm màhk hung* (known as *som tam* in Thailand), a salad of shredded green papaya mixed with garlic, lime juice, fish sauce, sometimes tomatoes, palm sugar, land crab or dried shrimp and, of course, chillies by the handful.

In lowland Lao areas almost every dish is eaten with *kòw nĕeo* (sticky rice), which is served in a small basket. Take a small amount of rice and, using one hand, work it into a walnut-sized ball before dipping it into the food.

In main centres, delicious French baguettes are a popular breakfast food. Sometimes they're eaten with condensed milk, or with *kai* (eggs) in a sandwich that also contains Lao-style pâté and vegetables.

Vegetarians & Vegans

Almost all Lao dishes contain some sort of animal product, be it fish sauce, shrimp paste or lard. There are very few dedicated vegetarian or vegan restaurants in Laos, but

traveller-oriented restaurants and cafes usually have some vegetarian dishes available. It is important to learn some basic food vocabulary in remote areas. The best all-round Lao phrase to learn is '*kòy gin đaa pak*' (I only eat vegetables).

Drinks

On the drinks front, Beerlao remains a firm favourite with 90% of the nation, while officially illegal *lòw-lów* (Lao liquor or rice whisky) is a popular drink among lowland Lao. It's usually taken neat and offered in villages as a welcoming gesture. International wine and spirits are widely available in big cities, though not in smaller towns and villages.

Drinking water is simply called *nâm deum*, whether it's boiled or filtered. All water offered to customers in restaurants or hotels will be purified, and purified water is sold everywhere. Check that the ice in any drink originated from purified water.

Juice bars proliferate around Vientiane and Luang Prabang, and smoothies are usually on the menu in most international cafes. Lao coffee is usually served strong and sweet. Lattes and cappuccinos are springing up across the country with pasteurised milk coming from Thailand.

Chinese-style green tea is the usual ingredient in *nâm sáh* or *sáh lôw*, the weak, refreshing tea traditionally served free in restaurants. For Lipton-style tea, ask for *sáh hôrn* (hot tea).

PRACTICALITIES

Media

Vientiane Times (www.vientianetimes.org.la) The country's only English-language newspaper follows the party line. Published Monday to Saturday.

Le Rénovateur (www.lerenovateur.la) A government mouthpiece in French; similar to the *Vientiane Times*.

Lao National Radio (LNR; www.lnr.org.la) Broadcasts sanitised English-language news twice daily.

Radio Short-wave radios can pick up BBC, VOA, Radio Australia and Radio France International.

TV Lao National TV is so limited that most people watch Thai TV and/or karaoke videos.

Smoking

While a large number of people smoke in rural Laos, towns and cities are becoming increasingly smoke free. Almost all hotels in Laos offer nonsmoking rooms and there is a ban on smoking in cafes and restaurants in Vientiane and Luang Prabang.

Weights & Measures

The metric system is used for measurements. Gold and silver are sometimes weighed in *baht* (15g).

If you stay away from anything you know to be illegal, you should be fine. If not, things might get messy and expensive. Drug possession and using prostitutes are the most common crimes for which travellers are caught, often with the dealer or consort being the one to inform the authorities. Sexual relationships between foreigners and Lao citizens who are not married are illegal; penalties for failing to register a relationship range from fines of US$500 to US$5000, and possibly imprisonment or deportation.

If you are detained, ask to call your embassy or consulate in Laos, if there is one. A meeting or phone call between Lao officers and someone from your embassy/consulate may result in quicker adjudication and release.

Police sometimes ask for bribes for traffic violations and other petty offences.

Insurance

A good travel-insurance policy, as always, is a wise investment. Laos is generally considered a high-risk area, and with limited medical services it's vital to have a policy that covers being evacuated (medivaced), by air if necessary, to a hospital in Thailand. Read the small print in any policy to see if hazardous activities are covered; rock climbing, rafting and motorcycling are often not.

If you undergo medical treatment in Laos or Thailand, be sure to collect all receipts and copies of the medical report, in English if possible, for insurance purposes.

Worldwide travel insurance is available at www.lonely planet.com/travel-insurance. You can buy, extend and claim online anytime, even if you're already on the road.

Internet Access

Free wi-fi is pretty standard these days and available in many guesthouses, hotels and cafes in the main tourist destinations around Laos. Internet cafes are still around but are increasingly rare. It's possible to get online in most provincial capitals, with prices ranging from 5000K per hour in popular centres to as much as 10,000K or more per hour in provincial backwaters.

Computers in most internet cafes have instant-messaging software and Skype, although headsets are not always available.

Legal Matters

Although Laos guarantees certain rights, the reality is that you can be fined, detained or deported for any reason, as has been demonstrated repeatedly in cases involving foreigners.

LGBTI Travellers

For the most part Lao culture is very tolerant of homosexuality, although lesbianism is often either denied completely or misunderstood. The gay and lesbian scene is not nearly as prominent as in neighbouring Thailand, but you might find something happening in Vientiane if you're lucky. Strictly speaking, homosexuality is illegal, though we haven't heard of police busting anyone in recent years. In any case, public displays of affection, whether heterosexual or homosexual, are frowned upon.

Sticky Rice (www.stickyrice.ws) Gay travel guide covering Laos and Asia.

Utopia (www.utopia-asia.com) Gay travel information and contacts, including some local gay terminology.

Money

The official national currency in Laos is the Lao kip (K). Although only kip is legally negotiable in everyday transactions, in reality three currencies are used for commerce: kip, Thai baht (B) and US dollars (US$).

ATMs

ATMs are now found all over Laos. But before you get too excited, ATMs dispense a maximum of 700,000K to 2 million K (about US$85 to US$250) per transaction, depending on the bank, not to mention a variable withdrawal fee. If you also have to pay extortionate charges to your home bank on each overseas withdrawal, this can quickly add up.

Credit Cards

A growing number of hotels, upmarket restaurants and gift shops in Vientiane and Luang Prabang accept Visa and MasterCard, and, to a much lesser extent, Amex and JCB. Outside of these main towns, credit cards are virtually useless.

Banque pour le Commerce Extérieur Lao (BCEL) branches in most major towns offer cash advances/withdrawals on MasterCard and Visa credit/debit cards for a 3% transaction fee. Other banks may have slightly different charges, so it might be worth shopping around in Vientiane.

Currency

Laos relies heavily on the Thai baht and the US dollar for the domestic cash economy. An estimated one-third of all cash circulating in Vientiane, in fact, bears the portrait of the Thai king, while another third celebrates US presidents. Kip is usually preferred for small purchases, while more expensive items and services may be quoted in kip, baht or dollars. Anything costing the equivalent of US$100 or more is likely to be quoted in US dollars.

The majority of transactions will be carried out in kip, however, so it's always worth having a wad in your pocket. Notes come in denominations of 500, 1000, 2000, 5000, 10,000, 20,000, 50,000 and 100,000 kip. Small vendors, especially in rural areas, will struggle to change 100,000K notes.

Moneychangers

After years of volatility the kip has in recent times remained fairly stable at about 8000K to the US dollar. Don't, however, count on this remaining the same.

Generally exchange rates are virtually the same whether you're changing at a bank or a moneychanger. Both are also likely to offer a marginally better rate for larger bills (US$50 and US$100) than smaller bills (US$20 and less). Banks in Vientiane and Luang Prabang can generally change UK pounds, euros, Canadian, US and Australian dollars, Thai baht and Japanese yen. Elsewhere most provincial banks usually change only US dollars or baht.

Licensed moneychangers maintain booths around Vientiane (including at Talat Sao) and at some border crossings. Their rates are similar to the banks, but they stay open longer.

There's no real black market in Laos and unless there's an economic crash that's unlikely to change.

Tipping

Tipping is not customary in Laos except in tourist-oriented restaurants, where 10% of the bill is appreciated, but only if a service charge hasn't already been added.

Opening Hours

Bars and clubs 5pm–11.30pm (later in Vientiane)

Government offices 8am–noon and 1pm–5pm Monday to Friday

Noodle shops 7am–1pm

Restaurants 10am–10pm

Shops 9am–6pm

Post

Sending post from Laos is not all that expensive and is fairly reliable, but people still tend to wait until they get to Thailand to send parcels. Heading to Cambodia, it's probably smarter to post any parcels from Laos.

When posting any package leave it open for inspection by a postal officer. Incoming parcels might also need to be opened for inspection; there may be a small charge for this mandatory 'service'.

The main post office in **Vientiane** (Map p136; ☏020-22206362; Th Saylom; ⊗8am-5pm Mon-Fri, to noon Sat & Sun) has a poste restante service.

Public Holidays

Schools and government offices are closed on the following official holidays, and the organs of state move pretty slowly, if at all, during festivals.

International New Year (1 January)

Army Day (20 January)

International Women's Day (8 March)

Lao New Year (14–16 April)

International Labour Day (1 May)

International Children's Day (1 June)

Lao National Day (2 December)

Safe Travel

Over the last couple of decades Laos has earned a reputation among visitors as a remarkably safe place to travel, with little crime reported and few of the scams often found in more touristed places such as Vietnam, Thailand and Cambodia. And while the vast majority of Laotians remain honest and welcoming, things aren't quite as idyllic as they once were. The main change has been in the rise of petty crimes, such as theft and low-level scams, which are more annoying than dangerous.

Queues

The Lao people follow the usual Southeast Asian method of queuing for services, which is to say they don't form a line at all but simply push en masse towards the counter or doorway. The system is 'first seen, first served'. Learn to play the game the Lao way, by pushing your money, passport, letters or whatever to the front of the crowd as best you can. That said, it is nowhere near as chaotic as in some of the bigger neighboring countries.

Road & River Travel

Better roads, better vehicles and fewer insurgents mean road travel in Laos is quite safe, if not always comfortable. However, while the scarcity of traffic in Laos means there are far fewer accidents than in neighbouring countries, accidents are still the main risk for travellers.

As motorbikes become increasingly popular among travellers, the number of accidents is rising. Even more likely is the chance of earning yourself a Lao version of the 'Thai tattoo' – that scar on the calf caused by a burn from a hot exhaust pipe.

The speedboats that careen along the Mekong in northern Laos are as dangerous as they are fast. We recommend avoiding all speedboat travel unless absolutely necessary.

Theft

While Lao people are generally trustworthy and theft is much less common than elsewhere in Southeast Asia, it has been on the rise in recent years. Most of the reports we've heard involve opportunistic acts that are fairly easily avoided.

Money or items going missing from hotel rooms is becoming more common, so don't leave cash or other tempting belongings on show. When riding a crowded bus, watch the luggage and don't keep money in loose trouser pockets. When riding a bicycle or motorcycle in Vientiane, don't place anything of value in the basket, as thieving duos on motorbikes may ride by and snatch a bag.

Motorcycle theft is a growing problem. Always lock up your bike when out in the countryside or at night, and pay for parking whenever you can.

Unexploded Ordnance (UXO)

Large areas of eastern and southern Laos are contaminated by UXO. According to surveys by the Lao National UXO Programme (UXO Lao) and other nongovernment UXO clearance organisations, the provinces of Salavan, Savannakhet and Xieng Khuang are the most severely affected, followed by Champasak, Hua Phan, Khammuan, Luang Prabang, Attapeu and Sekong.

Statistically speaking, the UXO risk for the average foreign visitor is low, but travellers should exercise caution when considering off-road wilderness travel in the aforementioned provinces. Stick only to marked paths. And never touch an object that may be UXO, no matter how old and defunct it may appear.

Shopping

Shopping opportunities in Laos continue to improve. There are a huge number of stores selling local textiles and handicrafts, as well as regional favourites from Thailand and Vietnam. Vientiane and Luang Prabang are the main shopping centres, and in these cities, it's easiest to compare quality and price. It is, however, always nice to buy direct from the producer, and in many villages that's possible.

Antiques

Vientiane and Luang Prabang each have a sprinkling of antique shops. Anything that looks old could be up for sale in these shops, including Asian pottery (especially porcelain from the Ming dynasty of China), jewellery, clothes, carved wood, musical instruments, coins and bronze statuettes.

There is a *total* ban on the export of antiques and Buddha images from Laos, although the enforcement of this ban is lax.

Carvings

The Lao people produce well-crafted carvings in wood, bone and stone. Subjects include anything from Hindu or Buddhist mythology to themes from everyday life. Authentic opium pipes can be found, especially in the north, and sometimes have intricately carved bone or bamboo shafts.

To shop for carvings, look in antique or handicraft stores. Don't buy anything made from ivory, as Laos has become a major centre for the trans-shipment of illegal wildlife products.

Fabric (Textiles)

Textiles are among the most beautiful, most recognisable and easiest items to buy while travelling in Laos. Unlike many handicrafts that are ubiquitous throughout Indochina, these are unmistakably Lao.

The best place to buy fabric is in the weaving villages themselves, where you can watch how it's made and get 'wholesale' prices. Failing this, you can find a decent selection and reasonable prices at open markets in provincial towns, including Vientiane's Talat Sao. Tailor shops and handicraft stores generally charge more and quality is variable.

Jewellery

Gold and silver jewellery are good buys in Laos, although you must search hard for well-made pieces. Some of the best silverwork is done by the hill tribes.

Telephone

With a local SIM card and a 3G or wi-fi connection, the cheapest option is to use WhatsApp or Skype via a mobile device.

International calls can be made from Lao Telecom offices or the local post office in most provincial capitals and are charged on a per minute basis, with a minimum charge of three minutes. Calls to most countries cost about 2000K to 4000K per minute. Office hours typically run from about 7.30am to 9.30pm.

Mobile Phones

Roaming is possible in Laos but is generally expensive. Local SIM cards and unlocked mobile phones are readily available.

COVERAGE & COSTS

Lao Telecom and several private companies offer mobile-phone services on the GSM and 3G systems. Competition is fierce and you can buy a local SIM card for as little as 10,000K from almost anywhere. Calls are cheap and recharge cards are widely available. Network coverage varies depending on the company and the region.

DIALLING CODES

The country code for calling Laos is ☑856. For long-distance calls within the country, dial ☑0 first, then the area code and number. For international calls dial ☑00 first, then the country code, area code and number.

All mobile phones have a ☑020 code at the beginning of the number. Similar to this are WIN satellite phones, which begin with ☑030.

Time

Laos is seven hours ahead of GMT/UTC. Thus, noon in Vientiane is 10pm the previous day in San Francisco, 1am in New York, 5am in London and 3pm in Sydney. There is no daylight saving time.

Toilets

While Western-style 'thrones' are now found in most midrange and top-end accommodation, budget travellers should expect the rather-less-royal squat toilet to be the norm when staying in some guesthouses and particularly homestays.

Even in places where sit-down toilets are installed, the plumbing may not be designed to take toilet paper. In such cases there will usually be a rubbish bin for used paper.

Public toilets are uncommon outside hotel lobbies and airports. While on the road between towns and villages it's perfectly acceptable to go behind a tree or use the roadside. Lao tour guides use the euphemism 'shooting rabbits' for men and 'picking flowers' for women in case you wonder what on earth they are talking about.

Tourist Information

The Lao National Tourism Administration (LNTA) has tourist offices all over Laos, with the ones in Vientiane and Luang Prabang particularly helpful.

Many offices are well-stocked with brochures and maps, and have easily understood displays of their provincial attractions and English-speaking staff to answer your questions. Offices in Tha Khaek, Savannakhet, Pakse, Luang Namtha, Sainyabuli, Phongsali and Sam Neua are all pretty good, with staff trained to promote treks and other activities in their provinces and able to hand out brochures and first-hand knowledge. They should also be able to help with local transport options and bookings. Alternatively, you can usually get up-to-date information from a popular guesthouse.

The LNTA also runs three very good websites that offer valuable pre-departure information:

Central Laos Trekking (www.trekkingcentrallaos.com)

Ecotourism Laos (www.ecotourismlaos.com)

Laos National Tourism Administration (www.tourismlaos.org)

Travellers with Disabilities

With its lack of paved roads or footpaths (sidewalks), Laos presents many physical obstacles for people with mobility impairments. Rarely do public buildings feature ramps or other access points for wheelchairs, nor do most hotels make efforts to provide access for the physically disabled, the few exceptions being at the top end in Vientiane and Luang Prabang. Most sights have no disabled access. Public transport is particularly crowded and difficult, even for the fully ambulatory.

For wheelchair users, any trip to Laos will require a good deal of advance planning. Fortunately a growing network of information sources can put you in touch with those who may have wheeled through Laos before.

Access-Able Travel Source (www.access-able.com)

Mobility International USA (www.miusa.org)

Society for Accessible Travel & Hospitality (www.sath.org)

Download Lonely Planet's free Accessible Travel guide from http://lptravel.to/accessibletravel.

Travel with Children

Like many places in Southeast Asia, travelling with children in Laos can be a lot of fun as long as you come prepared with the right attitude. The Lao people adore children and in many instances will shower attention on your offspring, who will readily find playmates among their Lao peers and a temporary nanny service at practically every stop.

Practicalities

Child-friendly amenities such as high chairs in restaurants, car seats, and changing facilities in public restrooms are virtually unknown in Laos. Parents have to be extra resourceful in seeking out substitutes or follow the example of Lao families, which means holding smaller children on their laps much of the time.

Baby formula and nappies (diapers) are available at mini marts in the larger towns and cities, but bring along a sufficient supply to rural areas.

For the most part parents needn't worry too much about health concerns, although it pays to lay down a few ground rules – such as regular hand-washing or using hand-cleansing gel – to head off potential medical problems. All the usual health precautions apply. Children should especially be warned not to play with animals encountered along the way, as rabies is disturbingly common in Laos.

Do not let children stray from the path in remote areas of Laos that were heavily bombed during the Second Indochina War. Bombies (tennis-ball-sized bomblets) remain an everyday threat in some regions and children are usually the most common victims, as the bombies resemble tennis balls.

Visas

Thirty-day tourist visas are readily available on arrival at international airports and most land borders.

Citizens of the Association of Southeast Asian Nations (ASEAN) – Japan, South Korea, Russia and Switzerland – enjoy visa-free access to Laos. Most other nationalities can obtain their visa on arrival, including EU citizens, North Americans and Australians. Citizens of some African and Middle Eastern countries must apply for a visa in advance.

Tourist Visa on Arrival

The Lao government issues 30-day tourist visas on arrival at all international airports and most international border crossings.

The whole process is very straightforward. You need between US$30 and US$42 in cash, one passport-sized photo and the name of a hotel or guesthouse. Those without a photo, or who are arriving on a weekend, holiday or after office hours, will have to pay an additional one or two dollars.

The visa fee varies depending on the passport of origin, with Canadians having to fork out the most (US$42) and most other nationalities paying between US$30 and US$35. Pay in US dollars as a flat rate of 1500B (around US$50) is applicable in Thai baht. No other foreign currencies are accepted.

Tourist Visa

For those not eligible for a visa on arrival, Lao embassies and consulates abroad offer 30-day tourist visas. The process involves roughly the same cost and documentation and generally takes three working days. In Bangkok you can get your visa on the same day for an additional 200B express fee.

Work Visa

Business visas, valid for 30 days, are relatively easy to obtain as long as you have a sponsoring agency in Laos. A business visa can be extended by up to a year.

Visa Extensions

The 30-day tourist visa can be extended an additional 90 days at a cost of US$2 per day, but only in major cities such as Vientiane, Luang Prabang, Pakse and Savannakhet.

Overstaying Your Visa

Overstaying a visa is not a major crime, but it is expensive. It costs US$10 for each day overstayed, paid at the immigration checkpoint on departure.

Volunteering

Volunteers have been working in Laos for years, usually on one- or two-year contracts that include a minimal monthly allowance. Volunteers are often placed with a government agency and attempt to 'build capacity'. These sort of jobs can lead to non-volunteer work within the non-governmental organisation (NGO) community.

The alternative approach to volunteering, where you actually pay to be placed in a 'volunteer' role for a few weeks or months, has yet to arrive in Laos in any great capacity. A couple of groups in Luang Prabang need volunteers occasionally, and there are also local projects in places as diverse as Huay Xai, Muang Khua and Sainyabuli.

The website **Stay Another Day** (www.stayanotherday.org) is a good resource for unpaid volunteer opportunities.

Australian Volunteers International (www.australianvolunteers.com) Places qualified Australian residents on one- to two-year contracts.

Global Volunteers (www.australianvolunteers.com) Places qualified Australian residents on one- to two-year contracts.

Voluntary Service Overseas (VSO; www.vsointernational.org) Places qualified and experienced volunteers for up to two years.

Women Travellers

Laos is an easy country for women travellers, although it is necessary to be more culturally aware or sensitive than in many parts of neighbouring Thailand. Laos is very safe and violence against women travellers is extremely rare. Everyday incidents of sexual harassment may be more common than they were a few years ago, but they're still much less frequent than in virtually any other Asian country.

The relative lack of prostitution in Laos, as compared with Thailand, has benefits for women travellers. While a Thai woman who wants to preserve a 'proper' image often won't associate with foreign males for fear of being perceived as a prostitute, in Laos this is not the case. Hence a foreign woman seen drinking in a cafe or restaurant is not usually perceived as 'available' as she might be in Thailand. This in turn means that there are generally fewer problems with uninvited male solicitations.

It's highly unusual for most Lao women to wear singlet tops or very short skirts or shorts. So when travellers do, people tend to stare. If you're planning on bathing in a village or river, a sarong is essential.

Traditionally women didn't sit on the roofs of riverboats, because this was believed to bring bad luck. These days most captains aren't so concerned, but if you are asked to get off the roof while men are not, this is why.

Transport

GETTING THERE & AWAY

Many travellers enter or exit Laos via the country's numerous land and river borders. Flying into Laos is a relatively easy option as there is only a small number of airlines serving Laos and prices don't vary much. Flights and tours can be booked online at www.lonely planet.com/bookings.

Entering the Country

Wattay International Airport (Map p132;☎021-512165; www.vientianeairport.com) Buses and jumbos (a motorised threewheeled taxi, sometimes called tuk-tuk) run to/from Vientiane's airport. Taxis/minibuses cost a flat fare of US$7/8.

Luang Prabang International Airport (☎071-212173; 📶)
Taxis to/from the airport cost a standardised 50,000K.

Savannakhet International Airport (Map p192;☎041-212140; Th Kaysone Phomvihane) Jumbos cost 30,000K from the airport, but drivers may start higher.

Pakse International Airport (Rte 13) A sǎhm-lór or tuk-tuk to the airport will cost about 50,000K.

Air

Laos has air connections with regional countries including Thailand, Vietnam, Cambodia, Malaysia, Singapore, China and South Korea. The most convenient international gateway to Laos is Bangkok and there are plenty of flights to the Thai capital. If heading to Laos for a shorter holiday, it is cheaper to take an indirect flight to Bangkok with a stop on the way. Once in Bangkok, there are planes, trains and buses heading to Laos.

Airports & Airlines

There are four international airports in Laos: **Wattay International Airport** (Map p132; ☎021-512165; www.vientianeairport.com) in Vientiane, **Luang Prabang International Airport** (☎071-212173; 📶), **Savannakhet International Airport** (Map p192; ☎041-212140; Th Kaysone Phomvihane) and **Pakse International Airport** (Rte 13).

Lao Airlines is the national carrier and monopolises the majority of flights in and out of the country.

Air Asia (Map p132; www. airasia.com; Wattay Airport International Terminal) Flights from Vientiane to Bangkok and Kuala Lumpur daily, plus Luang Prabang to Bangkok and Kuala Lumpur.

Bangkok Airways (www. bangkokair.com) Daily flights between Bangkok and Vientiane, Luang Prabang and Pakse, plus Chiang Mai to Luang Prabang flights.

CLIMATE CHANGE & TRAVEL

Every form of transport that relies on carbon-based fuel generates CO_2, the main cause of human-induced climate change. Modern travel is dependent on aeroplanes, which might use less fuel per kilometre per person than most cars but travel much greater distances. The altitude at which aircraft emit gases (including CO_2) and particles also contributes to their climate change impact. Many websites offer 'carbon calculators' that allow people to estimate the carbon emissions generated by their journey and, for those who wish to do so, to offset the impact of the greenhouse gases emitted with contributions to portfolios of climate-friendly initiatives throughout the world. Lonely Planet offsets the carbon footprint of all staff and author travel.

Laos Air Fares

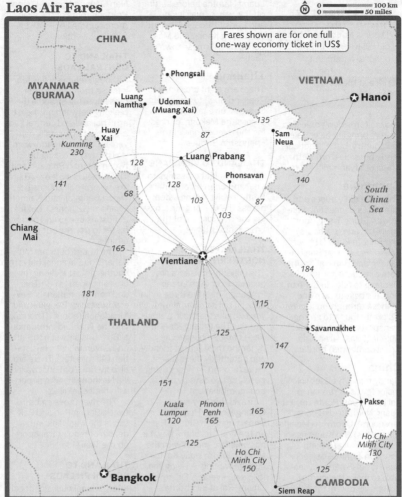

Fares shown are for one full one-way economy ticket in US$

0 — 100 km
0 — 50 miles

CHINA

MYANMAR (BURMA)

VIETNAM

• Phongsali

Luang Namtha •
Udomxai (Muang Xai)

✪ Hanoi

135

87

• Sam Neua

Huay Xai •

Kunming 230

128

• Luang Prabang

140

Phonsavan •

South China Sea

141

68

128

103

87

103

Chiang Mai

165

✪ Vientiane

184

181

115

THAILAND

125

• Savannakhet

147

170

151

Kuala Lumpur 120

Phnom Penh 165

165

• Pakse

Ho Chi Minh City 130

125

Ho Chi Minh City 150

CAMBODIA

✪ Bangkok

• Siem Reap

125

China Eastern Airlines (www. ce-air.com) Flies daily to Kunming and Nanning from Vientiane.

Korean Air (www.koreanair. com) Daily connections between Vientiane and Seoul.

Lao Airlines (www.laoairlines. com) National carrier. The extensive international flight network includes Vientiane to Bangkok, Chiang Mai, Guangzhou, Hanoi, Ho Chi Minh City, Kunming, Phnom Penh, Siem Reap and Singapore; Luang Prabang to

Bangkok, Chiang Mai, Hanoi and Siem Reap; Pakse to Bangkok, Danang, Ho Chi Minh City and Siem Reap; and Savannakhet to Bangkok and Danang.

Thai Airways (www.thaiairways. com) Vientiane and Luang Prabang to Bangkok daily.

Vietnam Airlines (www.vietnam airlines.com) Connects Vientiane with Ho Chi Minh City, Hanoi and Phnom Penh, plus Luang Prabang with Hanoi and Siem Reap.

Land

Laos shares land and/or river borders with Thailand, Myanmar (Burma), Cambodia, China and Vietnam. Border-crossing details change regularly, so ask around and check the Thorn Tree (lonely planet.com/thorntree) before setting off.

It's possible to bring a car or motorcycle into Laos from Cambodia and Thailand with the right paperwork and

DEPARTURE TAX

There is a departure tax of US$10 on all international flights, but it is included in the ticket price at the time of purchase.

Lao customs don't object to visitors bringing bicycles into the country, but it is not currently possible from Vietnam, China or Myanmar.

Cambodia

There are daily buses and minibuses connecting Pakse with Stung Treng (four hours), Kratie (six hours) and Phnom Penh (11 hours). These also stop at Ban Nakasang and Ban Hat Xai in both directions for travellers planning to relax in Si Phan Don. It's best to take one of these through-buses, as it's pretty tough to arrange transport at the Non Nok Khiene (Laos)/Trapaeng Kriel (Cambodia) border.

China

Handy through-buses link major towns in Yunnan to northern Laos. Routes include Luang Namtha–Jinghong (six hours), Udomxai–Mengla (five hours) and Kunming–Luang Prabang (around 24 hours on a Chinese sleeper bus). It's also perfectly feasible to make the journey in hops via Boten, the only China–Lao border crossing currently open to foreigners. From Móhān on the Chinese side it's around a two-hour minibus ride to Mengla, the nearest large town.

Myanmar (Burma)

The first Lao-Myanmar Friendship Bridge officially opened in May 2016 connecting Xieng Kok in Luang Namtha Province with Tachelik District in Shan State. However, border-demarcation disagreements have delayed it opening for international traffic. Check in Vientiane or Luang Namtha before setting off this way or play it safe and transit through Thailand, via Chiang Khong and Mae Sai, to the Burmese town of Tachilek.

Thailand

There are eight crossings to Thailand open to foreigners. Some involve taking a boat across the Mekong, or crossing the river on one of the Friendship Bridges.

THAILAND TO VIENTIANE

There are eight crossings to Thailand open to foreigners. Some involve taking a boat across the Mekong, or crossing the river on one of the Friendship Bridges.

THAILAND TO NORTHERN LAOS

The majority of visitors are heading to or from Luang Prabang. There are three main options but no route allows you to make the trip in a single journey. The Chiang Rai–Huay Xai–Luang Prabang route is by far the most tourist friendly and potentially the quickest route (around 24 hours using buses, or two days by bus-boat combination).

Travel this way is via Chiang Khong/Huay Xai. Departing from Chiang Rai on the first bus of the day it is possible to connect with the slowboat from Huay Xai to Luang Prabang, arriving the following evening. Or leave Chiang Rai at lunchtime and connect with the 5pm overnight bus (faster but not recommended when compared with the beautiful boat journey), arriving in Luang Prabang late next morning. Through-tickets from Chiang Mai or Chiang Rai agencies are generally overpriced.

Other possibilities are perfectly feasible but see almost no foreign tourists, so you'll need to be comfortable with local languages or sign language. These routes can also take several days due to limited transport and poor roads. Choose from the Nan–Muang Ngeun–Luang Prabang route or the even more remote Loei–Pak Lai–Sainyabuli option.

THAILAND TO CENTRAL LAOS

Although relatively few tourists use them, the border crossings that straddle the Mekong between northeastern Thailand and central Laos are almost universally convenient and straightforward.

The river crossing between Nakhon Phanom and Tha Khaek is a breeze. There are several daily buses between Bangkok and Nakhon Phanom (12 hours), but it's almost as cheap and much faster to use the budget airlines.

The bridge between Mukdahan and Savannakhet is the southernmost Mekong River crossing open to non-Thai and non-Lao nationals. Several buses link Bangkok and Mukdahan (about 10 hours), and the Thai-Lao International Bus runs between the latter and Savannakhet's bus station (45 minutes). There are also fly-drive options available via Nakhon Phanom airport with budget airlines.

The river crossing between Beung Kan and Paksan is the weak link with a dearth of regular transport on the Thai side.

THAILAND TO SOUTHERN LAOS

International buses connect Pakse with Ubon Ratchathani (four hours including crossing) via the Vang Tao (Laos) and Chong Mek (Thailand) border twice daily, plus there is one through service a day to Bangkok. Combination bus and train tickets can also be purchased in Pakse.

Vietnam

At the time of writing, foreigners could cross between Laos and Vietnam at seven different border posts. Laos issues 30-day tourist visas at all of these, but Vietnamese visas must be arranged in

Laos Border Crossings

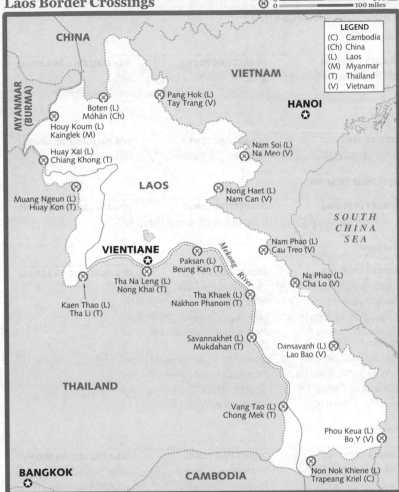

N

0 — 200 km
0 — 100 miles

LEGEND
(C)	Cambodia
(Ch)	China
(L)	Laos
(M)	Myanmar
(T)	Thailand
(V)	Vietnam

CHINA

MYANMAR (BURMA)

VIETNAM

HANOI

Boten (L)
Móhān (Ch)

Houy Koum (L)
Kainglek (M)

Pang Hok (L)
Tay Trang (V)

Huay Xal (L)
Chiang Khong (T)

Nam Soi (L)
Na Meo (V)

LAOS

Nong Haet (L)
Nam Can (V)

Muang Ngeun (L)
Huay Kon (T)

SOUTH
CHINA
SEA

VIENTIANE

Nam Phao (L)
Cau Treo (V)

Paksan (L)
Beung Kan (T)

Mekong River

Tha Na Leng (L)
Nong Khai (T)

Na Phao (L)
Cha Lo (V)

Tha Khaek (L)
Nakhon Phanom (T)

Kaen Thao (L)
Tha Li (T)

Savannakhet (L)
Mukdahan (T)

Dansavanh (L)
Lao Bao (V)

THAILAND

Vang Tao (L)
Chong Mek (T)

Phou Keua (L)
Bo Y (V)

BANGKOK

CAMBODIA

Non Nok Khiene (L)
Trapeang Kriel (C)

advance in Luang Prabang, Vientiane, Savannakhet or Pakse for some nationals. Exceptions are Association of Southeast Asian Nations (ASEAN) countries, Japan and South Korea, plus some European countries such as Scandinavia, France, Italy, Spain, Germany and the UK. In every case we recommend using a through-bus rather than trying to make the trip in hops, as it can be very difficult to arrange onward transport from the remote border posts.

VIETNAM TO NORTHERN LAOS

An increasingly popular alternative to the hellish 24-hour buses between Hanoi and Vientiane is to start from northwestern Vietnam and use the daily Dien Bien Phu–Muang Khua bus, crossing the border at Tay Trang, before arriving in fascinating Phongsali Province. Reaching Luang Prabang from Dien Bien Phu is possible in two days (one night in Muang Khua). Better is to take it slowly using the Nam Ou (Ou River) riverboats with a stop in Nong Khiaw.

Other decent alternatives start from the Vietnamese towns of Thanh Hoa and Vinh. Thanh Hoa–Sam Neua buses (daily), which pass through the border at Nam Soi, take a beautiful route and are ideal for visiting the memorable Vieng Xai Caves on a long overland trip to Luang Prabang.

Buses on the Vinh–Phonsavan route, which pass the border at lonely Nam Can, allow a visit to the

LAOS BORDER CROSSINGS

Cambodia

BORDER CROSSING	CONNECTING TOWNS	VISA AVAILABLE ON ARRIVAL
Non Nok Khiene (L)/Trapeang Kriel (C)	Si Phan Don (L), Stung Treng (C)	Yes

China

BORDER CROSSING	CONNECTING TOWNS	VISA AVAILABLE ON ARRIVAL
Boten (L)/Móhān (C)	Luang Nam Tha (L), Mengla (C)	Laos only

Myanmar (Burma)

BORDER CROSSING	CONNECTING TOWNS	VISA AVAILABLE ON ARRIVAL
Houy Koum (L)/Kainglek (M)	Luang Namtha (L), Tachilek (M)	No

Thailand

BORDER CROSSING	CONNECTING TOWNS	VISA AVAILABLE ON ARRIVAL
Tha Na Leng (L)/Nong Khai (T)	Vientiane (L), Nong Khai (T)	Yes
Paksan (L)/Beung Kan (T)	Paksan (L), Beung Kan (T)	No
Huay Xai(L)/Chiang Khong (T)	Huay Xai (L), Chiang Rai (T)	Yes
Tha Khaek(L)/Nakhon Phanom(T)	Tha Khaek (L), Nakhon Phanom (T)	Yes
Savannakhet (L)/Mukdahan (T)	Savannakhet (L), Mukdahan (T)	Yes
Vang Tao (L)/Chong Mek (T)	Pakse (L), Ubon Ratchathani (T)	Yes
Muang Ngeun (L)/Huay Kon (T)	Hongsa (L), Phrae (T)	Yes
Kaen Thao (L)/Tha Li (T)	Pak Li (L), Loei (T)	Yes

Vietnam

BORDER CROSSING	CONNECTING TOWNS	VISA AVAILABLE ON ARRIVAL
Dansavanh (L)/Lao Bao (V)	Savannakhet (L), Dong Ha (V)	Laos all/Vietnam some
Phou Keua (L)/Bo Y (V)	Attapeu (L), Kontum (V)	Laos all/Vietnam some
Na Phao (L)/Cha Lo (V)	Tha Khaek (L), Dong Hoi (L)	Laos all/Vietnam some
Nong Haet (L)/Nam Can (V)	Phonsavan (L), Vinh (V)	Laos all/Vietnam some
Nam Phao (L)/CauTreo (V)	Tha Khaek (L), Vinh (V)	Laos all/Vietnam some
Na Meo (L)/Nam Soi (V)	Sam Neua (L), Thanh Hoa (V)	Laos all/Vietnam some
Pang Hok (L)/Tay Trang (V)	Muang Khua (L), Dien Bien Phu (V)	Laos all/Vietnam some

enigmatic Plain of Jars but don't run daily.

VIETNAM TO VIENTIANE & CENTRAL LAOS
There are direct buses from both Hanoi and Ho Chi Minh City to Vientiane, but a more interesting alternative is to break up the trip in beautiful but seldom-visited central Laos.

Starting out in central Vietnam, there are a few different options. The border at Lao Bao, easily accessed from Dong Ha, is the largest and easiest of all crossings to/from Vietnam. Once in Laos, break the journey with stays in Sepon, visiting what's left of the Ho Chi Minh Trail, or in Savannakhet. Moving north, there's a crossing at Cha Lo, but virtually the only traffic is the buses that run between Dong Hoi and Tha Khaek. The most popular crossing is at Cau Treo, which is easily accessed via Vinh, and which is also the route that the direct buses between Vientiane and Hanoi use. Punctuate the journey with a visit to the spectacular underground river at Tham Kong Lor.

VIETNAM TO SOUTHERN LAOS

There is a daily bus service (in both directions) between Pakse and Kontum, passing through both Sekong and Attapeu, as well as the Phou Keua (Laos)/Bo Y (Vietnam) border. It takes about eight to nine hours to complete the entire journey or about half that between Attapeu and Kontum.

GETTING AROUND

Transport in Laos is generally very good value, but journeys can take a lot longer than distances on a map might suggest.

Air Laos has an extensive domestic flight network and this can save considerable time on a short visit.

Boat Rivers are the lifeblood of Laos, making boat journeys an important element of the transport network.

Bus Laos has some smart buses operating on major routes out of Vientiane, but venture into remote areas and vehicles are as old as the hills.

Car For those with a more flexible budget, a rented car with driver is the smoothest way to cover a lot of ground in a limited amount of time.

Air

Domestic flights to smaller airports suffer fairly frequent cancellations due to fog and, in March, heavy smoke during the slash-and-burn season. During the holiday season it's best to book ahead as flights can fill fast. At other times, when flights are more likely

to be cancelled, confirm the flight is still departing a day or two before.

Airlines in Laos

Lao Airlines (www.laoairlines. com) The main airline in Laos handling domestic flights, including between Vientiane and Luang Prabang, Luang Nam Tha, Pakse, Phonsavan, Savannakhet and Udomxai.

Lao Skyway (Map p132; ☑021-513022; www.laosky way.com; Domestic Terminal, Wattay International Airport; ☺8am-8pm) A newer domestic airline with flights from Vientiane to Udomxai, Luang Prabang, Huay Xai and Luang Namtha.

With the exception of the Lao Airlines' offices in major cities, where credit cards are accepted for both international and domestic tickets, it is necessary to pay cash in US dollars.

Bicycle

The stunningly beautiful roads and light, relatively slow traffic in most towns and on most highways make Laos arguably the best country for cycling in Southeast Asia.

Simple single-speed bicycles can be hired in most places that see a decent number of tourists, usually costing about 20,000K per day. Better mountain bikes will cost from 40,000K to 80,000K per day.

Boat

More than 4600km of navigable rivers are the highways and byways of traditional Laos, the main thoroughfares being the Mekong, Nam Ou (Ou River), Nam Khan (Khan River), Nam Tha (Tha River), Nam Ngum (Ngum River) and Se Kong (Kong River). The Mekong is the longest and most important route and is navigable year-round between Luang Prabang in the north and Savannakhet in the south. Smaller rivers accommodate a range of

smaller boats, from dugout canoes to 'bomb boats' made from war detritus.

Whether it's on a tourist boat from Huay Xai to Luang Prabang or on a local boat you've rustled up in some remote corner of the country, it's still worth doing at least one river excursion while in Laos.

River Ferries (Slowboats) & River Taxis

The slowboat between Huay Xai and Luang Prabang is the most popular river trip in Laos. It is still a daily event and relatively cheap at about 200,000K or US$25 per person for the two-day journey. From Huay Xai, these basic boats are often packed, while travelling in the other direction from Luang Prabang there seems to be more room. Passengers sit, eat and sleep on the wooden decks. The toilet (if there is one) is an enclosed hole in the deck at the back of the boat.

For shorter river trips, such as Luang Prabang to the Pak Ou Caves, it's usually best to hire a river taxi. The *héua hang nyáo* (longtail boats) are the most common and cost around US$10 an hour.

Along the upper Mekong River between Huay Xai and Vientiane, Thai-built *héua wái* (speedboats) are common. They can cover a distance in six hours that might take a ferry two days or more. Charters cost at least US$30 per hour, but some ply regular routes so the cost can be shared among passengers. They are, however, rather dangerous and we recommend taking one only if absolutely necessary.

Tours

With public boat routes becoming increasingly hard to find, tour companies are offering kayaking and rafting trips on some of the more scenic stretches of river. The best places to organise these

TYPES OF BOAT

Following are some of the *héua* (boats) that you may encounter in your adventures along Laos' many waterways:

Héua sáh (double-deck slowboats) Big, old boats; almost extinct.

Héua dooan (express boat) Roofed cargo boats, common on the Huay Xai–Luang Prabang route. Still slow, but faster than double-deck boats.

Héua wái (speedboat) These resemble a surfboard with a car engine strapped to the back: very fast, exhilarating, deafeningly loud, uncomfortable and rather dangerous. Not recommended.

Héua hăhng nyáo (longtail boat) Boats with the engine gimbal-mounted on the stern; found all over Laos.

Héua pái (row boat) Essentially a dugout; common in Si Phan Don.

are Luang Namtha, Luang Prabang, Nong Khiaw, Vang Vieng, Tha Khaek and Pakse.

For something a bit more luxurious, **Mekong Cruises** (www.mekong-cruises.com) and **Mekong River Cruises** (Map p44; ☑030-78600017, 071-254768; www.cruise mekong.com; 22/2 Th Sakkarin, Ban Xieng Thong, Luang Prabang; tours per person incl flights to/from Bangkok US$1650-2980) both offer multiday cruises along the Mekong on refurbished river barges.

Bus & Sŏrngtăaou

Long-distance public transport in Laos is either by bus or *sŏrngtăaou* (literally 'two rows'), which are converted pick-ups or trucks with benches down either side. Private operators have established VIP buses on some busier routes, offering faster and more luxurious air-con services that cost a little more than normal buses. Many guesthouses can book tickets for a small fee.

Sŏrngtăaou usually service shorter routes within a given province. Most decent-sized villages have at least one *sŏrngtăaou*, which will run to the provincial capital and back most days.

Car & Motorcycle

Driving in Laos is easier than it looks. Sure, the road infrastructure is pretty basic, but outside of the large centres there are so few vehicles that it's a doddle compared to Vietnam, China or Thailand.

Motorcyclists planning to ride through Laos should check out the wealth of information at **Golden Triangle Rider** (www.gt-rider.com). Doing some sort of motorbike loop out of Vientiane is becoming increasingly popular among travellers.

Bringing Your Own Vehicle

Bringing a vehicle into Laos is easy enough if you have proof of ownership and a carnet. Simply get the carnet stamped at any international border and there is no extra charge or permit required.

Coming from Thailand, which doesn't recognise the carnet system, an International Transport Permit, known in Thailand as the *lêm sée môoang* (purple book), is required. This is available at Nong Khai's **Land Transport Office** (☑042-411591, ext 103; ⊗8.30am-4.30pm). You'll need your vehicle's official registration book and tax receipts, your passport and

an international driving permit or Thai driver's licence.

On the Lao side you'll need all the documents mentioned above and will also need to arrange Lao vehicle insurance (about 300B for a week).

Exiting into Thailand or Cambodia is fairly hassle-free if your papers are in order. Vietnam is a different story and it is probably best not to even consider a crossing. Heading to China it's virtually impossible to drive a vehicle larger than a bicycle across the border.

Driving Licences

Officially at least, to drive in Laos a valid international driving permit is required. If you're only renting motorbikes you'll never be asked for any sort of licence.

Fuel & Spare Parts

At the time of writing, fuel cost about US$1 a litre for petrol, slightly less for diesel. Fuel for motorcycles is available from drums or Beerlao bottles in villages across the country, although prices are almost always higher than at service stations. Diesel is available in most towns. It's best to fuel up in bigger towns at big-brand service stations because the quality of fuel can be poor in remote areas.

Spare parts for four-wheeled vehicles are expensive and difficult to find, even in Vientiane.

Hire

Chinese- and Japanese-made 100cc and 110cc step-through motorbikes can be hired for approximately 40,000K to 100,000K per day in most large centres and some smaller towns, although the state of the bikes can vary greatly. No licence is required. Try to get a Japanese bike if travelling any distance out of town. In Vientiane, Luang Prabang, Vang Vieng, Tha Khaek and Pakse, 250cc dirt bikes are available from around US$25 to US$50 per day.

It's possible to hire a self-drive vehicle, but when you consider that a driver usually costs no more, takes responsibility for damage and knows where he's going, it looks risky. Costs run from US$40 to US$100 per day, depending on the route.

Vientiane-based **Avis** (Map p136; ☏021-223867; www.avis.la; Th Setthathirath; ⊗8.30am-6.30pm Mon-Fri, to 1pm Sat & Sun) is a reliable option for car hire. When it comes to motorbikes, try **Drivenbyadventure** (☏020-58656994; www.hochiminhtrail.org; rental per day US$38-95, tours per day US$160-200) or **Fuark Motorcycle Hire** (☏021-261970; fuarkmotor cross@yahoo.com) in Vientiane.

Insurance

Car-hire companies will provide insurance, but be sure to check exactly what is covered. Note that most travel-insurance policies don't cover use of motorcycles.

Road Conditions

While the overall condition of roads is poor, work over the last decade has left most of the main roads in reasonable shape.

Elsewhere, unsurfaced roads are the rule. Laos has about 23,000km of classified roads and less than a quarter are sealed. Unsurfaced roads are particularly tricky in the wet season when many routes are impassable to all but 4WD vehicles and motorbikes, while in the dry season the clouds of dust kicked up by passing traffic makes travel highly uncomfortable, especially in a *sŏrngtăaou* or by motorbike. Bring a face mask. Wet or dry, Laos is so mountainous that relatively short road trips can take forever.

Road Hazards

Try to avoid driving at dusk and after dark: cows, buffalo, chickens and dogs, not to mention thousands of people, head for home on the unlit roads, turning them into a dangerous obstacle course.

Road Rules

The single most important rule to driving in Laos is to expect the unexpected. Driving is on the right side, but it's not unusual to see Lao drivers go the wrong way down the left lane before crossing over to the right, a potentially dangerous situation if you're not ready for it. At intersections it's normal to turn right without looking left.

Motorcycle Tips

There are few more liberating travel experiences than renting a motorbike and setting off; stopping where you want, when you want. The lack of traffic and stunningly beautiful roads make Laos one of the best places in the region to do it. There are, however, a few things worth knowing before you hand over your passport as collateral to rent a bike.

The bike Price and availability mean that the vast majority of travellers rent Chinese 110cc bikes. No 110cc bike was designed to be used like a dirt bike,

TRANSPORT CAR & MOTORCYCLE

ROAD DISTANCES (KM)

	Attapeu	Luang Namtha	Luang Prabang	Muang Khong	Nong Haet	Pakse	Phongsali	Phonsavan	Sam Neua	Savannakhet	Tha Khaek	Udomxai	Vang Vieng
Luang Namtha	1400												
Luang Prabang	1130	270											
Muang Khong	190	1380	1110										
Nong Haet	1280	580	350	1260									
Pakse	210	1250	980	120	1130								
Phongsali	1550	360	410	1520	720	1390							
Phonsavan	1170	470	250	1150	110	1020	620						
Sam Neua	1350	450	460	1320	300	1190	590	180					
Savannakhet	410	1050	780	390	930	250	1190	820	990				
Tha Khaek	480	920	650	460	800	370	1070	690	870	130			
Udomxai	1290	110	180	1270	470	1140	250	360	440	940	820		
Vang Vieng	970	440	170	940	320	810	580	220	480	650	490	350	
Vientiane	810	680	390	790	470	660	810	380	620	500	330	580	150

but Japanese bikes deal with it better and are worth the extra few dollars a day.

The odometer Given that many roads have no kilometre stones and turn-offs are often unmarked, it's worth getting a bike with a working odometer. Most bike shops can fix an odometer in about 10 minutes for a few dollars. Money well spent, as long as you remember to note the distance when you start.

The gear Don't leave home without sunscreen, a hat, a plastic raincoat or poncho, a bandanna and sunglasses. Even the sealed roads in Laos get annoyingly dusty, so these last two are vital. A helmet is essential (ask for one if they don't offer), as is wearing trousers and shoes, lest you wind up with the ubiquitous leg burn.

The problems Unless you're very lucky, something will go wrong. Budget some time for it.

The responsibility In general, you can ride a motorbike in Laos without a licence, a helmet or any safety gear whatsoever, but for all this freedom you must take all the responsibility. If you have a crash, there won't be an ambulance to pick you up, and when you get to the hospital, facilities will be basic. Carrying a basic medical kit and phone numbers for hospitals in Thailand and your travel-insurance provider is a good idea. The same

goes for the bike. If it really dies you can't just call the company and get a replacement. You'll need to load it onto the next pick-up or *sŏrngtăaou* and take it somewhere they can fix it. Don't abandon it by the road, or you'll have to pay for another one.

Local Transport

Although most town centres are small enough to walk around, even relatively small settlements often place their bus stations several kilometres out of town.

Bus

Vientiane is the only city with a network of local buses; however, with the exception of a few key recommended routes, they're not much use to travellers.

Sŏrngtăaou, Jumbo, Săhm-Lór & Tuk-tuk

The various pick-ups and three-wheeled taxis found in Vientiane and provincial capitals have different names depending on where you are. Largest are the *sŏrngtăaou*, which double as buses in some areas and as local buses around bigger towns. Larger three-wheelers are called *jąmbǫh* (jumbo) and can hold four to six passengers on two facing

seats. In Vientiane they are sometimes called tuk-tuks as in Thailand (though traditionally in Laos this refers to a slightly larger vehicle than the jumbo). These three-wheeled conveyances are also labelled simply *taak-see* (taxi) or, usually for motor-cycle sidecar-style vehicles, *săhm-lór* (three-wheels). The old-style bicycle *săhm-lór* (pedicab), known as a *cyclo* elsewhere in Indochina, is an endangered species in Laos.

Taxi

Vientiane has a handful of taxis that are used by foreign business people and the occasional tourist, while in other cities a taxi of sorts can be arranged. They can be hired by the trip, by the hour or by the day. Typical all-day hire within a town or city costs between US$35 and US$50, subject to negotiations.

Train

Currently Laos has just 3km of railway line connecting Nong Khai to Vientiane Prefecture via the Friendship Bridge. Plans are underway to extend this line to central Vientiane, and eventually connect with a Chinese-funded railway line from Kunming to Vientiane via Luang Prabang, which is currently under construction.

Health

Dr Trish Batchelor
Health issues and the quality of medical facilities vary enormously depending on where and how you travel in Laos. Travellers tend to worry about contracting infectious diseases when in the tropics, but infections are a rare cause of serious illness or death in travellers. Pre-existing medical conditions such as heart disease and accidental injury account for most of the life-threatening problems. Falling ill in some way, however, is relatively common. Fortunately, most common illnesses can either be prevented with common-sense behaviour or be treated easily with a well-stocked traveller's medical kit.

Before You Go

Pack medications in their original, clearly labelled, containers. A signed and dated letter from your physician describing your medical conditions and medications, including generic names, is also a good idea. If carrying syringes or needles, be sure to have a physician's letter documenting their medical necessity.

If you happen to take any regular medication, bring double your needs in case of loss or theft. In Laos it can be difficult to find some newer drugs, particularly the latest antidepressant drugs, blood-pressure medications and contraceptive pills.

Insurance

Even if you are fit and healthy, don't travel without health insurance, as accidents do happen. Declare any existing medical conditions you have: the insurance company *will* check if your problem is pre-existing and will not cover you if it is undeclared. You may require extra cover for adventure activities such as rock climbing. If your health insurance doesn't cover you for medical expenses abroad, consider getting extra insurance: check www.lonely planet.com/travel-insurance for more information. If you're uninsured, emergency evacuation is extremely expensive.

Find out in advance if your insurance plan will make payments directly to providers or reimburse you later for overseas health expenditures. In Laos, most doctors expect payment in cash. If you have to claim later, keep all the documentation.

Medical Checklist

The following are some recommended items for a personal medical kit:

➡ antibacterial cream, eg Muciprocin

➡ antibiotics for diarrhoea, eg Norfloxacin or Ciprofloxacin; Azithromycin for bacterial diarrhoea; and Tinidazole for giardiasis or amoebic dysentery

➡ antifungal cream, eg Clotrimazole

➡ antihistamines for allergies, eg Cetrizine for daytime and Promethazine for night

➡ anti-inflammatories, eg Ibuprofen

➡ antinausea medication, eg Prochlorperazine

➡ antiseptic for cuts and scrapes, eg Betadine

➡ antispasmodic for stomach cramps, eg Buscopan

➡ contraceptives

➡ decongestant for colds and flus, eg Pseudoephedrine

➡ DEET-based insect repellent

➡ diarrhoea 'stopper', eg Loperamide

➡ first-aid items such as scissors, plasters (Band-Aids), bandages, gauze, thermometer (electronic, not mercury), sterile needles and syringes, and tweezers

➡ indigestion medication, eg Quick Eze or Mylanta

➡ iodine tablets to purify water

➡ oral-rehydration solution for diarrhoea, eg Gastrolyte

➡ paracetamol for pain

➡ permethrin (to impregnate clothing and mosquito nets) for repelling insects

➡ sunscreen and hat

RECOMMENDED & REQUIRED VACCINATIONS

The only vaccine required by international regulations is yellow fever. Proof of vaccination will only be required if you have visited a country in the yellow-fever zone within the six days prior to entering Southeast Asia.

Specialised travel-medicine clinics are the best source of information on vaccines and will be able to give tailored recommendations.

Most vaccines don't produce immunity until at least two weeks after they're given, so visit a doctor four to eight weeks before departure. Ask the doctor for an International Certificate of Vaccination (otherwise known as the yellow booklet), which will list all the vaccinations received.

The World Health Organization (WHO) recommends the following vaccinations for travellers to Southeast Asia, some of which do have side effects:

Adult diphtheria and tetanus Single booster recommended if you've had none in the previous 10 years.

Hepatitis A Provides almost 100% protection for up to a year; a booster after 12 months provides at least another 20 years' protection.

Hepatitis B Now considered routine for most travellers. Given as three shots over six months. A rapid schedule is also available, as is a combined vaccination with Hepatitis A. Lifetime protection occurs in 95% of people.

Measles, mumps and rubella Two doses of MMR required unless you have had the diseases. Many young adults require a booster.

Polio Since 2006, India, Indonesia, Nepal and Bangladesh are the only countries in Asia to have reported cases of polio. Only one booster is required as an adult for lifetime protection.

Typhoid Recommended unless the trip is less than a week and only to developed cities. The vaccine offers around 70% protection, lasts for two to three years and comes as a single shot.

→ throat lozenges

→ thrush (vaginal yeast infection) treatment, eg Clotrimazole pessaries or Diflucan tablet

Websites

There is a wealth of travel health advice on the internet.

World Health Organization (WHO; www.who.int/ith) WHO publishes a superb book called *International Travel & Health*, which is revised annually and is available online for free.

MD Travel Health (www.mdtravelhealth.com) Provides complete travel-health recommendations for every country and is updated daily.

Centers for Disease Control & Prevention (CDC; www.cdc.gov) Good general information.

Health Advisories

It's usually a good idea to consult your government's travel-health website before departure, if one is available.

Australia (www.smartraveller.gov.au)

Canada (www.travelhealth.gc.ca)

New Zealand (www.safetravel.govt.nz)

UK (www.fco.gov.uk/en/travel-and-living-abroad/staying-safe)

USA (www.cdc.gov/travel)

IN LAOS

Availability & Cost of Health Care

Laos has no facilities for major medical emergencies. The state-run hospitals and clinics are among the most basic in Southeast Asia in terms of the standards of hygiene, staff training, supplies and equipment.

For minor to moderate conditions, including malaria, Mahasot Hospital's **International Clinic** (Map p132; ☑021-214021; Th Fa Ngoum; ☺24hr) in Vientiane has a decent reputation. Some foreign embassies in Vientiane also maintain small but professional medical centres, including the **Australian Embassy Clinic** (Map p132; ☑021-353840; Th Tha Deua; ☺8.30am-5pm Mon-Fri) and the **Centre Médical de L'Ambassade de France** (French Embassy Medical Center; Map p132; ☑021-214150; cnr Th Khu Vieng & Th Simeuang; ☺8.30am-noon & 4.30-7pm Mon, Tue, Thu & Fri, 1.30-5pm Wed, 9am-noon Sat).

For any serious conditions, Thailand is the destination of choice. If a medical problem can wait until Bangkok, then all the better, as there are excellent hospitals there.

For medical emergencies that can't be delayed before reaching Bangkok, ambulances can be arranged from nearby Nong Khai or Udon Thani in Thailand. **Nong Khai Wattana General Hospital** (☎042-465201) in Nong Khai is the closest. The better **Aek Udon Hospital** (☎42 342555; Th Phosri) in Udon Thani is an hour further from the border by road.

Buying medication over the counter is not recommended, as fake medications and poorly stored or out-of-date drugs are common in Laos.

Infectious Diseases

Hepatitis A

A problem throughout the region, this food- and water-borne virus infects the liver, causing jaundice (yellow skin and eyes), nausea and lethargy. There is no specific treatment for hepatitis A, you just need to allow time for the liver to heal. All travellers to Southeast Asia should be vaccinated against hepatitis A.

Hepatitis B

The only sexually transmitted disease that can be prevented by vaccination, hepatitis B is spread by body fluids, including sexual contact. In some parts of Southeast Asia, up to 20% of the population are carriers of hepatitis B, and usually are unaware of this. The long-term consequences can include liver cancer and cirrhosis.

Hepatitis E

Hepatitis E is transmitted through contaminated food and water and has similar symptoms to hepatitis A, but it is far less common. It is a severe problem in pregnant women and can result in the death of both mother and baby. There is currently no vaccine; prevention is by following safe eating and drinking guidelines.

HIV

According to Unaids and WHO, Laos remains a 'low HIV prevalence country'. However, it's estimated that only about one-fifth of all HIV cases in Laos are actually reported. Heterosexual sex is the main method of transmission in Laos. The use of condoms greatly decreases but does not eliminate the risk of HIV infection.

Malaria

Many parts of Laos, particularly populated areas, have minimal to no risk of malaria, and the risk of side effects from the antimalaria medication may outweigh the risk of getting the disease. For some rural areas, however, the risk of contracting the disease far outweighs the risk of any tablet side effects. Remember that malaria can be fatal.

Malaria is caused by a parasite transmitted by the bite of an infected mosquito. The most important symptom of malaria is fever, but general symptoms such as headache, diarrhoea, cough or chills may also occur. Diagnosis can only be made by taking a blood sample.

Two strategies should be combined to prevent malaria: mosquito avoidance and antimalarial medications. Most people who catch malaria are taking inadequate or no antimalarial medication.

Travellers are advised to prevent mosquito bites by taking the following steps:

➡ Choose accommodation with screens and fans.

➡ Impregnate clothing with Permethrin in high-risk areas.

➡ Sleep under a mosquito net impregnated with Permethrin.

➡ Spray your room with insect repellent before going out for your evening meal.

➡ Use an insect repellent containing DEET on exposed skin.

➡ Wear long sleeves and trousers in light colours.

MALARIA MEDICATION

There are a variety of medications available. Lariam (Mefloquine) has received much bad press, some of it justified, some not. This weekly tablet suits many people. Serious side effects are rare but include depression, anxiety, psychosis and seizures. Anyone with a history of depression, anxiety, other psychological disorders or epilepsy should not take Lariam. It is around 90% effective in most parts of Southeast Asia, but there is significant resistance in parts of northern Thailand, Laos and Cambodia. Tablets must be taken for four weeks after leaving the risk area.

Doxycycline, taken as a daily tablet, is a broad-spectrum antibiotic that has the added benefit of helping to prevent a variety of tropical diseases. The potential side effects include photosensitivity (a tendency to sunburn), thrush in women, indigestion, heartburn, nausea and interference with the contraceptive pill. More serious side effects include ulceration of the oesophagus – you can help prevent this by taking your tablet with a meal and a large glass of water, and never lying down within half an hour of taking it. It must be taken for four weeks after leaving the risk area.

Malarone is a new drug combining Atovaquone and Proguanil. Side effects are uncommon and mild, most commonly nausea and headaches. It is the best tablet for those on short trips to high-risk areas. It must be taken for one week after leaving the risk area.

A final option is to take no preventive medication but to have a supply of emergency medication should you develop the symptoms of malaria. This is less than ideal, and you'll need to get to a good medical facility within 24 hours of developing a fever. If you choose this option the most effective and safest treatment is Malarone (four tablets once daily for three days).

Opisthorchiasis (Liver Flukes)

These are tiny worms that are occasionally present in fresh-water fish in Laos. The main risk comes from eating raw or undercooked fish. Travellers should in particular avoid eating uncooked ɓạh dàak (an unpasteurised fermented fish used as an accompaniment for many Lao foods) when travelling in rural Laos.

A rarer way to contract liver flukes is by swimming in the Mekong River or its trib-utaries around Don Khong in the far south of Laos.

At low levels, there are virtually no symptoms at all; at higher levels, an overall fatigue, low-grade fever and swollen or tender liver (or general abdominal pain) are the usual symptoms, along with worms or worm eggs in the faeces. Opisthor-chiasis is easily treated with medication.

Rabies

This uniformly fatal disease is spread by the bite or lick of an infected animal, most com-monly a dog or monkey. You should seek medical advice immediately after any animal bite and commence post-ex-posure treatment. Having a pre-travel vaccination means the post-bite treatment is greatly simplified. If an animal bites you, gently wash the wound with soap and water, and apply iodine-based an-tiseptic. If you are not vacci-nated you will need to receive rabies immunoglobulin as soon as possible.

STDs

Sexually transmitted diseas-es (STDs) most common in Laos include herpes, warts, syphilis, gonorrhoea and chlamydia. People carrying these diseases often have no signs of infection. Condoms will prevent gonorrhoea and chlamydia but not warts or herpes. If after a sexual encounter you develop any rash, lumps, discharge or pain when passing urine, seek immediate medical attention. If you have been sexually active during your travels, have an STD check on your return home.

Tuberculosis

Tuberculosis (TB) is very rare in short-term travellers. Medical and aid workers, and long-term travellers who have significant contact with the local population, should take precautions, however. Vaccination is usually only given to children under the age of five, but adults at risk are advised to get pre- and post-travel TB testing. The main symptoms are fever, cough, weight loss, night sweats and tiredness.

Typhoid

This serious bacterial infec-tion is spread via food and water. It gives a high, slowly progressive fever and head-ache, and may be accom-panied by a dry cough and stomach pain. It is diagnosed by blood tests and treated with antibiotics. Vaccination is recommended for all trav-ellers spending more than a week in Southeast Asia, or travelling outside of the major cities.

Traveller's Diarrhoea

Traveller's diarrhoea is by far the most common problem affecting travellers. Some-where between 30% and 50% of people will suffer from it within two weeks of starting their trip.

Traveller's diarrhoea is defined as the passage of more than three watery bow-el actions within 24 hours, plus at least one other symp-tom such as fever, cramps, nausea, vomiting or feeling generally unwell.

Treatment consists of staying well hydrated. Rehydration solutions like Gastrolyte are the best for this. Antibiotics such as Norfloxacin, Ciprofloxacin or Azithromycin will kill the bacteria quickly.

Loperamide is just a 'stop-per' and doesn't get to the cause of the problem, but it can be helpful when taking a long bus ride. Don't take Lop-eramide if you have a fever, or blood in your stools. Seek medical attention quickly if you do not respond to an appropriate antibiotic.

AMOEBIC DYSENTERY

Amoebic dysentery is very rare in travellers but is often misdiagnosed by poor-quality labs in Southeast Asia. Symptoms are similar to bacterial diarrhoea, ie fever, bloody diarrhoea and gener-ally feeling unwell. You should always seek reliable medical care if you have blood in your diarrhoea. Treatment involves two drugs: Tinidazole or Met-ronidazole to kill the parasite in your gut and then a second drug to kill the cysts. If left untreated complications such as liver or gut abscesses can occur.

GIARDIASIS

Giardia lamblia is a parasite that is relatively common in travellers. Symptoms include nausea, bloating, excess gas, fatigue and intermittent diarrhoea. The parasite will eventually go away if left untreated but this can take months. The treatment of choice is Tinidazole, with Metronidazole being a second-line option.

Environmental Hazards

Food

Eating in restaurants is the biggest risk factor for con-tracting traveller's diarrhoea. Ways to avoid it include eat-ing only freshly cooked food, and avoiding shellfish and food that has been sitting around in buffets. Peel all fruit and cook all vegetables. Eat in busy restaurants with a high turnover of customers.

WATER

→ Never drink tap water.

→ Bottled water is generally safe, but check the seal is intact at purchase.

→ Boiling water is the most efficient method of purifying it.

→ The best chemical purifier is iodine. It should not be used by pregnant women or people who suffer with thyroid problems.

→ Water filters should protect against viruses. Ensure your filter has a chemical barrier such as iodine and a small pore size.

Heat

Many parts of Southeast Asia are hot and humid throughout the year and it takes time to adapt to the climate. Swelling of the feet and ankles is common, as are muscle cramps caused by excessive sweating. Prevent these by avoiding dehydration and excessive activity in the heat.

Dehydration is the main contributor to heat exhaustion. Symptoms include feeling weak, headache, irritability, nausea or vomiting, sweaty skin, a fast, weak pulse and a normal or slightly elevated body temperature. Treatment involves getting out of the heat and/or sun, fanning the victim and applying cool wet cloths to the skin and rehydrating with water containing a quarter of a teaspoon of salt per litre. Recovery is usually rapid, though it is common to feel weak for some days afterwards.

Heatstroke is a serious medical emergency. Symptoms come on suddenly and include weakness, nausea, a hot dry body with a body temperature of over 41°C, dizziness, confusion, loss of coordination, seizures and eventually collapse and loss of consciousness. Seek medical help and commence cooling by getting the person out of the heat, removing their clothes, fanning them and applying cool wet cloths or ice to their body, especially to the groin and armpits.

Prickly heat is a common skin rash in the tropics, caused by sweat being trapped under the skin. The result is an itchy rash of tiny lumps. Treat by moving out of the heat and into an air-conditioned area for a few hours and by having cool showers. Locally bought prickly heat powder can be helpful.

Insect Bites & Stings

Bedbugs don't carry disease but their bites are very itchy. They live in the cracks of furniture and walls and then migrate to the bed at night to feed on you. You can treat the itch with an antihistamine.

Ticks are contracted during walks in rural areas. They are commonly found behind the ears, on the belly and in armpits. If you have had a tick bite and experience symptoms such as a rash, fever or muscle aches, then see a doctor. Doxycycline prevents tick-borne diseases.

Leeches are found in humid forest areas. They do not transmit any disease but their bites are often intensely itchy for weeks afterwards and can easily become infected. Apply an iodine-based antiseptic to any leech bite to help prevent infection.

Bee and wasp stings mainly cause problems for people who are allergic to them. Anyone with a serious bee or wasp allergy should carry an injection of adrenaline (eg an Epipen) for emergency treatment.

Skin Problems

Fungal rashes are common in humid climates. Watch out for moist areas that get less air, such as the groin, armpits and between the toes. The problem starts as a red patch that slowly spreads and is usually itchy. Treatment involves keeping the skin dry, avoiding chafing and using an antifungal cream such as Clotrimazole or Lamisil.

Cuts and scratches become easily infected in humid climates. Take meticulous care of any cuts and scratches to prevent complications such as abscesses. Immediately wash all wounds in clean water and apply antiseptic.

Snakes

Southeast Asia is home to many species of both poisonous and harmless snakes. Assume all snakes are poisonous and never try to catch one. Always wear boots and long pants if walking in an area that may have snakes. First aid in the event of a snake bite involves pressure immobilisation via an elastic bandage firmly wrapped around the affected limb, starting at the bite site and working up towards the chest. The bandage should not be so tight that the circulation is cut off, and the fingers or toes should be kept free so the circulation can be checked. Do not use tourniquets or try to suck the venom out.

Sunburn

Even on a cloudy day, sunburn can occur rapidly. Always use a strong sunscreen (at least factor 30), making sure to reapply after a swim, and always wear a wide-brimmed hat and sunglasses outdoors. Avoid lying in the sun during the hottest part of the day (from 10am to 2pm). If you are sunburnt stay out of the sun until you have recovered.

Women's Health

In the urban areas of Southeast Asia, supplies of sanitary products are readily available. Birth-control options may be limited though, so bring adequate supplies of your own form of contraception. Heat, humidity and antibiotics can all contribute to thrush. Treatment is with antifungal creams and pessaries such as Clotrimazole. A practical alternative is a single tablet of Fluconazole (Diflucan).

Pregnant women should receive specialised advice before travelling. The ideal time to travel is in the second trimester (between 16 and 28 weeks), when the risk of pregnancy-related problems are lowest and pregnant women generally feel at their best. Always carry a list of quality medical facilities available at your destination and ensure you continue your standard antenatal care at these facilities. Most of all, ensure travel insurance covers all pregnancy-related possibilities, including premature labour.

Malaria is a high-risk disease during pregnancy. None of the more effective antimalarial drugs are completely safe in pregnancy.

Traditional Medicine

Throughout Southeast Asia, traditional medical systems are widely practised. There is a big difference between these traditional healing systems and 'folk' medicine. Folk remedies should be avoided, as they often involve rather dubious procedures with potential complications. In comparison, traditional healing systems such as traditional Chinese medicine are well respected, and aspects of them are being increasingly used by Western medical practitioners.

All traditional Asian medical systems identify a vital life force, and see blockage or imbalance as causing disease. Techniques such as herbal medicines, massage and acupuncture are utilised to bring this vital force back into balance, or to maintain balance. These therapies are best used for treating chronic disease such as chronic fatigue, arthritis, irritable bowel syndrome and some chronic skin conditions. Traditional medicines should be avoided for treating serious acute infections such as malaria.

Language

The official language of Laos is the dialect spoken and written in Vientiane. As an official language, it has successfully become the lingua franca between all Lao and non-Lao ethnic groups in the country.

In Lao, many identical syllables are differentiated by their tone only. Vientiane Lao has six tones. Three of the tones are level (low, mid and high) while three follow pitch inclines (rising, high falling and low falling). All six variations in pitch are relative to the speaker's natural vocal range, ie one person's low tone is not necessarily the same pitch as another person's.

➡ **low tone** – Produced at the relative bottom of your conversational tonal range – usually flat level, eg dęe (good).

➡ **mid tone** – Flat like the low tone, but spoken at the relative middle of your vocal range. No tone mark is used, eg het (do).

➡ **high tone** – Flat again, this time at the relative top of your vocal range, eg héu·a (boat).

➡ **rising tone** – Begins a bit below the mid tone and rises to just at or above the high tone, eg săhm (three).

➡ **high falling tone** – Begins at or above the high tone and falls to the mid level, eg sôw (morning).

➡ **low falling tone** – Begins at about the mid level and falls to the level of the low tone, eg kòw (rice).

There is no official method of transliterating the Lao language, though the public and private sectors in Laos are gradually moving towards a more internationally recognisable system along the lines of Royal Thai General Transcription (RTGS), since Thai and Lao have very similar writing and sound systems. This book uses a custom system of transliteration.

In our coloured pronunciation guides, the hyphens indicate syllable breaks within words, eg ang-git (English). Some syllables are further divided with a dot to help you pronounce compound vowels, eg kěe·an (write).

The pronunciation of vowels goes like this: i as in 'it'; ee as in 'feet'; ai as in 'aisle'; ah as the 'a' in 'father'; a as the short 'a' in 'about'; aa as in 'bad'; air as in 'air'; er as in 'fur'; eu as in 'sir'; u as in 'put'; oo as in 'food'; ow as in 'now'; or as in 'jaw'; o as in 'phone'; oh as in 'toe'; ee·a as in 'lan'; oo·a as in 'tour'; ew as in 'yew'; and oy as in 'boy'.

Most consonants correspond to their English counterparts. The exceptions are đ (a hard 't' sound, a bit like 'dt') and ɓ (a hard 'p' sound, a bit like 'bp').

BASICS

Hello.	ສະບາຍດີ	sábąi-děe
Goodbye.	ສະບາຍດີ	sábąi-děe
Excuse me.	ຂໍໂທດ	kŏr tôht
Sorry.	ຂໍໂທດ	kŏr tôht
Please.	ກະລຸນາໆ	ga-lú-náh
Thank you.	ຂອບໃຈ	kòrp jąi
Yes./No.	ແມນ/ບໍ່	maan/bor

How are you?
ສະບາຍດີບໍ່ sábąi-děe bor

I'm fine, and you?
ສະບາຍດີ ເຈົ້າເດ sábąi-děe jôw dâir

WANT MORE?

For in-depth language information and handy phrases, check out Lonely Planet's *Lao Phrasebook*. You'll find it at **shop.lonelyplanet.com**, or you can buy Lonely Planet's iPhone phrasebooks at the Apple App Store.

What's your name?
ເຈົ້າຊື່ຫຍັງ jôw seu nyăng

My name is ...
ຂ້ອຍຊື່ ... kòy seu ...

Do you speak English?
ເຈົ້າປາກ jôw ɓàhk
ພາສາອັງກິດໄດ້ບໍ່ páh-săh ang-kít dâi bor

I don't understand.
ບໍ່ເຂົ້າໃຈ bor kòw jai

ACCOMMODATION

hotel ໂຮງແຮມ hóhng háam
guesthouse ທີ່ຮັບແຂກ hŏr hap káak

Do you have a room?
ມີຫ້ອງບໍ່ mée hòrng bor

single room
ຫ້ອງນອນຕຽງດຽວ hòrng nórn đěe·ang dee·o

double room
ຫ້ອງນອນຕຽງຄູ່ hòrng nórn đěe·ang koo

How much ...? ... ເທົ່າໃດ ... tow đại
  per night ຄືນລະ kéun-la
  per week ອາທິດລະ ạh-tit-la

air-con ແອເຢັນ ạa yen
bathroom ຫ້ອງນ້ຳ hòrng nâm
fan ພັດລົມ pat lóm
hot water ນ້ຳຮ້ອນ nâm hôrn

DIRECTIONS

Where is the ...?
... ຢູ່ໃສ ... yòo săi
Which (street) is this?
ບ່ອນນີ້ (ຖນົນ) ຫຍັງ born nêe (ta-nŏn) nyăng
How far?
ໄກເທົ່າໃດ kại tow đại
Turn left/right.
ລ້ຽວຊ້າຍ/ຂວາ lêe·o sâi/kwăh
straight ahead
ໄປຊື່ໆ ɓại seu-seu

EATING & DRINKING

What do you have that's special?
ມີຫຍັງພິເສດບໍ່ mée nyăng pi-sèt bor

I'd like to try that.
ຂ້ອຍຢາກລອງກິນເບິ່ງ kòy yàhk lórng gɪn berng

I eat only vegetables.
ຂ້ອຍກິນແຕ່ຜັກ kòy gɪn đaa pák

I (don't) like it hot and spicy.
(ບໍ່) ມັກເຜັດ (bor) mak pét

I didn't order this.
ຂ້ອຍບໍ່ໄດ້ສັ່ງແນວນີ້ kòy bor dâi sang náa·ou nêe

Please bring the bill.
ຂໍແຊ້ກແດ່ kŏr saak daa

Key Words

bottle ແກ້ວ kâa·ou
bowl ຖ້ວຍ tòo·ay
chopsticks ໄມ້ທູ່ mâi too
fork ສ້ອມ sôrm
glass ຈອກ jòrk
knife ມີດ mêet
menu ລາຍການ lái-gạhn
 ອາຫານ ạh-hăhn
plate ຈານ jạhn
spoon ບ່ວງ boo·ang

Meat & Fish

beef ຊີ້ນງົວ sèen ngóo·a
chicken ໄກ່ kai
crab ປູ ɓọo
fish ປາ ɓạh
pork ຊີ້ນໝູ sèen mŏo
seafood ອາຫານທະເລ ạh-hăhn ta-láir
shrimp/prawn ກຸ້ງ gûng

Fruit & Vegetables

banana ໝາກກ້ວຍ màhk gôo·ay
bean sprouts ຖົ່ວງອກ too·a ngôrk
beans ຖົ່ວ too·a
cabbage ກະລ່ຳປີ gá-lam ɓẹe
cauliflower ກະລ່ຳປີດອກ gá-lam ɓẹe dòrk
coconut ໝາກພ້າວ màhk pôw
cucumber ໝາກແຕງ màhk đạang
eggplant ໝາກເຂືອ màhk kĕua
garlic ຫົວຜັກທຽມ hŏo·a pák tée·am

green beans	ຖົ່ວຍາວ	too·a nyów
guava	ໝາກສິດາ	màhk sĕe-dạh
jackfruit	ໝາກມີ້	màhk mêe
lettuce	ຜັກສະລັດ	pák sá-lat
lime	ໝາກນາວ	màhk nów
longan	ໝາກຍຳໄຍ	màhk nyám nyái
lychee	ໝາກລິ້ນຈີ່	màhk lîn-jee
mandarin	ໝາກກ້ຽງ	màhk gêe·ang
mango	ໝາກມ່ວງ	màhk moo·ang
onion (bulb)	ຫົວຜັກບົ່ວ	hŏoa pák boo·a
onion (green)	ຕົ້ນຜັກບົ່ວ	đôn pák boo·a
papaya	ໝາກຫຸ່ງ	màhk hung
peanuts	ໝາກຖົ່ວດິນ	màhk too·a dịn
pineapple	ໝາກນັດ	màhk nat
potato	ມັນຝລັ່ງ	mán fa-lang
rambutan	ໝາກເງາະ	màhk ngo
sugarcane	ອ້ອຍ	ôy
tomato	ໝາກເລັ່ນ	màhk len
vegetables	ຜັກ	pak
watermelon	ໝາກໂມ	màhk móh

Other

bread (plain)	ເຂົ້າຈີ່	kòw jẹe
butter	ເບີ	bẹr
chilli	ໝາກເຜັດ	màhk pét
egg	ໄຂ່	kai
fish sauce	ນ້ຳປາ	nâm bạh
ice	ນ້ຳກ້ອນ	nâm gôrn
rice	ເຂົ້າ	kòw
salt	ເກືອ	gẹua
soy sauce	ນ້ຳສະອິ້ວ	nâm sá-éw
sugar	ນ້ຳຕານ	nâm-đạhn

Drinks

beer	ເບຍ	bẹe·a
coffee	ກາແຟ	gạh-fáir
draught beer	ເບຍສດ	bẹe·a sót
drinking water	ນ້ຳດື່ມ	nâm deum
milk (plain)	ນ້ຳນມ	nâm nóm
orange juice	ນ້ຳໝາກກ້ຽງ	nâm màhk gêe·ang

rice whisky	ເຫຼົ້າລາວ	lòw-lów
soda water	ນ້ຳໂສດາ	nâm sŏh-dạh
tea	ຊາ	sáh
yoghurt	ນມສົ້ມ	nóm sòm

EMERGENCIES

| **Help!** | ຊ່ວຍແດ່ | soo·ay daa |
| **Go away!** | ໄປເດີ້ | bại dêr |

Call a doctor!
ຊ່ວຍຕາມຫາໝໍ
ໃຫ້ແດ່
soo·ay đạhm hăh mŏr hài daa

Call the police!
ຊ່ວຍເອີ້ນຕຳລວດແດ່
soo·ay êrn đam-lòo·at daa

Where are the toilets?
ຫ້ອງນ້ຳຢູ່ໃສ
hòrng nâm yoo săi

I'm lost.
ຂ້ອຍຫຼົງທາງ
kòy lŏng táhng

I'm not well.
ຂ້ອຍບໍ່ສະບາຍ
kòy bor sá-bại

SHOPPING & SERVICES

I'm looking for ...
ຂ້ອຍຊອກຫາ ...
kòy sòrk hăh ...

How much (for) ...?
... ເທົ່າໃດ
... tow dại

The price is very high.
ລາຄາແພງຫລາຍ
láh-káh páang lăi

I want to change money.
ຂ້ອຍຢາກປ່ຽນເງິນ
kòy yàhk bee·an ngérn

bank	ທະນາຄານ	ta-náh-káhn
bookshop	ຮ້ານຂາຍປຶ້ມ	hâhn kăi beum
pharmacy	ຮ້ານຂາຍຢາ	hâhn kăi yạh
post office	ໄປສະນີ (ໂຮງສາຍ)	bại-sá-née (hóhng săi)

TIME & DATES

What time is it?
ເວລາຈັກໂມງ
wáir-láh ják móhng

this morning	ເຊົ້ານີ້	sôw nêe
this afternoon	ບ່າຍນີ້	bai nêe
tonight	ຄືນນີ້	kéun nêe

yesterday	ມື້ວານນີ້	mêu wáhn nêe
today	ມື້ນີ້	mêu nêe
tomorrow	ມື້ອື່ນ	mêu eun

Monday	ວັນຈັນ	wán jạn
Tuesday	ວັນອັງຄານ	wán ạng-káhn
Wednesday	ວັນພຸດ	wán put
Thursday	ວັນພະຫັດ	wán pa-hát
Friday	ວັນສຸກ	wán súk
Saturday	ວັນເສົາ	wán sŏw
Sunday	ວັນອາທິດ	wán ạh-tit

TRANSPORT

boat	ເຮືອ	héu·a
bus	ລົດເມ	lot máir
minivan	ລົດຕູ້	lot đôo
plane	ເຮືອບິນ	héu·a bǐn

airport
ສະຫນາມບິນ   sá-năhm bǐn
bus station
ສະຖານີລົດປະຈຳທາງໆ   sa-tăh-nee lot
ꞗá-jam táhng
bus stop
ບ່ອນຈອດລົດປະຈຳທາງໆ   born jòrt lot
ꞗá-jam táhng
taxi stand
ບ່ອນຈອດລົດແທກຊີ   born jòrt lot taak-sêe

I want to go to ...
ຂ້ອຍຢາກໄປ ...   kòy yàhk ꞗại ...
I'd like a ticket.
ຂ້ອຍຢາກໄດ້ປີ້   kòy yàhk dâi ꞗêe
Where do we get on the boat?
ລົງເຮືອຢູ່ໃສ   lóng héu·a yoo săi
What time will the ... leave?
... ຈະອອກຈັກໂມງ   ... já òrk ják móhng
What time does it arrive there?
ຈະໄປຮອດພຸ້ນຈັກໂມງ   já ꞗai hôrt pûn ják móhng
Can I sit here?
ນັ່ງບ່ອນນີ້ໄດ້ບໍ່   nang born nêe dâi bor
Please tell me when we arrive in ...
ເວລາຮອດ ...   wáir-láh hôrt ...
ບອກຂ້ອຍແດ່   bòrk kòy daa
Stop here.
ຈອດຢູ່ນີ້   jòrt yoo nêe

Numbers

1	ຫນຶ່ງ	neung
2	ສອງ	sŏrng
3	ສາມ	săhm
4	ສີ່	see
5	ຫ້າ	hàh
6	ຫກ	hók
7	ເຈັດ	jét
8	ແປດ	ꞗàat
9	ເກົ້າ	gôw
10	ສິບ	síp
11	ສິບເອັດ	síp-ét
12	ສິບສອງ	síp-sŏrng
20	ຊາວ	sów
21	ຊາວເອັດ	sów-ét
22	ຊາວສອງ	sów-sŏrng
30	ສາມສິບ	săhm-síp
40	ສີ່ສິບ	see-síp
50	ຫ້າສິບ	hàh-síp
60	ຫກສິບ	hók-síp
70	ເຈັດສິບ	jét-síp
80	ແປດສິບ	ꞗàat-síp
90	ເກົ້າສິບ	gôw-síp
100	ຮ້ອຍ	hôy
200	ສອງຮ້ອຍ	sŏrng hôy
1000	ພັນ	pán
10,000	ຫມື່ນ(ສິບພັນ)	meun (síp-pán)
100,000	ແສນ(ຮ້ອຍພັນ)	săan (hôy pán)
1,000,000	ລ້ານ	lâhn

I'd like to hire a ...
ຂ້ອຍຢາກເຊົ່າ ...   kòy yàhk sôw ...

bicycle	ລົດຖີບ	lot tèep
car	ລົດ(ໂອໂຕ)	lot (ŏh-đŏh)
motorcycle	ລົດຈັກ	lot ják
passenger truck	ສອງແຖວ	sŏrng-tăa·ou
pedicab	ສາມລໍ້	săhm-lôr
taxi	ລົດແທກຊີ	lot tâak-sêe
tuk-tuk	ຕຸກ ຕຸກ	đúk-đúk

GLOSSARY

ąahaan – food

anatta – Buddhist concept of nonsubstantiality or nonessentiality of reality, ie no permanent 'soul'

anicca – Buddhist concept of impermanence, the transience of all things

Asean – Association of South East Asian Nations

bâhn – the general Lao word for house or village; written Ban on maps

bąhsěe – sometimes spelt basi or *baci;* a ceremony in which the 32 *kwăn* (guardian spirits) are symbolically bound to the participant for health and safety

baht – *(bàht)* Thai unit of currency, commonly negotiable in Laos; also a Lao unit of measure equal to 15g

BCEL – Banque pour le Commerce Extérieur Lao; in English, Lao Foreign Trade Bank

bęea – beer; *bęea sót* is draught beer

bun – pronounced *bųn,* often spelt boun; a festival; also spiritual 'merit' earned through good actions or religious practices

corvée – enforced, unpaid labour

đàht –waterfall; also *nâm tók;* written Tat on maps

đalàht – market; *talàat sâo* is the morning market; *talàat mèut* is the free, or 'black' market; written Talat on maps

Don – pronounced *dąwn;* island

dukkha – Buddhist concept of suffering, unsatisfactoriness, disease

falang – from the Lao *falang-sèht* or 'French'; Western, a Westerner

fěr – rice noodles, one of the most common dishes in Laos

hăi – jar

héua – boat

héua hăhng nyáo – longtail boat

héua pái – row boat

héua wái – speedboat

hŏr đại – monastery building dedicated to the storage of the Tripitaka (Buddhist scriptures)

hùay – stream; written Huay on maps

Jataka – (Pali-Sanskrit) mythological stories of the Buddha's past lives; *sáa-dók* in Lao

jęen hór – Lao name for the Muslim Yunnanese who live in Northern Laos

jęhdii – a Buddhist stupa; also written Chedi

jumbo – a motorised three-wheeled taxi, sometimes called tuk-tuk

káan – a wind instrument devised of a double row of bamboo-like reeds fitted into a hardwood soundbox and made air-tight with beeswax

kanŏm – pastry or sweet

kip – pronounced *gèep;* Lao unit of currency

kòw – rice

kòw jee – bread

kòw něeo – sticky rice, the Lao staple food

kóo-bạh – Lao Buddhist monk

kwăn – guardian spirits

láhp – a spicy Lao-style salad of minced meat, poultry or fish

lák méuang – city pillar

lám wóng – 'circle dance', the traditional folk dance of Laos, as common at discos as at festivals

Lao Issara – Lao resistance movement against the French in the 1940s

lòw-lów – distilled rice liquor

Lao Loum – 'lowland Lao', ethnic groups belonging to the Lao–Thai Diaspora

Lao Soung – 'highland Lao', hill tribes who make their residence at higher altitudes, such as Hmong, Mien; also spelt Lao Sung

Lao Thoeng – 'upland Lao', a loose affiliation of mostly Mon-Khmer peoples who live on midaltitude mountain slopes

lingam – a pillar or phallus symbolic of Shiva, common in Khmer-built temples

LNTA – Lao National Tourism Administration

LPDR – Lao People's Democratic Republic

LPRP – Lao People's Revolutionary Party

maa nâm – literally, water mother; river; usually shortened to *nâm* with river names, as in Nam Khong (Mekong River)

meuang – pronounced *méuang;* district or town; in ancient times a city state; often written Muang on maps

moo bâhn – village

móoan – fun, which the Lao believe should be present in all activities

mŏr lám – Lao folk musical theatre tradition; roughly translates as 'master of verse'

Muang – see *meuang*

naga – *nâa-kha* in Lao; mythical water serpent common to Lao–Thai legends and art

náhng sée – Buddhist nuns

náirn – Buddhist novice monk; also referred to as *samanera*

nâm – water; can also mean 'river', 'juice', 'sauce': anything of a watery nature

NGO – nongovernmental organisation, typically involved in the foreign-aid industry

nibbana – 'cooling', the extinction of mental defilements; the ultimate goal of Theravada Buddhism

NPA – National Protected Area, a classification assigned to 20 wildlife areas throughout Laos

NVA – North Vietnamese Army

ʼbạh – fish

ʼbạh dàak – fermented fish sauce, a common accompaniment to Lao food

pa – holy image, usually referring to a Buddha; venerable

pàh – cloth

pàh bęeang – shoulder sash worn by men

pàh nung – sarong, worn by almost all Lao women

pàh salóng – sarong, worn by Lao men

Pathet Lao – literally, Country of Laos; both a general term for the country and a common journalistic reference to the military arm of the early Patriotic Lao Front (a cover for the Lao People's Party); often abbreviated to PL

Pha Lak Pha Lam – the Lao version of the Indian epic, the Ramayana

phúu – hill or mountain; also spelt phu

sǎhláh lóng tám – a sala (hall) where monks and lay people listen to Buddhist teachings

sǎhm-lór – a three-wheeled pedicab

sakai-làap – alternative name for jumbo in southern Laos due to the perceived resemblance to a space capsule (Skylab)

sala – pronounced sǎa-láa; an open-sided shelter; a hall

samana – pronounced sǎamanáa; 'seminar'; euphemism for labour and re-education camps established after the 1975 Revolution

samanera – Buddhist novice monk; also referred to as náirn

se – also spelt xe; Southern Laos term for river; hence Se Don means Don River and Pakse means pàak (mouth) of the river

sěe – sacred; also spelt si

shophouse – two-storey building designed to have a shop on the ground floor and a residence above

sǐm – ordination hall in a Lao Buddhist monastery; named after the sima, (pronounced siimáa) or sacred stone tablets, which mark off the grounds dedicated for this purpose

soi – lane

sǒrngtǎaou – literally two-rows; a passenger truck

taak-sée – taxi

tanǒn – street/road; often spelt Thanon on maps; shortened to 'Th' as street is to 'St'

tâht – Buddhist stupa or reliquary; written That on maps

tuk-tuk – see jumbo

UXO – unexploded ordnance

Viet Minh – the Vietnamese forces who fought for Indochina's independence from the French

vipassana – insight meditation

wat – Lao Buddhist monastery

wihǎhn – (Pali-Sanskrit vihara) a temple hall

Behind the Scenes

SEND US YOUR FEEDBACK

We love to hear from travellers – your comments keep us on our toes and help make our books better. Our well-travelled team reads every word on what you loved or loathed about this book. Although we cannot reply individually to your submissions, we always guarantee that your feedback goes straight to the appropriate authors, in time for the next edition. Each person who sends us information is thanked in the next edition – the most useful submissions are rewarded with a selection of digital PDF chapters.

Visit **lonelyplanet.com/contact** to submit your updates and suggestions or to ask for help. Our award-winning website also features inspirational travel stories, news and discussions.

Note: We may edit, reproduce and incorporate your comments in Lonely Planet products such as guidebooks, websites and digital products, so let us know if you don't want your comments reproduced or your name acknowledged. For a copy of our privacy policy visit lonelyplanet.com/privacy.

OUR READERS

Many thanks to the travellers who used the last edition and wrote to us with helpful hints, useful advice and interesting anecdotes:

Adrien Be, Aileen Gerloff, Alex Vrees, Allan Wood, Amy Larkins, Faith Kramer, Friederike Haberstroh, George Crook, Goedele Dupont, Hans Ohrt, Julia Henke, Katherine Shea, Lewis Levine, Lotte Clemminck, Madeline Oliver, Marie-Aline de Lavau, Marjolaine & Hanael Sfez, Mark Fisher, Max Pit, Montserrat Aguilera, Philip Worrall, Pieter Verckist, Tessa Godfrey, Thomas Wiser, Tim Greene, Torben Retboll, Werner Bruyninx, William Murray-Smith, Yvonne Wei

WRITER THANKS

Tim Bewer

A hearty *kòrp jại* to the many people along the way who answered my incessant questions or helped me out in other ways during this update. In particular, Nicolas Papon-Phalaphanh, Latanakone Keokhamphoui, Yves Verlaine, Khun Buasone and Prapaporn Sompakdee provided great assistance, while Laura, Nick, Rich and the rest of the Lonely Planet team were a pleasure to work with, as always. Finally, a special thanks to my wife, Suttawan, for help on this book and much more.

Nick Ray

A huge and heartfelt thanks to the people of Laos, whose warmth and humour, stoicism and spirit make it a happy yet humbling place to be. Biggest thanks are reserved for my wife, Kulikar Sotho, as without her support and encouragement the adventures would not be possible. And to our children, Julian and Belle, for signing up for some family adventures in new-look Vang Vieng.

Thanks to fellow travellers and residents, friends and contacts in Laos who have helped shaped my knowledge and experience in this country. Thanks also to my co-authors for going the extra mile to ensure this is a worthy new edition.

Finally, thanks to the Lonely Planet team who have worked on this title. The author may be the public face, but a huge amount of work goes into making this a better book behind the scenes, so thanks to everyone for their hard work.

Richard Waters

My special thanks to Elizabeth Vongsa, Adri Berger, Ivan Schulte, Harp, Saly Phimpinith, Dennis Ulstrup, Annabel and Josef, Agnes, Mr Vongdavone and Marco. Also thanks as usual to my extended family, the Lao people, from whom I seem to learn something every trip. Finally, special thanks to Laura Crawford, my long suffering Destination Editor, who keeps stoic when my technical skills fail to join the 21st century.

ACKNOWLEDGEMENTS

Climate map data adapted from Peel MC, Finlayson BL & McMahon TA (2007) 'Updated World Map of the Köppen-Geiger Climate Classification', Hydrology and Earth System Sciences, 11, 163344.

Cover photograph: Monks at Wat In Paeng, Vientiane, Travel Pix Collection/AWL©

THIS BOOK

This 9th edition of Lonely Planet's *Laos* guidebook was researched and written by Tim Bewer, Nick Ray and Richard Waters, and was curated by Kate Morgan. The previous edition was written by Nick Ray, Greg Bloom and Richard Waters. This guidebook was produced by the following:

Destination Editor Laura Crawford
Product Editor Jenna Myers
Book Designer Mazzy Prinsep
Assisting Editors Nigel Chin, Victoria Harrison, Gabrielle Innes, Lauren O'Connell, Charlotte Orr

Cartographers Michael Garrett, Diana Von Holdt
Cover Researcher Naomi Parker

Thanks to Bruce Evans, Jane Grisman, Liz Heynes, Catherine Naghten, Anthony Phelan, Martine Power, Vicky Smith, Professor Martin Stuart-Fox

Index

Map Legend

Sights

- Beach
- Bird Sanctuary
- Buddhist
- Castle/Palace
- Christian
- Confucian
- Hindu
- Islamic
- Jain
- Jewish
- Monument
- Museum/Gallery/Historic Building
- Ruin
- Shinto
- Sikh
- Taoist
- Winery/Vineyard
- Zoo/Wildlife Sanctuary
- Other Sight

Activities, Courses & Tours

- Bodysurfing
- Diving
- Canoeing/Kayaking
- Course/Tour
- Sento Hot Baths/Onsen
- Skiing
- Snorkelling
- Surfing
- Swimming/Pool
- Walking
- Windsurfing
- Other Activity

Sleeping

- Sleeping
- Camping

Eating

- Eating

Drinking & Nightlife

- Drinking & Nightlife
- Cafe

Entertainment

- Entertainment

Shopping

- Shopping

Information

- Bank
- Embassy/Consulate
- Hospital/Medical
- Internet
- Police
- Post Office
- Telephone
- Toilet
- Tourist Information
- Other Information

Geographic

- Beach
- Gate
- Hut/Shelter
- Lighthouse
- Lookout
- Mountain/Volcano
- Oasis
- Park
- Pass
- Picnic Area
- Waterfall

Population

- Capital (National)
- Capital (State/Province)
- City/Large Town
- Town/Village

Transport

- Airport
- Border crossing
- Bus
- Cable car/Funicular
- Cycling
- Ferry
- Metro/MRT/MTR station
- Monorail
- Parking
- Petrol station
- Skytrain/Subway station
- Taxi
- Train station/Railway
- Tram
- Underground station
- Other Transport

Note: Not all symbols displayed above appear on the maps in this book

Routes

- Tollway
- Freeway
- Primary
- Secondary
- Tertiary
- Lane
- Unsealed road
- Road under construction
- Plaza/Mall
- Steps
- Tunnel
- Pedestrian overpass
- Walking Tour
- Walking Tour detour
- Path/Walking Trail

Boundaries

- International
- State/Province
- Disputed
- Regional/Suburb
- Marine Park
- Cliff
- Wall

Hydrography

- River, Creek
- Intermittent River
- Canal
- Water
- Dry/Salt/Intermittent Lake
- Reef

Areas

- Airport/Runway
- Beach/Desert
- Cemetery (Christian)
- Cemetery (Other)
- Glacier
- Mudflat
- Park/Forest
- Sight (Building)
- Sportsground
- Swamp/Mangrove

OUR STORY

A beat-up old car, a few dollars in the pocket and a sense of adventure. In 1972 that's all Tony and Maureen Wheeler needed for the trip of a lifetime – across Europe and Asia overland to Australia. It took several months, and at the end – broke but inspired – they sat at their kitchen table writing and stapling together their first travel guide, *Across Asia on the Cheap*. Within a week they'd sold 1500 copies. Lonely Planet was born.

Today, Lonely Planet has offices in Franklin, London, Melbourne, Oakland, Dublin, Beijing and Delhi, with more than 600 staff and writers. We share Tony's belief that 'a great guidebook should do three things: inform, educate and amuse'.

OUR WRITERS

Kate Morgan

Having worked for Lonely Planet for over a decade now, Kate has been fortunate enough to cover plenty of ground working as a travel writer on destinations such as Shanghai, Japan, India, Zimbabwe, the Philippines and Phuket. She has done stints living in London, Paris and Osaka, but these days is based in one of her favourite regions in the world – Victoria, Australia. In between travelling the world and writing about it, Kate enjoys spending time at home working as a freelance editor.

Tim Bewer
Southern Laos

After university Tim worked as a legislative assistant before quitting capitol life to backpack around West Africa. It was during this trip that the idea of becoming a travel writer and photographer was hatched, and he's been at it ever since. He has visited over 80 countries, including most in Southeast Asia. His first journey to Laos was in 1997, before the highway from Vientiane to the south was paved, and he's returned nearly a dozen times since. He lives in Khon Kaen, Thailand.

Nick Ray
Vientiane, Vang Vieng & Around, Central Laos

A Londoner of sorts, Nick comes from Watford, the sort of town that makes you want to travel. He currently lives in Phnom Penh and has written for countless guidebooks on the Mekong region, including Lonely Planet's *Cambodia* and *Vietnam* books, as well as *Southeast Asia on a Shoestring*. When not writing, he is often out exploring the remote parts of the region as a location scout or line producer for the world of television and film, including anything from *Top Gear Vietnam* to *Tomb Raider*. Laos is one of his favourite countries on earth and he was thrilled to finally ride the Loop and explore the caves of Tha Khaek.

Richard Waters
Luang Prabang & Around, Northern Laos, Environment, People & Culture

Richard is based in the Cotswolds, close enough to get to London and, more importantly, only two hours from Devon's surf. For the last 12 years he's worked for Lonely Planet and *The Daily Telegraph*, *Sunday Times*, *Independent* and more as a travel writer and author. He sometimes shoots photos for his stories and is drawn toward wildlife and out of the way places.

Published by Lonely Planet Global Limited
CRN 554153
9th edition – Jun 2017
ISBN 978 1 78657 531 9
© Lonely Planet 2017   Photographs © as indicated 2017
10 9 8 7 6 5 4 3 2 1
Printed in China